Modernization and Accountability in the Social Economy Sector

Augusta Ferreira
University of Aveiro, Portugal

Rui Marques
University of Aveiro, Portugal

Graça Azevedo
University of Aveiro, Portugal

Helena Inácio
University of Aveiro, Portugal

Carlos Santos
University of Aveiro, Portugal

A volume in the Advances in Finance, Accounting, and Economics (AFAE) Book Series

IGI Global
DISSEMINATOR OF KNOWLEDGE

Published in the United States of America by
IGI Global
Business Science Reference (an imprint of IGI Global)
701 E. Chocolate Avenue
Hershey PA, USA 17033
Tel: 717-533-8845
Fax: 717-533-8661
E-mail: cust@igi-global.com
Web site: http://www.igi-global.com

Library of Congress Cataloging-in-Publication Data

Names: Ferreira, Augusta da Conceicao Santos, 1966- editor.
Title: Modernization and accountability in the social economy sector / Augusta Ferreira [and four others], editors.
Description: Hershey, PA : Business Science Reference, [2020]
Identifiers: LCCN 2018054597| ISBN 9781522584827 (hardcover) | ISBN 9781522584834 (ebook) | ISBN 9781522585046 (softcover)
Subjects: LCSH: Nonprofit organizations. | Charities. | Humanitarian assistance.
Classification: LCC HD2769.15 .M63 2020 | DDC 658/.048--dc23 LC record available at https://lccn.loc.gov/2018054597

This book is published in the IGI Global book series Advances in Finance, Accounting, and Economics (AFAE) (ISSN: 2327-5677; eISSN: 2327-5685)

British Cataloguing in Publication Data
A Cataloguing in Publication record for this book is available from the British Library.

For electronic access to this publication, please contact: eresources@igi-global.com.

Advances in Finance, Accounting, and Economics (AFAE) Book Series

Ahmed Driouchi
Al Akhawayn University, Morocco

ISSN:2327-5677
EISSN:2327-5685

Mission

In our changing economic and business environment, it is important to consider the financial changes occurring internationally as well as within individual organizations and business environments. Understanding these changes as well as the factors that influence them is crucial in preparing for our financial future and ensuring economic sustainability and growth.

The **Advances in Finance, Accounting, and Economics (AFAE)** book series aims to publish comprehensive and informative titles in all areas of economics and economic theory, finance, and accounting to assist in advancing the available knowledge and providing for further research development in these dynamic fields.

Coverage

- Taxes
- Economics of Migration and Spatial Mobility
- Finance
- Economic Downturn
- Ethics in Accounting and Finance
- Evidence-Based Studies
- Development Economics
- Interest Rates and Annuities
- Economic Policy
- Applied Accounting

IGI Global is currently accepting manuscripts for publication within this series. To submit a proposal for a volume in this series, please contact our Acquisition Editors at Acquisitions@igi-global.com or visit: http://www.igi-global.com/publish/.

The Advances in Finance, Accounting, and Economics (AFAE) Book Series (ISSN 2327-5677) is published by IGI Global, 701 E. Chocolate Avenue, Hershey, PA 17033-1240, USA, www.igi-global.com. This series is composed of titles available for purchase individually; each title is edited to be contextually exclusive from any other title within the series. For pricing and ordering information please visit http://www.igi-global.com/book-series/advances-finance-accounting-economics/73685. Postmaster: Send all address changes to above address.

Titles in this Series

For a list of additional titles in this series, please visit: www.igi-global.com/book-series

Foreign Business in China and Opportunities for Technological Innovation and Sustainable Economics
Anna Visvizi (Deree – The American College of Greece, Greece) Miltiadis Lytras (Deree – The American College of Greece, Greece) Xi Zhang (Tianjin University, China) and Jie Zhao (Anhui University, China)
Business Science Reference • copyright 2019 • 284pp • H/C (ISBN: 9781522589808) • US $195.00 (our price)

Handbook of Research on Global Issues in Financial Communication and Investment Decision Making
Hasan Dinçer (Istanbul Medipol University, Turkey) and Serhat Yüksel (Istanbul Medipol University, Turkey)
Business Science Reference • copyright 2019 • 540pp • H/C (ISBN: 9781522592655) • US $365.00 (our price)

Behavioral Finance and Decision-Making Models
Tripti Tripathi (Jiwaji University, India) Manoj Kumar Dash (Khallikote University, India) and Gaurav Agrawal (Indian Institute of Information Technology and Management Gwalior, India)
Business Science Reference • copyright 2019 • 333pp • H/C (ISBN: 9781522573999) • US $215.00 (our price)

Global Challenges in Public Finance and International Relations
Deniz Şahin Duran (Tokat Gaziosmanpaşa University, Turkey) Yusuf Temür (Tokat Gaziosmanpaşa University, Turkey) and Doğan Bozdoğan (Tokat Gaziosmanpaşa University, Turkey)
Business Science Reference • copyright 2019 • 304pp • H/C (ISBN: 9781522575641) • US $225.00 (our price)

International Financial Reporting Standards and New Directions in Earnings Management
Jonas da Silva Oliveira (Instituto Universitário de Lisboa (ISCTE-IUL), Portugal) Graça Maria do Carmo Azevedo (University of Aveiro, Portugal) and Augusta da Conceição Santos Ferreira (University of Aveiro, Portugal)
Business Science Reference • copyright 2019 • 342pp • H/C (ISBN: 9781522578178) • US $225.00 (our price)

Throughput Accounting in a Hyperconnected World
Ionica Oncioiu (European Academy of the Regions, Belgium)
Business Science Reference • copyright 2019 • 362pp • H/C (ISBN: 9781522577126) • US $195.00 (our price)

Organizational Auditing and Assurance in the Digital Age
Rui Pedro Marques (University of Aveiro, Portugal) Carlos Santos (University of Aveiro, Portugal) and Helena Inácio (University of Aveiro, Portugal)
Business Science Reference • copyright 2019 • 404pp • H/C (ISBN: 9781522573562) • US $225.00 (our price)

International Firms' Economic Nationalism and Trade Policies in the Globalization Era
Harish C. Chandan (Argosy University, USA) and Bryan Christiansen (Global Research Society, LLC, USA)
Business Science Reference • copyright 2019 • 299pp • H/C (ISBN: 9781522575610) • US $215.00 (our price)

IGI Global
DISSEMINATOR OF KNOWLEDGE

701 East Chocolate Avenue, Hershey, PA 17033, USA
Tel: 717-533-8845 x100 • Fax: 717-533-8661
E-Mail: cust@igi-global.com • www.igi-global.com

Anna Oppelmayer, *University of Klagenfurt, Austria*
Mirko Pečarič, *University of Ljubljana, Slovenia*
Daniela Preite, *Università del Salento – Lecce, Italy & SDA Bocconi – Milano, Italy*
Leire San-Jose, *University of the Basque Country, Spain & University of Huddersfield, UK*
Vilmar Antonio Gonçalves Tondolo, *Federal University of Pelotas, Brazil*

Table of Contents

Detailed Table of Contents

The aim of this chapter is to present a domain model that represents the informational needs of transparency (governance structure and accountability dimensions) in Portuguese cooperatives. A domain model is an abstract representation of a reality and a milestone in the development of a metadata application profile (MAP). A community of practice publishes linked open MAP-based data for these data to be interoperable; this means intelligent software/agents can aggregate these data, provide different types of visualizations, infer from the data, and ultimately provide new discoveries. This model was developed having as basis the information obtained from the accomplishment of a focus group, and the analysis of financial reports and websites of seven Portuguese cooperatives. The authors will continue to work on the domain model to include 1) other dimensions that also contribute for transparency in the organizations and 2) other types of entities of the social economy (SE). The final aim is to define a model representing the needs of transparency of all types of European SE entities.

Nonprofit organizations play a relevant role in Brazilian society. In recent years, Brazil has faced frequent allegations of mismanagement of resources and corruption in different administrative spheres, including state-owned and private enterprises. In this scenario, transparency is essential to nonprofit organizations. Resource mobilization is a key management activity of nonprofit organizations that provides the achievement of the social objective of the organization. This chapter aims to analyze the influence of transparency on the resource mobilization of Brazilian nonprofit organizations. In order to achieve this goal, a survey was developed. Data from 93 Brazilian non-profit organizations were collected. The main contribution of study is that transparency has significant impact on resource mobilization in Brazilian nonprofit organizations.

This chapter addresses the topic of accountability and reporting of social entities as concepts and instruments of governance that are used to demonstrate transparency and rigor regarding their activity to their stakeholders. The objective of this chapter is to understand how these instruments are used by social entities, and to establish whether this use brings about an increase in the trust created between theses entities and their funders with regards to the possibility of obtaining increased funding. With this in mind, two surveys were carried out, one for social entities and the other for funders, with some similar content, in order to enable a comparison of answers. This study enabled us to conclude that social entities have a formal and periodic relationship with their funders, that they believe that the current accountability and reporting (A&R) quality level is adequate, that social entities' A&R information, although not decisive, is important for funding decision making, and if social entities were to receive substantial funding, this would improve their social impact.

Chapter 6
The Influencers of Social Accounting and Reporting: Some Evidence.. 98
Ninel Ivanova Nesheva-Kiosseva, New Bulgarian University, Bulgaria

This chapter is an attempt at presenting some reliable factors that have a significant impact on the creation, development, and practice of social accounting and reporting. A part of the research is devoted to presenting the problem of the emergence of the views of social accounting and reporting and their development over time. Attention has been provided to the most influential generators of social accounting and reporting that shape the state of the art to the fullest extent. The text seeks to highlight the driving forces that impact the development of social accounting and reporting. The essay cannot be exhaustive enough as the vast variety of social reports that exist cannot be covered in detail. The study, without seeking full comprehensiveness, tries to systematize some key drivers of social accounting and accountability. It seeks to provide a practical and simple coordinate system in which those who wish to conduct social accounting and reporting should be guided by the diverse sources of social accountability models.

Chapter 7
The Potential Role of Social Reporting in the Decision-Making Process of Cooperatives................ 115
Fabio De Matteis, Università del Salento – Lecce, Italy
Daniela Preite, Università del Salento – Lecce, Italy & SDA Bocconi – Milano, Italy

Accountability in the social economy sector is very important because it is inherent in the nature of the organizations of this sector. The literature on the topic of social accounting and accountability is abundant and highlights the benefits and the criticisms of social reporting. The objective of the chapter arises from the literature review that highlights how more in-depth studies are needed on the characters and role of social accountability in decision-making processes. In order to answer the research question (How is social reporting performed and how does social information influence the decision making of the management in a cooperative?), the single case study methodology has been adopted, considering embedded units of analysis and focusing on the social report of an Italian retail cooperative (COOP Lombardia). Thanks to the analyzed case study, it is possible to conclude that the social report can represent a tool of accountability that also informs future decisions, realizing a circular relationship between results achieved and decisions to be taken.

This chapter was based on one of the largest Spanish cooperative groups, which is part of the social economy sector (SES). Added value is a useful concept; however, after analyzing this case, the authors found that social accounting provides additional information about the social value that companies generate. Then, by applying social accounting complemented by a value-added statement, these companies belonging to the SES can quantify, monetize, and compare their social value and added value, and demonstrate their contribution to society. Social accounting is necessary to demonstrate and understand the value of social economy companies, since their value is not always fundamentally centered on commercial activity; at least not only. They can monitor their effort in terms of specific social values that are not part of the market. Because of this, their value is not reflected in traditional financial statements.

This chapter provides an assessment of social return on investment (SROI) as an instrument of reporting the value that (non-profit) organizations in the social economy have created. After a general overview and comparison of two most widely referred SROI guidelines, a selection of SROI reports in practice is analyzed based on criteria of popular reporting. Popular reporting has emerged in the accounting discipline as a way of establishing an easy to understand, short enough to maintain attention document to different user groups (e.g., clients, citizens, decision makers). This new approach lending from the basic ideas of popular reporting allows researchers and practitioners alike to gain new insights into the current design as well as the potential of SROI reports as a key instrument of accountability for (non-profit) organizations in the social economy.

This chapter aims to assess how the Portuguese foundations manage and disclosure on their websites information on corporate social responsibility (CSR). The study performs the assessment of the sampled foundations holding a website accessible to the broad public and being members of the Portuguese Foundation Centre. The evidence of this study impacts therefore the literature review on three ways. Firstly, it sheds light on the diversity of CSR policies undertaken by foundations, through the scale perspective and the CSR content categories. Secondly, it claims how distinct CSR information trends can be triggered by needs of legitimacy towards the stakeholders unlike other types of organizations. Lastly, the evidence provided by this study suggests that there in not a significant influence of the dimension factor of the foundations on the amount of CSR information they disclose, which contradicts evidence of previous studies.

In Portugal, in order to make the management of public resources more accountable, regulations on financial disclosure have emerged. Currently, the Private Institutions of Social Solidarity, through the Decree-Law No. 172-A/2014, are required to publish the financial reporting on their websites from 2016. Given the diffusion of innovations and the institutional theory, based on coercive isomorphism, the IPSS may have already created the conditions to fulfill this requirement. This chapter intends to ascertain whether the IPSS have conditions to comply with the mandatory disclosure under the law. This research shows that there is very limited presence of IPSS on the internet, the websites reveal low maturity levels and are little sophisticated. Furthermore, the IPSS that disclose the financial reporting on their websites, are still a minority, even if required by law to do so. The value of this research are related to the recent innovations introduced by the legal framework. Thus, it is important to monitor the evolution of law compliance by these institutions.

The chapter objectives focus on mapping the sector of social economy in some states from South-Eastern Europe, presenting their role and impact due to the activities achieved in society. The theoretical part of the chapter comprises the evolution of social economy in Europe, in general, and in South-Eastern Europe, in particular, the identification of the types of organizations in this area. The case study identifies and presents the stages of development of the social enterprises in countries such as Romania, Bulgaria, Cyprus, Serbia, Slovenia, Croatia, Greece, Republic of Moldova, and explores, by comparative analysis the institutional frameworks, the regulations of social enterprises, the eligible judicial forms, presenting similarities and differences, as well as the contribution to social inclusion and impact on community in general. The chapter identifies and explains the influence of the European actors and presents the factors specific to each country which have influenced and supported the emergence of social enterprises as well as the challenges faced.

Citizens' interactions are at the center of open governments. When the latter use open structures and open processes to foster (technical) collaboration, citizens' wellbeing can be improved by observing what citizens (do not) publicly write about or search for. This chapter tries to compare the wellbeing and quality of life (the older terms are public value or solidarity) with public goods inside and outside of public services. This relationship can be achieved when people debate and governments listen to diverse alternatives. To test this relationship, the Google Trends application was used. Trends show that satisfied people do not write about effective, efficient, legal, and ethical things, so a temporary conclusion needed for further investigation is that the government's success in a certain field is present when people do not talk (on a large scale) about matters or topics in that field. Governments should, therefore, listen to or read what people (do not) say or write.

Italian cooperative organizations contribute sensibly to the national growth and development, pursuing a social function of economic redistribution. Since they are based on the mutuality principle, the related accountancy and taxation systems follow such logic, in particular as far as the patronage refunds discipline is concerned. The aim of the chapter is to advance the understanding of such flows; the scope is pursued through an accounting records' comparative analysis based on the main legislative acts and professional and scholar literature. The results converge into a cause-and-effect model built according to a system dynamics perspective.

The stewardship of resources for the good of the people is an ancient concept in India, practiced by revered kingdoms. This chapter discusses the original ideals of stewardship and how colonization caused a deterioration of this philosophy in favor of materialistic wealth generation. Colonization followed by the development of an industrialized and capitalistic leaning in the economy brought wealth and increased consumption for Indian people and also created multiple waste-related issues. These issues require a drastic overhaul of waste management practices, with particular attention to industrial ecology. Modern stewardship by India's CSR community is essential to prevent further environmental degradation due to poor waste management practices. The circular economy holds promise as a new economic system and philosophy that can refocus society towards the values of stewardship espoused by the nation's ancestors, while transitioning to a circular economy.

Preface

ABOUT THE SUBJECT

The Social Economy Sector (SES) emerged in a context of crisis and degradation of conditions. This sector is made up of a group of private entities, duly organized, with autonomy and freedom, which are created to satisfy the needs of the stakeholders, through the provision of goods and services, ensuring their financing. These entities share some characteristics, as for example: they are neither a part of the public sector nor controlled by it; they are entities that promote democracy and perform activities that meet the needs of individuals and their families. Thus, the SES has played an increasingly important socio-economic role in local, regional and national life, mitigating the negative impact of the current economic context. We could say that the SES is between the State and the market.

In organizations that belong to the SES, each value invested has as purpose a specific cause or goal for the benefit of society, taking into consideration the various gaps that the State alone cannot fill. And perhaps for this reason they are often also funded by the state. Hence, the SES entities face pressures for greater accountability (social and corporate managers) towards their funders, users and citizens, and a growing need to report good practices and the social, economic and financial impact that they have on the community. However, because they have very particular characteristics, SES entities often face difficulties related to the management model; to the lack of an accounting framework that allows them to properly disseminate the results of their activities; to the lack of indicators that allow to measure the social, economic and financial impact of the activities carried out; to the lack of resources to enable them to use information and communication technologies to support the work they are undertaking; and to the adoption of required control mechanisms. In this sense, this book aims to disseminate good practices that involve financial reporting; the assessment of their social, economic and financial impact; and the use of technologies and information systems, which promote the modernization of the SES and the improvement of its accountability, sustainability and operational performance.

EXPECTATIONS

The editors expect this book to be useful for regulatory authorities and researchers in the field of accounting, management, internal control, auditing and technologies in the SES. It also intends to be valuable to SES managers, making them aware and realize how the several tools can be used to ensure the accuracy and transparency of SES management acts and to improve the efficiency and effectiveness of SES management. Through the dissemination of the research findings on the SES, this publication will also be helpful to develop and inspire further research by students in post-graduate courses with research interests in public accounting and management.

This book aims to achieve the following main objectives:

- Disseminate methodologies that would allow SES entities to implement practices, consistent with values of ethics, rigor, transparency and accountability to promote accountable SES managers;
- Document the management and control practices that are being used by SES entities in order to increase their accountability;
- Review the processes/models of governance that allow promoting accountability and document those that are being used by managers in order to increase the management transparency for citizens and other stakeholders;
- Discuss and disseminate the processes of control and stress their importance for the reliability of financial reporting;
- Disseminate the successful adoption of information technologies in order to instigate the SES modernization.

ORGANIZATION OF THE BOOK

This book is organized into 15 chapters. The first four chapters are focused on the accountability and transparency of the social entities and talk about some mechanisms that can be used to promote them. Thus:

- **Chapter 1: Modernization and Accountability in the Social Economy – A Systematic Review** provides a systematic review of the literature on modernization and accountability practice in the social economy.
- **Chapter 2: Accountability via Financial Disclosures – An Exploration of the Public's Perceptions** explores the general public's perceptions of the relative importance of specific financial disclosures, which the public believes SES organizations should publish as part of their provision of accountability.
- **Chapter 3: A Domain Model for Transparency in Portuguese Cooperatives – The Governance Structure and Accountability Dimensions** presents a domain model that represents the informational needs of transparency (governance structure and accountability dimensions) in Portuguese cooperatives.
- **Chapter 4: Transparency and Resource Mobilization in Times of Crisis – An Analysis of the Brazilian Nonprofit Sector** aims to analyze the influence of transparency on the resource mobilization of Brazilian non-profit organizations.

  Chapters 5 to 9 provide some knowledge of reporting, namely social reporting, in the social economy:
- **Chapter 5: Accountability and Reporting in the Funding Decision Process of Social Economy** aims to provide knowledge of how accountability and reporting are used by social entities, and to establish whether this use brings about an increase in the trust created between these entities and their funders with regard to the possibility of obtaining increased funding.

- **Chapter 6: The Influencers of Social Accounting and Reporting – Some Evidence** intends to present some reliable factors that have a significant impact on the creation, development and practice of social accounting and reporting.
- **Chapter 7: The Potential Role of Social Reporting in the Decision-Making Process of Cooperatives** addresses the role of social reporting in decision-making processes.
- **Chapter 8: Social Accounting in the Social Economy – A Case Study of Monetizing Social Value** aims to compare the results from social accounting with the results from traditional accounting using a relevant case: Clade group.
- **Chapter 9: Reporting Value Using Social Return on Investment Reports – An Overview and Analysis of Reports in Practice** provides an assessment of Social Return on Investment (SROI) as an instrument of reporting the value that (non-profit) organizations in the SES have created.

The next two following chapters provide reflections on online accountability in the social economy. In this way:

- **Chapter 10: Disclosure of Corporate Social Responsibility on the Websites of Portuguese Foundations** aims to assess how the Portuguese foundations manage and disclosure information about Corporate Social Responsibility on their websites.
- **Chapter 11: Evaluation of the Online Accountability of the Portuguese Private Institutions of Social Solidarity** intends to ascertain whether the Private Institutions of Social Solidarity in Portugal have conditions to comply with the mandatory disclosure under the law.

The next four chapters focus on subjects such as the impact of the social economy sector, the accountancy and taxation systems as a promotion of the discipline of patronage refunds, and the circular economy as a promise that can refocus society towards the values of stewardship. Thus:

- **Chapter 12: Realities and Challenges of the Social Enterprises in South-Eastern European Countries – Comparative Analysis** focuses on mapping the sector of social economy in some states from South-Eastern Europe, presenting their role and impact due to the activities achieved in society.
- **Chapter 13: Public Services and the Power of (Non)Communication** tries to compare the well-being and quality of life (the older terms were public value or solidarity) with public goods inside and outside public services.
- **Chapter 14: Distributing Mutual Advantages in Italian Cooperatives – An Analysis of Patronage Refunds** based on the mutuality principle, as far as the patronage refunds' discipline is concerned, aims to understand whether the related accounting and taxation systems follow such logic.
- **Chapter 15: Circular Economy for India – Perspectives on Stewardship Principles, Waste Management, and Energy Generation** discusses the original ideals of stewardship and how colonization caused a deterioration of this philosophy in favor of materialistic wealth generations. The chapter advances that the circular economy holds promise as a new economic system and philosophy that can drive society towards the values of stewardship.

Augusta Ferreira
University of Aveiro, Portugal

Rui Marques
University of Aveiro, Portugal

Graça Azevedo
University of Aveiro, Portugal

Helena Inácio
University of Aveiro, Portugal

Carlos Santos
University of Aveiro, Portugal

Acknowledgment

The editors would like to thank the support of all the people involved in this project and, more specifically, the authors and reviewers who took part in the review process. Their effort was an outstanding contribution to this publication process. Without their support, this book would not have become a reality.

First, the editors would like to thank each of the chapters' authors who contributed with their time and expertise to this book.

Second, the editors wish to acknowledge the excellent and valuable work of the Editorial Advisory Board members regarding the improvement of quality, coherence, and content presentation of chapters which ensured the highest accuracy in the double-blinded review process. Most of the authors also served as referees; we highly appreciate their double task.

Augusta Ferreira
University of Aveiro, Portugal

Rui Marques
University of Aveiro, Portugal

Graça Azevedo
University of Aveiro, Portugal

Helena Inácio
University of Aveiro, Portugal

Carlos Santos
University of Aveiro, Portugal

Acknowledgment

Chapter 1
Modernization and Accountability in the Social Economy: A Systematic Review

Carlos Santos
https://orcid.org/0000-0001-9728-8538
University of Aveiro, Portugal

Rui Marques
https://orcid.org/0000-0001-8449-0526
University of Aveiro, Portugal

Augusta Ferreira
https://orcid.org/0000-0003-1659-3309
University of Aveiro, Portugal

Graça Azevedo
https://orcid.org/0000-0002-6346-4035
University of Aveiro, Portugal

Helena Inácio
https://orcid.org/0000-0003-1281-2156
University of Aveiro, Portugal

ABSTRACT

This chapter aims to systematically review the literature on modernization and accountability practice in the social economy. The collection of bibliography to support this systematic review was made in several scientific databases, only considering documents written in English. The criteria for researching the documents used in the development of this chapter are explained in the section that presents the methodology. It is possible to verify that only two articles published in the 20th century, 1997 and 1999, were identified, with all other articles published in the 21st century. This leads to the conclusion that the concern about the issue of accountability, particularly in social economy organizations, is relatively recent and has been of growing interest. The research is more focused on the accountability practice and not so much on modernization, although they are two inseparable issues.

DOI: 10.4018/978-1-5225-8482-7.ch001

INTRODUCTION

The accountability practice, associated with the social economy, questions the mechanisms of internal control (performance reports, program evaluations, improvement of legislative supervision, strengthening of audit mechanisms, etc.) implemented in organizations of this sector, which, in some way, are connected to the public administration. However, the concept itself is difficult to conceptualize and can be interpreted as the relation between ownership and control, justifying the efforts in the development of comparative analyses on the issue of the accountability practice in the different areas of the social economy (Brandsen, van Hout, Vrielink, & Schillemans, 2008; Eeckloo, Van Herck, Van Hulle, & Vleugels, 2004; Humphrey & Erickson, 1997; Schwartz & Sharkansky, 2000).

The accountability practice is, to a large extent, obviously related to modernization, which is often associated with the migratory flows of populations from small villages to large urban centers, seen as a paradigm of human development (Bakar, Arshad, Pauzi, Mamat, & Omar, 2017), and has, of course, an impact on the formation of new types of knowledge. According to Rotheroe and Richards (2007), as knowledge increases, so does the need to incorporate new mechanisms into the internal control organizational system with an impact on accountability and, consequently, on improving accuracy and transparency of organizational negotiation processes. Also, globalization and the growing involvement of social economy organizations in responding to various social needs associated to modernization have altered the traditional way of assessing and monitoring accountability in these organizations (Choudhury & Ahmed, 2002; Molnar, 2004).

In the context of modernization, new information and communication technologies (ICT) should not be forgotten. Their adoption has created new paradigms of relationships among different entities, people or organizations, naturally fostering their networking, with all the challenges that this organizational governance poses at a time when rigor and transparency are increasingly demanded. Thus, the new ICT, in providing new approaches and new challenges, also bring new requirements which materialize in the need to define and implement new organizational strategies, which maintain the rigor of internal control mechanisms and accountability practice (Williamson & Bond, 2014). The accountability practice can be considered from two perspectives: the internal perspective, whose objective is to verify whether the economic-financial balance is based on an internal control system associated with the organizational information system, implemented by the management body; and the external perspective, when it includes the participation of external auditing entities, with the objective of evaluating and monitoring the accountability practice carried out by the organization before the community, in which it is inserted, taking into account all the resources associated with their mission (Hoffman, 2009; Preite & De Matteis, 2014).

The better the supervisory mechanisms, the greater the compliance with the regulatory framework by organizations associated with the social economy. Considering that these mechanisms are perfected in function of the knowledge acquired about a given reality, it is not difficult to see that modernization has a great impact on the accountability practice and hence on the level of trust on the part of their stakeholders. If the level of compliance with the normative framework is low, problems with accountability practice tend to increase.

Accountability in non-profit organizations is not only a concern of nowadays. Humphrey and Erickson (1997) developed a study to evaluate the level of accountability practice in non-profit industrial development organizations. These organizations, important in the United States of America, act as channels through which high public funding is channeled to the communities and companies located there. In view of their status, these organizations are exempt from taxation. In addition, they may also receive private financial contributions, with specific deductions for their donors. Their financing represents a substantial public investment with the objective of strengthening social development, which is why the accountability practice, fostering a culture of rigor and transparency in the governance of these organizations, is fundamental to their stakeholders.

For a large number of non-profit organizations, some of the accountability issues, particularly with regard to the financial side of these entities, have been scrutinized and have resulted in significant changes in their practices. However, for many other organizations, including the social economy, in particular religious organizations, accountability is still taking its first steps in its development. Brown (2001) analyzes the internal and external forces that have driven the transformation of accountability practice associated with the tax side of religious organizations and the challenges they face as they attempt to implement the changes needed to improve accountability practice.

One of the aspects of non-profit organizations is that they can provide services to society through various works, namely social welfare, in order to facilitate the development of communities. These organizations can also provide disaster relief and support the most disadvantaged and needy populations. In order for this support to be implemented, these organizations need to secure various financial and non-financial support, usually provided by stakeholders. These stakeholders expect beneficiary organizations to provide rigorous and transparent information related to accountability practice (Atan & Zainon, 2009).

Social economy organizations need to identify the resources entrusted to them and which affect their performance. The management of these resources is important to ensure the accountability practice and, consequently, its sustainability (Roshayani Arshad, Samad, Kamaluddin, & Roslan, 2016). Thus, the accountability practice plays a decisive role in promoting the authenticity and moral foundations of effective leadership. Leadership with these characteristics may help avoid inappropriate organizational behavior, which does not follow the principles of rigor and transparency (Siddiq, Meyer, & Ashleigh, 2013).

Historically, the accountability practice in non-profit organizations has been imperfect or non-existent. In part, the difficulties in implementing and operating internal control mechanisms in this type of organization can result from the fundamental role of social, philosophical, moral or religious values shared by their stakeholders (McDonald, 1999). Nonetheless, the difference in values may exist, regardless of whether the accountability practice is being developed and implemented in a similar way, or the type of organization, whether for profit or not (Saita & Franceschelli, 2016).

Because they are organizations with a high motivational index and with an organizational structure with some specificity, social economy organizations are able to solve situations that the State and the private sector can not solve well and reliably. However, for these organizations the accountability practice has become an increasingly relevant issue for their functioning, because they must be concerned about obtaining and maintaining the trust of their beneficiaries, employees and other stakeholders (Atan & Zainon, 2009).

The social and environmental impact, in the development of the communities in which they are inserted, facilitated by the organizations associated with the social economy, should be duly evaluated and monitored. This evaluation and monitoring should be carried out by implementing adequate accountability practices, thus providing assurance to their financiers, who can always know how their support (public or private) has been used. The accountability practice should not be limited to the fulfillment of the minimum normative requirements, but rather go beyond them, in an attempt to satisfy their stakeholders (Conroy, 2005; Corazza & Cisi, 2012; Lorenz, 2008).

In order to identify the impact of globalization, Choudhury and Ahmed (2002) used a framework for the practice of multiple accountability, in which they crossed the regime normally associated with the social economy organizations based in the Northern Hemisphere, with the social economy organizations based in the Southern Hemisphere. These authors identified an emerging pattern involving compliance, negotiation, professionalism, and institutional strengthening relationships in both Hemispheres.

As can be seen, the issues that arise within organizations connected to the social economy sector are global and point to the need to develop a facilitating framework for the accountability of these organizations, both financially and non-financially, giving comfort to their potential patrons, as a good accountability practice offers rigor and transparency to the processes of organizational governance (Santos, Ferreira, Marques, & Azevedo, 2018; Tenbensel, Dwyer, & Lavoie, 2014)

METHODOLOGY

A systematic review is an appropriate methodology, within the context of a research on the organizations attached to the social economy sector. However, it is important that this review is made in a sufficiently comprehensive manner to respond to the research question posed (Kelly, 2011). Also according to Kelly (2011), a systematic review that offers rigor and replicability must include certain standards adequate for research, namely: a research protocol; the specificity of the question to be explored; identification of relevant literature; quality of the literature found, and synthesis of the results.

In this chapter, the authors seek to identify and evaluate the impact of modernization and accountability on the functioning of social economy organizations. The term "social economy" is not an absolutely consensual term, as there are several other terms that can be used in the same sense or closely associated with the social economy. Thus, after a brief review in the social economy, the following terms were considered as suitably framed in this thematic: "social economy"; "social solidarity"; "social capital"; and "social enterprise". In addition to these terms, the following terms were also taken into account: "third sector" and "non-profit". These terms were individually crossed with "accountability" and "modernization".

According to the protocol defined above, the authors have developed a systematic review work by carefully reading several scientific articles collected from the following repositories of scientific articles: library of online knowledge (b-on); Google Scholar; Dialnet; DOAJ (Directory of Open Access Journal); SCIELO (Scientific Electronic Library Online) and SSRN (Social Science Research Network). The collection of scientific articles in these repositories, with the research criteria identified above, took place during the months of May and June 2018, justifying the reduced number of articles published in 2018.

As already mentioned, research was conducted on each of the pairs of the aforementioned terms, placed in the title of the documents. Only documents written in English were considered, and all duplicate documents were excluded. This research process allowed 74 documents to be found and analyzed, and their distribution per year is shown in Figure 1.

In Figure 1, we can observe that the trend line (dashed line) indicates that there has been an increasing publication initiative on this subject. Of the 74 articles collected, only 10 are specifically oriented to issues of modernization, and the remaining ones are directed towards accountability practice.

Figure 1. Distribution of articles consulted per year

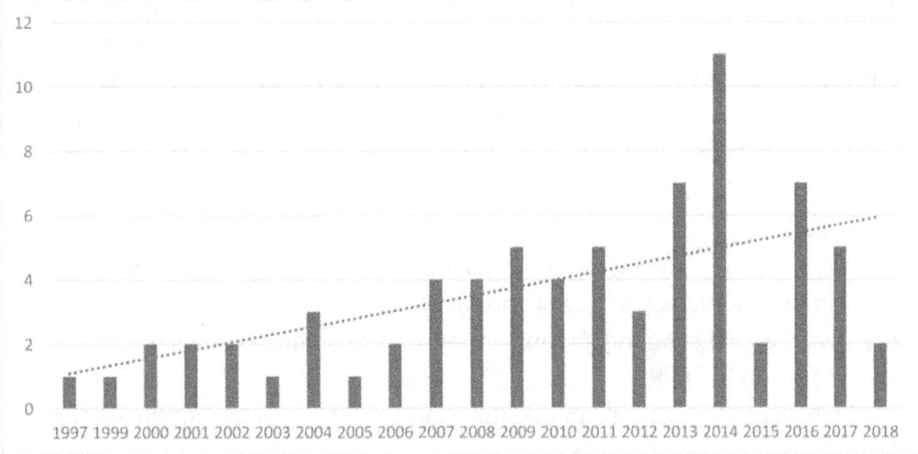

MODERNIZATION

Modernization has contributed decisively to the advances that have taken place in medicine, with a decisive impact on the average life expectancy, which has thus placed high social and political pressure on policy makers. One of the aspects of this pressure is that the performance of the organizations related to the social welfare of the elderly (belonging, therefore, to the social economy) should be evaluated and monitored with appropriate instruments. Kendall and Knapp (2000) evaluated the contribution of social economy organizations in the United Kingdom, focusing on social well-being and defined it in a comparative international context. This study concludes that those responsible for formulating public policies can not abandon or neglect social welfare. However, they should focus on the modernization and restructuring of social economy organizations.

Bisin and Guaitoli (2006) developed a study in order to analyze the dynamics of accumulation of human social capital through modernization processes and sought to explain how the growth of human capital can be accompanied by a loss of social capital (see concept at the end of the chapter). They also sought to identify the countries that have succeeded and those that have failed in this process and the respective reasons for such success or failure. To do so, the authors studied the social capital structure developed in rural and traditional economies, comparing it with the new role of social capital in urban environments, as a function of the index of modernization and development. The pattern of family socialization before and after modernization attempts played a key role in the analysis. This study led to the conclusion that human capital growth may, in fact, be accompanied by a loss of social capital.

Larsson (2007) suggested that modernization can have two antagonistic effects. It may be detrimental to social capital from the perspective of individualized trust (one entity can trust another in a given subject), and it can be beneficial to social capital from the perspective of generalized trust (one entity can rely on another even if unknown and in an extended context). This author concluded that there is a relatively strong relationship between modernization and trust, but it is not easily measurable.

Modernization is associated across all human activities, with enormous impact on social aspects. Mustafa and Qazi (2007) analyzed the social aspects associated with the water distribution system in Balochistan, province of Pakistan. In particular, they used social capital as a conceptual lens that allows us to perceive the dimensions of the social transition, which accompanies the change in the irrigation system used. The authors concluded that the modernization of the irrigation system in Balochistan may not only have had ecological and economic consequences but also social ones. These may be due to the social capital built around the new technique and, although they have not been evaluated yet, they are very likely to be negative.

At another level, political changes as part of modernization actions have had a significant impact on the role traditionally assumed by social economy organizations. For example, the United Kingdom has increasingly sought social economy organizations to engage in the provision of public services (Di Domenico, Tracey, & Haugh, 2009).

The recent speech on modernization, around the management capacity, commercialization and training leads to think about the need to modernize the organizations related to the social economy (Scott, 2010). This author focused on the importance of developing alternatives led by the social economy, with the aim of minimizing the existing asymmetries in the sector.

Ciftci (2010) sought to explain the determinants of the impact of modernization brought about by democratization in ten Muslim countries by testing two alternatives: social capital and Islamic values. This author concluded that the cultural attitudes generated by modernization and education have enormous explanatory power.

Tai (2011) intended to verify whether modernization in general leads to the decline of traditional social models in Kenyan rural villages. The analysis by Tai (2011) showed that, in part, modernization has an impact on the social capital of Kenyan rural communities.

The effects of different modernization processes between social capital and status acquisition in the Netherlands were studied by Sprok (2013). This author concluded that modernization processes seem to have a negative impact on established social relationships in a given community.

According to Titov (2013), in the context of the distribution of social capital as a condition for the modernization of Russian society, a relevant question arises concerning the presence or absence of a relationship between modernization as a process and "modernity" as a result on the one hand, and the factor of social capital on the other. Belyaeva (2014) examined issues that can be established between multiple modernization and social capital in Russia. Social capital is considered as a factor that determines the specificities and pace of modernization. This author says that societies with developed social capital, including a high level of trust, civic identity and positive social relations, have more favorable opportunities for modernization.

From the foregoing, modernization has a significant impact on all economic and social aspects, in particular on the functioning of social economy organizations. Thus, we must take advantage of modernization and implement new mechanisms that improve the accountability practice in social economy organizations. The improvement of this practice can bring great benefits to social economy organizations, considering that potential investors in these organizations will feel more comfortable deciding on this form of patronage.

ACCOUNTABILITY

Schwartz and Sharkansky (2000) explored the possibility, expressed in the literature, that social economy organizations can be a solution to solve the so-called crisis of accountability practice. This crisis originated in the difficulty experienced by public entities in being able to ensure complete rigor and transparency in their financial statements. These authors based their work on assessing a set of social economy organizations located in Israel. They also concluded that the work done in Israel can be replicated to other countries.

Some of the dysfunctions found in the accountability practice, according to Schwartz and Sharkansky (2000), may be due to the attempt to obtain direct and/or indirect benefits from some politicians, their relatives, friends and/or colleagues of party. These authors conclude that there is still much work to be done to make possible the characterization of the best types of accountability practices, which are appropriate to the specificities of the various organizational typologies within the social economy.

Schwartz (2001) stated that Israel's attempts to improve the accountability practice in social economy organizations, which collaborate with the public administration to meet social needs, were not successful. This because some of the actors involved have mutual interests to maintain some ambiguity about the rules of collaboration between those organizations and the State.

According to Goodin (2003), there are several strategic factors that advise social economy organizations to be rigorous and transparent, even in the absence of any formal or informal relationships in their accountability practice. Thus, these organizations must carry out their business processes with a level of rigor and transparency that is not yet commonplace in the profitable organizations sector.

Lee, Chen and Weiner (2004) aimed to find some link between wealth funds, the level of accountability practice, and service delivery to the community. In this study, a sample of health service providers located in the United States of America was used and the conclusions indicate that organizations with larger wealth funds do not necessarily implement more and better mechanisms to facilitate accountability practice.

From the perspective of Rotheroe and Richards (2007), sustainability is a dynamic concept, and it is fundamental that social economy organizations understand this fact. Thus, the increase of knowledge makes more evident the need to incorporate new mechanisms for accountability practice in the organizational structure. After establishing a theoretical framework to discuss this issue, these authors analyzed the social return on investment in an organization based in Liverpool, in the United Kingdom, based on conventional accounting principles. They identified some qualities of sustainability and concluded that the inclusion of stakeholders in the process is relevant to allow greater aptitude for accountability practice.

Aimers and Walker (2008a) analyzed several research papers from New Zealand between 1998 and 2008 that identified alternative models for accountability practice. This analysis aimed to evaluate the success of social economy organizations. After the analysis, the aforementioned authors systematized a set of tools with which social economy organizations can select the most adequate accountability model within their organizational practices, thus allowing a pluralistic approach to accountability practice.

Aimers and Walker (2008b) studied the problems of partnerships established between social economy organizations and the State that jeopardized their relationships with the community in which they were inserted. From the research emerged three models related to accountability practice observed in New Zealand organizations, which can help strengthen the insertion of social economy organizations in their communities. In this sense, the authors promoted the necessary adjustments so that the mentioned models were appropriate to the functioning of social economy organizations, enhancing the accountability practices.

Brandsen *et al.* (2008) considered that the practice of social accountability is difficult to define and their knowledge, at the time of the study, was still limited. These authors carried out several studies on this subject in the Netherlands, which culminated in an extensive comparative project in seven areas of social sciences. Despite still at a preliminary stage, the results suggest that although there are many tools and activities associated with social responsibility, and although that it can make a useful contribution to current governance systems, its effects are still limited.

Di Domenico *et al.* (2009) theorized about the political changes that led to the involvement of social economy organizations in the provision of public services in the United Kingdom. They criticized the arguments for this involvement and suggested that it could pose specific challenges in relation to community involvement and accountability. They concluded that the social economy emerged as an important force in the UK economy.

Claibourn and Martin (2007) verified whether the practice of political accountability (citizens' ability to hold the government accountable for the policies pursued) was reinforced by citizen participation in associative movements relevant to the social economy, and concluded that this participation facilitates, in fact, the practice of political accountability.

Over a period of ten to fifteen years, Nowland-Foreman (2009) studied the impact of external agents on accountability, especially in resource-dependent contexts. The study was based on the interaction with managers of social economy organizations in New Zealand and allowed to conclude that positive and negative aspects of the impact of external agents can be identified in the accountability practice. However, the prevailing experience of externally imposed requirements for accountability practice does not seem to have a relevant effect.

Awio, Northcott and Lawrence (2011) conducted a study which aimed to analyze how social economy organizations are responsible for their functioning and how the accountability practice places them before the citizens, who are beneficiaries of their services. This study concluded that by leveraging the status of social economy organizations associated with their social capital, these can complement the formal obligations of accountability by implementing a bottom-up approach associated with a group of stakeholders often neglecting the beneficiaries of the service.

Sangole, Kaaria, Njuki, Lewa and Mapila (2014) carried out a study in order to assess how participatory monitoring and evaluation by society, on the one hand, strengthens social capital and, on the other hand, affects the perception of performance, having an impact on accountability practice for resources, decision-making and leadership. The study corroborated the first two questions, not doing so in relation to the third question.

Zainon *et al.* (2014) discussed the principles of legitimacy and sustainability of social economy organizations in Malaysia, necessary for these organizations to carry out their mission with rigor and transparency (accountability practice).

Kamaluddin, Hasan, Arshad and Samah (2016) participated in a study to investigate the relationship between social capital and small and medium-sized enterprises in Malaysia. The results provided evidence that social capital, one of the key intangible assets of any organization, is vital to its functioning and sustainably influences its performance.

Irene and Dwiningrum (2016) explained the basic concepts of social capital and accountability practice and evaluated this practice, the quality of education and the role of social capital in the implementation of accountability practice in an educational institution. They concluded that the accountability practice in educational institutions needs to be socialized for the development of education. The accountability practice results from individual and institutional synergies.

Campos and Alcoforado (2018) conducted a study whose objective was to contribute to the analysis of the deficiencies and challenges of the Brazilian federal regulatory system, which regulates the access of social economy organizations to public financing and their role in the provision of services.

Barrett (2001) was concerned about responsiveness and accountability practice in non-profit organizations and stated that these organizations offer a wide range of services including sports, arts, culture and social services, and that the latter has been experiencing great growth.

Candler and Dumont (2010) studied a framework to facilitate the accountability practice in non-profit organizations. This framework was developed based on the broader scientific literature, which considers studies carried out not only in non-profit organizations but also in other sectors of the economy. The framework considered takes into account a comprehensive set of stakeholders to whom nonprofits must be accountable, as well as a set of resources for which they are also accountable.

The study of Conroy (2005) analyzed two frameworks proposed in previous studies on accountability practice and sought to know, to what extent, these frameworks can be applied to non-profit organizations, because the stakeholders of these organizations demand rigor and transparency in their governance. The study showed that the non-profit organizations should drop the idea that they are not subject to the rules of accountability practice increasingly demanded by their stakeholders. Furthermore, it also concluded that the frameworks analyzed are valid for all sectors of the economy.

Mullins (2006) analyzed the impact of accountability practice on the basis of its growth in the last 25 years, becoming a dimension to be addressed in the context of organizations dedicated to social housing. The author concluded that there has been a long process of significant political changes in which it was necessary to respond to an increase in the needs of social housing, maintaining the logic of accountability practice in this sector.

Gourdie and Rees (2009) reviewed the views of the managing bodies of three non-profit entities operating in the Waikato area of New Zealand to assess the challenges posed in the implementation of accountability mechanisms required by their stakeholders. This study, as noted, was limited to analyzing three non-profit organizations in the Waikato area of New Zealand and only the accountability practice between funders and beneficiary organizations. Thus, this analysis may not be broadly representative.

Costa, Ramus and Andreaus (2011) analyzed the accountability practice implemented in a particular type of non-profit organizations in Italy which provides services for voluntary associations. The objective of this research was to verify if the accountability practice adopted by those organizations responds to their information needs and fulfills the demands of their stakeholders. According to the authors, this study evaluated how accountability practice can affect the effectiveness and achievement of the mission of non-profit organizations. They stated that the accountability practice of the organizations studied is predominantly oriented to the economic-financial dimension and not to the social dimension, due to the difficulty found to objectively define the quantifiable variables for the social activities of the organizations studied and also given the pressure of funders and control bodies.

Arshad, Bakar, Thani and Omar (2013) developed a study in which they evaluated the influence of the composition of the management bodies at the level of the mechanisms, facilitating the accountability practice. This study was conducted within a group of non-profit organizations in Malaysia and provides relevant indications for understanding the relationships between the various governing bodies' compositions and the level of accountability practice.

In addition, Bakar, Arshad, Azman and Omar (2013) sought to find some impact of organizational characteristics on accountability practice in non-profit organizations. This study was also carried out with a sample of organizations in Malaysia and provides relevant indications for understanding the relationships between the various organizational characteristics and the level of accountability practice. This study is in line with other studies (Azman, Arshad, & Bakar, 2015; Bakar et al., 2014; Omar & Arshad, 2016).

Shuib, Said and Atan (2014) studied the impact of financial management practices, the level of accountability practice and the effectiveness of management bodies in the performance of non-profit organizations in Malaysia. The results obtained in this study showed that financial management practices and the effectiveness of management bodies have a significant impact on the financial performance of non-profit organizations. They also showed that the accountability practice has no significant impact on their financial performance.

Dainelli, Manetti and Sibilio (2013) analyzed the validity of stakeholder theory with a focus on accountability practice within the national museums located in the most developed countries: Australia; Canada; France; Germany; Italy and the United Kingdom. They concluded that stakeholder theory implies that the accountability practice depends on the strength and the number of stakeholders involved in the organizations.

Becker (2018) presented a conceptual framework that distinguishes four voluntary forms of the accountability practice in the scope of non-profit organizations, considering the context of agency theory. The main results of this study revealed considerable differences between the four forms of accountability practice in non-profit organizations.

Finnaly, Atan, Alam and Said (2017) examined the integrity of nonprofits and their impact on accountability practice. The results showed that organizational integrity contributed significantly to the accountability practice in non-profit organizations.

MODERNIZATION AND ACCOUNTABILITY

Modernization and accountability are synergistic and cross-cutting concepts across all sectors of the economy, including the social economy. The progressive increase in the level of knowledge originated by modernization has an impact on the development and implementation of more rigorous and transparent internal control mechanisms that correspond to an improvement in the accountability practice in the organizational structure. In this context, Molnar (2004) proposes a tool for self-evaluation that tests the conformity of the normative framework with the accountability practice in social economy organizations. This tool consists of the use, with appropriate methodology, of a properly structured questionnaire.

Education, a relevant factor in the modernization of society, can play a fundamental role in the development of accountability practice. It is in this assumption that Baylor and Page (2016), as well as Ciftci (2010), showed their concern about issues related to the teaching of accountability practice, with emphasis on non-profit organizations. Porumbescu (2016) organized various training actions for managers of non-profit organizations in Ghana, Nigeria and Burkina Faso. These sessions addressed the challenges faced by these organizations in the accountability practice. The results of these training actions suggest that the implementation of adequate mechanisms for a good accountability practice is not simple and that the commitment to education is one of the ways to consistently prepare social economy organizations and their stakeholders for accountability.

Maddocks, Novkovic and Smith (2011) presented the results of a joint social economy project between an independent education entity and its stakeholders. The project aimed to find ways to improve the communication and demonstration of the results of the teaching entity as part of the accountability practice between this institution and its stakeholders. These ways of improving communication and dissemination of results can be successfully implemented by using the new information and communication technologies that have had enormous development. The innovation that has occurred in the modernization of these technologies provides new functionalities that can be used with advantage in the implementation of mechanisms to facilitate accountability and for the communication and dissemination of financial and non-financial information.

Maddocks *et al.* (2011) concluded that all social economy organizations, aligned with democratic principles, could benefit from the involvement of their stakeholders and the development of specific processes, based on the practice of shared accountability. They also considered important the process of implementing an appropriate organizational structure that addresses the objectives of the organization, including the accountability practice.

Although there is research on the accountability practice in various types of organizations, both public and private sectors, Connolly and Kelly (2011) consider that the social economy organizations, comparatively to the others, have been given little attention, and therefore lack such studies. Given this gap, Connolly and Kelly (2011) proposed the use of a framework based on the accountability practice, the legitimacy and the needs of its users.

Baumüller and Haring (2014) compared the normative framework of accounting mechanisms used in German-speaking countries and described their similarities and differences. They found that stakeholders in social economy organizations rely on the financial statements of these organizations to support their decisions and that the normative framework has less impact than market mechanisms in defining the principles of accountability practice.

Donleavy and Ghoorah-Hurrychurn (2014) analyzed a set of papers on financial information disclosure in social economy organizations in Australia. On the basis of this analysis they sought to explain the reason behind the choice of information disseminated by those organizations and tried to find a pattern that would justify the differences. They concluded that the disclosure of financial information is undoubtedly related to the new information and communication technologies, highlighting the Internet as a valuable aid to improve accountability practice.

However, despite the substantial effort to address the concerns associated with accountability and to assume that this social practice is an important facilitator of third sector organizations, the concept of accountability, by disseminating the financial and non-financial information, and their role are not sufficiently specified or theorized (Nobari, 2015). Thus, this author developed a study in which he defined a practical model of accountability in the area of "social accounting", while exploring the concept of "social impact measurement" and its purpose within the organizational structure. This author also says that so far there is limited knowledge about the role that accountability practices play in the life of organizations and how that relationship can have an impact, for example, on their DNA. This study also responds to the limitation of studies that investigate organizational changes as a result of the social impact measurement exercise.

Karamoy, Pangemanan and Ilat (2017) conducted a study in the Netherlands in which they examined issues related to the performance of social economy organizations comparatively with the benefits they bring to the communities in which they operate. They also analyzed the influence of their stakeholders on their way of functioning and discussed their accountability practice. The results show that stakeholders need information on the efficiency and effectiveness of the activities carried out by social economy organizations, even though it is empirically shown that it is difficult to get all stakeholders to have full access to the financial statements of an organization.

Atan and Zainon (2009) analyzed the importance of some issues related to the mechanisms of accountability practice implemented in non-profit organizations. The study focused on a sample of organizations in Malaysia and sought to ascertain whether these organizations are concerned with accountability and, if so, what approaches are used to implement this practice. They concluded that the accountability practice has become an increasingly relevant issue, not only for business organizations and government agencies but also for non-profit organizations, which must have as their fundamental concern to capture and retain the trust of their stakeholders.

Basri and Siti-Nabiha (2010) analyzed a number of relevant issues in the area of accountability by non-profit organizations. They have done so in view of the particular nature of these organizations and also the relationship of trust and its impact on formal and informal models of accountability, specifically with regard to the use of financial reporting. They concluded that, over the last decades, concerns about the practice of non-profit sector accountability have been raised, with special emphasis on the adequacy of current reporting and supervision mechanisms. Stakeholders want to make sure that these organizations are managed properly. The importance of accountability practice in non-profit organizations, with emphasis on the adequate treatment of the resources entrusted to them, is well documented in the management and accounting literature.

Stone and Wilbanks (2012) carried out a study in which they analyzed the content of 96 institutional websites, belonging to non-profit organizations, with the objective of identifying and evaluating the levels of accountability practice existing in this type of organizations. The results obtained by these authors demonstrate that although most non-profit organizations provide information on their websites to attract funders and volunteers, this information is not sufficiently clear to assist potential funders in the decision making. This suggests that there are still improvements to be made regarding nonprofit accountability practice.

Boon, Greatbanks, Munro and Gaffney (2017) addressed the challenges related to the appropriate disclosure of financial information, namely regarding the quality of service and value to the various stakeholders. The authors concluded that although various accountability practices have been developed within the framework of non-profit organizations, tensions related to their practice continue to increase. For many nonprofits there are multiple entities, individuals, and organizations with diverse interests in the accountability practice.

Corazza and Cisi (2012) presented a case in which the organization seeked to increase its levels of rigor and transparency. For this purpose it decided to focus on an approach, in which the preparation of reports is more appropriate to be used by single-stakeholders (each of the stakeholders), based on non-financial data together with the traditional methods of producing the social report and financial statements. The authors verified that the report was effectively used in a single-stakeholder logic by interviewing the people to whom the report was sent.

The practice of social accountability, taking into account the aforementioned, can be associated with its governance processes and the environment in which the organizations are inserted. Jottier and Heyndels (2012) found a positive relationship between the quality of governance and the electoral results verified in the community. The authors believe that this relationship will be stronger in the communities with the highest index of social capital and that will translate into high accountability practice, leading to a better governance performance.

A study by Nannicini, Stella, Tabellini and Troiano (2013) sought to find evidence of the way in which social capital can improve the social and economic well-being of social economy organizations in Italy, as well as the practice of political accountability. Still, according to these authors, there is empirical evidence that shows that electoral punishment of behavioral deviations from governance is considerably higher in communities with higher social capital index.

Zainon *et al.* (2014) have developed a system that integrates financial information with non-financial information, in the perspective of being able to improve the quality and efficiency of disclosure of financial information, and thus promote the accountability practice. They concluded that the developed system could provide a relevant contribution to ensure sustainable practices as a complementary form of accountability practice.

Roslan, Arshad, Farahah and Pauzi (2017) analyzed in Malaysia the level of financial information and non-financial information disclosed in the annual reports of non-profit organizations, and concluded that the quality of this information can improve accountability in non-profit organizations.

The use of new information and communication technologies facilitated by the improvement of the educational levels of the communities in which the social economy organizations are inserted, as part of a modernization process, can be used to create institutional websites for social economy organizations, making this able to disclose financial and non-financial information. Hence, all their stakeholders can assess their performance and, consequently, improve their accountability.

As websites are used for the dissemination of information about the organization, the maturity of these websites is also an important matter. Santos *et al.* (2018) propose an index for periodic evaluation of institutional websites of the direct and indirect administration of the State, which should be reviewed periodically to evaluate the need to introduce improvements in the light of the technological advances and also of the evolution of legislative and regulatory framework related to e-government. This index can be adapted to evaluate and monitor the accountability practice of social economy organizations with many advantages.

The index proposed by Santos *et al.* (2018) has holistic characteristics as it encompasses the online presence of three relevant dimensions, associated with the accountability practice: online quality; online financial and performance reporting; and online services. In addition, it can be very useful to generate possible improvement actions on the institutional websites of social economy organizations and also a motivation for stakeholders. If stakeholders realize that the institutional websites of social economy organizations are of good quality, and that they provide a good financial and performance report online and online services, they will feel motivated to access those institutions through their website with all the advantages derived therefrom, not only for the stakeholders but also for the institutions concerned.

Measuring the level of accountability practice by assessing the maturity of institutional websites will help to improve the rigor and transparency of social economy organizations. This assessment is very important because social economy organizations have been pressured through specific legislation so that they are responsible for managing the resources that are attached to them.

FINAL REMARKS AND FUTURE WORK

In the light of what has been exposed in the previous sections, studies on the social economy are still in a small amount, but the trend is increasing, showing the growing interest in this research area. It is also concluded that modernization has an impact on the economic and social aspects of social economy organizations. Therefore, it is necessary to start with modernization to implement new mechanisms that improve the accountability practice in this type of organization. It was also evidenced that the accountability practice is an element of recognized merit for a good performance of social economy organizations. However, the absence of a framework that allows adequate implementation of mechanisms of accountability in its various dimensions is a limiting reality. As far as we could document, only Tenbensel *et al.* (2014) developed a framework that represents a considerable advance in this matter.

Considering the set of papers analyzed, it was also documented the need and the interest in combining modernization and accountability in order to enhance the sustainable growth of social economy organizations on the one hand, and to boost confidence of stakeholder groups of this type of organization on the other.

We should also note that a good accountability practice heavily depends on the quality of the internal control mechanisms. Thus, we conclude that modernization and accountability practice have a significant impact on the design of new internal control systems, which are crucial for the the functioning of organizations within the social economy. These conclusions fully justify a considerable effort to be made in the study of social economy organizations, in particular in the study of the accountability practice, which keeps the stakeholders aligned with the purpose that is given to the resources they manage. The integration of these organizations with the communities in which they are inserted allow the establishment of close relationships between their stakeholders and the institutions, resulting in great advantages for the development of the community, namely the establishment of new forms of relationship, favoring the personalized and individual relationship with each stakeholder, making them have a high level of relationship by interacting with high levels of trust.

Future work may be developed to enable further research into accountability and performance of social economy organizations, thereby making it possible to objectify the meaning of accountability by making it clear to all stakeholders, and thus facilitate their funding. A better understanding of social economy organizations and the existence of a consistent accountability practice with high levels of trust can facilitate the emergence of new patrons interested in funding these organizations. Further work can be developed in the future, with the aim of applying to social economy organizations the index proposed by Santos *et al.* (2018), which, having holistic characteristics, could be of great use to generate possible actions of improvement in institutional websites of social economy organizations, and also to motivate stakeholders.

REFERENCES

Aimers, J., & Walker, P. (2008a). Alternative models of accountability for third sector organisations in New Zealand. *Eighth International Conference of the International Society for Third Sector Research*. Retrieved from https://c.ymcdn.com/sites/istr.site-ym.com/resource/resmgr/working_papers_barcelona/Aimers.Walker.pdf

Aimers, J., & Walker, P. (2008b). Is community accoutability being overlooked as a result of government-third sector partnering in New Zealand. *Aotearoa New Zealand Social Work Review*, *XX*(3), 14–24.

Arshad, R., Bakar, N., Thani, N., & Omar, N. (2013). Board composition and accountability of non-profit organizations. *Journal of Applied Business Research*, *29*(4), 1021–1030. doi:10.19030/jabr.v29i4.7913

Arshad, R., Samad, N., Kamaluddin, A., & Roslan, N. (2016). Intellectual capital, accountability and sustainability in non-profit organizations. *Asian Journal of Scientific Research*, *9*(2), 62–70. doi:10.3923/ajsr.2016.62.70

Atan, R., Alam, M. M., & Said, J. (2017). Practices of corporate integrity and accountability of non-profit organizations in Malaysia. *International Journal of Social Economics*, *44*(12), 2271–2286. doi:10.1108/IJSE-09-2016-0260

Atan, R., & Zainon, S. (2009). In Defence of Non-Profit Accountability. Finance & Accounting, 29(40), 399–402. doi:10.1017/epi.2014.33

Awio, G., Northcott, D., & Lawrence, S. (2011). Social capital and accountability in grass-roots NGOs. *Accounting, Auditing & Accountability Journal*, *24*(1), 63–92. doi:10.1108/09513571111098063

Azman, N., Arshad, R., & Bakar, N. (2015). *Do Funding Resources Affect the Accountability Disclosure Of non-Profit Organizations*. Academic Press.

Bakar, N., Arshad, R., Azman, N., & Omar, N. (2013). Organisational characteristics and accountability in protecting risk exposures in non-profit organisations. *Journal of Energy Technologies and Policy*, *3*(11), 479–488. Retrieved from www.iiste.org

Bakar, N., Arshad, R., Azman, N., & Omar, N. (2014). Effective Governance Structure and Accountability in Managing Risks for Non-Profit Organizations. In *Proceedings of World Business And Economics Research Conference 24-25 February 2014* (pp. 1–16). Academic Press. Retrieved from http://www.ccsenet.org/journal/index.php/ibr/article/view/34859

Bakar, S., Arshad, R., Pauzi, N., Mamat, S., & Omar, N. (2017). Human Capital Management and Accountability of Social Enterprise. In *SHS Web of Conferences* (Vol. 36, p. 490). EDP Sciences.

Barrett, M. (2001). A Stakeholder Approach to Responsiveness and Accountability in Non-Profit Organisations. *Social Policy Journal of New Zealand*, (17), 36–51. Retrieved from http://www.msd.govt.nz/about-msd-and-our-work/publications-resources/journals-and-magazines/social-policy-journal/spj17/a-stakeholder-approach-to-responsiveness-and-accountability-in-non-profit-organisations.html

Basri, H., & Siti-Nabiha, A. K. (2010). Views on the issue of accountability in non-profit organizations. *Malaysian Management Journal*, *14*, 49–60.

Baumüller, J., & Haring, N. (2014). Enhancing Third Sector Accountability through Financial Accounting - Regulations and Practices in German-Speaking Countries. In International Society for Third-sector Research (ISTR) (pp. 1–20). Münster, Germany: Academic Press.

Baylor, A., & Page, D. F. (2016). *Developing a Pedagogy of Beneficiary Accountability in the Representation of Social* (Vol. 825). Academic Press.

Becker, A. (2018). An Experimental Study of Voluntary Nonprofit Accountability and Effects on Public Trust, Reputation, Perceived Quality, and Donation Behavior. *Nonprofit and Voluntary Sector Quarterly*, *47*(3), 562–582. doi:10.1177/0899764018756200

Belyaeva, L. A. (2014). On defining the problem: Regional social capital and multiple modernization in Russia. On defining the problem. *Economic and Social Changes: Facts, Trends, Forecast, 1*(31), 87–92. Retrieved from http://www.gurteen.com/gurteen/gurteen.nsf/id/L004680/

Bisin, A., & Guaitoli, D. (2006). *Social capital, modernization and growth*. Academic Press.

Boon, B., Greatbanks, R., Munro, J., & Gaffney, M. (2017). Service delivery under translation: Multi-stakeholder accountability in the non-profit community sector in New Zealand. *Health & Social Care in the Community, 25*(2), 402–413. doi:10.1111/hsc.12319 PMID:26710720

Brandsen, T., van Hout, E., Vrielink, M. O., & Schillemans, T. (2008). Social Accountability and the Third Sector: A Critical Appraisal. *International Workshop on Social Audit, Social Accounting and Accountability*, 1–22.

Brown, V. K. (2001). Non-profit accountability in faith-based organizations: Implications for philanthropy. *Journal of Ministry Marketing & Management, 7*(1), 1–8. doi:10.1300/J093v07n01_01

Campos, L., & Alcoforado, F. (2018). *Law, Government and Third Sector in Brazil: Improving deficient regulation to promote better accountability*. Academic Press.

Candler, G., & Dumont, G. (2010). A non-profit accountability framework. *Canadian Public Administration, 53*(2), 259–279. doi:10.1111/j.1754-7121.2010.00126.x

Choudhury, E., & Ahmed, S. (2002). The Shifting Meaning of Governance: Public Accountability of Third Sector Organizations in an Emergent Global Regime. *International Journal of Public Administration, 25*(4), 561–588. doi:10.1081/PAD-120013256

Ciftci, S. (2010). Modernization, Islam, or social capital: What explains attitudes toward democracy in the Muslim world? *Comparative Political Studies, 43*(11), 1442–1470. doi:10.1177/0010414010371903

Claibourn, M., & Martin, P. (2007). *The Third Face of Social Capital: How Membership in Voluntary Associations Improves Policy Accountability*. Academic Press. doi:10.1177/1065912907301766

Connolly, C., & Kelly, M. (2011). Understanding accountability in social enterprise organisations: A framework. *Social Enterprise Journal, 7*(3), 224–237. doi:10.1108/17508611111182386

Conroy, D. K. (2005). Non-profit organisations and accountability: A comment on the Mulgan and Sinclair frameworks. *Third Sector Review, 11*(1), 103–116.

Corazza, L., & Cisi, M. (2012). Accountability challenges in social enterprises and the implementation of a reporting standard an Italian case study. *The Journal of Social Business, 2*, 44–67.

Costa, E., Ramus, T., & Andreaus, M. (2011). Accountability as a Managerial Tool in Non-Profit Organizations: Evidence from Italian CSVs. *Voluntas, 22*(3), 470–493. doi:10.100711266-011-9183-7

Dainelli, F., Manetti, G., & Sibilio, B. (2013). Web-Based Accountability Practices in Non-profit Organizations: The Case of National Museums. *Voluntas, 24*(3), 649–665. doi:10.100711266-012-9278-9

Di Domenico, M., Tracey, P., & Haugh, H. (2009). Social economy involvement in public service delivery: Community engagement and accountability. *Regional Studies, 43*(7), 981–992. doi:10.1080/00343400701874180

Donleavy, G., & Ghoorah-Hurrychurn, U. (2014). Third Sector Accounting And Accountability In Australia: Anything But A Level Playing Field. *Australian Policy Online*. Retrieved from http://apo.org.au/node/52950

Eeckloo, K., Van Herck, G., Van Hulle, C., & Vleugels, A. (2004). From Corporate Governance to Hospital Governance. Authority, transparency and accountability of Belgian non-profit hospitals' board and management. *Health Policy (Amsterdam)*, *68*(1), 1–15. doi:10.1016/j.healthpol.2003.07.009 PMID:15033548

Goodin, R. E. (2003). Democratic Accountability: The Third Sector and All. In Crisis of Governance: The Nonprofit/Non-Governmental Sector. Academic Press. doi:10.2139srn.418262

Gourdie, J., & Rees, J. (2009). Financial Accountability Relationships between Donors and Recipients in the Non-profit Sector. *New Zealand Journal of Applied Business Research*, *7*(1), 41. Retrieved from http://search.ebscohost.com/login.aspx?direct=true&db=edsibc&AN=724680185512408&authtype=shib&site=eds-live&authtype=ip,cookie,shib%5Cnhttp://search.informit.com.au/documentSummary

Hoffman, S. (2009). Social Housing and Anti-social Behaviour: Issues of Community Engagement and Accountability for Non-profit Housing. European Network for Housing Research.

Humphrey, C. R., & Erickson, R. A. (1997). Public accountability in non-profit industrial development organisations. *Voluntas*, *8*(1), 39–63. doi:10.1007/BF02354180

Irene, S., & Dwiningrum, A. (2016). Social Capital and School Accountability. In *International Conference on Educational Research and Innovation (ICERI 2016)* (pp. 383–391). Academic Press.

Jottier, D., & Heyndels, B. (2012). Does social capital increase political accountability? An empirical test for Flemish municipalities. *Public Choice*, *150*(3–4), 731–744. doi:10.100711127-010-9727-1

Kamaluddin, A., Hasan, H. A., Arshad, R., & Samah, S. A. A. (2016). Social Capital and Innovation Capital: Accountability Towards Small Medium Enterprises' (SMEs) Sustainable Performance. *Malaysian Accounting Review*, *15*(1), 197–223. Retrieved from http://www.emeraldinsight.com/doi/10.1108/09513571111098063

Karamoy, H., Pangemanan, S., & Ilat, V. (2017). Accessibility, Accountability and The Impact of Social Enterprise. *Journal of Life Economics*, *4*(3), 1–12. doi:10.15637/jlecon.204

Kelly, E. (2011). Systematic and just: The use of a systematic review methodology in social work research. *Social Work & Social Sciences Review*, *15*(3), 72–85. doi:10.1921/095352212X657544

Kendall, J., & Knapp, M. (2000). The third sector and welfare state modernisation: Inputs, activities and comparative performance Civil Society Working Paper 14. *Health San Francisco*. Retrieved from http://eprints.lse.ac.uk/29055/

Larsson, D. (2007). *Social Capital, In spite of or due to modernization? An analysis of a two-dimensional concept*. Universiteteti Oslo.

Lee, S.-Y., Chen, W., & Weiner, B. (2004). Communities and Hospitals: Social Capital, Community Accountability, and Service Provision in U.S. Community Hospitals. *Health Services Research*, *39*(5), 1487–1509. doi:10.1111/j.1475-6773.2004.00300.x PMID:15333119

Lorenz, G. (2008). *The Implementation of Social Capital Features in Social Auditing Procedures to secure Community Accountability of Social Enterprises in the Third Sector*. Academic Press.

Maddocks, J., Novkovic, S., & Smith, S. M. (2011). Measuring Performance for Accountability of a Small Social Economy Organization: The Case of an Independent School. *Canadian Journal of Nonprofit and Social Economy Research, 2*(1), 45–60. doi:10.22230/cjnser.2011v2n1a59

McDonald, C. (1999). Internal Control and Accountability in Non-profit Human Service Organisations. *Australian Journal of Public Administration, 11*(22).

Molnar, M. (2004). *Accountability Model and Self-Assessment Initiative for Third Sector Organizations*. Academic Press.

Mullins, D. (2006). Competing Institutional Logics? Local Accountability and Scale and Efficiency in an Expanding Non-Profit Housing Sector. *Public Policy and Administration, 21*(3), 6–24. doi:10.1177/095207670602100302

Mustafa, D., & Qazi, M. U. (2007). Transition from Karez to Tubewell Irrigation: Development, Modernization, and Social Capital in Balochistan, Pakistan. *World Development, 35*(10), 1796–1813. doi:10.1016/j.worlddev.2007.06.002

Nannicini, T., Stella, A., Tabellini, G., & Troiano, U. (2013). Social capital and political accountability. *American Economic Journal. Economic Policy, 5*(2), 222–250. doi:10.1257/pol.5.2.222

Nobari, J. J. (2015). *Accountability and social impact measurement for a third sector supported housing organisation*. Newcastle University.

Nowland-foreman, G. (2009). The Challenge of Accountability, the Opportunity of Responsibility for Third Sector Organisations. In *6th International Society for Third Sector Research (ISTR) Asia Pacific Regional Conference*, (pp. 2–4). Taipei, Taiwan: Academic Press.

Omar, N., & Arshad, R. (2016). Effectiveness, Accountability and Understanding Board Characteristics of Non-Profit Organisations in Malaysia. *Malaysian Accounting Review, 15*(2), 127–150.

Porumbescu, G. A. (2016). Non-profit Accountability in Least Developed Nations: Lesson Learned from West Africa. *Public Administration Quarterly, 40*(2), 288–315. doi:10.1177/0149206309343469

Preite, D., & De Matteis, F. (2014). Non Profit Entities and Multi-Stakeholder Relations: Some Highlights on Accountability Management from the Italian "Pro-Loco" Organizations. *Procedia Economics and Finance, 15*(14), 176–183. doi:10.1016/S2212-5671(14)00474-2

Roslan, N., Arshad, R., Farahah, N., & Pauzi, M. (2017). Accountability and Governance Reporting By Non-Profit Organizations. *International Conference on Governance and Accountability 2016, 00041*, 1–15. 10.1051hsconf/20173600041

Rotheroe, N., & Richards, A. (2007). Social return on investment and social enterprise: Transparent accountability for sustainable development. *Social Enterprise Journal, 3*(1), 31–48. doi:10.1108/17508610780000720

Saita, M., & Franceschelli, M. V. (2016). Preparing financial statement : the restricted accountability of Non-profit organizations. Academic Press.

Sangole, N., Kaaria, S., Njuki, J., Lewa, K., & Mapila, M. (2014). Community based participatory monitoring and evaluation: Impacts on farmer organization functioning, social capital and accountability. *Journal of Rural and Community Development*, *9*(2), 128–148. Retrieved from http://journals.brandonu.ca/jrcd/article/view/749

Santos, C., Ferreira, A., Marques, R. P., & Azevedo, G. (2018). EAGLE_Index: Enhancement of an accountability guide for learning E-Government. In Handbook of Research on Modernization and Accountability in Public Sector Management. Academic Press. doi:10.4018/978-1-5225-3731-1.ch006

Schwartz, R. (2001). *Managing Government-Third Sector Collaboration: Accountability, Ambiguity, and Politics*. Academic Press.

Schwartz, R., & Sharkansky, I. (2000). Collaboration with the 'Third Sector' - Issues of Accountability: Mapping Israeli Versions of this Problematic. *Public Policy and Administration*, *15*(3), 92–106. doi:10.1177/095207670001500308

Scott, M. (2010). Critical reflections on a decade of third sector modernisation: Another sector is possible. *Local Economy*, *25*(5), 367–372. doi:10.1080/02690942.2010.526793

Shuib, N., Said, J., & Atan, R. (2014). The Influence of Financial management Practices, Board Effectiveness and accountability towards Performance: Empirical Test of Non-Profit Organization. *APMAJ Asia-Pacific Management Accounting Journal*, *8*(1), 43–63.

Siddiq, K., Meyer, E., & Ashleigh, M. (2013). What is the impact of authentic leadership on leader accountability in a non-profit context? *Proceedings of the International Conference on Management, Leadership and Governance*, 396–399.

Sprok, J. J. A. (2013). Status attainment in The Netherlands during the period 1851-1890 : The influence of social capital on status attainment in the context of. *Social Cosmos*, *4*(2), 152–166.

Stone, W. S., & Wilbanks, J. (2012). Transparency and Accountability: A Look at Non-Profit Internet Website Content. *Insights to a Changing World Journal*, (3), 79–86. Retrieved from http://nuncio.cofc.edu/login?url=http://search.ebscohost.com/login.aspx?direct=true&db=a9h&AN=83529732&site=eds-live%5Cnhttp://content.ebscohost.com/ContentServer.asp?T=P&P=AN&K=83529732&S=R&D=a9h&EbscoContent=dGJyMNHr7ESep7Q4zOX0OLCmr0yep69Ssqa4SreWxWXS&

Tăi, M. (2011). *The Nexus of Modernization and Social Capital : A Comparative Exploration of Two Kenyan Villages*. Wesleyan University.

Tenbensel, T., Dwyer, J., & Lavoie, J. (2014). How not to kill the golden goose. *Public Management Review*, *16*(7), 925–944. doi:10.1080/14719037.2013.770054

Titov, V. N. (2013). The Distribution of Social Capital as a Condition for the Modernization of Russian Society. *Sociological Research*, *52*(5), 40–58. doi:10.2753/SOR1061-0154520503

Williamson, A. L., & Bond, B. J. (2014). Making boston strong: Social capital, collaboration, and accountability lessons for public administrators in the twenty-first century. *Public Administration Review*, *74*(6), 693–695. doi:10.1111/puar.12302

Zainon, S., Ahmad, S. A., Atan, R., Wah, Y. B., Bakar, Z. A., & Sarman, S. R. (2014). Legitimacy and Sustainability of Social Enterprise: Governance and Accountability. *Procedia: Social and Behavioral Sciences*, *145*, 152–157. doi:10.1016/j.sbspro.2014.06.022

Zainon, S., Atan, R., Wah, Y., Ahmad, R., Othman, A., & Suhadak, N. (2014). An Integrated Ritual Effectiveness Accountability Reporting System (i-REARs) for Non-Profit Organizations. *International Business Research*, *7*(5), 156–165. doi:10.5539/ibr.v7n5p156

KEY TERMS AND DEFINITIONS

Accountability: Obligation of the organs to 1) account for its activities, 2) accept responsibility for these activities, and 3) disclose the results in a transparent manner.

Equity Funds: In nonprofits rather than equity capital, it is designated as equity funds. They are composed of donations whose value should be kept intact and invested to create a source of resources for the organization.

Financial Reporting: Includes all of a company's communication of financial information to people outside of the company.

Non-Profit Organizations: Also called not for profit organizations, are privately held entities that don't provide financial benefits for their members or stakeholders. In other words, they are privately incorporated groups with a charitable purpose of not profiting from the activities they carry.

Social Capital: It can be analyzed from two perspectives: accounting and sociology. As an accounting term, the share capital is the value of the assets or the money with which the members contribute to a company without right of return. Social capital implies the sociability of a human group, with the aspects that allow collaboration and its use. Sociologists emphasize that social capital is formed by social networks, by mutual trust and by effective norms, concepts that are not easy to define and which may vary depending on the analyst's point of view.

Social Economy: It is the sphere of the so-called third sector, including associativism, cooperativism, and mutualism as forms of organization of productive activity (NGO-autonomous organizations, aimed at improving social quality, social projects, and non-governmental organizations).

Sustainability: The ability to use natural, economic, and social resources to meet our current needs without compromising the ability of future generations to satisfy their own needs.

Chapter 2 Accountability via Financial Disclosures: An Exploration of the Public's Perceptions

Ushi Ghoorah
Western Sydney University, Australia

ABSTRACT

Social economy sector (SES) organizations are dependent on their funders and, similar to non-profit organizations, are vulnerable to the risk of mission drift as well as to concerns about the extent to which they are accountable for their fund flows. This chapter explores the general public's perceptions of the relative importance of specific financial disclosures which the public believes SES organizations should publish as part of their provision of accountability. Using a survey questionnaire administered to a sample of 400 Australian individuals, the chapter observes that the public perceives financial disclosures relating to sources of funds, mission-related expenses, and the financial sustainability of SES organizations as important. It is recommended that SES organizations cater to the general public's information needs as a way of improving their accountability, reducing information asymmetry, and eventually increasing general trust and confidence in their operations.

INTRODUCTION

Social economy sector (SES) organisations are primarily set up with the objective of promoting social welfare. These organisations operate following a business model to achieve their social or environment objectives, such as those related to the alleviation of poverty, wealth inequality and environmental damage. More specifically, SES organisations generate surpluses from their commercial activities and reinvest these funds into their social activities to increase welfare (Austin, Stenvenson & Wei-Skillern, 2012). SES organisations are neither pure commercial nor pure non-profit organisations, but are instead a combination of both (Ebrahim, Battilana & Mair, 2014). As such, SES organisations have dual objectives; namely, social welfare and profit maximisation (Santos, Pache & Birkholz, 2015). The fundamental purpose of SES organisations remains to pursue their social and/or environmental missions which

DOI: 10.4018/978-1-5225-8482-7.ch002

contribute to the social welfare of their beneficiaries (Barraket, Mason & Blain, 2016) and eventually, of the general public (Justice Connect, 2017a).

To carry out their activities, SES organisations receive support from their external environment in the form of funds from investors, government subsidies, charitable funds, donations (Bugg-Levine, Kogut & Kulatilaka, 2012), fundraising income, membership fees and government grants (Prakash & Gugerty, 2010; Zainon, Atan & Bee Wah, 2014). SES organisations are resource dependent on external funders, including the public at large. This dependence implies that SES organisations, similar to non-profit organisations, have a responsibility to spend their funds on the social causes which they promote to support (Dhanani & Connolly, 2012). SES organisations operate in an environment where trust and confidence are fundamental elements for their fund inflows (Hyndman & McConville, 2018) and ultimately, for the survival of individual organisations (Hyndman, 2017). Given the nature of SES organisations, there is a reasonable expectation that they can be trusted to use funds to maximise their social mission (Arshad, Bakar, Thani & Omar, 2013).

It can be challenging for SES organisations to manage their dual objectives (Canales, 2013) and satisfy all stakeholders' expectations. Within the SES context, stakeholders have different needs and expectations. For instance, investors, customers and commercial partners have expectations which are more focused on the financial performance and profit maximisation objectives of the organisation, as compared to donors, volunteers and social partners who are mainly interested in the social outcomes of the organisation. Though the dual objectives of SES organisations should complement rather than compete with each other (Ebrahim et al., 2014), this is not always the case. There have been concerns about the risk of mission drift within the sector, where an SES organisation moves its focus away from social outcomes to profit maximisation (Mair, Battilana & Cardenas, 2012). In the past, SES organisations have faced the problem of mission drifts where organisations have focused on their financial performance to the detriment of their social mission (Strom, 2010). An example of such mission drift is the commercialisation of the microfinance sector (Banerjee, Duflo, Glennerster & Kinnan, 2013).

The non-profit sector frequently deals with unfavourable media attention and given the close link between the non-profit and SES sectors, the latter sector is likely to be adversely impacted by spill-over effects from unfavourable media coverage. Well-known brands such as United Way in the United States (Handy & Russell, 2018), Oxfam in England (Crack, 2018) and the Returned and Services League (RSL) in Australia (Morris, 2018) have all experienced such effects. Coverage has included questions around the disproportionate amount of resources being allocated to non-mission activities (such as costs associated with administration and fundraising), allegations of fund misappropriation, and concerns about mission drift. As a result, the general public's level of trust and confidence in non-profit organisations has further declined and has fuelled their concerns about the extent to which these organisations discharge accountability (Dhanani & Connolly, 2012). SES organisations, being dependent on external funds to achieve their social missions (Ebrahim et al., 2014), also run the risk of making headlines about their allocation of funds.

Another problem the sector faces is the existence of information asymmetry between SES organisations and their different stakeholder groups, ranging from donors (individual and institutional), members and government agencies to the general public. Such asymmetry adds to concerns about the extent to which organisations misappropriate funds (Cordery & Baskerville, 2011), and in turn threatens the overall credibility and sustainability of these organisations (Yang, Northcott & Sinclair, 2017). As a result, SES organisations, similar to what is reported about non-profit organisations, face increasing pressure to justify their resource inflows (Kummer, Singh & Best, 2015) and improve their accountability (McDonnell, 2017).

Accountability, via disclosures and transparency, can play a fundamental role in building, retaining and repairing trust in SES organisations (Bryce, 2016). An SES organisation provides accountability to stakeholder groups who have a legitimate interest in its activities; it does so by publishing, amongst others, annual reports and financial statements (Ebrahim, 2003a). In producing financial statements, SES organisations are required to cater to report users' information needs, that is, provide information showing how well these organisations use funds to achieve their social mission (AASB, 2015).

The literature on SES organisations is still emerging and developing. While there is abundant literature on accountability in and by non-profit organisations (including Hyndman & McConville, 2018; McDonnell, 2017; Yasmin, Haniffa & Hudaib, 2014), few studies deal with accountability within the SES sector. Most studies have investigated accountability by focusing on communicated accountability - that is, accountability via disclosures and transparency (Yasmin et al., 2014), accountability from the perspective of the regulator (McDonnell, 2017) and the use of accountability mechanisms to address key stakeholders' perceived information needs and to build trust (Hyndman & McConville, 2018). Studies have also investigated donors' perspectives on accountability (Connolly & Hyndman, 2013) and how key funders extract the accountability information they need from SES organisations (Yang et al., 2017). Using data from semi-structured interviews, the study by Connolly and Hyndman found that funders were perceived as the main stakeholder to whom an organisation is accountable, but that funders may not necessarily find relevance in the publicly available information. The literature on the public's perceptions of specific disclosures within the SES sector is, however, scarce.

This chapter contributes to the existing literature by exploring the general public's perceptions of the relative importance of specific financial disclosures which SES organisations could publish as part of their provision of accountability. This chapter focuses on financial disclosures because funders perceive 'audited financial information' as a fundamental part of the disclosures made by an organisation (Connolly & Hyndman, 2013, p.273) and hence, as a key part in the accountability (discharged via disclosures) of an SES organisation. The chapter examines the public's perceptions of financial disclosures by considering accountability relationships in general (that is, it does not address a specific direction of these relationships). This is because an SES organisation can obtain legitimacy from both their upward (Ebrahim, 2003b) and downward accountability relationships (Goddard & Juma Assad, 2006). The chapter discusses accountability relationships and financial disclosures in a later section.

The findings reported in this chapter make three primary contributions. First, they contribute to the developing and emerging SES literature on financial disclosures and accountability. Second, the observations in this study will inform disclosure practices within the SES sector by providing insights into the general public's perceptions of financial disclosures, and hence, their information needs. Third, the results may revive discussions around financial disclosures within the SES sector and encourage regulators to introduce some mandatory minimum financial disclosure requirements which should apply uniformly across the sector.

The remainder of this chapter continues as follows: the next section discusses some key concepts related to accountability and financial disclosures within the SES context; the data and method of the chapter are then described; and finally, the results are discussed and conclusions are drawn.

KEY CONCEPTS

Accountability

Accountability is a concept which has no generally accepted definition (Sinclair, 1995; Tenbensel, Dwyer & Lavoie, 2014). That said, in broad terms, it refers to an organisation having to provide an account of its activities and performance to stakeholders (Dhanani & Connolly, 2012). In its examination of accountability within the SES context, the study by Guraieb Izaguirre (2015) argues that accountability is closely related to concepts like honesty, responsibility and transparency.

SES organisations are accountable for both their social mission and their financial performance (Ebrahim et al., 2014; Guraieb Izaguire, 2015). However, the reporting of social outcomes can be problematic in multiple ways given the ambiguity around the nature of social impact (Choi & Majumdar, 2014), the absence of a commonly agreed tool, benchmark or guideline for gauging social outcomes, and the limited comparability in the social outcomes of similar organisations (Ebrahim & Rangan, 2014). As recognised in the literature, the measurement and reporting of social outcomes is still developing (Ebrahim & Rangan, 2014). In contrast to social outcome measures, the measures of financial performance are relatively well-established (Ebrahim & Rangan, 2010). Therefore, in its exploration of accountability within the SES context, this chapter focuses on financial performance rather than social outcomes.

Accountability associated with the financial performance of an SES organisation can be classified into 'upward' and 'downward' relationships. The upward relationship is mainly with the funders, commercial partners and volunteers of an SES organisation, whereas the downward relationship is primarily with the beneficiaries of the organisation (Ebrahim, 2003a; Guraieb Izaguire, 2015). Accountability was initially established to be discharged by an organisation to its owners. Overtime, via stakeholder theory, the accountability relationship has been extended to other stakeholder groups as well (Gray, Meek & Roberts, 1995), to include employees, customers, and society at large. In other words, SES organisations have accountability relationships with different stakeholder groups who, in turn, have different interests (Ebrahim et al., 2014). For instance, investors tend to be interested in the financial performance of their SES organisation as compared to the beneficiaries who tend to be interested in the social outcomes of the SES organisation.

As for SES organisations themselves, they tend to mainly focus on accountability to their funders rather than downward to their beneficiaries. This emphasis on upward accountability is mainly driven by the resource dependence of an SES organisation and hence the need to minimise the risk that funders withdraw their support from the organisation if it does not perform as per funders' expectationss (Ebrahim et al., 2014). Mitchell, Agle and Wood (1997) explain that organisations prioritise their funders' accountability demands because this stakeholder group has salience, power and legitimacy. Also, SES organisations lack certainty in terms of how to engage and report with stakeholder groups other than their funders. This too may explain their focus on upward accountability (O'Dwyer & Unerman, 2008).

Trust Reporting

Accountability originates from the idea of reporting for 'trust or stewardship', which is part of the legal accountability of an organisation (Gross 1977, p. 66). The fundamental principle of trust accounting is to separate funds which have no legally abiding purpose from those which must be used as per the restrictions imposed by its funders (Ingram, 1986). Under trust reporting, the trustee (being the entity which controls the funds received by an SES organisation) accounts for the use of funds. Trust reporting is based on the idea that an SES organisation receives support from different funders because the latter trust the organisation and these funders are likely to experience a 'sense of betrayal' if an SES organisation misappropriates funds (van Staden & Heslop 2009, p. 45). Misappropriation of designated funds also entails a criminal act by the organisation. Trust accounting has overtime transformed into a specific form of accounting, namely fund accounting (van Staden & Heslop, 2009).

Fund Accounting

Fund accounting refers to the provision of different financial disclosures for each of the various funds held by an SES organisation, where 'funds' means resources which have been categorised based on the restrictions imposed by funders (Gross, McCarthy & Shelmon, 2005 p.19; McCarthy, Shelmon & Mattie, 2012). These funds are usually divided into restricted funds (that is, funds which can only be used for purposes specified by the funder) and unrestricted funds. Under fund accounting, all unrestricted fund inflows are categorised under one type of fund, and the restricted funds are grouped in different funds based on their restriction type (Gross et al., 2005). This categorisation of funds is closely related to trust reporting. Under fund accounting, there is a separate set of accounts for each type of restricted fund (Gross, 1977) and information is available about the purpose, the legal restriction imposed by funders, and the decision of the board about how to use each fund (Herzlinger & Sherman, 1980). Advocates of fund accounting argue that it is necessary to have separate accounts for restricted and unrestricted fund flows in order to allow funders to assess how well different funds perform (Herzlinger & Sherman, 1980).

However, fund accounting has been primarily criticised for the complexity of its financial statements (Ingram 1986), and also for its lack of contribution to informed analysis (Herzlinger & Sherman, 1980). For this reason, the chapter does not address the public's perceptions of fund accounting disclosures, but instead examines perceptions about financial disclosures more generally. The chapter takes the stance that there is a close link between fund accounting and financial reporting; because under financial reporting, SES organisations (similar to most organisations) are expected to at least provide an account of their fund inflows and of how they allocate funds to competing activities. For this reason, the chapter focuses on the financial accountability of SES organisations in its exploration of the public's perceptions of financial disclosures

Financial Accountability

Financial accountability can be of two types: internal and external. Internal accountability involves financial disclosures which meet the information needs of the employees, management and board of an organisation. External accountability pertains to financial disclosures which cater to the information needs of external stakeholders, such as resource providers, state, recipients of the goods and services provided by the reporting entity, and society at large (Raffer, 2004). In spite of the fact that funders are expected to primarily have an interest in the financial disclosures of an SES organisation (Connolly & Hyndman, 2013), they are unlikely to be the sole users of these information. Users may range from individual funders and volunteers to institutional grant providers and regulators. SES organisations owe accountability to a wide range of stakeholder groups in addition to their funders and it is not unreasonable to expect various stakeholder groups, including the general public, to have an interest in the financial disclosures published by these organisations.

To address the information needs of this range of stakeholder groups, SES organisations are expected provide accountability irrespective of whether or not stakeholders use the information (van Staden & Heslop, 2009). Accountability to multiple stakeholder groups is endorsed by established regulatory bodies. For instance, national regulators require organisations to discharge accountability to the general public in the form of financial disclosures that are prescribed and mandated by reporting frameworks. For instance, even though SES organisations deal with multiple and inconsistent reporting requirements, many of them are required to publish financial disclosures.

Financial Disclosures

An organisation publishes financial disclosures as part of its provision of financial accountability (O'Brien & Tooley, 2013) and these disclosures relate to a range of items, including the financial transactions, performance and position of an organisation (Mack & Ryan, 2006), the funds acquired by the reporting organisation, how it allocates funds to competing uses (González, 2010), and how as well as by how much the organisation is developing financially (Dhanani & Connolly, 2012).

In general, stakeholders rely on the financial disclosures of an organisation to make economic decisions (Keating & Frumkin, 2003) in terms of whether to provide funds to an organisation or to withdraw their support from the organisation (Parsons, 2007; Yetman & Yetman, 2012). The extent to which an organisation is considered to be financially accountable is directly influenced by the extent to which its financial disclosures facilitate decision-making (Hyndman, McKillop, Ferguson & Wall, 2004). In providing financial accountability, an SES organisation is expected to include enough financial disclosure to allow an assessment of its performance, as well as of the efficiency and effectiveness with which the organisation has used funds to achieve its social outcomes (O'Brien & Tooley, 2013; Zainon et al., 2014).

Financial disclosure represents a primary accountability mechanism that SES organisations use to engage with multiple stakeholder groups and remains, despite other means, a crucial part of its provision of accountability. Yet there are no current universal guidelines or requirements which regulate the SES sector (Ebrahim et al., 2014). Similarly, in Australia, there is no national representative body for SES organisations. Furthermore, these organisations operate across multiple states and/or territories and they adopt a range of structures (including that of companies, trust and incorporated associations) which in turn influences their report-keeping obligations (Justice Connect, 2017b) and hence their financial disclosures. As a result, these organisations face a range of financial disclosure requirements that vary depending on multiple factors, including their organisational structure and the state or territory in which they operate. Under this reporting framework, the financial disclosure practices of Australian SES organisations lack consistency and comparability.

DATA AND METHODS

Data and Sample

To explore the public's perceptions of specific financial disclosure items, this chapter collects data using a survey questionnaire. The questionnaire was pretested for any ambiguity as well as for the sequencing and wording of the items. Following feedback, the survey was finalised. It was conducted in the second half of 2017 and participants were not provided with any form of incentive. An initial email was sent to

1305 panellists. The email contained the survey web link and 522 panellists engaged with the survey. Incomplete responses and missing information which related to the respondents' demographic characteristics were removed. An eventual sample of 400 respondents was used for the purpose of this study. This represented a satisfactory response rate of 30.65%.

Consistent with demographic statistics published by the Australian Bureau of Statistics, the sample of 400 respondents is representative of the Australian population in terms of gender, age and distribution of the population by state or territory. The sample is divided between male (51.25%) and female (48.75%). Most of the respondents were aged between 18 and 54 years (80.75%), had at most a bachelor or equivalent (50.75%) and were employed (50.75%). A majority of the respondents lived in either New South Wales (30%) or Victoria (25.25%). These two states are the most populous places in Australia, both in terms of inhabitants as well as in terms of where SES organisations operate (Barraket et al., 2016). The sample was also fairly evenly divided between donors (48.50%) and non-donors (51.50%), where donors refer to past and present donors. To identify a respondent's donor status, the survey item *'Have you ever donated to any social economy sector (SES) organisation?'* was used and it was measured using a binary scale of 1 denoting *'yes'* and 0, if otherwise. The survey questionnaire did not differentiate between financial and in-kind donations. The characteristics of the sample are summarised in Table 1.

To assess the public's perceptions of financial disclosures within the SES sector, the study used disclosure items which relate primarily to the statement of financial performance, the statement of financial position, and the statement of cash flows. These disclosure statements are one of the most common tools which organisations use in their provision of accountability. Each of the survey items were adapted from the literature and included financial disclosure items such as *'Total revenue earned by the organisation'*, *'Breakdown of revenue sources of the organisation'*, *'Expenses associated with the mission promoted by the organisation'*, *'Salaries of senior staff'* and *'Cash inflows and outflows of the organisation'*. In addition, the questionnaire provided respondents with the following definition of SES organisation: *'A social economy sector organisation is an organisation which engages in commercial activities in order to address social and environmental issues. A social economy sector organisation, amongst others, enables employment opportunities to disadvantaged labour, addresses social needs using innovative products and provides educational supplies to children in need.'* Respondents were not asked to focus on any specific SES organisation. They instead were required to rate their perceptions about the relative importance of specific financial disclosure items which they believe SES organisations, in general, should publish.

RESULTS

Interest in Financial Disclosures

The survey assessed the general public's interest in financial disclosures using a 5-Likert scale, where 1 denoted *'Not Interested'*, 5 denoted *'Very Interested'* and 3 denoted *'Interested'*. The public were specifically asked the following: *'On a scale of 1 to 5, how would you rate your interest in financial disclosures?'*. The question was adapted from Goh, Schlegel, Tignor and Hall (2016). The study noted a mean of 3.25 for the public's overall interest in the financial disclosures published by SES organisation. The standard deviation and variance of the public' interest in financial disclosures were 1.21 and 1.48, respectively. Though 12% of the sample was not sure about their interest in financial disclosures made

Table 1. Characteristics of sample

	Frequency (%)		Frequency (%)
Gender		**Donor Status**	
Male	205 (51.25%)	Donor	194 (48.50%)
Female	195 (48.75%)	Non-Donor	206 (51.50%)
Age		**State/Territory where respondent resides**	
18-24 years	112 (28.00%)	New South Wales	120 (30.00%)
25-34 years	64 (16.00%)	Australian Capital Territory	7 (1.75%)
35-44 years	57 (14.25%)	Victoria	101 (25.25%)
45- 54 years	90 (22.50%)	Tasmania	9 (2.25%)
55-64 years	59 (14.75%)	Queensland	81 (20.25%)
65-74 years	17 (4.25%)	South Australia	33 (8.25%)
75-years	1 (0.25%)	Western Australia	46 (11.50%)
		Northern Territory & Others	3 (0.75%)
Educational Qualification		**Occupation status**	
Diploma or Lower	239 (59.75%)	Full Time (30+ hours per week)	134 (33.50%)
Bachelor or Equivalent	117 (29.25%)	Part Time (less than 29 hours per week)	69 (17.25%)
Master or Equivalent	40 (10.00%)	Home Duties (looking after dependents)	23 (5.75%)
PhD or Equivalent	4 (1.00%)	Student	58 (14.50%)
		Retired	72 (18.00%)
		Unemployed & Others	44 (11.00%)

n= 400. Note: The demographic information was collected using questions which have been adapted from ACNC (2013) and Rouf (2016).

within the SES sector, 67% of the respondents rated their interest in financial disclosures to be at least a 3, as reported in Figure 1.

Relative Importance of Specific Financial Disclosures

The public was asked *'How important is it for social economy sector organisations to make the following financial disclosures publicly available?'* and were given a list of specific financial disclosure items, such as *'Total revenue earned by the organisation'*, *'Breakdown of the revenue sources of the organisation'*, *'Expenses associated with the mission promoted by the organisation'* and *'Administration Expenses'*. Respondents rated their preference on a 5-Likert scale, where 1 denoted *'Not Important'*, 5 denoted *'Very Important'* and 3 denoted *'Important'*. The disclosures have been categorised into revenue, expenses and others, for the purpose of discussing the observations derived from the survey.

Revenue

Figure 2 shows that the revenue-related financial disclosure items with the highest mean scores being *'Revenue earned from donations'* (3.95) and *'Total revenue earned by the organisation'* (3.92). With

Figure 1. Interest in financial disclosures made by SES organisations

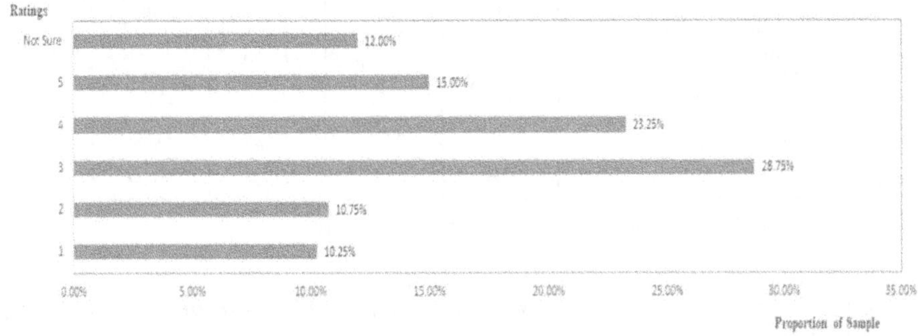

reference to the perceived relative importance of revenue-related financial disclosures which SES organisations should provide, Table 2 shows that over 75% of the respondents gave a score of at least 3 to each of the revenue-related financial disclosure items included in the survey questionnaire. This finding indicates that people have an interest in financial disclosures relating to the sources of fund inflows to SES organisations.

Expenses

The survey questionnaire included a range of expense items, such as *'Marketing expenses'*, *'Fundraising expenses'* and *'Employee expenses'*. As highlighted in Figure 3, the items with the highest mean scores were *'Salaries of senior staff'* (3.98), *'Fundraising expenses'* (3.90) and *'Administration expenses'* (3.84). Most respondents gave a score of at least 3 to *'Expenses associated with the provision of goods/ services which promote social welfare'* (80.45%), *'Expenses associated with the mission promoted by the organisation'* (79.19%) and *'Fundraising Expenses'* (79.19%), as shown in Table 3. This finding shows that most of the respondents perceived financial disclosures associated with the amount spent on the social mission of an SES organisation to be a relatively important disclosure that SES organisations should provide.

Figure 2. Mean of relative importance for specific revenue-related financial disclosures

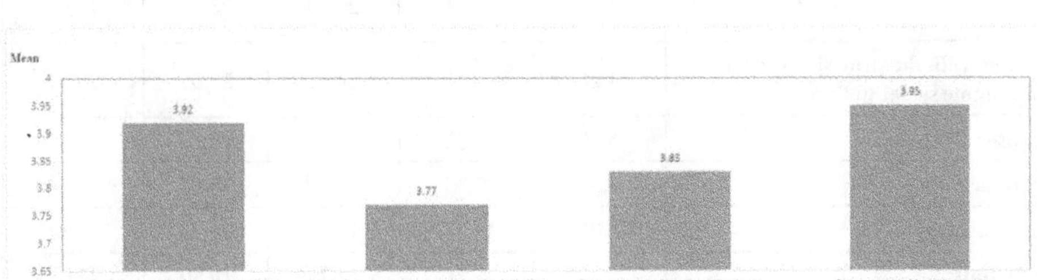

Table 2. Relative importance of revenue-related financial disclosures which SES organisations should provide

Responses (%)	1	2	3	4	5	Not Sure
Total revenue earned by the organisation	5.51	3.76	18.55	25.81	35.09	11.28
Breakdown of the revenue sources of the organisation	3.76	8.02	20.80	29.82	27.57	10.03
Revenue earned from the government	6.02	5.26	17.29	31.33	30.58	9.52
Revenue earned from donations	5.26	3.5	16.54	30.83	35.09	8.77

n = 400. Adapted from Mirshekary and Saudagaran (2005).

Figure 3. Mean of the relative importance for specific expense-related financial disclosures

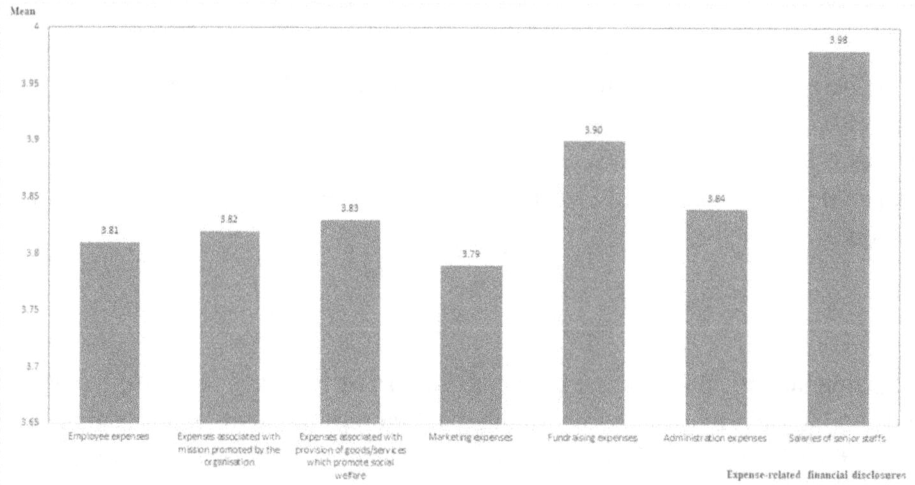

Table 3. Relative importance of expense-related financial disclosures which SES organisations should provide

Responses (%)	1	2	3	4	5	Not Sure
Employee expenses	4.26	9.02	18.80	24.31	32.58	11.03
Expenses associated with the mission promoted by the organisation	3.26	6.77	21.55	28.57	29.07	10.78
Expenses associated with the provision of goods/ services which promote social welfare	4.26	5.01	22.31	28.57	29.57	10.28
Marketing expenses	5.26	7.02	18.30	28.57	29.57	11.28
Fundraising expenses	4.51	5.76	17.04	28.82	33.33	10.53
Administration Expenses	5.01	8.27	17.29	24.56	34.84	10.03
Salaries of senior staff	5.76	5.51	15.79	19.80	42.61	10.53

n = 400. Adapted from Tooley and Hooks (2010).

'Other' Financial Disclosures

The 'other' financial disclosure items with the highest mean scores are *'Ability to pay debts when they fall due'* (3.99), *'Any surplus made by the organisation'* (3.93) and *'Cash inflows and cash outflows of the organisation'* (3.89), as shown in Figure 4. This finding suggests that the respondents have an interest in financial disclosures pertaining to the financial sustainability of the business. Further, as indicated in Table 4, at least 75% of the respondents scored a minimum 3 for all of the other financial disclosures included in the survey questionnaire. *'Money owed to creditors'* was perceived as being an important 'other' financial disclosure item by most respondents (80.95%) whereas *'Transactions with related parties'* was deemed the least important 'other' financial disclosure item by a majority of the respondents, although the proportion of respondents who ranked it 3 or above was still high at 76.20%.

Figure 4. Mean of relative importance for other specific financial disclosures

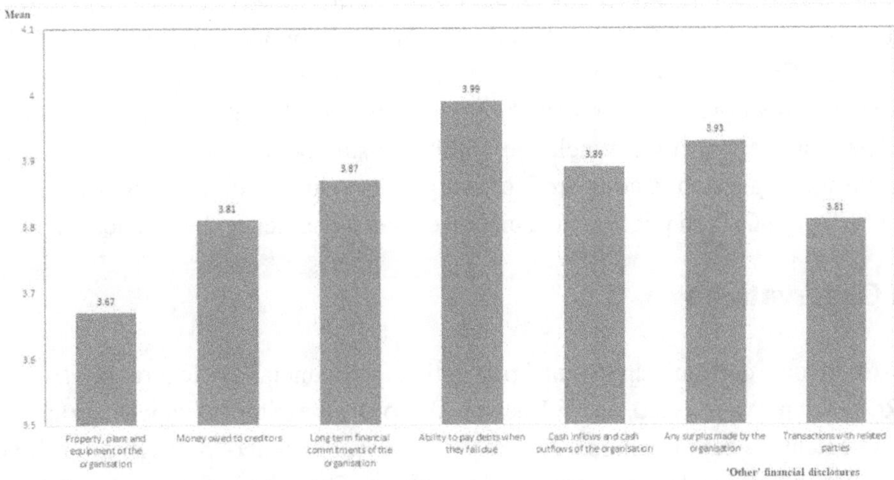

Table 4. Relative importance for SES organisations to make other specific financial disclosures

Responses (%)	1	2	3	4	5	Not Sure
Property, plant and equipment of the organisation	5.51	7.52	22.81	28.82	24.81	10.53
Money owed to creditors	5.01	4.76	20.55	32.33	28.07	9.27
Long term financial commitments of the organisation	4.01	6.02	19.30	29.07	31.33	10.28
Ability to pay debts when they fall due	3.26	3.76	18.80	29.07	35.34	9.77
Cash inflows and cash outflows of the organisation	5.51	4.26	16.79	31.08	32.08	10.28
Any surplus made by the organisation	4.51	5.26	16.29	28.82	34.34	10.78
Transactions with related parties	5.26	6.52	18.30	27.57	30.33	12.03

n = 400, Adapted from Magena, Kinman and Citron (2008).

Regression Analysis

A preliminary regression analysis was also run to examine the relationship between the respondents' individual characteristics and their perceptions of how important it is for SES organisations to publish specific financial disclosures. The analysis showed low R (below 0.3) and R^2 (less than 0.1) values for most of the models representing the relationship between respondents' perceptions of the relative importance of specific financial disclosure items (the dependent variable) and respondents' individual characteristics (the variables of interest). Hence, except for respondents' three individual characteristics (gender, donor status and age), the results of the regression analysis are not further elaborated in this chapter.

A regression analysis showed that gender has a statistically significant relationship (at a level of 0.01) with only one financial disclosure item, namely *'Administration expenses'*, as reported in Table 5. The relationship is inverse. This indicates that *'Administration expenses'* is perceived more by male respondents than female respondents to be a financial disclosure item which they believe SES organisations should publish. Also, respondents' donor status has statistically significant positive relationships with *'Marketing expenses'* and *'Salaries of senior staffs'* (both, at a level of 0.1). This shows that these two expenditure items are perceived more by donors than non-donors to be financial disclosure items which they believe SES organisations should publish. Additionally, the respondents' age has statistically significant and direct relationships with their perceptions of the relative importance of each of the financial disclosure items which were included within the survey questionnaires, as outlined in Table 5. These relationships suggest that, compared to younger respondents, older respondents perceive more important that SES organisation publish financial disclosures and hence, be financially transparent.

Additional Observations

The survey also collected data on respondents' perceptions of financial disclosures published by SES organisations. Respondents were asked, on a 5-Likert scale, to rate the extent to which they agree or disagree with specific statements; where 1 denoted *'Strongly disagree'*, 5 denoted *'Strongly agree'* and 3 denoted *'Agree'*. Each of these statements are summarised in Table 6. Over 80% of the respondents agreed with statements (that is, rated 3 or higher) '*It is important to be able to get any financial statement information you want from an SES organisation*', '*The public, in general, has a right to know about everything an SES organisation does*' and '*Financial transparency is key to fighting fraud by SES organisations*'. This observation suggests that the respondents feel there should be disclosures, transparency and accountability within the SES space. Additionally, Table 6 shows that most of the respondents (66.75%) agree that *'It is too much of a hassle to look at financial statement information published by Australian SES organisations'.* No specific definition of 'hassle' was provided to the respondents, although it is plausible to suggest that they took this to mean it was difficult or inconvenient for them to get access to the financial reports and/or interpret or understand financial statement disclosures.

Furthermore, the respondents' fairly poor financial knowledge scores support the speculation that 'hassle' is associated with their interpretation and/or understanding of financial statement disclosures. The study explored the respondents' level of knowledge of financial accounting concepts by including 10 multiple-choice questions. Each of these questions has been provided in Table 7 and they relate to basic accounting concepts as well as the Australian SES sector. Each correct answer was awarded a score of 1, and 0 if otherwise. The average score for most questions were below 0.5. Except for three of the multiple-choice questions, less than 50% of the respondents identified the right answer. The re-

Table 5. The relationship between respondents' selected individual characteristics and their perceptions of the relative importance of specific financial disclosures items which they believe SES organisations should publish

Financial disclosure items	Gender *t-value* *p-value*	Donor Status *t-value* *p-value*	Age *t-value* *p-value*
Total Revenue	–.048 .709	.030 .812	.129 .002***
Breakdown of total revenue	–.041 .714	.004 .971	.145 .000***
Revenue earned from the government	.021 .870	.096 .453	.114 .006***
Revenue earned from donations	– .043 .726	.092 .452	.109 .006***
Employee Expenses	– .165 .205	.032 .805	.176 .000***
Expenses associated with the mission promoted by the organisation	.026 .836	– .056 .653	.100 .013**
Expenses associated with the provision of goods/services which promote social welfare	.031 .802	061 .624	.098 .015**
Marketing expenses	– .123 .340	.249 .054*	.176 .000***
Fundraising expenses	– .124 .322	.086 .492	.129 .001***
Administration expenses	– .143 .000***	.126 .326	.213 .000***
Salaries of senior staff	– .083 .526	.252 .055*	.156 .000***
Property, plant and equipment	. – .043 .745	.172 .192	.087 .041**
Money owed to creditors	– .144 .241	.131 .286	.131 .001***
Long– term financial commitments of the organisation	– .025 .841	– .046 .713	.101 .012**
Ability to pay debts when they fall due	.010 .933	.078 .500	.146 .000***
Cash inflows and outflows of the organisation	– .188 .136	.047 .710	.093 .022**
Any surplus made by the organisation	– .055 .663	.112 .372	.080 .048**
Transactions with related parties	– .039 .766	.005 .970	.114 .007***

n = 400. *p<0.1, **p<0.05, *** p<0.01

Table 6. Perceptions of financial disclosures by SES organisations

Responses (%)	1	2	3	4	5	Not Sure
It is important to be able to get any financial statement information you want from an SES organisation	5.26	6.52	23.31	28.07	28.82	8.02
The public, in general, has a right to know about everything an SES organisation does	5.26	7.02	19.55	26.32	35.09	6.77
Every member of the public should have complete access to information about SES organisations	5.26	12.28	20.80	28.07	26.32	7.27
The records of an SES organisation belong to the public in general, not the SES organisation	5.76	9.77	24.31	28.07	23.31	8.77
Financial transparency is key to fighting fraud by SES organisations	3.76	5.51	17.04	22.56	42.36	8.77
It is nobody's business what SES organisations receive	31.08	21.80	14.54	13.28	10.78	8.52
It is nobody's business how SES organisations spend their money	33.83	18.30	15.79	13.28	10.53	8.27
It is too much of a hassle to look at financial statement information published by Australian SES organisations	9.25	13.00	29.50	23.50	13.75	11.00

n = 400. Adapted from Piotrowski and van Ryzin (2007).

spondents' level of knowledge of basic financial accounting concepts has an average total score of were 4.10 out of 10, as reported in Table 8. This implies that on average, a respondent may only understand around 41% of the disclosures provided within a financial statement; thereby rendering its full meaning of somewhat opaque.

DISCUSSION AND CONCLUSION

This chapter has explored the general public's perceptions of the relative importance of specific financial disclosures which it believes SES organisations should publish. Using a sample of 400 respondents and data collected from a survey questionnaire, it was found that the public perceives financial disclosures (which relate to sources of fund inflows, mission-related expenses and financial sustainability) to be relatively important disclosures and that these disclosures should be accessible to all.

A plausible explanation of these findings is that the public perceives SES organisations, similar to nonprofit organisations, as having an obligation to allocate funds to missions which increase social welfare (Dhanani & Connolly, 2012). Also, these findings suggest that the public feels that SES organisations have a duty to provide financial disclosures, transparency and accountability in the SES space. Given that SES organisations operate in an environment where trust is fundamental for its fund inflows (Hyndman & McConville, 2018), it is recommended that these organisations signal the legitimacy of their use of funds, and hence the legitimacy of their activities, by publishing financial disclosures associated with their fund inflows, their mission-related expenses and their financial sustainability. By making such disclosures publicly available, SES organisations will better cater to the public's information needs and

Table 7. Respondents' level of knowledge of basic financial accounting concepts

	Questions	Proportion of sample identifying correct answer	Average Score for each question
1	What is the basic accounting equation?	36.75%	0.22
2	Which financial statement presents a summary of the assets, liabilities, and owners' equity of a firm?	45.50%	0.46
3	Which authority oversees the social economy sector in Australia?	60.00%	0.60
4	In Australia, social economy sector organisations mainly operate as	37.00%	0.20
5	Subtracting expenses from revenues yields _____.	53.00%	0.84
6	Which accounting document keeps track of the cash receipts and cash payments of a business during a specific period?	39.50%	0.39
7	Under which type of cash flow statement activities should a social economy organisation record cash received from grants and donations?	32.00%	0.28
8	Total liabilities divided by total equity yields the _____.	56.00%	0.56
9	Which is the most popular method of accelerated depreciation?	26.00%	0.18
10	What is the name of the process of identifying each posting and journal entry?	37.75%	0.38

n = 400, Adapted from Sutton (2017). Figures have been rounded to 2 decimal places.

Table 8. Respondents' financial knowledge test score

	Average Total Score	Std. Error	Std. Deviation	Variance	Maximum	Minimum	Range
Test Score	4.10	0.10	1.97	3.90	8	0	8

n = 400. Figures have been rounded to 2 decimal places.

reduce the extent of information asymmetry which exists between SES organisations and the general public. As a result, this improved accountability (via financial disclosures) may increase the public's trust and confidence in SES organisations (Bryce, 2016), better inform their economic decisions, and eventually contribute to the sustainability of those SES organisations which effectively and efficiently allocates funds to activities that add to social and/or environmental welfare. Also, when publishing financial disclosures related to fund flows, SES organisations should provide sufficient detail to allow informed decisions by funders, other stakeholder groups and the general public. SES organisations need to ensure that they do not make their financial disclosures too complex; they should take a more accessible form to allow informed analysis by the general public (and more on this anon).

The chapter also observed that the majority of the members perceived *'Transactions with related parties'* as being the least important 'other financial disclosure' item which they believe SES organisations should publish. This is an interesting observation because related party transactions are one of the causes of scandals and it may suggest that when answering the survey questions, the respondents were unmoved by unfavourable media coverage. A reasonable interpretation is that the general public is not motivated in its perceptions by the actual behaviours of SES organisations but rather by the general principled concern that SES organisations should transparently act in accordance with their stated goals.

Further, from the regression analysis, it was observed that a respondent's age is a direct determinant of their perception of the relative importance of the financial disclosures which SES organisations publish. This finding implies that respondents who are older, compared to younger respondents, perceive more important that SES organisations make financial disclosures available to the general public.

Further, the chapter has found that the respondents have an interest in financial disclosures and their level of financial knowledge is unlikely to be sufficient to understand a majority of the disclosures provided within financial statements. However, at the same time, the study has noted that a majority of the respondents agree that financial statement information might be too much of a hassle to use. Taking these different findings into account, it is advised that SES organisations produce a one-page 'Snapshot Document' as a supplement to their publicly available full financial reports (Ghoorah, 2018). Such a 'Snapshot Document' should be tailored to the general public, rather than to any specific stakeholder group (such as funders) per se, in order to ensure the discharge of upward as well as downward accountability. Also, SES organisations should provide financial disclosures about their fund flows, their mission-related expenses and their financial sustainability using a format which is presented in a more user-friendly manner than the standardised format of financial statements. A way forward would be to use graphs, charts, colours and pictures to represent financial disclosure information. Furthermore, the 'Snapshot Document' should be made readily and easily available to the general public. By addressing the general public's information needs, simplifying the presentation of financial disclosures and making the information broadly available, an SES organisation will better fulfil its duty to be accountable and reduce the extent of information asymmetry (or at least the extent of perceived information asymmetry) with funders. As a result, both funders and the general public will have greater trust and confidence in SES organisations.

The findings and discussions of this chapter must be considered in light of its limitations. There are three primary limitations of this study. First, it does not explore the public's perceptions of the relative importance of non-financial disclosures, such as annual report, website and social media disclosures which SES organisations provide as part of their provision of accountability. Second, the study does not consider non-individual funders (such as institutional donors and grant providers) and how their perceptions of specific disclosure items differ from those of the general public. Last, given its focus on the Australian context, the findings and observations of the study cannot be generalised to contexts which are different from the Australian environment.

The limitations of the study represent avenues for future research. A longitudinal study may examine the evolution of different stakeholder groups' (such as funders', regulators', members') perception of the requirement for accountability. Such a study may further investigate how these perceptions change across age groups and with increasing age. Another study, a cross-cultural analysis study, may investigate whether there are differences in disclosure norms and perceptions of what is acceptable accountability 'standards' or practices for the general public. Such a study could help in providing preliminary input into establishing international disclosure standards for SES organisations globally. Another extension study may address the general public's specific normative conception of SES organisations' disclosures and accountability. The study may address questions like *'Does the general public think they have an absolute right to disclosures and accountability?'*, *'Does the public think that SES organisations have an absolute obligation to disclose?'* and *'Does the public believe that it is desirable, but not an obligation for SES organisations to disclose and be accountable?'*. The answer to these questions will give a more nuanced insight into the general public's perceptions and could inform future regulatory requirements and/or recommendations.

ACKNOWLEDGMENT

The author would like to thank two anonymous reviewers, Dr. Edward Mariyani-Squire and Associate Professor Maria Estela Varua for their comments on this chapter.

This research was supported by Western Sydney University, School of Business, Research Project Scheme 2017.

REFERENCES

AASB. (2015). *AASB 101 - Presentation of Financial Statements*. Australian Government.

ACNC. (2013). *Australian Charities and Not-for-profits Commission (ACNC) 2013 research: Public trust and confidence in Australian charities*. Commonwealth of Australia.

Arshad, R., Bakar, N. A., Thani, N. Y., & Omar, N. (2013). Board composition and accountability of non-profit organizations. *Journal of Applied Business Research*, *29*(4), 1021. doi:10.19030/jabr.v29i4.7913

Austin, J., Stevenson, H., & Wei-Skillern, J. (2012). Social and commercial entrepreneurship: Same, different, or both? *Revista ADM*, *47*(3), 370–384.

Banerjee, A., Duflo, E., Glennerster, R., & Kinnan, C. (2015). The miracle of microfinance? Evidence from a randomized evaluation. *American Economic Journal. Applied Economics*, *7*(1), 22–53. doi:10.1257/app.20130533

Barraket, J., Mason, C., & Blain, B. (2016). *Finding Australia's Social Enterprise Sector 2016: Final Report*. Centre for Social Impact. Swinburne University of Technology.

Bryce, H. J. (2016). The public's trust in nonprofit organizations: The role of relationship marketing and management. *The Nonprofit Quarterly*, *49*(4), 112–131.

Bugg-Levine, A., Kogut, B., & Kulatilaka, N. (2012). A new approach to funding social enterprises. *Harvard Business Review*, *90*(1/2), 118–123.

Canales, R. (2013). Weaving straw into gold: Managing organizational tensions between standardization and flexibility in microfinance. *Organization Science*, *25*(1), 1–28. doi:10.1287/orsc.2013.0831

Choi, N., & Majumdar, S. (2014). Social entrepreneurship as an essentially contested concept: Opening a new avenue for systematic future research. *Journal of Business Venturing*, *29*(3), 363–376. doi:10.1016/j.jbusvent.2013.05.001

Connolly, C., & Hyndman, N. (2013). Charity accountability in the UK: Through the eyes of the donor. *Qualitative Research in Accounting & Management*, *10*(3/4), 259–278. doi:10.1108/QRAM-02-2013-0006

Cordery, C. J., & Baskerville, R. F. (2011). Charity transgressions, trust and accountability. *Voluntas*, *22*(2), 197–213. doi:10.100711266-010-9132-x

Crack, A. (2018). The Oxfam scandal has taught us there's no reward for honest charities. *The Guardian*. Retrieved from https://www.theguardian.com/voluntary-sector-network/2018/mar/16/government-donors-reward-honest-charities-oxfam

Dhanani, A., & Connolly, C. (2012). Discharging not-for-profit accountability: UK charities and public discourse. *Accounting, Auditing & Accountability Journal*, *25*(7), 1140–1169. doi:10.1108/09513571211263220

Ebrahim, A. (2003a). Accountability in practice: Mechanisms for NGOs. *World Development*, *31*(5), 813–829. doi:10.1016/S0305-750X(03)00014-7

Ebrahim, A. (2003b). Making sense of accountability: Conceptual perspectives for northern and southern nonprofits. *Nonprofit Management & Leadership*, *14*(2), 191–212. doi:10.1002/nml.29

Ebrahim, A., Battilana, J., & Mair, J. (2014). The governance of social enterprises: Mission drift and accountability challenges in hybrid organizations. *Research in Organizational Behavior*, *34*, 81–100. doi:10.1016/j.riob.2014.09.001

Ebrahim, A., & Rangan, V. K. (2010). The limits of nonprofit impact: A contingency framework for measuring social performance (No. 10-099). Harvard Business School.

Ebrahim, A., & Rangan, V. K. (2014). What impact? A framework for measuring the scale and scope of social performance. *California Management Review*, *56*(3), 118–141. doi:10.1525/cmr.2014.56.3.118

Ghoorah, U. (2018). *Snapshot Document: A Tool to develop trust and confidence*. Pro Bono Australia Newsletter.

Goddard, A., & Juma Assad, M. (2006). Accounting and navigating legitimacy in Tanzanian NGOs. *Accounting, Auditing & Accountability Journal*, *19*(3), 377–404. doi:10.1108/09513570610670343

Goh, J. X., Schlegel, K., Tignor, S. M., & Hall, J. A. (2016). Who is interested in personality? The Interest in Personality Scale and its correlates. *Personality and Individual Differences*, *101*, 185–191. doi:10.1016/j.paid.2016.05.366

González, H. V. (2010). *The impact of nonfinancial performance on the financial performance of the United States investor-owned multihospital systems*. Rio Piedras: University of Puerto Rico.

Gray, S. J., Meek, G. K., & Roberts, C. B. (1995). International capital market pressures and voluntary annual report disclosures by US and UK multinationals. *Journal of International Financial Management & Accounting*, *6*(1), 43–68. doi:10.1111/j.1467-646X.1995.tb00049.x

Gross, M. J., Jr. (1977). Nonprofit accounting: The continuing revolution. *Journal of Accountancy*, *143*(6), 66-143.

Gross, M. J., McCarthy, J. H., & Shelmon, N. E. (2005). *Financial and accounting guide for not-for-profit organizations*. John Wiley & Sons.

Guraieb Izaguirre, G. A. (2015). *Social enterprises: Examining accountability for social and financial performance* (Doctoral dissertation). Queensland University of Technology.

Handy, F., & Russell, A. R. (2018). *Introduction: Why Ethics? Ethics for Social Impact*. Cham: Palgrave Macmillan. doi:10.1007/978-3-319-75040-8_1

Herzlinger, R. E., & Sherman, H. D. (1980). Advantages of fund accounting in'nonprofits'. *Harvard Business Review*, *58*(3), 94–105. PMID:10318498

Hyndman, N. (2017). The charity sector—Changing times, changing challenges. *Public Money & Management*, *37*(3), 149–153. doi:10.1080/09540962.2017.1281608

Hyndman, N., & McConville, D. (2018). Trust and accountability in UK charities: Exploring the virtuous circle. *The British Accounting Review*, *50*(2), 227–237. doi:10.1016/j.bar.2017.09.004

Hyndman, N., McKillop, D., Ferguson, C., & Wall, T. (2004). The financial accountability of Irish Credit Unions: An initial empirical study. *Financial Accountability & Management*, *20*(3), 253–279. doi:10.1111/j.0267-4424.2004.00385.x

Ingram, R. W. (1986). Tests of the fund accounting model for local governments. *Contemporary Accounting Research*, *3*(1), 200–221. doi:10.1111/j.1911-3846.1986.tb00634.x

Justice Connect. (2017a). *Social Enterprise Guide: Legal issues to consider when setting up a social enterprise*. Australia Not-for-profit Law Guide. Accessed 12 February 2019, https://www.nfplaw.org.au/sites/default/files/media/Social_Enterprise_Guide_Cth_1.pdf

Justice Connect. (2017b). *Running the organisation – Documents, records and requests for access*. Australia Not-for-profit Law Guide. Accessed 12 February 2019, https://www.nfplaw.org.au/recordkeeping

Keating, E. K., & Frumkin, P. (2003). Reengineering nonprofit financial accountability: Toward a more reliable foundation for regulation. *Public Administration Review*, *63*(1), 3–15. doi:10.1111/1540-6210.00260

Kummer, T. F., Singh, K., & Best, P. (2015). The effectiveness of fraud detection instruments in not-for-profit organizations. *Managerial Auditing Journal*, *30*(4/5), 435–455. doi:10.1108/MAJ-08-2014-1083

Mack, J., & Ryan, C. (2006). Reflections on the theoretical underpinnings of the general-purpose financial reports of Australian government departments. *Accounting, Auditing & Accountability Journal*, *19*(4), 592–612. doi:10.1108/09513570610679146

Magena, M., Kinman, R., & Citron, D. (2008). Investment analysts' perception of disclosure in UK interim financial reports. *Journal ofAppliedAccounting Research*, *8*(3), 146–185. doi:10.1108/96754260880001057

Mair, J., Battilana, J., & Cardenas, J. (2012). Organizing for society: A typology of social entrepreneuring models. *Journal of Business Ethics*, *111*(3), 353–373. doi:10.100710551-012-1414-3

McCarthy, J. H., Shelmon, N. E., & Mattie, J. A. (2012). *Financial and accounting guide for not-for-profit organizations*. John Wiley & Sons.

McDonnell, D. (2017). Improving Charity Accountability: Lessons from the Scottish Experience. *Nonprofit and Voluntary Sector Quarterly*, *46*(4), 725–746. doi:10.1177/0899764017692039

Mirshekary, S., & Saudagaran, S. M. (2005). Perceptions and characteristics of financial statement users in developing countries: Evidence from Iran. *Journal of International Accounting, Auditing & Taxation, 14*(1), 33–54. doi:10.1016/j.intaccaudtax.2005.01.001

Mitchell, R. K., Agle, B. R., & Wood, D. J. (1997). Toward a theory of stakeholder identification and salience: Defining the principle of who and what really counts. *Academy of Management Review, 22*(4), 853–886. doi:10.5465/amr.1997.9711022105

Morris, M. (2018). RSL Victoria admits 'inappropriate' gift to former boss partly paid with charity money. *ABC News*. Accessed 13 September 2018, http://www.abc.net.au/news/2018-06-28/former-rsl-victoria-boss-given-inappropriate-gift-probe-finds/9919012

O'Brien, E., & Tooley, S. (2013). Accounting for volunteer services: A deficiency in accountability. *Qualitative Research in Accounting & Management, 10*(3/4), 279–294. doi:10.1108/QRAM-09-2012-0037

O'Dwyer, B., & Unerman, J. (2008). The paradox of greater NGO accountability: A case study of Amnesty Ireland. *Accounting, Organizations and Society, 33*(7-8), 801–824. doi:10.1016/j.aos.2008.02.002

Parsons, L. M. (2007). The impact of financial information and voluntary disclosures on contributions to not-for-profit organizations. *Behavioral Research in Accounting, 19*(1), 179–196. doi:10.2308/bria.2007.19.1.179

Piotrowski, S. J., & Van Ryzin, G. G. (2007). Citizen attitudes toward transparency in local government. *American Review of Public Administration, 37*(3), 306–323. doi:10.1177/0275074006296777

Prakash, A., & Gugerty, M. K. (2010). Trust but verify? Voluntary regulation programs in the nonprofit sector. *Regulation & Governance, 4*(1), 22–47.

Raffer, K. (2004). International financial institutions and financial accountability. *Ethics & International Affairs, 18*(2), 61–77. doi:10.1111/j.1747-7093.2004.tb00468.x

Rouf, Md. (2016). Users' Perception on Corporate Voluntary Disclosure in Bangladesh. *Daffodil International University Journal of Business and Economics, 10*(1), 136–151.

Santos, F., Pache, A. C., & Birkholz, C. (2015). Making hybrids work: Aligning business models and organizational design for social enterprises. *California Management Review, 57*(3), 36–58. doi:10.1525/cmr.2015.57.3.36

Sinclair, A. (1995). The chameleon of accountability: Forms and discourses. *Accounting, Organizations and Society, 20*(2-3), 219–237. doi:10.1016/0361-3682(93)E0003-Y

Strom, S. (2010). Hybrid model for nonprofits hits snag. *New York Times*. Retrieved from https://www.nytimes.com/2010/10/26/business/26hybrid.html

Sutton, H. (2017). Boost your adult students' progress to degree with CLEP credit. *The Successful Registrar, 17*(6), 1–5. doi:10.1002/tsr.30326

Tenbensel, T., Dwyer, J., & Lavoie, J. (2014). How not to kill the golden goose: Reconceptualizing accountability environments of third-sector organizations. *Public Management Review, 16*(7), 925–944. doi:10.1080/14719037.2013.770054

Tooley, S., & Hooks, J. (2010). Public accountability: The Perceived usefulness of school annual reports. *Australasian Accounting. Business and Finance Journal, 4*(2), 39–59.

van Staden, C., & Heslop, J. (2009). Implications of Applying a Private Sector Based Reporting Model to Not-for-Profit Entities: The Treatment of Charitable Distributions by Charities in New Zealand. *Australian Accounting Review, 19*(1), 42–53. doi:10.1111/j.1835-2561.2008.00039.x

Yang, C., Northcott, D., & Sinclair, R. (2017). The accountability information needs of key charity funders. *Public Money & Management, 37*(3), 173–180. doi:10.1080/09540962.2017.1281649

Yasmin, S., Haniffa, R., & Hudaib, M. (2014). Communicated accountability by faith-based charity organisations. *Journal of Business Ethics, 122*(1), 103–123. doi:10.100710551-013-1759-2

Yetman, M. H., & Yetman, R. J. (2012). The effects of governance on the accuracy of charitable expenses reported by nonprofit organizations. *Contemporary Accounting Research, 29*(3), 738–767. doi:10.1111/j.1911-3846.2011.01121.x

Zainon, S., Atan, R., & Bee Wah, Y. (2014). An empirical study on the determinants of information disclosure of Malaysian non-profit organizations. *Asian Review of Accounting, 22*(1), 35–55. doi:10.1108/ARA-04-2013-0026

ADDITIONAL READING

Agyemang, G., O'Dwyer, B., Unerman, J., & Awumbila, M. (2017). Seeking "conversations for accountability" Mediating the impact of non-governmental organization (NGO) upward accountability processes. *Accounting, Auditing & Accountability Journal, 30*(5), 982–1007. doi:10.1108/AAAJ-02-2015-1969

Connolly, C., & Hyndman, N. (2013). Towards charity accountability: Narrowing the gap between provision and needs? *Public Management Review, 15*(7), 945–968. doi:10.1080/14719037.2012.757349

Furneaux, C., & Wymer, W. (2015). Public trust in Australian charities: Accounting for cause and effect. *Third Sector Review, 21*(2), 99.

Hall, M., & O'Dwyer, B. (2017). Accounting, non-governmental organizations and civil society: The importance of nonprofit organizations to understanding accounting, organizations and society. *Accounting, Organizations and Society, 63*, 1–5. doi:10.1016/j.aos.2017.11.001

Hyndman, N., & McConville, D. (2016). Transparency in reporting on charities' efficiency: A framework for analysis. *Nonprofit and Voluntary Sector Quarterly, 45*(4), 844–865. doi:10.1177/0899764015603205

McDonnell, D., & Rutherford, A. C. (2018). Promoting charity accountability: Understanding disclosure of serious incidents. *Accounting Forum*. doi:10.1016/j.accfor.2018.05.003

O'Dwyer, B., & Boomsma, R. (2015). The co-construction of NGO accountability: Aligning imposed and felt accountability in NGO-funder accountability relationships. *Accounting, Auditing & Accountability Journal, 28*(1), 36–68. doi:10.1108/AAAJ-10-2013-1488

Sinclair, R., Northcott, D., & Hooper, K. (2014). Can sector-specific standards enhance the comparability of Third sector organisations' financial statements? *Third Sector Review*, *20*(2), 27.

KEY TERMS AND DEFINITIONS

Accounting Information: Disclosures which give details about an entity in money terms. These disclosures are usually prepared and presented in a standardized format following reporting standards, guidelines, and/or generally accepted practices.

Economic Benefits: Advantages which can be measured in monetary value.

External Accountability: External accountability relates to the provision of disclosures which cater to the information needs of the external stakeholders of an organisation, such as funders, regulators, recipients of the goods and services provided by the entity, and society at large.

Information Asymmetry: A situation where, for two or more parties which have competing or common goals, at least one party possess "private" information unknown to but beneficial to the other party or parties.

Internal Accountability: Internal accountability involves the provision of disclosures which meet the information needs of the internal stakeholders of an organisation, such as its employees, management, and board.

Operational Capability: The ability of an entity to maintain a certain level of operation in the future.

Resource Dependence: Reliance which an organisation has on external supplies or inputs.

Social Economy Sector (SES) Organization: An organisation which operates a business model to achieve its social or environment objectives, such as those related to the alleviation of poverty, wealth inequality, and environmental damage.

Stewardship: The responsibility of managing and taking care of something on behalf of another party.

Transparency: The condition of not keeping secrets from another party by providing information and making disclosures.

Chapter 3
A Domain Model for Transparency in Portuguese Cooperatives:
The Governance Structure and Accountability Dimensions

Mariana Curado Malta
https://orcid.org/0000-0002-3512-931X
Polytechnic Institute of Porto, Portugal & University of Minho, Portugal

Deolinda Aparício Meira
Polytechnic Institute of Porto, Portugal

Ana Maria Bandeira
Polytechnic Institute of Porto, Portugal

Melanie Santos
Polytechnic Institute of Porto, Portugal

ABSTRACT

The aim of this chapter is to present a domain model that represents the informational needs of transparency (governance structure and accountability dimensions) in Portuguese cooperatives. A domain model is an abstract representation of a reality and a milestone in the development of a metadata application profile (MAP). A community of practice publishes linked open MAP-based data for these data to be interoperable; this means intelligent software/agents can aggregate these data, provide different types of visualizations, infer from the data, and ultimately provide new discoveries. This model was developed having as basis the information obtained from the accomplishment of a focus group, and the analysis of financial reports and websites of seven Portuguese cooperatives. The authors will continue to work on the domain model to include 1) other dimensions that also contribute for transparency in the organizations and 2) other types of entities of the social economy (SE). The final aim is to define a model representing the needs of transparency of all types of European SE entities.

DOI: 10.4018/978-1-5225-8482-7.ch003

INTRODUCTION

A Cooperative is a legal person that carries on any economic activity through the cooperation and mutual assistance of its members. These economic activities follow cooperative principles within the interests of its members where profit cannot be the ultimate purpose (article 2.1 of the PCC - 'Código Cooperativo Português')[1] (Fajardo et al., 2017). The primary purpose of cooperatives is to meet the economic, social and cultural needs of their members (mutuality) and not to make a profit (Bandeira, Meira, & Alves, 2016; Meira, 2009).

There are 12 branches of Cooperative in Portugal today: consumer, trade, agricultural, credit, housing and building, worker, crafts, fishery, cultural, services, education, and social solidarity (article 4 of the PCC).[2]

It is explicitly allowed that one Cooperative operates in areas covered by more than one branch: article 4.2 of the PCC distinguishes multi-purpose cooperatives (those covering more than one area of activity) from multi-sector cooperatives (those that carry out activities that are a feature of various types of cooperative within their sector).

The members of a cooperative can be cooperator members or investor members (art. 5 of the PCC). The cooperator members are 'users' of the cooperative enterprise, engaging in cooperative transactions with the cooperators. The investor members are contributors to the capital of the Cooperative enterprise (Meira & Ramos, 2014).

The value of transparency in governance is central to cooperatives, and it is inseparable from active participation in cooperative democratic control. Under the Portuguese law, cooperative governance is characterised as transparent among other characteristics. Members have the right to information, enshrined in the PCC, and have the right to control and supervise the Board of Directors through participation in the General Meeting and in the Supervisory Board (Münkner, 2015).

The structure of the governance bodies of Portuguese cooperatives can be characterised as hierarchical and tripartite. The bodies of a Cooperative are the General Meeting, the Board of Directors, and the Supervisory Board (art. 27.1 of the PCC).

The General Meeting is the highest body of a cooperative, and its decisions are bound to all the other bodies (art. 33.1 of the PCC). The Board of Directors is primarily an executive body (arts. 47 and 62 of the PCC), while the Supervisory Board is a body of control and supervision (arts. 53, 61, and 64 of the PCC).

Board members are elected from among members (with the exception of the Statutory Auditor) for a period of four years, unless a shorter period is provided in the cooperative's statutes (art. 29 of the PCC). The statutes of a Cooperative may limit the number of consecutive terms of the board of the General Meeting, of the Board of Directors, of the Supervisory Board, and any other Cooperative body (article 29.6 of the PCC).

According to art. 28 of the PCC, the management and supervisory board of a Cooperative may be structured in one of the following ways: (i) a Board of Directors and a Supervisory Board; (ii) a Board of Directors with an Audit Committee and an Auditor; or (iii) an Executive Board of Directors, a General and Supervisory Board, and an Auditor.

Each Cooperative chooses the management and supervision model that wishes to adopt, and this choice must be defined in the statutes of the cooperative (art. 16.1.d) of the PCC). In cooperatives with 20 or fewer members it is possible to have a sole Director (arts. 28.2 and 45 of the PCC) and a single Supervisor, insofar as this is provided in the statutes.

The General Meeting is the supreme body of cooperatives, and its decisions are bound to the remaining bodies (art. 33.1 of the PCC). Scrutiny of the performance of the Board of Directors and Supervisory Board by the General Meeting of a Cooperative occurs particularly at the time when the management report and accounts for the financial year are assessed (art. 38.b) of the PCC).

The PCC does not demand an external audit to cooperatives. In the case of cooperatives that are obliged to submit to statutory auditing, supervision will be entrusted to a Supervisory Board and to a Statutory Auditor who is not a member of the Supervisory Board (art. 51.1.c) of the PCC). In the models provided in art. 28.1, b) and c) of the PCC, a Statutory Auditor will always exist, but this person will not join the Supervisory Board (Meira, 2016).

In addition to the annual control, the General Meeting exerts over the Board of Directors, the cooperators may also exercise their right to information, individually or collectively (article 21.1.d) of the PCC).

The multiple obligations of the Cooperative's bodies, including the Board of Directors, to disclose facts and make documents related to the activities of the cooperative available are included in the passive component. Of note here is the significant duty of information that falls on the Board of Directors to make the management report, the financial year accounting documents, the business plan and the budget for the following financial year available to members at the cooperative's head office, accompanied by an expert opinion from the Supervisory Board (art. 47.a) of the PCC and art. 263.1 of the CSC, applicable by reference to article 9 of the PCC).

In addition to the duty to prepare accounting documents and records, the members of the Board of Directors are obliged to submit these documents to the competent bodies of the Cooperative, namely the General Meeting and the Supervisory Board, Audit Committee or a General and Supervisory Board.

Accounting documents and records that include the management report and accounts for the financial year (balance sheet, profit-and-loss account, notes, and other documents).

In the Portuguese legal system, cooperatives are not required to file their management reports and accounts for the financial year with the Commercial Registry. Article 4 of the Commercial Registration Code sets out the facts relating to cooperatives and registration, and they do not include those relating to accounts, as is expressly provided in the case of commercial companies (art. 3.n) of the Commercial Registration Code).

Cooperatives are also required to submit both their management reports and accounts to CASES – *Cooperativa António Sergio para a Economia Social* after obtaining approval from the respective General Meeting, as well as a Social Report, which is a prerequisite for obtaining credentials attesting to their legal incorporation and proper operation (arts. 116 and 117 of the PCC). In this context, CASES has allowed creditors of a Cooperative claiming a legitimate interest to query the accounting documents of cooperatives deposited there. The PCC does not, however, make it clear whether filing can be treated as a registration of cooperatives designed to make their legal status public; and therefore the question might be asked as to whether these documents are protected by confidentiality (in the sense that they were sent by the cooperative for the particular purpose of obtaining the credentials).

When preparing their accounts, cooperatives are subject to the SNC – *Sistema de Normalização Contabilística*[3] (Rodrigues, 2016).

Furthermore, in the SNC, the privileged user of the information disclosed in the financial statements is clearly the investor. The information prepared is based on assumptions that are very much conditioned by the logic of profitability and results distributed to investors, which is inadequate for the logic of cooperatives, which is based on a mutualist purpose, and where distributions of cooperative surpluses are made in proportion to the transactions carried out by each member.

Finally, income statements are dedicated to the economic and financial performance of the corporate entity at the expense of the economic and social performance which is a feature of cooperatives. This does not facilitate the capture of many of the objectives of cooperatives, which are alien to the logic of profit (Rodrigues, 2010).

The Supervisory Board, Audit Committee, or General and Supervisory Board (depending on the model adopted — arts. 28.1, 51, 56, 65 ff. of the PCC) will assess compliance with the law and the statutes, the formal audit (verification of the correctness of entries and accounting procedures), and the material audit (assessing the quality of management in relation to business objectives) of the cooperative (art. 53 of the PCC).

All this process has an amount of information that is available to the members of the Cooperative and to external individuals, organisations or governments, but it is organised in such a way that it can only be read by humans and not to be processed automatically by machines. For now, the civil society does not have access of any other type of information then pdf files (e.g. financial reports) or Web pages. The issue is that this information can be in fact captured and published as five stars linked open data in the semantic Web[4], assuring that the data from the Portuguese cooperative sector can become interoperable boosting the transparency in these organisations. This way data can be consumed by machines, can be processed and compared, and conclusions can be made out of a result of calculations of aggregated values from different organisations.

This problem is addressed by structuring this information in a common informational model (domain model) for the Portuguese Cooperatives. This chapter presents a domain model for the transparency of the Portuguese Cooperatives regarding two variables: governance structure and accountability. A domain model defines the concepts (and its properties) of a context, and how they relate. A domain model is the basis of a data structuring work in the context of developing a metadata application profile (MAP), a construct that enables the exchange of data in an automatic way, in other words interoperable data. A MAP is a construct of the Semantic Web, an ecosystem of linked open data (W3C, 2015). This domain model will be though a tool to enhance accountability transparency in the Portuguese cooperatives. This domain model was implemented based on a Focus Group with two accountability experts, and followed by a validation using real data extracted from the analysis of the 1) governance structure, 2) the accountability documents, and 3) the Websites of seven cooperatives from different branches of cooperatives and sizes.

This chapter is divided in six sections. The following section briefly presents the technological context, that is, the semantic web ecosystem and the metadata application profile construct, section three presents the methodology followed to develop the domain model. Section four presents in detail the model including the UML diagram (Rumbaugh, Booch, & Jacobson, 2017) of the model and a detailed description for each entity, relation and attribute of the model. Section five presents the limitations of the work, and section six concludes the chapter with some future perspectives of the work.

Semantic Web and Metadata Application Profile

The Semantic Web was a term firstly coined in the seminal article by Berners-Lee, Hendler & Lassila (2001) (revisited later in 2006) and it can be defined as a linked open data (LOD) (W3C, 2015) ecosystem and a set of different technologies that can reasoning over the data. This ecosystem, which is also called the Web of Data, lives side by side the Web of Documents we use every day. The data published as LOD are actually RDF graphs. The core of a RDF graph is a RDF triple which is composed by a

Subject, a *Predicate* and an *Object* (W3C, 2014a). Every part of the RDF triple can be defined as an IRI, a literal value or a blank node, but the IRI is the characteristic of the model that enhances the linking of the data. In fact, e.g. an *Object* can be described in a different server, with data that does not belong to the original dataset; this is the power of LOD: one can use other people's data to enrich its own data.

The *Predicate* of a triple is a property that makes explicit the relation between the *Subject* and the *Object*. A property is a term taken from a RDF vocabulary and it is what provides semantic to the statement (triple) (W3C, 2014b).

The Semantic Web has a great potential on the enhancement of interoperability between a community of practice because of its openness. Linked Open Data when accessible via SPARQL endpoints is openly available for any machine or intelligent agent, i.e. pieces of software, to make visualisations and infer over the data, even though these data are available in different servers. This is possible because of the semantic dimension that the *Predicate* gives to the RDF triple and ultimately to the RDF Graphs of the datasets. It is also imperative that the datasets of a same community of practice are structured in the same way.

The Dublin Core Metadata Initiative (DCMI) is a well-known and influential global initiative concerned with metadata. In order to provide "a foundation for the development of application-independent syntax specifications and constraint languages", DCMI developed the Dublin Core Abstract Model (DCAM) (c.f. Powell, Nilsson, Naeve, Johnston, & Baker (2009)). A DCAM defines the components and constructs used in DCMI metadata. One of these constructs is the Dublin Core Application Profile (DCAP) - "a generic construct for designing metadata records" (Coyle & Baker, 2009). A DCAP can also be called a metadata application profile (MAP). According to Nilsson, Baker, & Johnston, Pete (2009) a MAP is a very important construct to achieve interoperability. If a community of practice defines a MAP to express common data (common to the members of the community), it is in a sense declaring to the members of the community how the structure of the data should be, to be published as interoperable linked open data. Examples of MAPs are the DCAP-SSE developed by a group of the Social and Solidarity Economy (Curado Malta, Baptista & Parente, 2015), the MAP for the MODS community (Branan, 2019), or the MAP for archival descriptions (Matienzo, Roke, & Carlson, 2017).

The study here presented is integrated in a larger project that aims to define a MAP for the Portuguese Cooperatives. Ultimately the final aim is to define a MAP for the European entities of the social economy sector.

As far as the authors' understanding is concerned, in order to give rigor to this work it is essential to use a method to develop a MAP. The work here reported is using Me4MAP which defines as a milestone of the whole project the definition of a domain model with the informational needs of the context. A domain model is a construct that defines the things of the context (entities), how these "things" relate to each other (relations), and how these "things" are described (attributes). The Domain Model is developed using a graphical data modelling technique such as e.g. Entity-Relationship diagrams (ER) (Chen, 1976) or UML diagrams (Rumbaugh et al., 2017). The domain model will be the basis for the implementation of the MAP, where the entities correspond to the domains and ranges of the implementation and the attributes to the properties of the implementation.

Methodology

Me4MAP establishes that a MAP development team should be composed by different profile-members. It states that it is essential that such a team integrates experts in the context being modelled. The present context asks for experts in Cooperative Legislation and Cooperative Accountability. The team integrates one Cooperative expert in Legislation and one in Accounting, as well as one System Analyst and Semantic Developer expert.

Me4MAP also defines that the elicitation of the requirements can use different techniques, depending on the information made available by the context stakeholders.

The development of the model followed the workflow presented in Figure 1. The researchers used two sources of information to develop the model. The first source was a Focus Group held in the facilities of the Polytechnic of Porto Business School in July 24, 2018. Two experts in accounting participated in this Focus Group. They interacted with the system analyst of the research team to explain the components of a cooperative financial report so to identify the informational needs of such a report. After this first meeting the system analyst with the help of the context experts created a first version (V1) of the model.

The second source of information were 1) the financial reports of the cooperatives 2) the information provided by the Websites of the cooperatives. The work-team selected a sample of 42 Portuguese cooperatives for the study, from those 42, five had the information needed in their Websites. The other 37 were contacted by email, the researchers asked for the financial report for the study. From these 37, six replied to the email, but only two sent the financial report of 2017. The other four replied negatively, one said that they were in a phase of launching new projects, and for that they were moving for new facilities and reinforcing the technical team, so they did not have the time to send the financial report, other two said that they were not available since they were too busy, and the last one said that they were currently reviewing both the statutes of the cooperative and the annual chart of accounts, and that they did not feel comfortable in sending documents in the middle of a process of deep changes.

Table 1 presents the seven cooperatives used to do the validation of V1 of the domain model (from now on called "model"). The analysis of the websites and of the financial reports provided data that was used on this validation. V1 of the model was "implemented" in a stylesheet that served as template to be used in the validation process (all files available in http://github.com/marianamalta/domain-model-PT-coopertives[5]). This validation was done by a member of the team expert in accounting. After defining the files, some details were adjusted and V2 of the model was issued. V2 was validated before delivering the final version of the model. This validation took place again with the same experts that participated in the Focus Group I. This meeting took place in the facilities of the Polytechnic of Porto Business School in November 24, 2018: The experts discussed the V2 of the model with the researchers. Out of the discussion a third version was issued (V3) which is presented in the next section.

A Domain Model for the Portuguese Cooperatives

The model is presented in Figure 2 as an UML class diagram (see Rumbaugh, et al. (2017)) with entities that relate to each other, where each entity has attributes that define it.

The entities ENTITTY and ROC-SROC describe the dataset:

- **ENTITY**: Defines the year of the dataset, the name and the URL of the entity, the type of entity (in the present case all are "Cooperative" – this field will serve a future model with other type of Social Economy Entities) and the branch of the entity. As already said, there are 12 categorisations for branches in Portugal: consumer, trade, agriculture, credit, housing and building, worker, crafts, fishery, cultural, services, education, and social solidarity. A cooperative can work in more than one branch so the "Branch" attribute can be defined more than once. For instance, the Cooperative

Figure 1. Workflow of the work process

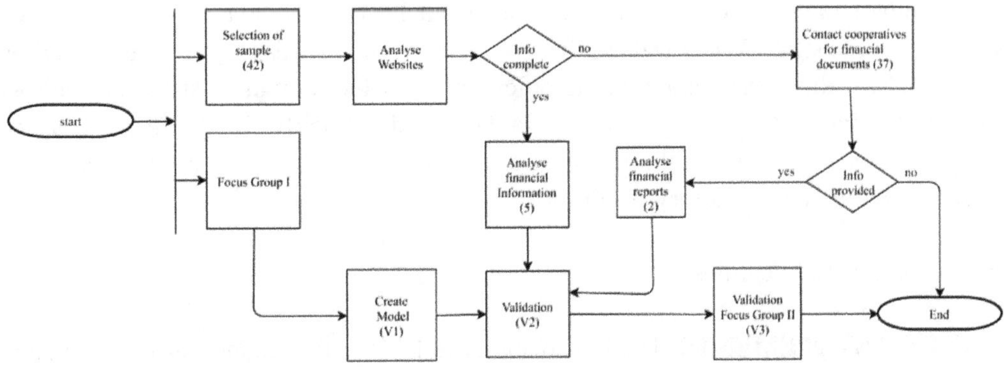

Table 1. List of cooperatives used to validate the model. Information from 2017

Name of cooperative	Industry	Number of Members	Revenue (€)	Total Assets (€)	URL
Cooperativa Agrícola de Barcelos, CRL	Farming Agriculture	8255	73.203.751,00	57.652.369,59	http://www.agribar.pt/
Cooperativa Social e Agro-Florestal de Vila Nova de Ceira, CRL	Farming, Agriculture, Social solidarity and services	n.a.	633.560,65	2.349.068,18	http://www.coopvnc.pt/
Cooperativa Agrícola de Alcobaça, CRL	Farming, Agriculture	4350 [6]	4.578.492,91	2.494.977,52	http://www.coopalcobaca.pt
Cooperativa de Habitação Económica Nova Morada, CRL	Construction,Housing	481	2.027,98	1.164.354,39	http://www.nova-morada.com/
CERCIFAF – Cooperativa de Educação e Reabilitação de crianças inadaptadas de Fafe, CRL	Social solidarity	n.a.	133.173,53	3.770.806,51	http://www.cercifaf.pt/
Coopérnico – Cooperativa de desenvolvimento sustentável, CRL	Renewable energy	820	78.787,62	788.092,55	https://www.coopernico.org/
Mútua de Pescadores, CRL	Insurance	n.a.	808.761,00	37.694.730,00	https://www.mutuapescadores.pt/

Figure 2: The domain Model for the Portuguese Cooperatives

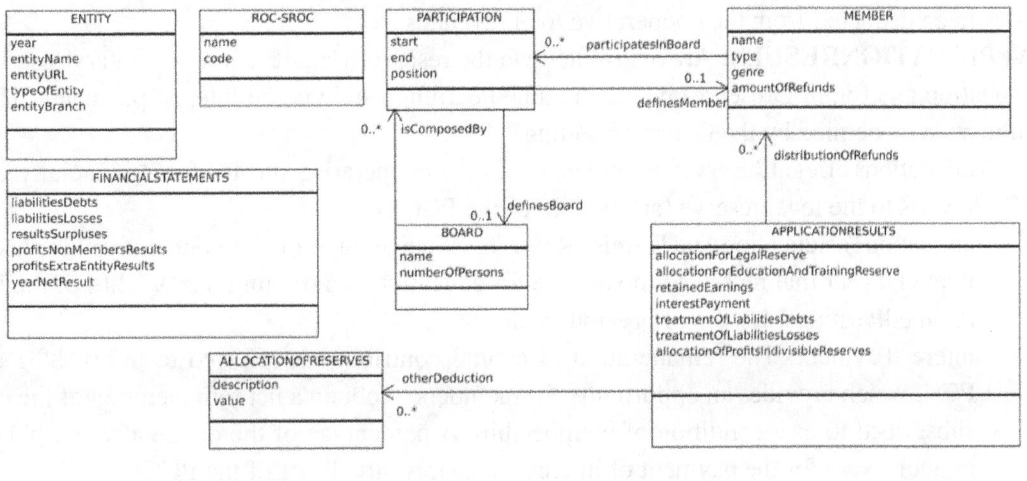

"Cooperativa Social e Agro-Florestal de Vila Nova de Ceira" acts in the field of Agriculture, Social Solidarity and Services. So the attribute "Branch" appears three times (see the file "Coop. SocialEAgroFlorestalDeVilaNovaDeCeira.xls" in the Github repository mentioned earlier).

- **ROC-SROC:** Defines the name and the official code of the individual statutory auditors (ROC – *Revisor Oficial de Contas*) or firms of statutory auditors (SROC – *Sociedades de Revisores Oficiais de Contas*) that signs the financial report (Law 140/2015 of 7 September 2015, which approved the Statute of Statutory Auditors).

The model has six more entities:

- **FINANCIALSTATEMENTS**: The information available in the balance sheet, the income statement, the cash-flow statement, the statement of changes inequity and in the annex to the financial statements.
  - liabillitiesDebts: Liability for the negative economic results from non-member cooperative transactions as well as from other extra-cooperative sources.
  - liabillitiesLosses: Liability for the negative economic results of cooperative transactions with members. Losses in member cooperative transactions are the excess of costs over revenues and are shown in the audited balance sheet.
  - resultsSurpluses: Positive economic results from member cooperative transactions. The cooperative surplus is defined as an amount that members pay to the cooperative in excess of what the cooperative owes to its members, in return for member participation in the cooperative's transactions (art. 100.1 of the PCC). Distribution of cooperative refunds among members is proportional to the business concluded by each of them with or for the cooperative during a given financial year.
  - profitsNonMemberResults: Positive economic results from non-member cooperative transactions (article 2.2 of the PCC). The economic results arising from transactions with non-members may not be shared by the cooperators (art. 100.1 of the PCC). They must be allocated to indivisible reserves (art. 99 of the PCC), as they are legally regarded as profits.
  - profitExtraEntityResults: Positive economic results from extra-entity sources. They must be allocated to indivisible reserves (art. 99 of the PCC), as they are legally regarded as profits.
  - yearNetResult: Amount remaining after all operating expenses, interests, and taxes that have been deducted from the cooperative total revenues.
- **APPLICATIONRESULS:** Are distributed via the reserves (legal reserve, voluntary reserve and education and training reserve), via the retained earnings and via the interest payments. This results must be defined by the General Meeting.
  - allocationToLegalReserve: A percentage of the cooperative surplus for a financial year that reverts to the legal reserve (art. 96.2.b) of the PCC).
  - allocationToEducationAndTrainingReserve: A percentage of the cooperative surplus for a financial year that reverts to the reserve for education and training (art. 97.2.b) of the PCC).
  - retainedEarnings: Losses of previous years.
  - interestPayment: The remuneration of capital contributions referred to in art. 88.1 of the PCC, which provides an opportunity for members to obtain a net remuneration of the capital subscribed to as a condition of membership. A percentage of the cooperative surplus for a financial year for the payment of interest on shares (art. 100.1 of the PCC).

- treatmentOfLiabilityDebts: Losses produced by activities with non-members and extra-co-operative activities. These losses are borne exclusively by the cooperative assets. The allocation to reserves must start with the voluntary reserves (art. 23 and art. 80 of the PCC).
- treatmentOfLiabilityLosses: Losses in member cooperative transactions that are covered by a decision of the General Meeting. These losses are covered by the cooperative 's reserves or by contributions of the cooperators. The allocation to reserves must start with the voluntary reserves. The distribution of losses among the members should be in proportion to the quantity and/or quality of their participation in the cooperative transactions (art. 96.5 PCC).
- allocationOfProfitsIndivisibleReserves: Profits that are allocated to indivisible reserves (articles arts. 99 and 114 of the PCC).

- **ALLOCATIONOFVOLUNTARYRESERVES:** Annual net surplus remaining. This remaining amount comes after the payment of interest on shares, after allocations for the various reserves, after payment of losses of previous years, and, when the legal reserves have been used to compensate for these losses, after the legal reserve has been reset at the level prior to its use (art. 100.2 of the PCC).
    - Description: The description of the allocation to voluntary reserve.
    - Value: The amount of the allocation (in Euros)
- **MEMBER:** the characteristics of the cooperator or investor member of the entity.
    - Name: The name of the member.
    - Type: The type of member (e.g. cooperator or investor member).
    - Genre: The genre of the member.
    - amountOfRefunds: The value of refunds the member receives in proportion to the quantity and/o quality of its participation in the cooperative transactions.
- **PARTICIPATION:** Defines the participation a member has on a specific Board.
    - Start: When the participation starts (a specific date or year)
    - end: when the participation ends (a specific date, a year)
    - Position: The position the member will assume on the board
- **BOARD:** A group of people (members of the entity) with specific functions in the entity.
    - Name: The name of the board (e.g. board of directors, supervisory board)
    - Number of Persons: The number of members that compose the board (integer)

Table 2 presents the relations among the entities.

LIMITATIONS OF THE STUDY

As far as the author see it, this work had two limitations:

- the researchers initially planned to carry out the work with data from 42 cooperatives but at the end of the study only seven were used. Thirty-five of the cooperatives (85%) were completely out of the study, a very high percentage.
- the information extracted from the reports and websites is scarce since many of the elements that compose the model did not have any information. In fact, if one looks at the files provided in Github (see section "Methodology"), many properties are empty, with no information.

Table 2. The relations between the entities of the model

Entity	Relation	Entity	Clarification
MEMBER	participatesInBoard	PARTICIPATION	Defines the participation of a member in a board
PARTICIPATION	definesMember	MEMBER	Defines the member that participates in a board *Note: This relation is the inverse of the previous one*
BOARD	isComposedBy	PARTICIPATION	Defines the composition of a Board
PARTICIPATION	definesBoard	BOARD	Defines the participation in a board *Note: This relation is the inverse of the previous one*
APPLICATIONREFUNDS	distributionOfRefunds	MEMBER	Defines how the refunds are distributed among the cooperator members
APPLICATIONREFUNDS	otherDeduction	VOLUNTARYRESERVES	Defines the allocation of voluntary reserves

Due to these limitations, the authors think this work needs another iteration, using more financial reports from other cooperatives. A bigger analysis will inform better the researchers so that they will be able to build a model that better responds to the informational needs of the community.

CONCLUSION AND FUTURE RESEARCH DIRECTIONS

This chapter presents a first approach to a domain model for transparency of the Portuguese Cooperatives. A domain model is a construct that presents the things of a certain context, and how they relate to each other; on the present case presents the things and relations related to the dimensions of governance and accounting of Cooperatives in Portugal.

The domain model here presented is part of a milestone of a greater project of building a Metadata Application Profile for the European Entities of the Social Economy Sector. A MAP is a construct of the Semantic Web, an ecosystem of Linked Open Data (LOD) that are supported by LOD technologies. The openness of the Semantic Web allows any organisation to develop intelligent software and use LOD datasets to build visualisations and infer over the data, allowing the access to new discoveries, ultimately to new knowledge. The Semantic Web also allows a community of practice to link its graphs to other graphs outside the community, thereby enhancing interoperability with neighboring communities of practice, which can be also interesting.

A cooperative is a legal person that carries on any economic activity, done by its members, through cooperation and mutual assistance. These economic activities follow cooperative principles within the interests of its members where profit cannot be the ultimate purpose. The value of transparency in governance is central to Cooperatives, and it is inseparable from active participation in the Cooperative democratic control. Under the Portuguese law, the Cooperative governance is characterised as transparent among other characteristics.

This model was developed first based in the information obtained from the accomplishment of a focus group with experts in accounting and law of Cooperatives, and then validated with information obtained from the analysis of financial reports and websites of seven Portuguese Cooperatives.

The model has limitations since the authors think that more information is needed to create the model. That is the reason why researchers envisage a new iteration of the process with more data from other Portuguese Cooperatives.

As future work the team will continue the definition of the domain model, with other iteration. After that, it will integrate other variables in the model that measure the transparency level of Cooperatives, such as financial information, promotion report of the needs of members, policies of education and training, sustainability and social cooperate responsibility reports, and audit reports. After defining the domain model for all dimensions, the team will work in the model in order to incorporate the informational needs of other entities of the social economy sector, such as associations and foundations. After all this work, the domain model will be finished.

Having defined the domain model, the team will follow the steps of Me4MAP (Curado Malta & Baptista, 2013) to develop the MAP for the European Social Economy sector.

In the future, entities of the Social Economy Sector in Europe will be able to publish LOD based on this MAP. Other entities such as public entities and universities will be able to use these data freely, and built software that will be able to compare parameters through visualisations, with different filters, and also build intelligent software that might infer from the data. The possibilities of crossing different dimensions of data and of inference will eventually open new knowledge that can be used by the entities' managers or policy makers to define new strategies and think the future of Social Economy in Europe.

ACKNOWLEDGMENT

The authors would like to thank all the cooperatives that provided the needed information. Without them this study would not have been possible.

REFERENCES

W3C. (2014a). *RDF 1.1 Concepts and Abstract Syntax*. Retrieved 21 November 2018, from https://www.w3.org/TR/rdf11-concepts/

W3C. (2014b). *RDF Primer*. Retrieved 10 November 2018, from https://www.w3.org/TR/rdf-primer/

W3C. (2015). *Data - W3C*. Retrieved 31 July 2018, from https://www.w3.org/standards/semanticweb/data

Bandeira, A. M., Meira, D., & Alves, V. (2016). Los diferentes tipos de resultados en las cooperativas portuguesas. Un estudio de caso múltiple. *REVESCO. Revista de Estudios Cooperativos*, *123*(0). doi:10.5209/REVE.54919

Berners-Lee, T., Hendler, J., & Lassila, O. (2001). The semantic web. *Scientific American*, *284*(5), 34–43. doi:10.1038cientificamerican0501-34 PMID:11396337

Branan, B. (2019). *MODS and RDF Descriptive Metadata*. Retrieved 29 March 2019, from https://wiki.duraspace.org/display/samvera/MODS+and+RDF+Descriptive+Metadata+Subgroup

Chen, P. P.-S. (1976). The Entity-relationship Model—Toward a Unified View of Data. *ACM Transactions on Database Systems*, *1*(1), 9–36. doi:10.1145/320434.320440

Coyle, K., & Baker, T. (2009). *DCMI: Guidelines for Dublin Core Application Profiles* (Working Draft). Retrieved 15 January 2018, from http://dublincore.org/documents/profile-guidelines/

Curado Malta, M., & Baptista, A. A. (2013). A method for the development of Dublin Core Application Profiles (Me4DCAP V0.2): detailed description. In *Proceedings on International Conference on Dublin Core and Metadata Applications* (pp. 90–103). Lisbon, Portugal: Dublin Core Metadata Initiative. Retrieved from http://dcpapers.dublincore.org/pubs/article/view/3674

Decree-Law no. 158/2009 of 13 July (Decreto-Lei 158/2009 de 13 de julho. Diário da República n.º 133/2009, Série I. Ministério das Finanças e da Administração Pública).

Fajardo, G., Fici, A., Henry, H., Meira, D., Münkner, H., & Snaith, I. (2017). *Principles of European Cooperative Law. Principles, Commentaries and National Reports*. Cambridge: Intersentia. doi:10.1017/9781780686073

Law no. 119/2015, of 31 August (Lei n.º 119/2015 de 31 de agosto. Diário da República n.º 169/2015, Série I. Assembleia da República).

Matienzo, M., Roke, E., & Carlson, S. (2017). Creating a Linked Data-Friendly Metadata Application Profile for Archival Description. *International Conference on Dublin Core and Metadata Applications*, 112–116.

Meira, D. (2009). O regime económico das cooperativas no direito português: o capital social. *Vida Económica*. Retrieved from http://recipp.ipp.pt/handle/10400.22/657

Meira, D. A., & Ramos, M. E. (2014). *Governação e regime económico das cooperativas*. Porto: VidaEconómica.

Meira, D. A. (2016). *A fiscalizaçao das cooperativas à luz do novo Código Cooperativo português*. Retrieved 6 November 2018, from https://dialnet.unirioja.es/servlet/articulo?codigo=5770310

Münkner, H. (2015). *Co-operative Principles and Co-operative Law* (2nd ed.). Zurich: Lit Verlag GmbH & Co. KG Wien.

Nilsson, M., Baker, T., & Johnston, P. (2009). *DCMI: Interoperability Levels for Dublin Core Metadata*. Retrieved 9 January 2018, from http://dublincore.org/documents/interoperability-levels/

Powell, A., Nilsson, M., Naeve, A., Johnston, P., & Baker, T. (2009). *DCMI: Abstract Model*. Retrieved 15 November 2018, from http://dublincore.org/documents/2007/06/04/abstract-model/

Rodrigues, A. M. (2010). Os novos desafios da Contabilidade para Organizações da Economia Social que aplicam o SNC - As Cooperativas. *Revista Cooperativismo e Economía Social*, *32*, 115–140.

Rodrigues, A. M. (2016). SNC- Sistema de Normalização Contabilística (3rd ed.). Almedina, Coimbra.

Rumbaugh, J., Booch, G., & Jacobson, I. (2017). *The unified modeling language reference manual*. Addison Wesley.

Shadbolt, N., Berners-Lee, T., & Hall, W. (2006). The semantic web revisited. *IEEE Intelligent Systems*, *21*(3), 96–101. doi:10.1109/MIS.2006.62

ADDITIONAL READING

Cracogna, D., Fici, A., & Henrÿ, H. (Eds.). (2013). *International Handbook of Cooperative Law*. Heidelberg: Springer. doi:10.1007/978-3-642-30129-2

Curado Malta, M., Baptista, A. A., & Walk, P. (Eds.). (2017). *Developing Metadata Application Profiles*. IGI Global. doi:10.4018/978-1-5225-2221-8

Gartner, R. (2016). *Metadata, Shaping knowledge from antiquity of the semantic web*. Springer.

Gray, R., Owen, D., & Adams, C. (1996). *Accounting & Accountability: Changes and Challenges in Corporate Social and Environmental Reporting*. Prentice Hall.

Zeng, M. L., & Qin, J. (2016). *Metadata* (2nd ed.). London, UK: Facet Publishing.

KEY TERMS AND DEFINITIONS

Accountability: Obligation of the organs to 1) account for its activities, 2) accept responsibility for these activities, and 3) disclose the results in a transparent manner.

Cooperative: Legal person that carries on any economic activity through the cooperation of its members, and in the interest of the members.

Domain Model: An informational model used to capture the "things" of a context. A domain model in the context of the Semantic Web is the basis of a metadata application profile. A domain model defines things that exist in the context (called entities) and the relations between the things (called relations). A domain model can also contain the properties of each thing (called attributes).

Governance: Direction and control of the cooperative enterprise.

Metadata Application Profile: A construct from the semantic web that enhances interoperability. A metadata application profile incorporates a data model and a set of rules that establish how a community of practice should publish linked open data in order to be interoperable among the members of the community.

Semantic Web: A paradigm of linked open data that together with linked open data technologies allows machines to inference from data and discovery new knowledge. The semantic web is a Web of data that uses the same basic principles of the World Wide Web (WWW). It does not exist to replace the WWW (or Web of Documents) but to leave beside it.

ENDNOTES

1 Law no. 119/2015, which was published on 31.08.2015 and came into force on 30.09.2015.

2 Decree-Law no. 335/99 of 20.08.1999 (agricultural cooperatives); Decree-Law no. 523/99 of 10.12.1999 (trade cooperatives); Decree-Law no. 522/99 of 10.12.1999 (consumer cooperatives); Decree-Law no. 24/91 of 11.01.1991, as amended by Decree-Law no. 230/95 of 12.09.1995, Decree-Law no. 320/97 of 25.11.1197, Decree-Law no. 102/99 of 31.03.1999 and Decree-Law no. 142/2009 of 16.06.2009 (credit unions); Decree-Law no. 313/81 of 19.11.1981 (cultural co-

operatives); Decree-Law no. 441-A/82 of 06.11.1982 (education cooperatives); Decree-Law no. 502/99 of 19.11.1999 (housing and building cooperatives); Decree-Law no. 312/81 of 18.11.1981 (fisheries cooperatives); Decree-Law no. 309/81 of 16.11.1981 (worker cooperatives); Decree-Law no. 323/81 of 04.12.1981 (service cooperatives); and Decree-Law no. 7/98 of 15.01.1998 (social solidarity cooperatives).

3 Accounting Normalisation System - Approved by Decree-Law no. 158/2009, 13.07.2009.

4 See https://5stardata.info/en/ - accessed in 28.03.2019.

5 Accessed 21 November 2018.

6 Information retrieved from the Website of the Cooperative. All the other information of number of members was retrieved from the financial reports.

Chapter 4
Transparency and Resource Mobilization in Times of Crisis:
An Analysis of the Brazilian Nonprofit Sector

Rosana da Rosa Portella Tondolo
Universidade Federal de Pelotas, Brazil

Vilmar Antonio Gonçalves Tondolo
Universidade Federal de Pelotas, Brazil

André Andrade Longaray
Universidade Federal do Rio Grande, Brazil

Maria Emilia Camargo
Universidade de Caxias do Sul, Brazil

Claudia Cristina Bitencourt
Universidade do Vale do Rio dos Sinos, Brazil

Gabriela Zanandrea
Universidade do Vale do Rio dos Sinos, Brazil

ABSTRACT

Nonprofit organizations play a relevant role in Brazilian society. In recent years, Brazil has faced frequent allegations of mismanagement of resources and corruption in different administrative spheres, including state-owned and private enterprises. In this scenario, transparency is essential to nonprofit organizations. Resource mobilization is a key management activity of nonprofit organizations that provides the achievement of the social objective of the organization. This chapter aims to analyze the influence of transparency on the resource mobilization of Brazilian nonprofit organizations. In order to achieve this goal, a survey was developed. Data from 93 Brazilian non-profit organizations were collected. The main contribution of study is that transparency has significant impact on resource mobilization in Brazilian nonprofit organizations.

DOI: 10.4018/978-1-5225-8482-7.ch004

INTRODUCTION

Nonprofit organizations play a relevant role in Brazilian society. They carry out several types of activities, contributing to the gross domestic product, as well as fomenting and giving access to different kinds of services to the Brazilian population. Recent data indicate the existence of 400 thousand nonprofit organizations in Brazil (IPEA, 2015).

In 1999, this sector moved more than 1 trillion dollars annually and mobilized more than 19 million paid employees (Salamon, Anheier, List, Toepler, & Sokolowski, 1999). Although information on the Brazilian nonprofit sector is outdated, the most recent national data being from 2013-2014, this sector presents strength and representativeness both in the number of jobs generated and in the volume of resources transacted.

However, the lack of recent data on the sector is not the only problem experienced in Brazil. It is also important to highlight the concern of Brazilians regarding processes that involve the public administration and the allocation of resources. In recent years, Brazil has faced frequent allegations of mismanaged resources and corruption in different administrative spheres, including the corruption of state-owned and private enterprises. This sequence of scandals causes incredulousness in both the country's population and in the foreign market, thus creating a national crisis.

The Brazilian crisis involves economic, political and moral aspects. In recent years, the Brazilian population has experienced a big crisis, which seems to have no end. According to the experts, this crisis is the worst since the economic recovery is slow when compared with the last eight crises reaching back to 1980 (Salomão, & Lima, 2018); but the economic aspect is not all. Brazil is experiencing a political crisis, with many cases of corruption. Many economic sectors and industries have been affected by the corruption and "agreements" among politicians and businessmen who represent the large companies in the country.

In addition, agreements between the Brazilian government and the governments of Latin American countries involve the financing of investments in other countries, but with the purpose to benefiting corrupt Brazilian companies that bribe corrupt politicians. These agreements were financed by a Brazilian Development Bank. The worst part is that a large amount of Brazilian money has financed investments and improvements abroad, while in Brazil, basic services such as education and health are in a deplorable state.

Brazilian nonprofit organizations have been impacted in different ways. First, poverty having increased over the last several years, they have more needs to address. Second, nonprofit organizations have few available resources to reach their goals, whether they are private or public. Third, the lack of trust in Brazilian organizations is impacting the mobilization of national and international resources.

In this view, it is important to analyze how Brazilian nonprofit organizations have adapted to this new scenario: scarce government funds and an atmosphere of distrust from both national and international partners and donors. This chapter has the premise that transparency is an essential management tool in the context of nonprofit organizations, not being an exclusive perception of the authors, but appearing in the results of several international research studies (Khieng, 2014; Valencia, Queiruga, & González-Benito, 2015; Gandía, 2011).

It is known that the performance of non-profit organizations has been a recurring aim of research in recent years. However, there are still few studies that demonstrate the relationship between transparency and economic efficiency (Valencia, Queiruga, & González-Benito, 2015). Given this gap, this study aims to contribute to the advancement of the state of the field, as the mobilization of resources can be understood as a measure of results or efficiency.

In this sense, this chapter aims to analyze the influence of transparency in the resource mobilization of Brazilian nonprofit organizations. In this chapter, the authors have sought to base their research stream basically on two previous studies which addressed the levels and dimensions of transparency for the Third Sector (Tondolo, Tondolo, Camargo, & Sarquis, 2016) and the exploratory research on the levels of transparency and resource mobilization (Dall'agnol, Tondolo, Tondolo, & Sarquis, 2017). At this point, it is tried to expand the research, analyzing a sample of 93 Brazilian social organizations from 14 Brazilian states using a quantitative approach.

The main contribution of this chapter is to identify the effect of transparency on resource mobilization, which will aid nonprofit organizations in understanding how to improve resources mobilization and the role of transparency for nonprofit organizations, and for their stakeholders. Additionally, this chapter contributes to understanding how different transparency levels affect resource mobilization. Reflecting on these contributions from the managerial perspective, they are important to spotlight the importance of transparency as an organizational practice. Transparency can show stakeholders and the community where resources are being invested, and, as a consequence, improve trust among stakeholders and the community in nonprofit organizations, as a result impacting resource mobilization.

BACKGROUND

The Crisis Scenario

The current Brazilian crisis started in 2014 and remains until the day of this writing. Some specialists emphasize that the current crisis is the worst since 1980. This title is attributed because economic recovery is slower than in other crises (Salomão, & Lima, 2018). This situation may originate from different perspectives, such as economic, political and moral.

The economic perspective refers to the reduction of economic growth. This started in 2013, basically in the manufacturing industry, and has gained huge proportions with the past of the years. As a result, this sector terminated many employees and many manufacturers stopped their activities. Thus, these events directly affected other sectors, which increased the unemployment rate and the closures of companies in the country.

Of course, that situation affected other areas, such as the public arena: reduced taxes received, increased unemployment insurance expenditures, and increased poverty levels, among others. The nonprofit organizations are affected by a corresponding reduction in public grants along with corporate and individual donations, while experiencing an increase in the number of potential beneficiaries.

However, the economic crisis is not the only crisis in Brazil at the moment. Since 2014, the number of corruption scandals involving politicians, public sector and big companies seems to have no end. These scandals involve a lot of people and a lot of money. The majority of politicians are involved in some corruption scandal. These scandals generate a generalized distrust in the country. As a result, a moral crisis has arisen in the country because all processes and all organizations (public or private) that appear legitimate are being investigated for some irregularity. Unfortunately, it seems that in 2019, this crisis is still far from over.

Although the crisis persists, the organizations continue, requiring nonprofit organizations to do something that involves the community and attracts more investors with the purpose of raising funds, increasing resources and improving services provided. In this sense, it is believed that a nonprofit organization being transparent to the public about its processes and investments can improve fundraising, legitimacy and the quality of services. Further, more transparent attitudes can strengthen nonprofit organizations in times of crisis.

Similarly, recent studies have emphasized the importance of understanding accountability in the new public management, and how this impacts issues of wider societal relevance, such as public services, crises, and social problems, as well as creation and maintenance of public value and democratic participation (Steccolini, 2019).

LITERATURE REVIEW AND HYPOTHESES DEVELOPMENT

Transparency in Resource Mobilization

Transparency has been a subject widely discussed in the academic environment in recent years (Murtaza, 2012; Tondolo et al., 2016). In this research, transparency should be understood as a procedural aspect of the organizational context, since transparency should not be limited to aspects related to accountability. Transparency should be related to the way organizational processes are viewed/performed, being a feature intrinsic to all organizational processes.

It is possible to identify in the non-profit literature that accountability, as a mechanism of transparency, that is presented in an erroneous or unclear way generates an environment of distrust, thus affecting the fundraising of the organization (Dall'agnol et al., 2017). Transparency in non-profit organizations can be understood under four aspects: a) transparency at the initial level of attendance; b) transparency in legal aspects; c) transparency in accountability; and d) transparency in management and results. The first aspect identifies evidence of transparency (elementary aspects); the second examines whether the organization meets the legal requirements; the third whether the organization presents practices related to accountability; and finally, the fourth whether the organization is transparent in management and organizational results (Tondolo et al., 2016).

Although transparency can be understood as a public capability (Heald, 2006), organizations still have difficulties articulating and interpreting how this transparency should be realized or for whom it should be intended. A classic example of this is that nonprofits have made efforts to be transparent, since they have efficient accountability mechanisms for donors and government, but accountability mechanisms for beneficiaries and the community are still extremely fragile (Murtaza, 2012).

Nonetheless, it is possible to find in the current literature a new approach that is focused on understanding accountability by phenomenological concepts, such as "empathy" and "communal emotions," based on Stein. In this line, Costa, Pesci, Andreaus, & Taufer (2019) use those concepts to understand legitimacy and accountability perspectives in voluntarily delivery and social environmental reporting, based on different levels of empathy towards different stakeholders.

From this, this chapter comprehends that the atmosphere of nonprofit organizations is composed of a complex multi-stakeholder nature (e.g. donors, beneficiaries, employees, volunteers, civil society, etc.), and each stakeholder has a peculiar behavior and is affected by different actions produced by non-profit organizations. Although it is a fertile field of research, the more important task is to comprehend how nonprofit organizations can manage this situation involving multiple stakeholders and their specific motivations for contributing to the cause in the practice. This manager "sensibility" is very important to nonprofit organizations business management (Costa et al., 2019; Tondolo et al., 2016).

According to Valencia, Queiruga and González-Benito (2015), transparency is the degree of information provided. It is influenced by variables such as organizational values, activity and recipients of the process, the participatory culture of the organization or the social environment. Three main aspects of transparency can be highlighted: (i) the stakeholders involved in the exchange of information; ii) the trust of volunteerism, civic engagement or donors in the organization; and (iii) the different dimensions of transparency, since the concept of transparency refers not only to the explanation of the organization's accounts, but is a multidimensional concept (Valencia, Queiruga, González Benito, 2015).

Transparency is one of the central mechanisms of organizational accountability. Accountability is the entity's obligation to report in detail and take responsibility for a particular action or set of actions and for the conscious use of its resources (Rapoport, 2011; Rosa 2013). It allows data reporting and information to flow to stakeholders. It provides donors with information about the use of fund-raised resources (Rapoport, 2011). For Koppell (2005), the accountability concept is understood through five dimensions: transparency, commitment, controllability, responsibility and receptivity. To demonstrate his method, the author presents five questions, one for each dimension:

- Transparency: Does the organization reveal the facts of its performance?
- Commitment: Does the organization face the consequences of its performance?
- Controllability: Does the organization do what is ordered by the managers?
- Responsibility: Does the organization follow the rules?
- Receptivity: Does the organization do the substantive expectation (demand / need)?

In this way, social accountability is implicated in the ethics and moral expectations. This is promoted through information accessibility to citizens and organizations, reinforcing the acts of monitoring and reducing management omissions. Accountability can be enhanced by improving transparency, measuring outcomes, increasing responsiveness, and ensuring that organizational priorities are aligned with citizens' concerns (Benjamin, 2012; Alves, 2014).

In the current literature, transparency can be understood through disclosure and compliance concepts. Some authors are highlighting the link between voluntary compliance and disclosure that is practiced by organizations with the boarder structure and mechanisms adopted by organizations (Al-Bassam, Ntim, Opong, & Downs, 2018). Others emphasize disclosure and accountability, seeking to identify the relationships among governance structure, voluntary disclosure in public accountability (Ntim, Soobaroyen, & Broad, 2017). This study finds that the interaction between executive team characteristics and governance variables enhances the level of voluntary disclosures. Also, findings provide support for the continued relevance of a shared leadership towards enhancing accountability and transparency in the context of Higher Education Institutions (Ntim, Soobaroyen, & Broad, 2017).

In the context of nonprofit organizations, this chapter takes resource mobilization as a capability, since resource mobilization seeks to "identify the resource and capability needed, articulate them, capture and implement them in social actions" (Tondolo, 2014, 53). In this way, resource mobilization is indispensable for these organizations since it acts as an articulator of the organizational strategy, promoting a sustainable environment through the effectiveness of its social objectives (Armani, 2008).

Along these lines, the authors understand that the transparency of nonprofit organization can affect the fundraising. Thus, the study's first hypothesis is that:

Hypothesis 1 (H1): Transparency of a nonprofit organization affects positively its resource mobilization.

Resource mobilization can be understood from four elements: resource types, resource articulation, resource mobilization, and resource sharing (Dall'agnol et al., 2017; Armani, 2008, Barney, 1991, 2001, Froelich, 1999, Tondolo, 2014). The type of resources involves identifying the resources of organizations, whether tangible or intangible; the articulation of resources encompasses the different forms of fundraising; the mobilization is related to the applicability and allocation of articulated resources; while sharing is the altruistic action of "donating" or developing a resource jointly.

However, if nonprofit organizations present low levels of transparency, they mobilize resources in a precarious way, and these resources are often insufficient for the development of the organization's activities. Based on the results of previous studies, the authors of this chapter understand that the different levels of transparency can contribute to resource mobilization (Dall'agnol et al., 2017, Tondolo et al., 2016). Therefore, the study's second hypothesis is that:

Hypothesis 2 (H2): The more nonprofit organizations show transparency, the more organizations show resource mobilization.

Nonprofit organizations that present high levels of transparency mobilize resources with excellence; these organizations have resources to apply to their activities and can improve service quality or increment new services (Dall'Agnol et al., 2017, Tondolo et al., 2016). This leads to the study's third hypothesis:

Hypothesis 3 (H3): A high level of transparency has a significant effect on resource mobilization.

RESEARCH DESIGN

This study used a quantitative approach in order to collect more data from Brazilian nonprofit organizations. In order to achieve the objectives proposed in this study, it was elaborated the data collection instrument composed of questions related to the characterization of the respondents, as well as two blocks of questions, based on scales previously validated, in order to measure the variables transparency and resource mobilization (Tondolo et al., 2016; Dall'agnol et al., 2017; Tondolo, Tondolo, Longaray, & Mello, 2017; Tondolo, Tondolo, Camargo, & Guerra, 2018). The transparency block comprises 15 questions about accountability, disclosure, activities monitoring and community participation/interaction, while resource mobilization includes 12 questions about fundraising, network to mobilize resources and sharing resources. The questionnaire is presented in the Appendix.

The data collection technique was the questionnaire, which was submitted to organizations in a virtual way. As criteria for the sample, it was used non-probabilistic convenience sampling. Data were collected from July to September of 2018, obtaining a sample of 93 Brazilian Social Organizations, which is described in the sequence. The authors chose multivariate statistics for data analysis, obeying the criteria of validity and reliability of data for the application of the chosen technique. It was used cluster and regression analysis to identify the influence of transparency on the resource mobilization of these organizations.

Cluster or conglomerate analysis aims at gathering objects which are classified according to similarities with others belonging to that group, and the resulting group classification should have a high degree of internal homogeneity and high external heterogeneity (Corrar, Paulo, & Dias, 2007). Regression analysis has as its purpose to determine mathematically the description of the behavior of variables, called dependent values, based on one or more variables, listed as independent (Cunha, & Coelho, 2007). The regression is multiple when two or more variables are independent (Hair, Anderson, & Black, 2005a).

EMPIRICAL RESULTS AND DISCUSSION

In the first step of data analysis, this chapter presents the main data of our sample composed by 93 organizations. Regarding location, our sample has data from 14 of 26 Brazilian states as shown in Table 1. The majority of the sample has more than 5 years of operation, and the main focus is social assistance.

Organizations of the sample have an average of 63 employees, 65 volunteers, and more than 22,000 beneficiaries, as shown in Table 2.

In order to verify the reliability of measures, it was used the Cronbach's alpha test. The results of alpha for the 15 items that measure transparency showed a value of 0.812, which is higher than the minimum of 0.7 indicted for Hair, Babin, Money, & Samouel (2005b). Thus, all 15 items remain in the measure of transparency.

I was also verified the reliability of the 14 items that measure resource mobilization. The results showed a value of 0.68, which as less than the expected minimum. In order to achieve a value of 0.7 or more, 2 items (variables 2 and 14) were dropped. The results showed a value 0.705, resulting in 12 items measured.

It was centralized the two constructs, transparency and resource mobilization, creating a new variable with the mean value of the respective measures. The general mean of transparency is 4.18 and resource mobilization is 3.49. Regarding age of organizations and mean values of transparency and resource mobilization, it was not possible to find significant difference among groups, as shown in Table 3. However, it is interesting to note that organizations with less than one year showed higher means of transparency and resource mobilization. Even though there are only three organizations in this category, it might suggest that new organizations are trying to start their operations with transparency and a focus on resources.

In order to identify the influence of transparency on the resource mobilization of these organizations, it was used multiple regression analyses. As Table 4 shows, the entire model is significant, and it predicts 17% of resource mobilization as the dependent variable. More importantly, only transparency has a significant impact on resource mobilization, with a standardized beta of 0.418. Other variables, inserted in the model as dummies, have no significant impact, emphasizing the role of transparency. Thus, it was found support to affirm that transparency has significant influence on the resource mobilization of Brazilian nonprofit organizations, providing empirical support to H1 and the findings of past studies that suggest that transparency is a multidimensional concept (Valencia, Queiruga, González Benito, 2015; Tondolo et al., 2016), considering accountability and disclosure as important aspects of understanding transparency (Benjamin, 2012; Alves, 2014; Dall'agnol et al., 2017; Ntim, Soobaroyen, & Broad, 2017; Al-Bassam et al., 2018; Costa et al., 2019). In this sense, transparency in the nonprofit organization context can be understood as a capability, given that it responsible for the access the resources, which is in line with Heald (2006) who suggested that transparency can be understood as a public capability.

In order to explore the results of the influence of transparency on resource mobilization, the sample was divided into two groups with different levels of transparency. Cluster analysis was employed using the 15 items of the transparency instrument. As a result, it was possible to find two clusters, one with 51 organizations and the other with 40 organizations. Two organizations were excluded by the method

Table 1. Sample frequencies

State of Location	Frequency	Percent
Bahia	.6	6.5
Distrito Federal	2	2.2
Espírito Santo	1	1.1
Goiás	1	1.1
Minas Gerais	7	7.5
Pará	1	1.1
Piauí	1	1.1
Paraná	6	6.5
Rio de Janeiro	2	2.2
Roraima	1	1.1
Rio Grande do Sul	37	39.8
Santa Catarina	7	7.5
Sergipe	1	1.1
São Paulo	20	21.5
Age of the organization		
5 years or more	81	87.1
1-3 years	3	3.2
3-5 years	6	6.5
less than 1 year	3	3.2
Sector		
Child	1	1.1
Civil Rights	5	5.4
Combat Hunger	1	1.1
Culture	6	6.5
Diverse	7	7.5
Economy Development	4	4.3
Education	12	12.9
Environment	6	6.5
Sports	1	1.1
Health	5	5.4
Microcredit	7	7.5
Religion	3	3.2
Social Assistance	33	35.5
Sustainability	1	1.1
Technology Development	1	1.1

Source: Study data

Table 2. Sample descriptive

	N	Minimum	Maximum	Mean
Number of employees	93	0	2,700	62.46
Number of volunteers	93	0	1,500	65.72
Number of beneficiaries	93	0	1,000,000	22,538.73

Source: Study data

Table 3. Age of organizations and means

Age of organization		mean transparency	mean mobilization
5 years or more	Mean	4.1967	3,4593
	N	81	81
	Std. Deviation	.52133	.64952
1-3 years	Mean	4.1778	3.8333
	N	3	3
	Std. Deviation	.39063	1.02402
3-5 years	Mean	3.9333	3.5139
	N	6	6
	Std. Deviation	.95963	.43912
Less than 1 years	Mean	**4.2222**	**4.1944**
	N	3	3
	Std. Deviation	.88024	.70874

Anova

			Sum of Squares	df	Mean Square	F	Sig.
mean transparency * Age	Between Groups	(Combined)	.393	3	.131	.414	.744
	Within Groups		28,202	89	.317		
	Total		28,595	92			
mean mobilization * Age	Between Groups	(Combined)	1,915	3	.638	1,502	.219
	Within Groups		37,816	89	.425		
	Total		39,731	92			

Source: Study data

of agglomeration because of missing data. It was named group 1 as "high level" and group 2 as "low level" according to results of the compares means procedure as Table 5 shows.

In addition, it was also verified the level of resource mobilization of the two groups. Table 6 presents that the high level group also shows significantly higher levels of mobilization. This result reinforces the impact of transparency on the resource mobilization of Brazilian nonprofit organizations, providing empirical support to H2 and the findings of past studies that suggest that different levels of transparency can contribute to resource mobilization (Dall'agnol et al., 2017, Tondolo et al., 2016). As a result,

Table 4. Regression Analysis results

Model	R	R Square	Adjusted R Square	Std. Error of the Estimate	Change Statistics					Durbin-Watson
					R Square Change	F Change	df1	df2	Sig. F Change	
1	.413[a]	.171	.133	.61197	.171	4.522	4	88	.002	1.588

Coefficients[a]

Model		Unstandardized Coefficients		Standardized Coefficients	t	Sig.
		B	Std. Error	Beta		
1	(Constant)	1.443	.494		2.922	.004
	mean transparency	.493	.117	.418	4.216	.000
	n. employees	.000	.000	-.048	-.472	.638
	n. volunteers	.000	.000	.065	.628	.532
	n. beneficiaries	-5.67	.000	-.126	-1.234	.221

Dependent Variable: mean mobilization
Predictors: (Constant), n. beneficiaries, n. employees, mean transparency, n. volunteers
Source: Study data

Table 5. Mean transparency clusters

Ward Method	Mean Transparency	N	Std. Deviation
High	4.4855	51	.33942
Low	3.7833	40	.54720
Total	4.1768	91	.56264

ANOVA

			Sum of Squares	df	Mean Square	F	Sig.
mean transparency * Ward Method	Between Groups	(Combined)	11.052	1	11.052	56.408	.000
	Within Groups		17.438	89	.196		
	Total		28.490	90			

Source: Study data

findings of this chapter are aligned with the framework presented earlier that represents the relationship between transparency and resource mobilization.

Finally in this study, two additional regression analyses were performed. For the first one, data from the 51 organizations in the high level transparency group were used. For the second one, data from the 40 organizations in the low level transparency group were used. As Table 7 presents, only regression with data from the high level group has a significant impact on resource mobilization. Based on this, the authors suggest that it is not just a matter of having or not some practice of transparency, but the intensity of the transparency of the organization that matters. This finding provided empirical support to H3 and the findings of past studies suggesting that nonprofit organizations that present high level of transpar-

Table 6. Mean mobilization clusters

Ward Method			Mean Mobilization	N		Std. Deviation		
High			3.6863	51		.70585		
Low			3.2551	40		.52193		
Total			3.4968	91		.66418		
ANOVA Table								
				Sum of Squares	df	Mean Square	F	Sig.
mean mobilization * Ward Method	Between Groups	(Combined)		4.167	1	4.167	10.438	.002
	Within Groups			35.535	89	.399		
	Total			39.702	90			

Source: Study data

ency mobilize resources with excellence (Dall'agnol et al., 2017, Tondolo et al., 2016). This practice contributes to organizations activities by improving service quality or by incrementing new services.

CONCLUSION

Brazilian nonprofit organizations are responsible for a myriad of "public" services that are provided in the Brazil. The current economic crisis has concerned these organizations because it has limited access to resources, for reasons such as: (i) the reduction of the availability of resources in the public sphere; (ii) the distrust that has been created in the country and consequently in their organizations, thus also impacting international resources; (iii) the reduction of individual donations because the future may be uncertain.

So, in the line with this concern around the crisis and corruption, this chapter recognizes that understanding the role of transparency and its influence on resource mobilization can contribute to reducing the distrust in this organizational sector and can improve the fundraising and the mobilization of resources as well for Brazilian nonprofit organizations.

Based on this, this study aimed to analyze the influence of transparency on the resource mobilization of Brazilian nonprofit organizations. Accordingly, 93 Brazilian nonprofit organizations were analyzed, and it was possible to identify that transparency has a significant impact on resource mobilization. Based on the findings, the authors understand that the development of high levels of transparency should be stimulated in nonprofit organizations, since high levels of transparency are related to resource mobilization.

This chapter identified support between the framework proposed in the previous pages and the findings, given that it was identified that nonprofit organizations with low levels of transparency do not show significant impact on resource mobilization. Conversely, the nonprofit organizations that presented with high levels of transparency showed significant impact on resource mobilization.

Table 7. Regression analysis by clusters

Model	R: Ward Method = High (Selected)		R Square	Adjusted R Square	Std. Error of the Estimate	Change Statistics: R Square Change	F Change	df1	df2	Sig. F Change	Durbin-Watson Statistic: Ward Method = High (Selected)
1	.361[a]		.130	.112	.66505	.130	7.322	1	49	,009	1.654

a. Predictors: (Constant), mean transparency

b. Unless noted otherwise, statistics are based only on cases for which Ward Method = High.

c. Dependent Variable: mean mobilization

Coefficients[a,b]

Model		Unstandardized Coefficients: B	Std. Error	Standardized Coefficients: Beta	t	Sig.
1	(Constant)	.323	1.246		.259	.797
	mean transparency	.750	.277	.361	2.706	.009

a. Dependent Variable: mean mobilization

b. Selecting only cases for which Ward Method = High

Model Summary[b,c]

Model	R: Ward Method = Low (Selected)		R Square	Adjusted R Square	Std. Error of the Estimate	Change Statistics: R Square Change	F Change	df1	df2	Sig. F Change	Durbin-Watson Statistic: Ward Method = Low (Selected)
1	.192[a]		.037	.012	.51888	.037	1.460	1	38	.234	2.016

a. Predictors: (Constant), mean transparency

b. Unless noted otherwise, statistics are based only on cases for which Ward Method = Low.

c. Dependent Variable: mean mobilization

Coefficients[a,b]

Model		Unstandardized Coefficients: B	Std. Error	Standardized Coefficients: Beta	t	Sig.
1	(Constant)	2.561	.580		4.413	.000
	mean transparency	.183	.152	.192	1.208	.234

Dependent Variable: mean mobilization

Selecting only cases for which Ward Method = Low

Source: Study data

Aside from that, is important to highlight the contribution of accountability and disclosure to understand the transparency idea. These terms are essential to understanding transparency in the nonprofit organization context because they provide the impression that all nonprofit organizations expose to community and stakeholders, such as providing access to legal documents and reports on where resources are invested, while invoking the community suggestions and accepting the participation of the community in decision-making.

The main contribution of this paper is to identify the effect of transparency on resource mobilization. That is a significant contribution given that nonprofit organizations can understand how to improve their resource mobilization through transparency. Additionally, the chapter contributes to understanding how different transparency levels affect resource mobilization. Reflecting on these contributions in the managerial aspect, they are important to highlight to nonprofit organizations the importance of transparency as an organizational practice because transparency shows stakeholders and the community where the resources are being invested, and, as a consequence, can improve the trust among stakeholders and the community in the nonprofit organization, consequently impacting resource mobilization.

Accordingly, considering the relevance of nonprofit organizations and the services they provide, the authors suggest that the results of this study encourage the creation of public policies aiming to promote the development and implementation of transparency mechanisms in nonprofit organizations. The creation of a public policy would help to increase the legitimacy of these organizations in society as well as resource mobilization, reducing future corruption scandals.

The several empirical implications are that Brazilian nonprofit organizations must invest in transparency because over the years only nonprofit organizations that are transparent will be in the market, by way of natural selection. Additionally, resource mobilization is a priority activity for nonprofit organizations because it leads to both improved service quality and quantity. Finally, transparency and resource mobilization development is a reciprocal model because the more transparent the nonprofit organization is, the greater resources mobilization, and the more resources the organization mobilizes the more it will need to be transparent. Therefore, these are some practices that Brazilian nonprofit organizations have to implement in their managerial process.

One of the study limitations is the small sample, which involved 93 organizations from 14 states, making it impossible to analyze each of the four levels of transparency. It is suggested that further studies investigate more organizations in the same context and can test the framework proposed considering the four levels of transparency and resource mobilization. Based on framework proposed, the authors also suggest further studies investigating the relationship between levels of transparency and resource mobilization in different research scenarios and contexts as well as investigating antecedents and contextual aspects that promote transparency, and outcomes from resource mobilization.

ACKNOWLEDGMENT

This research was supported by CNPq (Conselho Nacional de Desenvolvimento Científico e Tecnológico) [grant number 428197/2018-3].

REFERENCES

Al-Bassam, W. M., Ntim, C. G., Opong, K. K., & Downs, Y. (2018). Corporate boards and ownership structure as antecedents of corporate governance disclosure in Saudi Arabian publicly listed corporations. *Business & Society*, *57*(2), 335–377. doi:10.1177/0007650315610611

Alves, M. A. (2014). Social accountability as an innovative frame in civic action: The case of rede nossa São Paulo. *Voluntas*, *25*(3), 818–838. doi:10.100711266-013-9365-6

Armani, D. (2008). *Mobilizar para transformar: a mobilização de recursos nas organizações da sociedade civil.* São Paulo, SP: Peirópolis.

Barney, J. (1991). Firm resources and sustained competitive advantage. *Journal of Management*, *17*(1), 99–120. doi:10.1177/014920639101700108

Barney, J. (2001). Resource-based theories of competitive advantage: A ten-year retrospective on the resource-based view. *Journal of Management*, *27*(6), 643–650. doi:10.1177/014920630102700602

Benjamin, L. M. (2012). The potential of outcome measurement for strengthening nonprofits' accountability to beneficiaries. *Nonprofit and Voluntary Sector Quarterly*, *42*(6), 1224–1244. doi:10.1177/0899764012454684

Corrar, L. J., Paulo, E., & Dias Filho, J. M. (2007). *Análise Multivariada: para os cursos de administração, ciências contábeis e economia.* São Paulo, SP: Atlas.

Costa, E., Pesci, C., Andreaus, M., & Taufer, E. (2019). Empathy, closeness, and distance in non-profit accountability. *Accounting, Auditing & Accountability Journal*, *32*(1), 224–254. doi:10.1108/AAAJ-03-2014-1635

Cunha, J. V. A., & Coelho, A. C. (2007). Regressão linear múltipla. In L. J. Corrar, E. Paulo, & J. M. Dias Filho (Eds.), *Análise Multivariada: para os cursos de administração, ciências contábeis e economia* (pp. 131–231). São Paulo, SP: Atlas.

Dall'agnol, C. F. D., Tondolo, R. R. P., Tondolo, V. A. G., & Sarquis, A. B. (2017). Transparência e Prestação de Contas na Mobilização de Recursos no Terceiro Setor: Um estudo de casos múltiplos realizado no sul do Brasil. *Revista Universo Contábil*, *13*(2), 187–203.

Froelich, K. A. (1999). Diversification of revenue strategies: Evolving resource dependence in nonprofit organizations. *Nonprofit and Voluntary Sector Quarterly*, *28*(3), 246–268. doi:10.1177/0899764099283002

Gandía, J. L. (2011). Internet disclosure by nonprofit organizations: Empirical evidence of nongovernmental organizations for development in Spain. *Nonprofit and Voluntary Sector Quarterly*, *40*(1), 57–78. doi:10.1177/0899764009343782

Hair, J. F. Jr, Anderson, R. E., & Black, W. C. (2005a). *Análise multivariada de dados.* Porto Alegre, RS: Bookman.

Hair, J. F. Jr, Babin, B., Money, A. H., & Samouel, P. (2005b). *Fundamentos de métodos de pesquisa em administração.* Porto Alegre, RS: Bookman.

Heald, D. A. (2006). Varieties of transparency. *Proceedings of the British Academy, 135*, 25–43.

Instituto de Pesquisa Econômica Aplicada (IPEA). (2015). *Mapa das Organizações da Sociedade Civil - 2015*. Retrieved June, 2018, from https:// mapaosc.ipea.gov.br/dados-indicadores.html/

Khieng, S. (2014). Funding Mobilization Strategies of Nongovernmental Organizations in Cambodia. *Voluntas, 25*(6), 1441–1464. doi:10.100711266-013-9400-7

Koppell, J. G. S. (2005). Pathologies of accountability: ICANN and the challenge of "multiple accountabilities disorder". *Public Administration Review, 65*(1), 94–108. doi:10.1111/j.1540-6210.2005.00434.x

Murtaza, N. (2012). Putting the lasts first: The case for community-focused and peer-managed NGO accountability mechanisms. *Voluntas, 23*(1), 109–125. doi:10.100711266-011-9181-9

Ntim, C. G., Soobaroyen, T., & Broad, M. J. (2017). Governance structures, voluntary disclosures and public accountability: The case of UK higher education institutions. *Accounting, Auditing & Accountability Journal, 30*(1), 65–118. doi:10.1108/AAAJ-10-2014-1842

Rapoport, S. G. (2011). Transparencia y rendición de cuentas. *Revista Mexicana de Sociologia, 73*(2), 199–229.

Rosa, C. F. (2013). *Desafio de governança à sustentabilidade de organizações sociais: em análise o projeto desenvolvimento de princípios de prestação de contas e transparência da ONG Parceiros Voluntários* (Unpublished master's thesis). Universidade Federal do Rio Grande do Sul, Porto Alegre, RS.

Salamon, L. M., Anheier, H. K., List, R., Toepler, S., & Sokolowski, S. W. (1999). *Global civil society: Dimensions of the nonprofit sector*. Baltimore, MD: The Johns Hopkins Center for Civil Society Studies.

Salomão, A., & Lima, F. (2018). *Análise de crises passadas indica que Brasil vive pior retomada da história. Folha de São Paulo*. Caderno Mercado.

Steccolini, I. (2019). Accounting and the post-new public management: Re-considering publicness in accounting research. *Accounting, Auditing & Accountability Journal, 32*(1), 255–279. doi:10.1108/AAAJ-03-2018-3423

Tondolo, R. R. P. (2014). *Desenvolvimento de Capital Social Organizacional em um Projeto Interorganizacional no Terceiro Setor* (Unpublished doctoral dissertation). Universidade do Vale do Rio dos Sinos, São Leopoldo, RS.

Tondolo, R. R. P., Tondolo, V. A. G., Camargo, M. E., & Sarquis, A. B. (2016). Transparência no Terceiro Setor: Uma proposta de construto e mensuração. *Espacios Públicos, 19*(47), 7–25.

Tondolo, R. R. P., Tondolo, V. A. G., Longaray, A. A., & Mello, S. P. T. (2017). Implementação da Transparência em Organizações Sociais: Um estudo Multicaso. *Revista Eletrônica de Estratégia & Negócios, 10*(2), 81–98. doi:10.19177/reen.v10e2201781-99

Tondolo, V. A. G., Tondolo, R. R. P., Camargo, M. E., & Guerra, R. M. A. (2018). Capacidades Dinâmicas em Organizações Sem Fins Lucrativos: Uma proposta de mensuração para o terceiro setor. *Revista Eletrônica Científica do CRA-PR, 5*(1), 18–33.

Valencia, L. A. R., Queiruga, D., & González-Benito, J. (2015). Relationship between transparency and efficiency in the allocation of funds in nongovernmental development organizations. *Voluntas*, *26*(6), 2517–2535. doi:10.100711266-014-9527-1

KEY TERMS AND DEFINITIONS

Accountability: It refers to a practice of transparency.

Capability: Organization ability to perform a process or routine.

Crisis: It refers a period of time that a nation has problems which can be related to political, economic, and moral aspects.

Non-Profit Organizations: Organizations from civil society that does not have profit as the main goal.

Resource: Tangible or intangible asset of the organization.

Resource Mobilization: It refers to act of articulation, collecting, and application of resources.

Transparency: It refers to the way organizational processes are viewed/performed, being a feature intrinsic to all organizational processes.

APPENDIX

Survey Instrument

Aspects of Organization

1. City/State:
2. Year of foundation:
    a. () less than one year
    b. () 1 – 3 years
    c. () 4 – 5 years
    d. () more than 5 yeras
3. Main sector:
    a. () Social Assistance
    b. () Professional Associations
    c. () Culture and Recreation
    d. () Civil Rigths
    e. () Education
    f. () Housing
    g. () Environment
    h. () Religion
    i. () Health
    j. () Other: ______________
4. Number of employees hired by the organization:
5. Total number of volunteers in the organization:
6. Number of direct beneficiaries currently served (number of people, not households) (Table 8).

Regarding Management Processes of Your Organization

1. Your organization intends to disclose the Accounting Reports to stakeholders and the general community within the time frames required by law.
2. It is your organization's practice to disclose revenue and monthly receipts to stakeholders and the community at large.
3. Your organization has the practice of publicly disclosing its accounting reports and complementary reports on various types of media, such as newspapers, websites, blogs, facebook, among others.

Table 8.

Totally disagree	1	2	3	4	5	Fully agree

4. Your organization has the practice of accounting for the resources and actions taken whenever this is a requirement of the project financier.
5. Your organization makes available to stakeholders and the community at large the constituent documents of the organization, as well as statutes, minutes of the meeting and elections / appointment of chair and board.
6. Your organization makes available the stakeholders and the community at large the legislation that the organization is subject to.
7. Your organization uses social media (facebook, twitter, ...) to disseminate results and actions taken.
8. Your organization's practice is to account for the resources (financial, physical and human), as well as the practices carried out by the organization, stakeholders and the community at large.
9. Your organization provides an e-mail for community service.
10. Your organization uses Home Page (website and / or blog).
11. Your organization provides a space for criticism and input from stakeholders and the community at large.
12. Your organization has the practice of monitoring the activities carried out by its employees and volunteers in meeting its organizational objectives.
13. Your organization has the practice of monitoring the results and effectiveness of its actions in the community served.
14. Your organization has a central Ombudsman Office to assist beneficiaries, stakeholders and the community in general.
15. Your organization is committed to implementing suggestions received from beneficiaries, stakeholders, and the community at large.

Regarding Resources Mobilization of Your Organization

1. Your organization articulates, seeking partnerships and support from the community in general to capture and mobilize resources (financial, physical and human).
2. Your organization develops partnerships, partnerships and projects with public institutions.[x]
3. Your organization develops partnerships, partnerships and projects with private institutions and civil society.
4. In your organization fundraising in the last two years is more difficult.
5. In your organization fundraising in the last two years is easier because you realize that you have more resources available to be captured.
6. In your organization you realize that fundraising is directly linked to your organization's reputation vis-a-vis society
7. In your organization the mobilization of resources is important because it enables the fulfillment of the social mission.
8. Your organization has shared some kind of knowledge, information, tips, assets, and experience with other organizations in recent years.
9. Your organization has a habit of sharing donation resources with other social organizations, which will not be fully absorbed in your organization.
10. Your organization has a habit of sharing physical resources (equipment, furniture, ...) with other social organizations, which no longer have use in your organization.

11. Your organization has a habit of sharing human resources (employees and volunteers) with other social organizations, which are not fully utilized in your organization.
12. Your organization usually shares financial resources with other social organizations.
13. Your organization usually receives resources (of the most varied types) from other social organizations that have and will not use them.
14. Your organization has a shortage of resources, making it impossible to share them with other organizations.[x]

[x] Dropped variables by reliability analysis.

Chapter 5
Accountability and Reporting in the Funding Decision Process of Social Economy

António-Cardoso Pinto
University of Lisbon, Portugal

José Dias Lopes
University of Lisbon, Portugal

Pedro Verga Matos
University of Lisbon, Portugal

ABSTRACT

This chapter addresses the topic of accountability and reporting of social entities as concepts and instruments of governance that are used to demonstrate transparency and rigor regarding their activity to their stakeholders. The objective of this chapter is to understand how these instruments are used by social entities, and to establish whether this use brings about an increase in the trust created between theses entities and their funders with regards to the possibility of obtaining increased funding. With this in mind, two surveys were carried out, one for social entities and the other for funders, with some similar content, in order to enable a comparison of answers. This study enabled us to conclude that social entities have a formal and periodic relationship with their funders, that they believe that the current accountability and reporting (A&R) quality level is adequate, that social entities' A&R information, although not decisive, is important for funding decision making, and if social entities were to receive substantial funding, this would improve their social impact.

DOI: 10.4018/978-1-5225-8482-7.ch005

INTRODUCTION[1]

The main objective of this study is to understand the weight that the Accountability and Reporting (A&R) of Portuguese social entities currently has in their management, and what influence A&R has on their funding. At the same time, a characterisation of the relationship between social entities and funders was also studied, as well as what improvements could be made in the field of A&R.

The importance of this subject is derived from the current process of transformation following the public attention that social entities have been subject to, especially concerning both the use of public funding, or private funding (Maduro, Pasi & Misuraca, 2018). This increased attention on social entities has led to them to feel the need to become more effective in their mission of fund raising, as well as to become more rigorous with regards to their mechanisms of evaluation and control (Azevedo, 2013; OECD/EU, 2017) and to become more transparent about the positive and negative impacts of their activity in the communities (Jones & Mucha, 2014).

According to INE (2016), in Portugal the Social Economy represents 2.8% of the Portuguese gross added value (€4,206,000), 6% of employment, comprising 61,268 organisations from a very eclectic pool of entities (ranging from foundations to social care institutions, among others)[2]. Naturally, the current values may differ.

In order to answer the questions raised and to achieve the above-mentioned objectives, two surveys were carried out (one for social entities and the other for funders) - from which the relevant information was extracted.

This study is divided into five sections. Following the introduction, a review is made of the literature on the main subjects discussed in this study, where different contributions are highlighted and consequently an integration of the different perspectives and analysis is made, whilst at the same time the questions surrounding the main subject are outlined. In the next section, a description of the methodology used is made and the study proceeds with an analysis and review of the data gathered for each question. Lastly, the main conclusions are presented.

Litterature Review

The world of Social Economy is typically perceived as under watched in terms of rigor and transparency for its activities, including how organisations use their budgets and disclosure of the origins of their funds, as well as which objectives and results are proposed to be achieved, how this is to be done, and which results have genuinely been accomplished (Azevedo, 2013).

As such, performance measurement and the transparency of the accounting of social entities, together with the communication of that information, are elements which are increasingly being demanded either by public institutions (in Portugal, for example, the State represents nearly 40% of their revenue), private institutions, and even by society (Azevedo, 2013; OECD/EU, 2017). Therefore, this information regarding Accountability (to be accountable for their finances and activity) and Reporting (the use of transparency mechanisms) is thus of special interest for social entities, in particular for those concerned with their credibility and legitimacy when fund raising.

Definition and Principles of Accountability

In the debate about the meaning of accountability, Brown & Troutt (2007) identify a confrontation between performance accountability and procedures accountability, both of which are concepts that arise from the clash of the recent public management theory and the more traditional notions of accountability.

Procedures accountability is understood to be the obligation of the supported entity, due to hierarchical and legal obligations, to report to the funder how the funding was used, in accordance with established procedures. Brown & Troutt (idem) are critical of this situation, as it leaves little room for manoeuvre to either adopt new procedures or adapt to a new context.

The same authors (idem) view performance accountability from a "360º degrees" approach, where a relation is established between both parties (funders and financed entities) regarding the duty of reporting their activities, and also with regards to the communities that they deal with. In this way, total disclosure and communication about the activities of Non-Profit Organisations (NPOs) is assured, as well as how the funds are used.

When referring to accountability in NPOs, Brody (2001) and Geer et al., (2008) identify four key elements: (a) fiscal responsibility/avoidance of fraud; (b) good governance; (c) adherence to the mission and donor direction, and; (d) demonstration of the effectiveness of the organisation's programme. The main benefit of this elements, even though they are broad to some extent, is that they enable allow to be more readily measured, in terms of accountability.

Candler & Dumont (2010) adopt a more open and common-sense definition of accountability, describing it as being the "duty" to be accountable, in the context of being responsible to a third party. The authors state, however, that as NPOs are becoming increasingly subject to scrutiny, mainly by public authorities, which are becoming more inquisitive and have a bigger influence over NPOs governance – in line with the "new public management theory", identified by Brown & Troutt (2007). Using other accountability analysis models, the authors created an analysis table which attempts to answer two questions, namely: 1) accountable to whom? and, 2) accountable for what?

With regards to the first question, Candler & Dumont (2010) attempted to compile stakeholders' interests and concerns regarding NPOs in their table, and concerning the second question, the same authors focus on the topics that concern accountability, namely: internal consequences; consequences regarding NPOs' services to the exterior, and the level of quality of the formal aspects of accountability (such as: compliance with their mission, the legitimacy or fulfilment with legal procedures of NPOs).

Regarding the debate about the definition of accountability, Ebrahim (2003) points out the complexity and dynamics of the different theoretical perspectives in respect of NPOs (e.g.: the resource dependence theory, the organisation behaviour theory, and the agency theory). The author states that accountability can be defined as a mean through which individuals and organisations are responsible for their actions, and also as a mean through which organisations and individuals can assume their internal responsibility for the definition of their mission and values, as well as their transparency and the evaluation made of their performance.

The diversity and complexity of these different approaches for the definition of accountability and their different outlooks of analysis reveal the evolution that this subject has experienced in the field of NPOs, which is characterised by "growth pains", as mentioned in literature, which is related with profound changes in their political, social, legal, and economical contexts.

Weerawardena et al. (2010) mentioned that the competitive environment created by this attitude of change in social entities leads to the adoption of an organisation model which is extremely directed towards achieving results, which can diverge from their "social mission" and divert them from their organisational *raison d'être*. Another perspective considers that an outcome-based orientation will pressure social entities to increase their efficiency and managerial capabilities, mobilising new private players to the social sector (OECE/EU, 2017; Maduro, Pasi & Misuraca, 2018).

Wellens & Jegers (2014) state that the fact that different parties are interested in having influence at both the organisational level and planning of social entities affects its governance in particular, as these entities are facing an increasing demand to reveal more information and to be more accountable, resulting in a need to create mechanisms and structures that respond to the needs and interests of different stakeholders.

Nevertheless, this scenario has a positive effect, in that, through the correct use of these instruments of accountability, different groups and stakeholders of social entities are increasingly aware of the needs and interests of each other, and are thus able in this way to share information and ideas regarding which is the best operational model for the social entity, as well as for achieving the objectives in terms of performance.

Ebrahim (2003) studied in more depth the use of accountability mechanisms used by NPOs. By setting five broad methods, which he described as "processes" or "instruments" – reports and disclosure statements, performance assessments and evaluations, participation, self-regulation, and social audits – the author studied their actual use through three dimensions of accountability: "upward and downward"; internal and external; and functional and strategical.

Ebrahim states that "*the current emphasis among NGOs and donors regarding the upward and external dimensions of accountability is problematic in that it encourages the formation of relationships with highly imbalanced accountabilities. Similarly, the current emphasis on functional forms of accountability tends to reward NGOs for short term responses with quick and tangible impacts, while neglecting longer-term strategic responses that address more complex issues of social and political change.*"

In this way, the author proposes two fundamental changes. Firstly, a closer proximity and relationship between funders and organisations, which implies a reinforcement of the downward accountability mechanisms, whereby financing institutions and donors can be evaluated by the NPOs, in the perspective of discovering which funding sources are more convenient.

Secondly, the improvement of internal accountability mechanisms of NPOs, through regular social audits (where the stakeholders are involved, and a dialogue is established with the objective of discussing the organisation's issues) and also the development of mechanisms that promote self-regulation in particular situations (ex.: the creation of mechanisms at the sectorial level which address the common problems of the organisations).

Accountability and the Financing Decision

The direct relationship between A&R mechanisms and financing does not appear to have yet been widely developed in the academic literature, with a more notable connection between these instruments and the "professionalisation" of NPO's.

An interesting approach to this challenge was made by Carman (2008), who explores two growing trends in the world of philanthropy: the focus on adopting evaluation and performance measurement data mechanisms (see Epstein & Yuthas, 2017) and also the growing level of investment in training and in the efficiency of social entities.

Carman's opinion is that these trends focus on impact evaluation, performance, and efficiency, and that they are a result of the emergence of four factors that have been changing the social entities field, namely: wider public scrutiny; a growing concern with public image, due to some high-profile scandals; the benefits arising from significant fiscal exemptions, which gives more importance to the questions of accountability and transparency, and; a growing interest from donors/funders in knowing the mechanisms used by social entities to manage their activity.

However, the same author (idem) mentions that few studies on the evaluation activities of social entities exist, and accordingly her study focussed on presenting six hypotheses for monitoring, reporting, measuring, and evaluation of performance, together with their relationship with financing possibilities.

In their study about the measurement of efficiency in NPOs, Taysir & Taysir (2012) identify accountability to be the third most influent factor for the analysis of efficiency, indicating that transparency and information transmission, especially regarding how resources (financing resources) are made use of, is one of the reasons for justifying the necessity to measure the efficiency of NPOs, which is a consequence of increased transparency and that it is also an instrument of democratisation and community empowerment, as mentioned by Mueller-Hirth (2012).

Parsons (2007) concludes that voluntary disclosure of information has a positive correlation with the decision to finance NPO's, or on other words, there is a larger probability of donors/funders contributing financially if transparent financial information is disclosed during the fund-raising campaign. Parsons' study presents two important conclusions: first, it proves that transparent finance information has a direct impact on the decision making of funders, and secondly; that that the same information also positively affects the public image of the NPO in question.

Mitchell (2014) claims that in the case of NPOs, the adoption of measurement and evaluation mechanisms, together with assuming the duty to disclose their results should become increasingly-prevalent practices for those who finance and support such organisations, bearing in mind that a significant proportion of their donations and support comes from individuals and from non-economic areas of society.

Suárez (2010), however, finds a different reason for greater or less probability of funding NPOs, especially concerning governmental support, namely the funding record, where the author observes that previous funding from the State increases the probability of repeat funding.

The influence of donors/funders over the mechanisms of performance measurement and evaluation of NPOs, which reinforces the instruments of accountability and reporting, is more notable in the case of large-scale funders, whether they be public or private institutions, as suggested by Carman (2009) and Brown & Troutt (2007). The latter academics studied the way that relationships between governmental bodies and NPOs in the United States affect the adoption of accountability instruments, concluding that the way that financing agreements are drawn up result in it being more difficult to include accountability measures.

The Influence of Reporting

Suárez (2010) considers that profound changes exist regarding relations between NPOs and distinct groups of funders which support and finance these organisations, with consequences in terms of accountability (periodicity, contents, etc.)

Being accountable (*accountability*) is achieved through the use of an array of instruments and processes (*reporting*), whereby the demands of the latter can limit the quality/depth of the former. Brown & Troutt (2007) approach this issue, mentioning that the imposition of specific processes of *accountability* by external entities could narrow NPOs' capacity to report their activities, as the exercise of "accounting for" is sometimes subject to demands and is a waste of resources which otherwise could be used for the correct and timely disclosure of their reports. The effects of this demand for reporting, or the mismatch of the accountability criteria, can lead to the demotivation of the NPOs in fulfilling these requirements, with consequences for their social mission.

Othman & Ali (2012) studied the importance of the quality of reporting, and concluded that the adoption of regulation and supervision, which ensures that NPOs implement accountability and reporting processes, enhances the probability of the granting of donations by potential funders, both national and international.

For Azevedo (2013), individual donors are more aware of the activities of organizations to whom they donate their money, and how it is used to achieve the proposed objectives. Foundations and other philanthropic institutions have been attempting to assemble more information, beyond the quantitative reports which are disclosed by NPOs. Governmental authorities respectively try to introduce mechanisms and tools as they follow the activities of social entities, in order to better assess the benefits of contracting with these social entities, especially through the implementation of results-based evaluation metrics and other quantitative metrics (Maduro, Pasi & Misuraca, 2018).

Thornton & Belski (2010) deduce that the quality of reporting influences the decision of funders, who appreciate the imposition of transparency regarding the behaviour of the managers of NPOs and their conclusions are shared by Lammers (2003), who points out that the financial information of NPOs is more often being used as a support tool for funding decisions.

Reheul et al. (2014) mention the importance of the standardization of requirements and procedures for the disclosure of this kind of information, emphasizing that the potential changes in requirements may lead to delaying this disclosure. According to these authors, those NPOs that have a bigger dependency on donations or other kinds of funding, submit their reports quicker and have less probability in delaying their financial reports, which is consistent with the resources dependence theory.

Accountability Mechanisms and Governance

The "professionalization" of management and the adoption of good practices of accountability and reporting represent interesting challenges for the governance of NPOs, in line with the increasing responsibility required from different stakeholders.

Suárez (2010) notes that the adoption of planning strategies and annual audits are more frequent in NPOs, which implicates the hiring of more specialized human resources, and therefore changes the ancient *status quo* of almost exclusively using volunteers for this kind of work.

At the same level, Huang & Powell (2009) concluded that NPOs are now using more standardized practices and are more focused in issues related with efficiency and responsibility towards the stakeholders, and that this has increasingly become the driver.

Viader & Espina (2014) claim that business governance theories (the agency theory, resources dependence theory, administration theory, and hybrid theory) also apply to other organizational structures, namely NPOs. They add that the senior management of the NPOs that they studied tend to identify the need to manage and control operations and their financial performance which is very similar to the behaviour of most company managers.

Young (2011) identifies one obstacle related with the strong dependency of NPOs on voluntary work, even at management level, which can lead to the existence of not many incentives for modernization, due to the lack of financial and career perspectives. For, in the case of many NPOs, especially those that provide basic health care and social services, a fee for the service is not requested (or when this occurs, the fee is extremely low), which leads to the need to find other financing alternatives - such as fund raising or agreements with the State, which request managers to be more accountable, which is hard to achieve when the management itself is not professional.

Wellens & Jegens (2014) find another potential need for increasing professional levels at NPOs, by bringing to the debate the role of stakeholders in governance structures, who demand better accountability quality. The authors state that when taking into the account the worries and interests of these stakeholders in the decision process, they are obliged to adopt more professional management practices at NPOs.

On other hand, Lehn (2008) studies the problem from the perspective of risk management associated with the adoption of accountability mechanisms and their influence on the work and structural organization of NPOs. The author reached three conclusions: a) the work of NPOs requires more technical skills, with importance given to proximity and relational work; b) the obligation to evaluate NPOs' performance may enter into conflict with the development of their activity, and; c) it is necessary to know the respective implications by studying an analysis of the accountability of NPOs, in order to manage and distribute the risk in the situations of organizational redefinition.

By looking into the factors that imply responsibility within a NPO (between executive and management structures and the volunteers), McClusky (2007) highlights a relevant element for the debate on the governance structures of NPOs - due to the fact that there is much heterogeneity between NPOs, and despite many authors suggesting standardized analysis frameworks, the submission of a "pre-conceived model" is difficult to carry out, which makes accountability practices such an interesting exercise, as they have to be adapted to each case.

In summary, the academic literature shows that in the academic field there has been a growing interest in the accountability of NPOs, with some researchers studying good practices of transparency and the duty to be accountable and relating these with the funding decision process. Other authors relate the improvements in accountability and reporting with the "professionalization" process of NPOs' management structures, which has repercussions for the structures and models of governance and for the relationship between NPOs and stakeholders.

Methodology

The objective of this study is to acquire an understanding of the use made by social entities of the A&R mechanisms and their relationship with the funding decision process. In this context, it is intended to:

- Know the most common typology of the relationship between social entities and funders, and also to know whether there is any coordination between the information that may be of interest to funders and that which is transmitted;
- Understand which Accountability and Reporting elements have more influence in the funding process decision and which can increase the probability of funding;
- Know which information should be improved in a scenario of a significant increase of funding;

Table 1. Theoretical Framework Synthesis by themes, keywords and authors

Main Themes	Subthemes	Author(s)
Accountability	Definition of Accountability	Brown & Troutt (2007); Candler & Dumont (2010); Ebrahim (2003); Geer et al. (2008)
	Impact of Accountability in NPOs	Lehn (2008); Lehn (2010a); Moore & Ryan (2006); Taysir & Taysir (2012); Mueller-Hirth (2012)
	Relation between Accountability and Funding	Carman (2008); Mitchell (2014); Parsons (2007); Mueller et al. (2005); Trussel & Parsons (2008)
Reporting	Influence of Reporting in NPOs	Reheul et al. (2014); Thornton & Belski (2010); Jones & Mucha (2014)
	Reporting Tools	Othman & Ali (2012)
Governance	Governance Models	Bradshaw et al. (2007); Viader & Espina (2014); Smith (2010)
	Stakeholders' Role	Lehn (2010b); McClusky (2002); Manetti & Toccafondi (2014); Wellens & Jegers (2014)
	Impact of Governance Good Practices	Suárez (2010); Weerawardena et al, (2010); Young, D. (2011)
	Agency Theory in NPOs	Lehn (2008); Peterson (2010)

Source: Authors

- Know how social entities and funders evaluate certain elements of Accountability and Reporting in NPOs.

The methodology used is a survey, based on the literature review above, with closed answers, which was sent by email to social entities and funders. Meetings with social economy specialists also took place, which provided a more comprehensive analysis of the subject of this study.

The sample was comprised of entities that qualified as members of a convenience sample, after having considered the requirement that those managers consulted had to be familiar with the technical language being used. Furthermore, all the entities that participated in this study are Portuguese and are active organizations in the field of social economy in Portugal, this being a consequence of the regional scope of this study.

The survey questionnaire was mailed to 17 social entities, with 15 of them replying. Unfortunately, only 2 of 7 potential funders answered the funders' survey (one social business angel and one investment bank).

Being predominantly qualitative research, the sample of the study was reduced, as the focus was on those social entities that are usually involved with different funders and receive substantial funding by financing entities which are chosen for their record in supporting Social Economy.

The type of study described above made it necessary to create two questionnaires, one for social entities, and another for funders, with some common questions for both parties, while other questions are specific to each party.

Both surveys were carried out according to the following structural logic: initial questions regarding the amount of financial support received, and the level of financial support given (Questions 1 and 2); followed by questions designed to characterize the relationship between both parties (Questions 3 to 7); after these questions, questions were asked about the quality of information for accountability and reporting mechanisms and how they are perceived, in the light of the current funding models and whether any elements standout as potential leverage elements for increasing the probability of funding (Questions 8 to 12). To end, it was asked which improvements should take place (Question 13) and, in the cases of social entities, whether they would have the capability to implement them (Question 14), and finally, a score for the evaluation of the activity factors of social entities was requested (Question 15 for social entities, and Question 14 for funders).

The option for this system of asking questions - where some are common to both surveys, and others are differentiated - was due to the need to compare the opinions and realities from both parties regarding the same subjects regarding the importance that A&R information has in the funding decision process, thus making it possible to answer the "research questions" proposed in this study.

DATA ANALYSIS

All of the information collected was analysed and treated accordingly, using the answers received from the questionnaires that were sent to both social entities and funders.

Questions 1 and 2: Funding Characterization

Table 2 sums up the information gathered from the first two questions. It is perceptible that most social entities (53%) have between 1 to 10 funders, with a relative dispersion of the average funding value – ranging from small values (€0 to €10,000) to high values (€50,000 to €100,000). It is important to note the number of social entities that did not indicated any value.

These results allow us to state that there are two levels of funding – one which is characterized by social entities that typically receive funding between the value of €1,000 (or less) and €10,000, and others with values between €25,000 and €100,000. In the case of the latter, it is probable that the funds originate from collective donors/funders, such as companies, banks, foundations, or state funds.

This is not surprising, and is probably due to two facts: first, that some large private funders, such as banks or foundations, support (or give funds) social projects programs and select dozens of entities to whom they donate funding of thousands of euros. In terms of the high values of funding, the main reason for this occurring may relate to the preference of some funders for more important social entities, with whom funders have a track record and which are recognized as having a solid reputation in their field[3].

Table 2. Funders that support social entities (No.)

Nº of Funders	Social Entities Answers
0-5	4
6-10	4
11-20	1
20-50	3
+50	2
N.a.	1

Source: Questionnaire

Table 3. Average value of financial support

Average Value (€)	Social Entities Answers
0 - 1,000	1
1,000 - 5,000	3
5,000 - 10,000	2
10,000 - 25,000	0
25,000 - 50,000	1
50,000 - 100,000	3
+ de 100,000	1
N.a.	4

Source: Questionnaire

Questions 3 to 7: Relationship Between Social Entities and Funders

From Question 3 onwards, specific questions were introduced which helped to characterize the relationship between social entities and funders and the role of A&R mechanisms in the funding decision process.

Figure 1 presents a characterization of the dominant typology of the relationship between social entities and their funders – which mainly consists of "cooperation agreements", although some of the entities mentioned have different types of formal relationships with different funders.

The following question (Question 4) aims to understand the regularity with which social entities and funders usually meet and share information, where it is clear that, according to Figure 2, that annual meetings are more common[4], with relatively frequent periodical or *ad-hoc* meetings, which indicates that, besides the traditional annual review meeting, most social entities only meet with their funders when specific issues justifies such a meeting.

Figure 1. Typology of the relationship between social entities and funders
Source: Questionnaire

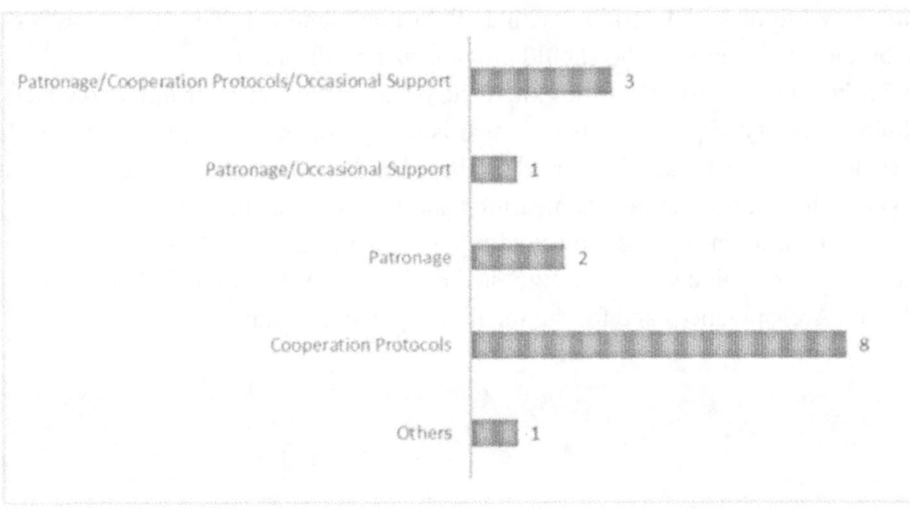

As most of these social entities are funded by companies and other large private organizations, the capacity (or interest) for follow-up by these funders is inferior to, for example, an investor such as a "business angel", which usually carries out a more constant and regular follow-up.

Question 5 aims to know, in the opinion of the managers of social entities, which financing entities typically give more importance to A&R information. The answers present a very scattered result, as can be seen in Figure 3, and it is impossible to pointing out one particular type of funder which could be predominant[5].

Figure 2. Meeting frequency between social entities and funders
Source: Questionnaire

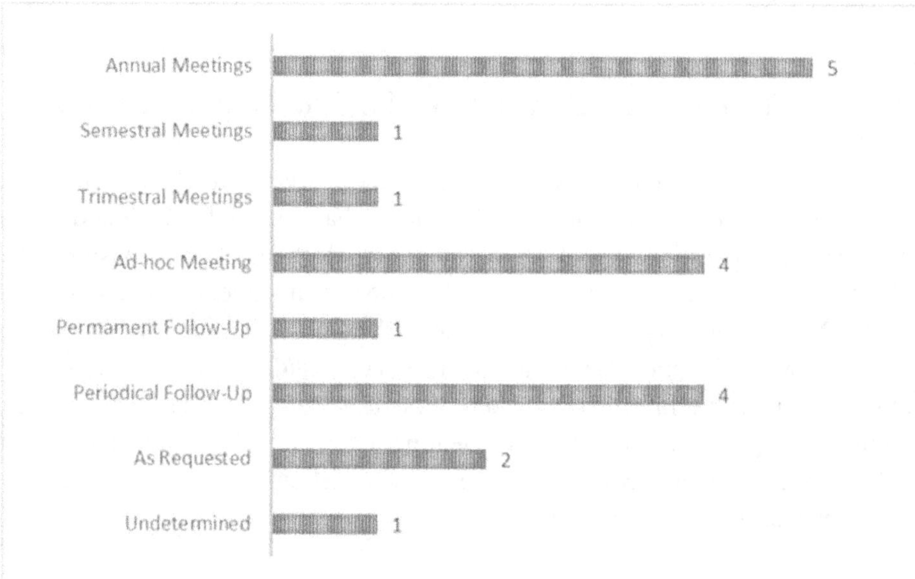

In the following question (Question 6), funders were asked whether they are aware of the financial needs and the daily life of social entities, with a slight dominance of "yes" as an answer (Figure 4), although doubt remains regarding who should provide such information.

Question 7 asked whether social entities knew the needs and interests of funders- which resulted in an overwhelming majority of positive answers, that is to say, that social entities consider that they are aware of what funders expect and wish for when they decide to fund their social causes. It would be interesting to know how this awareness is measured and how serious it is.

The coordination between social entities and funders regarding what the expectations and interests of both parties are, is a question which, as suggested by Candler & Dumont (2010), is important for the definition of good A&R practices and for the relationship between stakeholders.

Figure 3. Funders that give more importance do Accountability and Reporting information
Source: Questionnaire

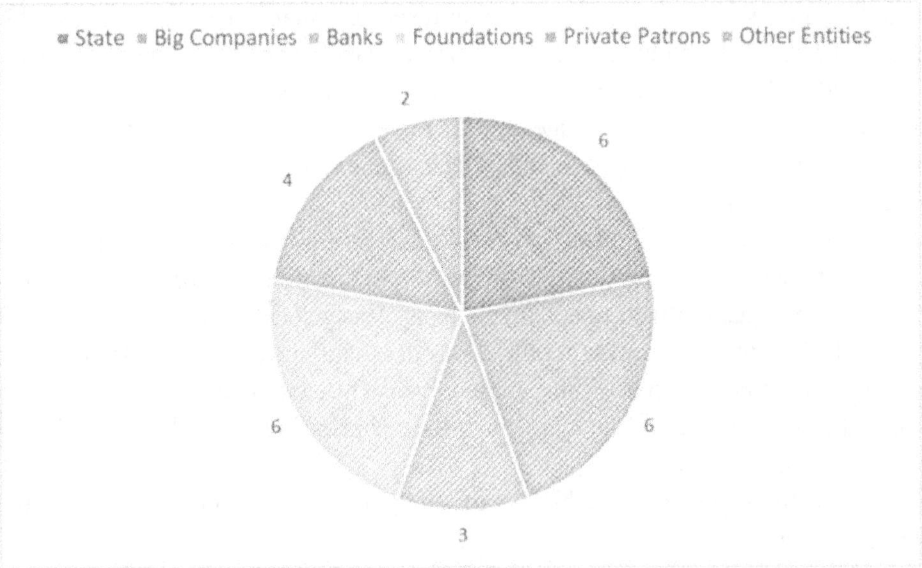

Figure 4. Funders' awareness of the financial needs and daily life of social entities
Source: Questionnaire (n. a. = non available)

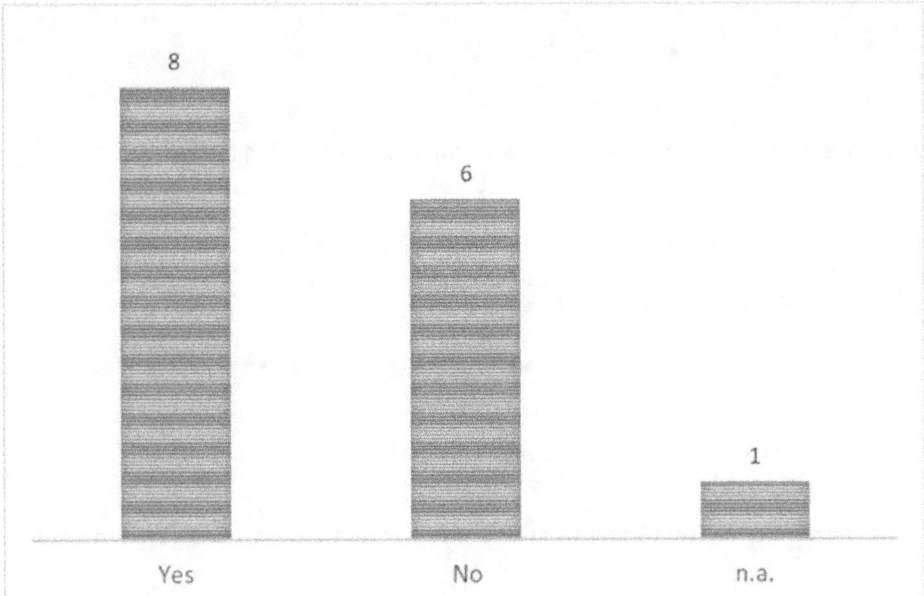

Questions 8 and 12: Accountability and Reporting and Funding

The answers to Question 8 – which enquired whether disclosed financial and non-financial information of social entities had in mind the interests and concerns of the different stakeholders, had a strong positive inclination, with only three social entities answering otherwise.

Question 9 asked for an evaluation judgement of the social entities, as the question asked, whilst knowing the average value of funding received, which element of information they considered fundamental to be disclosed to funders.

In this case, as in some previous questions, despite indications to the contrary, some entities chose to answer more than one hypothesis. Figure 5 shows the total chosen options - where the "Activities, General Objectives and Quantitative Impact" hypothesis clearly stands out.

Question 10 asked social entities whether they consider that the A&R information that they disclose is adequate, bearing in mind the level of funding received. Thirteen positive answers and two negative were received, which implies that a large majority of the social entities consulted consider this information to be sufficient and adequate.

Question 11 asked the social entities which factor, in their opinion, is more influential in the funding decision process of funders.

The factor which social entities sense are more influential in the decision process to financially support a social entity (or a related project) is the credibility and reputation that the entity has regarding Social Economy[6], with a special note regarding other options, such as: the credibility of the management team and the human resources and the CSR (Corporate Social Responsibility) of the funders.

Figure 5. Information to be disclosed, according to the current funding status
Source: Questionnaire

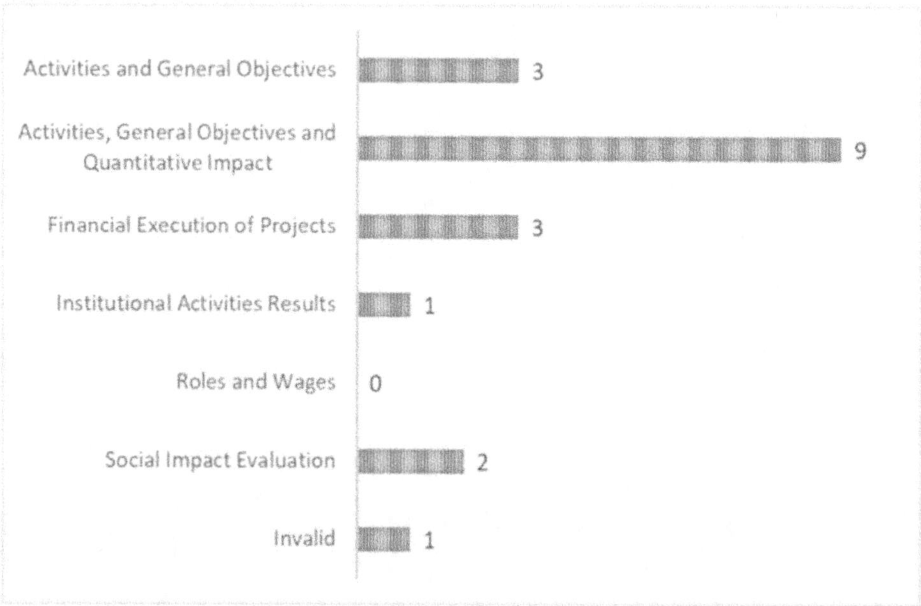

Figure 6. Influential factors of funding decision
Source: Questionnaire

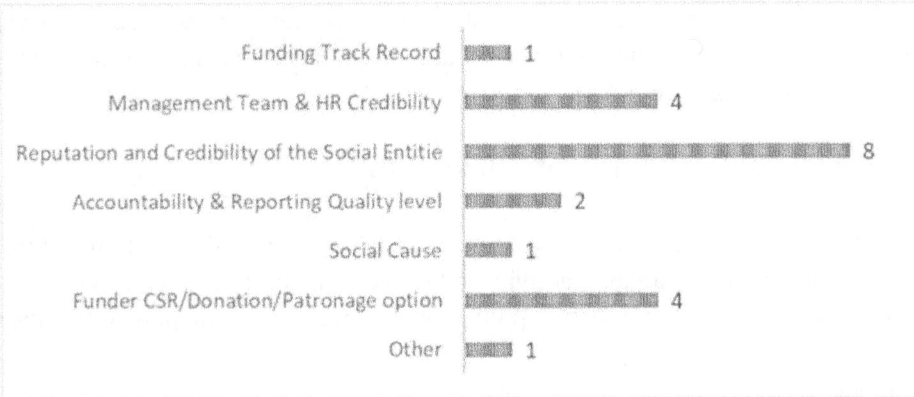

The objective of Question 12 was to know whether there is a direct relation between the quality of the financial and activities report of the social entities and the funding decision. The answers to this question were mostly affirmative (twelve out of fifteen answers received), with three negative answers.

Questions 13 and 14: Future Improvements and Funding

Question 13 asked whether, in the case of a social entity receiving a larger-than-usual level of funding, which elements related to their activity they believed should be improved. In this case, up to three options could be chosen.

According to the answers given, as summarized in Figure 7, social impact evaluation[7] stands out from the others that were possible to choose.

Figure 7. Elements to improve in a larger-than-usual funding scenario
Source: Questionnaire

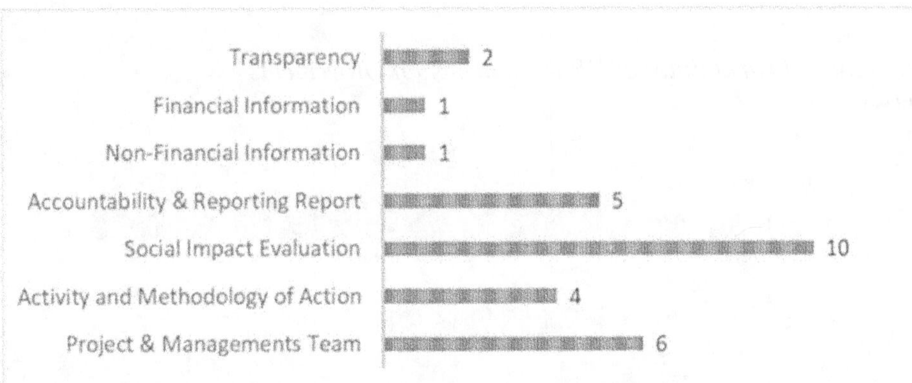

The objective of Question 14, which is related with the previous question, was to know the true capability of social entities to implement the above-mentioned improvements. According to the answers given, the majority of respondents believe they have human resources with the necessary technical skills to implement these improvements, although one should take notice of the number of social entities that answered to the contrary, as shown in Figure 8.

Question 15: Activity Evaluation of Social Entities

To conclude, in Question 15, social entities (and their managers) were asked to evaluate the quality of the following six factors related with their activity and the accountability and reporting information that they disclose (on a scale of 1 to 10, with 1 being the lowest degree of evaluation and 10 the highest):

- Transparency
- Financial Reporting
- Non-Financial Reporting
- Efficiency
- Performance Evaluation
- Social Impact Evaluation

The results presented in Figure 9 show that "Transparency" and "Financial Reporting" are both considered to be very important (with more than 9 points, on average), with "Social Impact Evaluation" being the factor of their activity which presents the least quality (with an average of just 5.5 points).

CONCLUSION

The answers collected from the social entities allowed us to conclude some important facts regarding the funding process of social entities and also their relationship with funders and the importance of A&R mechanisms and information in the funding decision process. In summary:

Figure 8. The technical capabilities of HR to implement improvements
Source: Questionnaire

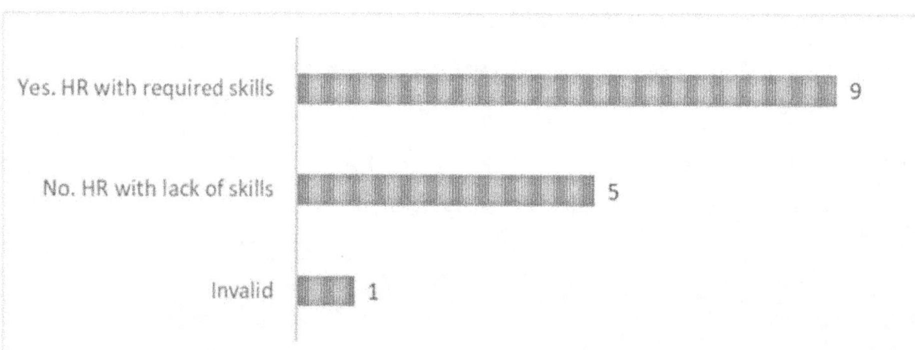

Figure 9. Social entities' evaluation of their accountability and reporting
Source: Questionnaire

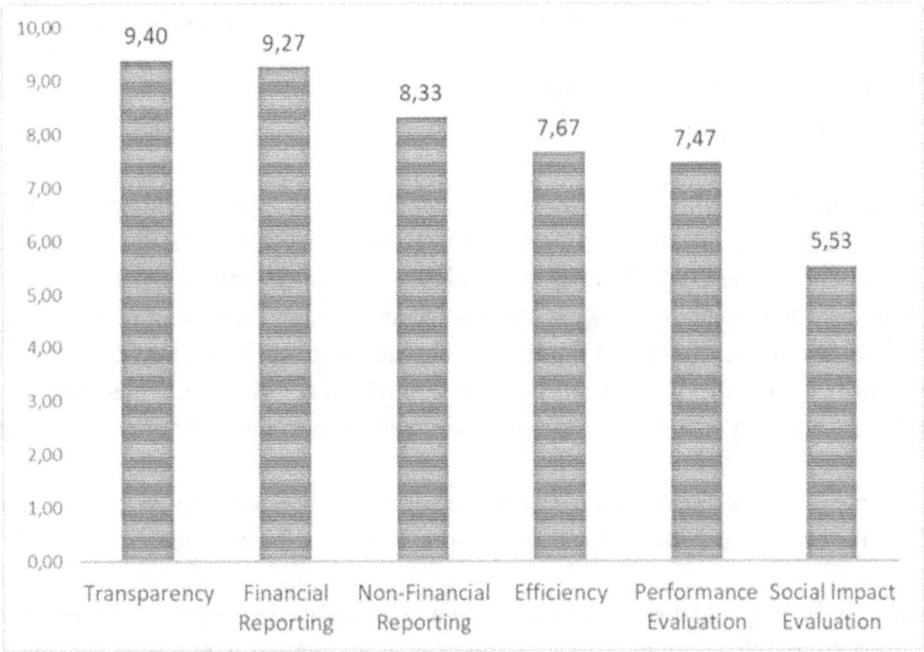

1. Formal Relationship and Annual and/or Periodical Follow-Up

According to the information received, the relationship between social entities and funders is usually made official through "cooperation agreements", with some social entities also signing patronage agreements. It is usual to celebrate more than one type of agreement with funders.

Another conclusion to be made from the characterization of the relationship between social entities and funders is the less common or sporadic follow-up by the funders of the social entities that they support.

2. Adequate Current Level of Accountability and Reporting

With regards to the current reality of the quality and degree of disclosure of information regarding their activity, the social entities consider that this is adequate, and that the important information that needs to be disclosed should focus on their activities, the objectives achieved, and the evaluation of the quantitative impact of their activity or their projects.

3. Relevant, but Not Decisive Accountability and Reporting Information

One of the most important conclusions, in line with Taysir & Taysir (2012) and Othman & Ali (2012), is that the information which social entities report regarding their accountability, and the way that they report this, is relevant to the funders, although it is not decisive.

According to the social entities, more important than this information is the credibility and reputation of the social entity in their field, which has a more decisive weight in the funding decision when comparing the track record between the social entities and funders, or the quality of Accountability & Reporting.

4. High Level of Transparency, but Need to Improve the Social Impact Evaluation

One of the main objectives of this study was to know which aspect of the control and evaluation of their activity social entities would like to improve if they were to receive substantially more funding, with a significant number of answers stating that this would improve their "social impact evaluation".

It was made clear that social entities would like to improve the evaluation of their impact on the communities with whom they work and the results that they achieve, going beyond the simple task of counting how many people they have reached out to through an activity or a project (as pointed out in Conclusion No. 3), and they also wanted to know the "how" more than the "how many" (quantitative impact).

In addition, the fact that transparency was the factor which received the best evaluation from the social entities may be related with the legal obligations that are subject to regarding the disclosure of their activity[8].

To conclude, we believe that these analysis could have important consequences for practitioners. According to our results, today Accountability and Reporting is an important, although not yet fundamental factor for the financing decision. However, the development in Portugal of a new approach to social innovation and the financial of social economy (Portugal Inovação Social) makes the accountabilty and reporting issues more relevant as (private) financiers and the state need more and better information (OECD/EU, 2017). The mobilisation of 150 million euros in EU structural funds (mainly from the European Social Fund), allocated among four funding programmes requeries a deeper relation among social entities, private funders and the Portuguese government, with better information, and a subsequent improvement in Accountability and Reporting mechanisms may increase the analysis and evaluation of programs and its outcomes. In addition, this study also presents the case for increasing the development of measuring social impact, as part of the Accountability and Reporting data to be presented to all players in the field, especially funders, which may encourage a more practical approach to the social impact measurement

REFERENCES

Azevedo, C. (2013). *Manual de Governo – O Desafio da Liderança nas Organizações do Terceiro Sector em Portugal*. Porto: Impulso Positivo.

Bradshaw, P., Hayday, B., & Armstrong, R. (2007). Nonprofit Governance Models: Problems & Prospect. *The Innovation Journal*, *12*(3), 1–22.

Brown, L. K., & Troutt, E. (2007). Reporting does not Equal Accountability! The Importance of Funding Characteristics and Process on Accountability. *International Journal of Public Administration*, *30*(2), 209–225. doi:10.1080/01900690601118240

Cabinet Office/Government of the United Kingdom. (n.d.). Available at: http://data.gov.uk/sib_knowledge_box/toolkit

Candler, G., & Dumont, G. (2010). A non-profit accountability framework. *Canadian Public Administration, 53*(2), 259–279. doi:10.1111/j.1754-7121.2010.00126.x

Carman, J. G. (2008). Nonprofits, Funders, and Evaluation: Accountability in Action. *American Review of Public Administration, 39*(4), 374–390. doi:10.1177/0275074008320190

Ebrahim, A. (2003). Accountability in Practice: Mechanisms for NGO's. *World Development, 31*(5), 813–829. doi:10.1016/S0305-750X(03)00014-7

Ebrahim, A., & Rangan, V. K. (2014). What impact? A framework for measuring the scale and scope of social performance. *California Management Review, 56*(3), 118–141. doi:10.1525/cmr.2014.56.3.118

Epstein, M. J., & Yuthas, K. (2017). *Measuring and improving social impacts: A guide for nonprofits, companies and impact investors*. Routledge. doi:10.4324/9781351276245

Geer, B. W., Maher, J. K., & Cole, M. T. (2008). Managing Nonprofit Organizations – The Importance of Transformational Leadership and Commitment to Operating Standards for Nonprofit Accountability. *Public Performance & Management Review, 32*(1), 51–75. doi:10.2753/PMR1530-9576320103

INE – Statistics of Portugal. (2016). *Conta satélite da economia social – 2013*. Author.

Jegers, M. (2009). "Corporate" Governance in Nonprofit Organizations – A Nontechnical Review of the Economic Literature. *Nonprofit Management & Leadership, 20*(2), 143–164. doi:10.1002/nml.246

Jones, K. R., & Mucha, L. (2014). Sustainability Assessment and Reporting for Nonprofit Organizations: Accountability "for the Public Good". *Voluntas, 25*(6), 1465–1482. doi:10.100711266-013-9399-9

Lazzarini, S. G. (2018). The measurement of social impact and opportunities for research in business administration. *RAUSP Management Journal, 53*(1), 134–137. doi:10.1016/j.rauspm.2017.12.010

Lehn, B. (2008). Bearing More Risk for Results – Performance Acountability and Nonprofit Relational Work. *Administration & Society, 39*(8), 959–983. doi:10.1177/0095399707309357

Lehn, B. (2010a). Funders as Principals - Performance Measurement in Philantropic Relationships. *Nonprofit Management & Leadership, 20*(4), 383–403. doi:10.1002/nml.20001

Lehn, B. (2010b). Mediating Accountability - How Nonprofit Fundind Intermediaries Use Performance Measurement and Why It Matter for Governance. *Public Performance & Management Review, 33*(4), 594–618. doi:10.2753/PMR1530-9576330404

Maduro, M., Pasi, G., & Misuraca, G. (2018). *Social impact investment in the EU. Financing strategies and outcome oriented approaches for social policy innovation: narratives, experiences, and recommendations*. Luxembourg: Publications Office of the European Union.

Manetti, G., & Toccafondi, S. (2014). Defining the Content of Sustainability Reports in Nonprofit Organizations: Do Stakeholders Really Matter. *Journal of Nonprofit & Public Sector Marketing, 25*(1), 35–61. doi:10.1080/10495142.2013.857498

McClusky, J. E. (2007). Re-Thinking Nonprofit Organization Governance Implications for Management and Leadership. *International Journal of Public Administration, 25*(4), 539–559. doi:10.1081/PAD-120013255

Mitchell, G. (2014). Why Will We Ever Learn - Measurement and Evaluation in International Development NGO's. *Public Performance & Management Review, 37*(4), 605–631. doi:10.2753/PMR1530-9576370404

Moore, M., & Ryan, W. (2006). *A Framework for analyzing Governance and Accountability Policies and Strategies.* The Hauser Center for Nonprofit Organizations - Harvard University, Working Paper nº 33.3.

Mueller, J., Williams, D., Higgins, A., & Tou, M. (2005). The Measurement of responsible governance and management of NPOs in New Zealand: An evaluation tool for NPOs, donors and government. "If you have no money – you have no mission. *Corporate Governance: The International Journal of Business in Society, 5*(2), 159–173. doi:10.1108/14720700510562730

Mueller-Hirth, N. (2012). If You Don't Count: Monitoring and Evaluation in South African NGOs. *Development and Change, 43*(3), 649–670. doi:10.1111/j.1467-7660.2012.01776.x

OECD/EU. (2017). *Boosting Social Enterprise Development: Good Practice Compendium.* Paris: OECD Publishing.

Othman, R., & Ali, N. (2012). NPO, Internal Controls, and Supervision Mechanisms in a Developing Country. *Voluntas, 25*(1), 201–224. doi:10.100711266-012-9335-4

Parsons, L. M. (2007). The Impact of Financial Information and Voluntary Disclosures on Contributions to Not-for-Profit Organizations. *Behavioral Research in Accounting, 19*(1), 179–196. doi:10.2308/bria.2007.19.1.179

Peterson, D. (2010). Agency Perspectives on NGO Governance. *Journal of Management Research, 2*(2), 1–11. doi:10.5296/jmr.v2i2.294

Rawhouser, H., Cummings, M., & Newbert, S. L. (2019). Social impact measurement: Current approaches and future directions for social entrepreneurship research. *Entrepreneurship Theory and Practice, 43*(1), 82–115. doi:10.1177/1042258717727718

Reheul, A.-M., Van Caneghem, T., & Verbruggen, S. (2014). Financial Reporting Lags in the Non-Profit Sector: Empirical Analysis. *Voluntas, 25*(2), 352–377. doi:10.100711266-012-9344-3

Smith, S. R. (2010). Hybridization and nonprofit organizations: The governance challenge. *Policy and Society, 29*(3), 219–229. doi:10.1016/j.polsoc.2010.06.003

Suárez, D. F. (2010). Collaboration and Professionalization: The Contours of Public Sector Funding for Nonprofit Organizations. *Journal of Public Administration: Research and Theory, 21*(2), 307–326. doi:10.1093/jpart/muq049

Taysir, E. A., & Taysir, N. K. (2012). Measuring Effectiveness in Nonprofit Organizations: An Integration Effort. *Journal of Transnational Management, 17*(3), 220–235. doi:10.1080/15475778.2012.706736

Thornton, J., & Belski, W. (2010). Financial Reporting quality and price competition among nonprofits firms. *Applied Economics, 42*(21), 2699–2713. doi:10.1080/00036840801964583

Trussel, J. M., & Parsons, L. (2008). Financial Reporting factors affecting donations to Charitable Organizations. *Advances in Accounting*, *23*, 263–285. doi:10.1016/S0882-6110(07)23010-X

Viader, M. I., & Espina, A. M. (2014). Corporate Governance - Are not-for-profits learning form for-profit organizations? A look into governance. *Corporate Governance*, *14*(1), 1–14. doi:10.1108/CG-11-2012-0083

WEB References Cooperativa António Sérgio para a Economia Social. Lei de Bases da Economia Social - (Lei n.º 30/2013 de 8 de maio) - e Estatuto das IPSS - (DL nº 119/83 de 25.02 (alterado pelos DLs n. os 9/85 de 9.01, 89/85 de 1.04, 402/85 de 1.10, e 29/86 de 19.02). (n.d.). Available at: www.cases.pt (consulted in September 12th, 2018)

Weerawardena, J., McDonald, R. E., & Mort, G. S. (2010). Sustainability of nonprofit organizations: An empirical investigation. *Journal of World Business*, *45*(4), 346–356. doi:10.1016/j.jwb.2009.08.004

Wellens, L., & Jegers, M. (2014). Effective Governance in nonprofit organizations: A literature based multiple stakeholder approach. *European Management Journal*, *34*(2), 223–243. doi:10.1016/j.emj.2013.01.007

Young, D. (2011). The Prospective Role of Economic Stakeholders in the Governance of Nonprofit Organizations. *Voluntas*, *22*(4), 566–586. doi:10.100711266-011-9217-1

ENDNOTES

1. The authors would like to thanks to collaboration of three experts in the field of Social Economy: Karen Frisch, independent consultant; Helena André, manager of Associação Entreajuda, and; Pedro da Silva Carvalho, former CEO of FSI – Finance for Social Impact and consultant. José Dias Lopes and Pedro Verga Matos also acknowledge the financial support received via ADVANCE-CSG, from the Fundação para a Ciência and Tecnologia (FCT Portugal) through the Multi-Year Funding Programme for R&D Units (UID/SOC/04521/2019).
2. https://www.cases.pt/contasatelitedaes/
3. In line with what was perceivable by the answers of question 11.
4. Some social entities indicated more than one possibility, with two of them mentioning *ad-hoc* meetings, as well as regular follow-up by their funders.
5. Despite indications suggesting otherwise, there were multiple answers from the same social entities.
6. In this question, more than one option was also chosen.
7. The terminology "Social Impact Evaluation" is commonly used throughout this study, and therefore a more detailed definition is required. "Social Impact Evaluation" is understood to be an evaluation of the impact that a certain social action (usually of a project) has on its beneficiaries, especially what improvements are made in their lives. As an example, in the case of a project which contributes to reducing the school failure rate in a disadvantaged community, potential future improvements could be better life conditions, a greater probability of completing full basic and secondary education, greater probability of being admited to a university, better wages, less (or none) problems with the law, amongst others. As an exemple, see "The HighScope Perry Preschool Program", https://

highscope.org/perrypreschoolstudy. See also Ebrahim & Rangan (2014), Epstein & Yuthas (2017), Lazzarini (2018) and Rawhouser, Cummings & Newbert (2019).

8 See Lei de Bases da Economia Social (Lei n.º 30/2013 de 8 de maio) and Estatuto das IPSS (DL nº 119/83 de 25.02 (alterado pelos DLs n. os 9/85 de 9.01, 89/85 de 1.04, 402/85 de 1.10, e 29/86 de 19.02).

APPENDIX

Table 4.

Question	Questionnaire for Social Entities	Questionnaire for Funders
Question 1	---	---
Question 2	---	---
Question 3	---	---
Question 4	Bradshaw et al. (2007); Espina (2014)	Bradshaw et al. (2007); Espina (2014)
Question 5	Candler & Dumont (2010); Carman (2008)	Espina (2014); Reheul et al. (2014); Peterson (2010); Bradshaw et al. (2007)
Question 6	Mueller et al. (2005); Ebrahim (2003)	Thornton & Belski (2010); Espina (2014)
Question 7	Mueller et al. (2005); Candler & Dumont (2010)	Reheul et al.; (2014), Ebrahim (2003); Mitchell (2014)
Question 8	Candler & Dumont (2010); Thornton & Belski (2010)	Parsons (2007), Reheul et al. (2014)
Question 9	Brown & Troutt (2007)	Brown & Troutt (2007); Carman (2008)
Question 10	Carman (2008); Thornton & Belski (2010)	Suárez (2010)
Question 11	Suárez. (2010); Lehn (2010a)	Wellens & Jegers (2014); Moore & Ryan (2006)
Question 12	Wellens & Jegers (2014); Moore & Ryan (2006)	FSI Report: Social Investment Strategic Options for Portugal - a focus on social enterprises
Question 13	Mueller et al. (2005); Carman (2008)	Mueller et al. (2005); Carman (2008)
Question 14	Geer et al. (2008); Lehn (2008); Suárez (2010); Weerawardena et al (2010)	Mueller et al. (2005); Espina (2014)
Question 15	Mueller et al. (2005); Espina (2014)	--

Chapter 6
The Influencers of Social Accounting and Reporting: Some Evidence

Ninel Ivanova Nesheva-Kiosseva
https://orcid.org/0000-0001-7163-0200
New Bulgarian University, Bulgaria

ABSTRACT

This chapter is an attempt at presenting some reliable factors that have a significant impact on the creation, development, and practice of social accounting and reporting. A part of the research is devoted to presenting the problem of the emergence of the views of social accounting and reporting and their development over time. Attention has been provided to the most influential generators of social accounting and reporting that shape the state of the art to the fullest extent. The text seeks to highlight the driving forces that impact the development of social accounting and reporting. The essay cannot be exhaustive enough as the vast variety of social reports that exist cannot be covered in detail. The study, without seeking full comprehensiveness, tries to systematize some key drivers of social accounting and accountability. It seeks to provide a practical and simple coordinate system in which those who wish to conduct social accounting and reporting should be guided by the diverse sources of social accountability models.

INTRODUCTION

Social accounting and reporting of the organizations has many names, forms and definitions - environmental accounting and reporting, as the environmental problems are in fact social problems; Environmental and Social accounting and reporting – accounts and reports for environmental and social performance of the organizations; Social reporting – the content of which is the same as the previous one, Report for corporate social responsibility, Ethical reports. They are often referred to with the generic name Non-financial Accounting and Reporting. These non-financial reports are usually placed under the term "accountability", a term used for the first time in the English language in 1750 in the sense it gives to social reporting in all its forms today. (Merriam-Webster's Collegiate Dictionary, 2019). Another defi-

DOI: 10.4018/978-1-5225-8482-7.ch006

nition of the term contains not only the meaning of "*responsibility to account*", but also "*to accept the consequences of one's actions*": "*The obligation of an organization or individual to account for activities and accept blame for the exploration of failures.*" (Spacey, 2016).

We can say that "*Accountability*" in the sense that accounting science gives it means "to have the dignity to account for and be accountable for your actions to society". The commitment to account for your own actions in front of society and bear responsibility for the consequences that your business has on stakeholders is the basis of social accounting and reporting in all its forms and diversity today.

Part of the Sustainability Reports, Strategic Reports and Integrated Reports also contain social accountability with a different focus on the needs they serve.

The effect behind this palette of social accounting and reporting is for organizations and profit-making companies to open towards society and create transparency and systematically account for the overall state of the company in front of their employees, not only for the financial indicators but for the non-financial indicators also - social, ethical, environmental. Such accounting aids the better management of companies, the more transparent relationships with state and local authorities, giving a more complete picture of their quantitative and qualitative performance metrics.

By conducting non-financial accounting and reporting, the company ceases to be a "closed black box", a world enclosed within itself. It shows its inner state and the impact it has on its affiliates and communities within and those outside.

BACKGROUND

It is assumed that social accounting and reporting should reflect the characteristics of different economies and organizations. They are not obligatory in the biggest part of countries. For these main reasons, social accounting and reporting have evolved and continue to develop on a national and corporate level with many features and variants. These leads to great difficulties in the systematization of scientific literature and professional practice on this subject. In this chapter we strive to outline big picture in which many important details can not find a place, trying to find the pillars of influential subjects in social accounting and accountability. The chapter includes a variety of sources dating from the 15th to the 21st century; from manuals and standards for social accounting and reporting, stock indices and daily practice to high scientific theory.

MAIN FOCUS OF THE CHAPTER

The study explores the most striking features of the author's concepts, circumstances and organizations that have shaped the contemporary diversity of social accounting. The main focus is on the underlying idea of social accounting and accountability and the major Influencers in its development - scientists and universities, professional accountancy companies, rating agencies, public service research centers, governmental, non-governmental and international organizations.

The Idea and Its Revival

There are some controversies about the emergence of Social Accounting and Reporting: when it started, who first proposed the term, whether it was due to economic or social reasons, how it originated in the separate countries.

Social accounting only looks like a new idea that has already made its way and reached a clear and orderly construction in many countries, but in others it is still experiencing difficulties in this respect. If the English term "accountability" was used in its current sense in England in 1750, then the concept of social accounting was present earlier in the past, according to us.

The idea that accounting is inherently social is contained in the philosophy of Luca Pacioli, father of contemporary dual accountancy, in his work "Particularis de computis et scripturis", 1494. In our opinion, it can be said that social accounting emerged with Luca Pacioli and that accounting is inherently social.

Pacioli writes thus: "*The goal of every merchant is to obtain a legitimate and relevant profit as a source of his existence.*" (Bauer, 1913, p. 3). *Therefore, merchants must proceed to their works in the name of God and at the beginning of each enrollment have their holy name in their minds.* (Pacioli/ Пачоли & Sokolov/ Соколов (Ed), 2001, p. 25).

Pacioli does not talk about maximization of the profit, but that the merchant receives only "*legitimate and relevant profit*", i.e. the amount of profit must not be the maximum, but on the contrary, it must meet the legal constraints accepted by society and the generally accepted supreme moral norms given by God, as well as to satisfy the merchant's vital needs - to correspond to what is needed for his livelihood but no more. Commercial activity, according to Pacioli, is generally responsible to society and God. Compliance with the social order and norms is a dominant thesis of Pacioli.

The purpose of the statement of accounts drawn up by the merchant in its dual form for L. Pacioli is above all informative - "*to conduct business transactions in the required order so as to obtain without delay any information about both debts and claims.*" (Pacioli/Пачоли & Sokolov/ Соколов (Ed), 2001, p. 24).

From this brief analysis of Pacioli's short texts, Pacioli's concept of accounting is that of contemporary social accounting - ethics, responsibility to society and supreme law, as well as informative. Such is the purpose and responsibility of companies presenting social reports today. It can be said that social accounting and accountability are embedded in the construction of modern accounting and accountability.

In the times after Pacioli, however, the idea that accounting along with its function of informative tendency of commercial affairs is also an activity of its own social nature in itself. It fades for a long time to be revived and developed in the times we are witnessing now.

By reading corporate social reports, we see that they are not constructed in the same way as the financial reports. They have a common sense basis, but the different companies construct them differently. These differences are due to several major reasons - the peculiarities of the economies of the countries in which companies operate, the severity and specificity of social factors in each country; the different focus that companies have on disclosing their social performance. However, they have a common base. The common base is what Pacioli had - ethical and informative.

Nowadays, according to the site Reporting Exchange, social reports have increased for a quarter of a century; provisions for non-financial reports around the world have risen from around 100 to about 1000 (https://www.reportingexchange.com/).

The development of contemporary social accounting and accountability has been described in a number of papers. According to Parker (2005) the bibliography on the social and environmental accounting is "voluminous". After "Accountability, Social Responsibility and Sustainability Accounting for Society and the Environment" by Rob Grey, Carol A. Adams and Dave Owen it is quite unlikely for anything to be added. The book of Gray, Adams and Owen not only systematically studies this story but also fills it with the content of the development of new types of accounts. For the purposes of this essay, we need to review this story briefly in order to track the emergence and spread of core social accounting and accountability centers that have exerted and influenced its current state.

Due to the fact that social accountability arises differently in different countries, and the fact that suprastate bodies, different states and different scientists have one topic but different angles from which they view it, social accountancy has been given a number of definitions.

"It is possible to view 'social accounting' as the universe of all possible accountings..." (Gray at al, 2014, p. 66).

We believe that the definition given by Rob Gray is the one that most accurately reflects the essence of social accounting: "*The process of communicating the social and environmental effects of organizations' economic actions to particular interest groups within society and to society at large. As such it involves extending the accountability to organizations (particularly companies), beyond the traditional role of providing a financial account to the owners of capital, in particular, shareholders. Such an extension is predicated upon the assumption that companies do have wider responsibilities than simply to make money for shareholders*". (Gray et al., 1996, p. 3).

The Principles of Social Accounting are known accounting principles: the Time principle, the Accrual principle, the Consistency principle, Economic entity principle, Revenue recognition, Reliability, Monetization, Cost principle, Materiality, Matching principle.

It is assumed that in the 1940s for the first time in the USA Theodore J. Kreps used the term "*social audit*" on the annual reports of the companies, which should also take into account their social commitments (Zadek, Pruzan, & Evans, 1997, pp. 16–17).

In the 50s of the 20th century, the so-called "social audit movement" appeared in the United Kingdom. The term "social audit" is attributed to George Goyder. (Pearce, 2005, 2012). George Goyder's book, "The Responsible Company", developed the thesis that the large companies, due to their importance in society, need a social audit more than they need a financial audit. (Goyder, 1961, p. 109)

The social audit movement in the UK goes beyond theory with the emergence of companies that start publishing social reports. "Social Audit Ltd" published reports in the early 70s of the 20th century about the impact of different companies on the communities and the impact of their business on the environment. (Pearce & Alan Kay updated (2012), 2005).

Most probably, in the USA the idea of social reporting proved to be serious and authoritative in the 60s of the 20th century not only among scholars of social science but also among economists. It is during this period that a large amount of innovative research comes out of print.

The initial urge was to look for indicators to measure socio-economic development by scientists such as Gary Becker, Raymond Bauer, Mancur Olson Jr., Eleanor Bernet Sheldon, Wilbert E. Moore, Bertram M. Gross and Jeffrey D. Straussman. *"The explicit normative use of aggregate statistics as social indicators began in response to the shortcomings of GDP as a welfare measure. Some representative references are U.S. Department of Health, Education, and Welfare D.C*; (Juster et al., 1969, pp. 6-7).

Gary Becker, later a Nobel memorial prize winner for Economics in 1992, published in 1964 "Human Capital: a theoretical and empirical analysis with a special reference to education", followed by other publications that expand the circle of researched economic science issues and provides new impetus to the tasks of economic science like A theory of the allocation of time" in The Economic Journal.

The second half of the 1960s and the early 1970s became a turning point for the imposition of the social theme in economic theory.

Are published "The Idea of Social Report" (1966) by Danel Bell under edition of Eleanor Bernet Sheldon and Wilbert E. Moore (1968), "Indicators of Social Change" by Mancur's, Jr., "Social Indicators and Social Accounts" (Olson, 1969b) and "The Plan and Purposes of Social Report" (Olson, 1969a); "The State Of The Nation: Social Systems Accounting" B Gross, (1972) in "Social Indicators" under edition of Raymond Bauer are published;

Leslie D. Wilcox, George Brooks, Beal and Gerald Klongan "Social Indicators and Societal Monitoring: An Annotated Bibliography (Palley, 1977); Bertram M. Gross and Jeffrey D. Straussman (1974), "The Social Indicators Movement, and many othrs.

In 1979, F. Thomas Juster, Paul N. Courant and Greg K. Dow published "Social Accounting and Social Indicators: A Framework for the Analysis of Well-Being". (Juster at al, 1979).

In 1981, a generalized work was published, edited by F. Thomas Juster and Kenneth C. Land, "Social Accounting Systems Essays on the State of the Art". (Juster & Land, 1981). It is the first attempt for clarifying the purposes of social accounting, its methods, focus and scale, on the basis of what has been achieved, and the discussions to date. Research is still underway in the field of economics, statistics, and sociology. But there is and discussion on the possibilities that some methods and concepts of Accounting science to be used for the creation of a new economic concept of well-being and its measurement.

The work is devoted to the problems of demography, national income, national accounting and macro-social indicators. Consideration is given to the fact that the accounting rules of the numerical presentation of events and double enrollment can be applied in demographic research.

Another important aspect of the study is "resource accounting" and its ability to provide analysis of the welfare of the people. (Juster & Land, 1981, p. 7).

Overall, the conclusion is that social accounting systems *"attempt to account for all uses of resources in society, including nonmarket time and (in Juster-Courant-Dow system) a greatly expanded concept of wealth, to trace the uses of these individual and societal resources in the production of intangible and tangible products, and ultimately to relate these outputs to the generation of well-being. The objective is a comprehensive resources and outcomes accounting system. ... By contrast, in the DA (demographic account) systems, data on market and nonmarket behavior are not put into a single accounting system."* (Juster & Land, 1981, p. 20).

The question of the importance of Intangible assets and the quality of the environment in the formation of human welfare, investment in other types of capital such as human, socio-political or environmental capital assets is being investigated. (Juster & Land, 1981, p. 44).

However, Nestor E. Terleckyj in his essay "A Social Production Framework for Resource Accounting" included in the book presents an attempt at using Cost accounting in the household welfare study. (Terleckyj, 1981, p. 110). He also proposes pollution control and more basic environmental improvements as "Goal Output Indicators." (Terleckyj, 1981, p. 110) to be included in the accounting system of "Resource accounting".

All these efforts are being made, with the ambition to create a more adequate welfare theory that integrates household production data, health costs, education and better lives into national statistics and to describe more fully, numerically the well-being of people by using certain "social indicators".

The role of accounting is still severely limited and subject to economic theory and the needs of statistics. For environmental accounting, such as" accounting " has not been said.

Movement has also been made in the field of theory of capital. In the book "Social Accounting And Social Indicators: A Framework for Analysis of Well-Being ", Thomas Juster, Paul N. Courant and Greg K. Dow systematized for the first time the concept of "six stocks" that create value for companies. Not only financial capital and not just financial capital is the driving force of business. These are already:

"1. *TK: Conventional stocks of tangible assets, such as machinery and houses. (Or tangible capital- Remark my);*
2. *KK (knowledge capital or intellectual capital- Remarks my): Stocks of abstract knowledge accumulated over time in society, not embodied in specific individuals or in specific tangible assets;*
3. *HK (human capital- Remark my): Human capital associated with specific individuals, such as health and skills;*
4. *OK (organizational capital- Remark my): Organizational stocks reflecting all networks of relationships among the particular people populating society. Types of networks include families, associations of friends and neighbors, public associations such as towns and state and federal governments, and voluntary organizations of various types;*
5. *SK (Social Capital- Remark my): Social-political capital stocks reflecting the institutional arrangements for the performance of collective or societal activities. These are distinct from OK in that they are institutional structures which tend to persist apart from the particular individuals playing roles within them. Examples include the legal system and the organization of production by firms or government;*
6. *EK (Environmental capital- Remark my): Environmental stocks reflecting the physical and biological surroundings of human society. These include the weather and the availability of natural resources." (Juster at al, 1981, p. 14).*

These stocks, called "capitals", will be presented in their original form given to Thomas Juster, Paul N. Courant and Greg K. Dow in the most recent, now generalized version of a financial-social report called Integrated Report, developed by the International Integrated Reporting Council (IIRC). (International Integrated Reporting Framework, 2013).

In the UK one of the first "environmental accounting" PhD studies was announced at the University of Saint Andrews in Scotland. The young accountant at KPMG, Robert Gray, is very intrigued by it and enters in the competition. Winning it, he is working on this new area of accounting science and creates the first self-sustaining ecological accounting and accounting system that continues to develop by bringing together environmental accounts with social accounts and accounts of economic and financial status, and the creation of social (environmental) accounting and sustainable development accounting. Prof. Rob Gray is also the founder of the CSEAR (Center for Social and Environmental Accounting Research) at the University of Saint Andrews, the world's largest social and environmental research center, around which national annual conferences with international participation take place to present progress in research in the individual countries.

The social theme is also becoming a focus for world organizations. This is the time when social accounting becomes a recognized field for scientific research and practical application. In Stockholm from 5 to 16 June 1972, was presented and adopted at a conference of the United Nations the "Declaration of the Human Environment. (United Nations, 1972).

The social theme also goes into corporations. In 1977, Leon Sullivan, as a member of the Board of directors of General Motors, formulated the "10 Global Sullivan Principles" that the organization must voluntarily accept and apply. They represent the basic principles of corporate social responsibility today: equality of workers on ethnic and racial grounds, equal rights for their development and the same working environment, equal pay for equal work, work to remove obstacles to equal treatment of people at work, equal conditions for learning, healthcare, transport, right of rest, developing training programs for workers. (Global Principles (GSP). (2006). For the first time, an influential transnational corporation accepts the voluntary application of human and ethical principles in its activity as a code of conduct.

Since then, Social Accountability has spread rapidly in market-economy countries.

The social theme, which is traditional to the public ideology of France, does not lag behind these processes. In the 1970s and in France, thanks to the Ministry of Work, Employment, Professional Training and Social Dialogue, is adopted "Bilan Social", which is a mandatory act. It requires companies with about 300 employees to prepare reports on the working conditions of their staff. (Ministry of Work, Employment, Professional training and Social dialogue, France, 2018)

The nation that gave Luca Pacioli and modern accounting to the world makes great strides in the direction of social accountability. In the 1980s, Italy's scientific concepts of social accounting and accountability appeared in the research by Antonio Matacena. (Baldarelli et al., 2017, p. 170)

Antonio Matacena sets up the foundations of the Italian School of Social Accountancy and Accountability, which is being developed today under its authoritative leadership in "Gruppo Bilancio Sociale" (GBS) - the Social Reporting Group) by numbering dozens of scientists. Antonio Matacena's research, published in the early 1980s and early 1990s, presented a complete concept of social accounting and social reporting, the accountability of the socially responsible enterprise and their practical application in non-profit and for-profit organizations. These are the studies of Prof. Matacena, published mainly in Italian: "Impresa e ambiente. Il "bilancio sociale", (1984); "Toward a "societal" information system" (Matacena, 1987); "Responsabilità sociale, cooperativa e sistema informative", (Matacena, 1991); "La cooperazione sociale ed i loro consorzi tra imprenditorialità e solidarietà sociale" (1992); "L'impresa cooperativa come 'ideal-tipo' di impresa socialmente responsabile" (1995) and others.

Also in the 1980s in Germany, dominated by the concept of the "state of social market economy" from the German Ordo-Liberalism, companies are to draw up the Social Report (*Sozialbericht*) a public voluntary report on the working conditions of employees.

The drive to highlight social accountability can be sought in different directions: the shift in the economies of the most developed countries, characterized by an active shift of workforce from the secondary, industrial, to tertiary services sector, in the "desperate" economic history high growth rates of the Soviet economy and the relative lagging behind in growth rates of the leading market economies.

The "Imperialism" of Social Accounting and Reporting

Owing to the talent of scientists, starting with Pacioli, scholars in universities have been the most influential factors that shape the concept, the theoretical and practical development of Social accountability.

They are the pioneers and generators of both the idea and its constructive shaping. Social accounting is a serious research topic for scientists worldwide.

There are a number of criticisms of the social and environmental accounting included in it. They are, for example, well summarized and meaningful by Crawford Spence, Javier Husillos and Carmen Correa-Ruiz (Spence, Husillos, & Correa-Ruiz, 2010). The main criticism is that social accounting is not based on a lean and homogeneous socio-economic theory. Critical remarks, however, do not diminish interest in it but contribute to its further development and adaptation to the practical needs of companies, countries and individuals.

Bolivia's unique "Global Green Accounting", which represents the first and only one to this moment annotated bibliography of national environmental accounting, has presented scientific research by almost all countries around the world, with the exception of several Asian, Central African and South American countries, including Wealth Accounting and Ecosystem Services (WAVES) (Fenton, Andersen, & Tracey, 2015, p. 20)

In a market economy of the liberal economic model the state (government) is not directly involved in the activities of the companies when it comes to their budget needs. In the East, however, the state has traditionally played a significant economic role.

In Russia, environmental accounting records are integrated to the financial ones in the statutory accounts required by the government from the companies. Initially, the government promoted social accountability. The Russian government organizes a national competition "Russian organizations with high social efficiency" for the first time in 2000, which since then has appeared on an annual basis. (Turkin /Туркин, n.d.)

But social accountability, which refers to labor indicators, arises at the initiative of some Russian corporations. The "Social Charter of Russian business" was developed by the Russian Union of Industrialists and Entrepreneurs. The Union is also developing an "Anti-Corruption Charter of the Russian Business", which extends its social commitments and responsibilities. (Russian Union of Industrials and Entrepreneurs/Российский союз промышленников и предпринимателей, n.d.)

In Japan, despite the fact that the large influential corporations are private, the Ministry of Industry, Economy and Commerce (METI) is involved in drafting guidelines for environmental reporting for corporations. It is not precisely known when compilation of environmental accounting and reporting in Japan started. The first Environmental Reporting Guidelines came into force in 2001. Currently, those from 2007 are in force. (Baldarelli et al., 2017, p. 393).

China's industrialization has been criticized by the world community for pollution and the Giant panda threatened with extinction, is a symbol of the struggle of environmentalists for the Chinese government to take action to protect the environment. The Chinese authorities seriously reacted to this ecological and essentially social problem by taking scientific and administrative measures. In this way China introduced Chinese Green Development Indices for the first time in 2010: the Province Green Development Index (PGDI) and the City Green Development Index (CGDI). China's GDIs are made by a huge team of university scholars but also with the great support and involvement of government departments such as the Policy Research Center for Environment and Economy, the China Economic Monitoring and Analysis Center and Relevant Research Institutes, the National Bureau of Statistics of China, China Economic Monitoring and Analysis Center. (Li & Pan, 2014, pp. iv-v)

Governments of countries with a European-style liberal economy prefer to work in the sphere of introducing social accounting and reporting with the help of independent research institutes.

In 1999, the British Standards Institution, together with Accountability and Forum for the Future, established the SIGMA Project (Sustainability Integrated Guidelines for Management, Sigma Guidelines). SIGMA creates a holistic approach to the management of 5 capitals: "*Natural capital - the environment; Social capital and social structures; Human capital - people; Manufactured capital - fixed assets;* (Sigma Project, 2003, p.3-4).

In the UK, the UK Government Working Group has been set up and is actively working.

The Australian Government is also committed to the introduction of standard in the field of mainly environmental accounting and reporting. (Water Accounting Standards Board, 2012).

The Italian Ministry of Labor and Social Policy has prepared special guidelines for the Social Report of Social Enterprises. (Ministry of Labor and Social Policy, Italy, 2008)

The non-governmental research organizations have a huge merit in the development of standards - voluntary and binding, with certification and not requiring certification like International Organization for Standardization (ISO), Institute of Social and Ethical (AccountAbility), Sustainability Accounting Standard Board (SASB), Global Reporting Initiative (GRI), Social Audit Network (SAN), Climate Disclosure Standard Board, International Integrated Reporting Council (IIRC), Gruppo di Studio de il Bilancio Sociale (Study Group for Social Reporting) (GBS) et cetera.

The Institute of Social and Ethical AccountAbility has developed 3 standards for social reporting and a Principles for Accountability:

1. The AccountAbility 1000 (AA1000) - AA1000 Series of Standards, based on the principle of accountability of triple bottom line, launched for the first time in 1999;
2. AA1000 Assurance Standard (AA1000AS, 2008) with 2018 Addendum AA 1000 AS. It sets out tests to conduct Sustainable Data. (Available at https://www.accountability.org/standards/);
3. AA 1000 Stakeholder Engagement Standard (SES) (https://www.accountability.org/wp-content/uploads/2016/10/AA1000SES_2015.pdf);
4. AA1000 Accountability Principles (AP), (2018) - which defines the general principles of social accountability. This is a *"principles-based framework and guidance that organizations can use to identify, prioritize and respond to sustainability challenges to improve long-term performance.*" (AccountAbility, 2018).

Sustainability accountability standards such as standards developed by the SASB also contains social reporting indicators for working conditions and ethics. (SASB, n.d.)

The International Social Accountability Standard 8000 (SA 8000) is a benchmark for social governance assessment that includes criteria for management's behavior regarding respect for human rights, working conditions, workers' rights, child labor regulation, etc. (Sustainability Accounting Standard Board (SASB), 1997)

Global Reporting Initiative (GRI) is an independent organization for the development of Sustainability Reporting Guidelines since 1997. Its standards for accounting and reporting of sustainability of the company including environmental and social accounting and accountability are one of the most influential and widely used in the world. (Global Reporting Initiative, 1997).

United Nations Global Compact) invites companies to base their work on the generally accepted principles of labor conditions, human rights, clean environment, the fight against corruption and work for sustainable development. (United Nations Global Compact, 2012). This program offers Integration of Sustainable Development Goals into Corporate Reporting. (United Nations Global Compact, 2012)

Verité Fair Labor Assessment Guidance for elimination of the bad labor practices and abuse of human rights at global level. (Verité, n.d.)

One of the most authoritative and recognized standards of social responsibility and accountability is the ISO 26000 International Organization for Standardization. ISO 26000 proclaimed "Seven core subjects and their related issues" and "Stakeholder engagement". (Nesheva-Kiosseva, 2018, p. 177).

Companies that voluntarily adhere to it are compiling reports on their social performance.

ISO 26000, Guidance on Social Responsibility, has been set up by the Social Responsibility Working Group at the Technical Council of ISO. Its text has been approved by many countries and 42 public and private sector organizations and was published in 2010. (International Organization for Standardization, 2014, p. 304). Standard IC CSR-08260008000 "Social Responsibility Requirements" was adopted the following year, complementing it. ISO 26000 covers all corporate social responsibility fields. It is built around "Seven Principles":

1. Accountability;
2. Transparency and disclosure;
3. Ethical behaviour;
4. Respect for the stakeholders' interests- Stakeholder engagement;
5. Respect for rule of law;
6. Respect for international norms of behaviour;
7. Respect for Human rights. (International Organization for Standardization, 2010, pp. 10–14).

Social accounting and reporting, which shows the social performance of companies, has become an influential factor in assessing the value of companies.

In the early 1970s, companies' ratings for their social and environmental performance began to rise, such as those in the United States of the "Council of Economic Priorities (CEP)"-a public service research organization. Other agencies and organizations are also starting to develop companies' rating methodologies for these social, ethical and environmental indicators that are based on organizations' reporting.

Companies like "Linowes", "Clark C. Abt"; "Eastern Gas" at 1972 and "Atlantic Richfield" (1974-1977) created and published social reports.

SBN Bank from Denmark issued the Ethical Accounting Statement in 1990.

The Shell (British-Dutch) outlines its core values and goals for sustainable development, including financial, environmental and social goals. (Gray et al., 1996, p. 102)

Ethical investments have come to the attention of society, the scientific community and the administration lastingly in the 80s of the 20th century.

Since the early 1990s, a number of stock indices have emerged to determine the degree of corporate social responsibility of companies, which includes the social performance of companies. Thus, social accounting and reporting has become an important component in the assessment of companies in financial markets. (Bravo et al., 2016, pp. 77-78; Bravo at al, 2015, pp. 75-108).

In our time there are a lot of guidelines, methodologies, manuals of social reporting and the assessment of the social performance of a number of exchanges.

Kazakhstan Stock Exchange has Methodology of preparing an Environmental, Social and Governance report; Taiwan Stock Exchange has Corporation Rules Governing the Preparation and Filing of Corporate Social Responsibility Reports by TWSE Listed Companies; Taipei Exchange - Rules Governing the Preparation and Filing of Corporate Social Responsibility Reports by TPEx Listed Companies;

Shanghai Stock Exchange - Notice of Improving Listed Companies' Assumption of Social Responsibilities; Santiago Exchange - Guidance for Environmental, Social and Corporate Governance Factors; Singapore Exchange- Guide to Sustainability Reporting Singapore Exchange, Appendix 27 and 20 for Environmental; Social and Governance Reporting Guide for Hong Kong Exchanges; Guidance for Annual Business Responsibility Reporting (ABRR) Securities and Exchange Board of India (SEBI). (World Business Council for Sustainable Development (WBCSD), n.d.)

The most influential among these indices, based on social accountability and special requirements for the social performance of companies, are FTSE4Good and Dow Jones Sustainability.

Dow Jones Sustainability indices (DJSI) are created in 1999 for measurement of public companies on the base of their financial, but also social and environmental performance. (Robeco SAM, 2018). FTSE4Good is established at 2001 to meet the demand for ethical investment. (Oulton, 2017). FTSE-4Good Index Series is a series of benchmark and tradable indexes for measurement of the quality of environmental, social and governance performance of the companies. (Russel Investment Group, n.d.). In 2007, Martin Curran and Moran found that the positive impact of the index on stock prices on market performance of the companies due to raising their reputation. (Martin Curran & Moran, 2007).

These indices primarily include large companies that due to their size and transnational operations have a serious impact on society. (Robeco SAM, 2018)

They use their own methodology but include economic, environmental and social dimensions. (RobecoSAM, n.d.)

With this, they have become one of the most influential users of social reports and have an impact on the development and improvement of social accounting and accountability.

Another important center of influence on the creation, application, dissemination and development of social accounting and reporting are the so-called "Big Four" because they encompass a large number of organizations around the world in the system of their accounting services and have an intellectual resource for theoretical and practical work in this field.

Large accounting and auditing firms like Deloitte, KPMG, Ernst & Young (EY), PriceWaterhouse Coopers (PwC) provide worldwide services for accounting and reporting corporate CSR and sustainability reports what included social accounts. For this reason, they largely determine the world practice in social accounting and accountability.

The CSR report is a variation of the Social Report. The definition of the CSR report also has many other interpretations, but for example, the one that deserves attention accurately and clearly defines the subjects of social accountability in terms of the needs of the accounting profession: "A *company's positive impact on, and amelioration of negative impacts against, society and the environment, through its operations, products or services and through its interaction with key stakeholders such as employees, customers, investors, communities and suppliers."* (Duff & Guo, 2010).

Deloitte gives serious evidence that they consider social accountability for accountability of particular importance to companies and emerging as the leader in social accounting and accountability among the four major. Deloitte published own, using GRI and AA1000 for its own social reporting. (Deloitte, 2010, p.7).

Deloitte's Corporate Responsibility and Sustainability services include non-financial reports and integrated reporting, accounting and reporting of social-environmental and economic impacts of companies, responsible sales, and ethical management. (Deloitte, https://www2.deloitte.com/ru/en/pages/risk/solutions/sustainability-and-csr.html Deloitte has also developed the Social Progress Index and has created a definition of social progress. "*Social progress is the capacity of a society to meet the basic hu-*

man needs of its citizens, establish the building blocks that allow citizens and communities to enhance and sustain the quality of their lives, and create the conditions for all individuals to reach their full potential." (Deloitte, 2015, p. 4)

In it the main groups of components are:

1. Basic Human Needs - Foundations of Wellbeing and Opportunity;
2. Health and Wellness and Ecosystem Sustainability. (Deloitte, 2015, p. 6).

According Angus Duff and Xin Guo, Big Four is concentrating its efforts on the following four areas: " *Community (how the firm's activities affect those communities in which it operates); Environmental actions (how the firm's operations affect the environment); Ethics and risk management (how the firm's operations affect its future wellbeing and standing in the marketplace); Human resource management (how the firm's policies affect its employees and partners in the workplace)*" (Duff & Guo, 2010, p. 6).

CONCLUSION

Social accounting and reporting has a difficult but fortunate fate. The benefit of fully taking into account the activities of organizations, including their social performance, though nonlinear and slow, has been assessed. Social accounting and accountability in all its diversity is one of the tools of a full valuation of companies, an important source of information for both corporate and individual investors and for all other stakeholders. They are also one of the risk management tools for companies and investors. The pioneers of social accounting are the scientists and the men of thought who have learned through practice. Every idea needs time to be perceived and applied by society, even if it is an idea that protects the public interest. Today, social accounting and reporting have many and influential centers for their development - in universities, large accounting and auditing companies, in financial markets, among many governmental and non-governmental organizations. Although social accounting has reached a noticeable extent, it faces new challenges. These new challenges are related to the forthcoming Fourth Industrial Revolution of Robotics and Artificial Intelligence. Research is already underway, asking questions about the ethics of the world from the Fourth Industrial Revolution, the rights of artificial intelligence, the ethical relationship between it (or him) and the human beings, and many more. Will Artificial Intelligence be included in social accounting and reporting and how? Will the social accounting influencers be changed and increased? As an interdisciplinary area to which these issues are also raised, social accounting and reporting will experience new changes and receive new chances.

REFERENCES

AccountAbility. (2018). *AccountAbility, Reporting Principles* (Standard). Retrieved from https://www.accountability.org/wp-content/uploads/2018/05/AA1000_ACCOUNTABILITY_PRINCIPLES_2018_Single_Pages.pdf

Accountability. (n.d.). In *Merriam-Webster's Collegiate Dictionary*. Retrieved from https://www.merriam-webster.com/dictionary/accountability

Baldarelli, M. G., Baldo, M. D., & Nesheva-Kiosseva, N. (2017). *Environmental Accounting and Reporting: Theory and Practice*. Cham, Switzerland: Springer International Publishing. doi:10.1007/978-3-319-50918-1

Bauer, A., (1913). Tractate Luca Pacioli. *Journal of Accounting*, 3.

Bauer, R. A. (1966). *Social Indicators*. Cambridge, UK: M.I.T. Press.

Becker, G. (1964). *Human Capital: a theoretical and empirical analysis, with special reference to education*. Chicago, IL: The University of Chicago Press.

Becker, G. (1965). A theory of the Allocation of Time. *Economic Journal (London)*, *75*(299), 493–517. doi:10.2307/2228949

Bell, D. (1969). The Idea of Social Report. *The Public Interest,* (15), 72–84.

Bravo, M., & Al, A. T. (2016). Socially Responsible Investment A Multi-Criteria Decision Making Approach. In E. Ballestero, B. Pérez-Gladish, & A. M. Garcia-Bernabeu (Eds.), *Measurement of Assets' Social Responsibility Degree* (pp. 77–78). Cham, Switzerland: Springer.

Bravo, M., Ruiz, A. B., Pla-Santamaria, D., & Méndez-Rodríguez, P. (2015). Measurement of Assets' Social Responsibility Degree. In E. Ballestero, B. Pérez-Gladish, & A. Garcia-Bernabeu (Eds.), *Socially Responsible Investment. International Series in Operations Research & Management Science* (Vol. 219). Cham: Springer; doi:10.1007/978-3-319-11836-9_4

Deloitte. (2010). *Corporate Social Responsibility Report (Vision, Values, Responsibility).* Retrieved from https://www2.deloitte.com/content/dam/Deloitte/global/Documents/About-Deloitte/gx-deloitte-2010-gir-cr-report.pdf

Deloitte. (2015). *Social Progress Index 2015*. Retrieved from https://www2.deloitte.com/content/dam/Deloitte/global/Documents/About-Deloitte/gx-cr-social-progress-index-executive-summary-2015.pdf

Duff, A., & Guo, X. (2010). *Corporate Social Responsibility and the Professional Accounting Firm: Insights from Firms' Disclosures: Briefing*. The Institute of Chartered Accountants in England and Wales. Retrieved from https://www.icaew.com/-/media/corporate/files/products/sustainability/tecpln9787-crs-briefing-16-dec-final.ashx

Fenton, I., Andersen, L., & Tracey, L. I. (Eds.). (2015). *Global Green Accounting*. Retrieved from https://www.inesad.edu.bo/en/2015/06/14/global-green-accounting-2015/

Global Principles (GSP). (2006). In *Sustainability Dictionary*. Retrieved from: https://sustainabilitydictionary.com/2006/02/17/the-global-sullivan-principles-gsp/

Global Reporting Initiative. (n.d.). *Global Reporting Initiative*. Retrieved February 17, 2019, from https://www.globalreporting.org/Pages/default.aspx

Goyder, G. (1961). *The responsible company*. Oxford, UK: Basil Blackwell.

Gray, R., Adams, C. A., & Owen, D. (2014). *Accountability, Social Responsibility and Sustainability: Accounting for Society and the Environment*. London, UK: Pearson Education Limited.

Gray, R., Owen, D., & Adams, C. (1996). *Accounting & Accountability: Changes and Challenges in Corporate Social and Environmental Reporting*. London, UK: Prentice Hall.

Gross, B. (1972). The State Of The Nation: Social Systems Accounting. In R. A. Bauer (Ed.), *Social Indicators* (pp. 154–271). London, UK: M.I.T. Press.

Gross, B., & Straussman, J. (1974, September). The Social Indicators Movement. *Social Policy*.

International Integrated Reporting Council (IIRC). (n.d.). *Integrated Reporting*. Retrieved February 17, 2019, from http://integratedreporting.org/

International Organization for Standardization. (2010). *International Standard ISO 26000*. Geneva, Switzerland: ISO.

International Organization for Standardization. (2014). *Economic Benefits of Standards*. Geneva, Switzerland: ISO.

Juster, T. H. F., Courant, P., & Dow, G. (n.d.). *Toward a Social Report*. Washington, DC: Government Printing Office.

Juster, T. H. F., Courant, P., & Daw, G. (1979). *Social Accounting and Social Indicators: A Framework for the Analysis of Well-Being*. The University of Michigan.

Juster, T. H. H., & Land, K. (Eds.). (1981). *Social Accounting Systems Essays on the State of the Art*. New York: Academic Press, Inc.

Li, X., & Pan, J. (2014). *China Green Development Index Report Regional Comparison*. Berlin, Germany: Springer.

Martin Curran, M., & Moran, D. (2007). Impact of the FTSE4Good Index on firm price: An event study. *Journal of Environmental Management*, *82*(4), 529–537. doi:10.1016/j.jenvman.2006.02.010 PMID:16678334

Matacena, A. (1984). *Impresa e ambiente. Il "bilancio sociale"*. Bologna, Italy: CLUEB.

Matacena, A. (1987). *Toward a "societal" information system. Economia Aziendale, Rivista dell'Accademia Italiana Di Economia Aziendale*. Milano: Giuffrè.

Matacena, A. (1991). Responsabilità sociale, cooperativa e sistema informative. *Relazione al Workshop Responsabilità sociale. Bilancio sociale e Cooperativa, 18*.

Matacena, A. (1992). Impresa e ambiente. Il "bilancio sociale". In La cooperazione sociale ed i loro consorzi tra imprenditorialità e solidarietà sociale. Roma, Italy: Istituto Italiano di Studi Cooperativi "L. Luzzati".

Matacena, A. (1995). *L'impresa cooperativa come «ideal-tipo» di impresa socialmente responsabile. Giornata di studi economici sulla cooperazione*. Bologna: Printer Editrice.

Ministry of Labor and Social Policy Italy. (2008). *Social Reporting (Guidelines for the Social Report of Social Enterprises)*. Retrieved from https://www.reportingexchange.com/reportingProvision/1825?entityVersionID=2665

Ministry of Work, Employment, Professional Training and Social Dialogue, France. (2018). *Social Reporting* (Article R 2323.17 Labor Code). Retrieved from https://www.reportingexchange.com/search?search=social%20report&filters=%5B%7B%22filterName%22:%22entity_type%22,%22filterItem%22:3%7D%5D

Nesheva-Kiosseva, N. (2018). Aspects of ISO26000 Related to Transaction and Environmental Costs. In S. O. Idowu, C. Sitnikov, & L. Moratis (Eds.), *ISO 26000 - A Standardized View on Corporate Social Responsibility: Practices, Cases and Controversies* (pp. 177–195). Cham, Switzerland: Springer International Publishing.

Olson, M. (1969a). The Plan and Purposes of Social Report. *The Public Interest*, (Spring): 85–97.

Olson, M. (1969b). Social Indicators and Social Accounts. *Socio-Economic Planning Science*, (2), 334–346.

Oulton, W. (2017). The Role of Activism The FTSE4Good Indices, In: Responsible Investment. In R. Sullivan & C. Mackenzie (Eds.), *Responsible Investment* (2nd ed.; pp. 196–205). New York: Greenleaf Publishing. doi:10.4324/9781351283441-17

Pacioli, L., & Sokolov, I. (Ed.). (2001). Particularis de computis et scripturis. Moscow: Finance and Statistics.

Palley, M. (1977). Social Indicators and Societal Monitoring: An Annotated Bibliography. By Leslie D. Wilcox, Ralph M. Brooks, George M. Beal, and Gerald E. Klongan. (San Francisco: Jossey-Bass Inc., 1972. Pp. 464. *The American Political Science Review*, *71*(3), 1162–1162. doi:10.1017/S0003055400265647

Parker, L. (2005). Social and environmental accountability research: A view from the commentary box. *Accounting, Auditing & Accountability Journal*, *18*, 842–860. doi:10.1108/09513570510627739

Pearce, J., & Kay, A. (2012). Brief History of Social Accounting and Audit. *Social Audit Network*. Retrieved February 20, 2019, from http://www.socialauditnetwork.org.uk/getting-started/brief-history-social-accounting-and-audit

Robeco, S. A. M. (2018, September 24). *Dow Jones*. Retrieved February 20, 2019, from https://www.robecosam.com/images/review-presentation-2018.pdf

Robeco, S. A. M. (n.d.). *We are Sustainability Investing*. Retrieved February 20, 2019, from https://www.robecosam.com/media/7/3/6/7368ef74b7d48a7e14ff0f22e3b78f57_csa-benefits-of-participation_tcm1011-14469.pdf

Russel Investment Group. (n.d.). *FTSE Russel Indexes* [Index]. Retrieved February 17, 2019, from https://www.ftse.com/products/indices/home/PageNotFound?aspxerrorpath=/Analytics/Factsheets/temp/4588a59d-deda-4d98-aa7e-cc5b93093f41.pdf

Russian Union of Industrials and Entrepreneurs. (n.d.). *Press room Committees and commissions Positions Analytics Social responsibility Social Charter of Russian Business*. Retrieved February 20, 2019, from http://www.rspp.ru/simplepage/474

Sheldon, E., Wilbert, B., & Moore, E. (Eds.). (1968). *Indicators of Social Change*. New York: Russell Sage.

Sigma Project. (2003). *Sigma Guidelines: Putting sustainable development into practice - A Guide for Organizations.* Retrieved February 20, 2019, from http://www.projectsigma.co.uk/default.asp

Spacey, J. (2016, April 13). *8 Examples of Accountability.* Retrieved February 20, 2019, from https://simplicable.com/new/accountability

Spence, C., Husillos, J., & Correa-Ruiz, C. (2010). Cargo cult science and the death of politics: A critical review of social and environmental accounting research. *Critical Perspectives on Accounting, 21*(1), 76–89. doi:10.1016/j.cpa.2008.09.008

Sustainability Accounting Standard Board (SASB). (1997). *SA8000 Standard.* Retrieved February 20, 2019, from http://www.sa-intl.org/index.cfm?fuseaction=Page.ViewPage

Sustainability Accounting Standard Board SASB. (n.d.). *Sustainability Accounting Standards Board.* Retrieved February 20, 2019, from https://www.sasb.org

Terleckyj, N. E. (1981). A Social production framework for resource accounting. In *Social Accounting Systems* (pp. 95–129). New York: Academic Press. doi:10.1016/B978-0-12-392550-3.50009-6

Terleckyj, N. E. (1981). A Social Production Framework for Resource Accounting. In *Social Accounting Systems, Essays on the State of the Art.* Academic Press, Inc.

Turkin, S. (n.d.). *How beneficial to be kind: Make your business socially responsible: Social Reporting and Social Audit.* Retrieved February 20, 2019, from http://uchebnik.online/prakticheskaya-psihologiya-treningi/sotsialnaya-otchetnost-sotsialnyiy-46286.html

United Nations. (1972). *Declaration of the United Nations Conference on the Human Environment* (From Report of the United Nations Conference on the Human Environment, Stockholm, June 1972). Retrieved from http://www.un-documents.net/unchedec.htm

United Nations Global Compact. (2012). *A Practical Guide to the United Nations Global Compact for Higher Education Institutions: Implementing the Global Compact Principles and Communications.* Retrieved from https://www.unglobalcompact.org/library/5628

Verité. (n.d.). *Verité | Fair Labor. Worldwide. | Knowledge and Tools to Eliminate Child Labor, Forced Labor, Human Trafficking and Gender Discrimination.* Retrieved February 20, 2019, from https://www.verite.org

Water Accounting Standards Board. (2012) *Australian Water Accounting Standards 1 Preparation and Presentation of General Purpose Water Accounting Reports.* Retrieved from http://www.bom.gov.au/water/standards/documents/awas1_v1.0.pdf

World Business Council for Sustainable Development (WBCSD). (n.d.). *The Reporting Exchange | Global resource for sustainability reporting.* Retrieved February 20, 2019, from https://www.reportingexchange.com/search?search=social%20report

Zadek, S., Pruzan, P., & Evans, R. (Eds.). (1997). Building corporate accountability: emerging practices in social and ethical accounting, auditing and reporting. London, UK: Earthscan.

KEY TERMS AND DEFINITIONS

Corporate Social Responsibility Report: A company's positive impact on and amelioration of negative impacts against society and the environment through its operations, products, or services and through its interaction with key stakeholders such as employees, customers, investors, communities, and suppliers.

Environmental Accounting and Reporting: A new stage in the development of accounting and reporting, based on the principle of traditional accounting and reporting, but recording, analyzing and reporting environmental costs and benefits for companies. A part of social accounting and reporting.

Luca Pacioli: Fra Luca Bartolomeo de Pacioli (n.d. 1445- 19.06.1517) was a mathematician, monk of the Order of the Franciscans, author of "Summa de arithmetica, geometria, proporciones et proporcionità" published in Venice, 1494. One of the founders of modern accounting science.

Social Accounting: Accounting systems, which records, measures, and analyzes the impact of organizations on the environment and society.

Social Indicators: Quantitative measures usually presented as indices, and qualitative indicators for measuring and tracking the status and changes of welfare of people and societies.

Social Report: An accounting report that reflects organizations' relationships with stakeholders in all material respects.

Standards for Social Accounting and Reporting: Adopted principles and procedures for registration and measurement of the impact of organizations' activities on the environment and society.

Chapter 7
The Potential Role of Social Reporting in the Decision-Making Process of Cooperatives

Fabio De Matteis
Università del Salento – Lecce, Italy

Daniela Preite
Università del Salento – Lecce, Italy & SDA Bocconi – Milano, Italy

ABSTRACT

Accountability in the social economy sector is very important because it is inherent in the nature of the organizations of this sector. The literature on the topic of social accounting and accountability is abundant and highlights the benefits and the criticisms of social reporting. The objective of the chapter arises from the literature review that highlights how more in-depth studies are needed on the characters and role of social accountability in decision-making processes. In order to answer the research question (How is social reporting performed and how does social information influence the decision making of the management in a cooperative?), the single case study methodology has been adopted, considering embedded units of analysis and focusing on the social report of an Italian retail cooperative (COOP Lombardia). Thanks to the analyzed case study, it is possible to conclude that the social report can represent a tool of accountability that also informs future decisions, realizing a circular relationship between results achieved and decisions to be taken.

INTRODUCTION[1]

Over the years, accountability has begun to increase its importance in many kinds of organizations. Particular attention received social accounting and reporting.

Different motivations can lead an organisation to undertake a report supporting accountability. The approval acquisition/maintenance of the most powerful stakeholders (Islam & Deegan, 2010); the desire to be responsible and accountable towards all that are affected by the organizations' activity (Salani, 2004); the necessity to respond to a variety of institutional pressures (Bebbington et al. 2009); and the importance of protecting and enhancing the value deriving from organizational reputation (Spence, 2009).

DOI: 10.4018/978-1-5225-8482-7.ch007

Accountability in the Social Economy Sector is very important because it is inherent in the nature of the organizations of this sector: in fact, for the non-profit managers the necessity to give an account has always been important, both within organizations and towards their donors (Candler & Dumont, 2010). The authors think that the importance of accountability is particularly relevant for the cooperatives (specific object of this chapter), where their mutualistic purpose should stress the internal accountability (towards cooperative's members, employees, management). In other words, for a cooperative, accountability should be considered as a duty deriving from its institutional purpose (mutualistic).

Moreover, recently, in Italy social reporting has assumed a special relevance in the Social Economy Sector because, in 2017, the obligation to draft the Social Report was introduced for all Third Sector organizations (starting for the fiscal year 2018, when the guidelines for the drawing up of the Social Report have been approved).

In this chapter, the authors consider a specific Social Economy Sector organization represented by the cooperatives that are going through a very critical period (Battaglia et al., 2015) dictated by the need to pursue the competitiveness of other cooperatives and other non-cooperative companies operating in the same sector, without betraying their traditional reference values (first of all that of mutuality).

The main purpose of the chapter is to highlight to potential role of the Social Report in supporting internal decision making, while much of the literature considers the Social Report as an external accountability document. Therefore, the contribution of the chapter is to propose a different point of view on this document: from basically external purpose tool, to both internal and external purpose document.

To this end, section 2 proposes some literature contributions on accountability and social report, highlighting the need to fill a gap in analyzing the role of social reporting in the decision making of cooperatives. In section 3, the authors define the research question and describe the research methodology. Section 4 contains the case study analysis, while section 5 is focused on some discussion deriving from the previous analysis. Finally, section 6 summarize some conclusive reflections.

ACCOUNTABILITY AND SOCIAL REPORT: SOME LITERATURE CONTRIBUTION

Literature provides numerous contributions aimed at outlining the concept of accountability, its articulation in different components and the evolution that accountability has highlighted over time.

In extreme synthesis, the concept of accountability (Steccolini, 2004) requires the presence of an activity of transferring information from the accountor (social economy sector organization) to the accountee (stakeholder) to whom the possibility of evaluation is recognized on the basis of the information obtained.

In particular, in order to apply the accountability concept, the availability of information is necessary, but not sufficient. In effect, the information must also have the character of reliability, comprehensibility, accessibility, distribution and dissemination (Herzlinger, 1996).

The theoretical and empirical analyses contained in the international literature on accountability, are distinguished by their initial and overwhelming focus on the social reporting aspects related to the for-profit sector (Linowes, 1972; Estes, 1976; Gray et al., 1987).

This kind of scientific contribution can be considered natural since the tools of social reporting were born and spread in companies and, only in more recent times, has there been an adaptation of the same to the context of public administration and the non-profit sector.

This aspect is considered particularly relevant and distinctive of social reporting: in fact, it arises for companies, responding, therefore, to certain purposes and logics.

The use of social reporting in non-profit organizations and in public administration implies an adaptation of the tool defined to be used in the for profit sector.

The adaptation must consider all the problems that an "adjustment" of this type may entail: the risk is to draw up a document that does not realize the accountability concept effectively.

During the last decades, different theories have been elaborated in an attempt to motivate the use and diffusion of various methods of social reporting:

1. the information usefulness approach for readers' decision making purposes (Gray et al. 1995). This approach considers as a priority the users' point of view: the accountability tools should be useful for the decision making process of their readers. A recent study states that a rational management must evaluate both the financial-economic results and the social impact of its activity, in order to achieve the maximum level of information in the decision making. Nonetheless, this approach needs a deep change in order to consider human being at the center of any theoretical model, to avoid the creation of unfairness and inequalities (Migliavacca et al., 2018);
2. the theory of legitimation (Dowling and Pfeffer, 1975). On the basis of this theoretical approach, the focus is represented by the point of view of the community: a company pursues the continuity of its activity by adopting behaviors deemed socially acceptable. This in order to obtain the social legitimation necessary for the company to remain in business;
3. the stakeholders' theory (Freeman, 1984), according to which each company has different interlocutors to which it is required to report on its activities in an appropriate manner;
4. the theory of the political economy of detection systems. On the basis of this approach, the company's information system can influence the perception that the civil society has of the company, influencing the citizens' expectations towards the company (Woodward et al., 2001);
5. the positive theory of detection systems (Watts & Zimmermann, 1978). It relates the definition of accounting principles and profit maximization objectives pursued by the management. An application of this theory to social reporting leads to considering it as a tool used by managers to achieve their goals of maximizing income in the short term (Milne, 2002).

In this chapter, the authors base their analysis on another theory, different from those above mentioned. It is the Resource Dependence Theory (Pfeffer & Salanicik, 1978), one of the most influential theory in organizational theory and strategic management. The Resource Dependence Theory recognizes the influence of external factors on organizational behavior and considers that managers can act to face external uncertainty and dependence.

This study uses the Resource Dependence Theory, specifically considering (as elements of this theory):

- Each organization is not autonomous, but it is constrained by a network of interdependencies with other subjects;
- The organization's interdependence, together with the uncertainity about the role undertaken by the other subjects, leads to a situation in which survival and long term success are uncertain;
- Each organization takes actions to manage external interdependencies, but such actions are never completely successful and produce new situations of dependence and interdependence.

In this chapter, the use of the Resource Dependence Theory leads the authors to considers (i) the interdependence between Social Economy organizations and their environment; (ii) the influence of external factors (social information) on Social Economy organizations; (iii) the managers' decisions undertaken to face interdependencies/uncertainties.

The variety of theoretical approaches and, in particular, the use of the Resource Dependence Theory, denotes the extent of the phenomenon of social accountability, which, from a documental point of view, can be related to the social report.

The social report aims to provide information on the social impacts of an organization's activity and on the relationship established between the organization and the society in which it operates (Matacena, 1984). In addition to the purposes of communication towards the outside stakeholders, the social report can also play an important role in internal decisions, both organizational and strategic (Hinna, 2002).

On the one hand, the international literature does not lack a critical approach to the dissemination of the social report. In fact, literature also emphasizes the need to consider some conceptual limitations of social reporting (Lehman, 2001), as this tool is conceived by literature. In particular, a criticism derives from the goals of social reporting: is it really oriented to providing a representation of the social effects of the allocation of resources, or does it lead to the definition of a report that constitutes a mere marketing device? Therefore, this highlights the risk of exploiting the use of social reporting techniques that, behind transparency and the transfer of information, hide or neglect actions of lesser appeal for the organization. In this way, a vision of accountability is supported, which justifies uncritical social reporting models that are not really oriented towards the dissemination of information on the social impact of the actions undertaken.

On the other hand, the literature on the topic of social accounting and accountability is abundant and also highlights the benefits and motivations supporting voluntary reporting. Among them, for example: the development of a more informed decision making system (Burrit, 2012), the maintenance of the stakeholders' approval (Adams & Zutshi, 2004), the management of the reputation and its value, also in terms of income generation (Spence, 2009).

In addition, some scientific contributions highlight the need for further studies to investigate the integration of social and environmental issues into decision making processes (Burrit & Shaltegger, 2010; Searcy, 2012). In fact, it is considered of particular interest to understand the ways in which the information contained in the voluntary reports does not remain an end in itself, but influences the decision making processes of their users.

Starting from a previous examination of social reporting that highlighted the diversity and detail within reporting approaches of both third sector and private sector organisations, Luke attempts to address the limitations of different social reporting approaches and promote the introduction of a single and comparable reporting framework. Luke's findings highlight the complexity of applying a single social reporting framework across sectors and the reluctance towards comprehensive reporting until positive results are achieved for third sector organizations (Luke, 2017).

More recent studies explore how and where social impact measurement for social enterprise and values-based organisations is developing (Dey & Gibbon, 2017) or show how, sometime, the concept of social reporting has developed into that more broad of sustainability reporting (Manetti et al., 2014; Gazzola et al., 2017).

Literature on cooperative's social reporting practices is limited, especially in more recent period. In effect, as above highlighted, the guidelines for the drawing up of the social report in Social Economy organizations have been approved only in 2018. From this, the opportunity to consider this chapter a starting point in filling this literature gap in analyzing the role of social reporting in the cooperatives.

RESEARCH QUESTION AND METHODOLOGY

The objective of the chapter arises from the literature review that highlights how more in-depth studies are needed on the characters and role of social accountability in decision making processes. In particular, this chapter contextualizes this research opportunity in a particular type of organization of the Social Economy Sector: the cooperative.

As a consequence, the research question that guides this work is: "How is social reporting performed and how does social information influence the decision making of the management in a cooperative?".

In other words, the authors try:

- To describe the social disclosures of a cooperative (in terms of social reporting structure and contents);
- To analyze the process followed to collect these social disclosures (in order to understand how a cooperative can define structure and content of the social report);
- To highlight the impact of the social reporting on the (strategic and/or operational) decision making process of the management in a cooperative.

The authors choose to investigate specifically social reporting given the particular nature of cooperative companies (characterized by the mutualistic purpose), which should bring these organizations to pay particular attention to the social consequences of their activities. Besides, the authors consider a specific category of stakeholders represented by the management, in order to decide if their decisions are affected by social disclosures.

In order to answer the research question and reach the aim of the chapter, considering that (i) the research question is explanatory, (ii) the authors intend to analyze a contemporary phenomenon in relation to which (iii) the main behaviors cannot be influenced by the researcher, the research methodology followed is the case study (Yin, 2009).

The case study methodology - which in this research is explanatory (Turrini, 2002) - leads to a theoretical generalization (Foster et al., 2000). In fact, the analyses of specific socio-economic organizations, considering the managerial choices made in the same, do not allow the researchers an empirical generalization related to an aggregate of elements because of the presence of several specific elements that characterize the analyzed organization (Gillham, 1999).

In particular, developing the research design, the single case study methodology has been adopted (Eisenhardt, 1989; Baxter & Jack, 2008).

The single case study option is chosen on the basis of the rationale for which there is a critical case in relation to the object of analysis (that is the cooperative's social report). Therefore, the authors choose "COOP Italia" because it is the largest Italian cooperative in the retail sector. "COOP Italia" is composed of seven cooperatives, and, among these, "COOP Lombardia" (consumers cooperative) is the only one to draw up and publish a document defined as a Social Report on its institutional website.

This is why the authors decide to analyze how Coop Lombardia faces social reporting and how the Social report impacts the internal decision making process.

The research design considers embedded units of analysis (see Table 1):

1. the first unit of analysis focuses on social reporting with specific attention to the structure and content of the document. The in-depth analysis of these aspects was achieved through a document

analysis (Corbetta, 2003) based on the Social Report. From a temporal point of view, the documents analyzed refer to the last two years;

2. the second unit of analysis examines the Social Report through the point of view of the management of Coop Lombardia involved in the social reporting process. The technique of data collection, for this unit, is represented by semi-structured interviews (Kvale & Brinkmann, 2009) that allow the authors (in addition to deepening some technical aspects revealed in the document analysis of the previous unit), to investigate some organizational aspects and the decision making repercussions of the Social Report. The interviews were carried out with two top management representatives and lasted about 45 minutes;
3. the third unit of analysis examines the Social Report in terms of phases implemented to realizing the social reporting process and subjects involved. The data and information concerning these aspects have been collected through the technique of direct observations (Bailey, 1994) of an unstructured and dissimulated type (in order not to condition the observed subjects).

This highlights how the case study allow us to analyze the research objects (social reporting and decision making process) from different points of view (integrating the collected data and information): the Social Report, carrying out a document analysis; the top management of Coop Lombardia, that represents the point of reference of the social reporting and the internal decision making processes, carrying out semi structured interviews; and the subjects involved in the social reporting through direct observations.

THE SOCIAL REPORT OF COOP LOMBARDIA

Coop Lombardia is a consumer cooperative operating in the Italian region named Lombardia. A cooperative is an organization that pursues a mutualistic purpose and operates without any goal of private speculation, as required by art. 45 of the Italian Constitution. The members participate in the management of the Cooperative through Assemblies, which deliberate on financial statements, plans, programs and regulations.

The main elements of the organizational structure involved in decision making are as follow:

- The Board of Directors, that is the executive body in charge of implementing the programs and objectives of the Cooperative;
- Board of Statutory Auditors, that supervises over the compliance with the Articles of the Association and the compliance with the principles of proper administration of the Cooperative;
- The Ethical Committee, that is the body that oversees the compliance with the ethical code;

Table 1. Research methodology: units of analysis

	Object	Information source
Units 1	Structure and contents of the Social Report	Document analysis (Corbetta, 2003): Social Report Analysis
Units 2	Management point of view	Semi-structured interviews (Kvale e Brinkmann 2009) of the management involved in social reporting
Units 3	Subjects involved in social reporting	Direct observations (Bailey, 1994) unstructured and dissimulated

- Members participate in the management of the Cooperative through the Assemblies;
- The Local Members Committees, (formed by volunteers democratically elected among the Members), these are structures for the participation in the cooperative life over the territory through sociocultural, educational and solidarity initiatives;
- The General Council of Members approves electoral regulations, appoints the Ethics Committee and has a say in the matter of financial statements, investments, development programs and commercial policies;
- The Members Council is formed by Members of the Local Committees and it has a say on topics of particular importance for the cooperative activity;
- The Supervisory Body ensures the supervision of the functioning and observance of the Organizational Model.

Coop Lombardia has 4.266 workers, 825.170 members and 55 stores throughout the Lombardia Region's territory.

For several years, Coop Lombardia, in order to demonstrate its increased respect for accountability and to guarantee ever greater participation by its members, has drawn up a Social Report. Through the drafting of the Social Report, the cooperative sets some objectives (Coop Lombardia, 2018): interpret the change in the interests of the stakeholders, analyzing the impact of the implemented activities and accounting for the value generated (from different points of view: economic, social, environmental and cultural); reflect on the achieved results and identify, in a shared way, future actions aimed at improving results.

In this sense, the Social Report of Coop Lombardia represents an innovative case study for two main reasons: 1. the measurement of the social activities carried out in terms of outcome, in a logic of integration with the data from financial statements (Fiorentini & Preite, 2000); 2. the stakeholder approach, in order to provide information to a wide range of stakeholders, both internal and external (Freeman, 1984; Coda, 1998; Rusconi, 2009).

The Social Report is prepared in two versions: Tabloid and Gold. The Tabloid version is a summarized variant of the document while the Gold version is more detailed and was presented to the General Assembly of Delegates.

Regarding the methodological approach, the preparation of the Social Report takes place through a working group representing all the organizational levels of the cooperative, which provide data and indicators aimed at reporting on social responsibility. In fact, members of the board of directors and top management belong to the working group, in addition to employees. The preparation of the Social report is a long and complex process, as it takes place over 12 months, following the presentation in the General Assembly of Delegates.

The interviews with the top management reveal that, thanks to the Social Report preparation process, the whole structure of COOP Lombardia perceived the relevance of the document and developed a greater participation in the process. This also thanks to the understanding of the repercussions of Social Report on COOP Lombardia's decision making.

However, top management also highlights a problem represented by the big amount of data and information that need to be processed to drawn up the Social Report. During the interviews the authors note that this problem has been solved with a rigorous procedure of constant monitoring of social reporting.

The social reporting process includes the following steps:

1. The drafting and reporting process is planned;
2. The Social Report of the previous year is analyzed, highlighting its strengths and weaknesses;
3. The achieved results are assessed, analyzing the impact of the pursued actions (following a multi-stakeholder accountability perspective);
4. The most relevant results are highlighted to support future decisions (these can be "to maintain/to modify/to cancel an action");
5. The structure for the Social rRport of the following year is proposed, also according to the message to be communicated to the stakeholders;
6. The Social Report is drawn up following a multi-stakeholder accountability approach;
7. The interlocutors are involved in the drawing up process;
8. The drawing up process is connected to other internal management systems (e.g. accounting).

The structure of the Social Report is based on international and national standards on Corporate Social Responsibility (CSR), as defined by the AccountAbility 1000 guidelines (ISEA, 1999), and by the GRI4 - Global Reporting Initiative (Global Reporting Initiative, 2015). Furthermore, the structure also considers the GBS model (the model defined by the Italian Social Reporting Group), which provides indications on the methodology for measuring added value (GBS, 2013).

During the interviews, the top management explains that the use of a mix of different models is a reasoned choice, aimed at capturing the strengths of each of the above mentioned models/standards.

The Social Report (Gold version) is divided into seven chapters.

In the first chapter, named "Identity and Values" the mission and the vision of the cooperative are presented, together with the founding values. The goal is to recognize the cooperative's social responsibility, in order to protect the interests of members and consumers. In this section, the specificity of the organization is clarified: the cooperative is a solidarity organization, without the purpose of private speculation. In fact, the resulting profit is mainly destined to (i) indivisible reserves for the cooperative's development and for future generations, (ii) promotion and cooperative solidarity, (iii) a limited remuneration of the social quota and to a rebate related to the purchases made.

Therefore, unlike for-profit companies that have a strictly economic dimension (Borgonovi, 2000; Garzoni, 2013; De Matteis & Preite 2016), the most important dimensions of a solidarity firm are specifically ethical, philanthropic, moral or social, and they represent the basis for an economic-functional development and the necessary conditions for social assessment. Therefore, if the raw dimensions are of non-economic type, the operating dimensions are purely economic. Following this approach, the economic activity becomes an instrument for the development of social purposes (Fiorentini & Preite, 2000).

The "Identity" highlights that the Coop-branded product is 70 years old. It embodies the same founding values that define the cooperative movement, responding to the consumers' needs: from the banishment of dyes in the eighties and GMOs in the nineties, to the elimination of palm oil in 2016 and the limitation of using antibiotics on farms. The Coop-branded product represents the synthesis of the cooperative's values in terms of safety (compliance with the law and checks on the supply chain), ethics (respect for workers' rights), ecology (sustainable production methods), goodness (the quality is approved by the members), convenience (best value for money) and transparency (clear labels on the origin of raw materials). The measurement of the impact of these values can be found in the chapters that follow the first one.

In the same chapter, the functioning of the governance and the Coop system is explained. A specific part is dedicated to the stakeholders that are represented by:

- Members, who are the owners of the cooperative and evaluate the strategies to be adopted;
- Workers, who ensure the operation of the network;
- Consumers, who are customers of the cooperative, but not members;
- Institutions, the public bodies with which the cooperative maintains partnerships;
- Suppliers, the subjects supplying goods and services;
- Community, considered as the social reality to which the cooperative addresses cultural and educational initiatives;
- Future generations, young people and schools to which particular attention is paid;
- Environment, as an ecological resource for humanity and territory.

In the chapters following the first, the accountability of Coop Lombardia is measured with specific sections:

1. Economic value, which illustrates the core business and the main commercial actions; in this section the added value table is presented;
2. Social value, where the impact of actions on workers, members, the community and suppliers is measured;
3. Environmental value, where the impact on the environment - through actions aimed at safeguarding it - is presented;
4. Cultural value, in which the actions supporting young stakeholders and Schools are described and measured

In the chapter on economic value, the Statement of Added Value and the outcomes measurement deserve particular attention.

Table 2 shows that, despite the decrease in net sales, the Overall gross added value rises from 201,403 to 202,473 thousand euro. The data on the economic value also highlights that sales to members in 2017 are far higher than those to third parties non-members (627,425 thousand against 188,863 thousand euros). This aspect shows the detection of the mutual activity carried out by the cooperative towards its members. In order to produce this data, the cooperative implements accurate detection and calculation criteria and the data is constantly monitored to ensure a correct social accountability.

Table 3 shows the distribution of the added value. Employees receive 71.16%, considering both the cost of personnel and the cost of training. The Public Sector receives 3.47% of the added value, while 0.25% is distributed to funders, 2.51% to members, 3.09% to the community, 0.63% to the cooperative system and almost 19% to the Cooperative.

In the chapter of the Social Report related to the social value, among others, the following activities and their impacts are reported:

- with regard to the workers (4,266 employees), many training activities were started (78,636 training hours) and safety actions that led to a reduction in the frequency and severity the rates of injuries, which respectively went from 21 in 2016 to 19 in 2017 and from 0.5 in 2016 to 0.4 in 2017;
- with regard to the members (825,170 members), different activities inspired by the values of mutuality, cooperation and participation were implemented, leading to the enrollment of 26,759 new members in 2017; while the renewal campaign of the Members' Local Committees led 56,585 members to vote, with the election of 456 new elected members;

Table 2. Statement of Added Value (€/000)

	2017	2016
Net sales GDO	816.328	825.462
- to Members	627.465	631.481
- to Third parties	188.863	193.981
Sales of fuel	65.593	60.395
Real estate and other revenue	37.900	45.354
Financial and Equity participations Net income	35.255	27.097
Tot. Sales, other income and financial income	**955.076**	**958.309**
Cost of goods	-611.032	-615.852
Costs for services	-111.438	-111.171
Costs for rent	-22.430	-18.509
Other costs	-4.801	-9.366
Provisions for risks and charges	-2.901	-2.009
Tot. Cost of goods, Services, Rents and other costs	**-752.602**	**-756.907**
GROSS OVERALL ADDED VALUE	**202.473**	**201.403**

Source: (Social Report of COOP Lombardia, 2017)

Table 3. Added value distribution (€/000)

The Added value is distributed as follow:				
	2017	%	**2016**	%
To Employees				
Training	1.484	0,73%	3.113	1,55%
Cost of personnel	142.597	70,43%	138.356	68,70%
To the Public Administration				
State	2.577	1,27%	3.634	1,80%
Local governments	4.455	2,20%	6.697	3,33%
To Funders				
Other funders	498	0,25%	527	0,26%
To Members				
Remuneration of the social loan	4.929	2,43%	7.105	3,53%
Institutional communication	156	0,08%	303	0,15%
To the Community				
Social and cultural activities, sponsorship, solidarity	6.247	3,09%	5.524	2,74%
To the Cooperative System				
ANCC Contribution	186	0,09%	101	0,05%
Mutual Fund to promote and develop Cooperation (L.59/92)	251	0,12%	180	0,09%
Membership fees	860	0,42%	1.192	0,59%
To the Cooperative				
Depreciation and amortization	30.128	14,88%	30.138	14,96%
Provision to reserve	8.107	4,00%	5.825	2,89%
TOTAL ADDED VALUE DISTRIBUTION	**202.473**	**100,00%**	**201.403**	**100,00%**

Source: (Social Report of COOP Lombardia, 2017)

- towards the community, 110 tons of goods were donated to 90 non-profit organizations; 400 elderly people were assisted by 180 volunteers; over 600,000 meals were donated to associations that take care of the animals;
- with regard to suppliers, 3,029,437 analyses were carried out on 500 Coop-branded product suppliers, to ensure the compliance with the strict production rules and in order to respect the high quality of the product.

In the chapter on the environmental value, the Coop Lombardia's Social Report highlights the impact on energy saving and on environmental sustainability. Coop was the first group in Europe to adhere to the Greenlight protocol, supported and promoted by the European Commission. The adherence to the protocol has allowed 56 points of sale to adopt the Greenlight technology, with an energy saving of 6.4 million kWh and avoiding the emission of 471 tons of carbon dioxide, thanks to the use of energy generated by the photovoltaic system.

The environmental value section highlights a sustainability and "non-waste" culture following a multi-stakeholder approach, i.e. towards employees, members, consumers, communities and institutions. In fact, different actions were carried out in 53 points of sale in order to increase the participation and the involvement of the stakeholders who become an active part of the environmental protection process. The results led to the recovery of 1,171 tons of food products, donated to 86 associations, which assisted thousands of people by producing over 2,343,325 full meals.

The environmental value has also been measured in relation to the 3R policy (reduction, reuse, recycling), which Coop has been following for years, i.e. using fewer quantities of packaging, favoring recyclable materials and reusing reusable packaging for the same use. The impact of these actions is the reduction of the emission of 8,100 tons of carbon dioxide into the atmosphere.

Finally, the cultural value was measured on the basis of the actions taken towards young people and schools. Among the various actions, the following results have been reported. The school involved 21,584 students and 1,793 teachers with 2,377 meetings on issues like the environment and sustainability, food and health, citizenship and cooperation. In addition, 1,600 hours of training were carried out and 7,260 products were donated for a value of € 1,134,870.

The last two chapters represent of the Social Report contain, respectively, a testimony on the values of Coop through interviews addressed to suppliers, and a mapping of the points of sale located throughout the territory.

The interviewed top management states that the data and the information contained in the Social Report have been used to support decision making in three main areas: member and social policies, employee policies, environmental policies. This allows the top management to use qualitative and quantitative (other than financial) data and information to have a more clear framework to make decisions. Top managers find particularly relevant the opportunity to know the point of view of both internal stakeholders (e.g. employees) and external stakeholders (e.g. suppliers).

Therefore, top management declares that the social reporting is a kind of shared decision making. In effect, top management explains that the Social Report of COOP Lombardia is presented in 48 separate budgetary Assemblies (attended by over 10,000 members), while the Gold version is more detailed and is presented to the General Assembly of Delegates (with about 700 delegated members) in order to gather observations. Top management, to decide on future policies, discusses these findings. This shows a substantial participation of the Social Report contents in the decision making.

DISCUSSION

The analysis conducted in the previous section, allows the authors it is possible to highlight that the analyzed document affects the decisions of board and the top management of COOP Lombardia (Gray et al., 1995).

In summary, on the basis of the results reported in the Social Report, some decisions were taken in the following areas.

Member and social policies. Thanks to the organization of summer camps for the cultivation of land confiscated from the mafia, there has been a considerable increase in the commitment of voluntary and employee members who participated in the summer camps. This initiative also led to the increase of sales related to the affected products, with a considerable commercial impact. This demonstrates how a joint action between members/social and commercial policies is fundamental in a cooperative highly focused on values. In this sense, the former have an impact on the latter.

Employee policies. In this context, to face a decline in the sense of belonging and the adhesion to the cooperative's values, training actions for the employees were taken. One is the so-called "Cantastorie": during promotional activities, some sellers are dedicated to explaining (to customers, members and other employees) the "story" of the COOP branded products. This contributes to increasing the sense of belonging and also has an impact on the sales of the COOP brand products. Another action is represented by the Career and Performance Management project, which focuses on managing careers through the valorization and promotion of the talents of Coop Lombardia's employees. The logic of the model is based on a managerial approach (meritocracy and results) as opposed to the bureaucratic approach (procedures and job descriptions). The career path, based on objectives and results, differs according to the period in which growth develops and uses the figure of a mentor, i.e. a person skilled in the subject. The mentor supports the process of learning and growth and contributes to the dissemination of organizational culture, facilitating the development process. This project allowed the cooperative to increase the sense of belonging of its employees.

Environmental policies. In this context, attention to the environment is growing in commercial development initiatives. In fact, there are plans to restructure points of sale, with particular attention to the definition and the redistribution of the spaces, redeveloping them and improving the quality of life in the neighborhood.

The examination of the Social Report of Coop Lombardia was carried out on the basis of the indications of the literature, according to specific coding rules (Steccolini, 2004; Milne & Adler, 1999; Guthrie et al., 2003) to ensure the reliability of the analysis. The analysis was conducted on the basis of three perspectives:

1. the structure, where the different sections of the document have been analyzed, in order to highlight the main points;
2. the style of presentation (Gray et al., 1987), in which the nature of the presented information emerges, which appears qualitative (Identity section and Testimonials section), quantitative (in the different section in which measurable results are presented), quantitative-accounting (statement of added value);
3. the reported performance dimensions, in which two perspectives emerge (Elkington, 1997; Kaplan & Norton, 2003; Niven, 2003):

a. internal, related to accounting information, to process efficiency and to innovation;
b. external, where impacts on economic, social, environmental and cultural value are presented.

In light of the analysis carried out, it can be stated that the Social Report of Coop Lombardia presents the following strengths, which reflect the standards of the AccountAbility 1000 (AA1000):

- the multi-stakeholder approach, which allows the author of the Social Report to identify the stakeholders at which the cooperative is aimed;
- the measurement of added value, as a quantitative indicator of the generated and distributed value;
- the use of quantitative information, useful to measure results and impacts;
- the quality and significance of the reported information, both qualitative and quantitative;
- the participation and involvement of the stakeholders;
- the social reporting frequency, as the Social Report is produced regularly every year;
- the availability of the document, both in paper and in digital formats;
- the integration of the information contained in the Social Report into the management systems, as it is used for decisions making;
- the continuous improvement, as the drafting process is checked and improved every year.

The case study analyses also highlights some points of weakness related to the social reporting of COOP Lombardia:

- the amount of data needed to draft the document (they are very numerous and complex to manage);
- the involvement of the whole structure and the external stakeholders in the process of collecting data and information (the involvement implies a high level of complexity of social reporting).

CONCLUSION

The accountability in Social Economy Sector is very important because it is inherent to the nature of the organizations of this sector (Candler & Dumont, 2010), and it is often realized through the use of the Social Report. Some scientific contributions highlight the need for further studies to investigate the integration of social and environmental issues into decision making processes (Burrit & Shaltegger, 2010; Searcy, 2012).

As a consequence, the research question that guides this work is: "How is social reporting performed and how does social information influence the decision making of the management in a cooperative?".

In order to answer the research question, the research methodology followed is the single case study (Yin, 2009), with embedded units of analysis, represented by the Social Report of COOP Lombardia (an Italian consumers cooperative).

Therefore, thanks to the empirical support of the analyzed case study, it is possible to conclude that the Social Report can represent a tool of accountability that realizes the cycle of planning and control. In effect, as highlighted, the final data contained in this tool - besides supporting internal and external reporting - informs future decisions, realizing a circular relationship between results achieved and decisions to be taken.

This is also highlighted by the interviews with the top management, especially where top management explains the process of discussion about Social Report and the use of the findings deriving from discussion in supporting top management's decision making.

Finally, thanks to the case study analysis, the authors can conclude that internal purpose of social reporting in terms of support to decision making, can be interpreted as an informative declination of the Resource Dependence Theory considered in this chapter. In effect, on the one hand, a large part of the data contained in the Social Report can be considered as external factors influencing the cooperative. On the other hand, the managers' decisions (based on the Social Report's contents) are the actions undertaken to face interdependencies and uncertainties.

REFERENCES

Adams, C. A., & Zutshi, A. (2004). Corporate social responsibility: Why business should act responsibly and be accountable. *Australian Accounting Review*, *14*(1), 31–39. doi:10.1111/j.1835-2561.2004.tb00238.x

Bailey, K. D. (1995). *Methods of social research*. New York: Maxwell Macmillan International.

Battaglia, M., Bianchi, L., Frey, M., & Passetti, E. (2015). Sustainability reporting and corporate identity: Action research evidence in an Italian retailing cooperative. *Business Ethics (Oxford, England)*, *24*(1), 52–72. doi:10.1111/beer.12067

Baxter, P., & Jack, S. (2008). Qualitative case study methodology: Study design and implementation for novice researchers. *Qualitative Report*, *13*(4), 544–559.

Bebbington, J., Higgins, C., & Frame, B. (2009). Initiating sustainable development reporting: Evidence from New Zealand. *Accounting, Auditing & Accountability Journal*, *22*(4), 588–625. doi:10.1108/09513570910955452

Borgonovi, E. (2000). Le aziende non profit e la trasformazione di "valori" individuali in "valore" economico e sociale: elementi di teoria aziendale. In A. Zangrandi (Ed.), *Aziende non profit: le condizioni di sviluppo*. Milano: Egea.

Burrit, R. L. (2012). Environmental performance accountability: Planet, people, profits. *Accounting, Auditing & Accountability Journal*, *25*(2), 370–405. doi:10.1108/09513571211198791

Burrit, R. L., & Schaltegger, S. (2010). Sustainability accounting and reporting: Fad or trend. *Accounting, Auditing & Accountability Journal*, *23*(7), 829–846. doi:10.1108/09513571011080144

Candler, G., & Dumont, G. (2010). A non-profit accountability framework. *Canadian Public Administration*, *2*(2), 259–279. doi:10.1111/j.1754-7121.2010.00126.x

Coda, V. (1998). Stakeholder. In M. Rispoli (Ed.), *La strategia aziendale*. Torino: Utet.

Coop Lombardia. (2018). *Bilancio Sociale 2017*. Pavia: Glifo.

Corbetta, P. (Ed.). (2003). *La ricerca sociale: metodologia e tecniche*. Bologna: Il Mulino.

De Matteis, F., & Preite, D. (Eds.). (2016). *Azienda non profit e relazioni interistituzionali per il management dei sistemi territoriali*. Napoli: Editorialc Scicntifica.

Dey, C., & Gibbon, J. (2017). Moving on from Scaling Up: Further Progress in Developing Social Impact Measurement in the Third Sector. *Social and Environmental Accountability Journal, 37*(1), 66–72. doi:10.1080/0969160X.2017.1285712

Dowling, J., & Pfeffer, J. (1975). Organizational legitimacy: Societal values and organizational behaviour. *Pacific Sociological Review, 18*(19), 122–136. doi:10.2307/1388226

Eisenhardt, K. M. (1989). Building theories from case study research. *Academy of Management Review, Vol., 4*(14), 532–550. doi:10.5465/amr.1989.4308385

Elkington, J. (1997). *Cannibals with forks: The triple bottom line of twentieth century business*. Oxford, UK: Capstone Publishing Ltd.

Estes, R. W. (1976). Socio-economic accounting and external diseconomies. *The Accounting Review, 50*(2), 284–290.

Fiorentini, G., & Preite, D. (2000). Azienda pubblica e azienda non profit: Il ruolo del bilancio sociale nel decentramento. *Azienda Pubblica, 2-3*, 253–288.

Foster, P., Gomm, R., & Hammersley, M. (2000). *Case Study Method. Key Issues*. London: Sage.

Freeman, R. (1984). *Strategic Management: A Stakeholder Approach*. Boston: Pitman.

Garzoni, A. (Ed.). (2003). *Il governo dell'impresa cooperativa*. Milano: Egea.

Gazzola, P., Ratti, M., & Amelio, S. (2017). CSR and Sustainability Report for Nonprofit Organizations. An Italian Best Practice. *Management Dynamics in the Knowledge Economy, 5*(3), 355–376. doi:10.25019/MDKE/5.3.03

GBS. (2013). *Il Bilancio Sociale. Standard. Principi di redazione del bilancio sociale*. Milano: Giuffrè.

Gillham, B. (1999). *Case Study Research Methods*. London: Continuum.

Global Reporting Initiative. (2015). GRI4 – Sustainability Reporting guidelines. Boston: Author.

Gray, R. H., Kouchy, R., & Lavers, S. (1995). Constructing a research database of social and environmental reporting by UK companies: A methodological note. *Accounting, Auditing & Accountability Journal, 8*(2), 78–101. doi:10.1108/09513579510086812

Gray, R. H., Owen, D., & Maunders, K. (1987). *Corporate social reporting: accounting and accountability*. London: Prentice-Hall.

Guthrie, J., Petty, R., Yongvanich, K., & Ricceri, F. (2003). *Intellectual Capital Reporting: Content approaches to data collection*. Paper presented at Performance Measurement Association Intellectual Capital Symposium, Cranfield.

Herzlinger, R. E. (1996, March). *Can Public Trust in Nonprofits and Governments Be Restored? Harvard Business Review*.

Hinna, L. (2002). Le fasi e le valenze del processo di rendicontazione sociale. In Il bilancio sociale. Milano: Il Sole 24 ore.

ISEA. (1999). *AccountAbility 1000 - Framework. Standard, guidelines and professional qualification.* Institute of Social and Ethical Accountability.

Islam, M. A., & Deegan, C. (2010). Media pressures and corporate disclosure of social responsibility performance information: A study of two global clothing and sports retail companies. *Accounting and Business Research*, *40*(2), 131–148. doi:10.1080/00014788.2010.9663388

Kaplan, R. S., & Norton, D. P. (2003). *Balanced Scorecard*. Torino: ISEDI.

Kvale, S., & Brinkmann, S. (Eds.). (2009). *InterViews: Learning the craft of qualitative researching interviewing*. London: Sage.

Lehman, G. (2001). Reclaiming the public sphere: Problems and prospects for corporate social and environmental accounting. *Critical Perspectives on Accounting*, *12*(6), 713–733. doi:10.1006/cpac.2001.0476

Linowes, D. F. (1972). Socio-economic accounting. *Journal of Accountancy*, *133*, 37–42.

Luke, B. (2017). Statement of Social Performance: Opportunities and Barriers to Adoption. *Social and Environmental Accountability Journal*, *37*(2), 118–136. doi:10.1080/0969160X.2017.1307129

Manetti, G., & Toccafondi, S. (2014). Defining the content of sustainability reports in nonprofit organizations: Do stakeholders really matter? *Journal of Nonprofit and Public Sector*, *26*(1), 35–61. doi:10.1080/10495142.2013.857498

Matacena, A. (Ed.). (1984). *Impresa e ambiente. Il bilancio "sociale"*. Bologna: Clueb.

Migliavacca, A., Rainero, C., Puddu, L., & Modarelli, G. (2018). Social impact and evaluation: A rational management theory approach. *African Journal of Business Management*, *12*(5), 92–102. doi:10.5897/AJBM2017.8458

Milne, M. R. (2002). Positive Accounting Theory, Political Costs and social Disclosure Analysis: A Critical Look. *Accounting, Auditing & Accountability Journal*, *12*, 369–395.

Milne, M. R., & Adler, R. W. (1999). Exploring the reliability of social and enviromental disclsures content analysis. *Accounting, Auditing & Accountability Journal*, *12*(2), 237–256. doi:10.1108/09513579910270138

Niven, P. R. (2003). Balanced Scorecard Step-by-Step for Government and Nonprofit Agencies. John Wiley & Sons Inc.

Pfeffer, J., & Salancik, G. R. (1978). *The external control of organizations: a resource dependence perspective*. New York: Harper & Row.

Rusconi, G. (2009). Stakeholder theory and business economics. *Economia aziendale 2000 web*, 3.

Salani, M. P. (2004). *Il bilancio sociale cooperativo e la responsabilità sociale d'impresa*. Firenze: Il Ponte Editore.

Searcy, C. (2012). Corporate Sustainability Performance Measurement Systems: A Review and Research Agenda. *Journal of Business Ethics*, *107*(3), 239–253. doi:10.100710551-011-1038-z

Spence, C. (2009). Social and the environmental reporting and the corporate ego. *Business Strategy and the Environment, 18*(4), 254–265. doi:10.1002/bse.600

Steccolini, I. (2004). *Accountability e sistemi informativi negli enti locali. Dal rendiconto al bilancio sociale*. Torino: Giappichelli.

Turrini, A. (2002). Lo studio dei casi come metodologia di ricerca in economia aziendale. *Azienda Pubblica, 1-2*, 67–85.

Watts, R. L., & Zimmermann, L. (1978). Toward a Positive Theory of the Determination of Accounting Standards. *The Accounting Review, 54*(1), 112–134.

Woodward, D., Edwards, P., & Birkin, F. (2001). Some evidence on executive's view of corporate social responsibility. *The British Accounting Review, 33*(3), 357–397. doi:10.1006/bare.2001.0165

Yin, R. K. (2009). Case Study Research. In Design and Methods. SAGE.

ENDNOTE

1 This chapter was prepared jointly by the two authors. However, it is possible to assign sections "Introduction", "Accountability and Social Report: some literature contribution" and "Research question and methodology" to Fabio De Matteis, and sections "The Social Report of COOP Lombardia", "Discussion" and "Conclusion" to Daniela Preite.

Chapter 8
Social Accounting in the Social Economy:
A Case Study of Monetizing Social Value

Larraitz Lazcano
University of the Basque Country (UPV/EHU), Spain

Leire San-Jose
University of the Basque Country (UPV/EHU), Spain & University of Huddersfield, UK

Jose Luis Retolaza
University of Deusto, Spain

ABSTRACT

This chapter was based on one of the largest Spanish cooperative groups, which is part of the social economy sector (SES). Added value is a useful concept; however, after analyzing this case, the authors found that social accounting provides additional information about the social value that companies generate. Then, by applying social accounting complemented by a value-added statement, these companies belonging to the SES can quantify, monetize, and compare their social value and added value, and demonstrate their contribution to society. Social accounting is necessary to demonstrate and understand the value of social economy companies, since their value is not always fundamentally centered on commercial activity; at least not only. They can monitor their effort in terms of specific social values that are not part of the market. Because of this, their value is not reflected in traditional financial statements.

INTRODUCTION

Social value and social impact are becoming increasingly important in business because the social value explains their contribution to the society in a holistic way. As a whole, society is becoming more concerned about social issues, developing a new social consciousness about the role of companies and their social legitimacy. Companies are in the spotlight: they are expected to generate not only economic value but also social value. Although hundreds of years of development and study have created a good

DOI: 10.4018/978-1-5225-8482-7.ch008

accounting system that provides good information and understanding of the economic-financial situation of an organization, this system cannot reflect in monetary units the social value generated by organizations. However, another powerful line of research exists in both the sociological (Hopwood & Miller, 1994; Miller, 2001) and economic (Gray et al., 1997; Gray, 2002) literature. Both lines of research have practical applicability in a social accounting model with some relatively similar principles as the economic-financial accounting model (Retolaza et al., 2015; 2016). The goal of this study was to determine the differences between the application of traditional accounting and this social-accounting model, which is based on economic-financial principles and using monetary units, when applied to the Social Economy Sector (SES).

BACKGROUND

From a classical perspective, several accounting paradigms exist (Belkaoui, 2004). In terms of selecting the social value analysis model, highlight that social accounting is based on the economy-information and the utility-decision paradigms. Beyond these characteristics, the connection of social accounting with stakeholder theory (Freeman, 1984) allows us to expand the scope of usefulness of social value measurement from the framework of agency theory (Jensen and Meckling, 1976) to a framework of fiduciary responsibility for stakeholders, where all stakeholders in the organization are interested in identifying the value that they perceive (Boatright, 2008). Social accounting is a new method capable of visualizing the value generated by companies and organizations in society. Social accounting is relevant for both type of companies: for those companies oriented toward social entrepreneurship, and for social economy (Yunus et al., 2010; Velamuri et al., 2015). Social accounting is a tool that can be used to address the Jensen paradox in the governance problem (Jensen, 2002) because social accounting could be the instrument for managing organizations that are oriented toward multiple stakeholders (Freeman et al., 2010).

With social accounting (Gray, 2002; Retolaza et al., 2016), it is possible to identify and quantify the distribution of value between the various stakeholders of an organization. Thus, the entities with an explicit social purpose may benefit from this type of accounting because it can be used to visualize the value of the non-market, which is ignored in the accounting techniques exclusively dedicated to market transactions. The aim of this study was to compare social accounting, which incorporates specific social value for stakeholders, with accounting based on economic and financial data using a group of social companies. A broad comparison between commercial and social companies, using the gap between economic and financial information and social accounting as an instrument, would be beneficial; however, this would require a significant number of companies of both types to implement social accounting. Although this may be feasible in the short-term, the data currently available (Retolaza & San-Jose, 2018) do not allow for the comparison.

Many entities in the Clade group, which refers to the social economy in Catalonia (Spain), are implementing social accounting, following the polyhedral model proposed by Retolaza et al. (2016). So, with these companies, it was possible to analyse the data produced by applying social accounting in Clade to identify whether the use of this model provides any different information in comparison with traditional accounting. This comparison would allow a differential analysis of the decision process to increase the created social value.

We did not attempt to test the accuracy of the social accounting, which has already been done (Retolaza et al., 2018). Our focus was on Clade determining if this accounting represents a different opportunity to show the effort focused not only on financial performance for companies with a social purpose, through a case study on the group of companies belonging to Clade that have implemented social accounting. Our hypothesis was that additional value would be generated by social accounting for this type of entity to the extent that social accounting provides new information in relation to traditional accounting. If so, then such entities should incorporate social accounting into their analyses and accountability practices.

Notably, social accounting does not replace other types of qualitative report generated by organizations, but is rather a complement that would lead to a common language, monetary and efficiency ratios, and a set of scattered indicators. As financial accounting requires complementary reports of a qualitative nature, social information that does not address both aspects would be unsuitable (Gray et al., 1997).

The polyhedral model proposed by Retolaza et al. (2015) considers two types of value (in the last proposal, the Emotional Value is included [see Retolaza and San-Jose, 2018] to understand more about Social & Emotional Accounting) market and non-market value. The polyhedral model takes the group of stakeholders of an organization as receivers of that value. This generates a multidimensional perspective of the value generated by the organizations and facilitates the understanding of the shared value (San-Jose et al, 2017).

The perspective management focus is translated from shareholders view to stakeholders, and it implies substituting the value-added statement (VAS), with the aim of understanding the value generated and distributed by a company. However, this perspective change can occur starting from traditional accounting, as shown by the contribution of AECA (Spanish Association of Accounting and Business Management) (Gonzalo & Pérez, 2017). Therefore, it is crucial to understand whether the incorporation of non-market value, not collected in the VAS, and the extension of perspective from the classical stakeholders to others interested groups such as users, clients, suppliers, or volunteers, are significantly different from the image presented by the VAS.

The rest of this paper is organized as follows. In the next section, we first review the theoretical phases and published literature of social accounting. Subsequently, social value is theorized, and then our methodology is explained. Next, we provide an empirical calculation produced by applying the methodology to a sample group of Spanish social enterprises. Finally, the results are provided with our conclusions, review of the study limitations, and recommendations for future research lines.

LITERATURE REVIEW

Although the demand to understand the value that the different organizations contribute or detract from society has increased after the global financial crisis in 2008, social accounting had already been in existence for more than 40 years. The first proposals can be traced back to the 1970s, when the goal of social accounting was to expand the factors considered in accounting, and to relate the financial statements to the stakeholders (Brandson, 2016, Estes, 1976, Linowes, 1968, 1973). Linowes (1968) coined the term "socio-economic accounting" to emphasize the sociological, political, and economic aspects that the classic accounting paradigm did not consider. The fundamental idea centered on social accounting superimposed on conventional financial accounting. As a consequence of this movement, in the 1980s, the French and Italian cooperatives developed the cooperative balance (Rihai-Belkaoui, 1984; Vaccari, 1997), which would later be incorporated by the large French companies and had some use in Spain, where BBVA (Spanish large bank) developed the method for several years. At present, this approach has been applied in the Social and Solidarity Economy Network..

In the later decades, the incorporation environmental information broadened (Bebbington, Gray, and Owen, 1992, Gray, Owen, and Adams, 1996, Mathews, 1997), materializing in the turn of the century in the triple bottom line (TBL; Elkington, 1997, 2001). In the first decade of the 21st century, the most widespread applications under the label of social accounting used qualitative data and descriptive statistics to assess the degree to which the organization fulfilled its mission and the expectations of its stakeholders (Sillanpää, 1998). However, the methodology continued to be a complement to financial statements in a different language from the financial verbiage, and far removed from basic accounting principles. An example of this type of methodology is the Global Reporting Initiative (GRI), which has experienced wide adoption in large companies.

In the early 1980s, the first systematization of Social Balance methodologies was highlighted; it was subsequently expanded to the environmental arena (TBL), in the 1990s. Its systematization within accountability occurred in the 2000s. The current closest approximation to the accounting field (socio-environmental), is that it is more in line with financial accounting, because of used principles and monetizing purpose.

In this study, we labeled different periods with specific names for ease of reference (Table 1). INTRO refers to the time when accounting was based only on the past and present but not on the future, disclosing little information, and the fundamental measuring system was cost-benefit analysis. INTRO acts as a reference period against which the results of social accounting in a company can be compared. The second period, START, refers to the period influenced by the social responsibility concept. During this period, companies knew it was important to show to society the responsibilities of the organizations after an analytical analysis. The social contract argument was the key to establishing a different view to show that organizations are more socially and environmentally responsible. To achieve this goal, for example, some regulations such as Environmental Protection Act 1990 (UK) were developed. In the next period, DEVELOP, the environmental issues gained relevance, auditing was included, and the voluntary criteria for incorporating this accounting were accepted.

The most important period for the social arena was the next period, labeled IMPACT, during which stakeholder engagement was the main goal. In this period, efforts were made using action research and case experiment is to show that social accounting is possible and useful. The last period, RELEVANCY, some of the social accounting issues from the previous periods were resolved. Not only social reporting, but social accounting was accepted; the difference between environment and social was clear; and neutrality, objectivity, and verifiability were necessary for social accounting. Some of the most important regulations were developed voluntarily but positively in different countries. For example, the Social Value Act in the U.K., the Norsk Hydro in Norway, and Environmental Profit and Loss in France. Table 1 provides a more complex review of the main issues in each period of social (and environmental) accounting.

Social accounting, since its origins in the 1970s, has evolved non-linearly. We are now possibly in a phase of new interest, and social accounting shows more promise, which requires more research about social accounting (Gray, 2002).

Table 1. Social accounting throughout history

SOCIAL (AND ENVIRONMENTAL) ACCOUNTING			
PERIOD	**UNDERSTANDING**	**FINDINGS / CONTRIBUTIONS**	**REGULATION**
1971-1980 **INTRO** *(Descriptive)*	• Descriptive view • Voluntary • Tentative • Frequently unreliable Unorganized • Social cost Analysis • Show inputs and outputs	✓ Few information (less than half page) ✓ Focus on social ✓ Focus on employees and products ✓ Past and Present no Future analysis ✓ Social externalities but no explain how measure them	The Corporate Report (Accounting Standards Steering Committee, 1975) UK Government Green Paper (HMSO, 1977),
1981-1990 **START** (Social Contract)	• Analytical improvement • Social effects are important • Focus on Interest groups (Stakeholders) • Responsibilities with stakeholders • Reduce subjectivity • Increase the replicability • Content Analysis	✓ Social Responsibility importance ✓ Social contract and organizational legitimacy to justify ✓ Economic (monetarized) vs. Accounting view (regularized-standardized)	The Comprehensive Environmental Response Compensation and Liability Act (CERCLA) Environmental Protection Act 1990 (UK) Union Europeene des Experts Comptables, Economiques et Financiers (UEC, 1983)
1991-2000 ***DEVELOP*** *(Environmental theories)*	• Sustainability interest • Voluntary disclosures • Show externalities • Public and Private organizations • Environmental Focus • Auditing is included	✓ Five-year period proposition i.e. ✓ Environmental accounting development (species survival) ✓ Underdeveloped subject ✓ Results are trivial and/or unreliable	Resource Management Act 1991 (New Zeland) Slow regulation in Europe
2000-2010 ***IMPACT*** *(Stakeholder engagement)*	• Include broader stakeholder • Engagement • Case-based experimentation • Action research • Measurement and reporting design • Policy development	✓ Reporting initiatives: Global Reporting Initiative and the International / Integrated Reporting Committee ✓ Social Change	** North American accounting journals which tend to ignore such research.
2010- ***RELEVAN-CY*** *(Sustainability)*	• Reporting vs. Accounting • Focus on stakeholders make informed decisions • Voluntary • Market-forced • Consolidation of Auditory • Risk-matrices • Neutrality • Objectivity • Verifiability	✓ Ontological perspective: distinction between environmental and social ✓ Sustainable development ✓ Accounting for Human Rights ✓ Green Accounting Development	Social Value Act (UK) Social Audit in the UK Norsk Hydro in Norway Kering (France) 'Environmental Profit and Loss' Climate Disclosure Standards Board role of the regulation

METHODOLOGICAL PROCESS AND SAMPLE

Methodology: Steps for Social Accounting

Social Value Integrated (SVI) is a novel indicator that integrates the economic and social results of an organization into a single measure of value. Just as there are financial indicators that serve to measure the economic performance of a company (for example, Earning Earnings Before Interest Taxes Depreciation and Amortization, Return on Equity, etc.), the SVI monetarily quantifies the social value generated by the commercial and social activities of an organization. The process of social accounting can be grouped into five steps.

A sixth phase exists, consisting of integrating the feedback obtained in the process in the following period, normally annually, with the aim of ensuring the social result in the organization is aligned with the purpose of the company. The process starts when the company's management decides to quantify the social value generated by the organization. Figure 1 outlines the process. The fundamental motivation to start the process is usually linked to reputation or communication, but once developed, the information becomes an important management resource. In this first phase, the work team and schedule are defined. When forming the work team, the company decides whether to address the process autonomously or if they will seek external support (a consulting company or a university). At least two people from the organization should participate: one from the social department and another from the financial area. This phase, called "Orientation", is finished when the work team and the schedule are approved.

Once the work team and schedule are validated, the map of the stakeholders of the organization is created. This map is not finished until consensus on the map is reached. A program for the elaboration of mental maps should be used (such as software called mindjet, freemind, novamind, etc.) to facilitate the process. Then, potential contacts must be identified in each stakeholders group; there must be at least one contact per group. This second phase is called the "Identification of Interest Groups", whose goal is to summarize and explain the stakeholder map.

Next, the dialogue with stakeholders begins. Normally, the interview is the technique, either in person, telephone, or video conference, or a questionnaire or survey could be used to obtain the information from many stakeholders in same group. A focus group could be used in the cases where the characteristics of the group are complex and hard to obtain. All these techniques are conducted to identify the valued variables. Once the interviews results have been collected, the explanations and references provided by the points of contact are managed and a set of value variables are identified. This next period is probably the most complex phase of the process, when variables must be reformulated into indicators that can be linked to measurable outputs, which, in turn, suggests that it is possible to determine proxies that enable the monetization of those outputs. This third phase is called "Identification of Value Variables", and visualized using a value variables matrix.

In the fourth phase, the outputs that correspond to the variable are identified, as well as the proxies that allow their quantification. Normally, there is no single proxy, but several. When choosing the most suitable proxy, the simplest method involves choosing the proxy that most resembles the generated output. The process is similar to the fair value applied in traditional accounting. All indicators and proxies are collected in a table. After identifying the calculation algorithm, a value is identified for the proxy and a total monetary value to each variable is calculated. This fourth phase is called "Identification and Monetization of Outcomes".

The fifth and last phase consists of the calculation and visualization of value. The economic benefit and social value are composed of three ecosystems: (1) the value generated by the company for the whole society, (2) the money that returns to the public authorities or administration, and (3) the specific social value generated for the different stakeholders. The integrated social value considers the global value generated and distributed among a set of stakeholders. Based on the monetary values determined, percentages or ratios are calculated to interpret the company's performance. An important ratio is the relationship between the public subsidies received and the value generated, thereby reflecting the return on each unit of currency contributed by the company. As the ratios are not absolute, they do provide much information if they cannot be compared. Two types of analyses can completed: comparing the annual evolution of the reference ratios and analyzing the existing balance in the distribution of value to the different stakeholders. Although organizations that approach social accounting usually do so from a reputational perspective, the monetization of social value allows introducing indicators into the management of the company that are at the same level as the financial indicators, being able to incorporate the social aspect into the core of the organization.

Table 2 outlines some of the most significant variables considered when calculating the generated social value and the socio-economic return that can be considered for public administration or government. It is the return to the public administrations or government which is the money that each company returns to the administration or government through either payments or savings

From another perspective, the socio-economic value generated by an organization is divided into four categories. (1) The first is direct value, generated through added value. The VAS emerged and was developed in the 1990s by the consulting firm Stern Stewart & Company in the search for an indicator that would visualize the creation of value for the shareholder and help internal management with decision-making and the establishment of compensation plans for managers. However, its origin dates

Table 2. Social accounting variables considered when calculating social value and socio-economic return

Social Accounting Ecosystems	Explanation of values	Variables to include
Economic value for government (EVG)	Payments to Government	VAT (Value Added Taxes) + Corporate tax + Other taxes
	Saving resources for the administration (assuming no service)	Reduction in expenses incurred by the administration if the entity does not exist/ceased to exist
	Management savings in outsourcing	Differential input/output relationship with the entity contracted in connection with the second highest bid
Socio-economic value (SEV)	Direct socio-economic value	Salaries Social Security for employees pay by company Income tax VAT Other taxes Investment Result
	Indirect socio-economic Value: Suppliers	Payment for suppliers in the Autonomy, State Turnover with Suppliers Personal Expenses Added value from operating results Corporate tax Reservations
	Indirect socio-economic value: Clients	Wage cost for the entity Turnover local customers Turnover with customers Induced Employment: personal expenses Value added Corporate tax
Specific social value (SSV)	Stakeholder map, dialogue with stakeholders (interviews), list of social variables, select objective proxies, establish monetized values	
Social value integrated (VASI)	Integration of all the detected social values, but without repetitions.	$\sum EVG + SEV + SSV - repetitions$

Source: adapted from Retolaza et al. (2016: p. 46) and Retolaza & San-Jose (2016: p. 172).

back to the key concept of "income or residual benefit" (Church, 1917). The VAS was developed with the intention of being a financial measure that would maximize the creation of wealth for shareholders, so the method did not consider the valuation of intangibles or other stakeholders; however, authors do defend its use for this purpose (Gonzalo and Perez, 2017). (2) Indirect (supplier) value is generated through the supplies purchased, where the total expenditure is not considered—only the added value according to the distribution: salaries, income tax, social security, taxes, profits, and added value not distributed that generated by suppliers. (3) Induced (customers) value is the value generated or transferred to customers. (4) Non-market value is generated and distributed without an explicit economic transaction, and therefore not included in the accounting.

To compare the results of traditional accounting, based on market transactions and the added-value, and the social value generated by an organization, the following social efficiency calculations and indexes have been established:

1. Social Value Returned to Government (SROI) from added-value shows the amount of generated added-value compared with the amount of social value generated for the government. A low percentage of taxes payment is expected, but taxes could be much higher depending on the type of activity. SROI is calculated as Economic Value for Government/Total Added Value Distributed.
2. Integrated Social Value (SVI) Set of social value generated and distributed, both through market and non-market.
3. Social efficiency index (SEI) is the SVI divided by the amount of business (sales invoices). (SVI/ Amount of Business or Turnover)
4. Social Plus Value Index (SPVI) is difference between social value and the amount of business (invoices) without considering the effect of income in the social value. SPVI is the social value generated by an entity in terms of market value apart from their turnover.(SVI–Amount of Business)/ Amount of Business or Turnover.
5. Social Equilibrium-Market Index (SEMI) is an index of equilibrium between the social and the commercial or market value. SEMI includes the social dimension of different organizations but the index is not monetized due to the non-market value of their activities. SEMI provides a value that it is not included in invoice and is calculated as SPVI/Integrated social value/Amount of Business or Turnover).

Case Analysis

The social economy, as defined by the International Co-operative Alliance (ICA in 1995):

is an autonomous association of persons united voluntarily to meet their common economic, social, and cultural needs and aspirations through a jointly-owned and democratically-controlled enterprise... is based on the values of self-help, self-responsibility, democracy, equality, equity, and solidarity. In the tradition of their founders, cooperative members believe in the ethical values of honesty, openness, social responsibility, and caring for others.

The principles of the social economy are: (1) voluntary and open membership; (2). democratic member control; (3). economic member participation; (4). autonomy and independence; (5). education, training, and information; (6). cooperation among cooperatives; and (7). concern for community. Apart from other considerations, the last three principles refer to the distribution of non-commercial value, or at least to the partners, the cooperative environment, and society in general. As such, social accounting could capture this complementary contribution to the value generated through the market, which is not adequately captured in regular financial accounting, since this contribution would be recorded as an expense.

In Spain, the eight largest business groups in the social economy employ more than 169,433 people: the Cajamar Cooperative Group, Atlantis Group, Espriu Foundation, Clade Group, Unide, Mondragón Corporation, Ilunion Group, and Gredos San Diego Group. The Clade Group is the first cooperative business group in Catalonia. Today, 12 companies form the Clade Group: 8 cooperatives, 2 foundations, 1 labor anonymous company, and 1 anonymous company. Each company is part of different sectors (education, culture, leisure, consumption, environment, music, service, etc.), but form a group of social enterprises sharing values and method of participation in the social economy framework. The group's main values are the participation of people in the company, social responsibility, and the desire to collaborate through inter-cooperation. In 2016, the Group included 5.866 people, 452 more than in 2015 (an increase of 8%). This represents 0.2% of the €2,741,500 people who compose the actively employed population in Catalonia (IDESCAT, 2016: www.idescat.cat). Of the 5.866 workers, 1.662 are working partners (the 28.8%). The group's income was €316,466,000 in 2016. This represents 0.15% of Catalonia's gross domestic product (GDP). Table 3 lists the different companies belonging to the Clade Group and their characteristics.

RESULTS

The monetization of social value is logical in this cooperative group since all the companies in the Group belong to the SES. Therefore, the social value generated and distributed among stakeholders is considerable. We hypothesized that there should be a large gap between the economic value generated by these companies in terms of profitability, and the social value returned to society, since the principles of the companies in this sector consider economic profitability as an instrument to reach their goal, which is people and their wellness. However, the goal or final objective is people and not profitability. When discussing people, the analysis is not only focused on workers, but all those who interact with the organization, including the stakeholders.

After applying social accounting to a sample of 5 of the 12 companies in the Clade Group, we determined the social value generated by each company and the average value generated by the five, which were Abacus, Blanquerna, Lavola, Sant Gervasi, and Suara. Various types of value are generated by organizations, the most obvious of which is the value generated through market activity. Through their activity, companies and other organizations generate jobs and consequently salaries. These salaries create contributions to social security or private pension plans, to the payment of personal taxes, and to a large proportion of purchasing power. The payment of salaries also generates taxes on profits and other types. Likewise, organizations stimulate business activity through the purchases of suppliers, in what could be considered a generation of induced social value through market transactions. This social market value is attributable to any type of organization, whether non-governmental organizations (NGOs) or public entities, but the value can also be generated by commercial companies of all kinds.

The main factor through which companies generate value is the employment factor (Table 4). The people in the company receive a return for the effort made for the generation of value. These five com-

Table 3. Clade Group companies

Company	Year of Constitution	Type	Sector	Partners	People attended	Work places	Income
Abacus Cooperativa	1968	Consumer cooperative	Education, culture, leisure	855,254 consumer partner,493 worker partners			€89,674,145
Comunidad Minera Olesana	1868	Water supply cooperative	Environment	10,274		10	
Cooperativa Plana De Vic	1966	Agrarian cooperative	Agriculture				
Corma	1981	Agrarian cooperative	Ornamental plants			210	
Escola San Gervasi	1970	Associated work cooperative	Education		2800 students		
Fundació Blanquerna	1948	University Foundation	Education		7230 students		
Som	2003	Cooperative Group	Communication and culture				
Lavola	1981	public limited company	Sustainability services	14			7.000.000 €
Suara Cooperativa	2008	Social initiative cooperative	Service	1074	40,344	3284	75.967.541 €
La Orquestra Simfònica Del Vallès	1987	Orquestra. Limited Annonymous Society	Culture and music		150 performance per season	53	7.000.000 €
Lafageda	1983	Working cooperative	Dairy products				
Grup Qualitat	1989	Foundation	Real estate promotion				

panies generated a distribution to the work factor of 55 to 62.9% with a mean of 61.53%. The capital factor in these social companies is the lowest of all key factors through which the companies can generate added value. This is probably due to the reduction in the dependency on financiers and their no-risk policy. Government is the second factor through which these companies generate value. The distribution to the government ranges from €24.2 to €32.9, with a differential of 8.7 points. This contribution to the government and society does not depend on the type of the company; the smallest and largest companies contribute similarly to the government and all the industries (from a library to a consultancy company) return a similar percentage of the added-value to the government.

There are at least two different perspectives of analysis of these results. First, from the most restrictive perspective of social value from traditional accounting, the social value of the funds generated for public administration or government it could be measured by the return of funds to the government. Second, from a broader perspective, social value with added value results is considered (see Appendix 1). In the first case, the generated value would range from 24.2% to 32.9% of the added value, and from 5.4% to 30.5% of the amount of business or turnover. This shows that there is no clear results. The means of these

Table 4. Value Added Statement of-Clade companies that use social accounting

Clade Company	**Abacus**		**Blanquerna**		**Lavola**	
VAS 2016	**Total (€)**	**%**	**Total**	**%**	**Total**	**%**
Distribution to the Work Factor	10,744,139	55..00%	21,137,742	62.78%	2,815,296	60.62%
Distribution to the Capital Factor	761,213	3.20%	167,232	0.50%	14,652	0.32%
Distribution to the Government	4,852,351	24.48%	10,670,076	31.69%	1,529,393	32.93%
Retained by the Company	3,594,261	17.32%	1,691,922	5.03%	284,640	6.13%
Total added value distributed	19,951,964	100.00%	33,666,972	100%	4,643,981	100%
Amount of business	*89,050,078*		*42,025,659*		*6,910,081*	
% Added value/ amount of business	5.4%		25.4%		22.1%	
Clade Company	**Sant Gervasi**		**Suara**		**TOTAL**	
VAS 2016	Total	%	Total	%	Total (€)	%
Distribution to the Work Factor	4,206,245	64.41%	42,962,476	62.9%	81,865,899	61.53%
Distribution to the Capital Factor	205,989	3.15%	138,635	0.2%	1,287,721	0.97%
Distribution to the Government	1,581,687	24.22%	22,061,862	32.3%	40,695,368	30.59%
Retained by the Company	536,035	8.21%	3,090,366	4.5%	9,197,224	6.91%
Total added value distributed	6,529,956	100%	68,253,340	100%	133,046,213	100%
Amount of business	*8,660,670*		*72,367,624*		*219,014,112*	
% Added value/ amount of business	18.3%		30.5%		18.6%	

two factors are 30.6% for the added-value, and 18.6% for the amount of business or turnover. The added value of a book company is different (less) than the added value generated by a service company. This relative added-value calculation shows the importance of the company in terms of generation of added value. Although the information obtained from this analysis is interesting and could help to establish the contribution of each company to the GDP and to the public treasury, it does not provide any additional information about the value generated through non-market mechanisms. This is important because the social value is more global.

In terms of social accounting, Table 5 briefly and theoretically explains the economic value generated for the government, the socio-economic value, the specific social value, and the integrated social value. Retolaza et al., 2016 provided a more exhaustive explanation of economic value and the applicability of these factors. Table 5 shows the social value generated by the different Clade Group companies. First, we provide the financial result, which is the economic result of each company determined using the traditional accounting. This value does not provide the social value generated. Next, we examined the return to the public administrations or government, which is the money that each company returns to the administration, through either payments or savings. To obtain the result, we added what the company contributes to the administration, the social security contribution of the company plus the social security contribution of the worker, income tax, other taxes, and the value added tax. The same was performed to calculate the amount the suppliers and companies invested that has been returned to the administration. The government received from €3 million to 24 million from each social economy company, depending on its size, industry, activity, and employees.

Socio-economic value is the value generated for the whole of society by each company through their economic activity. To obtain this result, we included the added value of the company, the added value of the suppliers, and the induced value of the companies with which the entity was involved. The monetary socio-economic values were the highest compared with other figures. The main reason for this is that the companies have market value, they generate social actions with their activity, and a large amount of their activity involves participation in the market, which means that transactions occur and those transactions are captured with traditional accounting. Then, the first result is that traditional accounting is a useful system in which the main key factors are included. However, as shown by the specific social value, non-market values and non-transactional activities exist but are not included in traditional financial accounting, not because they are not performed but because they do not directly involve money or cash.

The specific social value provided to the different stakeholders is the value of the non-market that each organization contributes to all the interest groups related to the company. To obtain these data, some valuable variables value were identified by the primary information collected by the representatives of each interest group. After the experts (academics with the approbation of all the team) provide a reference value (a proxy), the generated social value was monetized. The specific social value is specific for each company because it depends on the stakeholders, the dialogue, detected variables, and the monetization of the social values. The social value ranges widely amongst these five companies from 742,011€ to 87,786,138€,

The gross integrated social value is the sum of the economic social value and the specific social value. This value considers the joint value generated, which is the amount (represented with a currency) that can be used to show the social accounting of a company. For Table 6, we calculated some ratios to provide a comparison between added-value statement results and social accounting.

The social accounting data provides more information because it integrates indirect and induced funds. The ratio of contribution to government in relation to added value increases significantly from 36% to 117%. The ratio obtained by dividing the integrated social value (SVI) by the amount of business

Table 5. Social value of Clade companies that have incorporated social accounting (table in €)

Clade Company	Abacus	Blanquerna	Lavola	Sant Gervasi	Suara	Total
Results (Traditional Accounting)	566,309	1,018,652	229,598	257,637	2,138,192	4,210,388
Economic Value for Government	20,118,332	14,911,163	5,426,576	3,298,056	24,551,401	68,305,528
Socio-Economic Value	137,691,884	36,474,580	14,223,478	8,657,659	72,228,855	269,276,456
Specific Social Value	7,929,347	74,096,427	742,011	14,362,487	87,786,138	184,916,410
Integrated Social Value (Gross) SVI	144,214,740	107,630,158	14,770,667	22,937,146	158,096,531	447,649,242

Table 6. Comparison of added value and social accounting

Social Accounting Ecosystems	Clade Company					
	Abacus	Blanquerna	Lavola	Sant Gervasi	Suara	Total
Social Value Returned to Government from added-value	101%	44%	117%	51%	36%	51%
Level between Social Value Integrated (SVI) and Distributed Added-Value	722,8%	319,7%	318,1%	351,3%	231,6%	336,5%
Level between Social Value Integrated (SVI) and Amount of Business (invoices).	161,9%	256,1%	213,8%	264,8%	218,5%	204,4%
Social Plus Value Index (SPVI)	0,62	1,56	1,14	1,65	1,18	1,04
Social Equilibrium-Market Index (SEMI)	38,3%	61,0%	53,2%	62,2%	54,2%	51,1%

(billing) averaged of 204.4%, with scores ranging from 161.9% to 264.8%. This ratio has already been integrated in the added-value efficiency. If we considered the added value provided to the stakeholders in the analysis of the social value integrated (SVI), we could subtract the amount of the gross income from these percentages, obtaining the ratio called the Social Plus Value Index (SPVI). This index calculates the extra value generated by the organizations beyond what corresponds to the income received for this purpose. For these five companies, SPVI ranges between 0.62 and 1.65, with an average of 1.04.

Regardless of whether this indicator reflects a broader concept of value than traditional accounting indicators, social accounting provides a value that is, on average, 43.6 points higher. The information obtained is not directly related to the information obtained from VAS, thus refuting the null hypothesis that both types of information, although different in their amounts, would have some kind of proportionality. If so, we suggest that the information provided by social accounting provides more or different information compared to traditional economic accounting, contributing to the transparency of social value generated by the company that is not monetized in the market.

Based on the obtained data, a new index was created that would determine the part of the social value generated through commercial activity and through non-market actions. This index, called Social Equilibrium-Market Index (SEMI), identifies the social contributions of the organizations. The average for the sample companies was 51.1%, ranging from 38.3% to 62.2%. SEMI indicates that, in some companies, less than 50% of the generated value through market activity, and the rest occurred through complementary actions. This finding aligns with the double commercial and social dimension of Clade companies. We suppose that the ratio for mercantile companies would be significantly lower, and that of NGOs possibly higher, but further investigation is needed to confirm this hypothesis.

The results show that social accounting provides additional information, different from that of economic-financial accounting, without identifying any direct correlation between social accounting and VAS data provided from traditional accounting. Social accounting provides more complete information about the value generated by a company.

CONCLUSION

Based on the obtained results, no feedback exists between market value and non-market value, so social accounting provides different information, which can be extracted from traditional accounting. The problem of duplication of information is eliminated. Secondly, the variation between the results obtained only from market data and the integral social value does not affect all organizations equally. This means two things: the integral social value cannot be estimated using an algorithm linked only to traditional accounting data, and social accounting allows companies and organizations that generate value through non-market transactions to demonstrate their higher societal value.

Since the social economy has the purpose of generating social value in the non-market, social accounting enables the visualization of that value. The SPVI is a good tool to reflect this value. However, the identified increase in value is not homogeneous for all entities in the social economy, but instead depends on the extent to which they use or do not use market transactions as the main element for value distribution. Although social accounting is not a different accounting system for mercantile entities, social accounting allows these companies to demonstrate their value from the social perspective, as well as the commercial activity they have already developed. As such, social accounting allows dialogue for all types of companies and organizations, although social accounting particularly favours organizations that distribute their value through non-market mechanisms, such as the social economy, the third sector, or public entities.

SPVI is an appropriate instrument to capture the social value that organizations generate outside the market. As a working hypothesis, in general, social enterprises will have a higher index of social value added than commercial companies. Then, the social equilibrium index and SEMI can be used to discern the degree to which organizations distribute value through the market. In this sense, the utility of social accounting does not depend so much on the entities participating in the social economy, but on how to distribute the value. However, the social economy in general distributes a greater share of value through the non-market than the mercantile economy. A hypothesis could be the correlation of the out-of-market value distribution ratio with the SPVI. Both indices, SPVI and SEMI, and social accounting, in general, enable analyses of the market value and non-market value with similar criteria, so social accounting could serve to facilitate the understanding of the social value generated by all types of organizations, which was the aspiration of social accounting since its inception almost 50 years ago.

Finally, although most organizations approach social accounting from the perspective of communication, the generation of data naturally leads to data integration into the strategy and management of organizations. Then, social accounting data will be translated from the calculation of the social value of organizations to the optimization of the value.

The fundamental limitations our work due to the sample. Although our sample is representative within the framework of the social economy, it is small and localized, so this work is only exploratory in nature and cannot be extended to other areas or countries. Social accounting still needs to be standardized and dimensioned, so companies may apply social accounting in different ways, which obviously limits the interpretation and generalization of the data.

With regard to the lines of research, the analysis could be extended to a broader sample, and the hypothesis that are proposed in these conclusions could be explored: (1) the possibility of understanding the social value generated by social entities, commercial companies, and the public; (2) generalization of the index of social value added to understand the social value distributed externally to the market; (3) confirm the correlation between SEMI and SPVI; an (4) confirm the transition from communication to strategy among entities that adopt social accounting. It is possible to analyse the real interest that the various stakeholders have for this information to analyse the extent to which the information could facilitate their empowerment in their relationship with the entity, perhaps by guiding processes of governance with multiple stakeholders, or expanding social accounting to the emotional values.

REFERENCES

Bebbington, J., Gray, R., & Owen, D. (1999). Seeing the wood for the trees: Taking the pulse of social and environmental accounting. *Accounting, Auditing & Accountability Journal*, *12*(1), 47–52. doi:10.1108/09513579910259906

Belkaoui, A. (2004). *Accounting Theory.* Boston: Cengage Learning, EMEA.

Boatright, J. (2008). *Ethics in Finance.* Malden, MA: Blackwell. (Original work published 1999) doi:10.4135/9781412956260.n341

Branson, D. M. (2016). Corporate Behaviour and Sustainability. Doing Weel by Being Good. In A. Guler & C. Ingley (Eds.), *A parthway to corporate sustainability social accounting* (p. 138). London: Routledge.

Casadesus-Masanell, R., & Heilbron, J. (2015). The business model: Nature and benefits. In C. Baden-Fuller & V. Mangematin (Eds.), *Business models and modelling* (pp. 3–30). Emerald Group Publishing Limited. doi:10.1108/S0742-332220150000033002

Church, A. H. (1917). *Manufacturing costs and Accounts* (Vol. 4). New York: McGraw-Hill book Company.

Dumay, J., Guthrie, J., & Farneti, F. (2010). GRI sustainability reporting guidelines for public and third sector organizations: A critical review. *Public Management Review*, *12*(4), 531–548. doi:10.1080/14719037.2010.496266

Elkington, J. (1997). *Cannibals with forks. The triple bottom line of 21st century*. Oxford, UK: Capstone Publishing.

Elkington, J. (2001). The "Triple bottom line of 21st century business". In R. Starkey & R. Welford (Eds.), *The Earthscan reader in business & sustainable development* (pp. 20–43). London: Earthscan.

Estes, R. (1976). *Corporate and social accounting*. New York: Wiley.

Freeman, R. E. (1984). *Strategic Management: A Stakeholder Approach.* Boston: Pitman.

Freeman, R. E., Harrison, J. S., Wicks, A. C., Palmar, B. L., & Colle, D. E. S. (2010) Stakeholder Theory: The State of the Art. Cambridge, UK: Cambridge University Press.

Gonzalo, J. A., & Pérez, J. (2017). Una propuesta de normalización relativa al valor añadido como medida alternativa de rendimiento empresarial. *Especial XIX Congreso Internacional AECA*, 35-39.

Gray, R. (2002). The social accounting project and Accounting Organizations and Society Privileging engagement, imaginings, new accountings and pragmatism over critique? *Accounting, Organizations and Society*, *27*(7), 687–708. doi:10.1016/S0361-3682(00)00003-9

Gray, R., Dey, C., Owen, D., Evans, R., & Zadek, S. (1997). Struggling with the praxis of social accounting: Stakeholders, accountability, audits and procedures. *Accounting, Auditing & Accountability Journal*, *10*(3), 325–364. doi:10.1108/09513579710178106

Groth, J. C., Byers, S. S., & Bogert, J. C. (1996). Capital, economic returns and the creation of value. *Management Decision*, *24*(6), 21–20. doi:10.1108/00251749610121452

Hawkins, J. P., Roberts, C. M., Kooistra, D., Buchan, K., & White, S. (2005). Sustainability of scuba diving tourism on coral reefs of Saba. *Coastal Management*, *33*(4), 373–387. doi:10.1080/08920750500217518

Hopwood, A. G., & Miller, P. (Eds.). (1994). *Accounting as social and institutional practice* (Vol. 24). Cambridge, UK: Cambridge University Press.

Jensen, M. C. (2002). Value maximization, stakeholder theory, and the corporate objective function. *Business Ethics Quarterly*, *12*(2), 235–256. doi:10.2307/3857812

Jensen, M. C., & Meckling, W. H. (1976). Theory of the firm: Managerial behavior, agency costs and ownership structure. *Journal of Financial Economics*, *3*(4), 305–360. doi:10.1016/0304-405X(76)90026-X

Linowes, D. F. (1968). Socio-economic accounting. *Journal of Accountancy*, *126*(5), 37–42.

Linowes, D. F. (1973). The accounting profession and social progress. *Journal of Accountancy*, *136*(1), 32–40.

Mathews, M. R. (1995). Social and environmental accounting: A practical demonstration of ethical concern? *Journal of Business Ethics*, *14*(8), 663–671. doi:10.1007/BF00871347

Miller, P. (2001). Governing by numbers: Why calculative practices matter. *Social Research*, *62*(2), 379–396.

Retolaza, J. L., & San-Jose, L. (2016). Prevención y detección del fraude en la empresa. *Revista Contabilidad y Dirección*, *23*(1), 159–178.

Retolaza, J. L., & San-Jose, L. (2018). Contabilidad social para el bien común. *Revista de Responsabilidad Social de la Empresa*, *29*, 95–122.

Retolaza, J. L., San-Jose, L., & Ruiz-Roqueñi, M. (2015). Monetarizing the social value: Theory and evidence. *Revista de Economía Pública, social y cooperative. C.I.R.I.E.C. España*, *83*(1), 43–62.

Retolaza, J. L., San-Jose, L., & Ruíz-Roqueñi, M. (2016). *Social accounting for sustainability: Monetizing the social value*. Cham: Springer. doi:10.1007/978-3-319-13377-5

Retolaza, J.L., San-Jose, L., Ruiz-Roqueñi, M., Barrutia, J., & Bernal, R. (2013). *Metodología para la cuantificación del valor social generado por una organización. El caso de Lantegi Batuak*. Bilbao: Universidad del País Vasco e Instituto de Economía Aplicada a la Empresa.

Riahi-Belkaoui, A. (1984). *Socio- Economic Accounting*. London: Praeger Pub Text.

San-Jose, L., & Retolaza, J. L. (2015). *La generación de Valor Social como eje vertebrador de la Unión Europea*. Vitoria: Francisco de Landaburu Eurobask.

San-Jose, L., & Retolaza, J. L. (2016). *Contabilidad Social orientada a los stakeholders. Perspectiva de la Administración Pública*. Madrid: Pirámide.

San-Jose, L., Retolaza, J. L., & Freeman, R. E. (2017). Stakeholder Engagement at Extanobe: A Case Study of the New Story of Business. In R. E. Freeman, J. Kujala, & S. Sachs (Eds.), *Stakeholder Engagement: Clinical Research Cases* (pp. 285–310). Cham: Springer. doi:10.1007/978-3-319-62785-4_13

Sillanpää, M. (1998). The Body Shop values report-towards integrated stakeholder auditing. *Journal of Business Ethics, 17*(13), 1443–1456. doi:10.1023/A:1006099731105

Sitton, J. F. (2010). *Marx today. A Contribution to the Critique of Political Economy*. New York: Palgrave Macmillan.

Tapsuwan, S., & Asafu-Adjaye, J. (2008). Estimating the economic benefit of SCUBA diving in the Similan Islands, Thailand. *Coastal Management, 36*(5), 431–442. doi:10.1080/08920750802412908

Vaccari, A. (2013). Constructing the social balance: Consumer cooperative, Italy. In S. Zadek, P. Pruzan, & R. Evans (Eds.), *Building Corporate Accountability: Emerging Practice in Social and Ethical Accounting and Auditing* (pp. 171–189). London: Routledge.

Velamuri, S. R., Priya, A., & Vasantha, K. (2015). *Doing Well to Do Good: Business Model Innovation for Social Healthcare Business Models and Modelling* (Vol. 33, pp. 279–308). London: Emerald Group Publishing Limited.

Wongthong, P. (2013). *An integrated approach to sustainable management of reef-based SCUBA dive tourism: a case study of Koh Tao, Thailand* (Doctoral dissertation). Retrieved May 1, 2018 from https://hekyll.services.adelaide.edu.au

Yunus, M., Moingeon, B., & Lehmann-Ortega, L. (2010). Building Social Business Models: Lessons from the Grameen Experience. *Long Range Planning, 43*(2/3), 308–325. doi:10.1016/j.lrp.2009.12.005

Zhang, X., Song, H., & Huang, G. Q. (2009). Tourism supply chain management: A new research agenda. *Tourism Management, 30*(3), 345–358. doi:10.1016/j.tourman.2008.12.010

Zott, C., Amit, R., & Massa, L. (2011). The business model: Recent developments and future research. *Journal of Management, 37*(4), 1019–1042. doi:10.1177/0149206311406265

KEY TERMS AND DEFINITIONS

Market Social Value: It is the value that an organization generates or distributes to the whole of the company through its business activity. It basically consists of the net salaries, social security contributions, personal taxes, corporate taxes and taxes, and VAT. It is reflected in the accounting of the company.

Monetization of Social Value: It is the process that estimated in monetary units the utility of the whole social assets (those that provides well-being or discomfort to some group of members of society) generated by an organization.

Non-Market Social Value: It is the social value distributed outside the market, and therefore free of Price, or at least with a price that does not respond to the market. It is the value that an organization distributes to some of its stakeholders but in the absence of a monetary transaction, it is not reflected in the financial statements. Usually this value is only collected (when done), qualitatively. The main contribution of Social Accounting is to incorporate this value (hidden) to the social value integrated.

Social Accounting: It is a systematic process that provides information about the creation or destruction of social value to stakeholders, using accounting principles and monetary units. It is complementary to financial statements and it collects and shows non-financial information based on social aspects.

Social Equilibrium-Market Index (SEMI): It is an index of equilibrium between the social and the commercial or market value. SEMI includes the social dimension of different organizations, but the index is not monetized due to the non-market value of their activities. SEMI provides a value that it is not included in invoice and is calculated as SPVI/Integrated Social Value/Amount of Business or Turnover.

Social Plus Value Index (SPVI): It is difference between social value and the amount of business (invoices) without considering the effect of income in the social value. SPVI is the social value generated by an entity in terms of market value apart from their turnover. (SVI –Amount of Business)/Amount of Business or Turnover.

Social Value: Utility provided by the set of social assets generated by an organization for the stakeholders or interest groups related to the organization.

Social Value Integrated (SVI): Set of social value generated and distributed, both through market and non-market.

Socio-Emotional Value: It is the result of multiplying the Integrated Social Value (SVI), by the emotional corrector index (ratio). It reflects the total market value, non-market and emotional that an organization generates for the Company. It corresponds to the sum of the integrated social value and the emotional value.

APPENDIX

Table 7. Value-added Statement based on AECA

VALU ADDED STATEMENT (VAS)
Works factor distribution
Wages, salaries and assimilated
Provisions for employee compensation
Distribution to the capital factor
Own capital
Dividends
Foreign capital
Financial expenses
Distribution to the Government
Public Treasury
Taxes
Social charges
PIT(Personal Income Tax)
Taxes on profits
Retained by the Company
-Amortization of fixed assets
-Deterioration of merchandise, raw materials and other supplies
-Losses, impairment and variation of provisions for commercial operations
+Excesses of provisions
-Deteriorations of fixed assets
-Impairment of financial instruments
Applied to Reservations
TOTAL ADDED VALUE DISTRIBUTED

Chapter 9
Reporting Value Using Social Return on Investment Reports:
An Overview and Analysis of Reports in Practice

Sanja Korać
Alpen-Adria-Universitaet Klagenfurt, Austria

Anna Oppelmayer
Alpen-Adria-Universitaet Klagenfurt, Austria

ABSTRACT

This chapter provides an assessment of social return on investment (SROI) as an instrument of reporting the value that (non-profit) organizations in the social economy have created. After a general overview and comparison of two most widely referred SROI guidelines, a selection of SROI reports in practice is analyzed based on criteria of popular reporting. Popular reporting has emerged in the accounting discipline as a way of establishing an easy to understand, short enough to maintain attention document to different user groups (e.g., clients, citizens, decision makers). This new approach lending from the basic ideas of popular reporting allows researchers and practitioners alike to gain new insights into the current design as well as the potential of SROI reports as a key instrument of accountability for (non-profit) organizations in the social economy.

INTRODUCTION

Giving account of how (financial) resources are used to create value has been a long-standing issue in organizations across different sectors. Over time, performance measurement trends in the business sector have driven similar approaches in organizations in the non-profit sector and the social economy. Tools like benchmarking and the balanced scorecard have been adopted widely (Kaplan & Norton 1992; Keehley & Abercrombie 2008), but also more specific models, e.g. the multidimensional, integrated model of non-profit organizational effectiveness (MIMNOE) (Sowa, Selden, & Sandfort, 2004) or the public

DOI: 10.4018/978-1-5225-8482-7.ch009

value scorecard (Moore, 2003), have been developed to fit the needs of organizations that have a social mission and where performance is therefore not easy to measure. Many of these tools have focused on providing more clarity to the organization itself, e.g. in terms of the support that the organization relies on, about its organizational capacity, etc. However, facing increasing legitimation pressure and orientation towards efficiency and effectiveness (see Gray, Dillard, & Spence, 2010), organizations have put a higher emphasis on accounting for and reporting the performance and the value that is achieved to the broad spectrum of their stakeholders. While non-profit organizations have a long experience in reporting their social impact to stakeholders and the public at large, the orientation towards assigning a monetized value to the latter has become topical only about two decades ago (Mook, 2013).

As a consequence, 'social accounting' (and social audit) has taken a foothold in the not-for-profit realm. Considering a broader set of variables than those included in 'conventional' accounting (Mook, Quarter, & Richmond, 2007, p. 3) as well as a myriad of stakeholders, such as service recipients, employees, funders, governmental entities, media, and civil society, social accounting has been considered particularly suitable for non-profit organizations and organizations in the social economy that seek to disclose information on the economic and social value that they have generated for their communities of interest (Gray, Owen, & Adams, 1996; Mook et al., 2007; Nicholls, 2009; Osborne and Ball, 2010). In contrast to conventional accounting, social accounting uses stakeholder input and thus builds not only on (quantitative) financial data, but also on qualitative data and descriptive statistics to produce the accounting statement (see Richmond, Mook, & Quarter, 2003). Several models have been developed within the framework of social accounting; many organizations have particularly embraced the triad of the expanded value added statement, the socio-economic impact statement, and the socio-economic resource statement as social accounting statements. Resembling the three main financial statements in the business sector, these statements were expected to increase the acceptance of particularly those stakeholders that were used to yield information from conventional accounting. Other tools, for instance, include the social impact statement, the co-operative social balance, and the social return on investment (see Mook, 2007; Mook, 2014).

This chapter addresses the Social Return on Investment (SROI), a tool that aims to account for and report the social impact of an organization by involving stakeholders in the process of valuation of outcomes. In contrast to other social accounting tools, the SROI corrects for outcomes that may occur through actions of other organizations or also without any action by any organization. The chapter aims to (1) provide a general overview of the development, use and usability of SROI as an instrument of reporting the value that has been created by a non-profit organization or organization in the social economy at large. This step also comprises a comparison of the two most widely referred guidelines to the methodology of SROI and its calculation. Reflecting the design and content of SROI reports with the principles and guidelines of popular reporting, the chapter (2) combines the approach to reporting the creation of social value to a wider audience with the principles and best practices in communicating accounting information to non-professional stakeholders (popular reporting). Popular reporting has been widely discussed as a means to increase transparency, foster participative democracy, and promote accountability in the public sector (see e.g. Barbera, Borgonovi, & Steccolini, 2016; Cohen & Karatzimas, 2015), but similar attempts in the non-profit sector or the social economy are much less widespread. To the best of the authors' knowledge, no scholarly work exists so far that examines SROI reports using this approach. The findings of the SROI reports assessment from the perspective of popular reporting highlight aspects that warrant further attention in reporting the social value that has been created, and thus offer the basis for a brief outlook for which 'blind spots' (non-profit) organizations in the social economy need to address in order to strengthen the role of SROI as an instrument of user-centered reporting.

SOCIAL RETURN ON INVESTMENT (SROI): THE INSTRUMENT AT A GLANCE

Social Return on Investment (SROI) has been introduced to the non-profit arena in the 1990s, when stakeholders placed a greater emphasis on accountability and philanthropy has been increasingly approached from a social investment perspective. In recent years, SROI has emerged as a key concept of planning, monitoring, and evaluating the multifaceted value created by non-profit organizations (Lingane & Olsen, 2004; Maier, Schober, Simsa, & Millner, 2015; Olsen & Lingane, 2003). In addition to presenting the financial and economic value and costs, it encompasses also the environmental and social impact to society at large (see Mook, 2014; SROI-Network, 2009, SROI-Network, 2012). However, its particular elegance stems from its roots in the return on investment approach used in business analysis (Moody, Littlepage, & Paydar, 2015), where a monetary value is assigned to the social impact, and in addition, the latter is expressed as one indicator - the ratio of funds and other resources invested to the value or impact created. The SROI is expressed as a benefits-to-cost ratio, where e.g. a SROI of 5:1 indicates that an investment of 1 Euro delivers 5 Euros (or other currency) of social value. (Banke-Thomas, Madaj, Charles, & van den Broek, 2015).

Development of the SROI

The SROI methodology has been developed as a "modified discounted cash flow analysis in an effort to calculate the impact achieved through a foundation grant and [to] document the economic value of the social purpose enterprises the foundation had supported" by Jed Emerson and colleagues at the Roberts Foundation in the United States (Emerson, Wachowicz, & Chun, 2000, p. 133). Under a new initiative, the Roberts Enterprise Development Fund - REDF, both the approach towards the evaluation of impact and the calculation of a social return on investment have been improved. Other organizations joined the efforts, and the Hewlett Foundation, a working group of SROI practitioners, further broadened the scope of the calculation and updated the guidance in 2004. It was here that the aspects of including stakeholders and assuring the quality of reports have received increased attention (Nicholls, 2017).

The SROI has been refined especially in Anglo-Saxon regions, where different players joined forces to further develop the instrument (Kehl, Then, & Münscher, 2012). The new economics foundation (nef) for instance has looked at it not only from a reporting, but also from a management accounting perspective (see Moody et al., 2015), i.e. as an instrument to enhance planning and decision-making within an organization. Together with the nef SROI methodology, the blended value return created by the Roberts Enterprise Development Fund (REDF), and the Benefits Cost Ratio developed by the Robin Hood Foundation in New York City (Cooney & Lynch-Cerullo, 2014), the approach by the SROI Network in the UK is one of the most widely referred to in the field.

In 2008, the UK *Office of the Third Sector* started a three-year project to establish a standard measure of the social return on investment. Bringing together the SROI Network, the new economics foundation (nef), Charities Evaluation Services, the National Council for Voluntary Organisations and New Philanthropy Capital, the project gave practitioners in the public sector, the non-profit sector, and in the field of consulting a platform to share their experience and best practice examples in measuring social value and thereby contribute to the improvement of the SROI methodology (Arvidson, Lyon, McKay, & Moro, 2013; Nicholls, 2017; Ryan & Lyne, 2008). The result of this programme, the *Guide to SROI* was published in 2009 (and an updated version in 2012) and it has been translated into several languages since (Kehl et al., 2012; Nicholls, 2017). The increased attention paid towards the measurement of social impact has notably fostered collaborations between various organizations in the field, e.g. the Social Impact Analysts Association (SIAA), the Bertelsmann Foundation and New Philanthropy Capital that have jointly provided support for practitioners. The SIAA and the SROI Network even have merged in 2015, creating one of the key players in the field, the *Social Value* (Nicholls, 2017).

Calculation of the SROI

An SROI analysis can be carried out for the organization as a whole, or for one particular aspect and program of, or intervention by the organization. It can be either of an evaluative character, where the SROI is calculated in *retrospect*, based on investments (costs) and outcomes (benefits) that have already occurred, or present a *forecast*, where the costs and the value that will be generated if the intervention meets the intended outcomes are predicted (SROI-Network, 2009, SROI-Network, 2012). This prospective approach is useful as a tool for strategic planning, improving, and investment decisions within the organization. Carried out in retrospect, the SROI lives up to the expectations towards an instrument of reporting or impact communication (Nicholls, 2009). In both cases however, a favourable SROI can attract investment, i.e. funding from donors, government, or financing institutions.

The description of how to calculate the SROI that is presented below is based on the guidelines by nef and the SROI Network/Social Value. It needs to be pointed out that the most recent edition of the nef framework guideline has been published in 2008, before the organization joined the programme initiated by the Office of the Third Sector (see above). The Social Value guideline (published in 2009 and 2012) therefore has been developed based on the conceptual work and the experiences that nef has brought to the SROI Network. The guidelines by both organizations, nef as well as Social Value, however are still referenced by various organizations that embark on the process of calculating an SROI. Social Value even offers a quality assurance of SROI reports submitted to them. Both organizations provide a platform where the reports that are submitted to them for assessment are made available to the broader public. This is also the reason for these two platforms to be included in the search strategy for the present chapter.

The nef framework describes the process of conducting an SROI in 14 steps across four stages: boundary setting and impact mapping; collecting data; modelling and calculating; reporting and embedding. The Social Value approach follows 24 steps across six stages: establishing scope and identifying key stakeholders; mapping outcomes; evidence outcomes and giving them a value; establishing impact; calculating the SROI; reporting, using and embedding. The notable difference in the number of steps stems from the disaggregation of stages and steps that has occurred during the process of refining the SROI methodology, as well as from different clustering of steps into stages: the stage of *collecting data* and *modelling and calculating* in the nef approach spans across four stages in the Social Value approach, i.e. *mapping outcomes, evidence outcomes and giving them a value, establishing impact, calculating the SROI.*

When comparing the nef and the Social Value frameworks of SROI, readers are at first confronted with seemingly different frameworks. However, both approaches follow the same principles of involving stakeholders, understanding what changes (e.g. by developing a theory of change), valuing the things that matter and including only what is material, avoiding over-estimation or over-claiming, ensuring

Figure 1. Comparison of the nef and Social Value guides to SROI

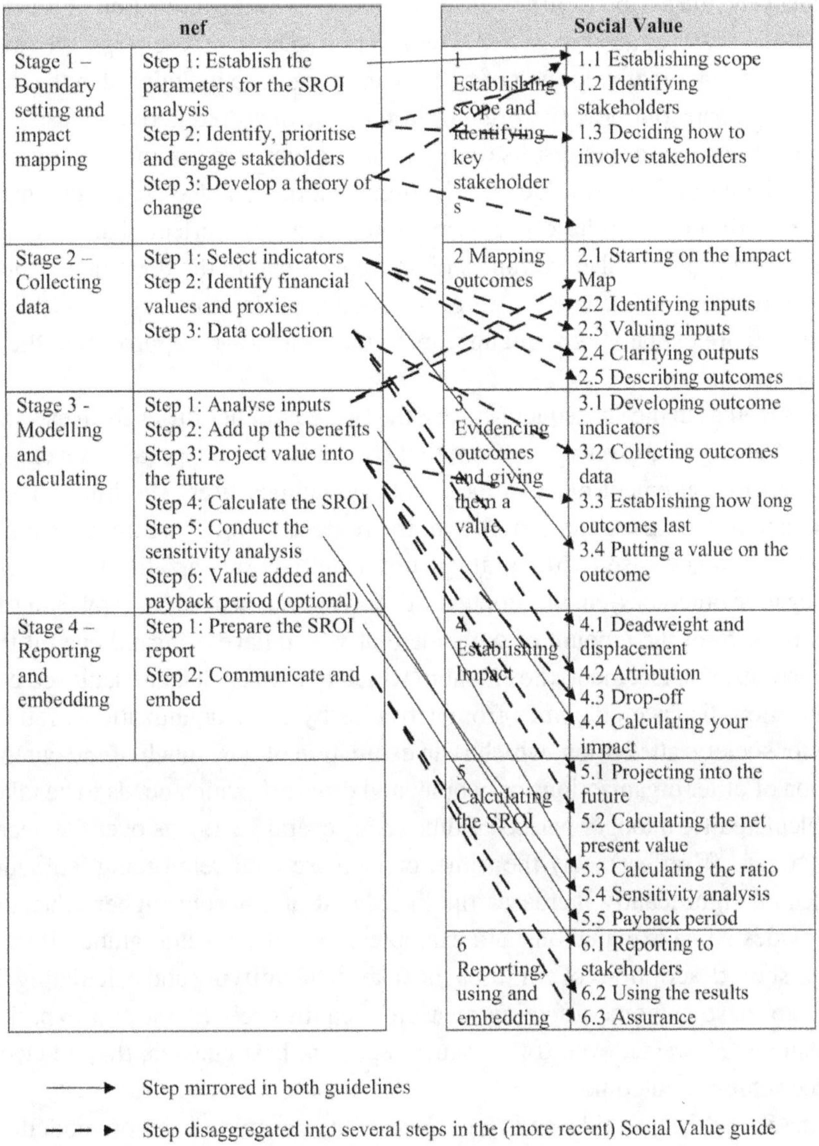

transparency, and verifying the result (nef, 2008; SROI-Network, 2009, SROI-Network, 2012). Although they structure the process differently and show a varying intensity in their explanations of the steps, both guidelines basically describe the same process (see Figure 1). The more extensive explanations in the Social Value guide appear to result from the experiences of practitioners in the field who have contributed to the SROI Network. The established guidelines seem to mirror their call for providing more clarification and more structure in certain aspects and stages of the process of calculating an SROI.

In both approaches, the *first stage* includes establishing the scope of the analysis and identifying key stakeholders. The scope of the analysis describes the purpose of the SROI, the audience of the analysis, the aims and objectives of the organization, the resources, the organization carrying out the analysis (e.g. the organization that creates value itself, or external consultants), the range of activities that will be included in the analysis, the period of time considered, as well as the indication of whether the analysis is an ex-ante SROI (forecast) or an ex-post SROI (evaluation). During these steps, the two organizations' frameworks differ only marginally. In the nef framework, stage one includes also the theory of change. The theory of change maps out how the organization or the analyzed activities use certain resources (inputs) to deliver activities or direct results (outputs) and longer-term, or more significant results (outcomes), as well as the part of social value that the organization can take credit for (impact). While the nef guide provides definitions for these key terms in the cause-and-effect chain that are then laid out in the impact map (and provides also examples of an impact map in the document), the impact map in the Social Value framework is discussed in *stage two*, and done so more extensively. The Social Value guide offers readers more explanations and appears to take a hands-on approach in the presentation of how to set up an impact map.

In this aspect as well as in the subsequent stages, the two guidelines differ from each other to a higher extent. The Social Value guide gives more room to the measurement approach, development of indicators, estimation, and measurement of outcomes. Both guidelines stress the importance of estimating how much of the outcome is due to the activities of the respective value creating organization, and how much outcome occurs in any case (without any action from any organization) or develops differently than expected (negative outcomes). In this context, several measures need to be taken into consideration: deadweight, the measure of the amount of outcome that would have occurred even if the organization did not take any actions; displacement, the extent to which outcomes that are achieved due to the activities of the organization displace outcomes from activities by other organizations, rather than creating additional value for society; attribution, which is an estimation of how much of the outcome was caused by the contribution of other organizations or people; and drop-off, which needs to be taken into account if the SROI is calculated for a longer period of time (e.g. several years), as over the years, the outcome could decrease ('wear off' effect), stay the same, or increase (self-reinforcing, e.g. education, where finishing high-school significantly increases the likelihood of entering higher education). While the nef guideline provides some explanations and examples, the Social Value guide offers more practical examples and also short descriptions of common mistakes in identifying and calculating these measures. Assigning values to these outcome-affecting measures requires relying on past experience, empirical studies, or estimations. However, even if the values represent best guesses, they reduce the likelihood of over-stating the achieved outcome.

Stage five in the *Social Value* guide, and *stage three* in the *nef* guide focus on modelling and calculating the SROI. The calculation is based on adding up the costs, and adding up the benefits, in order to assign one value for each of the two sides of the SROI coin (costs/investments, benefits/outcomes). Both guidelines lay out how values can be projected into the future (in case of an ex-ante SROI), i.e. how the net present value can be calculated, what the actual calculation of the ratio looks like, and subsequently, how the reporting organization can conduct a sensitivity analysis to check for the robustness of their earlier estimations. This step basically asks how the SROI ratio would change if particular estimations were altered, but also which assumptions have the greatest impact on the SROI. As a further step, an organization could also calculate the payback period of a certain investment. This step is described as optional in both guides. The latter is due to the fact that a shorter payback period may appear as desirable, but activities with higher social impact usually show a long payback period.

Both approaches present reporting, using and embedding as the *last stage* in the process of calculating an SROI. Social Value as well as nef present requirements for the (qualitative and quantitative) information that needs to be included in an SROI report:

- Information of the work, key stakeholders, and activities of the organization,
- A description of the scope of the analysis, the stakeholder involvement, the methods of data collection and any underlying assumptions and limitations,
- The impact map with indicators and proxies,
- Details of the calculations, the sensitivity analysis and a description of varied assumptions and their effects, as well as
- An audit trail for the decisions made, regarding which stakeholders, outcomes and indicators have been included and which not, including a rationale for those decisions,
- An executive summary, and
- Illustrations of particular findings, for example with case studies or quotes from participants.

However, it is also clearly stated that the most important part is using the results for changes within the organization, to enhance the quality of communication with investors, funders, principals (contracting authorities), and using the information that has been generated throughout the process of calculating the SROI to improve the activities with clients.

In practice, the SROI has been mainly applied by non-profit organizations, but it has been gradually transferred to different contexts and applied by different actors e.g. governmental entities, consultants, and social enterprises. Over the last years, the concentration of SROI expertise in the US and the UK is also slowly dispersing, and SROI networks are being established in a number of other countries (Nicholls, 2017). This picture is supported by looking at the SROI reports that are available on the websites of the two most widely known international platforms that audit SROI reports, nef and Social Value.

SROI REPORTS IN PRACTICE

This chapter aims to present an empirical assessment of SROI as an instrument of reporting in practice. A Google Scholar search conducted during the compilation of this chapter revealed that there are no scholarly contributions on the use of SROI reports by stakeholders of non-profit organizations or organizations in the social economy, and only little research on how stakeholders use performance information of non-profit organizations in general (for exceptions, see Barman & MacIndoe, 2012; Saxton & Guo, 2011). This stands in contrast to the quite extensive literature on the use of financial reports by shareholders in the business sector, or by citizens in the case of governmental entities. The search strategy used to select the SROI reports that, in a further step, are assessed from a popular reporting perspective, began with an initial Google web search with the terms "social return on investment" and "SROI", and was complemented with a more focused search in the databases of nef and Social Value. The latter approach is in line with considerations in a systematic review on the topic of SROI (Banke-Thomas et al., 2015), but limits the results to SROI reports that have been published in English[1].

Selection of SROI Reports

The search focused on SROI reports published between 2014 and 2018, thus covering almost five years. Reports that provide no indication of the year of publication, and where the year of publication could not be discerned from the period covered or through additional information on the website where it has been published are excluded from further analysis. This initial step yielded 63 SROI reports. The next inclusion criterion comprised the type of the organization. In line with the overarching theme of the book, the present chapter seeks to analyze SROI reports by organizations in the social economy, and in particular, non-profit organizations that are part of the social economy (i.e. have a clear social mission, and are engaged in producing social or merit goods in particular) (Monzon & Chaves, 2008).

Thus, reports by cooperatives, mutual societies, non-profit organizations, associations, and foundations, and – following the definition of social economy by the European Commission – also reports by social enterprises (European Commission, 2018) are included in the assessment. 17 reports have been excluded as they were either provided by governmental entities or professional associations where membership is mandatory (and that are therefore not part of the social economy), or by initiatives and voluntary networks (that do not meet the criterion of a formal organization/own legal status). Reports that presented the SROI of specific (social mission oriented) programmes by businesses, or refer to the SROI generated in a service field as a whole (e.g. HIV treatment in a country, delivered by dozens of different organizations) are also excluded from further analysis as they do not meet the criterion of an organization with an own legal status (a discernible characteristic of both organizations in the social economy as well as non-profit organizations). This led to the exclusion of additional 11 reports.

An Overview of the Included SROI Reports

Of the 35 included reports, 22 have been retrieved from the Social Value database, 11 from the Google web search, and 2 from the nef website. Again, it needs to be pointed out that nef's expertise in conducting and calculating the SROI has been brought into Social Value that specifically focuses on this topic, while nef covers a wider spectrum of think tank activities. The majority of the included reports (17) are of an evaluative character, 7 are ex-ante SROI reports that projects costs and benefits in the future, and in one case, the (short) report provided no clear information on whether the presented SROI was an ex-ante or an ex-post figure. The reports present SROIs for organizations in very different country contexts (see Table 1).

The time period of the activities or programs provided by the organization in the focus of the SROI report ranges from 6 months to 6 years, with an average of 25 months. Most of the reports calculate the SROI for a period of one year, and only 8 look at a time period that is longer than two years (see Table 2). In three of the 35 reports, the time period for the SROI calculation could not be identified.

The framework for the assessment of the design and content of the selected SROI reports comprises principles and guidelines of popular reporting, which is presented in the following. Lending from the basic ideas of popular reporting allows to gain new insights into the current design as well as the potential of SROI reports as a key instrument of accountability for organizations in the social economy.

Table 1. Number of reports per organization's country of origin

Organization's country of origin	No. of reports
United Kingdom	19
Ireland	5
Australia	3
United States	2
Brazil	1
Canada	1
Jordan	1
Nepal	1
Netherlands	1
Taiwan	1

Table 2. Time period of activities used for the SROI calculation in the reports

Time period of activities	No of reports
6 months	2
1 year	12
1 to 2 years	3
2 years	7
more than 2 years	8

INTRODUCING THE PERSPECTIVE OF POPULAR REPORTING

Popular reporting is a way of presenting financial and non-financial accounting information by providing a concise, comprehensive, and easy to read (avoiding the use of jargon or technical terms) report that is prepared with the information demand of non-accounting-professional users in mind (citizens, but also political decision makers/legislators, public sector employees, media) (Herrmann, 2011). Presenting accounting information in a simplified manner does not mean that popular reports are simplistic. In fact, the objective of providing an easy to process document for users that have low proficiency in (governmental) accounting, i.e. providing a 'translation' of financial reports (Lee, 2006), can be challenging to the preparers or suppliers of such reports. Popular reporting has been described as one of the key future developments in governmental accounting, as the reporting entity can enhance accountability towards stakeholders who seldom engage with financial reports (see e.g. Brusca & Montesinos, 2006). However, there appears to exist a discrepancy between the rhetoric on popular reporting and its actual implementation and *utilization* as means to increase transparency, foster participative democracy, and promote accountability (Barbera et al., 2016, p. 5). Governmental entities embarked on designing and preparing popular reports, and started competing for awards by professional associations (e.g. Governmental Finance Officers Association - GFOA), but they mainly fell short of an active dissemination to the primary target group of citizens (Yusuf, Jordan, Neill, & Hackbart, 2013).

So far, there have not been developed any agreed upon standards for popular reporting in the public sector (Shoulders & FreeMan, 2012, p. 801). Popular reporting therefore is mainly based on principles and (non-mandatory) guidelines, e.g. by the *Government Finance Officers Association (GFOA)*. Scholars in the field frequently refer to this Anglo-American association as a source for how popular reporting should be conducted, even if they investigate its implementation in different country contexts (Barbera et al., 2016; Cohen, Mamakou, & Karatzimas, 2016). In a similar vein, this chapter uses the GFOA guidelines as a starting point for the development of the criteria for the SROI reports assessment, but takes into account also guidelines and recommendations that have been put forth by other sources (FMCBC, 2004; Herrmann, 2011)[2].

ASSESSMENT CRITERIA

The included SROI reports are assessed on 21 criteria in five aspects: formal criteria, reader appeal, understandability, dissemination, and portrayal.

1. Formal Criteria

- **Timely publication:** The report is issued on a timely basis. For popular reports, this is no later than six months after the close of the fiscal year, in order to ensure relevance of the presented information (FMCBC, 2004; GFOA, 2006). Given that SROI reports are exceptional and not part of regular reporting in organizations, this criterion is considered non-applicable, but the publication of the SROI report within a period of six to twelve months after the end of the time period of activities is likely to represent a timely publication. In case of forecasts, the question whether the publication is timely depends on the timeliness of the collected data and the time period of the forecast, since forecasts of more than 3 years in the future are prone to higher uncertainty.
- **Clear Outline of Scope:** The report clearly outlines the scope of information presented (the focus, e.g. organization as a whole, certain service area, specific program, as well as the time period covered, e.g. the past year, certain time period of intervention/program). This helps users to understand in which context the report is prepared. The time period covered also establishes a baseline for timely publication. If the SROI report refers to the value of a program that has been carried out between 2011 and 2013, but the report is prepared in 2018, the timeliness of publication could be questioned.
- **Reference to Detailed Report/Executive Summary:** Popular reports need to focus on information that is crucial to set the context and explain the story behind the data. However, an explicit reference to the annual financial statement is needed to give interested users the possibility to obtain more detailed information (Herrmann, 2011). In the case of SROI, most reports are full reports and thus would not meet the general objective of presenting information in a short, easy-to-grasp manner. Those reports therefore should include a straight-forward executive summary with the most important information and results. If organizations present only short SROI reports, or refer to data that has been obtained from other reports, organizations should clearly refer to those (longer) documents with detailed information.

2. Reader Appeal

- **Length/Format:** The report needs to be short and focus on a few significant aspects. There exists no rule of thumb on the exact page length (range) that would be considered as short enough, thus, this criterion is dependent on the individual user's way of information processing, but also on the way information is structured and graphically designed. A clear structure and the use of graphic elements can provide easement of text overload and maintain user interest also in longer reports. The report format needs to be logical and easy to understand (GFOA, 2016). This could be accomplished with a clear introduction and an easy to follow style, e.g. introducing small sections, presenting short summaries to each section.
- **Readability of Typography:** The report's typography needs to be readable (Herrmann, 2011). While this is subjective, there is little point in using fonts that may appear less professional (e.g. *Comic Sans* may be appropriate for a birthday invitation but not for an SROI report), or typography in an ornament style.
- **Appeal of Typography:** The typography needs to be appealing to readers, thus the text could be placed also inside design elements or as action sub-headings to create an open and inviting layout (Herrmann, 2011).
- **Visuals:** The report should use charts, tabular format, graphics or other artwork to present summarized information, which can also facilitate comparison (e.g. across years) for the reader. Photographs/images should be used to present the organization, awake emotions, but also to inform and establish a connection between the organization (and its staff) and the report users (e.g. using photos of the board, volunteers, clients) (see GFOA, 2016; Herrmann, 2011).

3. Understandability

- **Clear Language:** The report should adopt a clear and concise writing style. This means using rather short sentences and short phrases, and avoiding jargon and technical language. Potentially confusing terms need to be explained (FMCBC, 2004; GFOA, 2016; Herrmann, 2011).
- **Content supporting use of graphs and charts:** This is a criterion that follows up on the visuals. The charts and graphs should support the readers' understanding of the text, and trigger their curiosity. All graphs need to be clear, fully explained, and should provide possibilities for comparison over time or with other, similar entities (GFOA, 2016; Herrmann, 2011).
- **Report Narrative:** A narrative should be used to explain (general trends of) financial data and to highlight significant items. The narrative should draw readers into the report and demand readership by the intended users. Generic titles for the SROI report should be avoided (GFOA, 2016; Herrmann, 2011). Graphic elements could underline the narrative (e.g. a heart symbol next to text that is referring to health outcomes).
- **Comparative Information:** The report should provide appropriate information on past trends, but also on similar organizations, so that report users receive a broader understanding of the organization's current position (GFOA, 2006). Relevant changes to the external environment can be included if it is supportive of the understandability of current results/outcomes (FMCBC, 2004).

- **Balanced presentation of information:** The report should minimize the potential for misinterpretations and the information should be presented in a balanced and objective manner (FMCBC, 2004; GFOA, 2006). Feel-good posturing should be avoided, problems (e.g. unexpected negative outcomes, negative trends in the social economy) should be tackled directly. This could also allow to demonstrate how the organization handled difficult situations (Herrmann, 2011).

4. Dissemination

- **Distribution - availability on website:** The report should be available on the organization's website (not only published on e.g. the nef or Social Value websites).
- **Distribution - retrieveability on website:** This refers to the level of effort needed to find and retrieve the report on the website. The retrieveability can be enhanced by e.g. clear indication of the SROI reports on the homepage; flip-through version of the report on the website; pdf download of the report directly with a link, avoiding mandatory registration or request via e-mail.
- **Feedback opportunity:** Report users should be encouraged to provide feedback, e.g. including a section with contact information for feedback, presenting a contact form next to the download link for the report.

5. Portrayal

- **Design by organization itself/by third party:** The SROI report either can be designed and prepared by the organization itself, or the organization can be supported by a third party in the process of measuring and reporting the value achieved, e.g. by a consulting firm. This criterion does not suggest that either one possibility is preferable. Rather, it aims to acknowledge the effort if an organization carries out and presents the SROI itself.
- **Innovation/Creativity:** The report should strive for an innovative and creative way of presenting information. However, it needs to be stressed that the report needs to present information in a balanced and objective manner to establish credibility with readers (see the criterion on a balanced presentation of information above).
- **Usefulness for service users:** The report needs to be useful to individuals who use the organization's services, so that they can make informed decisions about continuing or taking up relations to the organization.
- **Usefulness for professionals:** Similar to the above criterion, the SROI report should be useful to professionals, e.g. social investors, government officials, the media, so that the achieved value is easily portrayed to potential funders, decision-makers or watchdogs. The usefulness of the SROI report could enhance dissemination and thus contribute to a more positive image of the organization.
- **Image:** The report should make the organization more attractive to the intended readers or other interested parties. This could be achieved also by paying attention to the state of the art of presenting annual reports, e.g. leading with a letter by and a photograph of the CEO (or, in this case, a testimonial for the organization). In the letter, management should assume responsibility for the value achieved and the results of the SROI, especially in comparison to other organizations.

RESULTS AND FINDINGS

Eight of the presented criteria (executive summary in case of full reports, readability of typography, report narrative, comparative information, distribution – availability on website, feedback opportunity, design by organization itself/by third party, innovation/creativity) have been assessed dichotomously, i.e. a score of '1' is assigned if a criterion was met, '0' if it was not met. The other criteria are assed on a scale from 0 to 2, with '0' representing the case that a criterion has not been met, and '2' that more aspects of a criterion have been met (see Table 3). Results on the different criteria (Table 4) will be discussed together with the findings in the following.

1. Formal Criteria

The analysis of the SROI reports regarding the formal criteria shows that 22 reports have been published in due time after the analyzed time period. Half of these reports have been published the year after the last year observed (e.g. publication in 2015, observed time period 2011-2014, or in case of ex-ante SROI, forecasts of no more than 3 years after the publication date), and half of them look at very recent data (e.g. publication 2016, observed time period 2015/2016). Four reports have been published later than one year after the observed time period (in one case, three years after the observed period). Nine reports did not meet the criterion of timely publication, as either the year of publication was not provided in the report, or the time period has not been explicitly stated. Almost all (30 of 35) SROI reports have a clear outline of scope, i.e. the focus of the SROI (the activities of the organization as a whole, specific program) and the time period covered is clear. In four reports, the focus (either the organization as a whole or only certain programs) is clear but the covered time period was not - either it is not mentioned at all (seemingly with the assumption that it would be clear to the organizations' stakeholders which program or time period of a certain action the report is referring to), or the time period is indicated as five years, but the actual years are unclear. In one case the report did not explicitly indicate the focus but it appeared from information in the report that it considered the project as a whole. The majority of SROI reports are full reports (24 of 35). Of the 11 short reports, only two include a clear reference to the full report or other, more detailed reports that present useful information to the interested reader, providing also the links to those documents. Four reports include a reference to additional documents (annual report submitted to a funder/regulator, excel file) but the latter are not easily retrievable (available only upon e-mail request, presented only in documents for stakeholders). One report was a full report, but did not contain all information that should be covered in a SROI report. Five of the short SROI reports do not provide any indication of or reference to a full or detailed report. 19 of the 24 full reports provide an executive summary.

2. Reader Appeal

About two thirds (21) of the reports have a clear structure and a clear introduction/information on the objective of the report and the general methodology of the SROI, they are short and thus 'easily digestible' or make good use of graphic elements so that user awareness is maintained even throughout lengthy reports. Twelve reports of medium length and mainly a clear structure include information on the organization and the objectives and/or short information on the sections of the report, but show shortcomings in the design of the index (i.e. the format appears complex or not well structured), or

Table 3. Assessment criteria overview and scores

Assessment criteria	Score
Timely publication	0=publication not explicitly indicated or time period not clear; 1=publication more than one year after observed time period; 2=publication one year after the observed time period or less
Clear outline of scope	0= focus and time period unclear; 1=focus or time period unclear; 2=focus and time period clear
Reference to detailed report:	n.a.=the full report is being analyzed; 0=short report with no reference to full report; 1=reference to full report, but not easily retrievable; 2=reference to full report, available for download
Executive summary (in case of full report)	0=not provided; 1=provided
Length and format	0=long, unstructured reports; 1=clear structure, but not maintaining user awareness; 2=clear structure, info on organization/SROI/purpose; maintaining user awareness
Readability of typography	0=non-readable (e.g. fonts too small, overlapping); 1=readable
Appeal of typography	0=non-appealing typography, non-appealing colors, no text inside design elements; 1=no text inside design elements, non-aligned paragraphs, 'standard' font; 2=new font, appealing typography, appealing colors, text inside design elements
Visuals	0=no use of graphs, charts, illustrations, photos; 1= use of tables, illustrations, graphs etc. but appeal medium, use of only few visuals; 2=use of charts, graphs, tables, illustrations, photos, use of 'new' appealing fonts
Clear language	0=technical language; 1=clear language; 2=clear language and glossary provided
Content supporting use of visuals	0=visuals are not used in a supportive way, but are merely decorational; 1=visuals used supportively, but not throughout the report; 2=use of boxes, charts, illustrations, photos supports text (enhances the explanations given in text)
Report narrative	0=no narrative evident; 1=narrative evident ('slogan' for the report)
Comparative information	0=no comparative information on SROI; 1=comparative information on SROI provided (past SROI in the organization; similar organizations)
Balanced presentation of information	0=presentation of information non-balanced (lack of information on sensitivity analysis, data collection etc.); 1=sensitivity analysis/detailed information on data collection/deadweight not provided, but other aspects provided; 2=sensitivity analysis provided, data collection instruments provided, drop-off etc. discussed
Distribution – availability on website	0=not available on website; 1=available on website
Distribution – retrievability on website	0=not available on website, or not easily retrievable (only upon e-mail request, after log-in, only to stakeholders); 1=available, but not easy to find on website/only retrievable after designated Google search; 2=available, intuitively and clearly placed on website menu
Feedback opportunity	0=no feedback opportunity; 1=feedback opportunity (not general contact information, but indication of e.g. "further questions on this report")
Design by organization itself/by third party	0=external; 1=internal
Innovation/creativity	0=no special features; 1=innovative/creative elements in report
Usefulness for service users	0=not useful for service users, no executive summary provided; 1=executive summary provided, useful to service users, but no highlights; 2=useful to service users, much information on organization and its services, executive summary provided
Usefulness for professionals	0=not useful to professionals; 1=useful to professionals, conclusions general, no recommendations; 2=clear and structured recommendations
Image	0=no letter from management with photo; 1=letter from management with/without photo

do not use graphic elements (boxes, charts, illustrations) in a 'strategic' and diversified way so that it maintains user awareness. These reports meet the criterion of a balanced format and length to a satisfactory degree. Only two reports do not meet this criterion at all: one report includes no numbering for the chapters and no graphic elements are used, thus its structure appears less clear and in general, the full report appears very lengthy. The other builds extensively on 'graphic' elements, thus the sheer number of extensive tables is detrimental to user awareness. Only three of the 35 reports received no points with regards to typography. While the main text in these three reports was readable, there are issues with the text in graphs (that is non-readable due to its small size), or errors in typesetting that led to overlapping and thus result in non-readable text. When it comes to the appeal of typography however, the picture somewhat changes. Only seven reports meet this criterion to a high degree (score: 2). This is mainly due to the use of text inside design elements, an appealing design of quotes, column design of text, and an appealing, 'new' or non-standard font. In contrast, nine reports have rather little appealing typography, mainly due to non-alignment of paragraphs, the use of 'standard' font (i.e. Arial or Times New Roman that made the report appear rather usual), or a rather non-appealing choice of colors (score '0'). The majority of reports (19) exerted neither non-appealing nor particularly appealing typography and therefore are assigned a score of '1'. Ten reports use visuals (charts, graphs, illustrations, or photos) intensively but not overwhelmingly. Only two reports make poor use in this context (either extensive use of tables but little text, or no use of graphs, illustrations, or photos at all), and the majority (23) use visuals to a sufficient degree.

3. Understandability

While all analyzed SROI reports use a clear language, i.e. they adopt a clear and concise writing style, avoid overly long sentences, jargon and technical language, seven organizations paid particular attention to using a clear language and provide a glossary of terms that are used in the reports (mainly explanations of SROI terms that are probably new to the organizations' stakeholders, and even more so to non-professional users of the reports). 19 of the reports use the visuals (graphs, illustrations, charts, photos) in a supportive way, i.e. the visual elements enhance the descriptions and explanations in the text, 14 reports use these elements in a supportive, but sometimes in a purely decorative way (in particular, photos), and some illustrations appear too complex and thus do not enhance understandability of the text. Two reports seem to use graphs, illustrations, and charts rather coincidentally. Only three of the 35 reports exert a report narrative, mainly reflecting the intended impact on the organizations' clients, five provided comparative SROI information, three of which compared their SROI value with reports in past years, and two presented SROI values of similar organizations. Most reports meet the criterion of a balanced presentation of information; 15 of which provide extensive information on the sensitivity analysis, information on deadweight, drop-off, and financial proxies, as well as comprehensive information on the instruments of data collection (i.e. provide full questionnaires, interview or focus group questions in the appendix), or even regulatory assurance (beyond the Social Value UK assurance) of an objective presentation of information and prudent calculation of value (not over-claiming). Only six provide insufficient information on sensitivity analysis or data collection; they show a copy-paste approach in their estimations of deadweight and drop-off, or build on a very small sample (e.g. only one case study) and are therefore prone to over-claiming the SROI value, or in general, are at risk of presenting unbalanced information.

4. Dissemination

More than half (18) of the analyzed SROI reports are available on the platforms of Social Value UK and nef that were used in the report selection (see above) only (not available on the respective organizations' websites). In one of those cases, the report is available on one of the organization's main investor's website as the organization's website focuses only on presenting its services; and in another, the report is neither available for download nor upon request, but there is a short information on the SROI value on the organization's website under the menu point "about us". In two cases, the organizations at stake do not have websites (in one case it seemingly never existed and in one case the website expired). As a consequence, 20 reports received no points on the criterion of retrievability on the website. In two cases the SROI report is available on the website (and the respective report is rated '1' on availability on website), but the retrievability is rated '0' as the report is retrievable only after a distinct search via an integrated Google web search button on the organization's website. Thus, this case is distinct from the seven cases where the report is retrievable only after a distinct search via a search button that performs a search on the organization's website, only after numerous clicks on the organization's website (not easily identifiable on the website menu), or only upon request (mainly per e-mail) (these seven cases scored '1' on retrievability). Eight reports are easily retrievable via an intuitively identifiable menu point on the organizations' websites and with a direct download possibility. In one case, there is also a short information on the SROI and the SROI value on the organization's homepage. Only four of the 35 analyzed SROI reports provide a feedback opportunity, i.e. a distinct contact in case of questions on the report rather than a general website or contact address (e.g. info@..., contact@...).

5. Portrayal

Of the 35 analyzed reports, eleven were prepared by the organization itself. Three of which have been produced with help or advice by external organizations with expertise in the social economy. Six reports exert innovative or creative aspects, e.g. using black/white structures, creative illustrations, drawing elements, snapshots of media articles, or using a landscape or cubic format that allows a different structure and presentation of information. 26 reports are considered useful for service users, as they provide sufficient information on the organization, its services, and aims/mission/vision, and contain an executive summary with the key information of the report. However, there are also six reports seem highly useful (score '2') to service users, as they contain extensive information on the organization or provide a visually structured discussion on the outcomes for different client groups. In contrast, three reports appear rather non-useful for service users as they contain either an overwhelming amount of information (which also stems from the poor use of graphic elements), or too little and too generic information. The usefulness for professionals presents itself differently. 16 reports appear highly useful (score '2') for professionals since they present extensive conclusions and structure the recommendations by different themes. Twelve reports provide specific conclusions but no, or too general, recommendations (e.g. the recommendation to assure the SROI value by an external organization, or to increase the number of clients). Six reports offer no recommendations at all, and in addition, provide only general conclusions and insights. These were not necessarily the same reports that received no points on the usefulness for service users as these two groups will have different information demand when looking at SROI reports. Only one report scores '0' on both criteria of usefulness (for service users as well as for professionals) as it presents only general information that cannot be used for decision-making (using the organization's services as a client, or funding the organization/program, partnering with the organization etc.). Merely five reports present a letter from management with a photo of the executive/director/responsible, two present a letter from the management but no photo, one presents no letter from the management but uses a quote by a client with a photo instead, and one presents a letter from the author (an employee of the organization), but no photo of them. However, the latter case is peculiar as the report includes a statement that this individual is the sole author of the report, which somewhat undermines the identification with and accountability for the presented results.

CONCLUSION AND OUTLOOK FOR SROI REPORTS AS AN INSTRUMENT OF REPORTING CREATED VALUE

From a more general perspective, there are seven reports that achieve an overall score of 15 (out of 33 for short reports, 31 for full reports) or more. These are mainly reports that have a clear structure and clear introduction to the report. Also, the 'strategic' use of graphic elements in order to maintain user awareness appeared as a viable way of balancing the length of the document itself. Further, these reports have an appealing typography with text inside design elements, that are able to utilize visual elements such as charts, graphics, illustrations, and photos in a supportive manner, but need not necessarily exert innovative or creative aspects or elements. Rather, it is the retrievability on the organization's website and the usefulness for service users and for professionals that makes one SROI report more adhering to criteria of popular reporting than others. There are however also seven reports that achieve an overall score of less than 10. They, too, show a clear structure, information on the organization and the report itself. Some of them use visual elements and do so in a supportive way; their typography can be considered as appealing, and they could be assessed as useful for service users and professionals. From the analysis, no general tendencies emerged that would suggest distinct criteria characterizing these (lower scoring) reports. Thus, it seems that no one criteria discern reports that score higher on the adapted popular reporting criteria and those that score lower.

Some of the SROI reports' 'blind spots' (from a popular reporting perspective) appear unexpected, especially given that many of the analyzed reports have received a quality assurance by Social Value. A notable number of reports do not meet the criterion of a timely publication, either because there exists no information on the year of publication at all (indirectly, this also hampers the usefulness for service users), or much time has elapsed between the data collection and the publication of the SROI report. From an accountability perspective, it is advised to keep with the rule of thumb of six months to one year of time elapsed between the time period observed and the publication of the report. There is a mix of short and full SROI reports in the sample, which highlights different shortcomings. Only few of the short reports include a reference to the full SROI report or other, more detailed documents and reports (e.g. annual report, files presenting the financial proxies etc.), and not all of the full reports provide an executive summary, which would enhance the usefulness for the report users.

Comparing the SROI reports, a considerable number shows issues with providing sufficient information on the organization and its objectives, information on the sections of the report, and the use of graphic elements (boxes, charts, illustrations) that helps maintaining user awareness also in lengthy documents (which usually are more useful for service users and professionals). While almost all reports were considered readable, this is key to communicating professionality of the authoring as well as the reporting organization. Small typesetting errors or shortcomings in alignment of text can have a potentiated negative

Table 4. Overview of the assessment results

Report No.	Formal Criteria				Reader appeal				Understandability					Dissemination			Portrayal					TOTAL
	Timely publi-cation	Clear outline of scope	Refe-rence to detailed report	Execu-tive Summa-ry	Length / Format	Reada-bility of typo-graphy	Appeal of typo-graphy	Visuals (use of photographs, charts, graphics etc.)	Clear lan-guage	Suppor-ting use of graphs visuals	Report narra-tive	Compa-rative infor-mation	Balan-ced presen-tation of infor-mation	Distribution – availa-bility on website	Distribution – retrie-vability on website	Feed-back oppor-tunity	Design by organi-zation itself / by third party	Innovation / Creati-vity	Useful-ness for service users	Useful-ness for professionals	Image	
1	1	2	1	0	2	1	1	1	1	1	0	0	1	0	0	0	0	0	1	1	0	10
2	2	2	2	1	2	1	1	1	1	1	0	0	0	1	2	0	0	0	1	2	0	16
3	0	2	n.a.	1	1	1	0	1	1	1	0	0	1	0	0	0	0	0	1	1	0	7
4	2	2	n.a.	1	1	1	1	1	2	2	0	1	2	1	1	0	0	0	2	1	0	13
5	0	1	n.a.	0	2	1	2	2	2	1	1	0	2	1	2	0	0	1	1	1	0	12
6	2	2	n.a.	1	2	1	2	2	1	2	1	1	2	0	0	0	1	1	1	1	0	14
7	0	1	2	1	2	1	0	1	1	1	0	0	0	1	1	0	0	0	1	1	1	11
8	1	2	n.a.	0	2	1	0	1	1	1	0	0	1	0	0	1	0	0	0	2	0	9
9	2	2	0	0	2	0	1	1	1	2	0	0	0	0	0	0	0	0	1	0	0	8
10	2	2	n.a.	1	1	1	0	1	1	1	0	0	1	0	0	0	1	0	1	0	0	9
11	0	1	0	0	2	1	1	1	1	2	0	0	0	0	0	0	0	1	0	1	2	9
12	0	0	0	0	1	0	1	1	1	2	0	0	0	1	2	0	1	1	1	0	2	10
13	0	1	n.a.	1	0	1	0	0	1	0	0	0	1	0	0	0	0	0	0	0	0	3
14	2	2	n.a.	1	0	1	1	1	1	1	0	1	2	1	2	1	0	0	1	1	0	13
15	2	2	n.a.	1	2	1	1	1	1	2	0	0	2	0	0	0	1	0	2	2	0	14
16	2	2	n.a.	0	1	1	1	1	1	2	0	0	2	0	0	0	0	0	2	2	0	11
17	2	2	n.a.	1	1	1	1	1	1	2	0	1	1	1	2	0	0	0	2	2	0	15
18	2	2	n.a.	1	2	1	1	1	2	2	0	0	1	1	0	0	0	1	1	2	0	14
19	1	2	n.a.	0	1	1	1	1	2	2	0	0	1	0	0	0	0	0	1	2	1	10
20	0	2	0	1	2	1	1	2	1	1	0	0	1	1	1	0	1	0	1	1	0	12
21	2	2	n.a.	1	2	1	2	1	1	2	0	0	1	1	1	0	0	0	2	2	0	16

continued on following page

Table 4. Continued

Report No.	Formal Criteria				Reader appeal				Understandability					Dissemination			Portrayal						TOTAL
	Timely publi-cation	Clear outline of scope	Refe-rence to detailed report	Execu-tive Summa-ry	Length / Format	Reada-bility of typo-graphy	Appeal of typo-graphy	Visuals (use of photographs, charts, graphics etc.)	Clear lan-guage	Suppor-ting use of graphs visuals	Report narra-tive	Compa-rative infor-mation	Balan-ced presen-tation of infor-mation	Distribution – availa-bility on website	Distribution – retrie-vability on website	Feed-back oppor-tunity	Design by organi-zation itself / by third party	Innovation / Creati-vity	Useful-ness for service users	Useful-ness for professionals	Image	
22	2	2	n.a.	1	2	1	1	1	1	2	0	0	2	1	1	0	0	0	1	2	0	14
23	2	2	1	0	2	1	2	2	1	2	0	0	1	1	2	0	0	0	1	1	2	16
24	0	2	n.a.	1	2	0	2	2	2	2	0	0	1	1	1	1	1	1	1	2	2	17
25	2	2	n.a.	1	1	1	0	1	1	1	0	0	2	1	0	0	1	0	1	2	0	12
26	0	2	n.a.	1	1	1	0	1	1	1	0	0	2	0	0	0	0	0	1		0	6
27	2	2	n.a.	0	2	1	0	0	1	0	0	0	2	0	0	1	1	0	1	1	0	11
28	2	2	1	0	2	1	1	2	2	2	0	0	1	0	0	0	0	0	1	0	1	11
29	2	2	n.a.	1	1	1	0	1	2	1	0	0	2	1	2	0	1	0	1	2	1	15
30	2	2	1	0	2	1	2	1	1	2	0	0	0	0	0	0	0	0	1	0	0	11
31	2	2	n.a.	1	1	1	1	2	1	2	0	0	2	0	0	0	1	0	1	2	0	12
32	2	2	n.a.	1	1	1	1	2	1	2	0	0	2	0	0	0	1	0	1	2	0	12
33	1	2	0	0	2	1	2	2	1	2	0	0	1	1	1	0	0	0	1	1	0	12
34	2	2	n.a.	1	2	1	1	2	1	1	0	0	2	0	0	0	0	0	1	2	2	14
35	2	2	n.a.	1	2	1	1	1	1	1	1	1	2	1	2	0	0	0	2	2	0	16

effect on the overall perception of a report. Among the analyzed reports, there are a few well-designed documents that use 'new' appealing fonts, highlight quotes by clients or other stakeholders either in graphic designs or by using appealing colors and formatting. In general, they present text and numbers in design elements, use a column design of the text, and apply charts, graphs, illustrations, and photos in an intensive, but not an overwhelming manner. They also tend to use these elements 'strategically', i.e. to support the explanations in the text and enhance the report users' understanding of the content, rather than inserting these visual elements in a purely decorative manner.

While all analyzed SROI reports use a clear language (which seemingly also is due to the aspiration of meeting the Social Value UK assurance criteria), those reports that provided an additional glossary of terms (that are probably new to most report users) appear to be more user-oriented, i.e. more popular reporting oriented, than others. Only few SROI reports showed a report narrative, an aspect that may enhance the understanding of the report's importance and the perceived usefulness by the users. However, the narrative needs to be in line with the implicit narrative conveyed by the costs and benefits information in order not to frame the narrative in an unbalanced, less objective way. Many reports in the analyzed sample score high on the criterion of a balanced presentation of information; they provide extensive information in the sensitivity analysis, present the original data collection instruments in the appendix, and describe decisions on deadweight/drop-off/displacement in a transparent and detailed manner. Many however do not, and it is in particular the short reports that provide a less balanced view of information.

The results on the usefulness of the reports for service users and professionals need to be considered with caution. The two researchers conducting the analysis perceived the reports as generally useful, but those that provided extensive information as more useful than others. This may be the result of the researchers' bias due to their training and experience in (public and non-profit sector) accounting. However, it needs to be pointed out that usefulness - in general - is a highly subjective aspect of reporting, depending on the users' prior knowledge and experience, the use purpose, other available financial and non-financial information, as well as on the existence of comparable information. Comparisons of SROI values to prior values are few, and to an even lesser extent, the reports provide information on the SROI of similar organizations. Admittedly, due to the nature of the SROI itself, comparisons of SROIs across organizations (even organizations similar in size or with regards to their services) must be made with caution. The two reports that present comparisons of their SROI to the SROI of similar organizations also clearly indicate that this type of benchmarking needs to be viewed as purely informational and must not be taken as a basis for a prioritization/ranking of the cost-benefit-ratio.

Future preparers of SROI reports are well advised to include a dedicated e-mail address or contact details for feedback or questions on the report, and to encourage feedback by the report users. This may assist in establishing a real accountability relationship between the supply and demand side actors of the reports. Furthermore, it needs to be better communicated that the management of the reporting organizations takes ownership of and responsibility for the values reported in the SROI reports, even if the latter is prepared by an external organization (e.g. consulting firm). In the most visible manner, this could be accomplished by including a letter from the management and a photo of the executive/director/board. While this is a minor tweak to the report, it can be a powerful tool for establishing a reporting narrative, and even more importantly, an emotional connection to the report users.

In general, organizations in the social economy that wish to take the opportunities that popular reporting provides in terms of wider accountability may follow the strategy to publish easily available, retrievable, and also widely disseminated/communicated (e.g. via social media) short SROI reports (for example, following the AGA Citizen-Centric Reporting recommendations, see Association of Government Accountants, n.d.) that meet the formal criteria and the criteria of appeal according to suggestions in popular reporting, on the one hand. On the other hand, they may prepare full SROI reports that follow the same visual design but provide more extensive information to the interested reader. This would account for actual lending of the basic ideas of popular reporting presented in this chapter. However, these full reports need to be made easily available to the wider user group of such reports. The availability of full reports with detailed information on data collection, financial proxies, and the decisions made on the attribution of value to the activities of an organization is imperative for the usefulness of an SROI report, and thus its usefulness as an accountability instrument. So far, in many cases the full reports are published only on professional platforms or are available only upon distinct search. If the average user of SROI reports is however not aware of their existence, a dedicated/distinct search is unlikely.

ACKNOWLEDGMENT

This research received no specific grant from any funding agency in the public, commercial, or not-for-profit sectors.

REFERENCES

Arvidson, M., Lyon, F., McKay, S., & Moro, D. (2013). Valuing the social? The nature and controversies of measuring social return on investment (SROI). *Voluntary Sector Review*, *4*(1), 3–18. doi:10.1332/204080513X661554

Association of Government Accountants. (n.d.). *Citizen-centric reporting (CCR)*. Retrieved April 10, 2019, from https://www.agacgfm.org/ccr

Banke-Thomas, A. O., Madaj, B., Charles, A., & van den Broek, N. (2015). Social return on investment (SROI) methodology to account for value for money of public health interventions: A systematic review. *BMC Public Health*, *15*(1), 582. doi:10.118612889-015-1935-7 PMID:26099274

Barbera, C., Borgonovi, E., & Steccolini, I. (2016). Popular reporting and public governance: The case of "bilancio in arancio" in milan municipality. In A. Hinna, L. Gnan, & F. Monteduro (Eds.), Studies in Public and Non-Profit Governance: Vol. 5. Governance and Performance in Public and Non-Profit Organizations (pp. 3-30). Bingley, UK: Emerald Group Publishing Limited.

Barman, E., & MacIndoe, H. (2012). Institutional pressures and organizational capacity: The case of outcome measurement. *Sociological Forum*, *27*(1), 70–93. doi:10.1111/j.1573-7861.2011.01302.x

Brusca, I., & Montesinos, V. (2006). Are citizens significant users of government financial information? *Public Money & Management*, *26*(4), 205–209. doi:10.1111/j.1467-9302.2006.00526.x

Cohen, S., & Karatzimas, S. (2015). Tracing the future of reporting in the public sector: Introducing integrated popular reporting. *International Journal of Public Sector Management*, *28*(6), 449–460. doi:10.1108/IJPSM-11-2014-0140

Cohen, S., Mamakou, X., & Karatzimas, S. (2016, August). *IT enhanced popular reports: Is it the missing link in triggering citizens' interest?* Paper presented at the EGPA Conference, Utrecht, The Netherlands.

Cooney, K., & Lynch-Cerullo, K. (2014). Measuring the social returns of nonprofits and social enterprises: The promise and perils of the SROI. *Nonprofit Policy Forum*, *5*(2), 367-393.

Emerson, J., Wachowicz, J., & Chun, S. (2000). *Social Return on Investment: Exploring aspects of value creation in the nonprofit sector* (REDF Box Set No. Vol. 2). Retrieved March 13, 2019, from http://redf.org/app/uploads/2013/10/REDF-Box-Set-Vol.-2-SROI-Paper-2000.pdf

European Commission. (2018). *Social economy in the EU*. Retrieved March 13, 2019, from https://ec.europa.eu/growth/sectors/social-economy_en

FMCBC. (2004). *Recommended practice: Preparing popular reports*. Retrieved April 10, 2019, from https://www.nsmfc.ca/budgeting-and-financial-reporting/493-preparing-popular-reports/file.html

GFOA. (2006). *Popular reporting of financial information*. Retrieved April 10, 2019, from http://www.gfoa.org/popular-reporting-financial-information

GFOA. (n.d.). *Popular annual financial reporting award program: Judges's evaluation form*. Retrieved April 10, 2019, from http://www.gfoa.org/sites/default/files/u63/pafr-reviewers-checklist.pdf

Gray, R., Dillard, J., & Spence, C. (2010). A brief re-evaluation of "the social accounting project": Social accounting research as if the world matters. In A. Ball & S. P. Osborne (Eds.), *Routledge Critical Studies in Public Management: 5. Social Accounting and Public Management: Accountability for the Common Good* (pp. 11–22). New York, NY: Routledge.

Gray, R., Owen, D., & Adams, C. (1996). *Accounting and accountability: Changes and challenges in corporate social and environmental reporting*. London: Prentice-Hall.

Herrmann, K. R. (2011). Creating an excellent popular financial report. *Government Finance Review*, 41-44. Retrieved April 10, 2019, from https://www.gfoa.org/sites/default/files/GFR_OCT_11_41.pdf

Kaplan, R. S., & Norton, D. P. (1992, January). The balanced scorecard – measures that drive performance. *Harvard Business Review*, 71–79. PMID:10119714

Keehley, P., & Abercrombie, N. N. (2008). *Benchmarking in the public and nonprofit sectors. Best practices for achieving performance breakthroughs* (2nd ed.). San Francisco, CA: Jossey-Bass.

Kehl, K., Then, V., & Münscher, R. (2012). Social return on investment: Auf dem weg zu einem integrativen ansatz der wirkungsforschung. In H. K. Anheier, A. Schröer, & V. Then (Eds.), *Soziale Investitionen: Interdisziplinäre Perspektiven* (pp. 313–331). Wiesbaden: VS Verlag für Sozialwissenschaften. doi:10.1007/978-3-531-94105-9_12

Lee, M. (2006). The history of municipal public reporting. *International Journal of Public Administration*, *29*(4-6), 453–476. doi:10.1080/01900690500436982

Lingane, A., & Olsen, S. (2004). Guidelines for social return on investment. *California Management Review*, *46*(3), 116–135. doi:10.2307/41166224

Maier, F., Schober, C., Simsa, R., & Millner, R. (2015). SROI as a method for evaluation research: Understanding merits and limitations. *Voluntas, 26*(5), 1805–1830. doi:10.100711266-014-9490-x

Monzon, J. L., & Chaves, R. (2008). The european social economy: Concept and dimensions of the third sector. *Annals of Public and Cooperative Economics, 79*(3-4), 549–577. doi:10.1111/j.1467-8292.2008.00370.x

Moody, M., Littlepage, L., & Paydar, N. (2015). Measuring social return on investment: Lessons from organizational implementation of SROI in the netherlands and the united states. *Nonprofit Management & Leadership, 26*(1), 19–37. doi:10.1002/nml.21145

Mook, L. (2007). *Social and environmental accounting: The expanded value added statement* (Unpublished doctoral dissertation). University of Toronto, Toronto, Canada.

Mook, L. (2013). Social accounting for the social economy. In L. Mook (Ed.), *Accounting for Social Value* (pp. 5–28). Toronto: University of Toronto Press. doi:10.3138/9781442694453-003

Mook, L. (2014). An integrated social accounting model for nonprofit organizations. In E. Costa, L.D. Parker, & Andreaus, M. (Eds.), Advances in Public Interest Accounting: Vol. 17. Accountability and Social Accounting for Social and Non-Profit Organizations (pp. 197-221). Bingley, UK: Emerald Group Publishing Limited. doi:10.1108/S1041-706020140000017008

Mook, L., Quarter, J., & Richmond, B. J. (2007). What counts: Social accounting for nonprofits and cooperatives (2nd ed.). Medina, OH: Sigel.

Moore, M. H. (2003). *The public value scorecard: a rejoinder and an alternative to 'strategic performance measurement and management in non-profit organizations' by Robert Kaplan.* Hauser Center for Nonprofit Organizations, The Kennedy School of Government, Harvard University, Working Paper 18.

Nef. (2008). *Measuring value: a guide to social return on investment (SROI).* Nef.

Nicholls, A. (2009). 'We do good things, don't we?': 'Blended value accounting' in social entrepreneurship. *Accounting, Organizations and Society, 34*(6-7), 755–769. doi:10.1016/j.aos.2009.04.008

Nicholls, J. (2017). Social return on investment - development and convergence. *Evaluation and Program Planning, 64*, 127–135. doi:10.1016/j.evalprogplan.2016.11.011 PMID:27919435

Olsen, S., & Lingane, A. (2003). *Social return on investment: Standard Guidelines* (Working Paper Series). UC Berkeley.

Osborne, S. P., & Ball, A. (Eds.). (2010). *Social accounting and public management: Accountability for the public good.* Abingdon, UK: Routledge. doi:10.4324/9780203846070

Richmond, B. J., Mook, L., & Quarter, J. (2003). Social accounting for nonprofits: Two models. *Nonprofit Management & Leadership, 13*(4), 308–324. doi:10.1002/nml.2

Ryan, P. W., & Lyne, I. (2008). Social enterprise and the measurement of social value: Methodological issues with the calculation and application of the social return on investment. *Education, Knowledge & Economy, 2*(3), 223–237. doi:10.1080/17496890802426253

Saxton, G. D., & Guo, C. (2011). Accountability online: Understanding the web-based accountability practices of nonprofit organizations (First Published July 23, 2009). *Nonprofit and Voluntary Sector Quarterly*, *40*(2), 270–295. doi:10.1177/0899764009341086

Shoulders, C. D., & FreeMan, R. J. (2012). Government financial-reporting standards: Reviewing the past and present, anticipating the future. In R. D. Ebel & J. E. Petersen (Eds.), *The Oxford Handbook of State and Local Government Finance.* Oxford, UK: Oxford University Press.

Sowa, J. E., Selden, S. C., & Sandfort, J. R. (2004). No longer unmeasurable? A multidimensional integrated model of nonprofit organizational effectiveness. *Nonprofit and Voluntary Sector Quarterly*, *33*(4), 711–728. doi:10.1177/0899764004269146

SROI-Network. (2009). *A guide to social return on investment.* Author.

SROI-Network. (2012). *A guide to social return on investment.* Author.

Yusuf, J.-E., Jordan, M. M., Neill, K. A., & Hackbart, M. (2013). For the people: Popular financial reporting practices of local governments. *Public Budgeting & Finance*, *33*(1), 95–113. doi:10.1111/j.1540-5850.2013.12003.x

KEY TERMS AND DEFINITIONS

Accountability: An individual's or organization's obligation to account for their activities, the practice of assuming responsibility for the latter and disclosing the results of these activities in a transparent manner.

Impact Map: An illustration of the theory of change in a diagrammatic form.

Monetized Value/Monetary Value: The value that an item, service, or effect/outcome would have were it sold for money to a willing buyer. In functioning markets, this value would be the market price; in imperfect markets, the value is determined using financial proxies.

Popular Reporting: An approach of presenting financial and non-financial accounting information to non-accounting-professional users (e.g., citizens) in a concise, comprehensive, and easy-to-read report.

Proxies: Indirect measures of (one or more) desired indicator(s). Proxies are used when exact data or direct measures for an outcome are unavailable.

Report Narrative: An overarching story or theme to the financial figures and non-financial results presented in a financial (or popular) report in order to strengthen the presentation of an organization's activities and to put the results into perspective.

Sensitivity Analysis: The process of verifying the SROI results and rationalizing findings. The sensitivity analysis builds on an estimation of the extent to which the results would change if the underlying assumptions changed.

Social Return on Investment (SROI): A tool that allows accounting for and reporting the social impact of an organization by involving stakeholders in the process of valuation of outcomes.

Stakeholder: Any person or group of people that can affect, or is affected by, the activities of an organization, either in a positive or a negative way.

Theory of Change: A conceptualization of how the organization or the analyzed activities use certain resources (inputs) to deliver activities or direct results (outputs) and longer-term, or more significant results (outcomes), as well as the part of social value that the organization can take credit for (impact).

ENDNOTES

1. However, a random search using different configurations of Google search (language, region), using German, Spanish, and Italian retrieved no noteworthy results on SROI reports in different languages or from different country or regional contexts than those published in the Social Value and nef databases.
2. The present chapter however does not claim to, and also does not aim to provide an exhaustive overview of respective efforts, not least given a likely under-representation of international developments due to language barriers.

Chapter 10
Disclosure of Corporate Social Responsibility on the Websites of Portuguese Foundations

Rui Robalo
School of Management and Technology of Santarém, Portugal

Wilson Patrocínio
School of Management and Technology of Santarém, Portugal

ABSTRACT

This chapter aims to assess how the Portuguese foundations manage and disclosure on their websites information on corporate social responsibility (CSR). The study performs the assessment of the sampled foundations holding a website accessible to the broad public and being members of the Portuguese Foundation Centre. The evidence of this study impacts therefore the literature review on three ways. Firstly, it sheds light on the diversity of CSR policies undertaken by foundations, through the scale perspective and the CSR content categories. Secondly, it claims how distinct CSR information trends can be triggered by needs of legitimacy towards the stakeholders unlike other types of organizations. Lastly, the evidence provided by this study suggests that there in not a significant influence of the dimension factor of the foundations on the amount of CSR information they disclose, which contradicts evidence of previous studies.

INTRODUCTION

Corporate Social Responsibility (CSR) presents an integrated vision of social and environmental concepts in companies' operations and interactions with their stakeholders in a voluntary manner (Dincer & Dincer, 2010). CSR will be analyzed in this study by disseminating the quantity and typology of information disclosure on the websites of Portuguese foundations.

The literature on the analysis of CSR has been carried out predominantly through studies based mainly on companies, as are the cases of studies of Chaudhri & Wang (2007), Dincer & Dincer (2010), and Branco et al. (2014). However, more recent studies (e.g. Gálvez-Rodríguez et al., 2012, 2014; Tremblay-

DOI: 10.4018/978-1-5225-8482-7.ch010

Boire & Prakash, 2014) have already studied this subject through non-profit organizations, more precisely through non-governmental organizations. We intend to contribute empirically by using another type of non-profit organizations, specifically foundations, which we do not believe to have been the subject of studies by the scientific community, and which may provide different results on the commitment of this type of organizations in the dissemination of the quantity and quality of CSR disclosure.

The analysis of the disclosure tool itself also gains preponderance in this study. The fact that CSR dissemination analysis has evolved mainly through studies based on annual reports, raises the importance of analyzing the dissemination of other types of dissemination tools (Fifka, 2012). Therefore, we intend to study the dissemination of CSR through the *Internet,* another usual tool in the exposure of information in the context of social responsibility (e.g. Chapple & Moon, 2005; Chaudhri & Wang, 2007; Chen & Bouvain, 2009; Silva, 2015). For example, Silva (2015) says that it is relevant to study the use of Internet, in this study represented by the websites, to communicate the information related to CSR, as consumer awareness and the competitive environment exerts a certain amount of pressure to the benefit of the society in which they are placed so that the entities disclose CSR practices. In fact, non-profit organizations are strategically using their own personal website to present themselves to the public and share information (Lee & Blouin, 2017).

This study will be used as a methodology similar to those adopted in the studies of Chaudhri & Wang (2007), Dincer & Dincer (2010), and Branco et al. (2014) This will allow the comparison between studies that analyzed the dissemination of CSR in different temporal spaces, types of organizations and cultural contexts. With the purpose of supporting the analysis of the CSR theme between our study and the others, this study has as a theoretical support the theory of legitimacy and the theory of stakeholders, two theories connected to the corporate disclosure of information on social affairs.

In the next section we review the concept, objectives and tools of disclosure of CSR, as well as the underlying theories chosen to explain their dissemination, more specifically the theory of stakeholders and the theory of legitimacy. In the third section, we present the research methodology, including the definition of the study sample, the process of data collection and analysis. In the fourth section, the results are presented and discussed. Contributions, limitations and perspectives of future research are in the final section.

LITERATURE REVIEW

Conceptual Framework of CSR: Concept, Objectives and Dissemination Tools

Due to the importance that social and environmental issues have reached among the citizens, the organizations try to present, in addition to financial stability, a good image to the citizens of the society in which they are part of (Brown & Dacin, 1997). In turn, there has been a significant increase in the concern of citizens and consumers about the responsible management of companies and public institutions (Servera-French et al., 2015). Additionally, businesses have been increasingly confronted with greater demand for transparency in the behavior of business practices (Kolk, 2008; Pollach et al., 2009).

The introduction of reporting standards, as is the case with the Global Reporting Initiative, has provided to the organizations auxiliary mechanisms to determine the amount of information disclosed and, in turn, has created the potential to significantly develop the usefulness and quality of information disseminated by organizations on the impacts and performances in the face of the environment, society and the economy (Willis, 2003). In this way, the use of initiatives from organizations related to CSR, with the aim of receiving support from society and influencing consumer concerns, became more common (Birch, 2003). CSR is considered as a commitment of an organization to go beyond the economic priorities, to build a good relationship with the stakeholders and to maintain transparency and ethical behavior (Dincer & Dincer, 2010). However, there is also the prospect that disclosure of CSR may not be beneficial to the organization itself, as consumers may consider that organizations only disclose this information as a way of compensating for the mediocre performance of their activities (Coope, 2004).

Empirical studies on CSR tend to analyze in which proportions organizations disclose non-financial information, rather than merely financial information. Non-financial indicators complement financial information and facilitate better benchmarking of the organization's value and interest (Maines et al., 2002). According to Dincer & Dincer (2010) CSR is increasingly associated with a new management model focused on voluntary integration of economic, social and environmental responsibilities in the entire functional process of the organization. Consequently, several studies (e.g. Van der Laan et al., 2005; Dincer & Dincer, 2010; Fifka & Drabble, 2012) have noticed difference in the extension and the type of reporting followed in the various countries but the influence of cultural, social and economic specificities need to be more considered.

This study was based on the concept of CSR coherent with some perspectives evidenced in other studies (e.g. Branco et al., 2014; Gray et al., 2001). According to Branco et al. (2014), CSR is a concept that portrays the relationships between the organizations and the society in which they are inserted. The same authors consider that, to provide solutions to the objectives proposed by CSR, users of this type of information try to change their social and environmental behaviors according to the society in which they are inserted, in which the organizations are influenced and influence the society where they act. Thus, a greater interest of organizations is justified in disseminating information about CSR. Organizations must disclose their activities, aspirations, and public image with attention to the environment, community, employees and consumer-related issues (Gray et al., 2001). Although the literature evidences that organizations are increasingly encouraged to adopt standards about CSR, the current research on their adoption and impacts can still be considered limited.

Also, the scope of the CSR concept has been discussed. Wood (1991) considers that CSR covers the configuration of social responsibility principles, social sensitivity processes and policies, programs and observable results in relation to the company's social relations. The European Commission (2001) considers that CSR consists of practices through which companies voluntarily integrate social and environmental concerns in their business operations and interactions with stakeholders, contributing to their sustainable development. A Lifelong Learning Programme (2010) defines CSR as the general responsibility of companies for sustainable economic, ecological and social management, and this concept is designed to help companies voluntarily integrate social and ecological concerns in their business activities and relationships with their stakeholders. More recently, Servera-French et al. (2015) says that CSR allows companies to acquire a greater level of commitment to consumers and to society in general.

In relation to the business context of the CSR concept, Branco & Rodrigues (2008) claim that companies with a good reputation for CSR are interested in developing relations with external entities such as consumers, investors, bankers, suppliers and competitors. In addition, these entities consider that companies with good CSR practices also attract better employees and increase their motivation, commitment and loyalty, which translates into a financial increment for the companies that practice it.

The CSR theme is part of the non-financial information disseminated by the various companies (or other organizations). In general, companies in formulating their strategy should consider the satisfaction of the capital holders (shareholders), but also that of all groups or individuals that are affected or that can affect the achievement of the organization's objectives (Campos, 2006). To provide all kinds of information to their information users, the various organizations disclose financial and non-financial information. Regarding the information disclosed in a financial nature, all information on the financial position, expenditure and income related to the activities is usually presented. About the non-financial information of the organizations, documents such as sustainability reports and codes of conduct are highlighted. Van der Laan et al. (2005) says that literature on CSR can be portrayed as a subchapter of corporate financial disclosure. The study of Chen & Bouvain (2009) concluded that companies, such as Henkel, BHP and Johnson & Johnson, have a long tradition in reporting of non-financial information and in the disclosure of all the characteristics of its responsibility and business sustainability.

The dissemination of non-financial information has been studied through companies, but also from non-profit organizations (e.g. Torres & Pina 2003; Gálvez-Rodríguez et al., 2012, 2014; Tremblay-Boire & Prakash, 2014). Regarding studies on non-profit organizations, the Torres & Pina (2003) study concludes that there is a greater demand for financial and non-financial information on this type of organizations, either by the management bodies or by the other stakeholders. According to the same authors, the non-profit organizations usually have specific missions that usually do not fall directly into an economic-financial sphere. They are public and private organizations, which are directed not to the distribution of profits to shareholders, but to the realization of public interests (Junqueira, 2000). In another perspective, non-profit organizations are vulnerable to accounting problems derived from the activity and the institutional context in which they work (Silva & Burger, 2015).

This work investigates the CSR in the foundations, one of the types of non-profit organizations. Pratas (2009: 252) says that a foundation is a *"collective person whose fundamental element is a set of assets permanently affected to the realization of a particular purpose, of an altruistic nature"*. The philanthropic foundations, in a generic way, are defined as instruments of private wealth for public purposes, because these are non-governmental and non-profit organizations that have their own capital, and that exist to maintain or to carry out social, educational, charitable or other activities that meet the welfare of the society in general (Borges et al., 2007). To evaluate the non-financial information presented by the foundations, it is useful to analyze the dissemination tools used by organizations, more precisely the dissemination through the annual reports, sustainability reports, or Websites.

Over the last two decades, empirical research on the dissemination of CSR has evolved through work done in the emerging economies and developed countries but focusing on the annual business reports of the companies (Fifka, 2012). For example, the Van der Laan et al. (2005) study obtained the empirical data from the annual reports of 32 Norwegian and Danish companies and 26 English companies in the years 1998 and 1999, to analyze the disclosure on social issues. However, there are also studies that analyze disclosure through other documents which are also the main theme of CSR. For example, sustainability reports were also used in the Kolk Study (2004) to obtain evidence regarding the disclosure of documentation about CSR.

During technological developments, a new information dissemination tool was created. Internet has arisen as a fundamental means in the spread of information and communication, not only because of its interactivity and ability to disseminate information, but also because it is a bidirectional communication channel and universal access, in which communication is almost synchronous (Vilar, 2012). The fact that Internet being the cheapest and most effective dissemination tool of today, increases the interest of the present study, and its implications, although the great generality of the organizations still do not use the Internet as a disclosure tool (Dincer & Dincer, 2010). In business terms, the Internet is a communication tool in which companies can disseminate information of different natures. The use of Internet is now an excellent communication channel, widely used to sell products, disseminate information and connect people, among other features (Sousa & Wanderley, 2007). According to Branco et al. (2014) disclosure through this tool has evolved over the years, to the detriment of disclosure only from the annual reports. The authors investigated the dissemination of CSR practices via Internet of the largest companies in Sweden and Spain, to analyze the extent, and to ascertain whether there were differences in CSR communication practices in Websites of the companies in these two countries.

Motivations of Organizations to Disseminate CSR Information

At the point of view of theoretical justification, the motivations of organizations to disseminate CSR information have been explained mainly by theory of stakeholders and by the theory of legitimacy. Regarding the theory of Stakeholders, which according to Freeman & McVea (2001) arose in the mid-80, companies have obligations to a larger set of individuals than only owners (Freeman, 1984). Each non-profit organization by itself, such as the companies, relates and interacts with a set of stakeholders. These are affected or may affect the achievement of the objectives of the organization (Freedman & Reed, 1983).

According to the theory of stakeholders, companies seek to respond preferentially to the most important stakeholders and tend to ignore those less important (Roberts, 1992; Neu et al., 1998). Thus, it is ensured that the non-profit organizations tend to disseminate preferably the CSR information requested by its major stakeholders. This theory is based on the premise that companies from countries with a greater orientation for social affairs will have higher levels of quality in the disclosure of CSR in their annual reports (Van der Laan et al., 2005). However, companies from countries with greater guidance for their shareholders and with a lower emphasis on social affairs, they will present a lower level of disclosure of CSR (Van der Laan et al., 2005). The study of Branco et al. (2014) concludes that there are countries that have greater evidence of guidance for stakeholders. Thus, countries such as Spain present a lower level of guidance for the stakeholders than those that are normally considered to be countries targeted at stakeholders, as are the cases of Australia, Canada, New Zealand, or the United Kingdom (Dhaliwal et al., 2012).

Friedman & Miles (2006) state that the theory of stakeholders has served as a reference to several research and methodological developments around disclosure of CSR. The authors argue that in providing information to the outside of the organization efforts have been made in the sense that the reports produced serve the interests and needs of the various stakeholders of the organizations. They also refer to the need or advantage of the stakeholders having systematic information is not sufficiently treated by the literature. In turn, Chen & Bouvain (2009) state that the results and differences established in the extension and content of CSR reports may also be related to differences in the importance attributed to CSR issues by stakeholders in different countries. Van der Laan et al. (2005), Branco et al. (2014), and Tremblay-Boire & Prakash (2014) used the theory of stakeholders as a theoretical livelihood for their articles.

The theory of stakeholders is closely linked to the theory of legitimacy (Guthrie et al., 2004). This theory suggests that organizations seek the approval of the society in which they are part of, which is consistent with the concept of information disclosed to a greater number of stakeholders (O'Dwyer & Unerman, 2008). In short, these two theories have explained the results of several empirical studies around disclosure of CSR information. Many researchers studying the dissemination of information about CSR, using samples of non-profit organizations, have used the theory of legitimacy and theory of *stakeholders,* simultaneously or separately, to explain the disclosure of CSR information by the non-profit organizations (e.g. Barrett, 2001; Keating & Frumkin, 2003, Dainelli et al. 2012). Barrett's (2001) study found that one of the limitations in relation to the theory of stakeholders relates to the fact that it was developed primarily for liability issues in for-profit organizations. The author says that the theory of stakeholders is not the only theoretical framework that leads to the conclusion that the external parties play a crucial role in the success of an organization. Dainelli et al. (2012) analyzed non-profit organizations, more specifically museums in Australia, Canada, France, Germany, Italy, the United Kingdom and the United States of America, and, based on the theory of stakeholders, argue that in the absence of shareholders the disclosure of CSR practices is driven by the number and power of different stakeholders. The authors sought to validate in this way the theory of stakeholders.

Quantity and Typology of Information Disclosure on the Websites of Portuguese Foundations

For analysing the quantity and typology of information disclosure on the websites of Portuguese foundations, it is important to attend studies that investigated the dissemination of CSR practices by means of websites. In the dissemination of these practices, organizations can follow different strategies.

According to Guziana & Dobers (2013), presenting information about CSR on the homepage indicates that there is a recognition of the need and importance of the quality of the presentation of the corporate social commitment. Pollach (2005) considers that companies presenting information about CSR on the page for the section entitled "About Us", they do so to highlight the information presented in their websites. However, it is considered that companies that have a section dedicated exclusively to CSR gain a greater prominence than those presenting CSR information on the page entitled "About Us", or on another page of the website (Branco & Rodrigues, 2008; Branco et al., 2014).

The studies of Chaudhri & Wang (2007), Dincer & Dincer (2010), and Branco et al. (2014) presented different results in relation to the site of the website for the disclosure of CSR. Chaudhri & Wang (2007) provided evidence that approximately two thirds of the top 30 Indian sample companies had CSR information in the section "About Us", and the remaining third presented the information about CSR on the homepage, while 70 companies did not disclose information about CSR. In the analysis of Dincer & Dincer (2010), of the 410 Turkish companies surveyed, 297 companies do not disclose information about CSR. Of the 113 that disseminate, more than 40% (46 companies) presented information on their homepage while the other companies presented the information in the "About Us" section. More recently, Branco et al. (2014) noted that, from their sample of 27 Swedish companies and 29 Spanish companies, only 7% of the sample did not disclose information about CSR, and 75% disclosed the information about CSR on the homepage, and only 18% in the "About Us" section, or on another page of *the website.* Thus, to analyze the commitment of the Portuguese foundations to the provision of information of CSR, the following questions were formulated:

Q1: Do the Portuguese foundations disclose CSR information on any page of their websites?

Q1A: Do the Portuguese foundations disseminate information about CSR on the homepage of their websites?

Q1B: Do the Portuguese foundations disclose information about CSR on the page regarding the "About Us" section, or on another page of their websites?

It is therefore important to assess how much the foundations disseminate information about CSR in their websites. There has also been advocated by researchers that the number of pages is an indicator of the effort applied by an organization to disclose its commitment to the thematic of CSR (e.g. Chaudhri & Wang, 2007; Dincer & Dincer, 2010; Branco et al., 2014). Based on these studies, the theoretical lines concerning the amount of CSR information disclosed indicates that disclosures with more than three pages suggest companies' commitment to disseminate CSR information. According to the results obtained in the study of Chaudhri & Wang (2007), 43% of the sample companies only disclose between one to three pages, 37% of the sample discloses between four to ten pages and 20% of the sample discloses more than 10 pages about CSR in their websites. In turn, in the study of Dincer & Dincer (2010), 47% of the sample discloses one to three pages, 51% of the sample discloses between four to ten pages of CSR, and only 2% disseminate more than ten pages on CSR information in their websites. Branco et al. (2014) also concluded in their study that 12% of the sample companies disclose one to three pages of information on CSR, 17% spread between four to ten pages and 71% disclose more than ten pages of CSR on their websites. Based on these studies, the following questions were formulated:

Q2A: Do the Portuguese foundations disclose one to three pages about CSR information on their websites?
Q2B: Do the Portuguese foundations disclose four to ten pages about CSR information on their websites?
Q2C: Do the Portuguese foundations disclose more than ten pages about CSR information on their websites?

In addition to the different amount of CSR information disclosed in the websites of organizations, there may also be significant differences in the type of information disseminated, notably between organizations in different countries. Based on a sample of Spanish and Swedish companies, the study of Branco et al. (2014) indicates that there is a causality between the variety of CSR information derived and the characteristics of the two countries. These findings are in line with those of the study of Halme & Huse (1997), which found that the Nordic countries have traditionally demonstrated more commitment to protecting the environment than the countries of southern Europe, due essentially to political factors such as Norway's law drawn up in 1989, which requires that the companies include information in the annual report on emission levels, contamination, and measures envisaged and carried out by the entities to clean the environment. Thus, the CSR themes to be disseminated by the Portuguese foundations may be influenced by the cultural, political, social and economic characteristics of Portugal.

Moreover, the literature differs in the thematic on the CSR predominantly disseminated through the websites. Van der Laan et al. (2005) identified environmental practices as the most widely disseminated information typology in their study on 32 Danish and Norwegian companies, and 26 companies from the United States of America. These authors assessed that 55% of Norwegian and Danish companies disseminated information on environmental practices, 26% of the sample disseminated information on human resources, 7% disseminated information on products and consumers, and only 2% of the sample disseminated information on philanthropy and social involvement, while of the 26 American companies, 16% disseminated information on environmental practices, 26% disseminated information on human resources, 32% disseminated information about the products and consumers, and 26% disseminated information on philanthropy and social involvement. Branco et al. (2014) also obtained different results from their sample of Spanish and Swedish companies. Spanish companies mainly disseminated information about social and philanthropic involvement, while Swedish companies disseminated information about the environment, human resources or products and consumers. Thus, based on the studies of Van der Laan et al. (2005) and of Branco et al. (2014), we formulated the following questions:

Q3A: Do the Portuguese foundations disclose information about the environment on their websites?
Q3B: Do the Portuguese foundations disclose information about human resources on their websites?
Q3C: Do the Portuguese foundations disclose information about products and consumers on their websites?
Q3D: Do the Portuguese foundations disclose information about philanthropy and social involvement on their websites?

To further examine the content of disclosure about CSR, we also contemplate the dissemination of websites of CSR-related documents, such as the codes of conduct and sustainability reports. The analysis concerning the disclosure of the codes of conduct of foundations is justified by the need for organizations to demonstrate their commitment to CSR from the creation of codes of conduct and CSR policies, as well as to the subscription of letters of credible principles that provide some guidance as to the practices and behaviors considered acceptable and not acceptable in terms of CSR (Waddock, 2008). In relation to the results of the empirical studies that analyzed the dissemination of codes of conduct, Fifka & Drabble (2012) assessed in their study on the 100 largest companies in the UK and Finland, which 86% of the UK companies and 82% of the Finnish have published their code of conduct, as well as their guiding principles for the decision-making process concerning sustainability issues. Branco et al. (2014) analyzed this strand in their study and found that 83% of the sample released the code of conduct in their websites.

The analysis of sustainability reports is also justified, as this is a report drawn up according to the guidelines of the Global Reporting Initiative, and that addresses three following inter-related elements: the social, environmental and economic aspects of an organization. In relation to the results of the empirical studies that analyzed the dissemination of sustainability reports in the websites, Fifka & Drabble (2012) concluded that of the 50 largest companies for each country, 50% of the sample of UK companies released a sustainability report separately from another document, and 40% of Finnish companies released the sustainability report. Finally, the study of Branco et al. (2014) found that 83% of the sample released their sustainability reports in their websites. With the aim to analyzing the dissemination of sustainability reports and codes of conduct by the Portuguese foundations, we formulated the following questions:

Q4A: Do the Portuguese foundations disclose codes of conduct on their websites?
Q4B: Do the Portuguese foundations disclose sustainability reports on their websites?

Another important issue is the way the CSR information is disclosure in the websites. Chaudhri & Wang (2007) consider that the Internet offers organizations the ability to design the content of their websites, not being obliged to follow a traditional pattern. In their study, 50% of the Indian sample companies used the text contextualized with images to disseminate information about CSR, and 47% of the companies mainly used text, while 3% of the companies presented mainly images to disclose information about CSR. In turn, Dincer & Dincer (2010) also concluded in their study that 49% of the Turkish sample companies only disseminated information in text format, 50% disseminated information in contextualized text with images, while only 1% disseminated the information through images. Based on these studies, we decided to analyze the forms of presentation of the information about CSR according to the following three options: mainly text, mainly images, and text contextualized with Images. The analysis of these three options gave rise to the formulation of the following questions:

Q5A: Do the Portuguese foundations present the CSR information predominantly through text?
Q5B: Do the Portuguese foundations present the CSR information predominantly through images?
Q5C: Do the Portuguese foundations present the CSR information through contextualized text with images?

It is also known that organizations disclose information for various reasons. The study of Branco et al. (2014) argue that factors such as the size of the company may be empirically important in terms of the amount of disclosure of CSR practices. The interest of this factor is mainly due to two reasons. First, it has to do with the fact that the amount of information disclosed is done voluntarily by the large companies, derived from a more susceptible assessment by the public (e.g. Gray et al., 2001; Patten, 2002; Baldini et al., 2016). Second, the larger organizations are conducive to attracting more attention and, consequently, to disclose more information related to CSR practices (e.g. Saxton & Guo, 2011; Gálvez-Rodríguez et al., 2012). In turn, companies with a larger dimension will probably have more resources to create and maintain a website, being that they do it strategically (Saxton & Guo, 2011).

The relationship between the size of a company and the amount of disclosure has already been analyzed in some scientific studies. Some of these studies refer that the size of the entities is highly correlated with the level of financial disclosure in Internet (e.g. Gálvez-Rodríguez et al., 2012). Van der Laan et al. (2005) and Wanderley et al. (2008) argue that the largest companies disclose more CSR information in their annual reports and their websites, while smaller companies disclose less information. We want to see how the foundation's size affects the dissemination of CSR information and, thus, the following question has been formulated:

Q6: Do the larger Portuguese foundations disseminate more CSR information on their websites than those of smaller size?

From the whole of the above questions, we will proceed in the next section to the definition of the research methodology.

RESEARCH METHODOLOGY

Given that this study aims to analyze the quantity and variety of CSR disclosure on the websites of the Portuguese foundations, the collection of empirical data is based on foundations that have a page of Internet. More specifically, to be included in the initial sample of this study, the foundations had to be associated entities in the Portuguese Foundation Centre at the end of the year 2015 and have their page of Internet available for access to their information users.

The initial sample included all foundations in the Portuguese Foundation Centre on the date of 26 October 2015, available online at the following email address: http://www.cpf.org.pt/paginas/14/diretorio-de-associados/14/. The collection of sample data took place between 26 October and 2 December 2015.

Of an initial sample of 137 foundations, only 123 had websites. This final sample contemplates 84 private foundations, 28 public foundations of private law and 11 public private foundations.

The process of collecting empirical data was carried out through the digital observation of the websites of foundations, more specifically information on the quantity and variety of disclosure of CSR, referring to the formulated questions based on previous section. Empirical data concerning the questions Q1, Q1A, and Q1B were obtained through verification in websites the section where information about CSR is presented. Since another of the strands analyzed in this study was the number of pages with information about CSR disclosed by the foundations, with the objective of answering the questions Q2A, Q2B and Q2C of this study, the empirical data consisted in the count of the number of pages observed on CSR information disclosed in the websites of the foundations. The possible results of this count consisted in considering that CSR information in the *website* contemplated the disclosure between one to three pages, between four to ten pages or more than ten pages of CSR information.

In relation to the analysis of the thematic presented in websites, we collected the CSR information on the websites of the foundations to answer the questions Q3A, Q3B, Q3C and Q3D. Thus, to segregate the thematic of CSR information by the different subareas, we based this choice from the categories on social responsibility used in the study of Van der Laan et al. (2005), Chen & Bouvain (2009), and of Branco et al. (2014). The empirical data for these questions were obtained by observing the CSR information presented in the websites of foundations, and its corresponding framing in one of the following themes: environment, human resources, products and consumers, and philanthropy and social involvement.

Empirical data were also collected to assess whether the Portuguese foundations disseminate in their websites CSR-related documents. The possible results of this collection were the foundations did or did not disclose in their website: codes of conduct, sustainability reports or other CSR-related documents. This allows us to answer the questions Q4A and Q4B,

The quality of the presentation of information in the websites was also an object of analysis in this study. Thus, to obtain empirical data to answer the questions Q5A, Q5B and Q5C, we gathered the information of the dissemination format of CSR: predominantly in text, predominantly in images, or if it was in text contextualized with images.

About the collection of data to answer the question Q6, concerning the analysis of the relationship between the size of the foundation and the amount of information disclosed about CSR, it was necessary to advance the identification of the size of the inquired foundations. There are several ways of characterizing the organizations in relation to their size (Elsakit & Worthington, 2014). There are studies that have measured the dimension through the total assets of the organization (e.g. Hossain & Reaz, 2007; Branco & Rodrigues, 2008; Al-Shubiri et al., 2012), through the number of employees (e.g. Amran & Devi, 2008) and through sales (e.g. Deegan & Gordon, 1996). We considered that the total of the asset was the best criterion for the foundations, since the number of workers and sales do not illustrate with the utmost foresight the dimension of non-profit entities. To segregate the various foundations by different types of dimension, the criteria of distinction laid down in Decree-Law No. 98/2015 of 2 June, which adopts the total asset of the organizations. The total asset of the foundations was obtained by analyzing the accounts reports for the last year available in the websites of the foundations, having 2015 as a reference year. There were considered micro-foundations those ones that showed a total of assets less than 350000 euros and Small foundations those with a total of assets between 350000 and 4 million euros. In turn, the were considered as medium-foundations those with a total of assets greater than 4 million and less than 20 million euros, and as large-foundations those with a total of assets greater than 20 million euros. These different dimensions were related to the number of pages disclosed in the websites of the foundations.

Regarding the analysis of the data collected through the digital observation of the phenomena related to the questions, these will be carried out simultaneously with the descriptive research process. The results relating to the observation of the phenomena was expressed in quantitative data, particularly through the number of foundations of the sample in which the respective phenomenon was observed, and its corresponding percentage. The results arising from this analysis are presented in the next section.

PRESENTATION AND DISCUSSION OF RESULTS

In this section, we present and discuss the findings of this study. From the sample of 123 Portuguese foundations, 14 of the foundations (11.38%) disseminate information about CSR on their main pages, 57 of foundations (47.15%) transmit information about CSR on the page for the section "About Us" or on other pages of the websites, and 52 foundations (41.47%) do not place CSR information in their websites (see Table 1). We can consider that the percentage obtained from foundations that disclose information about CSR may be justified by the need for such organizations to provide non-financial information to their stakeholders. As evidenced by the study of Tremblay-Boire & Prakash (2014) in non-profit organizations, the Portuguese foundations intend to legitimize themselves to their stakeholders, thereby disseminating information about CSR.

The result obtained though the question Q1 indicates that 58.53% of the sample foundations report information about CSR in their websites (see Table 1). However, the results on the questions Q1A and Q1B refer that there is a greater predisposition of the Portuguese foundations to present CSR information on the page destined for the section "About Us" of their websites. The results obtained also indicate that of the 71 foundations that provide CSR information on the homepage, *o*nly about one-fifth (19.71%) discloses information about CSR on its main page, and approximately four-fifths (80.29%) discloses this type of information on the page for the section entitled "About Us".

The results obtained in the questions Q1, Q1A and Q1B of this study follow the same tendency as those obtained by Chaudhri & Wang (2007) and Dincer & Dincer (2010) but differ from those obtained by Branco et al. (2014). In the latter study, the authors report the existence of a higher percentage of Spanish companies, compared to Swedish companies, which disseminate CSR information on the main pages of their websites. The difference obtained by this study in relation to the study of Branco et al. (2014) can be explained by the type of organizations analyzed. The fact that their study was carried out based on the major Spanish and Swedish companies could entail a greater need for them to present greater commitment to social affairs, since they are in organizational contexts with greater emphasis on the stakeholders, evidenced by a higher percentage of companies presenting CSR information and disseminating it on the main page of their websites.

Regarding the questions Q2A, Q2B and Q2C, the results obtained indicate that 69.01% of the 71 foundations disclose between one to three pages of CSR information, 28.17% disclose between four to ten pages and 2.82% discloses more than ten pages (see Table 2). The results showed that most of the Portuguese foundations disclose only the CSR information that they consider most important. As in the study of Chaudhri & Wang (2007), we will not be able to say that the Portuguese foundations that disclose more than three pages of CSR information are more committed in social affairs than those that disclose

Table 1. Comparison between studies on the number of organizations that disseminate CSR information in their websites

Studies	Current study	Chaudhri & Wang (2007)	Dincer & Dincer (2010)	Branco et al. (2014)
Sample of each study	123 Foundations	100 Companies	410 Companies	56 Companies
They do not disclose CSR information in their *websites*	52 Foundations (41.47%)	70 Companies (70.00%)	297 Companies (72.44%)	4 Companies (7.14%)
They disclose CSR information on any page of their websites (Q1)	71 Foundations (58.53%)	30 Companies (30.00%)	113 Companies (27.56%)	52 Companies (92.86%)
They disclose information on the main page of their website*s* (Q1A)	14 Foundations (11.38%)	11 Companies (11.00%)	46 Companies (11.22%)	42 Companies (75.00%)
They disclose information on the page regarding the "About Us" or in another page of their *websites* (Q1B)	57 Foundations (47.15%)	19 Companies (19.00%)	67 Companies (16.34%)	10 Companies (17.86%)

only one to three pages. However, the reduced number of pages disclosed on CSR may indicate a lesser need for legitimacy by Portuguese foundations in relation to other types of organizations.

The empirical results obtained in this study do not follow the tendency of the studies of Chaudhri & Wang (2007), Dincer & Dincer (2010) and Branco et al. (2014), which differ mainly from the latter, as can be seen in Table 2. These may be justified by the type of analyzed organizations. Given that the largest Spanish and Swedish companies have been analyzed, it is to be admitted that these, by their nature and size, may have a higher commitment to disclose CSR information to legitimize themselves to their stakeholders and achieving a better competitive position than their competitors.

From the analysis of the empirical data related to the questions Q3A, Q3B, Q3C and Q3D, it was obtained evidence that 70.42% of the 71 foundations disclose information on philanthropy and social involvement, 14.08% disclose information about the environment, 12.68% disclose Information about the products and consumers and 16.90% disclose information on human resources (see Table 3). The theme of philanthropy and social involvement is very much associated with foundations and associations, as referred to in Branco et al. (2014). Thus, the results of a greater level of disclosure of philanthropic and social involvement issues found in this study are not surprising, as foundations are under analysis.

Table 2. Comparison between studies on the number of pages disclosed by organizations about CSR information in their websites

Studies	Current study	Chaudhri & Wang (2007)	Dincer & Dincer (2010)	Branco et al. (2014)
Sample organizations that disseminate CSR information in their *Websites*	71 Foundations	30 Companies	113 Companies	52 Companies
They disclose between one to three pages of CSR information in their websites (Q2A)	49 Foundations (69.01%)	13 Companies (43.33%)	53 Companies (46.90%)	6 Companies (11.54%)
They disclose between four to ten pages of CSR information in their websites (Q2B)	20 Foundations (28.17%)	11 Companies (36.67%)	58 Companies (51.33%)	9 Companies (17.31%)
They disclose more than ten pages of CSR information in their websites (Q2C)	2 Foundations (2.82%)	6 Companies (20.00%)	2 Companies (1.77%)	37 Companies (71.15%)

According to the results obtained in the studies of Van der Laan et al. (2005) and Branco et al. (2014), only the sample of Spanish entities of this last study disclosed essentially information about philanthropy and social involvement.

The results obtained in the questions Q4A and Q4B indicate that 63 Portuguese foundations disclose codes of conduct in their websites (see Table 4). In turn, the results also indicate that only 3 foundations use their websites to communicate their sustainability reports. The results suggest that most of the Portuguese foundations are concerned enough to disclose to their stakeholders their guiding principles concerning their decision-making processes of the phenomena related to the CSR practices. The Portuguese foundations appear to have a lesser experience in the disclosure of CSR information, and this is evidenced by the disclosure of codes of conduct to the detriment of the disclosure of sustainability reports. Nevertheless, it is expected that in the future more foundations develop and disclose sustainability reports.

It can be admitted that the experience of disclosure could influence the disclosure of sustainability reports. The results obtained on the disclosure of the sustainability reports indicate that these were disclosed only by a medium-sized foundation and two large foundations. Moreover, studies of Fifka & Drabble (2012) and Branco et al. (2014), when attending large companies in Finland, the United Kingdom, Spain and Sweden, found levels of disclosure of the sustainability reports rather than those presented in this study. This greater disclosure could be explained by these companies having already initiated the process of disseminating the sustainability report for longer and using them to achieve greater legitimacy with their stakeholders.

Table 3. Comparison of studies on CSR themes disclosed in Websites

Studies	Current study	Van der Laan et al. (2005)	Van der Laan et al. (2005)	Branco et al. (2014)
Sample organizations that disclose CSR information in their websites	71 Portuguese foundations	32 Norwegian and Danish Companies	26 North American Companies	52 Spanish and Swedish companies
They disclose information about the environment in their websites (Q3A)	14,08%	54,70%	16,30%	42,31%
They disclose information about human resources in their websites (Q3B)	16,90%	26,40%	26,10%	42,31%
They disclose information about products and consumers in their *websites* (Q3C)	12,68%	7,00%	32,10%	42,31%
They disclose information about philanthropy and social involvement in their *websites* (Q3D)	70,42%	1,60%	25,50%	40,38%

Table 4. Comparison of studies on codes of conduct and sustainability reports

Studies	Current study	Fifka & Drabble (2012)	Branco et al. (2014)
Sample organizations that disseminate CSR information in their *Websites*	71 Foundations	90 Companies	52 Companies
They disclose codes of conduct in their websites (Q4A)	63 Foundations (88.73%)	84 Companies (93.33%)	43 Companies (82.69%)
They disclose sustainability reports in their *websites* (Q4B)	3 Foundations (4.22%)	45 Companies (50%)	43 Companies (82.69%)

The results related to the questions Q5A, Q5B and Q5C showed that of the 71 foundations that disclose CSR information, there is a greater predisposition for the disclose of it based mainly on text, since 60.56% of these foundations disclose it predominantly through text, while 33.80% disclose it through text contextualized with images, and only 5.64% predominantly display it through images (see Table 5).

The empirical studies that had analyzed the disclosure of CSR information (Chaudhri & Wang, 2007; Dincer & Dincer, 2010), concluded that there is a uniformity of the language used of CSR, which translates into a constant use of the same text format and images. The dissemination solely through images is not much sought by the Portuguese foundations, as it is the case in other studies.

According to the data collected on the size of the sample foundations that disclose CSR information, 7 foundations fall within the parameters of micro, 22 in small, 29 in the medium and 13 in the large ones (see Table 6). In turn, the results obtained in relation to the question Q6 of this study show that the level of CSR information disclosure from these four sets of foundations is not proportionate to their respective dimensions. The results indicated that 100% of micro foundations disseminated between one to three pages of CSR information. Then, 62.82% of the 22 small foundations also disclose only between one to three pages, 27.27% between four to ten pages, and 9.91% disclose more than ten pages of CSR information. In turn, of the 29 major foundations, 65.51% disclose between one to three pages, while 34.49% of these foundations disclose between four to ten pages of CSR information. Finally, of the 13 major foundations, 69.23% of them disclose one to three pages, while 30.77% disclose four to ten pages of CSR information.

Surprisingly, the results also indicate that the foundations that disclose more than ten pages of CSR information are small-scale. There are two small foundations that disseminate more than ten pages of CSR information, focusing on topics of philanthropy and social involvement. These results contrast with those obtained in the studies of Van der Laan et al. (2005), Wanderley et al. (2008) and Gálvez-Rodríguez et al. (2012), which argue that organizations with greater size disseminate more CSR information. This study does not follow this logic of studies that also analyzed the relationship between the dimension and disclosure of CSR information in companies and non-profit organizations. It follows from this study that it is to be admitted that in certain organizational and/or cultural contexts the dimension factor may not be as decisive in the level of disclosure of CSR information.

Table 5. Comparison of studies on the forms of CSR information disclosure

Studies	Current study	Chaudhri & Wang (2007)	Dincer & Dincer (2010)
Sample organizations that disclosure CSR information in their *Websites*	71 Foundations	30 Companies	113 Companies
They disclose the CSR information predominantly through text (Q5A)	43 Foundations (60.56%)	14 Companies (46.60%)	55 Companies (48.67%)
They disclose the CSR information predominantly through images (Q5B)	4 Foundations (5.64%)	1 Company (3.30%)	1 Company (0.88%)
They disclose the CSR information through contextualized text with images (Q5C)	24 Foundations (33.80%)	15 Companies (50.00%)	56 Companies (49.55%)

Table 6. Relationship between the size and amount of CSR information disclosed

The size of the sample foundations that disclose CSR information in their websites	Micro (7 foundations)	Small (22 foundations)	Medium (29 foundations)	Large (13 foundations)	Total sample (71 foundations)
They disclose between one to three pages of CSR information in their websites	7 Foundations (100.00%)	14 Foundations (62.82%)	19 Foundations (65.51%)	9 Foundations (69.23%)	49 Foundations (69.01%)
They disclose between four to ten pages of CSR information in their websites	0	6 Foundations (27.27%)	10 Foundations (34.49%)	4 Foundations (30,77%)	20 Foundations (28.17%)
They disclose more than ten pages of CSR information in their websites	0	2 Foundations (9.91%)	0	0	2 Foundations (2.82%)

CONCLUSION

This study conducted an analysis of the disclosure of the quantity and typology of CSR information disclosed in the websites of Portuguese foundations. We intend to contribute empirically by using this type of non-profit organizations. The results obtained were compared with similar studies and analyzed in the light of the theory of *Stakeholders* and the theory of legitimacy.

Our study offers three contributions to the literature on CSR information disclosure. The first of these contributions has to do with the organizational context studied, foundations, a type of non-profit organizations that, according to our best knowledge, had not yet been studied. The study contributes thus to different practices of disclosure of CSR information, both in terms of the quantity and the variety of the CSR information themes disclosed.

The second contribution of this study results from the use of a methodology for the observation of information disclosed in websites of foundations used by other studies that focused their analysis on another type of organizations. These other studies particularly based on large companies belonging to different countries and, consequently, different cultures. The use of the same methodology has made it possible to find several differences that, although they can also be conditional on the national context in which the study took place, result from the different needs of legitimacy of the different types of organizations face to their stakeholders. Organizations operating in more competitive environments tend to have a greater need for legitimacy in the face of their stakeholders and may result in an increase, or at least, the maintenance of their competitive position against their competitors.

The third contribution of this study is related to the idea advocated, in other studies (e.g. Van der Laan et al., 2005; Wanderley et al., 2008; Gálvez-Rodríguez et al., 2012), that the organizations with larger size disclose more CSR information. In the case of the Portuguese foundations studied, the results do not suggest the existence of a significant influence between the dimension factor and the amount of CSR information disclosed by the foundations. Consequently, it could be admitted that in certain organizational and/or cultural contexts the dimension factor may not be so decisive in the level of disclosure of CSR information.

As in all research work, this study is not free of limitations. One of the limitations may be related to the fact that the sample consists only of Portuguese foundations. To overcome this limitation, it is suggested that future studies meet a sample of foundations from several countries. Another of the limitations of this study may be related to the fact that it was only to disclose CSR information exclusively through the websites of the Portuguese foundations. It is suggested that future studies incorporate other forms of CSR information disclosure and/or adopt a longitudinal approach. For example, adopting a longitudinal approach through multiple case studies would allow us to know the evolution of CSR information disclosure practices.

REFERENCES

Al-Shubiri, F., Al-Abedallat, A., & Orabi, M. (2012). Financial and non-financial determinants of corporate social responsibility. *Asian Economic and Financial Review*, *2*(8), 1001–1012.

Amran, A., & Devi, S. (2008). The impact of government and foreign affiliate influence on corporate social reporting: The case of Malaysia. *Managerial Auditing Journal*, *23*(4), 386–404. doi:10.1108/02686900810864327

Baldini, M., Dal Maso, L., Liberatore, G., Mazzi, F., & Terzani, S. (2016). Role of country-and firm-level determinants in environmental, social, and governance disclosure. *Journal of Business Ethics*, 1-20.

Barrett, M. (2001). A stakeholder approach to responsiveness and accountability in non-profit organizations. *Social Policy Journal of New Zealand*, *1*(17), 36–51.

Birch, D. (2003). Corporate social responsibility: Some key theoretical issues and concepts for new ways of doing business. *Journal of New Business Ideas and Trends*, *1*(1), 1–19.

Borges, J., Miranda, R., & Valdir, M. (2007). O discurso das fundações corporativas: Caminhos de uma "nova" filantropia? *Revista de Administração de Empresas*, *47*(4), 1–15.

Branco, M., Delgado, C., Sá, M., & Sousa, C. (2014). Comparing CSR communication on corporate web sites in Sweden and Spain. *Public Journal of Management*, *9*(2), 231–250.

Branco, M., & Rodrigues, L. (2008). Factors influencing social responsibility disclosure by Portuguese companies. *Journal of Business Ethics*, *83*(4), 685–701. doi:10.100710551-007-9658-z

Brown, T., & Dacin, P. (1997). The company and the product: Corporate associations and consumer product responses. *Journal of Marketing*, *61*(1), 68–84. doi:10.1177/002224299706100106

Calixto, L. (2013). The disclosure of sustainability reports in Latin America: A comparative study. *Revista de Administração (São Paulo)*, *48*(4), 828–842. doi:10.5700/rausp1124

Campos, T. (2006). Políticas para *stakeholders*: Um objetivo ou uma estratégia organizacional. *Revista de Administração Contemporânea*, *10*(4), 111–130. doi:10.1590/S1415-65552006000400006

Chapple, W., & Moon, J. (2005). Corporate social responsibility (CSR) in Asia: A seven-country study of CSR website reporting. *Business & Society*, *44*(4), 415–441. doi:10.1177/0007650305281658

Chaudhri, V., & Wang, J. (2007). Communicating corporate social responsibility on the internet. *Management Communication Quarterly*, *21*(2), 232–247. doi:10.1177/0893318907308746

Chen, S., & Bouvain, P. (2009). Is corporate responsibility converging? A comparison of corporate responsibility reporting in the USA, UK, Australia, and Germany. *Journal of Business Ethics*, *87*(1), 299–317. doi:10.100710551-008-9794-0

Dainelli, F., Manetti, G., & Sibilio, B. (2012). Web-based accountability practices in non-profit organizations: The case of national museums. *Voluntas*, *24*(3), 649–665. doi:10.100711266-012-9278-9

Decree-Law No. 98/2015. Journal of the Portuguese Republic, 1st series, No. 106, June 2, 3470-3493.

Deegan, C., & Gordon, B. (1996). A Study of the environmental disclosure practices of Australian corporations. *Accounting and Business Research*, *26*(3), 187–199. doi:10.1080/00014788.1996.9729510

Dhaliwal, D. S., Radhakrishnan, S., Tsang, A., & Yang, Y. (2012). Nonfinancial disclosure and analyst forecast accuracy: International evidence on corporate social responsibility disclosure. *The Accounting Review*, *87*(3), 723–759. doi:10.2308/accr-10218

Dincer, C., & Dincer, B. (2010). An investigation of Turkish small and medium-sized enterprises online CSR communication. *Social Responsibility Journal*, *6*(2), 197–207. doi:10.1108/17471111011051711

Elsakit, O., & Worthington, A. (2014). The impact of corporate characteristics and corporate governance on corporate social and environmental disclosure: A literature review. *International Journal of Business and Management*, *9*(9), 1–15. doi:10.5539/ijbm.v9n9p1

European Commission. (2001). *Promoting a European framework for corporate social responsibility – green paper. Luxemburg*. Office for Official Publications of the European Communities.

Fifka, M. S. (2012). The development and state of research on social and environmental reporting in global comparison. *Journal fur Betriebswirtschaft*, *62*(1), 45–84. doi:10.100711301-012-0083-8

Fifka, M. S., & Drabble, M. (2012). Focus and standardization of sustainability reporting – a comparative study of the United Kingdom and Finland. *Business Strategy and the Environment*, *21*(7), 455–474. doi:10.1002/bse.1730

Freeman, R. (1984). *Strategic management: a stakeholder approach*. Boston: Pitman.

Freeman, R., & McVea, J. (2001). A stakeholder approach to strategic management. Working-paper 01-02. Charlottesville, VA: Darden Graduate School of Business Administration. doi:10.2139srn.263511

Gálvez-Rodríguez, M., Caba-Perez, C., & López-Godoy, M. (2012). Responsabilidad social y transparencia on-line de las ONG: Análisis del caso español CIRIEC-España. *C.I.R.I.E.C. España*, *74*, 207–238.

Gálvez-Rodríguez, M., Caba-Perez, C., & López-Godoy, M. (2014). Drivers for the proactive online disclosure of information in the NGO sector: The Colombian case. *Online Information Review*, *38*(6), 769–787. doi:10.1108/OIR-05-2014-0113

Gray, R., Javad, M., Power, D., & Sinclair, C. (2001). Social and environmental disclosure and corporate characteristics: A research note and extension. *Journal of Business Finance & Accounting*, *28*(3-4), 327–356. doi:10.1111/1468-5957.00376

Guthrie, J., Petty, R., Yongvanich, K., & Ricceri, F. (2004). Using content analysis as a research method to inquire into intellectual capital reporting. *Journal of Intellectual Capital*, *5*(2), 282–293. doi:10.1108/14691930410533704

Guziana, B., & Dobers, P. (2013). How sustainability leaders communicate corporate activities of sustainable development. *Corporate Social Responsibility and Environmental Management*, *20*(4), 193–204. doi:10.1002/csr.1292

Halme, M., & Huse, M. (1997). The influence of corporate governance, industry and country factors on environmental reporting. *Scandinavian Journal of Management*, *13*(2), 137–157. doi:10.1016/S0956-5221(97)00002-X

Hossain, M., & Reaz, M. (2007). The determinants and characteristics of voluntary disclosure by Indian banking companies. *Corporate Social Responsibility and Environmental Management*, *14*(5), 274–288. doi:10.1002/csr.154

Junqueira, L. (2000). *Organizações sem fins lucrativos e redes sociais na gestão das políticas sociais. Caderno de Administração PUC- São Paulo, 3*. EDUC.

Keating, E., & Frumkin, P. (2003). Reengineering nonprofit financial accountability: Toward a more reliable foundation for regulation. *Public Administration Review*, *63*(1), 3–15. doi:10.1111/1540-6210.00260

Kolk, A. (2004). A decade of sustainability reporting: Development and significance. *International Journal of Environment and Sustainable Development*, *3*(1), 51–64. doi:10.1504/IJESD.2004.004688

Kolk, A. (2008). Sustainability, accountability and corporate governance: Exploring multinationals' reporting practices. *Business Strategy and the Environment*, *17*(1), 1–15. doi:10.1002/bse.511

Lee, R., & Blouin, M. (2017). Factors affecting web disclosure adoption in the non-profit sector. *Journal of Computer Information Systems*, 1–10. doi:10.1080/08874417.2017.1370988

Lifelong Learning Programme. (2010). *O que é a responsabilidade social empresarial? The project "InnoTrain CSR"*. Disponível em: http://www.csr-training.eu/en/csr-training/what-is-csr/

Maines, L., Bartov, E., Fairfield, P., Hirst, D., Iannaconi, T., Mallett, R., ... Vincent, L. (2002). Commentary - recommendations of disclosure of nonfinancial performance measures. *Accounting Horizons*, *16*(4), 352–362. doi:10.2308/acch.2002.16.4.353

Neu, D., Warsame, H., & Pedwell, K. (1998). Managing public impressions: Environmental disclosures in annual reports. *Accounting, Organizations and Society*, *23*(3), 265–282. doi:10.1016/S0361-3682(97)00008-1

O'Dwyer, B., & Unerman, J. (2008). The paradox of greater NGO accountability: A case study of Amnesty Ireland. *Accounting, Organizations and Society*, *33*(7), 801–824. doi:10.1016/j.aos.2008.02.002

Patten, D. M. (2002). Give or take on the internet: An examination of the disclosure practices of insurance firm web innovators. *Journal of Business Ethics*, *36*(3), 247–259. doi:10.1023/A:1014009229437

Pollach, I. (2005). Corporate self-presentation on the www strategies for enhancing usability, credibility and utility. *Corporate Communications*, *10*(4), 285–301. doi:10.1108/13563280510630098

Pollach, I., Scharl, A., & Weichselbraun, A. (2009). Web content mining for comparing corporate and third-party online reporting: A case study on solid waste management. *Business Strategy and the Environment, 18*(3), 137–148. doi:10.1002/bse.549

Pratas, A. (2009). *Dicionário Jurídico* (Vol. 1). Lisboa: Almedina.

Roberts, R. (1992). Determinants of corporate social responsibility disclosure: An application of stakeholder theory. *Accounting, Organizations and Society, 17*(6), 595–612. doi:10.1016/0361-3682(92)90015-K

Saxton, G., & Guo, C. (2011). Accountability online: Understanding the web-based accountability practices of nonprofit organizations. *Nonprofit and Voluntary Sector Quarterly, 40*(2), 270–295. doi:10.1177/0899764009341086

Servera-Francés, D., & Arteaga-Moreno, F. (2015). The impact of corporate social responsibility on the customer commitment and trust in the retail sector. *Ramon Llull Journal of Applied Ethics, 6*, 161–178.

Silva, B. (2015). Análise do consumidor consciente e do marketing ambiental: Reflexos do índice de sustentabilidade empresarial (ISE) na imagem das empresas. *REN-Revista Escola de Negócios, 2*(2), 78–97.

Silva, B., & Burger, R. (2015). *Financial vulnerability: an empirical study of Ugandan NGOs*. CIRIEC-Université de Liège.

Sousa, F. J. M., & Wanderley, L. S. O. (2007). Divulgação da responsabilidade social empresarial: Como os websites empresariais vêm sendo utilizados por empresas de energia e varejo. *Cadernos EBAPE.BR, 5*(2), 1–13. doi:10.1590/S1679-39512007000200008

Torres, L., & Pina, V. (2003). Accounting for Accountability and Management in NPOs. A comparative study of four countries: Canada, The United Kingdom, The USA and Spain. *Financial Accountability & Management, 19*(3), 265–285. doi:10.1111/1468-0408.00174

Tremblay-Boire, J., & Prakash, A. (2014). Accountability.org: Online disclosures by U.S. Nonprofits. *Voluntas, 26*(2), 693–719. doi:10.100711266-014-9452-3

Van der Laan, S. J., Adikhari, A., & Tondkar, R. H. (2005). Exploring differences in social disclosures internationally: A stakeholder perspective. *Journal of Accounting and Public Policy, 24*(2), 123–151. doi:10.1016/j.jaccpubpol.2004.12.007

Vilar, V. (2012). *Divulgação de responsabilidade social na internet – estudo descritivo das páginas de internet dos maiores Bancos mundiais. Dissertação de Mestrado*. Lisboa: Universidade Aberta.

Waddock, S. (2008). The development of corporate responsibility / corporate citizenship. *Organizational Management Journal, 5*(1), 29–39. doi:10.1057/omj.2008.5

Wanderley, L., Lucian, R., Farache, F., & Filho, J. (2008). CSR information disclosure on the web: A context-based approach analysing the influence of country of origin and industry sector. *Journal of Business Ethics, 82*(2), 369–378. doi:10.100710551-008-9892-z

Willis, A. (2003). The role of the Global Reporting Initiative's sustainability reporting guidelines in the social screening of investments. *Journal of Business Ethics, 43*(3), 233–237. doi:10.1023/A:1022958618391

Wood, D. (1991). Corporate social performance revisited. *Academy of Management Review*, *16*(4), 691–718. doi:10.5465/amr.1991.4279616

KEY TERMS AND DEFINITIONS

Code of Conduct: A document that aims to establish the rules and general principles of ethics and professional conduct of employees of a given organization.

Corporate Social Responsibility: A framework that aims to present an integrated vision of social and environmental organizations' operations and interactions with their stakeholders in a voluntary manner.

Foundation: Non-profit organizations that proactively contribute to social, educational, scientific, environmental, or cultural progress.

Philanthropy: Act of helping others, through various altruistic and supportive attitudes that collaborate with support for other human beings.

Portuguese Foundation Centre: A Private Association of public utility, formed by Portuguese foundations characterized by different origins, dimensions, purposes, and scopes of action.

Sustainability: The ability to use natural, economic, and social resources to meet our current needs without compromising the ability of future generations to satisfy their own needs.

Sustainability Report: A report published by an organization about the economic, environmental, and social impacts caused by its everyday activities.

Chapter 11
Evaluation of the Online Accountability of the Portuguese Private Institutions of Social Solidarity

Augusta Ferreira
https://orcid.org/0000-0003-1659-3309
University of Aveiro, Portugal

Carlos Santos
https://orcid.org/0000-0001-9728-8538
University of Aveiro, Portugal

Rui Marques
https://orcid.org/0000-0001-8449-0526
University of Aveiro, Portugal

Graça Azevedo
https://orcid.org/0000-0002-6346-4035
University of Aveiro, Portugal

Helena Carla Antunes Mendes
University of Aveiro, Portugal

ABSTRACT

In Portugal, in order to make the management of public resources more accountable, regulations on financial disclosure have emerged. Currently, the Private Institutions of Social Solidarity, through the Decree-Law No. 172-A/2014, are required to publish the financial reporting on their websites from 2016. Given the diffusion of innovations and the institutional theory, based on coercive isomorphism, the IPSS may have already created the conditions to fulfill this requirement. This chapter intends to ascertain whether the IPSS have conditions to comply with the mandatory disclosure under the law. This research shows that there is very limited presence of IPSS on the internet, the websites reveal low maturity levels and are little sophisticated. Furthermore, the IPSS that disclose the financial reporting on their websites, are still a minority, even if required by law to do so. The value of this research are related to the recent innovations introduced by the legal framework. Thus, it is important to monitor the evolution of law compliance by these institutions.

DOI: 10.4018/978-1-5225-8482-7.ch011

INTRODUCTION

Faced with the contexts of the globalization, the economic crisis and the aging population the State is becoming less able to directly address all social needs. The non-profit organizations, belonging to the non-profit sector, also called Third Sector, are making efforts to mitigate the impact of the economic environment, developing their activities, generating aid, producing goods and providing services in various social and economic areas. In Portugal, these organizations generally benefit from the declaration of public utility, declared by the State through Decree-Law No. 460/77 (Presidência do Conselho de Ministros, 1977) and some of their activity is financed by the General Government Budget. This financing is then understood to rationalize the financial resources of the State to improve services to citizens.

Being the non-profit organizations, namely the Private Institutions of Social Solidarity (IPSS), considered of public utility and financed, at least partially, by the General Government Budget, it is understandable that the State imposes the use of mechanisms of control and of assessment of the efficiency and effectiveness of the public resources allocated to them and that the accountability of that kind of organizations has an increasingly important role.

The mechanisms of accountability imposed recently on the IPSS are, in particular: disclosure of financial reporting and transparency. Regarding the disclosure of financial reporting, the IPSS became obliged to apply the Accounting Standardization System for Non-profit Entities (SNC-ESNL), approved by Decree-Law No. 36-A/2011 of 9 March (Ministério das Finanças e da Administração Pública, 2011). As regards transparency, as required by paragraph 2 of Article 14-A in Decree-Law 172-A/2014 (Ministério da Solidariedade, 2014) (establishes a new model for IPSS financial supervision): the financial reporting of the previous year must be disclosed on the institution's website until May 31st of the following year, that is, it imposes the disclosure of financial reporting to all stakeholders. This last requirement must be fulfilled, annually, since 2016, regarding the financial reporting of the immediately preceding year.

We have also verified that periodic evaluations of the websites of the Organizations of Direct or Indirect Administration by the State should be made (Presidência do Conselho de Ministros, 2001), in particular, to assess the maturity of websites. In this way, since IPSS are stated of public utility, and they should also be subjected to this evaluation, it is adequate to conduct a study with the following objectives: to assess whether the IPSS are able to comply with the requirement foreseen by Decree-Law No. 172-A/2014 (Ministério da Solidariedade, 2014), and if financial information is already disclosed on their websites. These two objectives will allow us to understand the concern of these institutions regarding accountability.

Notwithstanding the fact that this requirement must only be strictly fulfilled after 2016, the IPSS have been aware of it since November 2014, so, given the diffusion theory of innovation and the institutional theory, based on coercive isomorphism, the IPSS should already create the conditions to be able to disclose these data on their websites. However, a study by Ferreira, Marques, Santos, Azevedo and Mendes (2016), carried out with data from the year immediately prior to the mandatory disclosure of financial reporting, showed that only a minority of IPSS had a website and that, of those which had a website, only a small part disclosed financial information.

In this context, this work intends to assess whether the IPSS, after the obligation to disclose financial reports on their websites, already have the conditions to do so and, if so, to assess if they have been doing so. The evaluation that this chapter presents refers to the period between the situation highlighted by Ferreira *et al.* (2016) and the date of data collection also analyzed here. Thus, the present study address the following problem: after the obligation of disclose of financial reporting on their institutional website, do the IPSS have conditions to comply with these requirement?

The answer to this question requires that an evaluation should be made as to whether IPSS already have a website; whether those which have a website comply at least with the maturity level 1 (considered basic) and with the mandatory disclosure of financial reporting. This research is an analytical study and follows an inductive approach. Methodologically, it combines quantitative and qualitative research methods. Due to the large number of institutions, in this study we used a sample, determined by a stratified random sampling technique, which is composed of 340 IPSS and 80 equivalent institutions.

The results allow us to conclude that most IPSS do not have a website yet. Moreover, in the cases they do, we could verify that the websites are still at an early stage of development, complying only with some characteristics associated with low maturity levels. Finally, it was concluded that, even though it is mandatory to publish financial reports on their websites, some IPSS have disclosed very little financial information.

In addition to this introduction, this paper is divided into four other sections. The second section provides the literature review, enhancing methodologies to assess the institutions' online state and presence, showing the results of related works, describing theories which can underpin the existence of different maturity levels of websites, and presenting the IPSS legal framework in Portugal. In third section, the research problem, the research questions and the methodology are presented. In fourth section, the results are presented, analysed and discussed. Finally, in the last section we draw some conclusions and present some proposals for future work.

BACKGROUND

Theorical Literature Review

The methodology to assess the institutions' online state and presence is essential since it allows to understand and compare the results from different studies. Furthermore, it allows to assess to what extent the existing methodologies can be applied to different contexts.

The methodologies used generally include the definition of an indicator, a numeric indicator, which, according to García-Meca and Conesa (2004), is developed in two stages: first stage - choice of informative aspects or items to analyse; second stage – weighting of items according to their relative importance. Regarding the first stage, different models were identified, among them: Baum and Maio's model (Baum and Maio, 2000); eEurope 2002 model (eEurope-2002, 2002); UMIC model (UMIC, 2003), the Santos and Amaral's model (Santos and Amaral, 2005), the Pratas's model (2007), and the Soares, Amaral, Ferreira, and Leal's models (Soares *et al.*, 2014).

According to Almeida (2011), the Baum and Maio's model is developed based on four stages of ICT (Information and Communication Technologies) integration: presence, interaction, transaction and transformation, as each stage represents a greater ICT integration. The first stage, presence, aims to assess whether the institution complies with the disclosure of basic information to citizens, usually static content, not allowing any interaction. The second stage, interaction, assesses whether the website allows the citizen to interact, comprising the provision of: search engines; downloadable forms; links to other portals; as well as email customer support. The third stage, transaction, includes the complete execution of online tasks; and the fourth stage, transformation, comprises the use of Systems of Customer Relationship Management.

The eEurope 2002 model (eEurope-2002, 2002) initially foresees four levels of sophistication of online public services: information; one-way interaction; two-way interaction; and transaction. In 2007 a fifth level, personalization, was added. The four first levels correspond, in the same order, to the levels of the model of Baum and Maio (2000). The fifth level, personalization, introduces the concepts of pro-active services (use of functions that improve the service quality and usability and data integration, for example alerts and automatic messages, and the automatic filling of forms using data available in databases), and automatic services (services are provided automatically, i.e. without user request) (Almeida, 2011).

The Innovation and Knowledge Mission Unit (UMIC) is a Portuguese body of the central Government, which coordinates the implementation of the policy for the Information Society. The model UMIC includes 4 stages of development: presence; interaction; transaction/two-way interaction; and transformation (UMIC, 2003), being its description very similar to the model of Baum and Maio (2000).

The model of Santos and Amaral (2005) is adapted from eEurope 2002 model (eEurope-2002, 2002) and is based on four maturity levels, increasing value according to maturity. Level one corresponds to the provision of static information; level two to the provision of downloadable forms and basic services; level three to the possibility of performing a two-way interaction; and level four to the possibility of performing two-way transactions, which ultimately allow a whole process to be fully conducted online. This model is adapted to the Portuguese reality and since 1999 it has served as a basis to an assessment of the maturity level of websites of the Portuguese local governments, whose results are published every two years.

The model of Pratas (2007) has eight maturity levels, from zero to seven. In level zero, no administrative information is provided. In level one, little administrative information is provided (usually five references). In level two, some administrative information is provided (six or more references). In level three, information is provided, and it usually includes the planning options, the budget of the current financial year and the financial reporting of the previous financial year, and some decisions made by the entity. In level four, all the information to be published in a hard copy version is provided. In level five, all decisions of the entity's management bodies are provided. In level six, all decisions of the entity's bodies and the full access to the unreserved documents of, at least, 10 administrative processes are provided. At last, in level seven, all the unreserved administrative information is provided.

When a website evaluation is made, for each of the aforementioned levels, a set of items is established. These, along with the evaluation, provide the characterization of the websites regarding maturity.

In what concerns the weighting of items which make up the indicator, according to their relative importance, the studies differ. Some authors consider an equal distribution for each section and, within this one, an equal value for each item (Pérez *et al.*, 2005) whereas other authors (García & García, 2008; Gandía & Archidona, 2008) consider it is necessary to assign a weight to every observed item, thus resulting in a weighted index.

Recently, the EAGLE_Index was developed, which allows evaluating the accountability maturity of the websites of several types of public bodies or any type of public institution that works mostly with public capitals or capitals donated by other financiers (Santos *et al.*, 2018).

Practical Literature Review

There are several studies conducted in the public sector about the disclosure of financial information via the Internet, aiming to assess the online state and presence of different public entities, e.g the studies of Santos and Amaral (2005, 2006, 2008a, 2008b), Anes (2009), Almeida (2011), Olszak and Ziemba (2011), Dokhtesmai, Saberi and Moradi (2011) and Makoza (2013).

Santos and Amaral (2005, 2008b) used the eEurope 2002 model (eEurope-2002, 2002) to classify the websites of the parish councils according to the criteria which make up each of the maturity levels of the model. The study shows a very positive evolution of online presence of the parish councils, from 6.6% in 2004 to 28% in 2006. In the maturity ranking, a positive evolution was also observed. The study allowed us to conclude that there were structure constraints in the parish councils, which hindered the adoption of new technologies to modernize their services.

Santos and Amaral (2008a, 2008b) evaluated the websites of the Portuguese local governments in 2007 and in 2006, also following the eEurope 2002 model (eEurope-2002, 2002). They compared with the previous study and concluded that there was a clear evolution, with 153 local governments having a website in 1999, with a significant increase to 306 in 2007, and to 308 in 2012, comprising all the Portuguese municipalities (Soares *et al.*, 2014).

The study of Anes (2009), which assessed the maturity level of the websites of the local government of Bragança district, using the model of Santos and Amaral (2005), concluded that the websites of these municipalities had, in general, a maturity level equivalent to level 3 of the reference model.

Almeida's study (Almeida, 2011) based on a combination of models, allowed us to conclude that the maturity of the websites of the municipalities of Viseu district fall broadly into the 5 maturity levels. The majority, however, were placed in level 1 (presence) followed by stage 3 (consolidation/interaction).

The study of Olszak and Ziemba (2011), carried out in the Silesian region in Poland, had the objective to evaluate their maturity level of the websites of governmental entities, mainly to assess to what extent the enterprises and citizens would use the services provided online. The results showed that the websites were poor and that the situations in which the use of services occurred at the integrated or transaction level were quite rare.

The study carried out by Dokhtesmati *et al.* (2011) assessed the maturity of the websites of the Middle East ministries and the results showed that the maturity in these countries is still very low.

A study conducted by Makoza (2013) on the websites of Malawi's central government allowed to conclude that the websites were placed in the lowest maturity levels (presence and interaction) and that the websites maturity evolution rate is low.

A study by Ferreira *et al.* (2016), concluded that most IPSS did not have an institutional website in February 2016. It also allowed the conclusion that those that had website, did not fully comply with the maturity level 1, meaning that efforts have yet to be made to improve the quality of their websites. Finally, the study also concluded that a very small percentage of IPSS, although they are not yet been obligated, disclose financial information on their websites.

THEORIES WHICH CAN UNDERPIN THE EXISTENCE OF DIFFERENT LEVELS OF WEBSITE MATURITY

The diffusion of innovations theory can underpin studies related to the diffusion of innovations. Rogers (2003, p. 5) refers that diffusion is "the process by which an innovation is communicated through certain channels over time among the members of a social system. It is a special type of communication, in that the messages are concerned with new ideas". Thus, Rogers (2003) considers some of the attributes of technological innovation to explain its adoption at a large scale: relative advantage; compatibility; complexity; trialability and observability. However, Chen, Gillenson and Sherrell (2004), highlight that only the relative advantage, compatibility and complexity seem to be consistently associated with the adoption of technological innovation. In this way, the studies of Balasubramanian (2003), Wu and Chen (2005), among others, have been useful to explain the variations in the adoption level of systems made available online to users.

The institutional theory is based on the concept that organizations are led to integrate practices and procedures which prevail in the organizational environment and that are institutionalized in society, i.e. that become isomorphic with the context in which they develop their activity. Isomorphism can be: coercive, when it results from the mechanism through which organizations comply with the government regulations and with cultural expectations able to impose uniformity within organizations; mimetic, which occurs when the organizational technologies are poor, when the goals are ambiguous or when their context creates symbolic uncertainties, making organizations shape themselves and imitate others regarded as leaders; normative, arising from professionalization, formal education, dissemination of knowledge by experts, and from the definition of working methods to establish a legitimate knowledge-base.

In this way, institutional theory can be used as a theoretical basis to justify the level of disclosure financial reporting by IPSS on their websites.

Overview on Portuguese Non-Profit Organizations

The Social Economy arose, according to Catarino (2012, p. 1) "from the need felt by societies, during a crisis and deterioration of conditions, evincing a sector between the State and the market", and that "the Social Economy is made up of a group of private entities, properly organized, endowed with autonomy and freedom of membership, which are created to meet the needs of their members, through the provision of goods and services, ensuring their financing". The author adds that these entities share some characteristics, as for example: "They are not integrated into the public sector, nor are they controlled by it; they have the autonomy to elect and oust the social bodies which will control and structure the activities they perform; they have their own legal personality; the eventual distribution, regarding surpluses, is made in connection with the activities performed by each member within organizations; membership of this type of institution is not mandatory; they are entities which promote democracy and perform activities which allow to meet the needs of individuals and their families".

Regarding the Non-profit Organizations (NPOs), Santos, Raimundo and Lima (2012) states that despite the existing diversity, the NPOs share a very important characteristic, which is not shared by the Government or by any other for-profit organization: while the State seeks to control and the enterprises to provide goods and services, the NPOs represent a challenge in the way of thinking among individuals, spurring individual accountability within a community. The State benefits from the support provided to institutions of Social Economy, as these are capable of raising and managing funds and offer a guarantee in terms of democratic procedures.

The social and solidarity sector (holy mercy houses, institutions of social solidarity and mutual societies, i.e. Private Institutions of Social Solidarity) is given a prominent position in the establishment and development of a range of social responses in the whole national territory, grounded on the set of values of social solidarity, which reveals a more human approach, i.e. closer and more beneficial to the citizens and less costly to the State. Thus, aiming to implement the partnership and constant communication with this sector, the Government realized it would be of the utmost importance to provide the social and solidarity sector with its own identity and proper legal recognition, having implemented the Framework Law on Social Economy. Thus, in November 2014 legislation was introduced (Ministério da Solidariedade, 2014), aiming to ensure that this new cycle of social economy can rely on more solid and sustainable foundations, from the economic and financial point of view, and that the efforts and progresses already made can be safeguarded.

The aforementioned decree-law places more demand on financial reporting, as required by No.1 of Article 14-A "the financial reporting of institutions must comply with the Accounting Standards for the non-profit sector entities legally applicable and are subject to approval by the respective statutory bodies" and No. 2 of the same article states that "the financial reporting of the previous year must be disclosed on the institution's website until May 31st of the following year".

RESEARCH DISIGNE

Research Problem and Research Questions

From the literature review there is only one study, in the scope of organizations that are included in the so-called social economy, which assesses the online state and presence of these organizations through their websites. However, as aforementioned, this sector has been growing, both nationally and internationally, and, in Portugal, this is largely due to the work developed by the IPSS, which have been granted a proper framework (Ministério da Solidariedade, 2014). Thus, as the decree-law was issued in November 2014, the IPSS are for the first time required to disclose the financial reporting of 2015 until the end of May 2016.This requirement implies that the IPSS must have a website, and so the diffusion of innovations theory can be used to explain the differences regarding the creation of the website, and the different website maturity levels.

Furthermore, the fact that the requirement to publish the financial reporting falls over the one of 2015 and must only be fulfilled in 2016, the IPSS have had access to this information since November 2014, and thus, considering the institutional theory based on coercive isomorphism, they were supposed to have the necessary conditions to fulfil this requirement; and based on mimetic isomorphism, it's more likely that they imitate the institutions seen as leaders.

The literature review also shows that the models to assess the institutions' online state and presence are not only related to the content of websites, but also to other items which mainly aim to evaluate: update of contents, navigability, accessibility and easy access to websites. This evaluation becomes important as IPSS are largely financed by the State. In this framework the IPSS manage public resources which are made available to them, and thus they should provide information about the management of these resources, becoming, in this way, answerable to citizens.

Given this context, the research problem of this study is the following: after the obligation of disclose of financial reporting on their institutional website, do the IPSS have conditions to comply with these requirement?

In order to answer the research problem, the following research questions have been raised, as well as possible answers:

1. Do the IPSS already have a website on the Internet?
2. If the IPSS have a website, do its contents comply with a set of minimum indicators?
3. If the IPSS have a website, does the update its contents comply with a set of minimum indicators?
4. If the IPSS have a website, does its accessibility comply with a set of minimum indicators?
5. If the IPSS have a website, does its navigability comply with a set of minimum indicators?
6. If the IPSS have a website, does it provide easy access for disabled citizens?
7. If the IPSS have a website, do they disclose financial information on this website?

The research question 1 is answered by using search engines which allow, for every IPSS that makes up the sample, to verify whether there is a website. The research questions 2, 3, 4 and 5 is answered through the website analysis, collecting and analysing the necessary data. The research question 6 is answered using specific tools and the last question is answered through the online website analysis of every IPSS included in the sample, collecting the necessary data and analysing the results for dimension "contents-financial information" of the maturity index cited in the next section.

Methodology

The current research is classified as an analytical study (Collis and Hussey, 2005) and the approach method is inductive. From the observation of actual facts and phenomena, it is possible to see the relationship between both dimensions. Then, a generalization is made based on the observed relationship, with the aim to improve the underlying theoretical framework.

In what regards the research process this study is classified as both quantitative and qualitative as it aims to measure the studied phenomenon and to identify different realities regarding the state of IPSS websites. Finally, the data collection techniques consist of content analysis of the IPSS websites using and following the Maturity Index (MI) conceptualized by Ferreira *et al.* (2016), complementing it with statistical procedures.

The data for the calculation of the disclosure index were collected through direct access to the websites of the IPSS included in the sample using the content analysis technique. Such access occurred in February 2017 after the disclosure of financial information on their websites being mandatory.

The studied population is made up of 5069 IPSS, 155 cooperatives and 106 community centres (our study is based only on the cooperatives and community centres regarded as equivalent to IPSS). However, we used a sample determined by a stratified random sampling technique which is composed of 340 IPSS (221 associations, 66 parish centres, 23 holy houses of mercy, 16 foundations and 14 religious organizations), 40 cooperatives and 40 community centres.

The sample calculation was made using Software-Epi Info™ version 7.1.0.6 (Dean *et al.*, 1991). A confidence level of 95% and a confidence interval of 10% were adopted. The IPSS and the other equivalent institutions included in the sample were randomly selected, from each aforementioned group, using Microsoft Excel software, associating to each group a random number between 0 and 1 for each of the institutions within each group. Hereinafter, they were sorted out and the first elements concerning the sample were selected, as previously mentioned.

In this study the variables used are the ones defined in the Maturity Index (MI) Ferreira *et al.* (2016), composed by 6 dimensions. Each dimension is composing by indicators that are used to measure content (general and dissemination of financial information), content updating, accessibility, navigability, and ease of access to citizens with special needs.

Like in Ferreira *et al.* (2016), the maturity assessment methodology used was adapted from eEurope 2002 model (eEurope-2002, 2002), which is based on five maturity levels. The maturity levels are assessed based on the type of contents made available on the websites to the different stakeholders (APDSI, 2009) and can be classified as shown in Table 1.

Considering the different maturity levels, the MI is based on 6 dimensions that was developed with the objective of verifying whether the IPSS websites achieve maturity level 1. Like in the Ferreira *et al.* (2016) study, the dimensions considered were the following:

- Contents: general information (DIMgi);
- Contents: financial information (DIMfi);
- Update of contents (DIMup);
- Accessibility (DIMac);
- Navigability (DIMn);
- Access for disabled citizens (DIMa).

Considering that the objectives of this study is also make a comparison with the results obtained in Ferreira *et al.* (2016), and to verify if, after the obligation of disclosure of financial reporting in the website (required by the Decree-law No. 172-A/2014 (Ministério da Solidariedade, 2014)), the IPSS fulfil all conditions to do so, complying with the required by law.

Thus, this evaluation should imply to assess whether the website, in case there is one, complies, at least, with maturity level 1. To this end, and as aforementioned, the indicators were defined based in Ferreira *et al.* (2016) study and in the studies referred in the literature review, namely, Santos, Oliveira and Amaral (2003). Moreover, the present study also aims to assess if the IPSS started to disclose the financial information on the website as required by the Decree-law No. 172-A/2014 (Ministério da Solidariedade, 2014).

Table 1. Maturity levels (eEurope-2002, 2002)

Level	Characterization
5	Pro-active services and automatic services
4	Complete transaction, including payments
3	Online form filling and online access to information about processes
2	Provision of downloadable forms
1	General communication via web (provision of information)
0	No web presence

In Table 2, the MI is shown along with the indicators to be assessed in each dimension. The set of indicators in each dimension corresponds to the set of indicators considered as minimum. According to Santos *et al.* (2003) and Pérez *et al.* (2005), equal weight is assigned to each dimension. The weight of each indicator varies exclusively according to the number of indicators included in each dimensions of the MI.

Considering the previously mentioned, the weight to assign to each dimension is calculated using the formula (1) and the weight assigned to each indicator is calculated using formula (2).

$$WeightDim_i = \frac{100}{N} \tag{1}$$

Table 2. Maturity index (Ferreira et al., 2016)

IPSS Website Evaluation Grid

Qualitative Evaluation (Maturity level 0/1)

Level	Criteria (qualitative)	Weight	Indicators	Measures (Scale)	Weight
0			With active website	URL	n/a
			Without active website	0	n/a
1	Contents: General Information **DIMgi**	16.67%	Institutional Information	0/0.5/1	14.29%
			Organizational structure	1/0	14.29%
			Services provided	1/0	14.29%
			Contacts	0-5	14.29%
			Possibility of selecting contents in English	1/0	14.29%
			News feed	1/0	14.29%
			FAQ (Frequently Asked Questions)	1/0	14.29%
			DIMgi Index		**100.00%**
	Contents: Financial Information **DIMfi**	16.67%	Forecast maps	1/0	33.33%
			Budget execution maps	1/0	33.33%
			Other financial statements	1/0	33.33%
			DIMfi Index		**100.00%**
	Update of Contents **DIMup**	16.67%	Date of the website last update	0-4	25.00%
			Scheduled or ongoing events	1/0	25.00%
			Activities plan	1/0	25.00%
			Statistics, publications and studies	1/0	25.00%
			DIMup Index		**100.00%**
	Accessibility **DIMac**	16.67%	The website has an easily remembered URL	1/0	33.33%
			Compliance with browsers	1/0	33.33%
			Indexing in search engines	1-10	33.33%
			DIMac Index		**100.00%**
	Navigability **DIMn**	16.67%	There are navigation links in every page	0/0.5/1	25.00%
			A site map is available	1/0	25.00%
			There is a search engine for internal research	1/0	25.00%
			The different contents are clearly identified	1/0	25.00%
			DIMn Index		**100.00%**
	Access for Disabled Citizens **DIMa**	16.67%	Compliance with level "A", "AA" or "AAA"	0-3	50.00%
			Accessibility Symbol on the main page	1/0	50.00%
			DIMa Index		**100.00%**
	Maturity Index	100.00%	**MI=DIMgi*100/6+DIMfi*100/6+DIMup*100/6+DIMac*100/6+DIMn*100/6+DIMa*100/6**		

in which:

$WeightDim_i$ - weight assigned to dimension i;
N - number of dimensions included in the MI.

$$WeightInd_i = \frac{100}{T_i} \quad (2)$$

in which:

$WeightInd_i$ - weight assigned to the indicators in dimension i;
T_i - number of indicators considered in dimension i.

Once the weight of each indicator is calculated, the maximum value that each dimension can reach is one, and it is calculated through the following formula:

$$ValueDim_{ij} = \sum WeightInd_i * CA_{ij} \quad (3)$$

in which:

$ValueDim_{ij}$ - value for dimension i of IPSS j;
$WeightInd_i$ - weight assigned to the indicators in dimension i;
CA_{ij} - classification of compliance assigned to each indicator of dimension i and to each IPSS j according to the established scale.

The MI calculation is made as shown in formula (4).

$$MI_j = \sum_{i=1}^{6} WeightDim_i * ValueDim_{ij} \quad (4)$$

in which:

MI_j - maturity index for IPSS j;
$WeightDim_i$ - weight assigned to dimension i;
$ValueDim_{ij}$ - value for dimension i.

EMPIRICAL RESULTS AND DISCUSSION

As referred above, the analysis of the IPSS websites occurred in February 2017. This analysis allowed us to see, as presented in Table 3, that, overall, 159 IPSS, representing 37.86% of the sample, have an institutional website and 261 IPSS, representing 62.14% of the sample, do not have one. The Cooperatives and the Holy House of Mercy are those that represent the highest percentage of entities with institutional website (60.00% and 56.52%, respectively), unlike the Community Centre and the Parish Social Centre, which represent the highest percentage of entities without websites (72.50% and 69.70%, respectively). This results are very similar to those obtained by Ferreira *et al.* (2016).

Given the aforementioned results, the answer to the research question 1, “Do the IPSS already have a website on the Internet?”, shows that only a minority does. This answer can be extrapolated to the population, with a confidence level of 95%.

The answer to the remaining research questions depends on the analysis only made to the IPSS which had a website. Thus, in Table 4 the results concerning the disclosure index for the institutions with a website are presented.

Analysing Table 4, the total average of the MI is 0.26. The Holy Houses of Mercy have the highest average of MI, achieving 0.34, followed by the Associations with 0.31, Cooperatives with 0.28, the Foundations and the Religious Institutions or Organizations with 0.25, the Parish Social Centres with 0.22, and finally, the Community Centres with 0.21. Comparing with the results from Ferreira *et al.* (2016), we can verify that the MI increased for all types of IPSS.

Although the results show an improvement in the maturity index comparing with the results obtained by Ferreira *et al.* (2016), even so, the results seem to indicate that the IPSS website do not fully comply with maturity level 1, meaning that they still have to continue to make efforts to improve the quality of their websites.

Regarding the MI dimensions, we can see from analysis of Table 4 that, on average, the dimension accessibility (DIMac) is the one that achieves the highest value, 0.56. Nonetheless, it is just above half the value possible for this dimension. The dimension general information (DIMgi) with a value of 0.39 is the second-highest ranked. The dimension navigability (DIMn) presents a value of 0.28; the dimension update of contents (DIMup) has a score of 0.10; the dimension financial information (DIMfi) 0.23; and, at last, the dimension access for disabled citizens (DIMa) with 0.3. Comparing with the results obtained by Ferreira *et al.* (2016), we observe that the great variation found occurs in the dimension financial information (DIMfi), which rose from 0.09 to 0.23. while the remaining dimensions show substantially identical values.

Table 3. IPSS with and without a website in February 2017

Juridical nature	IPSS in the Sample	IPSS with a website		IPSS without a website	
	No.	No.	%	No.	%
Association	221	77	34.84%	144	65.16%
Community Centre	40	11	27.50%	29	72.50%
Parish Social Centre	66	20	30.30%	46	69.70%
Cooperative	40	24	60.00%	16	40.00%
Foundation	16	8	50.00%	8	50.00%
Religious Institution or Organization	14	6	42.86%	8	57.14%
Holy House of Mercy	23	13	56.52%	10	43.48%
Total	**420**	**159**	**37.86%**	**261**	**62.14%**

Table 4. MI mean and its dimensions

Juridical nature	Elements of the Sample with a Website	DI Mean	Contents		Update	Accessibility	Navigability	Access for disabled citizens
			DIMgi Mean	DIMfi Mean	DIMup Mean	DIMac Mean	DIMn Mean	DIMa Mean
Association	77	0,31	0,40	0,27	0,15	0,59	0,42	0,02
Community Centre	11	0,21	0,29	0,06	0,02	0,54	0,33	0,00
Parish Social Centre	20	0,22	0,33	0,22	0,06	0,43	0,20	0,07
Cooperative	24	0,28	0,48	0,20	0,18	0,55	0,27	0,01
Foundation	8	0,25	0,31	0,33	0,06	0,55	0,22	0,02
Religious Institution or Organization	6	0,25	0,41	0,22	0,17	0,53	0,13	0,03
Holy House of Mercy	13	0,34	0,49	0,28	0,08	0,72	0,42	0,06
Total	**159**	**0.26**	**0.39**	**0.23**	**0.10**	**0.56**	**0.28**	**0.03**

From the analysis of the different dimensions we can observe that in DIMgi the Holy Houses of Mercy are the ones with the highest value, with 0.49, and the Community Centres are the ones with the lowest value, with 0.29. In the remaining institutions, the value obtained ranges between 0.48 for the Cooperatives and 0.29 for the Community Centres. In the DIMfi, the Foundations present the highest value, with 0.33, followed by the Holy Houses of Mercy with 0.28, the Associations with 0.27, the Parish Social Centres and Religious Institutions or Organizations with 0.22, the Cooperatives with 0.20 and finally, the Community Centres with 0.06.

The results now obtained are much higher than those obtained by Ferreira *et al.* (2016), since at the date of data collection the disclosure of financial reporting in the institutional websites of the IPSS was already mandatory. Nevertheless, the results obtained for this dimension indicate that the IPSS do not disclose all the required financial information.

Considering the results obtained for the DIMfi, the answer to research question 7, “if the IPSS have a website do they disclose financial information on this website?”, is partially affirmative although only some IPSS disclose this type of information. This mean that they don’t comply with the law.

The DIMgi and the DIMfi refer to the contents, and according to the results just presented, on average, none of the institutions achieves the minimum value of 0.50, and thus the answer to the research question 2, “if the IPSS have a website, do its contents comply with a set of minimum indicators?”, is negative, considering a minimum number of indicators selected for this index. The results now obtained are much higher than those obtained by Ferreira *et al.* (2016).

In the DIMup, the Cooperatives are once again the ones with the highest value, with 0.18, followed by the Religious Institutions or Organizations with 0.17, the Associations with 0.15, the Holy Houses of Mercy with 0.08, the Parish Centres and Foundations with 0.06 and Community Centres in the lowest rank with 0.02. The compliance with the indicators in this dimension is generally very low. Therefore, the answer to the research question 3, “If the IPSS have a website, does the update of its contents comply with a set of minimum indicators?”, is negative. Once again, the answer takes into account a minimum number of indicators selected for this index. The results obtained by Ferreira *et al.* (2016) are similar, but, in general, a little higher. Regarding the DIMac, Table 4 shows that the values range between 0.72

for the Holy Houses of Mercy and 0.43 for the Parish Centres, being the latter the only ones which present a percentage lower than 0.50. Thus, the answer to the research question 4, "if the IPSS have a website, does its accessibility comply with a set of minimum indicators?", is negative, considering, as aforementioned, a minimum number of indicators selected for this index. The results obtained by Ferreira *et al.* (2016) are also similar.

The Associations and the Holy Houses of Mercy are the institutions with the highest score in DIMn with 0.42, and the Religious Institution or Organization are the ones in the lowest rank, with 0.13. Thus, the answer to the research question 5, "if the IPSS have a website, does its navigability comply with a set of minimum indicators?", is also negative given the minimum number of indicators selected for this index. The results obtained by Ferreira *et al.* (2016) are also very similar.

Finally, concerning the DIMa, all institutions, except Community Centres, score some points, contrary to the results obtained by Ferreira *et al.* (2016) in which only the Associations and the Cooperatives scored. Nevertheless, the highest score is obtained by the Parish Social Centre with 0.07. This result depicts that the overwhelming majority of institutions does not show any concern about meeting the needs of disabled users. Thus, the answer to the research question 6, "if the IPSS have a website, does it provide easy access for disabled citizens?", is also negative based on the minimum number of indicators selected for this index.

The answer to the research questions also allows to answer to the research problem - "after the obligation of disclose of financial reporting on their institutional website, do the IPSS have conditions to comply with these requirement?". Most IPSS do not have a website, meaning they already fail to comply with the requirement foreseen by Decree-Law No. 172-A/2014 (Ministério da Solidariedade, 2014).

Considering the diffusion of innovations theory and Rogers's adoption of innovation theory (Rogers, 2003), the results seem to indicate that the IPSS are not yet motivated to create a website and fulfil the requirement defined by law. However, according to the attributes which influence the rate of adoption of innovation by organizations, proposed by Rogers (2003), the growth rate for the creation of a website by the IPSS may be related to: the perception that a website can provide a greater relative advantage; the consistency of a website with existing values and previous experiences; with the demand of skilful use of the website by the user; the ability to understand possible uncertainties presented by the website; and finally, the ability to easily observe the website creation.

Indeed, some strategies should be developed in order to make the IPSS understand how they can improve and reach the citizen through a website. Regarding disclosing financial reporting, the IPSS still need to become aware of the importance of transparency in management and accountability both for citizens, in general, and the current and potential users of the IPSS services, in particular.

Responding to the institutional theory, based on coercive isomorphism, the IPSS should have created conditions of publishing financial reporting, as required. However, that has not happened yet.

SUMMARY AND CONCLUSION

In order to improve the transparency to the resources management, which are allocated to IPSS through the General Government Budget, these institutions are now required to disclose financial reporting on their institutional websites

However, this study states that most of them do not have an institutional website. In such conditions, these institutions fail in complying with the requirement foreseen by Decree-Law No. 172-A/2014 (Ministério da Solidariedade, 2014).

The results also demonstrate that some of the IPSS which have a website already disclose information on financial reporting, but do not fully comply, because these data are mainly incomplete.

Regarding the website maturity, in line with Ferreira *et al.* (2016), the results show a weak level of sophistication of the IPSS websites, and the maturity level 1is not even achieved by most of them.

Also in line with Ferreira *et al.* (2016), the results do not confirm the assumptions of the diffusion of innovations and the institutional theory and therefore they may be associated to factors such as resource shortage, namely financial resources, which do not allow the IPSS to have the funds to create a website. In the case of those IPSS which have a website, the resource shortage may be conditioning the adequate development of their website, hindering the possibility of achieving maturity level 1. It is to highlight that this maturity level is the lowest in the scale defined by eEurope 2002 (eEurope-2002, 2002) and that no website has achieved it. It can also mean that the web-design enterprises did not take into consideration the recommendations pursuant to eEurope 2002 (eEurope-2002, 2002). Another reason for these results might be related to the IPSS managers' level of schooling which may influence the decision to create a website in case it is low.

A possible future study to consider from the current research is the development of an index which will allow to assess whether the IPSS websites, despite not fully complying with the requirements of maturity level 1, comply with those of more advanced maturity levels. This is a relevant question which is related to the contribution of websites to the improvement of accountability in the IPSS.

Finally, following the diffusion of innovations theory, a study may be conducted with the aim of explaining the variations in the adoption level of systems made available online by the IPSS for their users.

REFERENCES

Almeida, F. (2011). *E-Government: Análise E Avaliação Dos Municípios No Distrito de Viseu.* Escola Superior de Tecnologia e Gestão de Viseu - Instituto Politécnico de Viseu. Available at: http://repositorio.ipv.pt/handle/10400.19/1096

Anes, A. (2009). *Estado de Maturidade Do E-Government Municipal No Distrito de Bragança.* Escola Superior de Tecnologia e Gestão - Instituto Politécnico de Bragança. Available at: https://biblioteca-digital.ipb.pt/handle/10198/2126

APDSI. (2009), *O Poder Local E a Sociedade Da Informação Em Portugal A Evolução Das Câmaras Municipais.* APDSI.

Balasubramanian, S., Konana, P., & Menon, N. M. (2003). Customer Satisfaction in Virtual Environments: A Study of Online Investing. *Management Science, 49*(7), 871–889. doi:10.1287/mnsc.49.7.871.16385

Catarino, L. (2012). *O Uso Do Orçamento Como Ferramenta de Gestão Nas IPSS.* Aveiro: Dissertação de Mestrado, Universidade de Aveiro.

Chen, L., Gillenson, M.L., & Sherrell, D.L. (2004). *Consumer acceptance of virtual stores: a theoretical model and critical success factors for virtual stores.* Academic Press.

Collis, J., & Hussey, R. (2005). Pesquisa. In *Administração: Um Guia Prático Para Alunos de Graduação E Pós-Graduação (2nd ed.)*. Porto Alegre: Bookman.

Dean, A.G., Dean, J.A., Burton, A.H., & Dicker, R.C. (1991). Epi Info: a general-purpose microcomputer program for public health information systems. *American Journal of Preventive Medicine*, 178-182.

Dokhtesmati, M., Saberi, M., & Moradi, S. (2011). The status of ministries' website of Middle Eastern countries in achieving e-government. *77th IFLA General Conference and Assembly.*

eEurope-2002. (2002). *E-Europe 2002 - Uma Sociedade Da Informação Para Todos*. Conselho da União Europeia - Comissão das Comunidades Europeias.

Ferreira, A., Marques, R.P., Santos, C., Azevedo, G., & Mendes, H. (2016). Avaliação da Presença na Internet das Instituições Particulares de Solidariedade Social Portuguesas. *Estudos Do ISCA*, 14. doi:10.1234/ei.v0i14.4730

García-Meca, E., & Conesa, I. M. (2004). Divulgación voluntaria de información empresarial: Índices de revelación. Partida Doble, 157, 66-77.

Makoza, F. (2013). The level of e-Government implementation: Case of Malawi. *Electronic Journal of E-Government, 11*(1), 267–278.

Ministério da Solidariedade, E. e S.S. (2014). Decreto-Lei 172-A/2014. *Diário da República, 221*(1). Available at: https://dre.pt/application/conteudo/58900566

Ministério das Finanças e da Administração Pública. (2011). Decreto-Lei 36-A/2011. *Diário da República, 48*(1). Available at: https://dre.pt/application/conteudo/647296

Olszak, C. M., & Ziemba, E. (2011). The Stage of E-Government Maturity in a Polish Region -- Silesia. *Journal of Economics & Management*, *7*, 87.

Pérez, C. C., Hernández, A. M. L., & Bolívar, M. P. R. (2005). Citizens' access to on-line governmental financial information: Practices in the European Union countries. *Government Information Quarterly, 22*(2), 258–276. doi:10.1016/j.giq.2005.02.002

Pratas, S. (2007). *Administração aberta e Internet. O caso dos municípios portugueses*. Lisboa: Revista de Administração Local.

Presidência do Conselho de Ministros. (1977). Decreto-Lei 460/77. *Diário da República, 257*(1). Available at: https://dre.pt/application/conteudo/277832

Presidência do Conselho de Ministros. (2001). Resolução do Conselho de Ministros n.º 22/2001. *Diário da República, 49*(1). Available at: https://dre.pt/application/conteudo/384669

Rogers, E. (2003). The Diffusion of Innovations (5th ed.). The Free Press.

Santos, C., Ferreira, A., Marques, R. P., & Azevedo, G. (2018). EAGLE_INDEX - Enhancement of Accountability Guide for Learning E-Government. In G. Azevedo, J. Oliveira, R. P. Marques, & A. Ferreira (Eds.), *Handbook of Research on Modernization and Accountability in Public Sector Management* (pp. 103–129). Hershey, PA: IGI-Global. doi:10.4018/978-1-5225-3731-1.ch006

Santos, J., Raimundo, J., & Lima, R. (2012). *Entidades do setor não lucrativo* (NCRF-ESNL e fiscalidade). Ordem dos Técnicos Oficiais de Contas.

Santos, L., & Amaral, L. (2005). *A Presença Na Internet Das Juntas de Freguesia Portuguesas: Estudo Comparativo Entre 2002 E 2004*. Guimarães, Portugal: Gávea – Laboratório de Estudo e Desenvolvimento da Sociedade da Informação. Universidade do Minho.

Santos, L., & Amaral, L. (2006). *A Presença Na Internet Das Câmaras Municipais Portuguesas 2005*. Guimarães, Portugal: Gávea – Laboratório de Estudo e Desenvolvimento da Sociedade da Informação. Universidade do Minho.

Santos, L., & Amaral, L. (2008a). *Presença Na Internet Das Câmaras Municipais Portuguesas Em 2007 : Estudo Sobre Local eGovernment Em Portugal, DSI - Sociedade Da Informação*. Gávea – Laboratório de Estudo e Desenvolvimento da Sociedade da Informação. Universidade do Minho, Guimarães. Available at: http://hdl.handle.net/1822/8443

Santos, L., & Amaral, L. (2008b). *Presença Na Internet Das Juntas de Freguesia Portuguesas Em 2006 : Estudo Sobre Local eGovernment Em Portugal*. Gávea – Laboratório de Estudo e Desenvolvimento da Sociedade da Informação. Universidade do Minho. Available at: http://hdl.handle.net/1822/8477

Santos, L., Oliveira, J., & Amaral, L. (2003). *Método de Avaliação Da Presença Na Internet Dos Organismos Da Administração Direta E Indireta Do Estado*. Unidade de Missão Inovação e Conhecimento da Presidência do Conselho de Ministros e Departamento de Sistemas de Informação da Universidade do Minho.

Soares, D., Amaral, L., Ferreira, L., & Leal, D. (2014). *Método de Avaliação Da Presença Na Internet Das Câmaras Municipais Portuguesas: Versão 4.0*. Guimarães: Gávea – Laboratório de Estudo e Desenvolvimento da Sociedade da Informação. Universidade do Minho.

UMIC. (2003). *Qualidade e eficiência dos serviços públicos : Plano de acção para o governo electrónico*. UMIC.

Wu, I.-L., & Chen, J.-L. (2005). An extension of trust and TAM model with TPB in the initial adoption of on-line tax: An empirical study. *International Journal of Human-Computer Studies*, *62*(6), 784–808. doi:10.1016/j.ijhcs.2005.03.003

KEY TERMS AND DEFINITIONS

Accountability: Obligation of the organs to 1) account for its activities, 2) accept responsibility for these activities, and 3) disclose the results in a transparent manner.

Financial Reporting: Includes all of a company's communication of financial information to people outside of the company.

Maturity: Indicating the final date for payment of principal and interest.

Non-Profit Organizations: Also called not for profit organizations, are privately held entities that don't provide financial benefits for their members or stakeholders. In other words, they are privately incorporated groups with a charitable purpose of not profiting from the activities they carry.

Online Presence: Is the process of presenting and drawing traffic to a personal or professional brand online.

Private Institutions of Social Solidarity: Are constituted as not-for-profit with the purpose of giving organized expression to the moral duty of solidarity and justice among individuals by private initiative.

Social Economy: It is the sphere of the so-called third sector, including associativism, cooperativism, and mutualism, as forms of organization of productive activity (NGO-autonomous organizations, aimed at improving social quality, social projects, and non-governmental organizations).

Chapter 12
Realities and Challenges of the Social Enterprises in South-Eastern European Countries:
Comparative Analysis

Ani Matei
National University of Political Studies and Public Administration, Romania

Corina-Georgiana Antonovici
National University of Political Studies and Public Administration, Romania

Carmen Săvulescu
National University of Political Studies and Public Administration, Romania

ABSTRACT

The chapter objectives focus on mapping the sector of social economy in some states from South-Eastern Europe, presenting their role and impact due to the activities achieved in society. The theoretical part of the chapter comprises the evolution of social economy in Europe, in general, and in South-Eastern Europe, in particular, the identification of the types of organizations in this area. The case study identifies and presents the stages of development of the social enterprises in countries such as Romania, Bulgaria, Cyprus, Serbia, Slovenia, Croatia, Greece, Republic of Moldova, and explores, by comparative analysis the institutional frameworks, the regulations of social enterprises, the eligible judicial forms, presenting similarities and differences, as well as the contribution to social inclusion and impact on community in general. The chapter identifies and explains the influence of the European actors and presents the factors specific to each country which have influenced and supported the emergence of social enterprises as well as the challenges faced.

DOI: 10.4018/978-1-5225-8482-7.ch012

INTRODUCTION

Three major forms of institutions are available to every society: private, governmental and non-profit. Within these three categories, the variety of institutional forms that may exist in a society is not fixed. New forms can be and are invented (Weisbrod, 1988, p. 16). Different institutional forms have different effects on society.

In time social and economic distress and enormous pressures on governmental budgets, the third sector and the private sector through social enterprises represent a "renewable resource" for social and economic problem - solving and civic engagement in Europe, not an alternative to government, but as a full-fledged partner in the effort to promote the European progress (Enjolras, 2018, p. 4).

The social economy, an increasingly expanding area has become a genuine concern at public policy making level when the states acknowledged their need for enhancing the capacity and resources in view to ensure social services for their citizens, to create wealth and to develop the social capital.

The social, political changes and the economic crises affecting in the latest decades the European states, as well as other countries all over the world, have imposed other types of solutions and state interventions.

Worldwide, the countries are facing a broad range of social problems, without still identifying or implementing efficient solutions. Low economic growth rates, migration of labour force, poverty, social exclusion or the development of technology have created new needs and require new services in society. In this context, the social enterprises have provided activities which adjusted the services to the needs of various vulnerable groups, supported the increase of living standard and equitable breakdown of incomes.

The social enterprises become a factor of change, due to their capacity to generate benefits for community, their important role in creating jobs, combating exclusion and poverty and identifying innovative solutions for increasing the life quality. Adaptability to social changes and the innovative potential represent the key features of the social enterprises. The innovative approaches proposed by social economy enterprises are designed to increase the social capital and to inspire people for deeper involvement in community.

The social economy plays an essential role in the European economy, combining profitability with solidarity, creating jobs, consolidating the social, economic and regional cohesion, generating social capital, promoting active citizenship, solidarity and a type of economy awarding priority to people, supporting sustainable development, social, technological, environment innovation (European Parliament, 2009, p. 6). The social enterprises contribute to a sustainable economic model: the primacy of the individual and the social objective over capital, voluntary and open membership, democratic control by membership, combination of the interests of members/users and/or general interest, the defence and application of the principle of solidarity and responsibility, autonomous management and independence from public authorities, most of the surpluses are used in pursuit of sustainable development objectives (European Parliament, 2009, p. 6) .

The emergence and evolution of the social enterprises at the European level have been influenced by the diversity of the countries, their own economic, social and cultural specificity as well as by external actors.

The social enterprises promoting the social change and innovation represent the main provider of services designed to change society by the social benefits generated, the concern for vulnerable groups, education, insertion on labour market, fair trade and environment protection.

Social enterprise means the enterprise whose primary objective is to achieve social impact rather than generate profit for owners and stakeholders. It operates in the market through the production of goods and services in an entrepreneurial and innovative way, and uses surpluses mainly to achieve social goals. It is managed in an accountable and transparent way, in particular by involving workers, customers and stakeholders affected by its business activity (European Commission, 2011, art. 2).

The social economy is neither considered an ideal model of economic and social organisation, nor a global alternative model, it represents an alternative model for certain situations in view to address certain needs (Bidet, 2000, p. 593).

The research methodology is qualitative, based exclusively on the study and analysis of the field literature (scientific papers, books), normative acts, documents, official reports accomplished at the European and national level.

The research aims a comparative analysis concerning the organisation and operation of the social enterprise in eight countries in South-Eastern Europe (Romania, Bulgaria, Cyprus, Serbia, Slovenia, Croatia, Greece, Republic of Moldova), approaching the following issues: legislative framework, legal forms, areas of activity, vulnerable groups and financing mechanisms.

The research aims to present the context of social economy and to identify its perspectives in the above mentioned countries.

The authors have chosen Romania, Bulgaria, Serbia, Slovenia, Croatia, Republic of Moldova, as there are important similarities in their historical past. During the post-socialist period the third sector and enterprises with social missions played a relevant role within transformative processes.

At the same time, when selecting the countries, the moment of their accession to the European Union (Greece in 1981, Cyprus and Slovenia in 1995, Romania and Bulgaria in 2007, Croatia in 2013, Serbia – is official candidate to the EU membership since 2012, while Republic of Moldova is a potential candidate) was taken into consideration. The social enterprises have been supported for set up and development at the European legislative and institutional level.

The research questions refer to: 1. How has the social enterprise sector developed in countries aiming the same purpose (accession to the EU), but with different speeds? 2. Which are the characteristics of the social enterprises in each country?

The limits of research have been determined by the analysis on the social economy sector only in certain states in South-Eastern Europe, thus hindering to generalise the research for the whole South-Eastern Europe. Also, the language spoken in the eight countries has represented a barrier (exception for Romania and Republic of Moldova) and has imposed inevitable limits for our research, taking into consideration the fact that only documents translated into English have been used.

CONCEPTUAL AND HISTORICAL DIMENSIONS OF THE SOCIAL ENTERPRISES IN EUROPE

The Social Economy. Emergence and Evolution of the Social Enterprises

The social economy comprises organisations with specific features, such as the benefit of communities or the benefit of the organisation's members. In a period characterized by inadequate responses of the state concerning social problem solving and the *private organisations* (Drucker, 2010, p. 267 addressed those issues, fulfilling social missions, crystallising in social enterprises, thus developing the social economy.

Schumpeter (1934) asserted that the economic development represented a process with new combinations in production, the entrepreneurs introducing changes at least by one of the following modalities: introducing a new type of product or new quality standards; introducing a new production method; opening new markets; purchasing new raw materials or reorganising a new sector of activity (Defourny, 2002, p. 4).

The social economy consists of private, formally-organised enterprises and networks that operate on the basis of democratic and participatory decision-making processes, producing market and nonmarket goods and services. In social economy initiatives, the distribution of profits or surpluses amongst members is not directly linked to the capital or the fee contributed by each member, but it is directed towards meeting the members' needs, through the production of goods and the provision of services, insurance and finance (Liger, Stefan, & Britton, 2016, p. 8).

The term of social enterprise was mentioned for the first time in 1990s in Italy, the concept being promoted in *Impresa sociale* (Defourny & Nyssens, 2012, p. 75) newspaper. The expression "new social economy" (nouvelle économie sociale) emerges, being used in view to describe new initiatives of "new actors, new requirements or new forms of organisation" (Favreau, 2005); new organisations emerged, such as the social cooperatives in Italy, replacing the traditional concept of cooperative (Bidet, 2000, p. 593).

The evolution of social enterprises was connected to the evolution of cooperatives, Italy adopting in 1991 (Cafaggi & Iamiceli, 2009, p. 32) a law on social cooperatives. *The specificity and general experience of the third sector* (Kerlin, 2012, p. 96) have played an essential role in the development of social enterprises. In countries such as Belgium, France or Germany, by the end of 1970s, the increase of the number of unemployed and the scarce resources for remuneration have imposed the implementation of *active measures* (Develtere & Defourny, 1999, p. 25), in view to support the integration on labour market. The associations and other organisations of the third sector have initiated active measures for professional counselling or reconversion. The associations promoting reintegration on the labour market through productive activities have been the precursors of social enterprises, at that time belonging to the *social economy or solidary economy* (Mendell & Nogales, 2009, p. 93). The term originates from France, which in 1980 adopted a law on solidarity based social economy. In the same year, relevant actors of the associative, mutual and cooperative sector adopted the *Charter of Social Economy*, document updated in 1995.

In the Nordic countries, characterised by a clear separation of the responsibilities of the state, private environment and civil society and a high level of social welfare, the social enterprises have emerged especially for meeting the needs of vulnerable groups. For Sweden, when the state reduced its intervention as *service provider* (Borzaga & Defourny, 2001, p. 6) in the child care system, *the parents' private initiatives* (Fazzi, 2010, p. 91), such as cooperatives and local groups have been developed in the education area.

Most initiatives concerning the development of social enterprises, respectively integration of vulnerable groups on labour market have benefited of the experience of Italy, Spain and Portugal, countries characterised by a *scanty social service system* (Fazzi, 2010, p. 92), with numerous needs solved inefficiently or unmet by the public institutions.

The social enterprise development on the European level has been influenced by the country diversity, the economic, social, cultural specificity. The development trends of the social enterprise sector have drawn the attention of researchers from several universities, so that in 1996, a network has been created aimed to study the emergence and evolution of social enterprises in the European Union Member

States. The Research Network for Social Enterprise – EMES (https://emes.net/) has elaborated three sets of indicators for three dimensions of social enterprises, attempting to establish a general framework for new organisations. Three indicators reflect the economic and entrepreneurial dimensions of social enterprises, three indicators encapsulate the social dimensions and three indicators reflect the participatory governance (Defourny & Nyssens, 2012, p. 77) (see Table 1).

The activity of producing goods and providing services represents a key element as the delivery of an economic activity constitutes a *vehicle for sustainability* (Mair & Marti, 2004, p.8). The high level of autonomy derives from the democratic control of the membership on activities and autonomous management and independence from the public authorities. The risk level specific to social enterprises could be explained by their financial viability depending on how the vital resources are ensured by members and employees, while job creation and insertion of vulnerable groups on labour market suggest a minimum number of employees.

The participatory nature is reflected by the representativeness of all stakeholders, service providers and direct beneficiaries. According to EMES approach, the explicit aim is to support community or a certain vulnerable group.

Those nine criteria have a double role, to support the identification of new entities and to include those older organisations adopting a *new internal dynamics* and developing as social enterprises (Defourny & Nyssens, 2012, p. 78). Influenced by the social, economic and cultural context, the organisations have developed differently, but the features highlighted by EMES researchers represent a valuable tool for better mapping the social economy sector.

The third sector and the social enterprises emerged and developed also in United States. The North American experience concerning the social enterprises is similar to the European one. Known as *businesses with social purposes, non-profit entrepreneurship, enterprises for community welfare* (Defourny & Nyssens, 2012, p. 40), the new initiatives were analysed in the framework of programmes such as *Social Enterprise Initiative,* developed by Harvard Business School in 1993.

Table 1. Indicators of the three dimensions of social enterprises

Dimension	Set of indicators
Economic and entrepreneurial dimensions	- continuous activity for production of goods or supply of services
	- high degree of autonomy
	- assuming a significant economic risk and minimum paid employees
Social dimension	- explicit aim to benefit the community
	- an initiative launched by a group of citizens or civil society organisations
	- limited profit distribution
Participatory governance	- high degree of autonomy
	- decision-making power not based on capital ownership
	- participatory nature

Source: Defourny, J., & Nyssens, M. (2012). Conception of social entreprise in Europe. A comparative perspective with the United States. In *Social Entreprises. An organizational perspective.* Edited by Yeheskel Hasenfeld and Benjamin Gidron. London: Palgrave Macmillan, p. 77, pp. 71-90

The analysis is based on the need of the non-profit sector entities to develop economic activities in view to finance their mission. Like in the European countries, the non-profit sector entities were involved in activities in education, health, social services, environment protection or fight against poverty and exclusion, and further the crisis in 1970-1980 they had to identify financing sources. The research of the social enterprises was accomplished by two schools of thought (Defourny & Nyssens, 2012, pp.40-41), *the earned income school* and *the social innovation school.*

The first North American school focused on activities while the second school highlighted the importance of entrepreneur. *The earned income school* emphasises the role of organisation in business management, generating resources for fulfilling the social objectives. *The social innovation school* highlights the role of social entrepreneur, who is dedicated to the mission in view to create and sustain the social value.

Considered as agent of change, the social entrepreneur *identifies and pursues new opportunities in view to serve the mission, is engaged in a process of continuous innovation, adaptation and learning and acts boldly without being limited by resources, and exhibits accountability to the constituencies served and for the outcomes created* (Dees, 2001).

The social enterprises represent important actors within the social innovation process through the products and services accomplished and especially their effects on the whole local development process (Borzaga & Tortia, 2009). According to the European Commission (2013), by social innovation, the social enterprises address the unmet needs, generate sustainable development, taking into consideration the impact on environment and the vision on long term, focus on people and social cohesion. The social enterprises are considered innovative business models, addressing economic and social objectives, contributing to integration on the labour market, social inclusion and economic development (Neguț, 2013, p. 41).

Concerning the innovative feature of the social enterprises, some authors consider that this feature derives from the tradition of entrepreneurship, other authors consider that innovation is rooted in the risks faced by social entrepreneurship. Other opinions highlight the requirements for creativity and innovation both for profit-designed entrepreneurship and social entrepreneurship, conceived for addressing social problems (Peattie & Morley, 2008, p. 92).

The main differences between the European and North American approaches derive from a different context. In the United States, the social enterprises have developed on entrepreneurial background while in Europe, the vulnerable groups and the social mission represented the main pillars. Europe promoted initially cooperatives, for example in Italy, while in the US, the foundations and associations were paramount. Moreover, in the European countries it is more obvious the connection between social enterprises and public policies, as the organisations are accomplishing a social mission and promote social accountability.

Social enterprises have been also supported at institutional level in the European Union, by documents and strategic programmes such as the Social Entrepreneurship Initiative (2011), the European Union Programme for social changes and social innovation (2011), European Union Programme for Employment and Social Innovation (2013), Regulation of the European Parliament and Council on the European Funds for Social Entrepreneurship (2013).

In full economic crisis, the European Parliament issues the resolution OJ 25.03.2009 requiring the European Commission to transpose the main features of social economy into the European legislation and policies of the Member States as well as to promote and support the new approaches for social economy (CIRIEC, 2017, p.37). The European economy continues its development and recently the representatives of eleven European governments signed *Madrid Declaration,* requiring a European Action plan in view to boost the social economy.

The European Union bodies award special attention to social economy and the activity of the social enterprises is considered a valuable resource in solving problems related to social development, social cohesion and inclusion, respecting the human rights and overcoming any form of discrimination (Vaculovschi & Antonov, 2016, p. 10).

Characteristics of Social Enterprises

Salamon et al. (2000, p. 4) established the most important criteria for characterisation of third sector entities, separation from the public and private sector, existence of structures with distinct legal statute and clear purposes, autonomy in setting the objectives, involvement of volunteers, developing activities that do not pursuit profit.

The analysis on the development of social economy concept in the United States and Europe is essential for establishing the characteristics of the third sector. Revealing a *parallel evolution* (Defourny & Nyssens, 2012, p. 75), especially after 1970s, in the US, several organisations formed the non-profit sector, while in Europe the French origin term is that of *social economy* (CIRIEC, 2017, p. 9).

Relevant studies (Borzaga & Defourny, 2001, pp.6-9) highlighted distinct elements as well as common features of those two concepts. The entities associated to the social economy sector aim to serve a community and not to pursuit the profit, have independent management, the decision-making process is democratic and award priority to the person in revenues distribution.

Thus the most popular definition of the third sector, as developed by the Johns Hopkins project, has an 'American bias' (Borzaga, 1998) because it is based on the criterion of non-distribution that underlies the American configuration of the sector (Table 2). This does not take into account the specific legal requirements of European countries for which the distinguishing criterion is the existence of limits on profit distribution. It is this criterion that separates third sector organisations from other productive organisations. Using a term such as 'non-profit sector' as equivalent to 'third sector' is clearly misleading. Given the European experience, with an influential 'social economy' besides charities, voluntary agencies and those associations that are primarily advocacy groups, one might say that all organisations in the third sector are 'not-for-profit', having a legal status that places limits on private, individual acquisition of profits (Evers & Laville, 2004, p.13).

Table 2. The organisations involved

'European' definition of the third sector	'American' definition of the third sector
Emphasis on analytical approach developing association typologies and changes as well as the development of the economic dimension of all not-for- profit social economy organisations.	Emphasis on a classificatory approach centred on a statistical interpretation of the importance of a sector comprising all non-profit organizations
Criterion of limits on private acquisition Non-distribution constraint central of profits: inclusion of cooperatives and exclusion of cooperatives and mutual aid societies.	Non-distribution constraint central, exclusion of cooperatives and mutual aid societies.

Source: Evers, A., & Laville, J.-L. (2004). Defining the third sector in Europe, p. 13

The non-profit organisations have distinct legal personality, display self-governance by own regulations and decision-making bodies, cannot distribute the profit to members, managers or owners, involve volunteers and donors. Common elements could be found in both descriptions, such as a formal structure, self-governance, activities that do not pursuit the profit. Concerning the differences related to social economy, the distinctive feature refers to the fact that the organisation has the mission to support community or a group that shares a well-defined need or aim. On the other hand, the non-profit organisations do not undertake explicitly a social aim and the attempt to maximize the profit is limited only by the principle of non-distribution. *The non-distribution constraint* (Hansmann, 1980, p. 838) establishes the interdiction to distribute the net revenues to the persons exercising control on the entity.

The civic participation represents an important pillar of the third sector. Therefore, the communities with strong civic engagement, states with powerful civil society trigger the development of an independent sector. Social trust and generalised mutuality lead to faster identification of solutions for the social problems, to a better life in community.

EMES defines the concept of the multi-stakeholder enterprise. The feature of being a multi-stakeholder organisation determines the democratic character of decision-making. Social enterprises are organisations that are governed by democratic criteria or at least, have circuits of participation not dependent on the contribution of financial capital to the organisation (Vidal, 2008, p. 314).

The features of the independent sector organisations represent the basis for highlighting their main functions in view to respond to the needs unmet by the state or the private sector both in Europe and the US. The social entities aim mainly to *promote the change and social innovations* (Dees, 2013, pp. 31-32), to support the economic system, social integration and to valorise the human potential. The general objective of social cohesion is ensured by *the development of stable social connections* (Grieco, 2015, p. 9), eliminating barriers for vulnerable groups, enabling access to education, labour market and medical services.

The EU characterizes social enterprise through the respect for common values – primacy of democracy, social stakeholders' participation, supremacy of individual and social objectives over the financial ones, solidarity and responsibility, democratic control by its members, voluntary and open membership (Matei & Sandu, 2016, p. 168).

Common characteristics of the social enterprises (Oatley, 1999, p. 339) could be also:

- Combination of objectives, economic, social and ethical values;
- Benefits for the community members;
- Focus on people, not on investment;
- Participative values;
- Independence and autonomy;
- The trade activities are only for reaching the purpose of the organisation.

Active component of the economic growth process (Matei & Sandu, 2011), the social enterprise supports the creation of new jobs, promotes innovation and a better relationship between the entity as provider of goods and services and the community.

Understanding the whole ensemble, the size of the social economy sector, its characteristics and functions represents the starting point for the analysis of social enterprises.

Legal Forms of Social Enterprises

Although there are differences across Europe, there are comparable organisations with the same features, even not described as belonging to the social economy sector or not legally regulated in all European countries.

The associations, foundations, cooperatives and mutual societies represent the main forms for organisation of social economy, being considered traditional forms in the national legislation of each state.

The associations are social-economic actors, activating not to obtain profit as they are dedicated to their members and the aim is to contribute to the general interest. Their activity is based on service delivery, militant activities, social security, integration, education.

The associations include charitable organisations, trade unions, professional or academic entities, associations of consumers, political parties, churches or religious organisations, cultural, leisure, educational, citizen organisations, social services, health care, environment entities, sport clubs, gathering a high number of organisations with millions of members (CIRIEC, 2017, p. 27).

The foundations are non-profit organisations, managed by a purpose and organised for the public benefit. The foundations focus on environment, social services, health, education, science, research, arts and culture.

The activity field is close related to their type. The foundations could be grouped in the following broad categories: independent foundations, composing the largest part of this sector; corporatist foundations; government supported foundations; community foundations on local/community level and other foundations for fundraising (European Foundation Centre, 2008).

The cooperatives are set up with the double purpose to obtain economic success and to respond to the social objectives (Cooperatives Europe). The main types of cooperatives operating in the European Union are agricultural, financial, retail, housing, manufacturing cooperatives. Other significant types refer to consumption cooperatives, pharmaceutical, production, women, fishery, health, education, tourism cooperatives, credit unions, banks.

The European Commission (2003) defines Mutuals as "voluntary groups of persons (natural or legal) whose purpose is primarily to meet the needs of their members rather than achieve a return on investment. These kinds of enterprise operate according to the principles of solidarity between members, and their participation in the governance of the business".

Depending on their main activity and the type of risk, the mutual societies are divided into two main categories. The first group includes provident type mutual societies, covering mainly the risks associated to health and social welfare of individuals and the second group comprises the insurance mutual companies (CIRIEC, 2017, p. 24).

The European Social Enterprise Law Association (2015, p. 21) identifies three main 'types' of Legal Forms used by Social Enterprises, namely (see Table 3):

Type 1: Non-Profit Organisations – which may be democratic or controlled by managers, do not distribute profit and trade in furtherance of a social purpose;

Type 2: Cooperatives – which are generally owned and controlled on a democratic basis by members, distribute profit from trading activities to members and may have a social purpose beyond benefitting members written into the constitution or carry out a service of general interest; and

Type 3: Share Companies – which are generally owned and controlled by shareholders on a pro rata basis and which may trade in furtherance of a social purpose and may have other governance features to subordinate profit to purpose.

COMPARATIVE ANALYSIS - ROMANIA, BULGARIA, CYPRUS, SERBIA, SLOVENIA, CROATIA, GREECE, REPUBLIC OF MOLDOVA

The Legal Framework of Social Economy and Social Enterprises

The concept of social economy is continuously developing in Europe. According to CIRIEG study (CIRIEC, 2017, pp. 33 - 34), countries could be divided into three categories depending on the level of recognition and acceptance of the concept of social economy in each country (by public authorities, social economy structures, academics, citizens). According to these categories there are: *1. countries in which the concept of the social economy is widely recognised, 2. countries in which the concept of the social economy enjoys a moderate level of recognition and 3. countries where there is little or no recognition of the concept of the social economy.*

Table 4 presents the categories of the countries analysed in the current chapter.

Peter Drucker asserts in his paper (Drucker, 2010, p. 283) the importance and need of the third sector in some countries, stating: *the need is maximum especially in the former communist countries where the community and citizens have been profoundly affected. In those countries the state was completely discredited and has become helpless*". His paper approaches some of the states analysed in the current chapter (except Greece and Cyprus).

The importance of a powerful civil society for state development and the difficulty to strengthen democracy in post-communist countries due to the *lack of tradition in expressing the civic spirit* (Putman, 1995) represent arguments for the need of activating and developing the third sector entities.

Table 3. Types' of legal forms used by social enterprises

Foundation	Association	Non-Profit Company	Certain Social Cooperatives	Cooperatives	Share Company
Type 1				Type 2	Type 3

Source: European Social Enterprise Law Association, 2015, p. 21

Table 4. National recognition of the concept of the 'social economy'

Category	Country
countries in which the concept of the social economy enjoys a moderate level of recognition	Romania (RO), Bulgaria (BG), Cyprus (CY), Greece (EL), Slovenia (SI)
countries where there is little or no recognition of the concept of the social economy	Croatia (HR), Serbia (SR), Republic of Moldova (MD)

Source: Authors, adapted after CIRIEG (2017)

Even if the social economy is paramount in the social development strategies of the European countries, not all countries dispose of a legislation that should contribute to adequate institutionalisation of the activity (Vaculovschi & Antonov, 2016, p. 10).

The Report of the International Research and Information Centre on Public, Social Economy and Cooperatives (CIRIEC, 2017, p. 67) acknowledges the progresses in the field of knowledge and legislation of social economy in the EU Member States.

Regulation of Social Economy/Social Enterprises in the Analysed States

Recently, the European states adopted special laws on social economy: in 2011, Spain and Slovenia, in 2011 and 2016 Greece, in 2013 Portugal, in 2014 France, in 2015 Romania, as well as laws at regional level in Belgium and Spain (see Table 5 concerning the regulation of social economy/social enterprises in the analysed states).

Taking into consideration the special normative regulations on social economy, the eight states could be classified into:

1. States with specific legislation for the social economy entities (Romania, Greece, Slovenia);
2. State which is on-going the adoption of specific legislation on social economy (Bulgaria);
3. States which did not adopt specific legislation on social economy (Cyprus, Croatia, Serbia, Republic of Moldova).

Analysing the legislative framework, Greece and Slovenia adopted laws since 2011, recently Romania (2015) and Republic of Moldova (2017) while Bulgaria, Cyprus and Serbia do not yet have special legislation for social economy/social enterprises.

Republic of Moldova has statutory provisions referring to social entrepreneurship and social economy organisations included in various laws.

Table 5. Special laws on social economy/social enterprises adopted in the analysed states

Country	Law
RO	Law 219/15 on the Social Economy, 23 July 2015 Ordinance on Methodological Norms for applying the Law of the Social Economy were adopted by Government Decision no. 585, 10 August 2016
BG	**Draft** Law on the Social Economy (2016)
CY	**No law** for Social Entrepreneurship or Social Enterprise
EL	Law 4430/2016 on Social and Solidarity Economy Social economy and social enterprises (2011) - **abolished**
SI	Act on Social Entrepreneurship no. 20 from 2011
HR	**No law** for Social Entrepreneurship or Social Enterprise
SR	**No law** for Social Entrepreneurship or Social Enterprise
MD	Law 845/1992 on entrepreneurship and enterprises, with amendments of law 223/02.11.2017, chapter VII (on social entrepreneurship and social enterprises)

Source: Authors

The focus on integration of the disadvantaged groups represents a common feature of the laws adopted in Greece, Romania, Slovenia and Republic of Moldova.

Noya (CIRIEC, 2017, p. 51) sustain that regulation of the social economy with new legal forms does not itself constitute an advance in fostering the social economy that goes beyond its institutional recognition. As with the European Cooperative Statute or the Spanish Law on the Social Economy, the effects could be too limited if the law is not accompanied by other measures.

Otherwise it risks becoming a soft law instead of a hard law that promotes the social economy (CIRIEC, 2017, p. 51), and policy narratives and discourses could move in a different direction to that of real public policies (CIRIEC, 2017, p. 51).

Strategies and Action Plans on Social Economy/ Social Enterprises in the Analysed States

The European Union supports the development of the social economy sector, the social enterprises through recommendations, programmes and projects dedicated both to the Member States and acceding countries. The official reports reveal the important role of the European funds in setting up and developing social enterprises in several EU Member States, imposing the states to adopt strategies and plans for the development of social economy/social enterprises.

Recently, the EU Member States and acceding countries designed and enforced strategies and action plans (see Table 6) based on the European funds, and accomplished Operational Programmes targeting the social economy.

Table 6. Strategies and action plans at national level

Country	Documents
RO	- "Solidar - Support for consolidating the Social Economy" programme, under POCU - Human Capital Operational Programme (2014-2020) - European Social Fund –Human Resource Development Operational Sectoral Programme POS DRU (2007-2013) *(Priority Axis 6 – Promoting the social inclusion, DMI 6.1 Social Economy Development)*
BG	- National strategy for reducing poverty and promoting social inclusion 2020 - Action plan for social economy (2014-2015; 2016-2017)
CY	- National Policy Statement for the Entrepreneurial Ecosystem (2015)
EL	- Strategy for the optimal use of European Structural and Investment Funds - Regional strategic plans for promoting social inclusion and combating poverty and discrimination (2015) - Strategic Plan for the Development of Social Entrepreneurship (2013)
SI	- Social entrepreneurship Strategy with Action plan (2013 – 2016) - European Social Fund, for the programming period 2007 – 2013, covering start-up phase of social enterprises and employment of disadvantaged groups of people.
HR	- Strategy for the Development of Social Entrepreneurship in the Republic of Croatia for the period of 2015 – 2020 (April, 2015)
SR	- Strategy for the Development and Promotion of Socially Responsible Business in the Republic of Serbia (2010 -2015) - Strategy for the support to development of small and medium-sized enterprises, entrepreneurship and the competition (2015)
MD	- Strategy for Civil Society Development (2018–2020) and Action Plan for implementing the Strategy for Civil Society Development (2018–2020) - Strategy for Civil Society Development (2012-2015)

Source: Authors

Romania, Bulgaria, Greece, Slovenia and Croatia have adopted strategies and plans for social economy development. Cyprus, Serbia and Republic of Moldova have strategies supporting entrepreneurship in general (Cyprus, Serbia), strategies for developing and promoting social responsibility (Serbia), strategies for civil society development in general, (Republic of Moldova), supporting also the social enterprise development.

It is worth to mention that the above countries have also national programmes sustaining social integration, social security, employment, integration of people with disabilities, child protection, Roma integration.

For the Non-European member states a great impact on national policies is represented by their status of candidates developing strategies for European Union Accession (Matei & Sandu, 2016, p. 201).

According to Table 6, all the countries, no matter they do have or not specific legislation, are implementing strategies, plans and projects specific for social economy development.

Beyond the legislation specific for social economy of some states, all countries have general legislation, applicable for various social economy entities. In most countries, the legislation refers to associations, foundations and cooperatives as well as to other entities such as protected units in Romania, humanitarian organisations in Croatia, vocational enterprises for disable persons (Matei & Sandu, 2016, p. 202) in Serbia, social cooperatives with limited liability (Koi.S.P.E.) in Greece.

Legal Forms of Social Enterprises in the Analysed States

Table 7 presents the Legal Forms most commonly used by Social Enterprises in the analysed countries in our chapter.

Table 7 reveals that in the analysed countries the ranking is as follows: non-profit organisations, cooperatives and share companies.

Table 7. The most common legal forms used by Social Enterprises in the analysed countries

Country	Legal Forms		
RO	Association	Mutual Help Associations for Employees	Mutual Help Associations for Pensioners
BG	Non-Profit Legal Entity (Associations and Foundations)	Cooperative of People with Disabilities	Specialised Enterprises For People With Disabilities
CY	Non-Profit Company	Association	Foundation
EL	Social Cooperative Enterprise	Limited Liability Social Co-operative	Third Legal Form not provided by Respondent
SI	Cooperative	Institutions	Share Company
HR	Share Company	Social Cooperative	Association
SR	Cooperative	Association	Enterprises for employment of persons with disability
MD	Association	Foundation	Cooperative

Source: Authors, adapted after European Social Enterprise Law Association, 2015, p. 53

Areas of Activity of the Social Enterprises

Depending on the social enterprise form there are several areas of activity.

In the analysed countries, the main areas of activity of the social enterprises are as follows: social security, paying special attention to the care of family, old persons and persons with disabilities, social inclusion, vocational training of unemployed or persons with risk of unemployment, research, education, medical security, ecological production, fair trade, protecting the natural and cultural heritage, tourism, non-professional sport activities, developing the local communities, supporting the environment for the social enterprises.

Social economy could be systematised according to activities and beneficiaries as follows (Foundation Together with You, 2011, p. 18):

1. Social economy generating jobs for vulnerable persons and activating in the economic field;
2. Social economy generating resources for social projects and activating in any economic field;
3. Social economy meeting the need of social services (and eventually products) and activating exclusively in the area of service delivery;
4. Any combination of the above.

The normative acts in the analysed states (especially the legal framework of the states with normative acts specific for social economy) stipulate the vulnerable groups that could be supported through the activity of social enterprises: youth in the child protection system, beneficiaries of guaranteed minimum income, beneficiaries of allowances for family support, asylum candidates, persons without shelter and any person under risk to lose the capacity of meeting subsistence. The social enterprises of insertion employ disadvantaged persons, belonging to vulnerable groups.

The social enterprise is considered an efficient instrument for fighting against social exclusion, by production of goods and services, all stakeholders' involvement such as volunteers, employees, beneficiaries, representatives of public and private bodies (OECD, 1999, p. 9).

The focus of social enterprises concerning re-integration of disadvantaged persons on labour market has triggered the emergence of social enterprises for insertion aiming especially the integration of unskilled persons, with high risk of exclusion, thus playing an essential role in job creation.

The mission of social entrepreneurship is directly linked to the possibilities of creating new jobs opportunities, of creating new goods and services for satisfying the social needs and it responds to the necessities of certain vulnerable groups (Matei & Sandu, 2016, p. 219).

The diversity of areas of activity, other than social services or insertion of vulnerable groups on labour market highlight the support of social mission in any sector of activity.

Funding Mechanisms of Social Enterprises

In Europe, the social enterprises could attract funding from national public funds, European funds, private funds or hybrid public-private systems.

Certain countries in Europe provide financing sources for social enterprises from national public funds, based on relevant policies, programmes and measures. This category include Belgium, Denmark, France, Italy, Luxembourg, Poland, Portugal, Spain, Sweden, Switzerland and the United Kingdom, as well as **Croatia, Slovenia** (European Commission, 2015, p. 67) and Cyprus (CIRIEC, 2017, p.52).

These examples should not be seen as "good practice" as evidence on what constitutes good practice in this area is currently lacking (European Commission, 2015, p. 67).

Some European countries have very limited or no publically funded schemes especially designed and targeting social enterprises. This is particularly the case in newer Member States, particularly from Eastern Europe - **Bulgaria**, Czech Republic, Estonia, Hungary, Latvia, Lithuania, Malta, **Slovenia**, Slovakia and **Romania** where ad hoc and fragmented initiatives have been funded through Structural Funds (European Commission, 2015, p. 68). The same situation is also present in **Serbia** and **Republic of Moldova**.

The EU structural funds have been used extensively in view to support social enterprises across the Member States. European Social Fund programmes in particular, have been instrumental in supporting the development of social economy and social enterprise concepts and models in many European countries. This is likely to continue with the increased emphasis on social enterprise in the new European Structural and Investment Funds Operational Programmes for 2014-2020, e.g. in Bulgaria, Croatia and Romania to name a few countries.

The European funds have been used on a large extent in view to support the social enterprises in the EU Member States. The European Social Fund has brought an important contribution to social economy development in several countries. For the time being, Bulgaria, Croatia, Romania, Slovenia benefit of the new Operational Programmes for the EU Structural and Investment Funds for 2014-2020.

In light to enhance the interest of private investors in social enterprises, Regulation 346/2013 on European social entrepreneurship funds was approved. It mainly established a new label (the EuSEF label) to identify European Social Entrepreneurship Funds. The label highlights the social impact of the beneficiaries of the funds, not their form or governance; a requirement is that at least 70% of the capital received from investors should be used in support of social businesses (CIRIEC, 2017, p. 44).

The mixed financial instruments for social enterprises with hybrid models are as follows (Damaschin-Ţecu & Etchart, 2016, pp. 17-19): credit lines; guarantees; debt/loan/convertible titles, individual investment; equity, financing in a combination of equity with borrowed capital (interim financing); hybrid instruments (combined financial instruments, usually public funds assuming a part of the risk or providing guarantee in view to attract the private capital); bonds with social impact; loans for trading purposes between individuals.

Those innovating instruments are often supported by private and public donors and investors focused on social aspects, are directed and validated before introducing them on a broader market. The developed markets use actively those instruments while the emergent and cross-border markets, such as those in Central and Eastern Europe adopt them slower (Damaschin-Ţecu & Etchart, 2016, p. 14).

The Impact of Social Enterprises on Community

The close link between the social enterprise and community is based on the social enterprise activity, providing economic benefits in disadvantaged communities, contributing to stability and vibration of local communities (Phillips, 2006 in Peattie & Morley, 2008, p. 40). In this context, two main areas have been identified: 1) access to managerial skills, based on the capacity to identify the local needs and to propose adequate solutions at local level; 2) infrastructure, by granting facilities and services, which support the establishment of an active community, such as income generating new enterprises or other local projects (Simon Clark Associates, 2002, in Peattie & Morley, 2008, p. 41) .

Social economy, comprising a rich variety of enterprise models, such as cooperatives, mutuals, associations, foundations and social enterprises, plays an important role in achieving several EU objectives, including smart, sustainable and inclusive growth, the creation of decent jobs, social cohesion and social innovation (European Union Council, 2015).

The economic data provide the existence of 2 million social enterprises in Europe (10% of total businesses in Europe), generating in 2017, 14.5 million jobs in the EU and 8% of the EU GDP. The social enterprises employ 11 million paid labour force, of which 70% work in non-profit associations, 26% in cooperatives and 3% in mutual societies (European Commission). CIRIEC (2017) Report highlights the fact that these jobs represent 6.3% of the working population of the EU and due to the economic crisis, there was recorded a drop from 6.5% to 6.3%. The growth potential is high, but the divide between the developed and former communist countries is present, so that the employment in the third sector entities amounts 9-10% in France, Belgium or Germany and under 2% in Slovenia, Croatia, Malta or Cyprus. In Romania, according to the analysed data the percentage is 1.7% and the number of contracts is decreasing.

The social economy provides a good example for job creation, support of social inclusion and promotion of participative economy.

Especially in the last decade, in Romania the social economy has drawn attention further financing by Structural Funds through Human Resource Development and Human Capital Operational Programmes. In Romania, the activities have aimed both the vulnerable groups and specialists in social service area, jobs have been generated, and the need for a law specific for this field has emerged.

The impact of the activities of social enterprises on the social-economic development comprises:

- Generation of new jobs in their areas of activity;
- Integration of disadvantaged persons on labour market, for certain social enterprises;
- Development of new forms for labour organisation;
- "Internalisation" of the economic growth for the community benefit (the community dimension enables adaptation to local context and resources);
- Contribution to increasing social cohesion and social capital (providing goods/services with powerful social potential, adopting institutional inclusive and participative structures).

Development Trends of Social Enterprises and Challenges

According to the above statistic data, in all eight states the social economy entities are in continuous progress, while the pace and manner of development are different.

There is general consensus that social economy represents a pole of social utility, as it provides a significant contribution to social problem solving, recording a higher weight among the economic sectors.

The analysed countries are facing the following main challenges in developing the social economy: institutional barriers; low level of recognition of social entrepreneurship; lack of a specific legislative framework at national level in some countries; limited access to funding.

The question for future is if the social economy entities could continue their missions for the benefit of community on medium and long term without clear public policies concerning the legal framework, access to funding and support fiscal measures.

SOLUTIONS AND RECOMMENDATIONS

The main solutions to address the above challenges refer to: adopting the legislative framework specific for social economy (social economy is a distinct field of the economic activity and it should be recognised as such in the legislation regulating the businesses); providing activities to promote the concept of social entrepreneurship and good practices; identifying and developing support mechanisms for social economy entities; strengthening the institutional capacity of the social economy organisations by access to training, consultancy and funding.

The support and development of social economy in all South-Eastern European countries should be considered an opportunity to better address several essential needs at the same time: generating new jobs, enhancing social inclusion as well as improving the quality and efficiency of the social services.

An integrated approach could lead to enhancing the economic growth in future years.

FUTURE RESEARCH DIRECTIONS

In Romania, the social enterprises have developed and have gained acknowledgement in the last decade in close connection with projects financed from Structural Funds. Mentioned in country programmes, firstly as structures of social economy, at the end of 2007-2013 financing period, the law on social economy was adopted during the process of validation of the indicators and finalisation of the reports corresponding to the Operational Programmes.

The normative act provided to the social economy entities, set up within the projects the requirement to obtain certificates of social enterprises or social enterprises of insertion, if complying with the definition and principles of social economy. Taking into consideration the fact that criteria were not provided, problems concerning the documents have emerged. There was no clarification concerning the obligation of the social economy entities, set up within projects in order to obtain the certificate during the sustainability period (Dâmbovița County Agency for Employment, 2017).

As future research direction, the authors would like to analyse the social enterprises and social enterprises of insertion that require the certificate or the social brand, since August 2016, moment when the norms for implementing the social economy were issued. The entities already activating in the social economy sector and those set up further the implementation of projects financed from Structural Funds have followed a procedure for submitting a request in view of certification, accompanied by relevant documents at the departments of social economy, set up within the county agencies for employment. The research will aim to emphasise the factors influencing the emergence of the legal framework, the process of certification, types of certified entities, the areas of activity, the impact on community, social change and innovation as key elements of social economy.

CONCLUSION

Although neither the size nor the dynamics of the social economy sector across the eight states do not inscribe in the category of a very developed sector, the social economy structures have become known especially due to implementation of projects financed from Structural Funds.

The study on national legislations has highlighted a legislative context favourable to fulfilling the function of social enterprises of training and integration on the labour market in all eight countries. Those states have adapted the legislative framework complying with the European Union directives.

Supporting the social economy development represents a solution to the new and complex problems in the social field as well as to sustainability, quality and flexibility of social services.

The social enterprises reveal key features as adaptability to social changes and innovating potential. The enlargement and improvement of services in traditional fields such as employment and social services have been the first initiatives demonstrating the innovation capacity of the new entities through job creation for disadvantaged persons, and specific measures in view to enhance the working conditions.

It is worth to mention that the social economy has not enjoyed the same level of interest and acknowledgement in all European countries. CIRIEC (2012) Report highlights a broad acceptation of the notion of social economy in Spain, France, Portugal, Ireland and Greece. In Italy, Cyprus, Denmark, Finland, Luxembourg, Sweden, Latvia, Malta, Poland, United Kingdom, Bulgaria and Iceland, the notion of social economy is known but it co-exists with other concepts, such as non-profit sector, voluntary sector, social enterprises. Austria, Czech Republic, Estonia, Germany, Hungary, Lithuania, the Netherlands, Slovakia, Romania, Croatia and Slovenia have the lowest acknowledgement level. In CIRIEC (2012) research, the cooperatives, mutual organisations, associations and foundations represent organisations acknowledged as belonging to social economy. The exceptions refer to the companies with social purpose in Belgium, the organisations for integration in Spain, the centers of socio-economic integration in Poland or protected units in Romania

Further our analysis, the authors assert that the social economy sector is in a development stage. The actual statistical data concerning the number of social enterprises, the number of jobs created and maintained and the impact on environment are hard to be obtained.

The social enterprises in those eight countries analysed are developing business models, combining the economic activity with the social mission. The authors have identified dynamism in the social economy sector across the eight countries, and despite the EU attempts for uniformisation of the social enterprise characteristics, the definition and regulation at national level are different, but based on an identic social economy development model, focused on social benefit, employment.

Taking into consideration the global challenges, the social economy actors have understood the significance of approaches in terms of innovation, sustainability and competitiveness.

REFERENCES

Bidet, E. (2000). Économie sociale, nouvelle économie sociale et sociologie économique. *Sociologie du Travail*, *42*(4), 587–599. doi:10.1016/S0038-0296(00)01103-1

Borzaga, C., & Defourny, J. (2001). *The Emergence of Social Entreprise*. London: Routledge.

Borzaga, C., & Tortia, E. C. (2009). Social enterprises and local economic development. In E. Clarence & A. Noya (Eds.), *The Changing Boundaries of Social Enterprises*. Paris: OECD Publishing. doi:10.1787/9789264055513-6-en

Cafaggi, F., & Iamiceli, P. (2009). New frontiers in the legal structure and legislation of social entreprises in Europe. A comparative Analysis. In A. Noya (Ed.), *The Changing Boundaries of Social Enteprises* (pp. 25–86). Paris: OECD Publishing. doi:10.1787/9789264055513-3-en

CIRIEC - International - Centre international de recherches et d'information sur l'économie publique, sociale et coopérative. (2012). *The Social Economy in The European Union.* Retrieved from https://www.eesc.europa.eu/sites/default/files/files/qe-04-17-875-en-n.pdf

CIRIEC - International - Centre international de recherches et d'information sur l'économie publique, sociale et coopérative. (2017). *Study Recent evolutions of the Social Economy in the European Union.* Retrieved from http://www.ciriec.uliege.be/wp-content/uploads/2015/12/EESC_CIRIECReport2012_EN.pdf

Cooperatives Europe. (n.d.). Retrieved from http://www.co-opseurope.co-op/spip.php?rubrique19

Damaschin-Ţecu, R., & Etchart, N. (2016). *Case of Romania. Developing the industry of social investments in Central and Eastern Europe.* NESsT.

Dâmboviţa County Agency for Employment. (2017). *Activity Report on monitoring the social enterprise activity and social enterprises of insertion certified for 2016.* Available at: www.dambovita.anofm.ro

Dees, J. G. (2001). *The meaning of social entrepreneurship.* Retrieved from https://entrepreneurship.duke.edu/news-item/the-meaning-of-social-entrepreneurship/

Dees, J. G. (2013). Toward an open-solution society. *Standford Social Innnovation Rewiew,* 31-32. Retrieved from https://ssir.org/articles/entry/toward_an_open_solution_society

Defourny, J. (2002). *Social Enterprise in an Enlarged Europe: Concept and Realities.* EMES European Research Network.

Defourny, J., & Nyssens, M. (2012). Conception of social entreprise in Europe. A comparative perspective with the United States. In Y. Hasenfeld & B. Gidron (Eds.), Social Entreprises. An organizational perspective (pp. 71-90). London: Palgrave Macmillan.

Develtere, P., & Defourny, J. (1999). The social economy: The worldwide making of a third sector. In J. Defourny, P. Develtere, & B. Fonteneau (Eds.), Social Economy – North and South. KULeuven: HIVA.

Drucker, P. (2010). *The essential Drucker: selection of management papers of Peter F. Drucker.* Bucharest: Meteor Press.

Enjolras, B. (2018). Introduction. In B. Enjolras, L. M. Salamon, K. H. Sivesind, & A. Zimmer (Eds.), *The Third Sector as a Renewable Resource for Europe. Concepts, Impacts, Challenges and Opportunities* (pp. 1–5). Palgrave Macmillan. doi:10.1007/978-3-319-71473-8_1

European Commission. (2003). *Mutual Societies in an enlarged Europe.* Consultation Document. Retrieved from file:///C:/Users/CA/Downloads/mutuals-consult-doc-en.pdf

European Commission. (2011). Proposal for a Regulation of the European Parliament and of the Council on a European Union Programme for Social change and Innovation. Retrieved from http://eurlex.europa.eu/LexUriServ/LexUriServ.do?uri=COM:2011:0609:FIN:RO:PDF

European Commission. (2013). *The Social Business Initiative of the European Commission*. Available at: http://ec.europa.eu/internal_markct/social_business/docs/201205 sbi leaflet_ en.pdf

European Commission. (2015). *A Map of Social Enterprises and their Eco-Systems in Europe Synthesis Report*. Retrieved from file:///C:/Users/CA/Downloads/Synthesis%20report%20FINAL%20(1).pdf

European Foundation Centre. (2008). *Report Foundations in the European Union - Facts & Figures Across*. Retrieved from http://www.efc.be/programmes_services/resources/Documents/EFC-RTF_EU%20 Foundations-Facts%20and%2-Figures2008.pdf

European Parliament – Commission for Employment and Social Affairs. (2009). *Report on social economy* (2008/2250INI). Author.

European Social Enterprise Law Association. (2015). *Social Enterprise in Europe. Developing Legal Systems which Support Social Enterprise Growth*. Retrieved from http://providus.lv/article_files/3058/original/ESELA_Legal_Mapping_Publication_250915_(3)-1.pdf?1444030170

European Union Council. (2015). Retrieved from http://www.europarl.europa.eu/sides/getDoc.do?pubRef=-//EP//TEXT+OQ+O-2017-000070+0+DOC+XML+V0//EN

Evers, A., & Laville, J.-L. (2004). Defining the third sector in Europe. In A. Evers & J.-L. Laville (Eds.), The Third Sector in Europe. Globalization and welfare. Cheltenham, UK: Edward Elgar.

Favreau, L. (2005). Qu'est-ce que l'économie sociale? Synthèse introductive. *Cahiers du Crises, Collection études théoriques*.

Fazzi, L. (2010). The provision of welfare and general-interest services. In C. Borzaga & L. Becchetti (Eds.), *The Economics of Social Responsability. The world of social entrepreses* (pp. 88–104). London: Routledge Advances in Social Economics.

Foundation Together with You. (2011). *Policies, practices and trends in the social economy in Romania and the European Union*. Retrieved from https://ec.europa.eu/epale/ro/resource-centre/content/politici-practici-si-tendinte-economia-sociala-romania-si-uniunea-europeana

Grieco, C. (2015). *Assesing Social Impact of Social Entrepises. Does one size really fit all?* Heidelberg, Germany: Springer Briefs in Business.

Hansmann, H. (1980). The Role of nonprofit enterprise. *The Yale Law Journal*, *5*(5), 835–901. doi:10.2307/796089

Kerlin, J. A. (2012). Defining social entreprise across diffrent context: a conceptual framework based on institutional factors. In Y. Hasenfeld & B. Gidron (Eds.), Social Entreprises. An organizational perspective (pp. 91-120). London: Palgrave Macmillan.

Liger, Q., Stefan, M., & Britton, J. (2016). *Social Economy, Study*. Directorate General For Internal Policies, Policy Department A: Economic And Scientific Policy. Retrieved from http://www.europarl.europa.eu/RegData/etudes/STUD/2016/578969/IPOL_STU(2016)578969_EN.pdf

Mair, J., & Marti, I. (2004). *Social entrepreneurship research: a source of explanation, prediction and delight*. Working paper no. 546. IESE Business School- University of Navarra.

Matei, L., & Sandu, C. (2011). *A social entreprise: An empirical Study for Romania*. Paper presented at the 10 International Congress of the International Association on Public and Nonprofit Marketing. Retrieved from SSRN: http://ssrn.com/abstract=1805770

Matei, L., & Sandu, C. (2016). Social Enterprise – an important pillar in Producing and Providing Public goods and services. In L. Matei, M. Meneguzzo, C. Mititelu, & B. Berceanu (Eds.), Business Government relations and social enterprises. Lessons and experiences from South-Eastern Europe (pp. 167-222). Brussels: Bruylant.

Mendell, M., & Nogales, R. (2009). Social Entreprises in OECD member countries. What are the financial streams. In A. Noya (Ed.), *The Changing Boundaries of Social Enteprises* (pp. 89–138). Paris: OECD Publishing. doi:10.1787/9789264055513-4-en

Neguț, A. (2013). Social capital, social economy and local development. In *Social economy in the context of local development*. Iași: Editura Polirom.

Oatley, N. (1999). Developing the Social Economy. *Local Economy*, *13*(4), 339–345. doi:10.1080/02690949908726461

OECD. (1999). *Social Enterprises*. Paris, France: OECD Publications.

Peattie, K., & Morley, A. (2008). Eight paradoxes of the social enterprise research agenda. *Social Enterprise Journal*, *4*(2), 91–107. doi:10.1108/17508610810901995

Peattie, K., & Morley, A. (2008). *Social Enterprises: Diversity and Dynamics, Contexts and Contributions. A Research Monograph*. ESRC Centre for BRASS, Cardiff University.

Phillips, M. (2006). Growing Pains: The sustainability of social enterprises. *Entrepreneurship and Innovation*, *7*(4), 221–230.

Putman, R. (1995). Bowling Alone: America's Declining Social Capital. *Journal of Democracy, 6*(1), 65-78.

Research Network for Social Enterprise. (n.d.). Retrieved from https://emes.net/

Salamon, L. M., Leslie, C. H., & Chinnock, H. (2000). *The nonprofit sector: for what and for whom*. Working Papers of the Johns Hopkins Comparative Nonprofit Sector Project. Baltimore, MD: The Johns Hopkins Centre for Civil Society Studies. Retrieved from https://www.sociedadenaccion.cl/wp-content/uploads/2015/06/Salamon-L.-Hems-L.-Chinnock-K.-2000.-The-Non-Profit-Sector.-For-What-and-for-Whom.pdf

Simon Clark Associates. (2002). The Social Economy: A Literature Review, a report to Communities, Simon Clark Associates Ltd, Scotland. In *Social Enterprises: Diversity and Dynamics, Contexts and Contributions. A Research Monograph*. ESRC Centre for BRASS, Cardiff University.

Vaculovschi, D., & Antonov, V. (2016). *Developing the social economy in Republic of Moldova by promotion of gender equal opportunities*. Policy Brief, IDIS "Viitorul". Retrieved from http://www.antreprenoriatsocial.md/media/files/Studiu_IDIS_Viitorul_policy_brief.pdf

Vidal, I. (2008). The role of social enterprises in Europe: a core element or a distraction in the provision of public services? In S. P. Osborne (Ed.), *The Third Sector in Europe. Prospects and challenges*. Oxon, UK: Routledge. doi:10.4324/9780203932827.pt8

Weisbrod, B. A. (1988). *The Nonprofit Economy*. Cambridge, MA: Harvard University Press.

ADDITIONAL READING

Antonovici, C., G., Săvulescu, & C., Sandu, C. (2015). The Agricultural Cooperatives in Romania: From Conceptual Framework to Profitable Local Production. *Journal of Public Administration, Finance and Law*, Issue 8, 7-15.

Antonovici, C. G., Săvulescu, C., & Sandu, C. (2015). Social Enterprise in Public Governance. The Early Stage for the Romanian Case. *Acta Universitas Danubius Administratio*, *7*(2), 43–60.

Grieco, C. (2015). *Assessing Social Impact of Social Enterprises Does One Size Really Fit All?* London: Springer.

Matei, A., Săvulescu, C., & Antonovici, C. G. (2016). From Public Services to Networks of Social Enterprises: Strategic Trends for South-Eastern Europe. *Theoretical and Applied Economics*, *23*(2), 103–116.

Matei, L., Meneguzzo, M., Mititelu, C., & Berceanu, B. (Eds.), *Business Government relations and social enterprises. Lessons and experiences from South-Eastern Europe* (pp. 167–222). Brussels: Bruylant.

Terziev, V., Bencheva, N., Arabska, E., Tepavicharova, M., Nichev, N., & Stoeva, T. (2016, June) *Social Entrepreneurship in Bulgaria: Barriers to Growth*. Paper presented at the Ninth International Scientific Conference, Durres, Republic of Albania. 10.2139srn.3157985

Zbuchea, A., Antonovici, C., & Pînzaru, F. (2016). Networked social enterprises. *In Proceeding of the 9th International Conference for Entrepreneurship, Innovation and Regional Development, Responsible entrepreneurship vision, development and ethics*, (pp. 210-217), Bucharest: Editura comunicare.ro.

Zoehrer, K. (2017 July). *Social Entrepreneurship in South- Eastern Europe – Comparative Analysis of the Cases of Croatia, Serbia and Greece*. Paper presented at the 6th EMES International Research Conference on Social Enterprise *Social enterprise for sustainable societies*, Université Catholique de Louvain, Louvain-la-Neuve, Belgium.

KEY TERMS AND DEFINITIONS

Non-Profit Company: Form of company set up for non-profit purpose, which may or may not be enforced to support a social purpose, not able to distribute profit through dividends.

Non-Profit Organization: Organization with legal personality which does not allow profit distribution, able to deliver economic activities in view to promote and support a social purpose (for example associations, foundations).

Share Company: Form of company used especially for commercial purpose to distribute profit to shareholders, owned by shareholders, distributing the profit proportional to shareholders' shares.

Social Cooperative: Organization with legal personality, set up legally as cooperative with an economic and social purpose. It may distribute profit according to certain provisions in the law.

Social Enterprise of Insertion: A social enterprise with full-time employees belonging to the vulnerable group, employed in certain conditions according to the law, ensuring them accompanying measures (such as information, counselling, access to vocational training, adjusting the job description to persons' skills, job accessibility depending on the persons' needs, etc.) in view to ensure professional and social insertion.

Vulnerable Group: Persons or families under risk to lose the capacity to meet the daily living needs.

Chapter 13
Public Services and the Missed Values of (Non)Communication

Mirko Pečarič
https://orcid.org/0000-0002-0551-5682
University of Ljubljana, Slovenia

ABSTRACT

Citizens' interactions are at the center of open governments. When the latter use open structures and open processes to foster (technical) collaboration, citizens' wellbeing can be improved by observing what citizens (do not) publicly write about or search for. This chapter tries to compare the wellbeing and quality of life (the older terms are public value or solidarity) with public goods inside and outside of public services. This relationship can be achieved when people debate and governments listen to diverse alternatives. To test this relationship, the Google Trends application was used. Trends show that satisfied people do not write about effective, efficient, legal, and ethical things, so a temporary conclusion needed for further investigation is that the government's success in a certain field is present when people do not talk (on a large scale) about matters or topics in that field. Governments should, therefore, listen to or read what people (do not) say or write.

INTRODUCTION

People must not only abide administrative law that affects everyone from the cradle to the grave but also other similar activities touch our daily lives, although the latter does not use public power on the same level. The main focus in this chapter will be given on activities related to the birth of children, to their care in kindergartens, to primary and secondary schools (in some countries also to higher education), on the research, basic health and social care, public urban and railway transport, water supply and sewerage, on public roads and other public infrastructure. Also, the private sector depends on these activities as much as the public one. These activities are named public services, and form the spine of all modern countries, which addresses not only the national social model but also the infrastructure for economic prosperity. Public services (within the European Union named as the Services of General Economic Interest or SGEIs[1]) are activities whose supplier is entrusted by a public authority with specific missions of

DOI: 10.4018/978-1-5225-8482-7.ch013

general interest. These services, therefore, include non-economic and economic services like education, healthcare, social care or water, energy, public transport, postal services, telecommunications, energy and so on. Although these activities do not involve a direct element of public power (*iure imperii*), we face them in a much more numerical and everyday sense (as soon as we wake up in the morning, we turn on the light, open water, see if there is any mail, etc.) than with the authoritative tasks of the state. Public services of now seen not only as services to protect the national interest but also as vital parts of the European integration project (Szyszczak, Davies, Andenæs, & Bekkedal, 2013), although the change of the State's role from providing services to providing only the legal framework and supervising the provision of services represents not only an apparent loss of powers (Nistor, 2013) but also of accountability that became more dispersed due to numerous public service providers. Despite these changes, public services still present the characteristics of market failure which cannot deliver services to customers in an affordable manner, and it is of utmost importance to have methods by which such activities can be managed and controlled. The information revolution combined with transparency can empower public service users and/or citizens to demand accountability from public services, but there must be present a method or a framework that can influence public services' performance. Despite the availability of some very simple but potentially effective tools there is a lack of systemic and effective quality control, accountability and responsibility for high-quality service delivery (Bauby & Similie, 2010); public service providers must be accountable to users and taxpayers for the quality of service and the outcomes they achieve (HM Government, 2014), and one way by which public services can work better is when they are designed and delivered in partnership with citizens in order to harness their interest, energies, expertise and ambitions (OECD, 2011). Public services should be – given the reason for whom they are established and provided in the first place – more accountable to users through deliberation, participation or even implementation, rather than through classic bureaucratic accountability to central government, which is of limited value due to the still persistent "red tape" principle that still dominates in this sphere. The government can promote accountability by increasing transparency and allocation of information about public services, so users can judge the implementation and successfulness of public service providers to make more informed decisions. "Accountability can be *explanatory* (that is a person is called on to explain their conduct or proposals) and it may also entail the imposition of *sanctions*" (Sueur, Sunkin, & Murkens, 2016, p. 285). In this chapter, a practical way will be examined in which accountability can be achieved through explanation, not by public service providers or public servants, but by public service users and/or citizens, who can give facts about ways on which some public service is done or experienced. The beauty of the presented approach is in its free availability to everyone, who is interested in the people's talks. In the next two sections arguments are given for users' voices to assure the legitimacy of public services in a similar way the public power activity is achieved, that is by the right of expression or defense within a procedure. People's voices or the expressions of opinions will be tested within a relationship between the rule of law index *vis-à-vis* debate on the public services, public goods and public utilities to be able to reach a conclusion that can be per se contra-intuitive, but still very practical. Everyone can use it immediately.

WELL-BEING AND PUBLIC SERVICE

Official statements many times prevail simply because they are official: the vast majority of legislative proposals (above 90%) are initiated by the government in Great Britain, Croatia, Finland, Hungary,

Macedonia, Romania and Slovenia (Kasemets, 2001). It is therefore of crucial importance how they establish relations between facts and evidence because the latter can – by using political power – often disregard the former, but still count as the truth. This sentence had reflected official reality until the Internet sprang on all sides of the world. For Maine, one of Hobbes' great insights was in understanding freedom as "political power divided into small fragments" (Maine, 1976, p. 89). But could these small fragments be now Internet users? If left to their own matters, people pay no attention to these pieces, but they can be skilfully used for good purposes, for open government that cooperates with people. The accumulation of power fragments usually in history did not contribute to the openness and transparency of public authority, but to people's *uncertainty:* in "the process of the creation and institutionalisation of power inequality is based on manipulation with uncertainty as the key tool of power" (Bauman, 2013, p. 36). In the light of Maine's fragmentation of political power, exercising one's freedom requires strong solidarity (Bauman, 2013); the latter is contrary to individualisation as the demand on the labour market where "people demand the right to develop their own perspective on life and to be able to act upon it ... but today it is also becoming apparent that such processes of individualization can be quite precarious... distant from traditional support networks and increasingly dependent on the amount of income, social security and the existence of employment" (Beck, 1992, p. 92). How can traditional support networks support solidarity? Beck sees the solution mainly in democratisation, in "the opening of the political", in the institutionalisation of self-criticism, in the controversial and alternative discussions, or interdisciplinary public spheres that should be institutionally-created,[2] but to us, a solution could be present in *public services*, which could open the political. Public services add total value around 30% of whole economy employment,[3] they largely contribute to GDP and the providers of SGIs contribute significantly to the EU workforce by employing more than 64 million persons in the EU-27, corresponding to 30.1% of the workforce (CEEP, 2010). It is estimated that just opening and reusing public-sector information can potentially create economic gains up to € 40 billion a year in the EU (European Commission, 2011b). In this chapter, we are on a quest to overcome uncertainty based on solidarity – present in public services; solidarity is many times mentioned with public services (Neergaard, Szyszczak, Gronden, & Krajewski, 2012; Sauter, 2015; Szyszczak et al., 2013), and we will try to bridge this gap with the help of public services, being at the same time – with the collective mechanisms of people and other resources – very similar with the power *per se* that 'corresponds to the human ability not just to act but to act in concert. Power is never the property of an individual; it belongs to a group and remains in existence only so long as the group keeps together' (Arendt, 1972, p. 143). Public services are similar to acts in concert, i.e. to collective acts and with Luhmann's notion of power:

The ruler's power is greater if, in exercising his power, he can choose between several different decisions; furthermore, it is greater when he can do so in relation to a partner who also has several different alternatives at his disposal. Power increases with freedom on both sides ... this means that, in order to compare the positions of power, society itself must develop substitutes that themselves become a factor of power (Luhmann, 2013, p. 15).

The power of public services is not hidden but is open to public scrutiny. In the presence of alternatives represented in the different forms of citizens' self-help, co-production, co-decision, media and markets the presuppositions of power on both sides are mutually weighted. With the rise of potential powers, both sides (the people and the country) *see alternatives* the realisation of which they wish to avoid: "the exercise of power only happens when the attitude of those involved towards their undesired alternatives is differently structured so that the power-inferior wishes to avoid his alternative ... *before* the power-superior does so ... the power code must [therefore] provide the possibility of a relationship between the two relationships" (Luhmann, 2013, pp. 28–29). In this theoretical stance, power occurs when the inferior behaves so as to avoid (so that it will avoid) the sanction in the manner assumed by the ruler, without explicitly ordering him to do so, keeping in mind that both of them are aware of this.[4] This predisposition is relevant for this paper due to a focus on the passivity of one or other side despite known solutions or actions and *vice versa*: activity (here talks on the Internet) and unknown solutions.

This contribution will be built on two common-sense predispositions: *when a realm of freedom shrinks, a desire to defend grows.* This common-sense inference usually stands in a presence of (even imaginary) fear, but not always: if there are more subtle approaches/alternatives present outside/inside the public arena (campaign contributions, lobbyists, hired experts, lawyers, PR campaigns), the majority of people will not defend itself (in the classical meaning) but *amplify* their *possibilities.* And the same could be true for public services: in the frame of economic and budgetary pressures, a solution is not to defend obtained rights but to enlarge possibilities, to innovate new alternatives. Another common-sense inference is that *public decisions should reflect the judgments, values and wishes of a majority of people.* There is increased pressure on public services to open additional communication channels for servicing and informing the public. This could be effective only when the public has the clear and understandable *data* (see Article 12 of GDPR: the controller shall take appropriate measures to provide any information…and any communication…in a concise, transparent, intelligible and easily accessible form, using clear and plain language') which decisions or wished are formed. Without them, it is possible to see everything and its opposite. These predispositions allow us to infer that people and countries are the most powerful when they have alternatives when the first do *not* use the basic public services (when people are so empowered they can self-help, *i.e.* autonomously solve their own problems) and the second when they are the most at hand. Countries with the highest rule of law scores (e.g. Denmark, Belgium, Finland, Netherlands) have the above-average share of public services in whole-economy value (Cambridge Econometrics, 2013), so it is interesting to know how much people debate about public services in these countries. Based on this open question and both mentioned common-sense, predispositions will be used to test the below hypothesis:

Hypothesis: Countries with the highest rule of law scores continuously maintain debate about public services, public goods and public utilities.

Well-being and the public service form four combinations, and it is obvious they both can stand alone. It may be that government is not the only possible provider of public service or well-being is achieved in ways outside of public service, but the government is always responsible at least for supporting the realization of *public value* or the *well-being* of citizens. Governments generate it when they deliver a set of social, economic and technological issues, aligned with the citizens', customers' and environmental priorities in a cost-effective and responsive manner. The purpose of this research is to show connections (or absence of them) between well-being and public services. Contrary to the above-given hypothesis people usually talk about problems when they perceive them as such. From this intuitive standpoint, public services could be the best when people do not talk about them. Public participation is a multidimensional phenomenon that can demonstrate exactly the opposite of what it shows at first sight. This understanding has important implications for the decision-makers and designers of participation processes.

PUBLIC SERVICE: THE INVOLVEMENT OF PUBLIC IN SERVICE

Already for Duguit the content of public services always varies, it is always in a state of flux; he defines public service as “any activity that has to be governmentally regulated and controlled because it is indispensable to the realisation and development of social solidarity…so long as it is of such a nature that it cannot be assured save by governmental intervention” (1921, p. 48). Nowadays the state’s intervention is mostly indirect by legal and technical control over the provision of services done by the public and private sector. But while this control is mostly done occasionally, there is a better way, a way by which control is done every day: this is the public services users’ way. “The best and most sustainable way to improve the responsiveness of public services is to improve the expectations and entitlements of service users” (Mayo in Greener, Simmons, & Powell, 2009, p. xiii). Similarly, for Reich the income and wealth increasingly depend on who has the power to set the rules of the game, so “the solution is not to create more or less government. The problem is not the size of government but whom the government is *for*” (2016, p. xv). We have to change our thinking about the public services, because “we become so accustomed to thinking about education, health care, child care, and public transportation as government *spending* that we don’t see the obvious: In the new global economy where financial capital is footloose, these are critical public *investments* … They mark the only path to a sustained and shared prosperity” (R. B. Reich, 2003, p. 115). A solution for him is to stop the growing inequality by the more *active engagement* of the middle class in the political life: “the only way back toward a democracy and economy that work for the majority is for the majority to become politically active once again, establishing a new countervailing power” (R. Reich, 2016, p. 182). His proposal is similar to Beck’s; in the field of public service it means a wider scope of stakeholders; governments can ensure public value also through cooperation with others. This participatory element is not the *sine qua non* of public service, but it is for public goods. Although public value was already mentioned, it can be even more concretely defined with the notion of public goods.[5]

The basic works on public service do not include the involvement of people in providing services, and this (more or less) holds also for the EU level: “there is no such thing as an EU law concept called public service. The concept of services of general interest (SGI)…comes closest to a functional equivalent, but has so far rarely been used in a legal context” (Sauter, 2015, p. 9). Services of general economic interest are an open concept of services for the EU Member States because they can assert this status for any set of services they wish as long as they provide proportionate constraints on the applicability of the Treaty’s competition rules. The EU terminology for public services could be useful due to multiple meanings of public services. Due to the lack of clarity on terminology and interchangeably and inaccurately used concepts on services of general interest the European Commission in 2011 issued Communication (*A Quality Framework for Services of General Interest in Europe*) in which defined SGI and SGEI:

Services of general interest (SGI) are services that public authorities of the Member States classify as being of general interest and, therefore, subject to specific public service obligations (PSO). The term covers both economic activities...and non-economic services. Services of general economic interest (SGEI) are economic activities which deliver outcomes in the overall public good that would not be supplied (or would be supplied under different conditions in terms of quality, safety, affordability, equal treatment or universal access) by the market without public intervention. The PSO is imposed on the provider by way of entrustment and on the basis of a general interest criterion which ensures that the service is provided under conditions allowing it to fulfil its mission (European Commission, 2011a, p. 3).

The Commission's definitions of SGEI do not directly include also public authority, on which could be inferred due to the words public intervention and imposed. This kind of powers usually does not include administrative public powers (like the one the state administrative agencies or other state agencies are obligated to observe when they in administrative matters, by directly applying regulations, adjudicate the rights, obligations or legal interests of citizens, legal persons or other parties). Services of general interest are the state or local government's activities, which in the public interest permanently and without suspension – but neither with *iure imperii* nor *iure gestionis vi-a-vis* citizen as a consumer – provide goods (public goods). Their objective is the adequate and qualitative provision of public goods available and affordable to all users under equal (qualitative and quantitative) conditions. SGI could be connected with *acta iure imperii*, if a service provider has at the same time a public authorisation to perform activities, issue permits or general acts for the exercise of public authority, but this authorisation is not *sine qua non* for SGI (the authorisation is given to SGI's provider solely due to fact of a more efficient and expedient performance of administrative tasks outside the public administration, where permanent and immediate supervision over the performance of tasks is not necessary or appropriate due to the nature of the tasks). In such cases, the SGI's providers are also obligated to abide by the General Administrative Procedure Act when adjudicating administrative matters in the performance of public powers. The SGI provider could also be connected with *acta iure gestionis* or the commercial activities, which aim is to offer a service for remuneration, but this activity constitutes service within the meaning of Article 57 TFEU, and not SG(E)I, while neither of them is not specifically focused in people's involvement.

PUBLIC SERVICE VIS-À-VIS PUBLIC GOOD

Well-being is connected with questions like what services should the government provide? How should we pay for them? How much of what government now provides could and should be provided outside the government? Well-being is by its content connected with public goods and public services, and we think the first fits into a category of public good, being just another name for the same thing.[6] If public good is defined clearly then also well-being is defined simultaneously. The public good is a wide concept into which can be put different goods as long as they fulfil the above-mentioned two classical conditions of non-excludability and non-rivalry. In Slovenia, terminological confusion is present in this regard, mainly due to the fact that public good is directly connected (only) with the natural, environmental or space elements (air, mountains, sea, lakes, hills).[7] These elements are connected directly with national assets or natural resources, or indirectly through the built public goods (roads, railways, harbours, highways, hydropower plants) that are put on some landscape. In the latter case, we are talking also about the public infrastructure that is maintained or organised through public utilities (public companies) as a public service. But public good – within the meaning of the fulfilment of non-rivalry and non-excludability (Samuelson, 1954) – can also be public broadcasting, public education, knowledge, basic research, museums, rare cultural monuments, libraries. Nowadays also the Internet could be a public good that provides services.

Law is the typical public good, but it is also public service. The latter is usually the (formal, institutional) mean by which the former (substantial goal) is delivered (public roads, health, schools, emergency services) or not (nature, wildlife, sea, lakes, mountains). Public goods as goals can be therefore connected with public services as means, but both can also stand alone: public goods do not need public services, because the former can be already present, while the latter could deliver services outside public goods

– this holds if we divide public services on those that are authoritative (they use public power, *iure imperii, e.g.* a notary public), and those without authority (they are still the public acts of government, but without public power; they are also not pure *ius gestionis* or the private, commercial acts of the government, because they can be provided for an affordable price, but also through taxes). In both cases, public services provide services or goods based on a social consensus that certain services should be available to all, regardless of income, physical ability and/or mental acuity. The public services in a narrower sense in the non-authoritative ones could be divided into economic (public utilities, water, electricity, wastewater management, water drainage, postal services, telecommunications) or infrastructure-based utilities and welfare services (public schools, healthcare, childcare, retirement homes, education, training and employment services). The former is directed more towards the general public, while the latter is more focused on the individual.

For Grand (2007) a good public service is run efficiently, responsive to the needs and wants of users, accountable to taxpayers, and equitable in its treatment of users and workers. There are four means or models for delivering public services to attain these ends: "*trust* (in professionals), *command-and-control* (hierarchy), *voice* (expressing dissatisfaction) and *user choice*. The hard price of a service is not the money that was spent on providing it, but the *other lost* opportunities that could have been exploited if resources had not been used for the chosen service (opportunity cost). One way to discover well-being is to establish machinery to record individual preferences and test new mechanisms outside government" (Seldon, 2005, p. 102). "Given sufficient knowledge, the optimal decisions can always be found by scanning over all the attainable states of the world and selecting the one which according to the postulated ethical welfare function is best. The solution exists; the problem is how to find it. One could imagine every person in the community being indoctrinated to behave like a parametric decentralized bureaucrat who reveals his preferences by signalling in response to price parameters or multipliers, to questionnaires, or to other devices" (Samuelson, 1954, p. 389). Social scientific research can for Piketty "by patiently searching for facts and patterns and calmly analysing the economic, social, and political mechanisms that might explain them, inform democratic debate and focus attention on the right questions. It can help to redefine the terms of the debate, unmask certain preconceived or fraudulent notions, and subject all positions to constant critical scrutiny" (2014, p. 3). This approach can be used also in a relationship between public services and public value: "in an open government model the question is not only about who produces public services, but also about how to distribute public value in society in an optimal way and about how responsibilities can be best shared" (European Commission, 2013, p. 10). It seems that solidarity and democracy, *i.e.* the more active engagement of the middle class in the political life or the opening of the political are focused on citizens and/or public participation, but one, a simpler step could be done that uses the political but turned upside down. This could be done with citizens as the Internet users who present/post their meanings as free information regarding public services or any other field of interest. Collective wisdom could be thus brought more to the fore in government administration because of its ability to provide a more objective, unbiased and at times more complete and professional information than any expert could ever do alone (Pečarič, 2016). Their searches and open comments can serve as citizens' voices that address governmental operations in a relevant field.

METHODS AND PROCEDURE

Based on the above-given observations the hypothesis will be tested. To test it, the rule of law scores will be from the World Bank's Worldwide Governance Indicators (Kaufmann & Kraay, 2015) taken for those countries which *Google Trends* will record high enough searches of their citizens for "public service", "public good" and "public utility". For these data, statistical calculations will be made to establish relations between the notions. From *Google Trends*[8] we look at all Google searches in the world in the past 5 years (Feb. 2012 – Feb. 2017) for the words "public good, public service, public utility". Data came from millions of searches people made with these words. Based on collected data some trends and/or relations between rule(s) and principle(s) among countries emerge:

Based on Google Trends explanation "numbers represent search interest relative to the highest point on the chart for the given region and time. A value of 100 is the peak popularity of the term. A value of 50 means that the term is half as popular. Likewise, a score of 0 means the term was less than 1% as popular as the peak". The rule of law scores – obtained from the World Bank's results – were in the upper graph put for easier comparison with the Google Trends results of the searched notions. Correlation between public service and rule of law shows strong negative relationship (r= - 0,56), moderate

Table 1. Rule of law vis-à-vis public utility/good/service

	Public good	Public utility	Public service	Rule of law
Denmark	0	11	2	99,04
New Zealand	37	0	5	98,08
Netherland	0	11	1	97,12
Singapore	69	21	10	96,63
Canada	39	32	20	95,19
Hong Kong	0	14	3	94,71
Australia	56	12	13	94,23
United Kingdom	25	20	5	93,75
Ireland	31	0	15	93,27
Germany	3	3	1	92,79
United States	49	100	9	90,38
Belgium	0	10	9	88,94
France	2	2	35	88,46
Malaysia	35	9	6	71,63
South Africa	57	8	18	59,13
India	23	10	17	55,77
Thailand	0	17	1	53,85
Philippines	34	16	5	42,31
Kenya	100	0	65	36,54
Pakistan	0	6	70	23,56
Nigeria	75	0	19	12,98

Source: Google Trends, 2017

Figure 1. Linear regression lines between the rule of law and public service/good/utility
Source: own

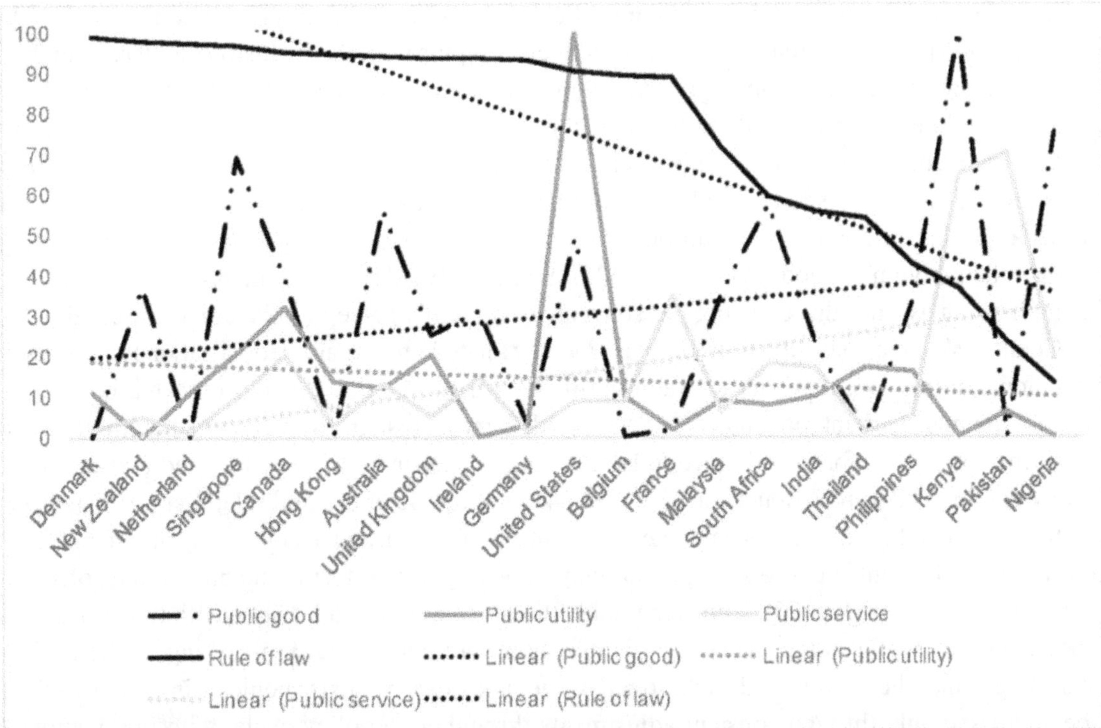

between public good and rule of law (r= - 0,31), and weak between public good and public service (r= 0,28) and between public utility and rule of law (r= 0,23). We used the standard two-tail test with α = 0.05, where the null hypothesis is rejected when p < .05 and *vice versa* when p > .05. In the first/second/third/fourth case p-values are= 1,0885E-09/8,18991E-06/0,065/1,07323E-09. The null hypotheses are rejected except in the third case; in the first, second and fourth case, there *is* a relationship between measured phenomena. Anova analysis (two-factor without replication) found Singapore as the best, although there is no statistically significant difference between countries (rows) (p-value= 0,789). There is a statistically significant difference between the scores of three variables (p-value= 6,86334E-11). Looking at the means the public utility scores are the lowest (302), although the public service scores only slightly better (329), then follows the public good (635) and the rule of law (1578). A conclusion from these means and from the trend lines are: *when talks about the public goods and public services are on the rise, but not for public utilities, the smallest is the country's rule of law.* Based on the results the hypothesis is rejected: *countries (i.e. citizens as the Internet users) with the highest rule of law scores do not debate on a large scale about the public services, public goods and public utilities.* Google Trends show that in the past 12 months: a) well-being is mostly debated in South Africa, Philippines and New Zealand, b) quality of life in Nepal, Mauritius and Ethiopia c) public services in Ireland, Tanzania and Uganda. *Google Correlate* shows *e.g.* for the United Kingdom public administration correlates with licenses and licensing law, Ireland (and Canada) with the university. An answer to problems if they are really present, can give people themselves.

SOLUTIONS AND RECOMMENDATIONS

So far, the problems of state flexibility in connection with normative interventions were mainly solved with soft law; the paper's approach is based on collective inputs with the inclusion of a large number of people. In the present research, findings show connections between the searched terms (or the absence of them) on the Internet and the rule of law. Conclusions from the mentioned four means and from the trend lines are made based on the people's searches in the included countries. Although there are differences among countries' scores, readers should be aware "there is no universal agreement on what counts as a problem and what as a solution, or when the point is reached where the solution becomes worse than the problem" (Hood, 1998, pp. 24–25). Some analysed score can be higher in one state vis-à-vis another, but as said, this does not per se mean a problem's perception is larger despite the larger score. Countries' values have much to do here. Geert Hofstede has examined variations in values and organisational norms over three decades across fifty countries. A cultural perspective has quite a lot to do with public management reform because "Hofstede's measures…reflect the broad cultural climates in which management reforms will have to be announced, interpreted, promoted, and resisted in each particular country" (Pollitt & Bouckaert, 2011, p. 64). In the style of cultural relativism, Hofstede et al. claim that "we cannot change the way people in a country think, feel, and act by simply importing foreign institutions…Each country has to struggle through its own type of reforms, adapted to the software of its people's minds" (2010, p. 25). The same holds the other way around. Citizens' interactions on the Internet and other public forums can be a valuable input into public decision-making, while for better substantive grounds the institutional background, values and other contexts should be included. Problems can be addressed only through constant adjustments throughout a policy cycle, with implications for how institutions, processes, skills and actors are organized. The proposed approach can be a first sign of a public institution's preparedness to be responsive to citizens' or users' opinions. To upgrade this research also the culture, legal and administrative framework within which individuals, companies, and governments interact to achieve their goals should be included.

FUTURE RESEARCH DIRECTIONS

The highest countries in the rule of law very little debate about the public services, public goods and public utilities. They obviously just do it (a trademark of shoe company Nike). Thoughts and facts are tightly connected, but they do not have to be publicly proclaimed on the highest levels. What is common-sense (that people speak about public services) is not always actual and *vice versa.* A problem emerges when we have actual, but it is based on *irrational.* Countries many times enact, change or amend regulations *a la* Alice in Wonderland, who just wanted to go from one place so long as she gets somewhere. This behaviour is spotted when regulators do not connect ideas with facts and *vice versa,* when they are always on the move, always regulate (do) something, but they basically do not know what they (will) cause, despite even knowable, legally determined goals. The results from Google Trends show *people do not talk about things that are effective, efficient, legal and ethical.* They have no need to do it.[9] A gist of the negative thinking is seen in Ellenberg's the missing bullet holes story:[10] you can find the weakest spot negatively by searching for missing bullets. A rough assumption on which public administrations could enhance the public well-being and growth is, therefore, to look for the most used words/searches in their countries because they show where problems are present and vice versa: people do not talk about effective public things or services. Citizens will participate when bureaucratic responsiveness will be present at the firstly stated problem.[11] Findings show public participation as a multidimensional phenomenon that can say the opposite of what it shows at first sight. If the function of law is to produce *expectations* (Luhmann, 2004), disappointments could call for new legal enactments. The paper's findings thus call for further research based on Luhmann's statement to which "the *expectation of disappointment* … is the core reason for communicating expectations in a normative style" (2004, p. 241). This research path could give new implications for decision-makers and designers of participation processes. If the government is understood as responsive when it acts on citizens' demands, then a simple application like Google Trends can be the first sign of this goal. For more thorough research on relations between the people's talks/silence and the (un)successfulness of an area of interest, additional research methods will be needed.

The studied approach can be seen as a soft outcome measurement approach that serves for the identification of problematic areas, provision of information to public officials to improve services in the terms of quality, quantity, benefits and affordability to citizens, but also of smart budgeting that services and their resources are distributed in ways most likely to produce the maximum benefits to citizens, and nonetheless – when services became better due to public deliberation on them – it can increase the public's trust in the government. On overall, this simple approach can make public bodies more accountable for results to elected functionaries and the public. There is a need for deeper analysis of the Internet communications, which could not be of help only to tame the spread of diseases (Cook, Conrad, Fowlkes, & Mohebbi, 2011; Ginsberg et al., 2009; Wilson & Brownstein, 2009; Yang, Horneffer, & DiLisio, 2013), but also to advance public services to be more effective, efficient and accountable. The recent scandals about Facebook vis-à-vis Cambridge Analytica, fake news, online hate speech, etc. question the aspects of security, privacy and other human rights. If the information is not clearly understood and relevant for a discussed topic than no Internet or classical participation will not be effective. Even in clear information, Internet results should be tested with other data and other available research methods.

CONCLUSION

Based on the fact that the rule of law is compared with data from Google Trends it can be said that countries in which there is less talk about public goods and public services have the highest rule of law. It can be inferred that the best public goods and services are in the absence of talks about them: *acta non verba* is, therefore, the right call for countries with the numerous talks about public goods and services, but with no relevant actions. They have the lowest rule of law scores and are in a desperate need to do something. They should do something, and the first step is to *listen to their citizens*. Governments should support also efforts in building participation and collaboration platforms, in making open data and accessible information, but if they do not listen to a first step, all others are irrelevant. They should listen to what people have to say because they not only have the freedom of expression and of assembly but also, know many things that could help governments to be more innovative at ensuring the well-being of people. If governments want is seen as responsive to citizens' demands, then a simple application like Google Trends can be the first sign of this goal. Governments should support efforts in building participation and collaboration platforms, in making open data and accessible information, but if they do not listen in a first step, all others are irrelevant. They should listen to what people say because the latter not only have the freedom of expression and of assembly but also know many things that could help governments to be more innovative at ensuring the well-being of people. The usual system of institutional checks and balances built into government structures does not incorporate the principle of good governance that empowers also public service users or citizens to motivate public bodies and policymakers to be better every day on a path of excellence. All-encompassing public-sector management must balance economic development with social equity and/or finances with fairness and inclusiveness. Then it can be said the public organisations are accountable to the people and by the people because their services are done for the people.

REFERENCES

Arendt, H. (1972). *Crises of the Republic: Lying in Politics, Civil Disobedience on Violence, Thoughts on Politics, and Revolution*. Harcourt Brace Jovanovich.

Bauby, P., & Similie, M. M. (2010). Public Services in the European Union & In the 27 Member States. *CEEP*. Retrieved from http://ceep.eu/images/stories/pdf/Mapping/CEEP_mapping%20experts%20report.pdf

Bauman, Z. (2013). Družbena neenakost v globalni dobi (K. Vidmar Horvat, Ed.). Ljubljana: Znanstvena založba Filozofske fakultete Univerze v Ljubljani.

Beck, U. (1992). *Risk Society: Towards a New Modernity*. London: SAGE Publications Ltd.

Bon, G. L. (2002). *The Crowd: A Study of the Popular Mind*. Mineola, NY: Dover Publications, Inc.

Cambridge Econometrics. (2013). Mapping evolutions in Public Services in Europe: towards increased knowledge of industrial relations. *Cambridge Trust for New Thinking in Economics*. Retrieved from http://www.ceep.eu/wp-content/uploads/2014/07/Mapping-Public-Services-project_final-experts-report_May-2013.pdf

CEEP. (2010). *Public Services in the European Union & In the 27 Member States: Statistics, Organisation and Regulations*. Retrieved from http://www.epsu.org/sites/default/files/article/files/MappinReportDefEN.pdf

Cook, S., Conrad, C., Fowlkes, A. L., & Mohebbi, M. H. (2011). Assessing Google Flu Trends Performance in the United States during the 2009 Influenza Virus A (H1N1) Pandemic. *PLoS One*, *6*(8), e23610. doi:10.1371/journal.pone.0023610 PMID:21886802

Duguit, L. (1921). *Law in the Modern State* (F. Laski & H. Laski, Trans.). London: George Allen & Unwin Ltd.

Ellenberg, J. (2014). *How Not to Be Wrong : The Power of Mathematical Thinking*. New York: Penguin USA.

European Commission. (2011a). Communication from the Commission to the European Parliament, the Council, the European Economic and Social Committee and the Committee of the Regions: A Quality Framework for Services of General Interest in Europe (COM(2011)900 final). Brussels: Author.

European Commission. (2011b). Communication from the commission to the European parliament, the council, the European economic and social committee and the committee of the regions Open data engine for innovation, growth and transparent governance /* COM/2011/0882 final */. Retrieved from http://eur-lex.europa.eu/legal-content/EN/TXT/HTML/?uri=CELEX:52011DC0882&from=EN

European Commission. (2013). *A vision for public services*. Retrieved from https://ec.europa.eu/digital-single-market/en/news/vision-public-services

Ginsberg, J., Mohebbi, M. H., Patel, R. S., Brammer, L., Smolinski, M. S., & Brilliant, L. (2009). Detecting influenza epidemics using search engine query data. *Nature*, *457*(7232), 1012–1014. doi:10.1038/nature07634 PMID:19020500

Government, H. M. (2014). *Open Public Services 2014*. Retrieved from https://assets.publishing.service.gov.uk/government/uploads/system/uploads/attachment_data/file/291854/Open_Public_Services_Progress_Report_2014.pdf

Grand, J. L. (2007). *The Other Invisible Hand: Delivering Public Services through Choice and Competition*. Princeton University Press.

Greener, I., Simmons, R., & Powell, M. (Eds.). (2009). *The Consumer in Public Services: Choice, Values and Difference*. Policy Press.

Hegel, G. W. F. (1998). *Fenomenologija duha*. Ljubljana: Analecta.

Hofstede, G., Hofstede, G. J., & Minkov, M. (2010). *Cultures and Organizations: Software of the Mind* (3rd ed.). Maidenhead, UK: McGraw-Hill.

Hood, C. (1998). *The Art of the State: Culture, Rhetoric, and Public Management*. Oxford University Press.

Kasemets, A. (2001). Impact Assessment of Legislation for Parliament and Civil Society: a Comparative Study. *Proceedings of ECPRD Seminar*. Retrieved from https://www.riigikogu.ee/rva/ecprd/04_part_2.pdf

Kaufmann, D., & Kraay, A. (2015). *The Worldwide Governance Indicators: Methodology and Analytical Issues*. Retrieved from http://info.worldbank.org/governance/wgi/index.aspx#home

Luhmann, N. (2004). *Law as a Social System* (F. Kastner, R. Nobles, D. Schiff, & R. Ziegert, Eds.; ZiegertK. A., Trans.). Oxford, UK: Oxford University Press.

Luhmann, N. (2013). *Oblast*. Ljubljana: Krtina.

Maine, S. H. S. (1976). *Popular Government: An Inquiry into the Conditions Necessary for the Success of Representative Government by the Author of Ancient Law*. Indianapolis, IN: Liberty Classics.

Neergaard, U., Szyszczak, E., van de Gronden, J. W., & Krajewski, M. (2012). *Social Services of General Interest in the EU*. Springer Science & Business Media.

Nistor, L. (2013). *Public Services and the European Union: Healthcare, Health Insurance and Education Services* (2011 edition). The Hague, The Netherlands: T.M.C. Asser Press.

OECD. (2011). *Together for Better Public Services: Partnering With Citizens and Civil Society*. OECD Publishing.

Pečarič, M. (2016). Can a group of people be smarter than experts? *The Theory and Practice of Legislation*, 1–25. doi:10.1080/20508840.2016.1259823

Piketty, T. (2014). *Capital in the Twenty-First Century* (T. Goldhammer, Trans.). Cambridge, MA: Harvard University Press. doi:10.4159/9780674369542

Pollitt, C., & Bouckaert, G. (2011). *Public Management Reform: A Comparative Analysis - New Public Management, Governance, and the Neo-Weberian State* (3rd ed.). Oxford, UK: Oxford University Press.

Reich, R. (2016). *Saving Capitalism: For The Many, Not The Few*. London: Icon Books Ltd.

Reich, R. B. (2003). *I'll Be Short: Essentials for a Decent Working Society*. Boston: Beacon Press.

Samuelson, P. A. (1954). The Pure Theory of Public Expenditure. *The Review of Economics and Statistics*, *36*(4), 387–389. doi:10.2307/1925895

Sauter, W. (2015). *Public Services in EU Law*. Cambridge, UK: Cambridge University Press.

Seldon, A. (2005). *Introducing Market Forces Into 'Public' Services*. Indianapolis, IN: Liberty Fund.

Sjoberg, F. M., Mellon, J., & Peixoto, T. (2017). The Effect of Bureaucratic Responsiveness on Citizen Participation. *Public Administration Review*, *77*(3), 340–351. doi:10.1111/puar.12697

Sueur, A. L., Sunkin, M., & Murkens, J. E. K. (2016). *Public Law: Text, Cases, and Materials* (3rd ed.). Oxford, UK: Oxford University Press. doi:10.1093/he/9780198735380.001.0001

Szyszczak, E., Davies, J., Andenæs, M., & Bekkedal, T. (Eds.). (2013). *Developments in Services of General Interest* (2011 edition). The Hague, The Netherlands: T.M.C. Asser Press.

Taleb, N. N. (2014). *Antifragile: Things That Gain from Disorder*. Random House Publishing Group.

Theopedia. (2016). *Negative theology*. Retrieved 2 March 2016, from http://www.theopedia.com/negative-theology

Wilson, K., & Brownstein, J. S. (2009). Early detection of disease outbreaks using the Internet. *CMAJ : Canadian Medical Association Journal*, *180*(8), 829–831. doi:10.1503/cmaj.1090215 PMID:19364791

Yang, Y. T., Horneffer, M., & DiLisio, N. (2013). Mining Social Media and Web Searches For Disease Detection. *Journal of Public Health Research*, *2*(1), 17–21. doi:10.4081/jphr.2013.e4 PMID:25170475

ADDITIONAL READING

Bauby, P., & Similie, M. M. (2010). Public Services in the European Union & In the 27 Member States. Ceep. Retrieved from http://ceep.eu/images/stories/pdf/Mapping/CEEP_mapping%20experts%20report.pdf

Chase, R. (2015). *Peers Inc: How People and Platforms Are Inventing the Collaborative Economy and Reinventing Capitalism*. New York: PublicAffairs.

Landemore, H., & Elster, J. (Eds.). (2012). *Collective Wisdom: Principles and Mechanisms*. New York: Cambridge University Press. doi:10.1017/CBO9780511846427

Loeffler, E., & Bovaird, T. (2016). User and Community Co-Production of Public Services: What Does the Evidence Tell Us? *International Journal of Public Administration*, *39*(13), 1006–1019. doi:10.1080/01900692.2016.1250559

Sauter, W., & Schepel, H. (2009). *State and Market in European Union Law: The Public and Private Spheres of the Internal Market Before the EU Courts*. Cambridge: Cambridge University Press. doi:10.1017/CBO9780511626647

Selloni, D. (2017). *CoDesign for Public-Interest Services*. Cham: Springer. doi:10.1007/978-3-319-53243-1

Sjoberg, F. M., Mellon, J., & Peixoto, T. (2017). The Effect of Bureaucratic Responsiveness on Citizen Participation. *Public Administration Review*, *77*(3), 340–351. doi:10.1111/puar.12697

Szyszczak, E. (2007). *The Regulation of the State in Competitive Markets in the EU*. Oxford: Hart Publishing.

Tapscott, D., & Williams, A. D. (2008). *Wikinomics: How Mass Collaboration Changes Everything*. New York: Portfolio.

KEY TERMS AND DEFINITIONS

Economic Public Services: Economic public services provide material public goods as products and services whose permanent and uninterrupted production in the public interest is provided by the state, the municipality or other local community in order to meet public needs when and insofar as they cannot be (or not to wider extent and with affordable price) provided on the market.

Google Trends: A public web facility of Google Inc., based on Google Search, that shows how often a particular search term is entered relative to the total search volume across various regions of the world, and in various languages.

Non-Economic (Social) Public Services: Non-commercial public services that provide through education, science, culture, sports, health, social care, disability insurance and other non-economic (social) activities the intangible public goods.

Public Good: A wide concept into which can be put different goods as long as they fulfil two classical conditions of non-excludability and non-rivalry. The public good is good or service that allows the implementation of public interest. It is also good for shared use, it is a thing or good that is publicly owned, it is a thing or good that guarantees equal access. If we want to establish the essence of the public good, we must therefore proceed from the implementation of public interest, shared use, public property and guaranteed equal access.

Public Interest: Activities that are in favor of a group of people, such as the prevention of danger to life and human health, ensuring public order and peace, preventing a threat to public security or property of greater value. In addition to the aforementioned, the public interest is a well-founded interest, which was registered in a democratic process, where the interests of the majority of citizens were harmonized.

Public Power: An authoritative exercise of public competences in the name of public interest; the characteristic of legal relationships in which the competent authority, without negotiation and agreement with the addressee of the norm, unilaterally takes a decision on the basis of the law and its borders.

Public Service: It represents activities which in a given society is understood to be necessary for the provision of the most important goods and services, which, therefore, is provided in the public interest by the state, local community or private contractor. The provision of these goods takes place in accordance with the principles of continuity and flexibility, equity or impartiality, accessibility and equal quality, where it cannot be, or not equally, ensured on the market, with the basic purpose of not gaining profit but providing a person with decent conditions for his life.

Public Utilities: They are basic public facilities and objects that allow economic activity within a particular community; they are basic installations that form the basis for the operation of the public system.

ENDNOTES

1 The first intrusion in the Member States' control over their public services came already in 1957, when Article 90(2) EEC created an exemption for services of general economic interest from the full application of the EEC Treaty rules.

2 That means that the preserving, settling, discursive functions of politics could become the core of its tasks ... legal and institutional conditions should enable ongoing processes of social learning and experimentation to continue against existing restrictions. Such processes include the development of new forms of living in the course of individualization processes, or pluralization and criticism within professions (Beck, 1992, p. 235).

3 In 2010, public services in the EU27 accounted for just over 26% of total value added, around 30% of whole-economy employment and around 22% of all investment. By comparison, if we apply broadly the same definition and take data from the same sectors for the US, Norway and FYR Macedonia, public services accounted for 26-27% of whole-economy value added in 2010. In Iceland it was closer to 30% and in Switzerland public services accounted for 22% of whole-economy value added (Cambridge Econometrics, 2013, p. 11). The contribution of SGIs sectors to GDP is 24,4% (CEEP, 2010, p. 26).

4 Power is a sort of medium of communication that affects both sides, much like Hegel's in/dependence of self-consciousness that places it between the master and the slave: self-consciousness can only arise with another self-consciousness and vice versa – one defines the other, one is independent (the master), the other is not (the slave), one, as an independent entity, "turns to the other, enjoying its independent entity, leaving its aspect of independence for the slave to cultivate ... The truth of independent consciousness is then the slave consciousness" (Hegel, 1998, p. 107).

5 When we are talking about public goods, we are accustomed to speaking about two main elements of non-excludability and non-rivalry, while both incorporate a mass of people. Samuelson is usually credited as the first economist who has developed the theory of public goods (he named the latter as the collective consumption goods) "where each individual's consumption of such a good leads to no subtraction from any other individual's consumption of that good" (1954, p. 387). While Samuelson gives the emphasis on non-rivalry, Seldon gives it on non-excludability. The essential characteristic of public goods is for him "they cannot be refused to people who refuse to pay, and who would otherwise have a free ride if they were not required to pay. Public goods, to be produced

at all, cannot, therefore, be produced in response to individual specification in the market: they must be financed collectively by the method known as taxation" (2005, p. 108).

6 Le Bon, as the pioneer of the new psychological crowd entity, warns against new images as being only a disguise of old ones: "one of the essential functions of statesmen consists, in baptizing with popular or, at any rate, indifferent words things the crowd cannot endure under their old names" (Bon, 2002, p. 64).

7 The land is a public good only if is by the nature of things intended for general use of all under the same conditions, or whether the legislature (by the law) expressly defines it as a public good. The decision of the Constitutional Court of Slovenia, no. U-I-176/94 of 5. 10. 1995, at 11.

8 Google Trends is a public web facility of Google Inc., based on Google Search, that shows how often a particular search term is entered relative to the total search volume across various regions of the world, and in various languages.

9 In the history of human thought this is known as an apophatic approach, known from apophatic (negative) theology, which describes God by negation, speaking only in terms of what God is not (gr. apophanai, "to deny") rather than presuming to describe what God is (Theopedia, 2016). When Michelangelo was asked by the pope about the secret of his genius, particularly in regards to the statue of David, largely considered to be the greatest sculpting masterpiece of all time. Michelangelo responded by saying, "It's simple. I just remove everything that is not David". (Taleb, 2014). The negative approach is present also in the *effet utile* doctrine: Article 10 EC provides a fidelity or solidarity clause which obliges the Member States to cooperate in a positive way to facilitate the objectives of the EC Treaty and, in a negative way, not to harm or obstruct the realisation of the EC Treaty objectives: "the Member States shall take all appropriate measures, whether general or particular, to ensure fulfilment of the obligations arising out of this Treaty or resulting from action taken by the institutions of the Community. They shall facilitate the achievement of the Community's tasks. They shall abstain from any measure which could jeopardise the attainment of the objectives of this Treaty".

10 The optimal protection of the U.S. army planes in WWII was about protecting the most vulnerable parts. An optimum amount of armour would be in the midpoint between not getting planes to get shot down by enemy fighters and not making the plane too heavy, less manoeuvrable and less fuel efficient. The military wanted – in a rational manner – to put more armour on the parts with the most numerous holes when Abraham Wald (the member of classified statistical research group) asked: "Where are the missing holes"? The missing bullet holes were on the missing planes. The reason planes were coming back with fewer hits to the engine was that planes that got hit in the engine weren't coming back. Armour should be put on spots with no holes (Ellenberg, 2014).

11 Sjoberg, Mellon and Peixoto (2017) developed a calculus of participation based on a large amount of data (n= 399,364) from the online application Fix My Street. They found users whose first reported the problem was fixed are 57 per cent more likely to send at least one more report.

Chapter 14
Distributing Mutual Advantages in Italian Cooperatives:
An Analysis of Patronage Refunds

Francesca Costanza
University of Palermo, Italy

Pietro Fontana
Unicoop Palermo, Italy

ABSTRACT

Italian cooperative organizations contribute sensibly to the national growth and development, pursuing a social function of economic redistribution. Since they are based on the mutuality principle, the related accountancy and taxation systems follow such logic, in particular as far as the patronage refunds discipline is concerned. The aim of the chapter is to advance the understanding of such flows; the scope is pursued through an accounting records' comparative analysis based on the main legislative acts and professional and scholar literature. The results converge into a cause-and-effect model built according to a system dynamics perspective.

INTRODUCTION

The global cooperative movement, accounting for 2.6 million of cooperative societies, more than 1 billion of members and a combined turnover of 3 trillion US-$, can be considered one of the largest organization in the world (Grace 2014), providing employment to many more people than all multinational companies taken together (Schwettmann, 2014)

Several researches (Birchall & Hammond Ketilson, 2009; Zevi, Zanotti, Soulage, & Zelaia, 2011; Accornero & Marini, 2011; Zamagni, 2012; Zanotti, 2013) show that since 2008 the cooperatives have performed anti-cyclically, in particular in countries where this form of organization has long-term and stable tradition (Roelants, Dovgan, Eum, & Terrasi 2012).

DOI: 10.4018/978-1-5225-8482-7.ch014

Italy is one of these countries, characterized by a cooperative sector able to deal purposefully with the financial crisis, contributing sensibly to the economic growth and registering a greater impact on the social sector, services and agri-food (Alleanza delle Cooperative Italiane, 2018, May 15).

Some comparative analyses cooperatives-corporations (for example, Fontanari & Borzaga, 2013), explain the cooperatives' anticyclical behavior looking inside the organizations and highlighting two elements: first, the diversity of objectives; second, the proprietary forms. Indeed, since the goal of cooperatives is to provide services or work to their members, they will tend to keep high levels of activity even putting the profit margins aside (Moore, 2000). Abate (2018) reports about the ability of agricultural cooperative organizations to *develop 'countervailing power' and internalizing transaction costs.* Thomson (2015) remarks worker cooperatives' wider ability to develop productive knowledge than conventional firms. Altman (2016) looks at the demand side and argues that, contrary to what's predicted by conventional economics, non-economic variables like consumer well-being in purchasing cooperative products, are relevant in the cooperative sector, so that the reactivity of the demand to the price for products sold by cooperatives is lower than for the ones sold by non-cooperatives.

Because of good performances of cooperatives in comparison with corporations, the attention of scholars and institutions towards the cooperative sector is growing and it emerges the need to further develop the knowledge of the phenomenon.

This chapter addresses the Italian case because this is among the countries with a well rooted cooperative tradition (Roelants et al., 2012), so that the cooperatives enjoy constitutional recognition (article 45 of the Constitution).

The relevance of cooperative organizations in Italy is undiscussed as far as the number of entities, members and economic contribution are concerned. With a production value exceeding 108 billion, the cooperative economy accounts for 8.5% of Italian GDP (Borzaga, 2015). Indeed, such legal form of organization is a legitimate alternative to the corporation, pursuing a social function of economic redistribution whenever private lucrative purposes cannot be qualified as the main businesses' objectives. Due to the mutual scope, cooperatives benefit of a favorable taxation regime, which represents one of the main incentives to the cooperative in comparison with the corporate form.

According to the Italian legislation, the cooperative organizations have to hold mutual purposes, i.e., to focus the needs of their members, called cooperators, so that the goods and services produced are mainly devoted to them. Regarding the accountancy and taxation system, the mutuality takes place also in the discipline of the patronage refunds, meaning the distribution of a certain percentage of profits to restitute a part of the price of the goods and services acquired by the members, or as additional remuneration for the goods and services provided by them.

The accounting of these economic flows can take place in two ways: through a direct charge in the income statement or by mean of profit allocation to the shareholders/cooperators. Although both accounting methods are allowed by the regulations, they affect the informative value of the balance sheet, the achievement of a certain level of "prevalent mutuality" to benefit of special tax supportive measures, the economic and financial situation of the gainer.

The aim of the chapter is to advance the understanding of cooperative patronage refunds by mean of an extensive document analysis based on the main legislative acts and professional and scholar literature about the cooperatives' taxation and accountancy, together with numerical and accounting simulations. The results converge into a stock-and-flow model built according to a system dynamics perspective (Sterman, 2000).

The structure of the chapter will be as follows: after this introduction about the main characteristics of the cooperative organization in the Italian system and the aims of the study, there will be a brief review of the main differences in the fiscal rules and accounting requirements for cooperatives and for corporations, focusing the peculiarity of the patronage refunds. Starting from that, a comparative analysis of the patronage refunds' alternative accounting records will be undertaken. The chapter ends with the proposal of a system dynamics-based model depicting the allocation of each option on the cooperative financial system.

BACKGROUND

The Italian Cooperative Organizations at Time of Crisis

According to the Second and Third Italy Reports on Cooperation (Foontanari & Borzaga, 2013; Borzaga, 2015), coherently with the global trends, the cooperative sector in Italy gained countercyclical results. In particular, in the years of crisis (2008-2013), cooperation has achieved a growth in the value of production of 14%, continuing to hire people and creating new stable jobs: in this arch of time, the number of working positions in cooperatives at the end of December of each year increased, by 80,575 units, equal to 6.8%, and in the 2013 the 68.1% of the jobs' activations were permanent positions. Putting cooperatives in relation to other forms of enterprises, in the period of crisis the cooperatives have constantly increased their contribution to public finance, while public limited companies have decreased it: in 2013 the total tax burden over the production value was higher for cooperatives (7.7%) than for Limited Liability Companies, (6.8%). The performance of cooperatives has been better in all sectors, even in those with declining employment.

Recent researches (Fontanari & Carini, 2017), confirm the previous cooperative trends also for the two-year period 2013-2014. In this regard, the authors also remark an increase in income from employment, privileged in the distribution of income to the detriment of the management surplus and the level of capitalization. They also highlight a reduction of the operating result, confirming that the cooperatives are willing to sacrifice the profit to increase or at least not to reduce the level of production.

The Alliance of Italian Cooperatives (Alleanza delle Cooperative Italiane, 2018, May 15) reported to the Italian Parliament the good performance also in the quality of the Italian cooperation, as far as modernity and social cohesion are concerned. Indeed, at the end of 2017, there were: 19,299 female active cooperatives, with a 23.8% incidence over the total; 7,195 youth active cooperatives, equal to the 8.9% of total assets in Italy; and 5,315 foreign cooperatives (made by migrants), representing a + 3.5% increase in comparison to the previous year.

The Institutional Framework

Italy recognizes the cooperative as an organizational form not having private speculation purposes as main objective, which could provide a social function of redistributing economic productivity away from large corporations, with minimal barriers to participation in trading activities (Jensen, Patmore, & Tortia, 2015) Indeed, the Italian Civil Code (CC), at the article 2511, defines cooperatives as variable capital companies with a mutual purpose, where mutuality consists of providing goods or services or working conditions directly to the members of the organization at more advantageous conditions than those obtainable from the market. This principle is also guaranteed by the article 45 of the Italian Constitution, which states that the Republic recognizes the social function of cooperation with character of mutuality and without the purpose of private speculation. The law promotes and fosters their development with the most suitable means and ensures, with appropriate controls, the cooperative character and purpose (Dulcamare, 2016).

The Italian cooperative law details the conditions of formation, membership, purpose, governance, acquisition of capital and taxation treatment (article 2519 CC and followings).

The presence of cooperative organizations into the Italian Constitution and the provision of a complete legal framework into the civil legislation, are the signs of how the cooperative sector is embedded into national socio-economics and constitute a high incentive to cooperative start-ups. The core difference between cooperative laws and the ones pertaining other corporate forms is the requirement of an organization pursuing a 'mutual purpose', that is, satisfying the interests of its members, the cooperators/shareholders, as users of the goods and services provided by the cooperative. In addition, cooperatives' characteristics have to respect the International Cooperative Alliance (ICA) standards.

In particular, the legal framework related to cooperatives is based on principles such as: *voluntary and open membership, democratic and active membership status, equitable contributions to the operation of cooperatives, enhancing cooperation amongst cooperatives, and the economic benefit to society derived from promoting such organizational forms* (Jensen et al., 2015).

According to the article 2522 of CC, in Italy it is required a minimum number of nine members in order to form a cooperative, with the exceptional cases of three cooperators in specific situations. The regulations impose initial meetings of members to fix governing rules agreed upon by majority. Afterwards, the cooperatives submit an application for registration to the Chamber of Commerce (art. 2522, par 3 CC). As far as the governance is concerned, in order to avoid mechanisms of concentration of control, there is a one member-one vote rule. Notwithstanding, specific corps of rules deviating from the general ones can be established within each cooperative, still under the respect of a set of governance standards. In any case, the Italian cooperatives are subject to reporting and auditing standards, the majority of cooperative directors need to be members of the cooperative (articles 2542, paragraph 2 CC), and this provision ensures that they keep fulfilling their fiduciary duties.

Although there is no legal obligation, cooperatives are encouraged to adhere to a cooperative federation, i.e. a recognized representative organization, to permit the latter to gather influence on policy makers' decisions. If cooperatives decide not to be part to a federation, the Ministry of Economic Development automatically receives control of them.

The federations (and the Ministry in case of independent cooperatives) have two specific tasks: supervision of their member cooperatives and the collection of their 3 per cent annual profits.

The supervision (regulated by Legislative Decree n. 220 of 2002), regards the financial statements and various organizational aspects, and basically verifies the respect of the mutualistic aims, the effectiveness of the member base, the member participation in the firm's life, the mutualistic exchange, the absence of lucrative aims and the fulfilment of requirements to benefit of fiscal and social benefits. They also advise cooperatives' managerial and administrative bodies how to improve management practices and internal democracy in terms of member participation. These tasks are called 'ordinary revisions' and are carried out (in general every two years) by the recognized representative organizations for their member cooperatives or by the Ministry for Economic Development for independent cooperatives. On the contrary, the Ministry is the only subject in charge of conducting the extra-ordinary revisions.

The second task of the cooperative federations is to collect money from their members to enhance the cooperative sector. In particular, Italian cooperatives are obliged to provide 3 per cent of their total annual profits to the cooperative movement via the federations (Law 57 of 1992), or to the State if they do not belong to any federation. These funds (called 'mutualistic funds', or 'mutual funds'), also fed by any residual capital remaining after the conversion of cooperatives to other organizational forms, have been used by the federations or the Ministry to spread the cooperative model by supporting existing organizations and promoting new ones; for example, stimulating joint projects for loans' guaranteeing, project financing researches, training activities, also in university contexts (Jensen et al. 2015).

TAX REGULATION

The cooperatives and their consortia are taxable persons for corporate income tax, therefore the rules of the Italian Law on Income Tax (TUIR) apply to them. Furthermore, The Italian cooperative organizations benefit of fiscal advantages, consisting of tax supportive measures provided by special laws, which dictate general rules and norms contemplated for specific categories of cooperatives. This favourable regime only applies to 'prevalently mutual cooperatives', i.e. cooperatives that act prevalently with their members and that remunerate member capital contributions only up to a certain extent. The Civil Code actually distinguishes two main categories of cooperatives: 'prevalently mutual cooperative' and 'non-prevalently mutual', which is often referred to as 'other cooperatives' (articles 2512-2514 CC).

The distinction above only serves to differentiate the tax treatment of cooperatives, as their regulation is identical with regard to all the other aspects (excluding conversion to other organizational legal forms). Therefore, a cooperative not interested in joining this specific tax treatment could well be established as 'other cooperative'.

The resulting regime basically consists of reductions in the corporate income tax (Imposta sul reddito delle società, or IRES) taxable amount, and the discipline of patronage refunds (DPR 601/1973). These last facilities are allowed only if prevalent mutuality conditions are fulfilled. If the mutualistic purpose belongs by definition to the generality of the cooperatives, the prevalent mutuality character belongs only to the cooperatives that meet certain requirements. In particular:

- The presence of a mutual purpose;
- The compliance with the mutual prevalence parameters referred to in articles 2512 and 2513 of the Civil Code for some types of cooperatives (whilst others are exempted from demonstrating prevalence);
- The cooperative bylaws must include: the prohibition to distribute dividends in excess of the maximum interest of the postal savings bonds, increased by two and a half points compared to the capital actually paid; the prohibition to remunerate the financial instruments offered in subscription to the cooperative members by more than two points compared to the maximum limit for dividends; the prohibition of distribution of reserves among the members; in the event of dissolution of the company, the obligation to devolve the entire company assets, deducting only the share capital and any dividends accrued, to the mutual funds for the promotion and development of cooperation;
- The record in the section dedicated to the 'prevalently mutual cooperatives' within the register of cooperative companies;

- The fulfilment of the obligation to pay 3% of annual net profits to mutual funds for the promotion and development of cooperation.

Such conditions have to be respected not only in the fiscal period under analysis, but also in the previous five ones. Furthermore, the tax benefits stop if the cooperative does not make the payment to mutualistic funds required by law.

Finally, according to the ruling of the Italian supreme judge, the Tax Administration can avoid the application of tax benefits whenever it can demonstrate that the mutual form of cooperatives is just a formality to hide a corporation covering a normal entrepreneurial activity, even for just one fiscal period (Dulcamare, 2016).

The formulas to calculate the prevalent mutuality indexes according to the Civil Code are summarized in the following table.

On the basis of the current legislation, the following table shows the IRES tax regime for the prevalent mutuality cooperatives:

Figure 1. Formulas to calculate the mutuality indexes according to Italian civil code

TYPE OF COOPERATIVE	MUTUALITY INDEX
a) Consumption and user cooperatives	(Revenues from sales towards cooperative members/ total revenues from sales and services)*100>50
b) Labour cooperatives	(Cost of cooperative members' labour/Total cost of labour)*100>50
c) Conferral cooperatives	(Purchasing cost of raw materials from members/Total purchasing cost of raw materials)*100>50
d) Service cooperatives	(Cost for the provision of services from members/ Total costs for services)*100>
e) Mixed cooperatives	(Revenues from sales towards cooperative members+ Purchasing cost of raw materials from members+ Cost of cooperative members' Labour past services+ Cost for the provision services from members) /(Total revenues from sales and services +Total purchasing cost of raw materials + Total cost of Labour related to mutuality+ Total costs for services related to the mutual relationship)*100>50

Figure 2. IRES Taxable amounts for prevalent mutuality cooperatives

Prevalent mutuality cooperatives	Taxable amount in IRES tax basis	Non-Taxable amount in IRES tax basis
Social cooperatives	3%	97%
Agriculture/Small-scale fishing	23%	67%
Consumption	68%	32%
Others	43%	57%

It is also worth mentioning that, under the respect of the minimum taxable profit above, according to the article 12 of Law n. 904 of 1977, n. 904, the profits allocated by the cooperative to indivisible reserves (which in turn can be compulsory or voluntary) are exempt from the corporate income tax. These reserves may be used to cover financial losses, without this producing the loss of the tax measure, but only as long as the profits are not distributed.

The prospectus in figure 3 summarises IRES calculations for Labour Cooperative and a Limited Liability Company, starting from the same pre-taxes net income (accounting data from a real Italian cooperative for which the authors have managed the accounting service). By comparing the results, it is possible to have a numerical confirmation of the tax advantages of the cooperatives.

However, the table does not consider that the cooperative's profit before taxes can be further lowered by the patronage refunds, which will be discussed in the next heading.

Patronage Refunds

Another significant tax provision for mutually prevalent cooperatives consists on the possibility to benefit of the patronage refunds' discipline and that the sums distributed to members as patronage refunds is exempt from taxation, also if they are assigned to members as free shares of the cooperative capital.

The patronage refunds correspond to the share of the total operating surplus, deriving from the mutual activity carried out with the cooperators, attributed to the same in proportion to the quality and quantity of mutual trade (relationships) with the cooperative during the year.

Notwithstanding, cooperative members can be subject to taxation for the sums received as patronage refunds, which is postponed when these refunds are assigned as free shares of capital.

As far as the criteria for determining them are concerned, the legislator granted the cooperatives ample discretionarily in terms of statutory autonomy, under the respect of the principles of proportionality, fairness and equal treatment.

The prerequisite for the disbursement of the patronage refunds is therefore the existence of a documented surplus deriving from the mutual activity, which represents the maximum limit of the refunds shares distributable among the cooperative members that can never be higher than the profit previously determined for the year. In the labour cooperatives, a further limit is represented by 30% of the total labour remuneration treatments.

According to the type of cooperative, patronage refunds represent:

Figure 3. Comparison of IRES calculations for a limited liability company and a labour cooperative

	Limited Liability Company (S.r.l.)	Labour Cooperative
Net income before taxes	12.925,05	12.925,05
Variation of net income due to fiscal rules	816,74	816,74
Sub-total	13.741,79	13.741,79
Maxi-amortization (tax benefits 2017/2018)	(214,86)	(214,86)
IRES tax basis	13.526,93	6.159,65
IRES tax liability	3.719,91	1.693,90

- The increase in members' compensations for the transfer of goods or services (conferral cooperatives);
- The increase in remuneration for the subordinate and non-subordinate work performed by the members (labour and service cooperatives);
- The return to the shareholders of a part of the price paid to acquire services (consumption and user cooperatives).

Comparing Accounting Options

There are two options to account the patronage refunds that can be freely chosen by cooperatives:

- First method: the patronage refunds are registered as economic components representing a cost or a lower revenue for the cooperative. With this method the accounting entries vary according to the type of coverage. This accounting option is suggested by the National Council of Chartered Accountant (CNDCEC) and by the main trade organizations;
- Second method: consider the patronage refunds as a share of profit to be distributed to the cooperators in liquid form or as free shares of capital.

Figure 4 presents the double-entry registrations according to both methods. As it noticeable, for the first method the account debited depends on the type of cooperative.

In the perspective of the cooperative organization, the two methods lead to indifferent results for the calculation of IRES and IRAP (regional tax on productive activity). From the cooperators' point of view, with the second method, the portion of patronage refund attributable is lower, as the accrued shares are deducted from the total profit which also takes into account the contribution of the shareholders (in practice a portion of the refunds is also set aside).

With the first method, the refunds are still deductible from the income of the cooperative, whilst they are taxed in the hands of the members.

Figure 4. Double-entry registrations for alternative accounting methods of patronage refunds

TRANSACTIONS – ACCOUNT NAMES	Debit	Credit
First Method		
Consumption and User Cooperatives		
Sales revenues	X	
Payable to cooperators for patronage refunds		X
Labour Cooperatives		
Personnel cost	X	
Payable to cooperators for patronage refunds		X
Conferral Cooperatives		
Purchasing cost of raw materials	X	
Payable to cooperators for patronage refunds		X
Service Cooperatives		
Cost for services (non-subordinate labour)	X	
Payable to cooperators for patronage refunds		X
Second Method (for all the types of cooperatives)		
Net income	X	
Indivisible capital reserve		X
…..		X
Payable to cooperators for patronage refunds		X

In the event that the refunds are distributed by means of an increase in share capital and not in liquid form, there will be a special "tax suspension" regime, according to subsection 2, article 6, Law Decree 63/2002.

BUILDING A SYSTEM DYNAMICS CONCEPTUAL MODEL

In this section of the chapter, the patronage refunds accountancy treatments are inserted into a causal model built according to the perspective of system dynamics (SD), a computer-aided methodology to represent the causal structure of a system through stock-and-flow, feedback structures and computer simulations regarding the accumulation of materials, information, people, and money (Forrester, 1961; Sterman, 2000; 2014). The scope of the methodology is to build conceptual or simulation models to support learning, policy design and analysis. The potential applications are several, since it is suitable to capture any dynamic problem or issue within systems characterized by interdependence, mutual interaction, information feedback, and circular causality.

The stock-and-flow diagrams are constructed by utilizing three elements: stocks (level of a resource within the system at a certain time); flows (rates of change of the stocks' level, expressed by quantities per units of time); auxiliary (variables aiding calculus or acting as exogenous parameters or constants).

Stocks accumulates their inflows less their outflows, thus mathematically SD models are systems of integrals and differential equations (Sterman, 2000).

The combination of SD and accountancy systems is not new for the field (Lyneis, 1982, Bianchi 1996; Yamaguchi, 2003; Nair & Rodrigues, 2013). Looking at financial accounting from the SD point of view *would allow for the elevation of the accounting system as merely a tool for record keeping (of 'past success') to a general-purpose system for strategic planning, management control and accounting* (Melse, 2008).

So far, only a couple of scientific work have addressed cooperative organizations' performance (Protil & Barreiros, 2012; Protil & Kugeratski, 2012), but none of them focused the cooperative accounting rules regarding the Italian system.

Figure 5. An example of stock-and-flow structure

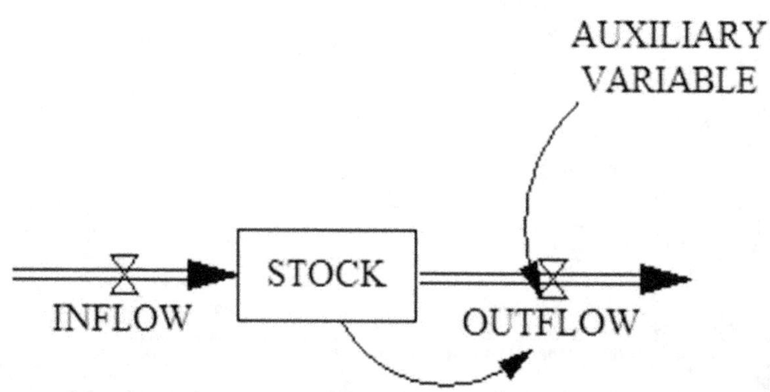

Model Description

The patronage refunds' accounting dynamic model presented in this heading is a stock-and-flow structure built by using a SD simulation software (Vensim by Ventana). In order to give rise to it, it was firstly analysed relevant system dynamics background literature to select model procedures suitable for the scope of the study. Beside this activity, the relevant relationships to be captured by the model were isolated and sketched in a simplified conceptual map (figure 6), representing the core 'actors' (the cooperative companies and their cooperators/shareholders) and their exchanges (patronage refunds vs services in case of a service cooperative). Going backward to the accountancy rules' causal tissue, it was possible to highlight the key candidate variables to include into the model.

The resulting model builds on Yamaguchi (2003) who presents general rules to integrate system dynamics and accounting. The author specifically applies SD to model corporate financial statements (income statement, balance sheet and cash flow statement) and sustains the usefulness of SD dynamic modeling and simulation skills to help in understanding financial statements, making them *more friendly*.

In order to foster the understanding of financial accounting system, he puts in relation the key SD principles (stock, flow and their relations) with the financial statement items, thus the latter can be expressed in light of system dynamics terms. In particular, balance sheet is tackled as a collection of stocks, while income statement and cash flow statement are made of inflows and outflows of the stocks in balance sheet. The paper also states that *the dynamic accounting system mostly depends on the parameters of transaction data obtained outside the system.*

Such approach was tailored to the patronage refunds' accounting within the Italian context, and it was considered the case of a service cooperative characterized by prevalent mutuality, a compulsory requisite to be fulfilled in order to benefit of the patronage refunds' discipline.

The model is proposed into two version: figure 7 represents the first accounting method and figure 8 the second one. In both structures, the 'net income' was modelled as an economic stock resulting from the feeding activity from 'revenues' and the draining by a number of outflows.

Regarding the first method, the outflows from the stock 'net income' are the following:

- **'Income Taxes':** Calculated on the taxable income according to the Italian Law on Income Tax (TUIR);

Figure 6. Conceptual map

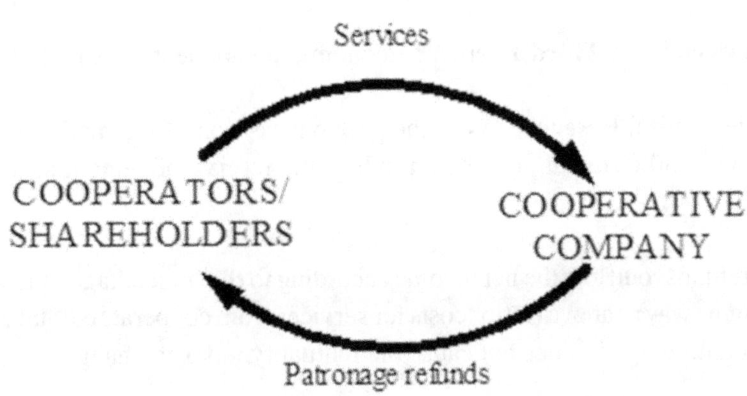

- **'To National Mutual Funds':** It is the compulsory destination flow of 3% annual profit to an indivisible capital reserve, as legislated by Italian Civil Code;
- **'Cost for Services From Cooperators':** Economic components representing the mutual transactions. The accounting of patronage refunds takes place through an increase of these costs;
- **'Cost for Services From Third Parties':** Economic components not included into the mutual transactions;
- **'To Indivisible Capital Reserve':** It is the compulsory destination flow of 30% annual profit to an indivisible reserve of capital, as legislated by Italian Civil Code.

In the model, each outflow converges in a stock accumulating its value over the time. Thus, the 'mutual fund' and the 'income taxes' flows feed respectively the 'account payable to representative federation' and the 'account payable to tax system'; while the flow 'to indivisible capital reserve' fills the stock 'indivisible capital reserve' to increase in turn the 'net assets'. In this figure, the stock of debt towards the cooperators, namely the 'account payables to cooperators', is directly fed by the flow of costs at their manifestation, whilst the stock of 'account payables to third parties' is fed by the flow of 'costs for services from third parties'.

The patronage refunds are proportional to the auxiliary variable 'percentage of mutuality', calculated through the ratio between the 'costs for services from cooperators' and 'total cost for services' (the sum of services from cooperators and third parties). In this case the attribution of the patronage refunds, provoking an increase in the 'costs for services from cooperators', causes the 'percentage of mutuality' to raise. Then the patronage refunds' pathway is twofold: (1) they can be paid by cash, then depleting the 'bank account/cash', or (2) they can be devoted to capital stock, then making the net asset to rise.

The next figure portrays the second method of patronage refunds' accounting. The core structure of the model is the same as the one previously presented, except for the determination of the patronage refunds.

The outflows from the stock 'net income' are the following:

- **'Income Taxes':** Calculated again on the taxable income according to the Italian Law on Income Tax (TUIR);
- **'To National Mutual Funds':** It is still the compulsory destination flow of 3% annual profit to an indivisible capital reserve, as legislated by Italian Civil Code;
- **'Patronage Refunds':** In this case they are not considered as an economic component but as a share of profit;
- **'Cost For Services From Cooperators':** Economic components representing the mutual transactions.
- **'Cost for Services from Third Parties':** Economic components not included into the mutual transactions;
- **'To Indivisible Capital Reserve':** As in the previous version of the model, it is the compulsory destination flow of 30% annual profit to an indivisible reserve of capital, as legislated by Italian Civil Code.

The 'patronage refunds' outflow the net income according to the 'percentage of mutuality'. The latter is calculated in the same way as above (ratio 'costs for services from cooperators/total costs for services'), but this second accounting option does not cause the mutuality index to change.

Figure 7. Stock-and- flow structure of the first accounting method

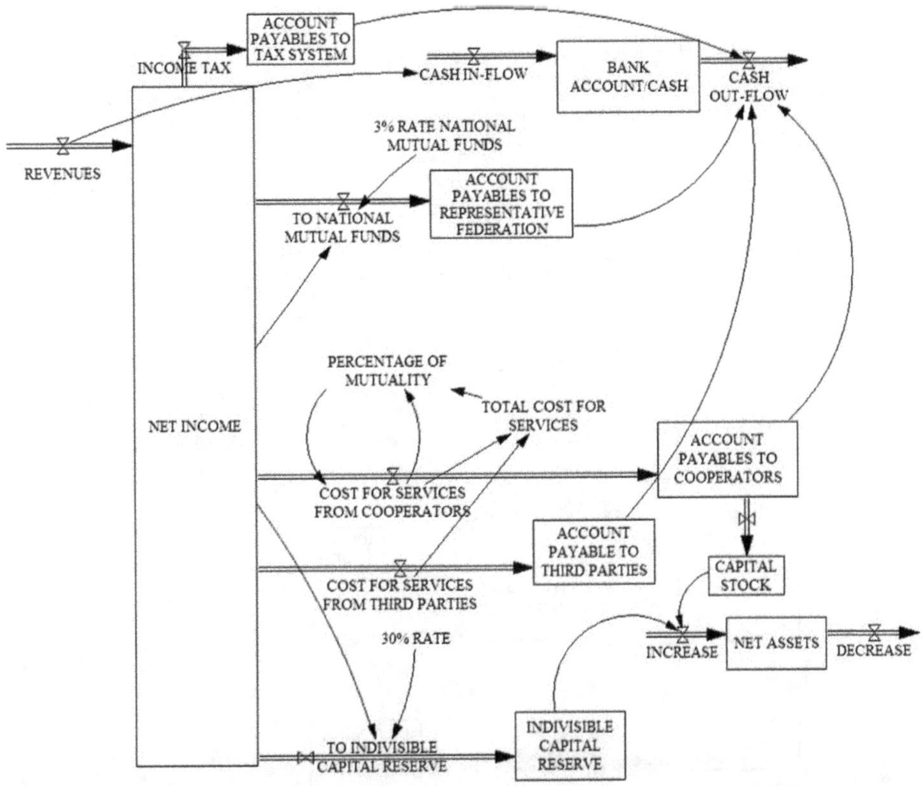

As it possible to notice, both versions of the model capture the compulsory destination of annual profits according to Italian Civil Code, by including the outflows from the 'net income' of 30% annual profits to legal reserve and 3% of annual profits to mutual funds. The model also tracks two alternative "routes" of patronage refunds, however recorded: the distributions to the cooperators and the assignation as free shares of capital.

SOLUTIONS AND RECOMMENDATIONS

This work was developed to contribute in the understanding of cooperative organizations' dynamics, then supporting the Italian policy makers' concern to stimulate the development of this sector.

For the purpose, the chapter addressed the cooperative patronage refunds' tax and accounting issues by mean of a mixed accountancy and system dynamics approach. The resulting model has the merit to depict the economic and financial interrelationships dynamically and in a more intuitive manner.

This approach could have a double use: on the one hand, it can have a managerial validity if efforts are devoted in integrating the cooperatives' accountancy systems with system dynamics models. The model presented in the chapter still lays at a qualitative stage, namely, structural equations have not been built and simulations cannot be run yet. Once the model formalization will be completed and the integration of the cooperative system dynamics model with a real cooperative firm's accounts will be completed,

Figure 8. Stock-and- flow structure of the second accounting method

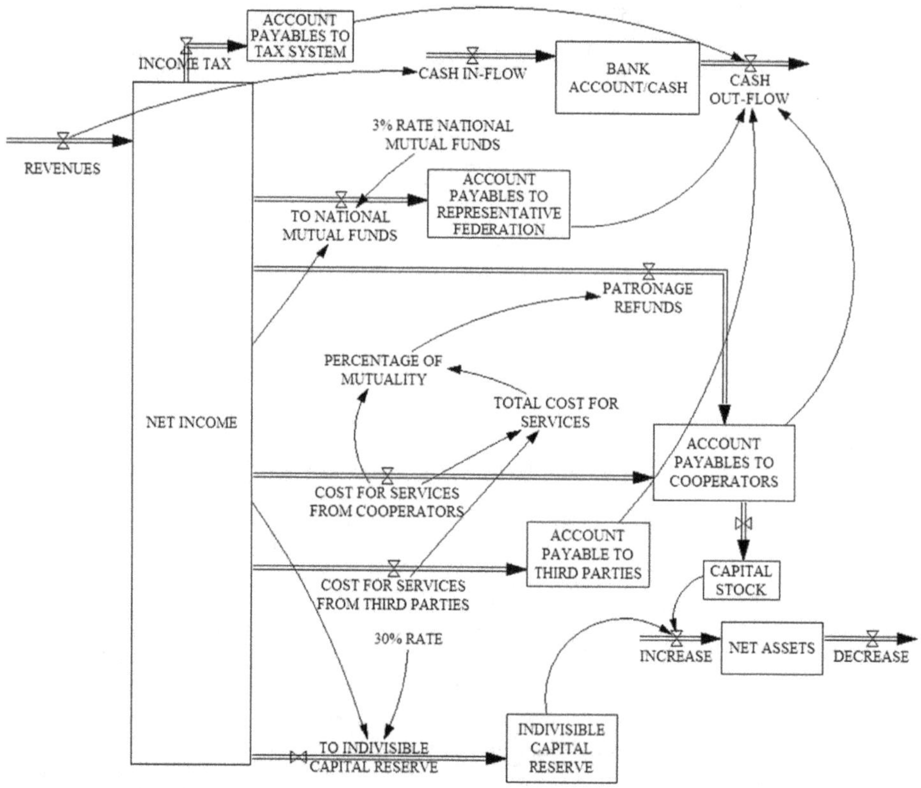

it will be possible to simulate relevant key-variables' behavior patterns to contribute to strategic, tactic and operational decision-making.

However, the model built is already a useful instrument to visualize and analyze complex accounting processes. Then the SD model can have a second use, i.e. to serve learning purposes in training classes and also in informal learning contexts. The teaching of accountancy topics is traditionally based on static models, still necessary and not to be set aside, but not always easy to understand for the learners. Pairing traditional teaching tools with system dynamics model can improve the understanding both of the accounting system as a whole and of specific transactions, also connecting the accountancy with other firms' subsystems like planning and control, general management, operation management, marketing management and logistics.

Looking at the whole system allows to identify, for instance, if the desired effect of a policy undertaken in a certain area finds unfavorable compensations by other dynamics happening elsewhere in the system, not immediately recognizable (Sterman, 2000). For example, if in a consumption cooperative the recording of the patronage refunds take place with the first method, i.e. through an accounting adjustment in the revenues from sales to cooperators, this reduction can impact the respect of the mutuality index (compulsory to benefit of the favorable tax regime) by mean of the reduction of the entire sales basis (the denominator of the fraction). Such risk, far from hard to be recognized in a non-complex context of decisions and actions, can be underestimated or even neglected considering the number of variables and issues that a firm faces. But a system dynamic simulation can help in detecting these mechanisms, thereby inducing to reconsider the accounting method to be preferred. Other possible trade-offs could be highlighted through simulators, for example non-physiological processes of sales/purchasing and corresponding receivables/liabilities and cash movements, as well as the potential effect of hiring measures in specific areas can be tested before implementation and disbursements. A comprehensive models could also force the creation of a better coordination of the organizational areas and a shared view of processes from the cooperators, thereby enhancing motivation and a more efficient and effective entrepreneurial action. The instrumental view (Bianchi, 2012) which make explicit how to improve the objects of the performance management system, is likely to empower cooperative members and scholars (which are potential cooperators) to feel more aware of the operative mechanisms interacting within the firm's structure. This way they could feel more accountable for the expected results coming from activating this or that policy levers, so that they could better understand if, how and where to move organizational resources, in order to lead the organizations towards the desired direction.

FUTURE RESEARCH DIRECTIONS

The chapter addressed the cooperatives' patronage refunds by presenting accounts' analyses and a qualitative system dynamics model. The latter is based on several assumptions regarding the boundaries of the relevant system and the variables' inclusion and links. The model portrayed just a type of cooperative, namely the service cooperative, so it could be adapted to capture the dynamics of other typologies of cooperative organizations. The focus was just on specific dynamics useful to capture the patronage refunds' accounting methods, thus neglecting other areas of the organizational structure (e.g. inventory and the sales management), which could be included in future versions of the model.

The modelling still lays at a qualitative stage, since no structural equations have already been built, so that it is not currently possible to run simulations of the economic and financial patterns of an existing cooperative organization. Next developments of this study will provide the mathematical formalization of the core variables' relations and the inserting of accounting data sets chosen from a real cooperative case. Then future works will present computer simulations, giving the SD tool the opportunity to capture behaviour patterns over the time in response to alternative policies' activation. In the same simulation software used so far, the stock-and-flow structures will be specified with a list of equations representative of decision rules and behavioural relationships. This support is likely to allow decision makers to undertake experiments with models representing real world-like systems (Pidd, 2004), giving them the opportunity to gain deep insights about the investigated problems.

Next versions of the model can include enlargements to other aspects of the cooperative management, such as governance and quality assurance procedures. These additions would imply for the modelers to make interviews to the members of a case-study cooperative firm in order to capture their mental perceptions and eventually to detect organizational issues and criticalities. In this direction, it would be interesting to verify the links between their mutual activity, their personal satisfaction and their commitment to the cooperation principles.

CONCLUSION

The cooperative sector in the Italian context is so relevant from the socio-economic point of view that it was cemented through the incorporation of cooperative principles into the Italian Constitution. In the mindset of the legislator, the cooperatives are seen as important vehicles for promoting economic growth as well as the democratization of ownership and work. For this reason, it is important the diffusion of cooperative culture and knowledge about managerial, accountancy and fiscal rules regulating this particular form of organization. This study tried to make a contribution in this sense. After a hint about cooperative countercyclical performances in comparison to corporations, the chapter have shown the main characteristics of the legislative framework in which they are embedded and have given specific attention to the favorable tax regime. In this respect a numerical simulation demonstrated that, under the respect of prevalent mutuality law requirements, the income tax level for cooperative organizations is sensibly lower, ceteris paribus, than the corporations' one. Afterwards, the analysis faced a specific aspect of the cooperative discipline, the patronage refunds. They were investigated as far as definition, tax regime and accounting rules are concerned. Double-entry transactions were presented according to different registering options, making proper distinctions for specific types of cooperatives within the Italian framework. Taking the case of a service cooperative, it was built a simplified qualitative system dynamics model depicting two possible accounting options for patronage refunds. The model, consisting of a stock-and-flow causal structure, was considered as a useful representation of the financial dynamics occurring within a cooperative and is likely to aid learning and training processes as well as cooperative members' insights. These purposes will be better served once the model will be enriched by the quantitative part. Indeed, the equations of the model structure, integrated by real-company datasets, will allow to experiment in a risk-free environment the potential impacts of alternative measures, thereby conducting to a greater awareness of the firms' performance causal tissue and better decision making.

ACKNOWLEDGMENT

Although both authors significantly contributed to this research, the following headings (and the related sub-headings) are to be attributed to Francesca Costanza: 'Introduction', 'Background', 'Building a System Dynamics Conceptual Model', 'Solutions and Recommendation', and 'Future Research Directions'; whilst the heading 'Tax Regulation' is ascribable to Pietro Fontana. Finally, the headings 'Patronage Refunds' and 'Conclusions' are the result of the authors' joint effort.

This research received no specific grant from any funding agency in the public, commercial, or not-for-profit sectors.

REFERENCES

Abate, T. G. (2018). Drivers of agricultural cooperative formation and farmers' membership and patronage decisions in Ethiopia. *Journal of Co-operative Organization and Management*, *6*(2), 53–63. doi:10.1016/j.jcom.2018.06.002

Accornero, A., & Marini, D. (2011). Le cooperative alla prova della crisi. Quaderni FNE - Collana Ricerche, n. 61. Mestre, Italy: Fondazione Nord Est.

Alleanza delle Cooperative Italiane. (2018, May 15). *Audizione dell'Alleanza delle Cooperative Italiane nell'ambito dell'esame del Documento di Economia e Finanza 2018 dinanzi alle Commissioni Speciali Senato della Repubblica e Camera dei deputati*. Retrieved February 11, 2019, from https://www.senato.it/application/xmanager/projects/leg18/attachments/documento_evento_procedura_commissione/files/000/000/081/ALLEANZA_DELLE_COOPERATIVE.pdf

Altman, M. (2016). Is there a co-operative advantage? Experimental evidence on the economic and non-economic determinants of demand. *Journal of Co-operative Organization and Management*, *4*(2), 66–75. doi:10.1016/j.jcom.2016.08.003

Bianchi C. (1996). *Modelli contabili e modelli 'dinamici' per il controllo di gestione in un'ottica strategica*. Milano: Centro Universitario Studi Aziendali - Collana di studi economico-aziendali.

Bianchi, C. (2012). Enhancing Performance Management and Sustainable Organizational Growth through System Dynamics Modeling. In Systemic Management for Intelligent Organizations: Concepts, Model-Based Approaches, and Applications, (pp. 143-161). Heidelberg, Germany: Springer.

Birchall, J., & Hammond Ketilson, L. (2009). Resilience of the Cooperative Business Model in Times of Crisis. Geneva, Italy: ILO.

Borzaga, C. (2015). Economia cooperativa. Rilevanza, evoluzione e nuove frontiere della cooperazione italiana. Trento, Italy: Euricse Edizioni.

Dulcamare, V. (2016). *Il regime fiscale delle cooperative*. Retrieved August, 20, 2018, from http://www.odcec.matera.it/files/formazione-regolamenti/slide%20DULCAMARE.pdf

Fontanari, E., & Borzaga, C. (2013). La cooperazione italiana negli anni della crisi. Trento, Italy: Euricse Edizioni.

Fontanari, E., & Carini, C. (2017). Le cooperative italiane sono fuori dalla crisi? Crescita, valore generato ed occupazione tra il 2013 e il 2014. Trento, Italy: Euricse Edizioni.

Forrester, J. W. (1961). *Industrial Dynamics*. Boston, MA: The MIT Press.

Grace, D. (2014). *Measuring the Size and Scope of the Cooperative Economy*. New York, NY: UN DESA.

Jensen, A., Patmore, G., & Tortia, E. (2015). *Cooperative Enterprises in Australia and Italy Comparative analysis and theoretical insights. Strumenti per la didattica e la ricerca 172*. Firenze, Italy: Firenze University Press.

Lyneis, J. M. (1982). *Corporate planning and policy design: a system dynamics approach*. Boston: MIT Press/Wright-Allen series in system dynamics.

Melse, E. (2008). The Financial Accounting Model from a System Dynamics' Perspective. MPRA Paper 7624. Munich, Germany: University Library of Munich.

Moore, M. H. (2000). Managing for Value: Organizational Strategy in For-Profit, Nonprofit and Governmental Organizations. *Nonprofit and Voluntary Sector Quarterly, 29*(1), 183–204. doi:10.1177/089976400773746391

Nair, G. H., & Rodrigues, L. L. R. (2013). Dynamics of Financial System: A System Dynamics Approach. *International Journal of Economics and Financial Issues, 3*(1), 14–26.

Pidd, M. (2004). *Systems modelling: Theory and practice*. Oxford, UK: John Wiley & Sons.

Protil, R., & Barreiros, R. (2012). *Strategic Control of Agro-Industrial Cooperatives: A Strategic Map Proposal*. Paper presented at the 30th International Conference of the System Dynamics Society, San Gallen, Switzerland.

Protil, R., & Kugeratski, S. (2012). *Economic Evaluation of Agronomic Research In Agricultural Cooperatives: Proposal of a Dynamic Scorecard Model*. Paper presented at the 30th International Conference of the System Dynamics Society, San Gallen, Switzerland.

Roelants, B., Dovgan, D., Eum, H., & Terrasi, E. (2012). *The Resilience of the Cooperative Model - How Worker Cooperatives, Social Cooperatives and Other Worker-owned Enterprises Respond to the Crisis and its Consequences*. Brussels, Belgium: CECOP-CICOPA Europe.

Schwettmann, J. (2014). The role of cooperatives in achieving the sustainable development goals - the economic dimension. Geneva, Italy: ILO.

Sterman, J. D. (2000). *Business Dynamics. System thinking and modeling for a complex world*. Boston, MA: Mc Graw-Hill.

Sterman, J. D. (2014). Interactive web-based simulations for strategy and sustainability: The MIT Sloan LearningEdge management flight simulators, Part I. *System Dynamics Review, 30*(1-2), 89–121. doi:10.1002dr.1513

Thomson, S. (2015). Towards a social theory of the firm: Worker cooperatives reconsidered. *Journal of Co-operative Organization and Management, 3*(1), 3–13. doi:10.1016/j.jcom.2015.02.002

Yamaguchi, K. (2003). *Principle of accounting system dynamics – modeling corporate financial statements*. Paper presented at the 21st International Conference of the System Dynamics Society, New York, NY.

Zamagni, V. (2012). Interpreting the Roles and Economic Importance of Cooperative Enterprises in a Historical Perspective. *JEOD, 1*(1), 21–36. doi:10.5947/jeod.2012.002

Zanotti, A. (2013). *Le performance delle cooperative di servizi durante la crisi: un'analisi nel periodo 2009-2011*. Euricse Working Paper, n. 51.

Zevi A., Zanotti, A., Soulage, F., & Zelaia, A. (2011). *Beyond the Crisis: Cooperatives, Work, Finance - Generating Wealth for the Long Term*. Brussels, Belgium: CECOP-CICOPA Europe.

KEY TERMS AND DEFINITIONS

Cooperative Federations: Representative organizations for cooperative societies. They supervise member cooperatives' financial and organizational aspects, and seek to stimulate the diffusion of the cooperative model.

Cooperative Societies: Variable capital companies with a mutual purpose (i.e., providing goods, services, or working conditions directly to the members of the organization at more advantageous conditions than those obtainable from the market).

Cooperators: The members of a cooperative organization.

Mutual Purpose: it is the requirement for cooperative organizations to focus the needs of their members, so that the goods and services produced are mainly devoted to them.

Patronage Refunds: The distribution of a certain share of operating surplus to restitute a part of the price of the goods and services acquired by the members, or additional remuneration for the goods and services provided by cooperators.

Stocks and Flows: Building blocks of a system dynamics model structure, considering the level of resources within a complex system (stock variables) and their rate of change over the time (flow variables).

System Dynamics: Methodology to build conceptual or simulation models depicting the causal structure of a complex system.

Chapter 15
Circular Economy for India:
Perspectives on Stewardship Principles, Waste Management, and Energy Generation

Saravan Krishnamurthy
https://orcid.org/0000-0003-4993-2215
Symbiosis International University (Deemed), India

Geoffrey Fudurich
https://orcid.org/0000-0001-7376-0500
Ryerson University, Canada

Prakash Rao
Symbiosis International University (Deemed), India

ABSTRACT

The stewardship of resources for the good of the people is an ancient concept in India, practiced by revered kingdoms. This chapter discusses the original ideals of stewardship and how colonization caused a deterioration of this philosophy in favor of materialistic wealth generation. Colonization followed by the development of an industrialized and capitalistic leaning in the economy brought wealth and increased consumption for Indian people and also created multiple waste-related issues. These issues require a drastic overhaul of waste management practices, with particular attention to industrial ecology. Modern stewardship by India's CSR community is essential to prevent further environmental degradation due to poor waste management practices. The circular economy holds promise as a new economic system and philosophy that can refocus society towards the values of stewardship espoused by the nation's ancestors, while transitioning to a circular economy.

DOI: 10.4018/978-1-5225-8482-7.ch015

INTRODUCTION

Learning from historical examples is essential for progress. This chapter intends to uncover lessons from ancient Indian kingdoms to develop modern views on stewardship for solving urgent issues plaguing the nation today. To prevent further degradation of our collective environment, upgrading waste management (WM) policy and practices in India is essential. However, several challenges confront the current administrations in India, posing barriers to complete change. In this context, this chapter proposes Circular Economy (CE) as a far-reaching solution.

The chapter is organized as follows: Section 1 begins with a definition of stewardship, an ancient India example to re-learn stewardship and outlines modern social issues in WM. Section 2 briefly outlines the transitions of the Indian economy in the preceding centuries and decades. Section 3 elaborates on current WM issues in India such as municipal solid waste, landfill issues, and policy instruments. Section 4 expounds on the industrial ecology issues and prospects of waste to energy generation. Section 5 Discusses the proposal for economic stewardship by CSR, aiding environmental stewardship, and the role of CSR in CE. Section 6 conclusion.

BACKGROUND: A BRIEF HISTORY OF INDIA RELEVANT TO STEWARDSHIP

A seminal research proposed a definition for stewardship:

Stewardship is the responsible use (including conservation) of natural resources in a way that takes full and balanced account of the interests of society, future generations, and other species, as well as of private needs, and accepts significant answerability to society. (Worrell & Appleby, 2000).

Stewardship is a willingness to be deeply accountable for a larger body than ourselves and puts leadership in the background (Block, 1993). While our current governance systems continue to be plagued by some form of colonialism, it is desirable to explore both worldly and religious interpretations (Block, 1993; Worrell & Appleby, 2000). Stewardship aims towards collective-serving rather than self-serving behavior (Davis et al., 1997). Even within business corporations, empirical evidence lends some support to stewardship theory (Donaldson & Davis, 1991). Stewardship, while keeping opportunistic tendencies in check, maximizes the potential performance of the system as a whole. Another seminal research reminds us of the great threats of modern times, global warming and finite fossil fuels, and implores us to pursue the much-needed cross-disciplinary flow of ideas (Chapin et al., 2009). This chapter explores cross-disciplinarily, beginning with a historical example, and arriving at recommendations for stronger accountability in adopting the modern method of circular economy.

Temples as Socio-Economic Centers in Ancient India

An example of trusteeship was highlighted during the discovery of Padmanabhaswamy temple treasures in Kerala, India. Ancient Indian temples were prominent organizations entrusted with the well-being of the people. Literature from as early as 500 BC, quote descriptions of a temple in Travancore that received contributions from neighboring kingdoms collecting unimaginable wealth (Aiyangar, 1940; Induchudan, 1969; Parthasarathy, 1993; Subramanian, 2011). In 1931, when one of the temple vaults was opened, the last King of Travancore stated that all the wealth paid as taxes belonged to the temple (Ganesh, 2013; Srivathsan, 2011). The King demonstrated scrupulousness in governance values, a key stewardship value. Where economic wisdom was practiced well, the king undertook himself as the 'Servant of God' and a caretaker of the people, an ascendance from temple wealth to a source of social power (Ganesh, 2013). In 2012, more than a trillion dollars' worth of treasures were discovered in the temple vaults, causing media excitement over the newly ordained richest institution of the world (Doshi, 2016; Mishra, 2017; Sasidharan, 2011; Sugden, 2012).

The Padmanabhaswamy temple treasures discovery news helps to remind and redeem sound governance with a sense of moral and social responsibility. Deliberating on governance (Davis, Schoorman, & Donaldson, 1997; Donaldson & Davis, 1991), the identification of kings with their kingdom is conceivable, owing to their long tenures. Citing the agency theory (Donaldson et al. 1991; Eisenhardt, 1989), such an association could have stimulated the individual's ego, ultimately breeding immoral behavior such as spoiling oneself with excesses, but in fact, it didn't. The ideals demonstrated in ancient governance also reappears in the modern stewardship theory for CEOs and corporations, formed some 2500 years later (Davis et al., 1997; Donaldson et al. 1991). Stewardship places high demands of integrity upon the individual's conduct. India had begun the right stewardship pathways for its leaders, in its early post-colonial era (Bose, 2004). But after decades of disappointment following constitutionalizing, regrettably, Indian people have formed a mistrust of the 'system as a whole' (Gifford, 2011; Harriss, 2015; Motwani, 2001). Contrastingly, deep-seated values of stewardship have been demonstrated by private organizational leaders in India (Benjamin, 2016; Sarukkai, 2012). A few corporations stand out in their evolvement from trusteeship to stewardship (Basu & Sharma, 2014; Benjamin, 2016). Such modern corporate kingdoms transcend geographical boundaries, are active in promoting societal well-being among Indian people, and involve their employees with a sense of belonging (Fox, Ward, & Howard, 2002; Narwal & Singh, 2013; Pradhan et al., S. 2016).

Divergent views on the failure of trusteeship in India were expressed in the late 1700s by an Irish political theorist, Edmund Burke (Siraj, 2002; Conniff, 1993; Burke, 1785). Burke condemned the British East India company for its destruction of real Indian traditions, pointing out deficiencies of new replacement customs. Naturally concurring with Adam Smith on economic issues (Smith, 1976; West, 1969), Burke fine-tuned historians' awareness to the cultural dismantling of India. Lasting influences of such destructions, echo in the 21st century, visible in post-colonial nations' bureaucracies and their inability to change. The uniqueness of the Indian approach to Management is a concept that seems to mystify academicians and the corporate community (Panda & Gupta, 2007; Virmani, 2005). The common efforts of the educated in India, is attempting to administrate based on Western values. When anticipated results are under-achieved, they are frustrated. Highly contextualized indigenous studies with unique characteristics and history of a place may provide essential stimulus for decision-making processes and effective management (Azuma, 1984; Millenium, 2005; Rajaram & Das, 2006; Tsui, 2004;). It can be understood that India is a land of strong religious sentiments and the inclusion of the divine appears to fuse into matters of administration.

Social Issues in Waste Management

The concept of CE presents opportunities to develop alternate means to address waste as a source of wealth (UNEP, 2006; Webster, 2015) the updated definition of Circular Economy:

A regenerative system in which resource input and waste, emission, and energy leakage are minimized by slowing, closing, and narrowing material and energy loops. This can be achieved through long-lasting design, maintenance, repair, reuse, remanufacturing, refurbishing, and recycling. (Nancy & Jan, 2017)

In contrast to the earlier stated history, culture and religious sentiments prevalent in India, the modern notion of a CE of 'waste to wealth' is radically dissimilar to traditional Indian beliefs. Such culturally-preset minds might disagree about CE's promise of 'finding wealth in the garbage.' Although scientifically sound, many modern concepts need to be de-alienized for Indian people, and the Indian people's conversion from linear waste generation to a CE is now essential. Recollecting a much-debated past norm of the caste system in India, caste-based professions are disintegrating in modern India. Subtle manifestations frequently surface, and still a controversial topic to discuss (Dumont, 1980; Pruthi, 2004; Silverberg, 1968). During medieval times, the lowest caste was considered to be people in service of higher castes, an unfathomable contrast from the original ancient text *Arthasastra* (Rangarajan, 1992; Shamasastry, 1915). Arthasastra encourages lowest caste members to convert to a higher caste of peasants, expounded in literature as a forgotten transformation (Bamshad et al., 2001; Dirks, 2011). Consequently, the workers cleaning up the trash in India may still be perceived as 'unclean' people.

In modern times, the caste has lost definitive bearing on one's chosen profession, a significant socio-economic improvement from previous decades (Carswell & De Neve, 2014; Jodhka, 2017). Emancipating new mindsets by virtue of 'dignity of labor' is the antidote to persisting prejudices on caste-based discriminations. Implementing the internationally acclaimed Social Accountability 8000 (Rasche & Gilbert, 2012) can ensure recycling industry workers receive the same dignity as factory workers. Considered a corporate socially responsible outlook until now, freedom of association, collective bargaining, and rights against discrimination need to include transparent reporting of present-day schemes. Synergistic convergence of standards amongst the public, private and Union-based organizations aiming 'beyond compliance standards' becomes necessary (Fox et al., 2002; Gautam & Singh, 2010; Krishnamurthy. S & Pradhan. V (2018b); O'Rourke, 2003). Sustainability standards like SA 8000 address integrating the social dimensions and individual well-being, not a mere business case for the private sector (Frey and Stutzer, 2001; Nancy & Jan, 2017; Murray et al., 2015). Unlike modern consumption-waste patterns, recycling principles were not required in and ancient times. This exceptionally post-industrialization challenge of mass-manufactured-non-biodegradable products has very few historical antecedents. Therefore, an unprecedented attention becomes essential for designing recyclable products and urban landfills.

Preceding Transitions of the Indian Economy

In the exalted example of ancient stewardship, the well-being of a kingdom, its micro-communities were all aligned with the spiritual growth of people. Such kingdoms were ill-prepared for calamitous changes in political landscapes and military invasions (Crowder, 1964). As military pressures and economic trends morphed, socio-political changes within the kingdoms arose. Entire kingdoms were persuaded towards new capitalistic trends, a significant drift from noble leadership wherein human advancement became concomitant with materialistic values (Du Pisani, 2006). The industrial revolution exerted tremendous pressure upon colonies as the dominant thinking was 'to make more for their imperial kingdoms, exploit more from the colonies' (Siraj, 2002; Conniff, 1993; Crowder, 1964). Post world wars, further pressures of poverty pushed humanity further away from noble pursuits.

Until the 1990s, the Indian economy was stabilizing on the world stage, simultaneously dominated by the linear economy mode of industrialization. India was compelled to transition towards the ways of the future, viz, liberalization, privatization, and globalization of many sectors (Goyal, 2006). Impelled into vigorous socio-economic transitions, the internet, new inter-continental trade connections, a rise in production and services economy ensued (Batra, 2009; Chandrasekhar et al., 2006). A newly-found wealth for the average middle-class Indians prompted a sudden rise in consumerism, very pleasing to the middle and above class citizens. These socioeconomic changes were not accompanied by matching policy changes in eco-friendly measures, particularly the urban landscape. It took more than 300 years of complex transitions to change the Indian economy from exalted nobility to a country well-connected into the miseries and commercial delights of the world (Kapoor, 2004; Kapur, 1982). To make a U-turn, society urgently needs appropriate change initiations. To avoid a repetition of errors, consider "Those who cannot remember the past are condemned to repeat it" (Santayana, 1905).

The disintegration of Indian traditions and rising consumerism coincides with attempts to implant a modern economy upon ancient socio-cultural foundations, ignoring the Indian socio-cultural contexts (Channa, 2004; Panda & Gupta, 2007). Devoid of new learning, this path of replicating modernization re-induces linear economy dependencies. Such replications are digressions from abundant possibilities of non-linear functioning (Jawahir & Bradley, 2016; MacArthur, 2013). To sustain linear economies, planned obsolescence was practiced during the earlier economic crashes and world wars (Andrews, 2015). Such transitions mimicked wasteful linear economies but also served useful introductions to tighter 3Rs practice. If such developments are closely followed by legislated, incentivized adoptions of CE, the current proliferation of consumption patterns could be expected to convert to CE simultaneously (Andrews, 2015; MacArthur, 2013). Therefore, changes need to be made in conjunction with existing linear patterns. If history has taught us well, such a unification of purpose can generate enough goodwill to the planet's cause.

CURRENT WASTE MANAGEMENT ISSUES IN INDIA

Overview of Municipal Solid Waste

As discussed, waste management is becoming an increasingly pressing environmental issue for India as the country's population and economy continue to grow. While India still lags behind developing countries in terms of per capita waste produced, given the size of the population, increase in demand for consumer products, and the fact that few cities have a comprehensive recycling system, this waste is cause for concern (Nandy et al., 2015; Seetharaman, 2017; Vij, 2012; Yaduvanshi et al., 2016). Given these influences, particularly the use of more packaged material, it is estimated that India's per capita waste generation is increasing by about 1.3% annually (Asnani, 2006; Sharholy et al., 2008).

Within the broad picture of waste in India, Municipal Solid Waste (MSW) is one of the most pressing issues. 31% of India's population is urban; this ratio continues to increase due to migration from rural areas (CPHEEO, 2016; Sharholy et al., 2008). Continued urbanization will lead to growing MSW. Municipal corporations manage the collection, transportation, and disposal of MSW in India; however, many do not have the necessary financial resources, capacity or technology which results in an insufficient collection of waste, and waste buildups (Sharholy et al., 2008; Vij, 2012). Estimates of MSW composition vary depending on the source. The data in Table 1 published by the government in the 2016

SWM guidelines are generally in line with other estimates (Burge & Gangurde, 2015; Chatrath & Patil, 2017). The category "other" includes hazardous and e-waste, while "inert" refers to waste that's "not bio-degradable, recyclable or combustible. It includes the non-recyclable fraction of construction and demolition waste, street sweeping or dust and silt removed from the surface drains" (CPHEEO, 2016, p. 537).

A significant change in the subcategories of dry waste is the growth of plastics. Plastics have grown from less than 1% of the global waste stream in 1960 to 19% in 2014 (Satapathy, 2017). They are ubiquitously used in consumer goods with approximately 50% of plastics designed for single-use disposable applications (Satapathy, 2017). Currently, India produces much less plastic waste per capita than developed countries (a tenth of a U.S. resident), and about 70% is recovered for recycling (Nandy et al., 2015; Seetharaman, 2017). However, given the population size and the fact that few cities have a comprehensive recycling system, this plastic waste is becoming a growing issue for many municipalities (Seetharaman, 2017).

Glass is another recyclable commonly found in the waste stream. Improper disposal of glass can be hazardous as the shards of glass can be very dangerous to waste pickers, while sorting waste and if littered on the roadside as pedestrians, children and animals can be harmed by broken glass, and it lead to punctured tires (TNN, 2016a). Somewhat encouragingly though, previous research suggests that most glass bottles produced for consumption in India are recovered, and reused or recycled (Nandy et al., 2015). Up to 90% of newspaper waste in India is recovered by households and either reused or recycled. Paper is also often used as packaging material for roadside hawkers (Rana, Ganguly, & Gupta, 2015), suggesting it is already subject to the informal recycling system in India. Paper, along with glass and metal appear to have higher shares of MSW mix as population increases (Rana, Ganguly, & Gupta, 2015; Sharholy, Ahmad, Mahmood, & Trivedi, 2008), meaning that as urbanization continues, the share of recyclables in the waste stream will likely grow as well. This will require new and powerful technologies that can recover and reuse these products, especially plastics given their widespread use and lower recovery rate.

Wet waste (organic waste) is the largest category of MSW across many cities in the country (Burge & Gangurde, 2015; Chatrath & Patil, 2017; CPHEEO, 2016; Dahiwal, 2017; Gidde et al., 2008;). There are several examples of organic waste reuse in India ranging in scale, from composting at home (TNN, 2016b) to the use of biogas generators or power generation at the municipal level (PCMC, 2017). E-waste is globally one of the fastest growing forms of waste, due to the rapid pace of technological change and resultant short lifespan of electronic products; and due to economic growth and increases in penetration of electronics, e-waste in India is set to substantially increase over the coming years (Dwivedy & Mittal, 2012). This is concerning as e-waste usually contains very toxic materials that if not disposed of properly can be a significant health risk to humans; prolonged exposure to the heavy metals found

Table 1. Estimates of municipal solid waste mix in India

Year	Composition (%)							
	Biodegradables	Paper	Plastic/ Rubber	Metal	Glass	Rags	Other	Inert
1996	42.21	3.63	.60	.49	.60	-	-	45.13
2005	47.43	8.13	9.22	.50	1.01	4.49	4.016	25.16

Source: (CPHEEO, 2016, p. 43)

in e-waste can cause damage to the nervous system, brain, kidneys, blood and a number of other body functions (Bhat & Patil, 2014; Dwivedy & Mittal, 2012). E-waste products usually contain metals and high-value materials recyclable into new products, thus making them a lucrative recycling opportunity (Bhat & Patil, 2014; Dwivedy & Mittal, 2012).

One of the biggest challenges to recycling is non-segregation at the source. Segregation in India is usually done after disposal by waste pickers, who tend to avoid soiled objects, including plastics and paper, thus omitting them from the recycling process (Nandy et al., 2015; Seetharaman, 2017). Waste segregation at the source could help avoid this mixing of recyclable and non-recyclable waste, thus improving the recovery rate (CPHEEO, 2016; Das & Bhattacharyya, 2014). Sharholey et al. (2008) suggest that due to the challenges of operating an MSW management program "*the informal policy of encouraging the public to separate MSW and market it directly to the informal network appears to be a better option*" rather than direct management of all aspects of a municipal corporation. Local waste is often also littered by residents, which appears to be partly due to a focus on keeping one's environment clean (Sachs, 2014). Garbage is cleared from the house and doorstep as it may be seen as a threat to one's dignity or status; it doesn't matter where it is cleared as long as it is out of the house (Sachs, 2014; Vij, 2012). Such behavior leads to refuse to build up along streets and in other public areas. Other areas with a high density of street vendors or shops may not have access to a public garbage bin or the one in use is not emptied frequently, leading to a buildup of trash (Das & Bhattacharyya, 2014), thus contributing significantly to the litter problem. This littering can cause damage to infrastructure by clogging drainage systems (Rana, Ganguly, & Gupta, 2015).

Inadequate Landfill Planning

The WM issue is worthy of great concern, especially because major municipal landfills are at or already over capacity (Bhatia, 2017). The majority of major cities in India send over 75% of their waste to landfills (Vij, 2012). These landfills are generally poorly designed and managed, lacking a control system for byproducts like leachate and gas, and are often open which results in unhygienic conditions (Mani & Singh, 2016; Sharholy, Ahmad, Mahmood, & Trivedi, 2008); in fact, nearly half of major cities do not have sanitary landfills, including Greater Mumbai and Delhi (Vij, 2012). According to the 2016 MSW Rules, these landfills are only meant to contain non-biodegradable and inert waste, commingled waste (mixed waste) not found suitable for waste processing, pre-processing and post-processing rejects from waste processing sites, and non-hazardous waste not being processed or recycled (CPHEEO, 2016). However, given the issues with segregation, in many municipalities all types of waste make their way to landfills.

Waste Policy Instruments

To address the MSW issue, the Government of India in 2016 released a Municipal Solid Waste Manual as part of its Swachh Bharat Mission, intended to provide information and guidance to municipal bodies regarding "planning, design, implementation, and monitoring of MSW management systems" (CPHEEO, 2016). The manual contains a thorough description of WM issues and considerations and includes information on segregation, collection, transportation, treatment, landfills, public education, and several other aspects critical to the management of MSW (CPHEEO, 2016). These guidelines reference the solid waste management (SWM) rules, which recommend three basic categories for waste segregation, specifically dry waste, wet waste, and hazardous materials (CPHEEO, 2016; Mani & Singh,

2016). The guidelines also specify waste to energy as a guiding principle and preferable practice to landfilling (CPHEEO, 2016). The government also released a set of Plastic Waste Management rules in 2016, mandating that local bodies "shall be responsible for developing and setting up of infrastructure for segregation, collection, storage, transportation, processing and disposal of the plastic waste either on its own or by engaging agencies or producers" (MoEFCC, 2016). These rules include implementing by-laws regarding the plastic collection and that the system must be set up as of one year of the publication of the new rules on March 18, 2016 (MoEFCC, 2016). However, some cities have been accused of shirking these laws (Mehta, 2014).

Some cities have also pursued improved WM processes as part of the Smart City initiative, as sanitation and solid waste management are core infrastructure elements in Smart City guidelines (MOUD, 2015). However, the Smart City initiative, focuses on more than just WM, as can be seen in its mission statement "The Smart Cities Mission is a bold new initiative to drive economic growth and improve the quality of life of people by enabling local development and harnessing technology as a means to create smart outcomes for citizens" (PCMC, n.d.,). It has been suggested many of the cities participating in the smart cities initiative are having challenges with WM, possibly because issues like infrastructure and development have received more attention (Banerjee, 2016).

An emphasis on social and political will to change has been debated well in India. This will to change is morphing into determined action today, with bold new schemes like Swaccha Bharat Abhiyaan addressing culture and behavioral change (Mission, 2007; Sinha, 2016; Teltumbde, 2014). The pathway may have begun well, but the determination to see the end of the change process has to be continually reinforced. The nation-state does not will itself unless there is an adequate consensus among many types of stakeholders. Instead of romanticizing the traditional rural communities, policy change needs to develop adequate consensus to traverse from 'solidarity networks' of traditional small industries to 'innovation networks' sharing knowledge and technology (Woolcock & Narayan, 2000; Barr 1998; Van Dijk, 1997).

CIRCULAR ECONOMY AND INDUSTRIAL ECOLOGY

Overview of the Circular Economy

The Circular Economy concept aims to minimize waste and include non-renewable energy use through the redesign of products and processes (Mathews, Tang, & Tan, 2011; Murray et al., 2017). As pointed out by Murray et al. (2017), the name alone suggests it is emphatically positioned as the opposite to the linear economy; where the linear economy turns raw materials into waste, CE uses waste as an input thereby attempting to have no impact on the environment (Yaduvanshi et al., 2016; Murray et al., 2017). Figure 1 illustrates CE using waste as an input.

The redesign of systems to minimize waste is pivotal, especially in a country like India where many jurisdictions do not have adequate waste disposal or recycling systems in place (Sharholy et al., 2008). This waste builds up rapidly, not only fueled by growing wealth and consumerism (Nandy et al., 2015; Seetharaman, 2017; Yaduvanshi et al., 2016) but because of the product design itself. It has been suggested by Paul Hawken that "over 90% of the original materials used in the production of, or contained within, the goods made in the US become waste within six weeks of sale" (Cohen-Rosenthal, 2004) which leads to 3200 pounds of waste for every 100 pounds of product produced (Cohen-Rosenthal, 2004). A focus on the reduction of waste at the source will minimize waste that enters the waste stream.

Figure 1. Circular economy illustration
Source: Ellen MacArthur Foundation (n.d)

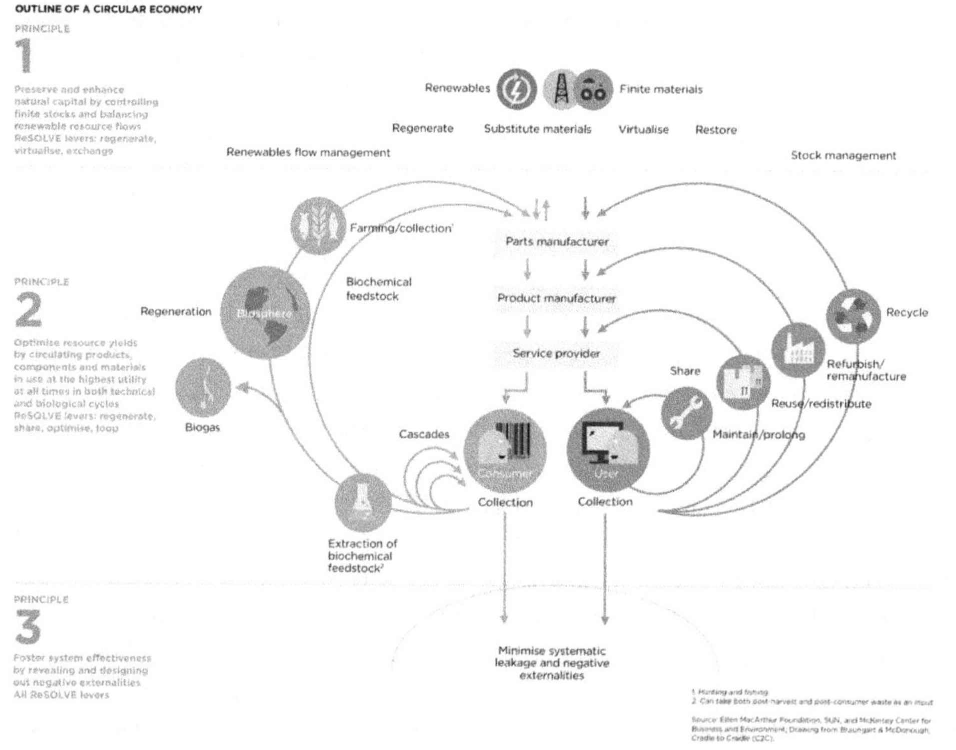

Principles of CE are already being exercised to some extent at the household and municipal level in cities such as Pimpri Chinchwad. As of May 2017, the Pimpri Chinchwad Municipal Corporation (PCMC) began requiring that households separate wet waste, dry waste, hazardous materials and e-waste (Dahiwal, 2017), and residents are being encouraged to use their wet waste as fertilizer in their home (TNN, 2016b). Additionally, large producers of waste like hotels and are required to collect wet waste separately from dry waste (Chatrath & Patil, 2017), and it appears the city also has plans to route wet waste from hotels to a biogas generator (PCMC, 2017). In nearby Pune, the Pune Municipal Corporation (PMC) has pursued multiple initiatives, all aimed at reducing the amount of waste going to landfills, including the operation of biogas converts and bio-methane plants for food waste (Dalal, 2016; PMC, n.d.).

The Role of Industrial Ecology in a Circular Economy

The concept of waste recycling is also a defining component of the theory of industrial ecology. Similar to CE, industrial ecology proposes the idea of a closed loop system that mimics natural ecosystems to minimize waste (Gibbs & Deutz, 2007; Singhal & Kapur, 2002). Korhonen (2001) referred to this concept as round put, described as cycling of matter and energy between actors; an extension of the idea first proposed by Frosch and Gallopoulos (1989). Key to this concept is the idea that "processes and industries are seen as interacting systems rather than comprising isolated components in a system of linear flows" (Gibbs & Deutz, 2007, p. 1684). Also referred to as industrial symbiosis, this concept has been attempted to be made a reality in eco-industrial parks around the world (Gibbs & Deutz, 2007;

Mathews et al., 2011; Singhal & Kapur, 2002). This has been attempted in many countries globally, but the most popular and successful example is that of Kalundborg Eco-Industrial Park (EIP) in Denmark (Gibbs & Deutz, 2007; Korhonen, 2001). This EIP creates value from waste by using the by-products of one company's operations as an input into the other. For example, heat from the power generating stations is used for warming nearby homes as well as in a local fish farm, and by-products from a health-care research facility are processed into fertilizers for local farmers (Ehrenfeld & Gertler, 1997; IISD, n.d.).

Criticisms have been made of Kalundborg, particularly regarding its use of fossil fuels as the primary inputs given that the two of the major participants are an oil refinery and a coal-fired power plant (Korhonen, 2001). However, much like with CE, the concept of industrial ecology is in its early stages, and the implementation of these ideas will have to co-exist with the linear economy until such a time that renewable energy is a viable input and the replacement of the old system with the new is complete. As with CE, industrial ecology may exist at multiple levels, from the individual firm to a cluster of companies, up to a regional or global level (Gibbs & Deutz, 2007; Roberts, 2004). Activities at the inter-firm level though, especially of firms nearby (e.g., eco-industrial parks) provide greater the opportunity for economies of scale to be achieved (Roberts, 2004).

Policy Considerations for a Circular Economy in India

One of the main barriers to industrial ecology and the cycling of waste in the U.S. is the regulatory framework surrounding the disposal of waste (Gibbs & Deutz, 2007). Research from the U.S. found that waste regulations, particularly surrounding hazardous, constricted the amount of waste reuse due to potential legal issues (Gibbs & Deutz, 2007). While a problem in developed countries like the U.S., the regulatory framework for waste disposal and industrial ecology in India is immature by comparison and less enforced (Mani & Singh, 2016; Singhal & Kapur, 2002; Zhu et al., 2008). This presents an opportunity for India to build regulations that can facilitate industrial symbiosis; however, this must be done before continued globalization and interconnectedness results in the country developing static, linear systems similar to developed economies (Ellen MacArthur Foundation, 2016). Similar to developed countries in the 1960s, India is now entering a stage of rapid economic growth and consumerism, leading to increased waste. As such, the country is at risk of implementing similarly linear waste management processes. However, if principles of CE are successfully adopted, this could present India the opportunity to "leapfrog" developed nations into a progressive age of waste minimization based on closed loop systems. It has been argued that for industrial ecology to further blossom in India, state, and the central government must develop coordinated policies that target WM, without restricting innovation or the ability to be flexible to meet this pressing demand (Ashton & Shenoy, 2015). These cooperative efforts are required for ambitious projects in India to succeed (Krishnamurthy et al., 2017). India could follow the role of China, where laws, funding, and policy were all directed towards industrial ecology and CE (Mathews et al., 2011).

Policies in India are needed to encourage cycling of waste and CE (Ashton & Shenoy, 2015). With the passing of the 74th Constitutional Amendment, Urban Local Bodies (ULBs), as opposed to states, became responsible for MSW management (GoI, 2008). To aid the transition, the government produced a list of MSW rules in 2000, which was followed by an updated set of rules in 2016 as part of its Swachh Bharat Mission (CPHEEO, 2016). The rules are intended to provide information and guidance to municipal bodies regarding "planning, design, implementation, and monitoring of MSW management systems" (CPHEEO, 2016). Despite the publication of these rules though, compliance with the rules of disposal is estimated to be less than 5% (GoI, 2008), with open landfills (GoI, 2008; Sharholy et al., 2008). This indicates that there is still a large gap between proposed solutions and the successful implementation of those solutions; however, it also indicates a massive opportunity, as it demonstrates that there is not an established system or collection of infrastructure that needs to be overcome to adopt new and creative waste treatment options. There are several reasons suggested for this including improper segregation, insufficient funding, outdated equipment and technology, poor planning, and opposition to siting of new facilities (GoI, 2008; Sharholy et al., 2008; Vij, 2012). Though another reason suggested by the government, as part of the National Action Plan on Climate Change (NAPCC) released in 2008, is that the MSW rules were too prescriptive and focused on specific treatment options (GoI, 2008). As would be echoed by Ashton and Shenoy (2015), the report suggests focusing the MSW rules on performance as opposed to prescribing specific technologies or processes, including the sharing of infrastructure across regions to enable economies of scale (GoI, 2008). Additional suggestions include recognition of the informal sector (i.e. rag-pickers) as a significant player in the WM process and removal of incentives and regulations that encumber the optimal utilization of non-hazardous materials (GoI, 2008), many of which have been echoed by other researchers (Vij, 2012; Mani & Singh, 2016). This action plan is set to be updated in 2017, and one of the purported focus areas will be waste-to-energy (Hindu, 2017). If the political establishment can craft a regulatory framework that encourages innovation, access to technology, and the reuse of materials, CE may begin to gain traction. However, previous policies have been ignored for WM, and lessons must be learned from those failures.

Industrial ecology has gained a foothold both at the firm level and inter-firm level in India. At the individual firm level, companies like Tata have invested in waste recycling during steel production; at the inter-firm level there are a handful of examples of industrial symbiosis where by-products from one process are used by another industry (Chiu & Yong, 2004), such as in Nanjangud where agricultural by-products are used in place of coal (Ashton & Shenoy, 2015).

Prospects of Waste-to-Energy Solutions

Waste-to-energy incineration technology fits seamlessly into the vision and principles of industrial ecology (Roberts, 2004). These technologies disrupt the linear waste model and help to close the loop so that waste can be used as an input. Various types of incineration exist, including Mass Burn/RDF incineration technology, Gasification technology, pyrolysis technology, and plasma arc gasification technology (Saini, Rao, & Patil, 2012). Incineration of waste holds promise in India given its potential to convert large volumes of waste to energy every day, and because of the existing energy market (Pillai, 2005, as cited in Saini, Rao, & Patil, 2012; Ghosh, 2016). Additionally, research by Saini, Rao, and Patil (2012) determined that, based on the volume of MSW created in India, by 2020 incineration based waste-to-energy technologies could generate over 3000 MW. While this amount of electricity produced represents less than 1% of the installed energy capacity of India (Ministry of Power, 2017), the value is not strictly on the energy produced, but in the reuse and elimination of landfill waste. A prime example is the case of Delhi. In March of 2017, India's largest waste-to-energy incineration plant was launched in North Delhi, with the capacity to turn 2,000 metric tonnes of waste to 24 MW of energy daily (Sharma, 2017). The plant will use waste from the Narela-Bawana landfill, the only one of Delhi's four landfills that are not overflowing, and will help control the waste accumulation at that site (Sharma, 2017). Such a perfect example illustrates the pressing need to build more similar plants to address landfill waste.

The Ministry of New and Renewable Energy (MNRE) has already developed policies to support the recovery of energy from waste. The MNRE provides financial support up to Rs. 10 crores per project as a capital subsidy, and the Power Ministry has agreed to increase their purchase price of energy from WTE plants (Mani & Singh, 2016). However, the costs of mitigating emissions from these plants remain high and represent a barrier to development (Mani & Singh, 2016), though new technologies appear able to control emissions (Ghosh, 2016) better. These plants though also usually need well-segregated waste, as high moisture contents can make incineration challenging (Narayana, 2009; Sharholy, Ahmad, Mahmood, & Trivedi, 2008; Zhu, Asnani, Zurbrugg, Anapolsky, & Mani, 2008). As discussed, the largest category of MSW in India is food waste or wet waste, and as the name implies, this waste has a high moisture content making it less attractive for incineration. Therefore, the policies spelled out in the SWM rules could have a significant impact on the viability of waste-to-energy incineration. Nevertheless, it is a promising sign, which the government has stated that waste-to-energy will be adopted as a focus area in the NAPCC, as it may represent a solution to addressing India's overflowing landfills.

DISCUSSION: MAKING A CASE FOR ECONOMIC STEWARDSHIP BY CSR AIDING ENVIRONMENTAL STEWARDSHIP IN INDIA

The Philosophy of 'Determination to Change'

Although capitalism had made the world rich from the exploitation of natural resources, it has unfortunately ignored the long-term effects on the ecological, social and multilateral characteristics of each country. Learning from history, bargaining for one set of gains with another set of hindrances, with the hope of a future adjustment or adaptation, had led to disastrous long-term transitions for the world. To avoid such unfavorable transitions in the future, envisioning wholesome changes are necessary. Therefore, a few positive changes happening within a few circles of the economy is an incomplete success. The role of higher education institutions in leading research and learning by action is essential (Krishnamurthy & Pradhan, 2018a; Krishnamurthy & Pradhan, 2018b; Rao et al., 2017). We posit that the best approaches include: participation of all at the community, state, and continent levels; long-term commitment of many states; implementing to enable a snow-balling effect towards CE. The framework for this discussion is illustrated in Figure 2.

The Role of CSR in a Circular Economy

Ancient governance values strong emphasized on respecting and living in co-existence with nature (Curtie, 1998; Dutt et al., 2015). Ancient Indian literature preaches "It is our duty to protect the environment, conserve natural resources and maintain ecological balance." (Baranwal, 2011; Dutt et al., 2015). Whereas, modern India has transformed into service and industrial economy governed by democracy principles (Eichengreen & Gupta, 2011; Mehrotra et al., 2014; Gaur et al., 2014). With the embedded modern kingdoms of business corporations already practicing stewardship in social responsibility, the call for CSR actions to address WM by CE is the need of the hour. A majority of CSR actions pertain to critical issues of national development such as education, watershed development, rural development, addressing familiar critical issues within Sustainable Development Goals (SDGs) (Gupta, 2007; Majumdar & Saini, 2016; Mehta & Aggarwal, 2015). From a CSR viewpoint, waste management is seen

Figure 2. Circular economy for India: representative model for steering actions in 'waste-to-energy' domain (Compiled by: Authors)

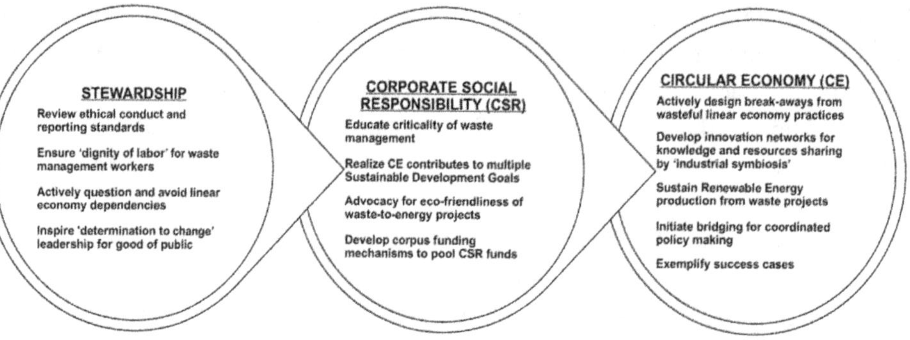

as primarily an urban issue, with waste generated by the middle and upper socio-economic sections (Appadurai, 2001; Benjamin, 2000). We contend that, although waste management may not be directly addressing chronic issues such as poverty eradication or rural development, the urgency of environmental degradation is colossal.

Additionally, the UN SDGs support the case for more active WM practices in India. (Watal, Advisor, & Aayog, 2017; Verbruggen et al., 2010; Morrissey & Browne, 2004; Baud et al., 2001). In the order of relevance, SDG 9: Industry, Innovation and Infrastructure, SDG 11: Sustainable Cities and Communities, SDG 17: Partnering for the goals, SDG 15: Life on land, SDG 12: Responsible consumption and production, SDG 7: Affordable and clean energy, SDG 8: Decent work and Economic growth. Considering the alarming proportions of urban waste and inadequate WM practices in India (Garlapati, 2016; Paul, Dutta, & Krishna, 2014; Regina Dube, 2014; Yaduvanshi et al, 2016), Urban Local Bodies are grievously outmatched in comparison to volume of waste generated (Saini, Rao, Patil, 2012). Modern technologies such as high-quality incinerators are capital-intensive. They do not propose a strong case for civic authority in India, given priority for historically chronic issues of poverty and rural development (Dube et al., 2014; Joshi & Ahmed, 2016; Kumar et al., 2009).

However, if the waste is not treated appropriately today and ranked below other issues, it is likely to scale up to dangerous problems in the future, one where our collective living environment is irreparably damaged. A 'short-term benefits' approach would result in a 'catch-up' game to battle against environmental degradation. Short-term approaches would create stronger dependencies on even more expensive modern technology, thus losing any economic sensibility. If we are to avoid the hazardous future consequences of waste build-up, we have to invest more in modern technology. We posit that capital-intensive investments in SWM could find enthusiastic sponsors among businesses ready to fund CSR actions. A key challenge in many CSR actions is allocating funds to sustainable social responsibility actions (GoI, 2013; Majumdar & Saini, 2016; Desai et al., 2015; Singh & Verma, 2014). Many corporations partner with NGOs to identify project engagement and continue with funding to recipients to 'give back to society.' The commitment of workers, a plethora of social issues and sustenance of interest in such project are the usual challenges (Gupta, 2007; Jammulamadaka, 2013; Kansal, 2012; Narwal & Singh, 2013). Many WM CSR actions about demonstrations of *Swachh Bharat Abhiyaan* are endearing examples, but couldn't address the urgent reality of piling tonnes of urban waste.

Also, most of the corporations shy away from high capital WM investments, apprising us of the need for spreading WM awareness in the CSR community, and enrich next level policy-think on CSR law. We posit that key discussions should be about: 'Does corporate investment in an incinerator in an urban area count as a profit-motivated investment or CSR? Does the salary and wages of WM employees count as CSR expenses of the funding organization? How can the existing expertise on the high-tech waste treatment of a company be shared for the public good? Why are CSR funding for incinerators an urgent need for urban India environment?' We contend that: multi-company CSR funds for environmental sustainability, already swelling into massive sums, need to focus on urgent needed urban WM projects. A centralized CSR corpus funds generation linked to on-ground implementation enables bulking of financial resources and simultaneously accounting for national and international reporting standards (GoI, 2011; Kilby, 2013: Hamschmidt & Pirson, 2018). Only half of the India companies have formed their CSR committee, and Significant sums of mandatory CSR funds remained unspent (TOI, 2018). Such funds could be used to develop CE-based WM companies within the social economy sector, avoiding sporadic or ceremonial investments (Singh 2014; Mitra et al., 2018). WM companies aspiring to leapfrog over older technologies need to establish high tech incinerators, robust waste collection fleet of lorries and address energy intensive reclaim processes such as recycling plastic wastes (Seetharaman, 2017; MoEFCC, 2016).

Literature critiques CSR as a tortured concept (Jamali et al., 2015; Godfrey & Hatch, 2007, p. 87), with many controversies (Jamali et al., 2015; Matten & Moon, 2008). Occasionally the very accountability of accounting standards is questioned (Behnam & Maclean, 2012). A seminal cross-disciplinary research, while comparing the early and late phases of diffusion in sustainability assurance reporting, notably criticizes that "several MNCs project a decoupled or symbolic image of accountability through sustainability assurance, thereby undermining the credibility of this verification practice" (Perego and Kolk, 2012). We observe that sometimes mere reporting takes precedence over concrete social responsibility action. In these evolving contemplations about credible accounting for an organizations' social responsibility, we recommend that ethical conduct needs to be rigorously reviewed before the policy-making process. For democracies such as the Indian Government, accountability towards society has been embedded within the CSR amendment to Companies Act (GoI, 2013). This chapter aims to re-inspire stewardship values, to support healthy debating for policy think tanks, to steer firmer ethics and better accountability, for the companies presently in the first phase of adherence to CSR law. In the next phase of policy upgrades and CSR practices diffusion, the hesitation of accountants to draw precise conclusions from sustainability assurances can be precluded, and decoupling of ethical standards and CSR practices can be avoided, thus enhancing legitimacy (Perego and Kolk, 2012; Behnam & Maclean, 2012; GoI, 2013).

Deconstruction of the Old Economy

Deconstruction of the old linear economy is essential for the evolvement to a circular economy. The stasis of prevailing methods may reach indolence until 'unwillingness to change' becomes an established mindset. Power sharing, loss of control for ULBs and political risks may pose major threats (Joshi & Ahmed, 2016). To buoy out of this wicked problem, destruction of old methods becomes a necessary evil. Envisioning CE methods will be scant without envisioning the deconstruction of the old. Given the solutions discussed, the deconstruction-redirection-reconstruction process requires careful planning as listed in Table 2. Additionally, we recommend future research directions to explore into: funding pat-

Table 2. **Summary of issues, trends and recommendations**

No.	Issue / Problem	Current Trends	Recommendations/ Solutions
STEWARDSHIP, HISTORIC, and SOCIAL PERSPECTIVES			
1	Loss of Stewardship values over long history	Few modern corporations demonstrate stewardship very well	**A)** Inspire review of existing stewardship principles, in the context of following newly implemented CSR law in India. **B)** Extend This key for strategic planning to modern standards such as Circular Economy (CE)
2	Prejudice by caste-based discrimination	Social Accountability 8000 standards is internationally accepted	**A)** Advocacy for generating new mindsets by virtue of 'dignity of labor' by awareness and employment programs **B)** Adherence to SA 8000 standards to pro-actively prevent discrimination and intervene in timely manner **C)** Periodic evaluation of WM employees' empowerment
3	Replicating modernization re-induces linear economy dependencies	New sporadic attempts for Circular Economy in India	**A)** Develop standards for CE, verifying and updating CE indicators on par with international standards. **B)** Develop rethink programs for manufacturers
WASTE MANAGEMENT IN INDIA, AS OF 2018			
4	Philosophy of 'Determination to Change'	Enthusiasm in India's development in many sectors, including WM	**A)** Envision wholesome changes **B)** Encourage role of higher education institutions in leading research and learning by action
5	Many municipal corporations' inadequate finances, capacity, technology for solid waste	Modernizing India with policies like Swachh Bharat Mission	**A)** Developing adequate funding and capacities for municipal corporations **B)** Encourage further adherence to MSW Manual **C)** Encourage stakeholders to meaningfully challenge, adequately modify norms for better performance
6	Non-segregation at the source of waste	Sporadic adoptions of segregation at home, and segregation at municipal level waste disposal	**A)** Mandating strict rules for waste segregation and 3Rs practices **B)** Periodical Impacts evaluations study
7	Matching waste to disposal of organic waste	Sporadic adoptions of composting at home, and biogas power generation at municipal level	**A)** Developing accountability standards **B)** Verifying adherence and revising on annual basis to ensure rigor in standards
8	Inappropriate disposal of e-waste	Enhanced awareness programs for e-waste disposal, collection campaigns. E-waste rules updated in 2016	Persuade manufacturers to adopt better e-waste collection standards, encourage CE adoption by re-designing products
9	Inadequate Landfill Planning, SWM rules	New SWM rules, specifying waste to energy as a guiding principle and preferable practice to landfilling	**A)** Developing stronger accountability standards **B)** Verifying adherence and annual review/ revision to ensure rigor in standards **C)** Building capacity processes for key stakeholders of the waste chain **D)** Program evaluation
10	Some Indian cities have been accused of shirking these Plastic Waste Management rules of 2016	Plastic waste regulation recently amended in 2018; Evolving regulation find inconsistent adoption among cities; Patchy improvements in WM processes as part of the Smart City initiative	**A)** Mandating plastic waste segregation and 3Rs practices **B)** Encourage CE practices and aspirations to be a smart city
CIRCULAR ECONOMY AND INDUSTRIAL ECOLOGY			
11	Weak counteraction against existing linear economy	Few success stories in India; Learning from other countries about CE practices	**A)** Educate CE principles and advocacy for adoption of CE practices **B)** Persuade with chances to "leapfrog" into a progressive age of waste minimization and closed loop systems
12	Industrial systems with isolated components, linear flows of energy and matter	Industrial ecology is still in early stages, and co-exist with the linear economy; is still a 'solidarity networks' of traditional industries	**A)** Develop 'innovation networks' for sharing knowledge, technology regarding cycling of matter and energy between industries instead of isolated components **B)** Build regulations that can facilitate industrial symbiosis
13	Regulatory framework for waste disposal and industrial ecology in India is immature in comparison to developed countries	Govt of India MSW rules were updated in 2016 as part of its Swachh Bharat Mission. Guidance given to municipal bodies on planning, design, implementation, and monitoring of MSW management systems	With a 'will to change', pursue the cycles in needs assessment-policy design-regulations development-implementation-measure impacts-feedback to policy-correction
14	Viable renewable energy generation from India's overflowing landfills is not well supported in policy	Few success cases such as North Delhi, Pune of waste-to-energy technologies. Active support by Ministry of Renewable Energy (MNRE) policies, financial support, agreement to purchase renewable energy	**A)** Pursue coordinated policy making and joint action responses within the National Action Plan on Climate Change and renewable energy bodies **B)** Building capacity by sharing of renewable energy generation infrastructure across regions to enable economies of scale
15	Role of CSR investments for high-tech incinerators is an urgent but unaddressed need	Currently discussed by policy think tanks in India. Removal of barriers is being considered	**A)** Advocacy for the critical need of SWM among CSR funders **B)** A centralized approach for investment to generate corpus funding linked to on-ground implementation is suitable, enabling bulking of financial resources and simultaneously accounting for national and international reporting standards **C)** Most importantly, creating new government departments specific to SWM for enhancing accountability throughout the waste chain

terns, particularly the barriers for corpus funding; CSR relevant corporate governance for small firms; hindrances for bridging on-ground hi-tech WM implementations and CSR fund channels.

Deconstruction of old methods hold a promising future for India. Ellen Macarthur Foundation suggests that pursuing CE based development, India could realize annual financial benefits of 40 lakh crore rupees by 2050, primarily by costs reduction in the areas of transportation, food, and construction (Ellen MacArthur Foundation, 2016). Environmental benefits abound, such as national GHG emissions reductions of 44%, in-line with the Paris Agreement and a 38% reduction in the use of non-renewable resources (Ellen MacArthur Foundation, 2016). A few successful CE entrepreneurs in India illustrate modern-day feasibility. *Banyannation* is a company that pioneered in closed loop recycling initiative enabled by Internet of Things (IoT) and cloud technology to connect last mile collectors in the informal sector of plastic waste chains (Yadagiri, 2018). Another well-known company *Geocyle* has applied CE to WM, avoids landfilling and fosters industrial symbiosis (Prabhune, 2018). Both examples illustrate the new expanding employment opportunities (Siddhartha, 2018).

CONCLUSION

This chapter elaborated a proposal for Circular Economy (CE) as a far-reaching solution for modern India's urban waste management issues. Such solutions can be made meaningful when imbued with the lessons drawn from history, culture, social issues and reminders from India's past economic transitions. An ancient Indian principle was presented as a persuasive example of stewardship. Such stewardship practices eroded over time, during transitions to capitalistic linear economic models. Linear waste generations and CE as a solution was discussed elaborately to encourage new-think for renewable energy generation. A refocus on ethical conduct and stewardship, underpinned by industrial ecology and waste-to-renewable-energy, promises an escape from catastrophic waste accumulation. Active support from many stakeholders such as policymakers, CSR community and technologists is essential. Importantly, a meaningful adoption of CE will require deconstruction of old methods. As nature has taught us, from death comes new life.

REFERENCES

Ahmed, S. (2002). The Theater of the Civilized Self: Edmund Burke and the East India Trials. *Representations (Berkeley, Calif.)*, *78*(1), 30. doi:10.1525/rep.2002.78.1.28

Aiyangar, S. K. (1940). *Seran Vanji: Vanji, the Capital of the Cheras. Superintendent.* Cochin Government Press.

Andrews, D. (2015). The circular economy, design thinking and education for sustainability. *Local Economy*, *30*(3), 305–315. doi:10.1177/0269094215578226

Appadurai, A. (2001). Deep democracy: Urban governmentality and the horizon of politics. *Environment and Urbanization*, *13*(2), 23–43. doi:10.1177/095624780101300203

Ashton, W., & Shenoy, M. (2015). Industrial ecology in India: converging traditional practice and modern environmental protection. In P. Deutz, D. I. Lyons, & J. Bi (Eds.), *International Perspectives on Industrial Ecology* (pp. 12–29). Cheltenham, UK: Edward Elgar Publishing Limited. doi:10.4337/9781781003572.00010

Asnani, P. U. (2006). Solid Waste Management. In A. Rastogi (Ed.), *India Infrastructure Report, 2006: Urban Infrastructure* (pp. 160–189). Oxford University Press.

Azuma, H. (1984). Psychology in a non-western country. *International Journal of Psychology, 19*(1-4), 45–55. doi:10.1080/00207598408247514

Bamshad, M., Kivisild, T., Watkins, W. S., Dixon, M. E., Ricker, C. E., & Rao, B. B. (2001). Genetic evidence on the origins of Indian caste populations. *Genome Research, 11*(6), 994–1004. doi:10.1101/gr.GR-1733RR PMID:11381027

Banerjee, P. (2016, February). Gone to waste: How India is drowning in garbage. *Hindustan Times.*

Baranwal, S. (2011). Concern for Environment in Ancient India. *Renewable Research Journal, 1*, 1-9. Accessed in Sep 2017 at www.rexjournal.org.managewebsiteportal.com/files/documents/Concern-for-Environment-in-Ancient-India--Shamik-Baranwal.pdf

Barr, A. (1998). *Enterprise Performance and the Functional Diversity of Social Capital.* Working Paper Series 98-1. Institute of Economics and Statistics, University of Oxford.

Basu, S., & Sharma, A. (2014). Exploring Stewardship as an Antecedent Behavioural Trait of Social Entrepreneurs. *The Journal of Entrepreneurship, 23*(1), 19–33. doi:10.1177/0971355713513347

Batra, S. (2009). Strengthening human capital for knowledge economy needs: An Indian perspective. *Journal of Knowledge Management, 13*(5), 345–358. doi:10.1108/13673270910988150

Baud, I. S. A., Grafakos, S., Hordijk, M., & Post, J. (2001). Quality of life and alliances in solid waste management: Contributions to urban sustainable development. *Cities (London, England), 18*(1), 3–12. doi:10.1016/S0264-2751(00)00049-4

Behnam, M., & MacLean, T. L. (2011). Where is the accountability in international accountability standards?: A decoupling perspective. *Business Ethics Quarterly, 21*(1), 45–72. doi:10.5840/beq20112113

Benjamin, N. (2016, July-December). JRD TATA (1904-93) and India's Economic Aspirations. Jharkhand Journal of Development and Management Studies. *XISS, Ranchi, 14*(3 & 4), 7111–7712.

Benjamin, S. (2000). Governance, economic settings and poverty in Bangalore. *Environment and Urbanization, 12*(1), 35–56. doi:10.1177/095624780001200104

Bhat, V., & Patil, Y. (2014). E-waste Consciousness and Disposal Practices among Residents of Pune City. *Procedia: Social and Behavioral Sciences, 133*(May), 491–498. doi:10.1016/j.sbspro.2014.04.216

Bhatia, A. (2017, April). *The Weight Of Waste In India: The Need For "One Nation, One Policy."* Banega Swachh India.

Block, P. (1993). *Stewardship: Choosing service over self-interest.* Berrett-Koehler Publishers.

Bose, S. (2004). Decolonization and state building in South Asia. *Journal of International Affairs*, 95–113.

Burge, N., & Gangurde, S. (2015). Solid Waste Management in PCMC (3R's Principle). *International Journal of Science and Research, 4*(5), 476–481.

Burke, E. (1785, February 28). *Speech on "The Nabob of Arcot's Debts"*. Burke delivered a now-famous speech, wherein he condemned the damage to India by the East India Company.

Carswell, G., & De Neve, G. (2014). T-shirts and tumblers: Caste, dependency and work under neoliberalisation in south India. *Contributions to Indian Sociology, 48*(1), 103–131. doi:10.1177/0069966713502423

Chandrasekhar, C. P., Ghosh, J., & Roychowdhury, A. (2006). The 'demographic dividend' and young India's economic future. *Economic and Political Weekly*, 5055–5064.

Channa, S. M. (2004). Globalization and modernity in India: A gendered critique. *Urban Anthropology, 33*(1), 37–71.

Chapin, F. S. III, Kofinas, G. P., & Folke, C. (Eds.). (2009). *Principles of ecosystem stewardship: resilience-based natural resource management in a changing world.* Springer Science & Business Media.

Chatrath, H., & Patil, Y. (2017). Waste management in the Pimpri Chinchwad, Pune, India. *Green Chemistry and Technology Letters, 3*(1), 1–8. doi:10.18510/gctl.2017.311

Chiu, A. S. F., & Yong, G. (2004). On the industrial ecology potential in Asian developing countries. *Journal of Cleaner Production, 12*(8–10), 1037–1045. doi:10.1016/j.jclepro.2004.02.013

Cohen-Rosenthal, E. (2004). Making sense out of industrial ecology: A framework for analysis and action. *Journal of Cleaner Production, 12*(8–10), 1111–1123. doi:10.1016/j.jclepro.2004.02.009

Conniff, J. (1993). Burke and India: The Failure of the Theory of Trusteeship. *Political Research Quarterly, 46*(2), 291–309. doi:10.1177/106591299304600205

CPHEEO. (2016). Central Public Health and Environmental Engineering Organization (CPHEEO). Municipal Solid Waste Management Manual, Part II. *Man.*

Crowder, M. (1964). Indirect rule—French and British style. *Africa, 34*(03), 197–205. doi:10.2307/1158021

Curtie, B. (1998). OP Dwivedi, India's Environmental Policies, Programmes and Stewardship. *Contemporary South Asia, 7*, 98–99.

Dahiwal, A. (2017, May). Now, PCMC Puts New System in Place for Waste Segregation. *Pune Mirror.*

Dalal, S. (2016, July). 4 Reasons Why Pune Scores in Waste Management. *Moneylife.*

Das, S., & Bhattacharyya, B. K. (2014). Estimation of Municipal Solid Waste Generation and Future Trends in Greater Metropolitan Regions of Kolkata, India. *Journal of Industrial Engineering and Management Innovation, 1*(1), 31–38. doi:10.2991/jiemi.2014.1.1.3

Das Gupta, A. (2007). Social responsibility in India towards global compact approach. *International Journal of Social Economics, 34*(9), 637–663. doi:10.1108/03068290710778642

Davis, J. H., Schoorman, F. D., & Donaldson, L. (1997). Toward a stewardship theory of management. *Academy of Management Review*, *22*(1), 20–47. doi:10.5465/amr.1997.9707180258

Desai, N., Pingali, V., & Tripathy, A. (2015). *Is 2% the Solution?* Experimental Evidence on the New CSR Rule in India.

Dirks, N. B. (2011). *Castes of mind: Colonialism and the making of modern India*. Princeton University Press.

Donaldson, L., & Davis, J. H. (1991). Stewardship theory or agency theory: CEO governance and shareholder returns. *Australian Journal of Management*, *16*(1), 49–64. doi:10.1177/031289629101600103

Doshi, V. (2016), Indian royals in row over missing temple treasures, India - The Observer. *The Guardian*. Available at: https://www.theguardian.com/world/2016/sep/24/former-maharajahs-accused-over-temple-treasures

Du Pisani, J. A. (2006). Sustainable development–historical roots of the concept. *Environmental Sciences*, *3*(2), 83–96. doi:10.1080/15693430600688831

Dube, R., Nandan, V., & Dua, S. (2014). Waste incineration for urban India: Valuable contribution to sustainable MSWM or inappropriate high-tech solution affecting livelihoods and public health? *International Journal of Environmental Technology and Management*, *17*(2-4), 199–214. doi:10.1504/IJETM.2014.061792

Dumont, L. (1980). *Homo hierarchicus: The caste system and its implications*. University of Chicago Press.

Dutt, A. K., Noble, A. G., Costa, F. J., Thakur, S. K., Thakur, R. R., & Sharma, H. S. (Eds.). (2015). Spatial Diversity and Dynamics in Resources and Urban Development: Vol. 1. Regional Resources. Springer.

Dwivedy, M., & Mittal, R. K. (2012). An investigation into e-waste flows in India. *Journal of Cleaner Production*, *37*, 229–242. doi:10.1016/j.jclepro.2012.07.017

Ehrenfeld, J., & Gertler, N. (1997). Industrial Ecology in Practice. *Journal of Industrial Ecology*, *1*(1), 67–79. doi:10.1162/jiec.1997.1.1.67

Eichengreen, B., & Gupta, P. (2011). *The service sector as India's road to economic growth (No. w16757)*. National Bureau of Economic Research. doi:10.3386/w16757

Eisenhardt, K. M. (1989). Agency theory: An assessment and review. *Academy of Management Review*, *14*(1), 57–74. doi:10.5465/amr.1989.4279003

Fox, T., Ward, H., & Howard, B. (2002). *Public sector roles in strengthening corporate social responsibility: A baseline study*. The World Bank.

Frey, B. S., & Stutzer, A. (2001). *Happiness and Economics: How the Economy and Institutions Affect Human Well-Being*. Princeton, NJ: Princeton University Press.

Ganesh, K. N. (2013). To Whom Does Temple Wealth Belong? A Historical Essay on Landed Property in Travancore. *Review of Agrarian Studies*, *3*(1). Retrieved from http://ras.org.in/to_whom_does_temple_wealth_belong_a_historical_essay_on_landed_property_in_travancore

Garlapati, V. K. (2016). E-waste in India and developed countries: Management, recycling, business and biotechnological initiatives. *Renewable & Sustainable Energy Reviews*, *54*, 874–881. doi:10.1016/j.rser.2015.10.106

Gaur, A. S., Kumar, V., & Singh, D. (2014). Institutions, resources, and internationalization of emerging economy firms. *Journal of World Business*, *49*(1), 12–20. doi:10.1016/j.jwb.2013.04.002

Gautam, R., & Singh, A. (2010). Corporate social responsibility practices in India: A study of top 500 companies. *Global Business and Management Research: An International Journal*, *2*(1), 41–56.

Ghosh, S. K. (2016). Sustainable SWM in Developing Countries Focusing on Faster Growing Economies, India and China. *Procedia Environmental Sciences*, *35*, 176–184. doi:10.1016/j.proenv.2016.07.073

Gibbs, D., & Deutz, P. (2007). Reflections on implementing industrial ecology through eco-industrial park development. *Journal of Cleaner Production*, *15*(17), 1683–1695. doi:10.1016/j.jclepro.2007.02.003

Gidde, M. R., Kokate, K. K., & Todkar, V. V. (2008). Municipal Solid Waste Management in Emerging Mega Cities: A case study of Pune City. In *Indo Italian Conference on Green and Clean Environment* (pp. 441–450). Academic Press.

Gifford, R. (2011). The dragons of inaction: Psychological barriers that limit climate change mitigation and adaptation. *The American Psychologist*, *66*(4), 290–302. doi:10.1037/a0023566 PMID:21553954

Godfrey, P. C., & Hatch, N. W. (2007). Researching corporate social responsibility: An agenda for the 21st century. *Journal of Business Ethics*, *70*(1), 87–98. doi:10.100710551-006-9080-y

GoI. (2008). *National Action Plan on Climate Change*. Author. doi:10.1111/j.1746-1561.1993.tb06065.x

GoI. (2011). *Guidelines for appraisal and approval of projects/schemes eligible for financing under the National Clean Energy Fund*. New Delhi: Department of Expenditure, Ministry of Finance.

GoI. (2013). *Companies Act, 2013*. Accessed in June 2018 at: www.mca.gov.in/Ministry/pdf/CompaniesAct2013.pdf

Goyal, K. A. (2006). Impact of Globalization on Developing Countries (with special reference to India). *International Research Journal of Finance and Economics*, *5*, 166–171.

Hamschmidt, J., & Pirson, M. (Eds.). (2018). *Case studies in social entrepreneurship and sustainability: the oikos collection* (Vol. 2). Routledge.

Harriss, J. (2015). Hindu Nationalism in Action: The Bharatiya Janata Party and Indian Politics. *South Asia*, *38*(4), 712–718. doi:10.1080/00856401.2015.1089826

Hindu. (2017). Climate change plan to get new missions. *The Hindu*. Retrieved from http://www.thehindu.com/news/national/Climate-change-plan-to-get-new-missions/article17090498.ece

IISD. (n.d.). International Institute for Sustainable Development. *Kalundborg*.

Induchudan, V. T. (1969). *The Secret Chamber: A Historical, Anthropological & Philosophical Study of the Kodungallur Temple*. Cochin Devaswom Board.

Jamali, D., Lund-Thomsen, P., & Khara, N. (2017). CSR institutionalized myths in developing countries: An imminent threat of selective decoupling. *Business & Society*, *56*(3), 454–486. doi:10.1177/0007650315584303

Jammulamadaka, N. (2013). The responsibility of corporate social responsibility in SMEs. *The International Journal of Organizational Analysis*, *21*(3), 385–395. doi:10.1108/IJOA-Mar-2012-0566

Jawahir, I. S., & Bradley, R. (2016). Technological elements of circular economy and the principles of 6R-based closed-loop material flow in sustainable manufacturing. *Procedia CIRP*, *40*, 103–108. doi:10.1016/j.procir.2016.01.067

Jodhka, S. (2017). *Caste in contemporary India*. Routledge.

Joshi, R., & Ahmed, S. (2016). Status and challenges of municipal solid waste management in India: A review. *Cogent Environmental Science*, *2*(1), 1139434. doi:10.1080/23311843.2016.1139434

Kansal, M., & Singh, S. (2012). Measurement of corporate social performance: An Indian perspective. *Social Responsibility Journal*, *8*(4), 527–546. doi:10.1108/17471111211272101

Kapoor, R. (2004). Plural dreams: India in the 21st century. *Futures*, *36*(6/7), 637–653. doi:10.1016/j.futures.2003.12.007

Kapur, J. C. (1982). *India*. New Delhi: An Uncommitted Society, Vikas Publishing House.

Kilby, P. (2013). Waste Recycling and the Household Economy: The Case of the Pune Waste-Pickers' Response to the Changing 'Rules of the Game. In *The Global Political Economy of the Household in Asia* (pp. 211–226). London: Palgrave Macmillan. doi:10.1057/9781137338907_14

Korhonen, J. (2001). Four ecosystem principles for an industrial ecosystem. *Journal of Cleaner Production*, *9*(3), 253–259. doi:10.1016/S0959-6526(00)00058-5

Krishnamurthy, S., Joseph, S., Pradhan, V., & Rao, P. (2017). Empowering Women of Rural India for Renewable Energy Adoption–An Exploratory Factor Analysis. *Indian Journal of Science and Technology*, *10*(37), 1–10. doi:10.17485/ijst/2017/v10i37/95576

Krishnamurthy, S., & Pradhan, V. (2018a). Anecdotes of Action Learning: Initiations of Sustainability Lessons by an Indian B-School. In *Cross-Disciplinary Approaches to Action Research and Action Learning*. IGI. doi:10.4018/978-1-5225-2642-1.ch007

Krishnamurthy, S., & Pradhan, V. (2018b). Anecdotes of Action Learning: Realizations of an Indian B-School's Sustainability Lessons. In *Cross-Disciplinary Approaches to Action Research and Action Learning*. IGI. doi:10.4018/978-1-5225-2642-1.ch008

Kumar, S., Bhattacharyya, J. K., Vaidya, A. N., Chakrabarti, T., Devotta, S., & Akolkar, A. B. (2009). Assessment of the status of municipal solid waste management in metro cities, state capitals, class I cities, and class II towns in India: An insight. *Waste Management (New York, N.Y.)*, *29*(2), 883–895. doi:10.1016/j.wasman.2008.04.011 PMID:18595684

MacArthur, E. (2013). *Towards a Circular Economy—Economic and Business Rationale for an Accelerated Transition*. Cowes, UK: Ellen MacArthur Foundation.

Majumdar, S., & Saini, G. K. (2016). CSR in India: Critical Review and Exploring Entrepreneurial Opportunities. *Journal of Entrepreneurship and Innovation in Emerging Economies*, *2*(1), 56–79. doi:10.1177/2393957515619719

Mani, S., & Singh, S. (2016). Sustainable Municipal Solid Waste Management in India: A Policy Agenda. *Procedia Environmental Sciences*, *35*, 150–157. doi:10.1016/j.proenv.2016.07.064

Mathews, J. A., Tang, Y., & Tan, H. (2011). China's move to a Circular Economy as a development strategy. *Asian Business & Management*, *10*(4), 463–484. doi:10.1057/abm.2011.18

Matten, D., & Moon, J. (2008). "Implicit" and "explicit" CSR: A conceptual framework for a comparative understanding of corporate social responsibility. *Academy of Management Review*, *33*(2), 404–424. doi:10.5465/amr.2008.31193458

Mehrotra, S., Parida, J., Sinha, S., & Gandhi, A. (2014). Explaining employment trends in the Indian economy: 1993-94 to 2011-12. *Economic and Political Weekly*, *49*(32), 49–57.

Mehta, A. (2014). PCMC officials get notice for waste management. *Daily News & Analysis.*

Mehta, D., & Aggarwal, M. (2015). Making Corporate Social Responsibility Mandatory in India-Prospects and Problems. *International Journal of Research in Business Management*, *3*(5), 21–30.

Millennium. (2005). *Millennium ecosystem assessment synthesis report, a report of the millennium ecosystem assessment*. accessed May 2017 at http://www.millenniumassessment.org/en/Products.Synthesis.aspx

Ministry of Power. (2017). *Power Sector at a Glance - All India*. Government of India.

Mishra, P. N. (2017). *Mismanagement Of Wealth In Shri Padmanabhaswamy Temple: Amicus Seeks SIT Probe, Report on May 3, 2017*. available at: http://www.livelaw.in/mismanagement-wealth-shri-padmanabhaswamy-temple-amicus-seeks-sit-probe-read-report/

Mission, R. (2007). *S-14011/2/2015-SBM, Swachh Bharat Mission (Gramin)*. Accessed in Sep 2017 at http://www.mdws.gov.in/sites/default/files/PMC_publication_of_contract_0.pdf

MoEFCC. (2016). Plastic Waste Management Rules 2016. New Delhi, India: Author.

Morrissey, A. J., & Browne, J. (2004). Waste management models and their application to sustainable waste management. *Waste Management, 24*(3), 297-308.

Motwani, R. (2001). *The Sociology of Indian Politics*. Cosmo Publications.

MOUD (2015). *Smart City: Mission Statement and Guidelines*. Author.

Mridula & Sinha. (2016). *Swachh Bharat - A Clean India*. Prabhat Prakashan.

Murray, A., Skene, K., & Haynes, K. (2017). The Circular Economy: An Interdisciplinary Exploration of the Concept and Application in a Global Context. *Journal of Business Ethics*, *140*(3), 369–380. doi:10.100710551-015-2693-2

Nancy, M. P., & Jan, E. (2017). *The Circular Economy – A new sustainability paradigm?* Academic Press. doi:10.1016/j.jclepro.2016.12.048.Abstract

Nandy, B., Sharma, G., Garg, S., Kumari, S., George, T., Sunanda, Y., & Sinha, B. (2015). Recovery of consumer waste in India - A mass flow analysis for paper, plastic and glass and the contribution of households and the informal sector. *Resources, Conservation and Recycling*, *101*, 167–181. doi:10.1016/j.resconrec.2015.05.012

Narayana, T. (2009). Municipal solid waste management in India: From waste disposal to recovery of resources? *Waste Management (New York, N.Y.)*, *29*(3), 1163–1166. doi:10.1016/j.wasman.2008.06.038 PMID:18829290

Narwal, M., & Singh, R. (2013). *Corporate social responsibility practices in India: a comparative study of MNCs and Indian companies. Social Responsibility Journal.* doi:10.1108/SRJ-11-2011-0100

O'Rourke, D. (2003). Outsourcing regulation: Analyzing nongovernmental systems of labor standards and monitoring. *Policy Studies Journal: the Journal of the Policy Studies Organization*, *31*(1), 1–29. doi:10.1111/1541-0072.00001

Panda, A., & Gupta, R. K. (2007). Call for developing indigenous organisational theories in India: Setting agenda for future. *International Journal of Indian Culture and Business Management*, *1*(1-2), 205–243. doi:10.1504/IJICBM.2007.014478

Parthasarathy, R. (1993). *The Cilappatikāram of Iḷaṅko Aṭikaḷ: An Epic of South India.* Columbia University Press.

Paul, K., Dutta, A., & Krishna, A. P. (2014). A comprehensive study on landfill site selection for Kolkata City, India. *Journal of the Air & Waste Management Association*, *64*(7), 846–861. doi:10.1080/10962247.2014.896834 PMID:25122958

PCMC. (2017). PCMC proposes to generate biogas from hotel waste. *Pune Mirror.* Accessed in July 2017 at http://punemirror.indiatimes.com/pune/civic/pcmc-proposes-to-generate-biogas-from-hotel-waste/articleshow/59761295.cms

PCMC. (n.d.). *Pimpri Chinchwad Smart City. PCMC.*

Perego, P., & Kolk, A. (2012). Multinationals' accountability on sustainability: The evolution of third-party assurance of sustainability reports. *Journal of Business Ethics*, *110*(2), 173–190. doi:10.100710551-012-1420-5

PMC. (n.d.). *Zero Garbage Model.* PMC.

Prabhune, T. (2018). *Times of India.* Accessed at: https://timesofindia.indiatimes.com/city/ahmedabad/gujarat-tops-in-putting-plastic-to-cleaner-use/articleshow/64954235.cms

Pradhan, V., Sharma, R., & Krishnamurthy, S. (2016). Analyses of Factors Affecting Employee Perception on Organizational Corporate Social Responsibility. *SCIT Journal, 16*(1).

Pruthi, R. K. (2004). *Indian caste system.* Discovery Publishing House.

Rajaram, T., & Das, A. (2006). Need for participatory and sustainable principles in India's EIA system: Lessons from the Sethusamudram Ship Channel Project. *Impact Assessment and Project Appraisal*, *24*(2), 115–126. doi:10.3152/147154606781765237

Rana, R., Ganguly, R., & Gupta, A. K. (2015). An assessment of solid waste management system in Chandigarh City, India. *The Electronic Journal of Geotechnical Engineering*, *20*(6), 1547–1572.

Rangarajan, L. N. (Ed.). (1992). *The Arthashastra*. Penguin Books India.

Rao, P., Patil, Y., Bhat, V., & Ketkar, M. (2017). Building Energy, Environment and Sustainability Linkages in Management Education in India—An Innovative Curriculum Based Approach. In Curricula for Sustainability in Higher Education (pp. 61-76). Springer International Publishing.

Rasche, A., & Gilbert, D. U. (2012). Social Accountability 8000 and socioeconomic development. *Business Regulation and Non-State Actors: Whose Standards? Whose Developments*, 68-79.

Roberts, B. H. (2004). The application of industrial ecology principles and planning guidelines for the development of eco-industrial parks: An Australian case study. *Journal of Cleaner Production*, *12*(8–10), 997–1010. doi:10.1016/j.jclepro.2004.02.037

Sachs, N. (2014, June). Garbage Everywhere: What refuse in India's streets reveals about America's hidden trash problem. *Atlantic*.

Saini, S., Rao, P., & Patil, Y. (2012). *City based analysis of MSW to energy generation in India, calculation of state-wise potential and tariff comparison with EU*. Academic Press. doi:10.1016/j.sbspro.2012.03.306

Santayana, G. (1905). Reason in Common Sense. In The Life of Reason (vol. 1, p. 284). Academic Press.

Sarukkai, S. (2012). *JRD Tata and the Idea of Trusteeship*. Academic Press.

Sasidharan, K. (2011), A Sree Padmanabhaswamy Sovereign Fund? *Wall Street Journal*. Available at: https://blogs.wsj.com/indiarealtime/2011/07/19/india-journal-a-sree-padmanabhaswamy-sovereign-fund/

Satapathy, S. (2017). An analysis of barriers for plastic recycling in the Indian plastic industry. Benchmarking. *International Journal (Toronto, Ont.)*, *24*(2), 415–430. doi:10.1108/BIJ-11-2014-0103

Seetharaman, G. (2017, June). India wants to double consumption of cheap material in 5 yrs, what about its plastic waste? *The Economic Times*.

Shamasastry, R. (1915). *Kautilya's Arthashastra*. Academic Press.

Sharholy, M., Ahmad, K., Mahmood, G., & Trivedi, R. C. (2008). Municipal solid waste management in Indian cities–A review. *Waste Management, 28*(2), 459-467.

Sharholy, M., Ahmad, K., Mahmood, G., & Trivedi, R. C. (2008). Municipal solid waste management in Indian cities - A review. *Waste Management (New York, N.Y.)*, *28*(2), 459–467. doi:10.1016/j.wasman.2007.02.008 PMID:17433664

Sharma, V. (2017). India's largest solid waste-to-energy plant launched at Delhi's at Narela. *Hindustan Times*.

Siddhartha, K. (2018). For a Greener Tomorrow. *The Hindu*. Accessed at https://www.thehindu.com/education/for-a-greener-tomorrow/article24953545.ece

Silverberg, J. (1968). *Social mobility in the caste system in India*. Academic Press.

Singh, A., & Verma, P. (2014). *CSR@ 2%: A new model of corporate social responsibility in India*. Academic Press.

Singhal, S., & Kapur, A. (2002). Industrial estate planning and management in India—An integrated approach towards industrial ecology. *Journal of Environmental Management*, *66*(1), 19–29. doi:10.1006/jema.2002.0571 PMID:12395584

Smith, A. (1976). An inquiry into the nature and causes of the wealth of nations (R. H. Campbell, A. S. Skinner, & W. B. Todd, Eds.). Academic Press.

Srivathsan, A. (2011, July 7) When the vault was opened in 1931, Kerala. *The Hindu*.

Subramanian, T. S. (2011). Eclectic architecture, exquisite features. *The Hindu*. Accessed in May 2017 from: http://www.thehindu.com/opinion/op-ed/eclectic-architecture-exquisite-features/article2236138.ece

Sugden, J. (2012). Why a Deity Should Be on 'India's Richest' List. *Wall Street Journal*. Available at: https://blogs.wsj.com/indiarealtime/2012/12/25/why-a-deity-should-be-on-indias-richest-list/

Teltumbde, A. (2014, November 8). No Swachh Bharat without Annihilation of Caste. *Economic and Political Weekly*.

TNN. (2016a, January). Glass waste dumping. *The Times of India*.

TNN. (2016b, January). Nod to zero waste plan in PCMC ward. *The Times of India*.

TOI. (2018). *Times of India*. Accessed at: https://timesofindia.indiatimes.com/business/india-business/no-takers-for-rs-1717-cr-of-csr-funds-in-fy18-report/articleshow/66832211.cms

Tsui, A. S. (2004). Contributing to global management knowledge: A case for high quality indigenous research. *Asia Pacific Journal of Management*, *21*(4), 491–513. doi:10.1023/B:APJM.0000048715.35108.a7

UNEP. (2006). *Circular Economy. An alternative model for economic development*. Paris: United Nations Environment Programme.

Van Dijk, M. P., & Rabellotti, R. (Eds.). (2005). *Enterprise clusters and networks in developing countries* (Vol. 7). Routledge. doi:10.4324/9780203988114

Verbruggen, A., Fischedick, M., Moomaw, W., Weir, T., Nadaı, A., Nilsson, L. J., … Sathaye, J. (2010). *Renewable energy costs, potentials, barriers: Conceptual issues*. Academic Press. doi:10.1016/j.enpol.2009.10.036

Vij, D. (2012). Urbanization and Solid Waste Management in India: Present Practices and Future Challenges. *Procedia: Social and Behavioral Sciences*, *37*, 437–447. doi:10.1016/j.sbspro.2012.03.309

Virmani, B. R. (2005). *Cultural Dilemma in Indian Management*. Academic Press.

Watal, R. P., Advisor, P., & Aayog, N. (2017). *Strategy Paper on Resource Efficiency*. Academic Press.

Webster, K. (2015). *The Circular Economy: A Wealth of Flows*. Isle of Wight, UK: Ellen MacArthur Foundation.

West, E. G. (1969). *Adam Smith*. New York: Arlington House.

Woolcock, M., & Narayan, D. (2000). Social capital: Implications for development theory, research, and policy. *The World Bank Research Observer, 15*(2), 225–249. doi:10.1093/wbro/15.2.225

Worrell, R., & Appleby, M. C. (2000). Stewardship of natural resources: Definition, ethical and practical aspects. *Journal of Agricultural & Environmental Ethics, 12*(3), 263–277. doi:10.1023/A:1009534214698

Yadagiri, S. (2018). *Banyan Nation: Living sustainably is the only way forward*. Accessed at http://www.newindianexpress.com/cities/hyderabad/2018/oct/13/banyan-nation-living-sustainably-is-the-only-way-forward-1884733.html

Yaduvanshi, N. R., Myana, R., & Krishnamurthy, S. (2016). Circular Economy for Sustainable Development in India. *Indian Journal of Science and Technology, 9*(46). doi:10.17485/ijst/2016/v9i46/107325

Zhu, D., Asnani, P. U., Zurbrugg, C., Anapolsky, S., & Mani, S. (2008). *Improving Municipal Solid Waste Management in India: A Sourcebook for Policy Makers and Practitioners*. World Bank Institute. doi:10.1596/ 978-0-8213-7361-3

KEY TERMS AND DEFINITIONS

3Rs: The three terms used to address waste are reduce, reuse, and recycle. Reducing is cutting back on the amount of waste, reusing is finding a new way to use waste material, and recycling is using waste material to remake new goods that can be sold or used again.

Agency Theory: Agency theory in political science mentions the "agent", who can make decisions on behalf of another person or people (i.e., "principal"). The dilemma occurs where the agent is motivated to act in his/her own best interests, which are contrary to those of the principal, thus becoming a moral hazard.

***Arthashastra*:** An ancient Indian treatise on statecraft, economic policy and military strategy, written in Sanskrit, in 2nd century BCE. The book *Arthashastra* has a broader scope, including the nature of government, law, civil and criminal court systems, ethics, economics, markets and trade, theories on war, nature of peace, and the duties and obligations of a king.

Freedom of Association: Is the right for coming together with other individuals to collectively express, promote, pursue or defend common interests. Freedom of Association is both an individual right and a collective right, guaranteed by all modern and democratic legal systems.

Incinerator: A special large container for burning waste at very high temperatures. This thermal treatment of waste materials converts the waste into ash, flue gas and heat (which can be recovered as an energy source).

Indigenous Studies: Studies in the academic field that examines the history, culture, politics, contemporary issues, and experiences of Native peoples of the land. Considering the people regarded as the original inhabitants of an area, as opposed to settlers from elsewhere.

Linear Economy: Raw materials used to make product, after use, culminate in a landfill. In economies based on recycling, such waste materials are reused.

Social Power: The degree of influence that an individual or organization has among their peers and within their society as a whole. The social power can be credited to the level of eminence or knowledge that they possess in a field.

Urban Local Bodies (ULB): Urban local government implies the governance of an urban area by the people through their elected representatives. Government of India, 74th Constitutional Amendment Act, 1992 provided constitutional status to local urban bodies.

Compilation of References

AASB. (2015). *AASB 101 - Presentation of Financial Statements*. Australian Government.

Abate, T. G. (2018). Drivers of agricultural cooperative formation and farmers' membership and patronage decisions in Ethiopia. *Journal of Co-operative Organization and Management*, *6*(2), 53–63. doi:10.1016/j.jcom.2018.06.002

Accornero, A., & Marini, D. (2011). Le cooperative alla prova della crisi. Quaderni FNE - Collana Ricerche, n. 61. Mestre, Italy: Fondazione Nord Est.

AccountAbility. (2018). *AccountAbility, Reporting Principles* (Standard). Retrieved from https://www.accountability.org/wp-content/uploads/2018/05/AA1000_ACCOUNTABILITY_PRINCIPLES_2018_Single_Pages.pdf

Accountability. (n.d.). In *Merriam-Webster's Collegiate Dictionary*. Retrieved from https://www.merriam-webster.com/dictionary/accountability

ACNC. (2013). *Australian Charities and Not-for-profits Commission (ACNC) 2013 research: Public trust and confidence in Australian charities*. Commonwealth of Australia.

Adams, C. A., & Zutshi, A. (2004). Corporate social responsibility: Why business should act responsibly and be accountable. *Australian Accounting Review*, *14*(1), 31–39. doi:10.1111/j.1835-2561.2004.tb00238.x

Ahmed, S. (2002). The Theater of the Civilized Self: Edmund Burke and the East India Trials. *Representations (Berkeley, Calif.)*, *78*(1), 30. doi:10.1525/rep.2002.78.1.28

Aimers, J., & Walker, P. (2008a). Alternative models of accountability for third sector organisations in New Zealand. *Eighth International Conference of the International Society for Third Sector Research*. Retrieved from https://c.ymcdn.com/sites/istr.site-ym.com/resource/resmgr/working_papers_barcelona/Aimers.Walker.pdf

Aimers, J., & Walker, P. (2008b). Is community accoutability being overlooked as a result of government-third sector partnering in New Zealand. *Aotearoa New Zealand Social Work Review*, *XX*(3), 14–24.

Aiyangar, S. K. (1940). *Seran Vanji: Vanji, the Capital of the Cheras. Superintendent*. Cochin Government Press.

Al-Bassam, W. M., Ntim, C. G., Opong, K. K., & Downs, Y. (2018). Corporate boards and ownership structure as antecedents of corporate governance disclosure in Saudi Arabian publicly listed corporations. *Business & Society*, *57*(2), 335–377. doi:10.1177/0007650315610611

Alleanza delle Cooperative Italiane. (2018, May 15). *Audizione dell'Alleanza delle Cooperative Italiane nell'ambito dell'esame del Documento di Economia e Finanza 2018 dinanzi alle Commissioni Speciali Senato della Repubblica e Camera dei deputati*. Retrieved February 11, 2019, from https://www.senato.it/application/xmanager/projects/leg18/attachments/documento_evento_procedura_commissione/files/000/000/081/ALLEANZA_DELLE_COOPERATIVE.pdf

Almeida, F. (2011). *E-Government: Análise E Avaliação Dos Municípios No Distrito de Viseu*. Escola Superior de Tecnologia e Gestão de Viseu - Instituto Politécnico de Viseu. Available at: http://repositorio.ipv.pt/handle/10400.19/1096

Al-Shubiri, F., Al-Abedallat, A., & Orabi, M. (2012). Financial and non-financial determinants of corporate social responsibility. *Asian Economic and Financial Review*, *2*(8), 1001–1012.

Altman, M. (2016). Is there a co-operative advantage? Experimental evidence on the economic and non-economic determinants of demand. *Journal of Co-operative Organization and Management*, *4*(2), 66–75. doi:10.1016/j.jcom.2016.08.003

Alves, M. A. (2014). Social accountability as an innovative frame in civic action: The case of rede nossa São Paulo. *Voluntas*, *25*(3), 818–838. doi:10.100711266-013-9365-6

Amran, A., & Devi, S. (2008). The impact of government and foreign affiliate influence on corporate social reporting: The case of Malaysia. *Managerial Auditing Journal*, *23*(4), 386–404. doi:10.1108/02686900810864327

Andrews, D. (2015). The circular economy, design thinking and education for sustainability. *Local Economy*, *30*(3), 305–315. doi:10.1177/0269094215578226

Anes, A. (2009). *Estado de Maturidade Do E-Government Municipal No Distrito de Bragança*. Escola Superior de Tecnologia e Gestão - Instituto Politécnico de Bragança. Available at: https://bibliotecadigital.ipb.pt/handle/10198/2126

APDSI. (2009), *O Poder Local E a Sociedade Da Informação Em Portugal A Evolução Das Câmaras Municipais*. APDSI.

Appadurai, A. (2001). Deep democracy: Urban governmentality and the horizon of politics. *Environment and Urbanization*, *13*(2), 23–43. doi:10.1177/095624780101300203

Arendt, H. (1972). *Crises of the Republic: Lying in Politics, Civil Disobedience on Violence, Thoughts on Politics, and Revolution*. Harcourt Brace Jovanovich.

Armani, D. (2008). *Mobilizar para transformar: a mobilização de recursos nas organizações da sociedade civil*. São Paulo, SP: Peirópolis.

Arshad, R., Bakar, N., Thani, N., & Omar, N. (2013). Board composition and accountability of non-profit organizations. *Journal of Applied Business Research*, *29*(4), 1021–1030. doi:10.19030/jabr.v29i4.7913

Arshad, R., Samad, N., Kamaluddin, A., & Roslan, N. (2016). Intellectual capital, accountability and sustainability in non-profit organizations. *Asian Journal of Scientific Research*, *9*(2), 62–70. doi:10.3923/ajsr.2016.62.70

Arvidson, M., Lyon, F., McKay, S., & Moro, D. (2013). Valuing the social? The nature and controversies of measuring social return on investment (SROI). *Voluntary Sector Review*, *4*(1), 3–18. doi:10.1332/204080513X661554

Ashton, W., & Shenoy, M. (2015). Industrial ecology in India: converging traditional practice and modern environmental protection. In P. Deutz, D. I. Lyons, & J. Bi (Eds.), *International Perspectives on Industrial Ecology* (pp. 12–29). Cheltenham, UK: Edward Elgar Publishing Limited. doi:10.4337/9781781003572.00010

Asnani, P. U. (2006). Solid Waste Management. In A. Rastogi (Ed.), *India Infrastructure Report, 2006: Urban Infrastructure* (pp. 160–189). Oxford University Press.

Association of Government Accountants. (n.d.). *Citizen-centric reporting (CCR)*. Retrieved April 10, 2019, from https://www.agacgfm.org/ccr

Atan, R., & Zainon, S. (2009). In Defence of Non-Profit Accountability. Finance & Accounting, 29(40), 399–402. doi:10.1017/epi.2014.33

Atan, R., Alam, M. M., & Said, J. (2017). Practices of corporate integrity and accountability of non-profit organizations in Malaysia. *International Journal of Social Economics*, *44*(12), 2271–2286. doi:10.1108/IJSE-09-2016-0260

Austin, J., Stevenson, H., & Wei-Skillern, J. (2012). Social and commercial entrepreneurship: Same, different, or both? *Revista ADM*, *47*(3), 370–384.

Awio, G., Northcott, D., & Lawrence, S. (2011). Social capital and accountability in grass-roots NGOs. *Accounting, Auditing & Accountability Journal*, *24*(1), 63–92. doi:10.1108/09513571111098063

Azevedo, C. (2013). *Manual de Governo – O Desafio da Liderança nas Organizações do Terceiro Sector em Portugal*. Porto: Impulso Positivo.

Azman, N., Arshad, R., & Bakar, N. (2015). *Do Funding Resources Affect the Accountability Disclosure Of non-Profit Organizations*. Academic Press.

Azuma, H. (1984). Psychology in a non-western country. *International Journal of Psychology*, *19*(1-4), 45–55. doi:10.1080/00207598408247514

Bailey, K. D. (1995). *Methods of social research*. New York: Maxwell Macmillan International.

Bakar, N., Arshad, R., Azman, N., & Omar, N. (2014). Effective Governance Structure and Accountability in Managing Risks for Non-Profit Organizations. In *Proceedings of World Business And Economics Research Conference 24-25 February 2014* (pp. 1–16). Academic Press. Retrieved from http://www.ccsenet.org/journal/index.php/ibr/article/view/34859

Bakar, S., Arshad, R., Pauzi, N., Mamat, S., & Omar, N. (2017). Human Capital Management and Accountability of Social Enterprise. In *SHS Web of Conferences* (Vol. 36, p. 490). EDP Sciences.

Bakar, N., Arshad, R., Azman, N., & Omar, N. (2013). Organisational characteristics and accountability in protecting risk exposures in non-profit organisations. *Journal of Energy Technologies and Policy*, *3*(11), 479–488. Retrieved from www.iiste.org

Balasubramanian, S., Konana, P., & Menon, N. M. (2003). Customer Satisfaction in Virtual Environments: A Study of Online Investing. *Management Science*, *49*(7), 871–889. doi:10.1287/mnsc.49.7.871.16385

Baldarelli, M. G., Baldo, M. D., & Nesheva-Kiosseva, N. (2017). *Environmental Accounting and Reporting: Theory and Practice*. Cham, Switzerland: Springer International Publishing. doi:10.1007/978-3-319-50918-1

Baldini, M., Dal Maso, L., Liberatore, G., Mazzi, F., & Terzani, S. (2016). Role of country-and firm-level determinants in environmental, social, and governance disclosure. *Journal of Business Ethics*, 1-20.

Bamshad, M., Kivisild, T., Watkins, W. S., Dixon, M. E., Ricker, C. E., & Rao, B. B. (2001). Genetic evidence on the origins of Indian caste populations. *Genome Research*, *11*(6), 994–1004. doi:10.1101/gr.GR-1733RR PMID:11381027

Bandeira, A. M., Meira, D., & Alves, V. (2016). Los diferentes tipos de resultados en las cooperativas portuguesas. Un estudio de caso múltiple. *REVESCO. Revista de Estudios Cooperativos*, *123*(0). doi:10.5209/REVE.54919

Banerjee, P. (2016, February). Gone to waste: How India is drowning in garbage. *Hindustan Times*.

Banerjee, A., Duflo, E., Glennerster, R., & Kinnan, C. (2015). The miracle of microfinance? Evidence from a randomized evaluation. *American Economic Journal. Applied Economics*, *7*(1), 22–53. doi:10.1257/app.20130533

Banke-Thomas, A. O., Madaj, B., Charles, A., & van den Broek, N. (2015). Social return on investment (SROI) methodology to account for value for money of public health interventions: A systematic review. *BMC Public Health*, *15*(1), 582. doi:10.118612889-015-1935-7 PMID:26099274

Baranwal, S. (2011). Concern for Environment in Ancient India. *Renewable Research Journal, 1*, 1-9. Accessed in Sep 2017 at www.rexjournal.org.managewebsiteportal.com/files/documents/Concern-for-Environment-in-Ancient-India--Shamik-Baranwal.pdf

Barbera, C., Borgonovi, E., & Steccolini, I. (2016). Popular reporting and public governance: The case of "bilancio in arancio" in milan municipality. In A. Hinna, L. Gnan, & F. Monteduro (Eds.), Studies in Public and Non-Profit Governance: Vol. 5. Governance and Performance in Public and Non-Profit Organizations (pp. 3-30). Bingley, UK: Emerald Group Publishing Limited.

Barman, E., & MacIndoe, H. (2012). Institutional pressures and organizational capacity: The case of outcome measurement. *Sociological Forum, 27*(1), 70–93. doi:10.1111/j.1573-7861.2011.01302.x

Barney, J. (1991). Firm resources and sustained competitive advantage. *Journal of Management, 17*(1), 99–120. doi:10.1177/014920639101700108

Barney, J. (2001). Resource-based theories of competitive advantage: A ten-year retrospective on the resource-based view. *Journal of Management, 27*(6), 643–650. doi:10.1177/014920630102700602

Barr, A. (1998). *Enterprise Performance and the Functional Diversity of Social Capital*. Working Paper Series 98-1. Institute of Economics and Statistics, University of Oxford.

Barraket, J., Mason, C., & Blain, B. (2016). *Finding Australia's Social Enterprise Sector 2016: Final Report*. Centre for Social Impact. Swinburne University of Technology.

Barrett, M. (2001). A Stakeholder Approach to Responsiveness and Accountability in Non-Profit Organisations. *Social Policy Journal of New Zealand*, (17), 36–51. Retrieved from http://www.msd.govt.nz/about-msd-and-our-work/publications-resources/journals-and-magazines/social-policy-journal/spj17/a-stakeholder-approach-to-responsiveness-and-accountability-in-non-profit-organisations.html

Barrett, M. (2001). A stakeholder approach to responsiveness and accountability in non-profit organizations. *Social Policy Journal of New Zealand, 1*(17), 36–51.

Basri, H., & Siti-Nabiha, A. K. (2010). Views on the issue of accountability in non-profit organizations. *Malaysian Management Journal, 14*, 49–60.

Basu, S., & Sharma, A. (2014). Exploring Stewardship as an Antecedent Behavioural Trait of Social Entrepreneurs. *The Journal of Entrepreneurship, 23*(1), 19–33. doi:10.1177/0971355713513347

Batra, S. (2009). Strengthening human capital for knowledge economy needs: An Indian perspective. *Journal of Knowledge Management, 13*(5), 345–358. doi:10.1108/13673270910988150

Battaglia, M., Bianchi, L., Frey, M., & Passetti, E. (2015). Sustainability reporting and corporate identity: Action research evidence in an Italian retailing cooperative. *Business Ethics (Oxford, England), 24*(1), 52–72. doi:10.1111/beer.12067

Bauby, P., & Similie, M. M. (2010). Public Services in the European Union & In the 27 Member States. *CEEP*. Retrieved from http://ceep.eu/images/stories/pdf/Mapping/CEEP_mapping%20experts%20report.pdf

Baud, I. S. A., Grafakos, S., Hordijk, M., & Post, J. (2001). Quality of life and alliances in solid waste management: Contributions to urban sustainable development. *Cities (London, England), 18*(1), 3–12. doi:10.1016/S0264-2751(00)00049-4

Bauer, A., (1913). Tractate Luca Pacioli. *Journal of Accounting*, 3.

Bauer, R. A. (1966). *Social Indicators*. Cambridge, UK: M.I.T. Press.

Bauman, Z. (2013). Družbena neenakost v globalni dobi (K. Vidmar Horvat, Ed.). Ljubljana: Znanstvena založba Filozofske fakultete Univerze v Ljubljani.

Baumüller, J., & Haring, N. (2014). Enhancing Third Sector Accountability through Financial Accounting - Regulations and Practices in German-Speaking Countries. In International Society for Third-sector Research (ISTR) (pp. 1–20). Münster, Germany: Academic Press.

Baxter, P., & Jack, S. (2008). Qualitative case study methodology: Study design and implementation for novice researchers. *Qualitative Report*, *13*(4), 544–559.

Baylor, A., & Page, D. F. (2016). *Developing a Pedagogy of Beneficiary Accountability in the Representation of Social* (Vol. 825). Academic Press.

Bebbington, J., Gray, R., & Owen, D. (1999). Seeing the wood for the trees: Taking the pulse of social and environmental accounting. *Accounting, Auditing & Accountability Journal*, *12*(1), 47–52. doi:10.1108/09513579910259906

Bebbington, J., Higgins, C., & Frame, B. (2009). Initiating sustainable development reporting: Evidence from New Zealand. *Accounting, Auditing & Accountability Journal*, *22*(4), 588–625. doi:10.1108/09513570910955452

Becker, A. (2018). An Experimental Study of Voluntary Nonprofit Accountability and Effects on Public Trust, Reputation, Perceived Quality, and Donation Behavior. *Nonprofit and Voluntary Sector Quarterly*, *47*(3), 562–582. doi:10.1177/0899764018756200

Becker, G. (1964). *Human Capital: a theoretical and empirical analysis, with special reference to education*. Chicago, IL: The University of Chicago Press.

Becker, G. (1965). A theory of the Allocation of Time. *Economic Journal (London)*, *75*(299), 493–517. doi:10.2307/2228949

Beck, U. (1992). *Risk Society: Towards a New Modernity*. London: SAGE Publications Ltd.

Behnam, M., & MacLean, T. L. (2011). Where is the accountability in international accountability standards?: A decoupling perspective. *Business Ethics Quarterly*, *21*(1), 45–72. doi:10.5840/beq20112113

Belkaoui, A. (2004). *Accounting Theory*. Boston: Cengage Learning, EMEA.

Bell, D. (1969). The Idea of Social Report. *The Public Interest*, (15), 72–84.

Belyaeva, L. A. (2014). On defining the problem: Regional social capital and multiple modernization in Russia. On defining the problem. *Economic and Social Changes: Facts, Trends, Forecast*, *1*(31), 87–92. Retrieved from http://www.gurteen.com/gurteen/gurteen.nsf/id/L004680/

Benjamin, L. M. (2012). The potential of outcome measurement for strengthening nonprofits' accountability to beneficiaries. *Nonprofit and Voluntary Sector Quarterly*, *42*(6), 1224–1244. doi:10.1177/0899764012454684

Benjamin, N. (2016, July-December). JRD TATA (1904-93) and India's Economic Aspirations. Jharkhand Journal of Development and Management Studies. *XISS, Ranchi*, *14*(3 & 4), 7111–7712.

Benjamin, S. (2000). Governance, economic settings and poverty in Bangalore. *Environment and Urbanization*, *12*(1), 35–56. doi:10.1177/095624780001200104

Berners-Lee, T., Hendler, J., & Lassila, O. (2001). The semantic web. *Scientific American*, *284*(5), 34–43. doi:10.1038 cientificamerican0501-34 PMID:11396337

Bhatia, A. (2017, April). *The Weight Of Waste In India: The Need For "One Nation, One Policy."* Banega Swachh India.

Bhat, V., & Patil, Y. (2014). E-waste Consciousness and Disposal Practices among Residents of Pune City. *Procedia: Social and Behavioral Sciences*, *133*(May), 491–498. doi:10.1016/j.sbspro.2014.04.216

Bianchi C. (1996). *Modelli contabili e modelli 'dinamici' per il controllo di gestione in un'ottica strategica.* Milano: Centro Universitario Studi Aziendali - Collana di studi economico-aziendali.

Bianchi, C. (2012). Enhancing Performance Management and Sustainable Organizational Growth through System Dynamics Modeling. In Systemic Management for Intelligent Organizations: Concepts, Model-Based Approaches, and Applications, (pp. 143-161). Heidelberg, Germany: Springer.

Bidet, E. (2000). Économie sociale, nouvelle économie sociale et sociologie économique. *Sociologie du Travail*, *42*(4), 587–599. doi:10.1016/S0038-0296(00)01103-1

Birchall, J., & Hammond Ketilson, L. (2009). Resilience of the Cooperative Business Model in Times of Crisis. Geneva, Italy: ILO.

Birch, D. (2003). Corporate social responsibility: Some key theoretical issues and concepts for new ways of doing business. *Journal of New Business Ideas and Trends*, *1*(1), 1–19.

Bisin, A., & Guaitoli, D. (2006). *Social capital, modernization and growth.* Academic Press.

Block, P. (1993). *Stewardship: Choosing service over self-interest.* Berrett-Koehler Publishers.

Boatright, J. (2008). *Ethics in Finance.* Malden, MA: Blackwell. (Original work published 1999) doi:10.4135/9781412956260.n341

Bon, G. L. (2002). *The Crowd: A Study of the Popular Mind.* Mineola, NY: Dover Publications, Inc.

Boon, B., Greatbanks, R., Munro, J., & Gaffney, M. (2017). Service delivery under translation: Multi-stakeholder accountability in the non-profit community sector in New Zealand. *Health & Social Care in the Community*, *25*(2), 402–413. doi:10.1111/hsc.12319 PMID:26710720

Borges, J., Miranda, R., & Valdir, M. (2007). O discurso das fundações corporativas: Caminhos de uma "nova" filantropia? *Revista de Administração de Empresas*, *47*(4), 1–15.

Borgonovi, E. (2000). Le aziende non profit e la trasformazione di "valori" individuali in "valore" economico e sociale: elementi di teoria aziendale. In A. Zangrandi (Ed.), *Aziende non profit: le condizioni di sviluppo.* Milano: Egea.

Borzaga, C. (2015). Economia cooperativa. Rilevanza, evoluzione e nuove frontiere della cooperazione italiana. Trento, Italy: Euricse Edizioni.

Borzaga, C., & Defourny, J. (2001). *The Emergence of Social Entreprise.* London: Routledge.

Borzaga, C., & Tortia, E. C. (2009). Social enterprises and local economic development. In E. Clarence & A. Noya (Eds.), *The Changing Boundaries of Social Enterprises.* Paris: OECD Publishing. doi:10.1787/9789264055513-6-en

Bose, S. (2004). Decolonization and state building in South Asia. *Journal of International Affairs*, 95–113.

Bradshaw, P., Hayday, B., & Armstrong, R. (2007). Nonprofit Governance Models: Problems & Prospect. *The Innovation Journal*, *12*(3), 1–22.

Branan, B. (2019). *MODS and RDF Descriptive Metadata.* Retrieved 29 March 2019, from https://wiki.duraspace.org/display/samvera/MODS+and+RDF+Descriptive+Metadata+Subgroup

Branco, M., Delgado, C., Sá, M., & Sousa, C. (2014). Comparing CSR communication on corporate web sites in Sweden and Spain. *Public Journal of Management*, *9*(2), 231–250.

Branco, M., & Rodrigues, L. (2008). Factors influencing social responsibility disclosure by Portuguese companies. *Journal of Business Ethics, 83*(4), 685–701. doi:10.100710551-007-9658-z

Brandsen, T., van Hout, E., Vrielink, M. O., & Schillemans, T. (2008). Social Accountability and the Third Sector: A Critical Appraisal. *International Workshop on Social Audit, Social Accounting and Accountability*, 1–22.

Branson, D. M. (2016). Corporate Behaviour and Sustainability. Doing Weel by Being Good. In A. Guler & C. Ingley (Eds.), *A parthway to corporate sustainability social accounting* (p. 138). London: Routledge.

Bravo, M., & Al, A. T. (2016). Socially Responsible Investment A Multi-Criteria Decision Making Approach. In E. Ballestero, B. Pérez-Gladish, & A. M. Garcia-Bernabeu (Eds.), *Measurement of Assets' Social Responsibility Degree* (pp. 77–78). Cham, Switzerland: Springer.

Bravo, M., Ruiz, A. B., Pla-Santamaria, D., & Méndez-Rodríguez, P. (2015). Measurement of Assets' Social Responsibility Degree. In E. Ballestero, B. Pérez-Gladish, & A. Garcia-Bernabeu (Eds.), *Socially Responsible Investment. International Series in Operations Research & Management Science* (Vol. 219). Cham: Springer; doi:10.1007/978-3-319-11836-9_4

Brown, L. K., & Troutt, E. (2007). Reporting does not Equal Accountability! The Importance of Funding Characteristics and Process on Accountability. *International Journal of Public Administration, 30*(2), 209–225. doi:10.1080/01900690601118240

Brown, T., & Dacin, P. (1997). The company and the product: Corporate associations and consumer product responses. *Journal of Marketing, 61*(1), 68–84. doi:10.1177/002224299706100106

Brown, V. K. (2001). Non-profit accountability in faith-based organizations: Implications for philanthropy. *Journal of Ministry Marketing & Management, 7*(1), 1–8. doi:10.1300/J093v07n01_01

Brusca, I., & Montesinos, V. (2006). Are citizens significant users of government financial information? *Public Money & Management, 26*(4), 205–209. doi:10.1111/j.1467-9302.2006.00526.x

Bryce, H. J. (2016). The public's trust in nonprofit organizations: The role of relationship marketing and management. *The Nonprofit Quarterly, 49*(4), 112–131.

Bugg-Levine, A., Kogut, B., & Kulatilaka, N. (2012). A new approach to funding social enterprises. *Harvard Business Review, 90*(1/2), 118–123.

Burge, N., & Gangurde, S. (2015). Solid Waste Management in PCMC (3R's Principle). *International Journal of Science and Research, 4*(5), 476–481.

Burke, E. (1785, February 28). *Speech on "The Nabob of Arcot's Debts"*. Burke delivered a now-famous speech, wherein he condemned the damage to India by the East India Company.

Burrit, R. L. (2012). Environmental performance accountability: Planet, people, profits. *Accounting, Auditing & Accountability Journal, 25*(2), 370–405. doi:10.1108/09513571211198791

Burrit, R. L., & Schaltegger, S. (2010). Sustainability accounting and reporting: Fad or trend. *Accounting, Auditing & Accountability Journal, 23*(7), 829–846. doi:10.1108/09513571011080144

Cabinet Office/Government of the United Kingdom. (n.d.). Available at: http://data.gov.uk/sib_knowledge_box/toolkit

Cafaggi, F., & Iamiceli, P. (2009). New frontiers in the legal structure and legislation of social entreprises in Europe. A comparative Analysis. In A. Noya (Ed.), *The Changing Boundaries of Social Enteprises* (pp. 25–86). Paris: OECD Publishing. doi:10.1787/9789264055513-3-en

Calixto, L. (2013). The disclosure of sustainability reports in Latin America: A comparative study. *Revista de Administração (São Paulo), 48*(4), 828–842. doi:10.5700/rausp1124

Cambridge Econometrics. (2013). Mapping evolutions in Public Services in Europe: towards increased knowledge of industrial relations. *Cambridge Trust for New Thinking in Economics*. Retrieved from http://www.ceep.eu/wp-content/uploads/2014/07/Mapping-Public-Services-project_final-experts-report_May-2013.pdf

Campos, L., & Alcoforado, F. (2018). *Law, Government and Third Sector in Brazil: Improving deficient regulation to promote better accountability*. Academic Press.

Campos, T. (2006). Políticas para *stakeholders*: Um objetivo ou uma estratégia organizacional. *Revista de Administração Contemporânea, 10*(4), 111–130. doi:10.1590/S1415-65552006000400006

Canales, R. (2013). Weaving straw into gold: Managing organizational tensions between standardization and flexibility in microfinance. *Organization Science, 25*(1), 1–28. doi:10.1287/orsc.2013.0831

Candler, G., & Dumont, G. (2010). A non-profit accountability framework. *Canadian Public Administration, 53*(2), 259–279. doi:10.1111/j.1754-7121.2010.00126.x

Carman, J. G. (2008). Nonprofits, Funders, and Evaluation: Accountability in Action. *American Review of Public Administration, 39*(4), 374–390. doi:10.1177/0275074008320190

Carswell, G., & De Neve, G. (2014). T-shirts and tumblers: Caste, dependency and work under neoliberalisation in south India. *Contributions to Indian Sociology, 48*(1), 103–131. doi:10.1177/0069966713502423

Casadesus-Masanell, R., & Heilbron, J. (2015). The business model: Nature and benefits. In C. Baden-Fuller & V. Mangematin (Eds.), *Business models and modelling* (pp. 3–30). Emerald Group Publishing Limited. doi:10.1108/S0742-332220150000033002

Catarino, L. (2012). *O Uso Do Orçamento Como Ferramenta de Gestão Nas IPSS*. Aveiro: Dissertação de Mestrado, Universidade de Aveiro.

CEEP. (2010). *Public Services in the European Union & In the 27 Member States: Statistics, Organisation and Regulations*. Retrieved from http://www.epsu.org/sites/default/files/article/files/MappinReportDefEN.pdf

Chandrasekhar, C. P., Ghosh, J., & Roychowdhury, A. (2006). The 'demographic dividend' and young India's economic future. *Economic and Political Weekly*, 5055–5064.

Channa, S. M. (2004). Globalization and modernity in India: A gendered critique. *Urban Anthropology, 33*(1), 37–71.

Chapin, F. S. III, Kofinas, G. P., & Folke, C. (Eds.). (2009). *Principles of ecosystem stewardship: resilience-based natural resource management in a changing world*. Springer Science & Business Media.

Chapple, W., & Moon, J. (2005). Corporate social responsibility (CSR) in Asia: A seven-country study of CSR website reporting. *Business & Society, 44*(4), 415–441. doi:10.1177/0007650305281658

Chatrath, H., & Patil, Y. (2017). Waste management in the Pimpri Chinchwad, Pune, India. *Green Chemistry and Technology Letters, 3*(1), 1–8. doi:10.18510/gctl.2017.311

Chaudhri, V., & Wang, J. (2007). Communicating corporate social responsibility on the internet. *Management Communication Quarterly, 21*(2), 232–247. doi:10.1177/0893318907308746

Chen, L., Gillenson, M.L., & Sherrell, D.L. (2004). *Consumer acceptance of virtual stores: a theoretical model and critical success factors for virtual stores*. Academic Press.

Chen, P. P.-S. (1976). The Entity-relationship Model—Toward a Unified View of Data. *ACM Transactions on Database Systems, 1*(1), 9–36. doi:10.1145/320434.320440

Chen, S., & Bouvain, P. (2009). Is corporate responsibility converging? A comparison of corporate responsibility reporting in the USA, UK, Australia, and Germany. *Journal of Business Ethics, 87*(1), 299–317. doi:10.100710551-008-9794-0

Chiu, A. S. F., & Yong, G. (2004). On the industrial ecology potential in Asian developing countries. *Journal of Cleaner Production, 12*(8–10), 1037–1045. doi:10.1016/j.jclepro.2004.02.013

Choi, N., & Majumdar, S. (2014). Social entrepreneurship as an essentially contested concept: Opening a new avenue for systematic future research. *Journal of Business Venturing, 29*(3), 363–376. doi:10.1016/j.jbusvent.2013.05.001

Choudhury, E., & Ahmed, S. (2002). The Shifting Meaning of Governance: Public Accountability of Third Sector Organizations in an Emergent Global Regime. *International Journal of Public Administration, 25*(4), 561–588. doi:10.1081/PAD-120013256

Church, A. H. (1917). *Manufacturing costs and Accounts* (Vol. 4). New York: McGraw-Hill book Company.

Ciftci, S. (2010). Modernization, Islam, or social capital: What explains attitudes toward democracy in the Muslim world? *Comparative Political Studies, 43*(11), 1442–1470. doi:10.1177/0010414010371903

CIRIEC - International - Centre international de recherches et d'information sur l'économie publique, sociale et coopérative. (2012). *The Social Economy in The European Union.* Retrieved from https://www.eesc.europa.eu/sites/default/files/files/qe-04-17-875-en-n.pdf

CIRIEC - International - Centre international de recherches et d'information sur l'économie publique, sociale et coopérative. (2017). *Study Recent evolutions of the Social Economy in the European Union.* Retrieved from http://www.ciriec.uliege.be/wp-content/uploads/2015/12/EESC_CIRIECReport2012_EN.pdf

Claibourn, M., & Martin, P. (2007). *The Third Face of Social Capital: How Membership in Voluntary Associations Improves Policy Accountability*. Academic Press. doi:10.1177/1065912907301766

Coda, V. (1998). Stakeholder. In M. Rispoli (Ed.), *La strategia aziendale*. Torino: Utet.

Cohen, S., Mamakou, X., & Karatzimas, S. (2016, August). *IT enhanced popular reports: Is it the missing link in triggering citizens' interest?* Paper presented at the EGPA Conference, Utrecht, The Netherlands.

Cohen-Rosenthal, E. (2004). Making sense out of industrial ecology: A framework for analysis and action. *Journal of Cleaner Production, 12*(8–10), 1111–1123. doi:10.1016/j.jclepro.2004.02.009

Cohen, S., & Karatzimas, S. (2015). Tracing the future of reporting in the public sector: Introducing integrated popular reporting. *International Journal of Public Sector Management, 28*(6), 449–460. doi:10.1108/IJPSM-11-2014-0140

Collis, J., & Hussey, R. (2005). Pesquisa. In *Administração: Um Guia Prático Para Alunos de Graduação E Pós-Graduação (2nd ed.)*. Porto Alegre: Bookman.

Conniff, J. (1993). Burke and India: The Failure of the Theory of Trusteeship. *Political Research Quarterly, 46*(2), 291–309. doi:10.1177/106591299304600205

Connolly, C., & Hyndman, N. (2013). Charity accountability in the UK: Through the eyes of the donor. *Qualitative Research in Accounting & Management, 10*(3/4), 259–278. doi:10.1108/QRAM-02-2013-0006

Connolly, C., & Kelly, M. (2011). Understanding accountability in social enterprise organisations: A framework. *Social Enterprise Journal, 7*(3), 224–237. doi:10.1108/17508611111182386

Conroy, D. K. (2005). Non-profit organisations and accountability: A comment on the Mulgan and Sinclair frameworks. *Third Sector Review*, *11*(1), 103–116.

Cook, S., Conrad, C., Fowlkes, A. L., & Mohebbi, M. H. (2011). Assessing Google Flu Trends Performance in the United States during the 2009 Influenza Virus A (H1N1) Pandemic. *PLoS One*, *6*(8), e23610. doi:10.1371/journal.pone.0023610 PMID:21886802

Cooney, K., & Lynch-Cerullo, K. (2014). Measuring the social returns of nonprofits and social enterprises: The promise and perils of the SROI. *Nonprofit Policy Forum*, *5*(2), 367-393.

Coop Lombardia. (2018). *Bilancio Sociale 2017*. Pavia: Glifo.

Cooperatives Europe. (n.d.). Retrieved from http://www.co-opseurope.co-op/spip.php?rubrique19

Corazza, L., & Cisi, M. (2012). Accountability challenges in social enterprises and the implementation of a reporting standard an Italian case study. *The Journal of Social Business*, *2*, 44–67.

Corbetta, P. (Ed.). (2003). *La ricerca sociale: metodologia e tecniche*. Bologna: Il Mulino.

Cordery, C. J., & Baskerville, R. F. (2011). Charity transgressions, trust and accountability. *Voluntas*, *22*(2), 197–213. doi:10.100711266-010-9132-x

Corrar, L. J., Paulo, E., & Dias Filho, J. M. (2007). *Análise Multivariada: para os cursos de administração, ciências contábeis e economia*. São Paulo, SP: Atlas.

Costa, E., Pesci, C., Andreaus, M., & Taufer, E. (2019). Empathy, closeness, and distance in non-profit accountability. *Accounting, Auditing & Accountability Journal*, *32*(1), 224–254. doi:10.1108/AAAJ-03-2014-1635

Costa, E., Ramus, T., & Andreaus, M. (2011). Accountability as a Managerial Tool in Non-Profit Organizations: Evidence from Italian CSVs. *Voluntas*, *22*(3), 470–493. doi:10.100711266-011-9183-7

Coyle, K., & Baker, T. (2009). *DCMI: Guidelines for Dublin Core Application Profiles* (Working Draft). Retrieved 15 January 2018, from http://dublincore.org/documents/profile-guidelines/

CPHEEO. (2016). Central Public Health and Environmental Engineering Organization (CPHEEO). Municipal Solid Waste Management Manual, Part II. *Man*.

Crack, A. (2018). The Oxfam scandal has taught us there's no reward for honest charities. *The Guardian*. Retrieved from https://www.theguardian.com/voluntary-sector-network/2018/mar/16/government-donors-reward-honest-charities-oxfam

Crowder, M. (1964). Indirect rule—French and British style. *Africa*, *34*(03), 197–205. doi:10.2307/1158021

Cunha, J. V. A., & Coelho, A. C. (2007). Regressão linear múltipla. In L. J. Corrar, E. Paulo, & J. M. Dias Filho (Eds.), *Análise Multivariada: para os cursos de administração, ciências contábeis e economia* (pp. 131–231). São Paulo, SP: Atlas.

Curado Malta, M., & Baptista, A. A. (2013). A method for the development of Dublin Core Application Profiles (Me4DCAP V0.2): detailed description. In *Proceedings on International Conference on Dublin Core and Metadata Applications* (pp. 90–103). Lisbon, Portugal: Dublin Core Metadata Initiative. Retrieved from http://dcpapers.dublincore.org/pubs/article/view/3674

Curtie, B. (1998). OP Dwivedi, India's Environmental Policies, Programmes and Stewardship. *Contemporary South Asia*, *7*, 98–99.

Dahiwal, A. (2017, May). Now, PCMC Puts New System in Place for Waste Segregation. *Pune Mirror*.

Dainelli, F., Manetti, G., & Sibilio, B. (2013). Web-Based Accountability Practices in Non-profit Organizations: The Case of National Museums. *Voluntas, 24*(3), 649–665. doi:10.100711266-012-9278-9

Dalal, S. (2016, July). 4 Reasons Why Pune Scores in Waste Management. *Moneylife.*

Dall'agnol, C. F. D., Tondolo, R. R. P., Tondolo, V. A. G., & Sarquis, A. B. (2017). Transparência e Prestação de Contas na Mobilização de Recursos no Terceiro Setor: Um estudo de casos múltiplos realizado no sul do Brasil. *Revista Universo Contábil, 13*(2), 187–203.

Damaschin-Ţecu, R., & Etchart, N. (2016). *Case of Romania. Developing the industry of social investments in Central and Eastern Europe.* NESsT.

Dâmboviţa County Agency for Employment. (2017). *Activity Report on monitoring the social enterprise activity and social enterprises of insertion certified for 2016.* Available at: www.dambovita.anofm.ro

Das Gupta, A. (2007). Social responsibility in India towards global compact approach. *International Journal of Social Economics, 34*(9), 637–663. doi:10.1108/03068290710778642

Das, S., & Bhattacharyya, B. K. (2014). Estimation of Municipal Solid Waste Generation and Future Trends in Greater Metropolitan Regions of Kolkata, India. *Journal of Industrial Engineering and Management Innovation, 1*(1), 31–38. doi:10.2991/jiemi.2014.1.1.3

Davis, J. H., Schoorman, F. D., & Donaldson, L. (1997). Toward a stewardship theory of management. *Academy of Management Review, 22*(1), 20–47. doi:10.5465/amr.1997.9707180258

De Matteis, F., & Preite, D. (Eds.). (2016). *Azienda non profit e relazioni interistituzionali per il management dei sistemi territoriali.* Napoli: Editoriale Scientifica.

Dean, A.G., Dean, J.A., Burton, A.H., & Dicker, R.C. (1991). Epi Info: a general-purpose microcomputer program for public health information systems. *American Journal of Preventive Medicine*, 178-182.

Decree-Law no. 158/2009 of 13 July (Decreto-Lei 158/2009 de 13 de julho. Diário da República n.º 133/2009, Série I. Ministério das Finanças e da Administração Pública).

Decree-Law No. 98/2015. Journal of the Portuguese Republic, 1st series, No. 106, June 2, 3470-3493.

Deegan, C., & Gordon, B. (1996). A Study of the environmental disclosure practices of Australian corporations. *Accounting and Business Research, 26*(3), 187–199. doi:10.1080/00014788.1996.9729510

Dees, J. G. (2001). *The meaning of social entrepreneurship.* Retrieved from https://entrepreneurship.duke.edu/news-item/the-meaning-of-social-entrepreneurship/

Dees, J. G. (2013). Toward an open-solution society. *Standford Social Innnovation Rewiew*, 31-32. Retrieved from https://ssir.org/articles/entry/toward_an_open_solution_society

Defourny, J., & Nyssens, M. (2012). Conception of social entreprise in Europe. A comparative perspective with the United States. In Y. Hasenfeld & B. Gidron (Eds.), Social Entreprises. An organizational perspective (pp. 71-90). London: Palgrave Macmillan.

Defourny, J. (2002). *Social Enterprise in an Enlarged Europe: Concept and Realities.* EMES European Research Network.

Deloitte. (2010). *Corporate Social Responsibility Report (Vision, Values, Responsibility).* Retrieved from https://www2.deloitte.com/content/dam/Deloitte/global/Documents/About-Deloitte/gx-deloitte-2010-gir-cr-report.pdf

Deloitte. (2015). *Social Progress Index 2015*. Retrieved from https://www2.deloitte.com/content/dam/Deloitte/global/Documents/About-Deloitte/gx-cr-social-progress-index-executive-summary-2015.pdf

Desai, N., Pingali, V., & Tripathy, A. (2015). *Is 2% the Solution?* Experimental Evidence on the New CSR Rule in India.

Develtere, P., & Defourny, J. (1999). The social economy: The worldwide making of a third sector. In J. Defourny, P. Develtere, & B. Fonteneau (Eds.), Social Economy – North and South. KULeuven: HIVA.

Dey, C., & Gibbon, J. (2017). Moving on from Scaling Up: Further Progress in Developing Social Impact Measurement in the Third Sector. *Social and Environmental Accountability Journal*, *37*(1), 66–72. doi:10.1080/0969160X.2017.1285712

Dhaliwal, D. S., Radhakrishnan, S., Tsang, A., & Yang, Y. (2012). Nonfinancial disclosure and analyst forecast accuracy: International evidence on corporate social responsibility disclosure. *The Accounting Review*, *87*(3), 723–759. doi:10.2308/accr-10218

Dhanani, A., & Connolly, C. (2012). Discharging not-for-profit accountability: UK charities and public discourse. *Accounting, Auditing & Accountability Journal*, *25*(7), 1140–1169. doi:10.1108/09513571211263220

Di Domenico, M., Tracey, P., & Haugh, H. (2009). Social economy involvement in public service delivery: Community engagement and accountability. *Regional Studies*, *43*(7), 981–992. doi:10.1080/00343400701874180

Dincer, C., & Dincer, B. (2010). An investigation of Turkish small and medium-sized enterprises online CSR communication. *Social Responsibility Journal*, *6*(2), 197–207. doi:10.1108/17471111011051711

Dirks, N. B. (2011). *Castes of mind: Colonialism and the making of modern India*. Princeton University Press.

Dokhtesmati, M., Saberi, M., & Moradi, S. (2011). The status of ministries' website of Middle Eastern countries in achieving e-government. *77th IFLA General Conference and Assembly*.

Donaldson, L., & Davis, J. H. (1991). Stewardship theory or agency theory: CEO governance and shareholder returns. *Australian Journal of Management*, *16*(1), 49–64. doi:10.1177/031289629101600103

Donleavy, G., & Ghoorah-Hurrychurn, U. (2014). Third Sector Accounting And Accountability In Australia: Anything But A Level Playing Field. *Australian Policy Online*. Retrieved from http://apo.org.au/node/52950

Doshi, V. (2016), Indian royals in row over missing temple treasures, India - The Observer. *The Guardian*. Available at: https://www.theguardian.com/world/2016/sep/24/former-maharajahs-accused-over-temple-treasures

Dowling, J., & Pfeffer, J. (1975). Organizational legitimacy: Societal values and organizational behaviour. *Pacific Sociological Review*, *18*(19), 122–136. doi:10.2307/1388226

Drucker, P. (2010). *The essential Drucker: selection of management papers of Peter F. Drucker*. Bucharest: Meteor Press.

Du Pisani, J. A. (2006). Sustainable development–historical roots of the concept. *Environmental Sciences*, *3*(2), 83–96. doi:10.1080/15693430600688831

Dube, R., Nandan, V., & Dua, S. (2014). Waste incineration for urban India: Valuable contribution to sustainable MSWM or inappropriate high-tech solution affecting livelihoods and public health? *International Journal of Environmental Technology and Management*, *17*(2-4), 199–214. doi:10.1504/IJETM.2014.061792

Duff, A., & Guo, X. (2010). *Corporate Social Responsibility and the Professional Accounting Firm: Insights from Firms' Disclosures: Briefing*. The Institute of Chartered Accountants in England and Wales. Retrieved from https://www.icaew.com/-/media/corporate/files/products/sustainability/tecpln9787-crs-briefing-16-dec-final.ashx

Duguit, L. (1921). *Law in the Modern State* (F. Laski & H. Laski, Trans.). London: George Allen & Unwin Ltd.

Dulcamare, V. (2016). *Il regime fiscale delle cooperative*. Retrieved August, 20, 2018, from http://www.odcec.matera.it/files/formazione-regolamenti/slide%20DULCAMARE.pdf

Dumay, J., Guthrie, J., & Farneti, F. (2010). GRI sustainability reporting guidelines for public and third sector organizations: A critical review. *Public Management Review*, *12*(4), 531–548. doi:10.1080/14719037.2010.496266

Dumont, L. (1980). *Homo hierarchicus: The caste system and its implications*. University of Chicago Press.

Dutt, A. K., Noble, A. G., Costa, F. J., Thakur, S. K., Thakur, R. R., & Sharma, H. S. (Eds.). (2015). Spatial Diversity and Dynamics in Resources and Urban Development: Vol. 1. Regional Resources. Springer.

Dwivedy, M., & Mittal, R. K. (2012). An investigation into e-waste flows in India. *Journal of Cleaner Production*, *37*, 229–242. doi:10.1016/j.jclepro.2012.07.017

Ebrahim, A., & Rangan, V. K. (2010). The limits of nonprofit impact: A contingency framework for measuring social performance (No. 10-099). Harvard Business School.

Ebrahim, A. (2003a). Accountability in practice: Mechanisms for NGOs. *World Development*, *31*(5), 813–829. doi:10.1016/S0305-750X(03)00014-7

Ebrahim, A. (2003b). Making sense of accountability: Conceptual perspectives for northern and southern nonprofits. *Nonprofit Management & Leadership*, *14*(2), 191–212. doi:10.1002/nml.29

Ebrahim, A., Battilana, J., & Mair, J. (2014). The governance of social enterprises: Mission drift and accountability challenges in hybrid organizations. *Research in Organizational Behavior*, *34*, 81–100. doi:10.1016/j.riob.2014.09.001

Ebrahim, A., & Rangan, V. K. (2014). What impact? A framework for measuring the scale and scope of social performance. *California Management Review*, *56*(3), 118–141. doi:10.1525/cmr.2014.56.3.118

Eeckloo, K., Van Herck, G., Van Hulle, C., & Vleugels, A. (2004). From Corporate Governance to Hospital Governance. Authority, transparency and accountability of Belgian non-profit hospitals' board and management. *Health Policy (Amsterdam)*, *68*(1), 1–15. doi:10.1016/j.healthpol.2003.07.009 PMID:15033548

eEurope-2002. (2002). *E-Europe 2002 - Uma Sociedade Da Informação Para Todos*. Conselho da União Europeia - Comissão das Comunidades Europeias.

Ehrenfeld, J., & Gertler, N. (1997). Industrial Ecology in Practice. *Journal of Industrial Ecology*, *1*(1), 67–79. doi:10.1162/jiec.1997.1.1.67

Eichengreen, B., & Gupta, P. (2011). *The service sector as India's road to economic growth (No. w16757)*. National Bureau of Economic Research. doi:10.3386/w16757

Eisenhardt, K. M. (1989). Agency theory: An assessment and review. *Academy of Management Review*, *14*(1), 57–74. doi:10.5465/amr.1989.4279003

Eisenhardt, K. M. (1989). Building theories from case study research. *Academy of Management Review, Vol.*, *4*(14), 532–550. doi:10.5465/amr.1989.4308385

Elkington, J. (1997). *Cannibals with forks. The triple bottom line of 21st century*. Oxford, UK: Capstone Publishing.

Elkington, J. (1997). *Cannibals with forks: The triple bottom line of twentieth century business*. Oxford, UK: Capstone Publishing Ltd.

Elkington, J. (2001). The "Triple bottom line of 21st century business". In R. Starkey & R. Welford (Eds.), *The Earthscan reader in business & sustainable development* (pp. 20–43). London: Earthscan.

Ellenberg, J. (2014). *How Not to Be Wrong : The Power of Mathematical Thinking*. New York: Penguin USA.

Elsakit, O., & Worthington, A. (2014). The impact of corporate characteristics and corporate governance on corporate social and environmental disclosure: A literature review. *International Journal of Business and Management*, *9*(9), 1–15. doi:10.5539/ijbm.v9n9p1

Emerson, J., Wachowicz, J., & Chun, S. (2000). *Social Return on Investment: Exploring aspects of value creation in the nonprofit sector* (REDF Box Set No. Vol. 2). Retrieved March 13, 2019, from http://redf.org/app/uploads/2013/10/REDF-Box-Set-Vol.-2-SROI-Paper-2000.pdf

Enjolras, B. (2018). Introduction. In B. Enjolras, L. M. Salamon, K. H. Sivesind, & A. Zimmer (Eds.), *The Third Sector as a Renewable Resource for Europe. Concepts, Impacts, Challenges and Opportunities* (pp. 1–5). Palgrave Macmillan. doi:10.1007/978-3-319-71473-8_1

Epstein, M. J., & Yuthas, K. (2017). *Measuring and improving social impacts: A guide for nonprofits, companies and impact investors*. Routledge. doi:10.4324/9781351276245

Estes, R. (1976). *Corporate and social accounting*. New York: Wiley.

Estes, R. W. (1976). Socio-economic accounting and external diseconomies. *The Accounting Review*, *50*(2), 284–290.

European Commission. (2001). *Promoting a European framework for corporate social responsibility – green paper. Luxemburg*. Office for Official Publications of the European Communities.

European Commission. (2003). *Mutual Societies in an enlarged Europe*. Consultation Document. Retrieved from file:///C:/Users/CA/Downloads/mutuals-consult-doc-en.pdf

European Commission. (2011). Proposal for a Regulation of the European Parliament and of the Council on a European Union Programme for Social change and Innovation. Retrieved from http://eurlex.europa.eu/LexUriServ/LexUriServ.do?uri=COM:2011:0609:FIN:RO:PDF

European Commission. (2011a). Communication from the Commission to the European Parliament, the Council, the European Economic and Social Committee and the Committee of the Regions: A Quality Framework for Services of General Interest in Europe (COM(2011)900 final). Brussels: Author.

European Commission. (2011b). Communication from the commission to the European parliament, the council, the European economic and social committee and the committee of the regions Open data engine for innovation, growth and transparent governance /* COM/2011/0882 final */. Retrieved from http://eur-lex.europa.eu/legal-content/EN/TXT/HTML/?uri=CELEX:52011DC0882&from=EN

European Commission. (2013). *A vision for public services*. Retrieved from https://ec.europa.eu/digital-single-market/en/news/vision-public-services

European Commission. (2013). *The Social Business Initiative of the European Commission*. Available at: http://ec.europa.eu/internal_market/social_business/docs/201205-sbi-leaflet_ en.pdf

European Commission. (2015). *A Map of Social Enterprises and their Eco-Systems in Europe Synthesis Report*. Retrieved from file:///C:/Users/CA/Downloads/Synthesis%20report%20FINAL%20(1).pdf

European Commission. (2018). *Social economy in the EU*. Retrieved March 13, 2019, from https://ec.europa.eu/growth/sectors/social-economy_en

European Foundation Centre. (2008). *Report Foundations in the European Union - Facts & Figures Across*. Retrieved from http://www.efc.be/programmes_services/resources/Documents/EFC-RTF_EU%20Foundations-Facts%20and%2-Figures2008.pdf

European Parliament – Commission for Employment and Social Affairs. (2009). *Report on social economy* (2008/2250INI). Author.

European Social Enterprise Law Association. (2015). *Social Enterprise in Europe. Developing Legal Systems which Support Social Enterprise Growth*. Retrieved from http://providus.lv/article_files/3058/original/ESELA_Legal_Mapping_Publication_250915_(3)-1.pdf?1444030170

European Union Council. (2015). Retrieved from http://www.europarl.europa.eu/sides/getDoc.do?pubRef=-//EP//TEXT+OQ+O-2017-000070+0+DOC+XML+V0//EN

Evers, A., & Laville, J.-L. (2004). Defining the third sector in Europe. In A. Evers & J.-L. Laville (Eds.), The Third Sector in Europe. Globalization and welfare. Cheltenham, UK: Edward Elgar.

Fajardo, G., Fici, A., Henry, H., Meira, D., Münkner, H., & Snaith, I. (2017). *Principles of European Cooperative Law. Principles, Commentaries and National Reports*. Cambridge: Intersentia. doi:10.1017/9781780686073

Favreau, L. (2005). Qu'est-ce que l'économie sociale? Synthèse introductive. *Cahiers du Crises, Collection études théoriques*.

Fazzi, L. (2010). The provision of welfare and general-interest services. In C. Borzaga & L. Becchetti (Eds.), *The Economics of Social Responsability. The world of social entrepreses* (pp. 88–104). London: Routledge Advances in Social Economics.

Fenton, I., Andersen, L., & Tracey, L. I. (Eds.). (2015). *Global Green Accounting*. Retrieved from https://www.inesad.edu.bo/en/2015/06/14/global-green-accounting-2015/

Ferreira, A., Marques, R.P., Santos, C., Azevedo, G., & Mendes, H. (2016). Avaliação da Presença na Internet das Instituições Particulares de Solidariedade Social Portuguesas. *Estudos Do ISCA*, 14. doi:10.1234/ei.v0i14.4730

Fifka, M. S. (2012). The development and state of research on social and environmental reporting in global comparison. *Journal fur Betriebswirtschaft*, *62*(1), 45–84. doi:10.100711301-012-0083-8

Fifka, M. S., & Drabble, M. (2012). Focus and standardization of sustainability reporting – a comparative study of the United Kingdom and Finland. *Business Strategy and the Environment*, *21*(7), 455–474. doi:10.1002/bse.1730

Fiorentini, G., & Preite, D. (2000). Azienda pubblica e azienda non profit: Il ruolo del bilancio sociale nel decentramento. *Azienda Pubblica*, *2-3*, 253–288.

FMCBC. (2004). *Recommended practice: Preparing popular reports*. Retrieved April 10, 2019, from https://www.nsmfc.ca/budgeting-and-financial-reporting/493-preparing-popular-reports/file.html

Fontanari, E., & Borzaga, C. (2013). La cooperazione italiana negli anni della crisi. Trento, Italy: Euricse Edizioni.

Fontanari, E., & Carini, C. (2017). Le cooperative italiane sono fuori dalla crisi? Crescita, valore generato ed occupazione tra il 2013 e il 2014. Trento, Italy: Euricse Edizioni.

Forrester, J. W. (1961). *Industrial Dynamics*. Boston, MA: The MIT Press.

Foster, P., Gomm, R., & Hammersley, M. (2000). *Case Study Method. Key Issues*. London: Sage.

Foundation Together with You. (2011). *Policies, practices and trends in the social economy in Romania and the European Union.* Retrieved from https://ec.europa.eu/epale/ro/resource-centre/content/politici-practici-si-tendinte-economia-sociala-romania-si-uniunea-europeana

Fox, T., Ward, H., & Howard, B. (2002). *Public sector roles in strengthening corporate social responsibility: A baseline study.* The World Bank.

Freeman, R. E., Harrison, J. S., Wicks, A. C., Palmar, B. L., & Colle, D. E. S. (2010) Stakeholder Theory: The State of the Art. Cambridge, UK: Cambridge University Press.

Freeman, R., & McVea, J. (2001). A stakeholder approach to strategic management. Working-paper 01-02. Charlottesville, VA: Darden Graduate School of Business Administration. doi:10.2139srn.263511

Freeman, R. (1984). *Strategic management: a stakeholder approach.* Boston: Pitman.

Freeman, R. (1984). *Strategic Management: A Stakeholder Approach.* Boston: Pitman.

Frey, B. S., & Stutzer, A. (2001). *Happiness and Economics: How the Economy and Institutions Affect Human Well-Being.* Princeton, NJ: Princeton University Press.

Froelich, K. A. (1999). Diversification of revenue strategies: Evolving resource dependence in nonprofit organizations. *Nonprofit and Voluntary Sector Quarterly, 28*(3), 246–268. doi:10.1177/0899764099283002

Gálvez-Rodríguez, M., Caba-Perez, C., & López-Godoy, M. (2012). Responsabilidad social y transparencia on-line de las ONG: Análisis del caso español CIRIEC-España. *C.I.R.I.E.C. España, 74*, 207–238.

Gálvez-Rodríguez, M., Caba-Perez, C., & López-Godoy, M. (2014). Drivers for the proactive online disclosure of information in the NGO sector: The Colombian case. *Online Information Review, 38*(6), 769–787. doi:10.1108/OIR-05-2014-0113

Gandía, J. L. (2011). Internet disclosure by nonprofit organizations: Empirical evidence of nongovernmental organizations for development in Spain. *Nonprofit and Voluntary Sector Quarterly, 40*(1), 57–78. doi:10.1177/0899764009343782

Ganesh, K. N. (2013). To Whom Does Temple Wealth Belong? A Historical Essay on Landed Property in Travancore. *Review of Agrarian Studies, 3*(1). Retrieved from http://ras.org.in/to_whom_does_temple_wealth_belong_a_historical_essay_on_landed_property_in_travancore

García-Meca, E., & Conesa, I. M. (2004). Divulgación voluntaria de información empresarial: Índices de revelación. Partida Doble, 157, 66-77.

Garlapati, V. K. (2016). E-waste in India and developed countries: Management, recycling, business and biotechnological initiatives. *Renewable & Sustainable Energy Reviews, 54*, 874–881. doi:10.1016/j.rser.2015.10.106

Garzoni, A. (Ed.). (2003). *Il governo dell'impresa cooperativa.* Milano: Egea.

Gaur, A. S., Kumar, V., & Singh, D. (2014). Institutions, resources, and internationalization of emerging economy firms. *Journal of World Business, 49*(1), 12–20. doi:10.1016/j.jwb.2013.04.002

Gautam, R., & Singh, A. (2010). Corporate social responsibility practices in India: A study of top 500 companies. *Global Business and Management Research: An International Journal, 2*(1), 41–56.

Gazzola, P., Ratti, M., & Amelio, S. (2017). CSR and Sustainability Report for Nonprofit Organizations. An Italian Best Practice. *Management Dynamics in the Knowledge Economy, 5*(3), 355–376. doi:10.25019/MDKE/5.3.03

GBS. (2013). *Il Bilancio Sociale. Standard. Principi di redazione del bilancio sociale.* Milano: Giuffrè.

Geer, B. W., Maher, J. K., & Cole, M. T. (2008). Managing Nonprofit Organizations – The Importance of Transformational Leadership and Commitment to Operating Standards for Nonprofit Accountability. *Public Performance & Management Review*, *32*(1), 51–75. doi:10.2753/PMR1530-9576320103

GFOA. (2006). *Popular reporting of financial information*. Retrieved April 10, 2019, from http://www.gfoa.org/popular-reporting-financial-information

GFOA. (n.d.). *Popular annual financial reporting award program: Judges's evaluation form*. Retrieved April 10, 2019, from http://www.gfoa.org/sites/default/files/u63/pafr-reviewers-checklist.pdf

Ghoorah, U. (2018). *Snapshot Document: A Tool to develop trust and confidence*. Pro Bono Australia Newsletter.

Ghosh, S. K. (2016). Sustainable SWM in Developing Countries Focusing on Faster Growing Economies, India and China. *Procedia Environmental Sciences*, *35*, 176–184. doi:10.1016/j.proenv.2016.07.073

Gibbs, D., & Deutz, P. (2007). Reflections on implementing industrial ecology through eco-industrial park development. *Journal of Cleaner Production*, *15*(17), 1683–1695. doi:10.1016/j.jclepro.2007.02.003

Gidde, M. R., Kokate, K. K., & Todkar, V. V. (2008). Municipal Solid Waste Management in Emerging Mega Cities: A case study of Pune City. In *Indo Italian Conference on Green and Clean Environment* (pp. 441–450). Academic Press.

Gifford, R. (2011). The dragons of inaction: Psychological barriers that limit climate change mitigation and adaptation. *The American Psychologist*, *66*(4), 290–302. doi:10.1037/a0023566 PMID:21553954

Gillham, B. (1999). *Case Study Research Methods*. London: Continuum.

Ginsberg, J., Mohebbi, M. H., Patel, R. S., Brammer, L., Smolinski, M. S., & Brilliant, L. (2009). Detecting influenza epidemics using search engine query data. *Nature*, *457*(7232), 1012–1014. doi:10.1038/nature07634 PMID:19020500

Global Principles (GSP). (2006). In *Sustainability Dictionary*. Retrieved from: https://sustainabilitydictionary.com/2006/02/17/the-global-sullivan-principles-gsp/

Global Reporting Initiative. (2015). GRI4 – Sustainability Reporting guidelines. Boston: Author.

Global Reporting Initiative. (n.d.). *Global Reporting Initiative*. Retrieved February 17, 2019, from https://www.globalreporting.org/Pages/default.aspx

Goddard, A., & Juma Assad, M. (2006). Accounting and navigating legitimacy in Tanzanian NGOs. *Accounting, Auditing & Accountability Journal*, *19*(3), 377–404. doi:10.1108/09513570610670343

Godfrey, P. C., & Hatch, N. W. (2007). Researching corporate social responsibility: An agenda for the 21st century. *Journal of Business Ethics*, *70*(1), 87–98. doi:10.100710551-006-9080-y

Goh, J. X., Schlegel, K., Tignor, S. M., & Hall, J. A. (2016). Who is interested in personality? The Interest in Personality Scale and its correlates. *Personality and Individual Differences*, *101*, 185–191. doi:10.1016/j.paid.2016.05.366

GoI. (2008). *National Action Plan on Climate Change*. Author. doi:10.1111/j.1746-1561.1993.tb06065.x

GoI. (2011). *Guidelines for appraisal and approval of projects/schemes eligible for financing under the National Clean Energy Fund*. New Delhi: Department of Expenditure, Ministry of Finance.

GoI. (2013). *Companies Act, 2013*. Accessed in June 2018 at: www.mca.gov.in/Ministry/pdf/CompaniesAct2013.pdf

González, H. V. (2010). *The impact of nonfinancial performance on the financial performance of the United States investor-owned multihospital systems*. Rio Piedras: University of Puerto Rico.

Gonzalo, J. A., & Pérez, J. (2017). Una propuesta de normalización relativa al valor añadido como medida alternativa de rendimiento empresarial. *Especial XIX Congreso Internacional AECA*, 35-39.

Goodin, R. E. (2003). Democratic Accountability: The Third Sector and All. In Crisis of Governance: The Nonprofit/ Non-Governmental Sector. Academic Press. doi:10.2139srn.418262

Gourdie, J., & Rees, J. (2009). Financial Accountability Relationships between Donors and Recipients in the Non-profit Sector. *New Zealand Journal of Applied Business Research*, *7*(1), 41. Retrieved from http://search.ebscohost.com/login.aspx?direct=true&db=edsibc&AN=724680185512408&authtype=shib&site=eds-live&authtype=ip,cookie,shib%5Cn http://search.informit.com.au/documentSummary

Government, H. M. (2014). *Open Public Services 2014*. Retrieved from https://assets.publishing.service.gov.uk/government/uploads/system/uploads/attachment_data/file/291854/Open_Public_Services_Progress_Report_2014.pdf

Goyal, K. A. (2006). Impact of Globalization on Developing Countries (with special reference to India). *International Research Journal of Finance and Economics*, *5*, 166–171.

Goyder, G. (1961). *The responsible company*. Oxford, UK: Basil Blackwell.

Grace, D. (2014). *Measuring the Size and Scope of the Cooperative Economy*. New York, NY: UN DESA.

Grand, J. L. (2007). *The Other Invisible Hand: Delivering Public Services through Choice and Competition*. Princeton University Press.

Gray, R. (2002). The social accounting project and Accounting Organizations and Society Privileging engagement, imaginings, new accountings and pragmatism over critique? *Accounting, Organizations and Society*, *27*(7), 687–708. doi:10.1016/S0361-3682(00)00003-9

Gray, R. H., Kouchy, R., & Lavers, S. (1995). Constructing a research database of social and environmental reporting by UK companies: A methodological note. *Accounting, Auditing & Accountability Journal*, *8*(2), 78–101. doi:10.1108/09513579510086812

Gray, R. H., Owen, D., & Maunders, K. (1987). *Corporate social reporting: accounting and accountability*. London: Prentice-Hall.

Gray, R., Adams, C. A., & Owen, D. (2014). *Accountability, Social Responsibility and Sustainability: Accounting for Society and the Environment*. London, UK: Pearson Education Limited.

Gray, R., Dey, C., Owen, D., Evans, R., & Zadek, S. (1997). Struggling with the praxis of social accounting: Stakeholders, accountability, audits and procedures. *Accounting, Auditing & Accountability Journal*, *10*(3), 325–364. doi:10.1108/09513579710178106

Gray, R., Dillard, J., & Spence, C. (2010). A brief re-evaluation of "the social accounting project": Social accounting research as if the world matters. In A. Ball & S. P. Osborne (Eds.), *Routledge Critical Studies in Public Management: 5. Social Accounting and Public Management: Accountability for the Common Good* (pp. 11–22). New York, NY: Routledge.

Gray, R., Javad, M., Power, D., & Sinclair, C. (2001). Social and environmental disclosure and corporate characteristics: A research note and extension. *Journal of Business Finance & Accounting*, *28*(3-4), 327–356. doi:10.1111/1468-5957.00376

Gray, R., Owen, D., & Adams, C. (1996). *Accounting & Accountability: Changes and Challenges in Corporate Social and Environmental Reporting*. London, UK: Prentice Hall.

Gray, R., Owen, D., & Adams, C. (1996). *Accounting and accountability: Changes and challenges in corporate social and environmental reporting*. London: Prentice-Hall.

Gray, S. J., Meek, G. K., & Roberts, C. B. (1995). International capital market pressures and voluntary annual report disclosures by US and UK multinationals. *Journal of International Financial Management & Accounting*, *6*(1), 43–68. doi:10.1111/j.1467-646X.1995.tb00049.x

Greener, I., Simmons, R., & Powell, M. (Eds.). (2009). *The Consumer in Public Services: Choice, Values and Difference*. Policy Press.

Grieco, C. (2015). *Assesing Social Impact of Social Entrepises. Does one size really fit all?* Heidelberg, Germany: Springer Briefs in Business.

Gross, B., & Straussman, J. (1974, September). The Social Indicators Movement. *Social Policy*.

Gross, M. J., Jr. (1977). Nonprofit accounting: The continuing revolution. *Journal of Accountancy, 143*(6), 66-143.

Gross, B. (1972). The State Of The Nation: Social Systems Accounting. In R. A. Bauer (Ed.), *Social Indicators* (pp. 154–271). London, UK: M.I.T. Press.

Gross, M. J., McCarthy, J. H., & Shelmon, N. E. (2005). *Financial and accounting guide for not-for-profit organizations*. John Wiley & Sons.

Groth, J. C., Byers, S. S., & Bogert, J. C. (1996). Capital, economic returns and the creation of value. *Management Decision*, *24*(6), 21–20. doi:10.1108/00251749610121452

Guraieb Izaguirre, G. A. (2015). *Social enterprises: Examining accountability for social and financial performance* (Doctoral dissertation). Queensland University of Technology.

Guthrie, J., Petty, R., Yongvanich, K., & Ricceri, F. (2003). *Intellectual Capital Reporting: Content approaches to data collection*. Paper presented at Performance Measurement Association Intellectual Capital Symposium, Cranfield.

Guthrie, J., Petty, R., Yongvanich, K., & Ricceri, F. (2004). Using content analysis as a research method to inquire into intellectual capital reporting. *Journal of Intellectual Capital*, *5*(2), 282–293. doi:10.1108/14691930410533704

Guziana, B., & Dobers, P. (2013). How sustainability leaders communicate corporate activities of sustainable development. *Corporate Social Responsibility and Environmental Management*, *20*(4), 193–204. doi:10.1002/csr.1292

Hair, J. F. Jr, Anderson, R. E., & Black, W. C. (2005a). *Análise multivariada de dados*. Porto Alegre, RS: Bookman.

Hair, J. F. Jr, Babin, B., Money, A. H., & Samouel, P. (2005b). *Fundamentos de métodos de pesquisa em administração*. Porto Alegre, RS: Bookman.

Halme, M., & Huse, M. (1997). The influence of corporate governance, industry and country factors on environmental reporting. *Scandinavian Journal of Management*, *13*(2), 137–157. doi:10.1016/S0956-5221(97)00002-X

Hamschmidt, J., & Pirson, M. (Eds.). (2018). *Case studies in social entrepreneurship and sustainability: the oikos collection* (Vol. 2). Routledge.

Handy, F., & Russell, A. R. (2018). *Introduction: Why Ethics? Ethics for Social Impact*. Cham: Palgrave Macmillan. doi:10.1007/978-3-319-75040-8_1

Hansmann, H. (1980). The Role of nonprofit enterprise. *The Yale Law Journal*, *5*(5), 835–901. doi:10.2307/796089

Harriss, J. (2015). Hindu Nationalism in Action: The Bharatiya Janata Party and Indian Politics. *South Asia*, *38*(4), 712–718. doi:10.1080/00856401.2015.1089826

Hawkins, J. P., Roberts, C. M., Kooistra, D., Buchan, K., & White, S. (2005). Sustainability of scuba diving tourism on coral reefs of Saba. *Coastal Management*, *33*(4), 373–387. doi:10.1080/08920750500217518

Heald, D. A. (2006). Varieties of transparency. *Proceedings of the British Academy*, *135*, 25–43.

Hegel, G. W. F. (1998). *Fenomenologija duha*. Ljubljana: Analecta.

Herrmann, K. R. (2011). Creating an excellent popular financial report. *Government Finance Review*, 41-44. Retrieved April 10, 2019, from https://www.gfoa.org/sites/default/files/GFR_OCT_11_41.pdf

Herzlinger, R. E. (1996, March). *Can Public Trust in Nonprofits and Governments Be Restored? Harvard Business Review*.

Herzlinger, R. E., & Sherman, H. D. (1980). Advantages of fund accounting in'nonprofits'. *Harvard Business Review*, *58*(3), 94–105. PMID:10318498

Hindu. (2017). Climate change plan to get new missions. *The Hindu*. Retrieved from http://www.thehindu.com/news/national/Climate-change-plan-to-get-new-missions/article17090498.ece

Hinna, L. (2002). Le fasi e le valenze del processo di rendicontazione sociale. In Il bilancio sociale. Milano: Il Sole 24 ore.

Hoffman, S. (2009). Social Housing and Anti-social Behaviour: Issues of Community Engagement and Accountability for Non-profit Housing. European Network for Housing Research.

Hofstede, G., Hofstede, G. J., & Minkov, M. (2010). *Cultures and Organizations: Software of the Mind* (3rd ed.). Maidenhead, UK: McGraw-Hill.

Hood, C. (1998). *The Art of the State: Culture, Rhetoric, and Public Management*. Oxford University Press.

Hopwood, A. G., & Miller, P. (Eds.). (1994). *Accounting as social and institutional practice* (Vol. 24). Cambridge, UK: Cambridge University Press.

Hossain, M., & Reaz, M. (2007). The determinants and characteristics of voluntary disclosure by Indian banking companies. *Corporate Social Responsibility and Environmental Management*, *14*(5), 274–288. doi:10.1002/csr.154

Humphrey, C. R., & Erickson, R. A. (1997). Public accountability in non-profit industrial development organisations. *Voluntas*, *8*(1), 39–63. doi:10.1007/BF02354180

Hyndman, N. (2017). The charity sector—Changing times, changing challenges. *Public Money & Management*, *37*(3), 149–153. doi:10.1080/09540962.2017.1281608

Hyndman, N., & McConville, D. (2018). Trust and accountability in UK charities: Exploring the virtuous circle. *The British Accounting Review*, *50*(2), 227–237. doi:10.1016/j.bar.2017.09.004

Hyndman, N., McKillop, D., Ferguson, C., & Wall, T. (2004). The financial accountability of Irish Credit Unions: An initial empirical study. *Financial Accountability & Management*, *20*(3), 253–279. doi:10.1111/j.0267-4424.2004.00385.x

IISD. (n.d.). International Institute for Sustainable Development. *Kalundborg*.

Induchudan, V. T. (1969). *The Secret Chamber: A Historical, Anthropological & Philosophical Study of the Kodungallur Temple*. Cochin Devaswom Board.

INE – Statistics of Portugal. (2016). *Conta satélite da economia social – 2013*. Author.

Ingram, R. W. (1986). Tests of the fund accounting model for local governments. *Contemporary Accounting Research*, *3*(1), 200–221. doi:10.1111/j.1911-3846.1986.tb00634.x

Instituto de Pesquisa Econômica Aplicada (IPEA). (2015). *Mapa das Organizações da Sociedade Civil - 2015*. Retrieved June, 2018, from https:// mapaosc.ipea.gov.br/dados-indicadores.html/

International Integrated Reporting Council (IIRC). (n.d.). *Integrated Reporting*. Retrieved February 17, 2019, from http://integratedreporting.org/

International Organization for Standardization. (2010). *International Standard ISO 26000*. Geneva, Switzerland: ISO.

International Organization for Standardization. (2014). *Economic Benefits of Standards*. Geneva, Switzerland: ISO.

Irene, S., & Dwiningrum, A. (2016). Social Capital and School Accountability. In *International Conference on Educational Research and Innovation (ICERI 2016)* (pp. 383–391). Academic Press.

ISEA. (1999). *AccountAbility 1000 - Framework. Standard, guidelines and professional qualification*. Institute of Social and Ethical Accountability.

Islam, M. A., & Deegan, C. (2010). Media pressures and corporate disclosure of social responsibility performance information: A study of two global clothing and sports retail companies. *Accounting and Business Research*, *40*(2), 131–148. doi:10.1080/00014788.2010.9663388

Jamali, D., Lund-Thomsen, P., & Khara, N. (2017). CSR institutionalized myths in developing countries: An imminent threat of selective decoupling. *Business & Society*, *56*(3), 454–486. doi:10.1177/0007650315584303

Jammulamadaka, N. (2013). The responsibility of corporate social responsibility in SMEs. *The International Journal of Organizational Analysis*, *21*(3), 385–395. doi:10.1108/IJOA-Mar-2012-0566

Jawahir, I. S., & Bradley, R. (2016). Technological elements of circular economy and the principles of 6R-based closed-loop material flow in sustainable manufacturing. *Procedia CIRP*, *40*, 103–108. doi:10.1016/j.procir.2016.01.067

Jegers, M. (2009). "Corporate" Governance in Nonprofit Organizations – A Nontechnical Review of the Economic Literature. *Nonprofit Management & Leadership*, *20*(2), 143–164. doi:10.1002/nml.246

Jensen, A., Patmore, G., & Tortia, E. (2015). *Cooperative Enterprises in Australia and Italy Comparative analysis and theoretical insights. Strumenti per la didattica e la ricerca 172*. Firenze, Italy: Firenze University Press.

Jensen, M. C. (2002). Value maximization, stakeholder theory, and the corporate objective function. *Business Ethics Quarterly*, *12*(2), 235–256. doi:10.2307/3857812

Jensen, M. C., & Meckling, W. H. (1976). Theory of the firm: Managerial behavior, agency costs and ownership structure. *Journal of Financial Economics*, *3*(4), 305–360. doi:10.1016/0304-405X(76)90026-X

Jodhka, S. (2017). *Caste in contemporary India*. Routledge.

Jones, K. R., & Mucha, L. (2014). Sustainability Assessment and Reporting for Nonprofit Organizations: Accountability "for the Public Good". *Voluntas*, *25*(6), 1465–1482. doi:10.100711266-013-9399-9

Joshi, R., & Ahmed, S. (2016). Status and challenges of municipal solid waste management in India: A review. *Cogent Environmental Science*, *2*(1), 1139434. doi:10.1080/23311843.2016.1139434

Jottier, D., & Heyndels, B. (2012). Does social capital increase political accountability? An empirical test for Flemish municipalities. *Public Choice*, *150*(3–4), 731–744. doi:10.100711127-010-9727-1

Junqueira, L. (2000). *Organizações sem fins lucrativos e redes sociais na gestão das políticas sociais. Caderno de Administração PUC- São Paulo, 3*. EDUC.

Juster, T. H. F., Courant, P., & Dow, G. (n.d.). *Toward a Social Report*. Washington, DC: Government Printing Office.

Juster, T. H. F., Courant, P., & Daw, G. (1979). *Social Accounting and Social Indicators: A Framework for the Analysis of Well-Being*. The University of Michigan.

Juster, T. H. H., & Land, K. (Eds.). (1981). *Social Accounting Systems Essays on the State of the Art*. New York: Academic Press, Inc.

Justice Connect. (2017a). *Social Enterprise Guide: Legal issues to consider when setting up a social enterprise*. Australia Not-for-profit Law Guide. Accessed 12 February 2019, https://www.nfplaw.org.au/sites/default/files/media/Social_Enterprise_Guide_Cth_1.pdf

Justice Connect. (2017b). *Running the organisation – Documents, records and requests for access*. Australia Not-for-profit Law Guide. Accessed 12 February 2019, https://www.nfplaw.org.au/recordkeeping

Kamaluddin, A., Hasan, H. A., Arshad, R., & Samah, S. A. A. (2016). Social Capital and Innovation Capital: Accountability Towards Small Medium Enterprises' (SMEs) Sustainable Performance. *Malaysian Accounting Review, 15*(1), 197–223. Retrieved from http://www.emeraldinsight.com/doi/10.1108/09513571111098063

Kansal, M., & Singh, S. (2012). Measurement of corporate social performance: An Indian perspective. *Social Responsibility Journal, 8*(4), 527–546. doi:10.1108/17471111211272101

Kaplan, R. S., & Norton, D. P. (1992, January). The balanced scorecard – measures that drive performance. *Harvard Business Review*, 71–79. PMID:10119714

Kaplan, R. S., & Norton, D. P. (2003). *Balanced Scorecard*. Torino: ISEDI.

Kapoor, R. (2004). Plural dreams: India in the 21st century. *Futures, 36*(6/7), 637–653. doi:10.1016/j.futures.2003.12.007

Kapur, J. C. (1982). *India*. New Delhi: An Uncommitted Society, Vikas Publishing House.

Karamoy, H., Pangemanan, S., & Ilat, V. (2017). Accessibility, Accountability and The Impact of Social Enterprise. *Journal of Life Economics, 4*(3), 1–12. doi:10.15637/jlecon.204

Kasemets, A. (2001). Impact Assessment of Legislation for Parliament and Civil Society: a Comparative Study. *Proceedings of ECPRD Seminar*. Retrieved from https://www.riigikogu.ee/rva/ecprd/04_part_2.pdf

Kaufmann, D., & Kraay, A. (2015). *The Worldwide Governance Indicators: Methodology and Analytical Issues*. Retrieved from http://info.worldbank.org/governance/wgi/index.aspx#home

Keating, E. K., & Frumkin, P. (2003). Reengineering nonprofit financial accountability: Toward a more reliable foundation for regulation. *Public Administration Review, 63*(1), 3–15. doi:10.1111/1540-6210.00260

Keehley, P., & Abercrombie, N. N. (2008). *Benchmarking in the public and nonprofit sectors. Best practices for achieving performance breakthroughs* (2nd ed.). San Francisco, CA: Jossey-Bass.

Kehl, K., Then, V., & Münscher, R. (2012). Social return on investment: Auf dem weg zu einem integrativen ansatz der wirkungsforschung. In H. K. Anheier, A. Schröer, & V. Then (Eds.), *Soziale Investitionen: Interdisziplinäre Perspektiven* (pp. 313–331). Wiesbaden: VS Verlag für Sozialwissenschaften. doi:10.1007/978-3-531-94105-9_12

Kelly, E. (2011). Systematic and just: The use of a systematic review methodology in social work research. *Social Work & Social Sciences Review, 15*(3), 72–85. doi:10.1921/095352212X657544

Kendall, J., & Knapp, M. (2000). The third sector and welfare state modernisation: Inputs, activities and comparative performance Civil Society Working Paper 14. *Health San Francisco*. Retrieved from http://eprints.lse.ac.uk/29055/

Kerlin, J. A. (2012). Defining social entreprise across diffrent context: a conceptual framework based on institutional factors. In Y. Hasenfeld & B. Gidron (Eds.), Social Entreprises. An organizational perspective (pp. 91-120). London: Palgrave Macmillan.

Khieng, S. (2014). Funding Mobilization Strategies of Nongovernmental Organizations in Cambodia. *Voluntas*, *25*(6), 1441–1464. doi:10.100711266-013-9400-7

Kilby, P. (2013). Waste Recycling and the Household Economy: The Case of the Pune Waste-Pickers' Response to the Changing 'Rules of the Game. In *The Global Political Economy of the Household in Asia* (pp. 211–226). London: Palgrave Macmillan. doi:10.1057/9781137338907_14

Kolk, A. (2004). A decade of sustainability reporting: Development and significance. *International Journal of Environment and Sustainable Development*, *3*(1), 51–64. doi:10.1504/IJESD.2004.004688

Kolk, A. (2008). Sustainability, accountability and corporate governance: Exploring multinationals' reporting practices. *Business Strategy and the Environment*, *17*(1), 1–15. doi:10.1002/bse.511

Koppell, J. G. S. (2005). Pathologies of accountability: ICANN and the challenge of "multiple accountabilities disorder". *Public Administration Review*, *65*(1), 94–108. doi:10.1111/j.1540-6210.2005.00434.x

Korhonen, J. (2001). Four ecosystem principles for an industrial ecosystem. *Journal of Cleaner Production*, *9*(3), 253–259. doi:10.1016/S0959-6526(00)00058-5

Krishnamurthy, S., Joseph, S., Pradhan, V., & Rao, P. (2017). Empowering Women of Rural India for Renewable Energy Adoption–An Exploratory Factor Analysis. *Indian Journal of Science and Technology*, *10*(37), 1–10. doi:10.17485/ijst/2017/v10i37/95576

Krishnamurthy, S., & Pradhan, V. (2018a). Anecdotes of Action Learning: Initiations of Sustainability Lessons by an Indian B-School. In *Cross-Disciplinary Approaches to Action Research and Action Learning*. IGI. doi:10.4018/978-1-5225-2642-1.ch007

Krishnamurthy, S., & Pradhan, V. (2018b). Anecdotes of Action Learning: Realizations of an Indian B-School's Sustainability Lessons. In *Cross-Disciplinary Approaches to Action Research and Action Learning*. IGI. doi:10.4018/978-1-5225-2642-1.ch008

Kumar, S., Bhattacharyya, J. K., Vaidya, A. N., Chakrabarti, T., Devotta, S., & Akolkar, A. B. (2009). Assessment of the status of municipal solid waste management in metro cities, state capitals, class I cities, and class II towns in India: An insight. *Waste Management (New York, N.Y.)*, *29*(2), 883–895. doi:10.1016/j.wasman.2008.04.011 PMID:18595684

Kummer, T. F., Singh, K., & Best, P. (2015). The effectiveness of fraud detection instruments in not-for-profit organizations. *Managerial Auditing Journal*, *30*(4/5), 435–455. doi:10.1108/MAJ-08-2014-1083

Kvale, S., & Brinkmann, S. (Eds.). (2009). *InterViews: Learning the craft of qualitative researching interviewing*. London: Sage.

Larsson, D. (2007). *Social Capital, In spite of or due to modernization? An analysis of a two-dimensional concept*. Universiteteti Oslo.

Law no. 119/2015, of 31 August (Lei n.º 119/2015 de 31 de agosto. Diário da República n.º 169/2015, Série I. Assembleia da República).

Lazzarini, S. G. (2018). The measurement of social impact and opportunities for research in business administration. *RAUSP Management Journal*, *53*(1), 134–137. doi:10.1016/j.rauspm.2017.12.010

Lee, M. (2006). The history of municipal public reporting. *International Journal of Public Administration*, *29*(4-6), 453–476. doi:10.1080/01900690500436982

Lee, R., & Blouin, M. (2017). Factors affecting web disclosure adoption in the non-profit sector. *Journal of Computer Information Systems*, 1–10. doi:10.1080/08874417.2017.1370988

Lee, S.-Y., Chen, W., & Weiner, B. (2004). Communities and Hospitals: Social Capital, Community Accountability, and Service Provision in U.S. Community Hospitals. *Health Services Research*, *39*(5), 1487–1509. doi:10.1111/j.1475-6773.2004.00300.x PMID:15333119

Lehman, G. (2001). Reclaiming the public sphere: Problems and prospects for corporate social and environmental accounting. *Critical Perspectives on Accounting*, *12*(6), 713–733. doi:10.1006/cpac.2001.0476

Lehn, B. (2008). Bearing More Risk for Results – Performance Acountability and Nonprofit Relational Work. *Administration & Society*, *39*(8), 959–983. doi:10.1177/0095399707309357

Lehn, B. (2010a). Funders as Principals - Performance Measurement in Philantropic Relationships. *Nonprofit Management & Leadership*, *20*(4), 383–403. doi:10.1002/nml.20001

Lehn, B. (2010b). Mediating Accountability - How Nonprofit Fundind Intermediaries Use Performance Measurement and Why It Matter for Governance. *Public Performance & Management Review*, *33*(4), 594–618. doi:10.2753/PMR1530-9576330404

Lifelong Learning Programme. (2010). *O que é a responsabilidade social empresarial? The project "InnoTrain CSR"*. Disponível em: http://www.csr-training.eu/en/csr-training/what-is-csr/

Liger, Q., Stefan, M., & Britton, J. (2016). *Social Economy, Study*. Directorate General For Internal Policies, Policy Department A: Economic And Scientific Policy. Retrieved from http://www.europarl.europa.eu/RegData/etudes/STUD/2016/578969/IPOL_STU(2016)578969_EN.pdf

Lingane, A., & Olsen, S. (2004). Guidelines for social return on investment. *California Management Review*, *46*(3), 116–135. doi:10.2307/41166224

Linowes, D. F. (1972). Socio-economic accounting. *Journal of Accountancy*, *133*, 37–42.

Linowes, D. F. (1973). The accounting profession and social progress. *Journal of Accountancy*, *136*(1), 32–40.

Li, X., & Pan, J. (2014). *China Green Development Index Report Regional Comparison*. Berlin, Germany: Springer.

Lorenz, G. (2008). *The Implementation of Social Capital Features in Social Auditing Procedures to secure Community Accountability of Social Enterprises in the Third Sector*. Academic Press.

Luhmann, N. (2004). *Law as a Social System* (F. Kastner, R. Nobles, D. Schiff, & R. Ziegert, Eds.; ZiegertK. A., Trans.). Oxford, UK: Oxford University Press.

Luhmann, N. (2013). *Oblast*. Ljubljana: Krtina.

Luke, B. (2017). Statement of Social Performance: Opportunities and Barriers to Adoption. *Social and Environmental Accountability Journal*, *37*(2), 118–136. doi:10.1080/0969160X.2017.1307129

Lyneis, J. M. (1982). *Corporate planning and policy design: a system dynamics approach*. Boston: MIT Press/Wright-Allen series in system dynamics.

MacArthur, E. (2013). *Towards a Circular Economy—Economic and Business Rationale for an Accelerated Transition*. Cowes, UK: Ellen MacArthur Foundation.

Mack, J., & Ryan, C. (2006). Reflections on the theoretical underpinnings of the general-purpose financial reports of Australian government departments. *Accounting, Auditing & Accountability Journal, 19*(4), 592–612. doi:10.1108/09513570610679146

Maddocks, J., Novkovic, S., & Smith, S. M. (2011). Measuring Performance for Accountability of a Small Social Economy Organization: The Case of an Independent School. *Canadian Journal of Nonprofit and Social Economy Research, 2*(1), 45–60. doi:10.22230/cjnser.2011v2n1a59

Maduro, M., Pasi, G., & Misuraca, G. (2018). *Social impact investment in the EU. Financing strategies and outcome oriented approaches for social policy innovation: narratives, experiences, and recommendations*. Luxembourg: Publications Office of the European Union.

Magena, M., Kinman, R., & Citron, D. (2008). Investment analysts' perception of disclosure in UK interim financial reports. *Journal of Applied Accounting Research, 8*(3), 146–185. doi:10.1108/96754260880001057

Maier, F., Schober, C., Simsa, R., & Millner, R. (2015). SROI as a method for evaluation research: Understanding merits and limitations. *Voluntas, 26*(5), 1805–1830. doi:10.100711266-014-9490-x

Maine, S. H. S. (1976). *Popular Government: An Inquiry into the Conditions Necessary for the Success of Representative Government by the Author of Ancient Law*. Indianapolis, IN: Liberty Classics.

Maines, L., Bartov, E., Fairfield, P., Hirst, D., Iannaconi, T., Mallett, R., ... Vincent, L. (2002). Commentary - recommendations of disclosure of nonfinancial performance measures. *Accounting Horizons, 16*(4), 352–362. doi:10.2308/acch.2002.16.4.353

Mair, J., & Marti, I. (2004). *Social entrepreneurship research: a source of explanation, prediction and delight*. Working paper no. 546. IESE Business School- University of Navarra.

Mair, J., Battilana, J., & Cardenas, J. (2012). Organizing for society: A typology of social entrepreneuring models. *Journal of Business Ethics, 111*(3), 353–373. doi:10.100710551-012-1414-3

Majumdar, S., & Saini, G. K. (2016). CSR in India: Critical Review and Exploring Entrepreneurial Opportunities. *Journal of Entrepreneurship and Innovation in Emerging Economies, 2*(1), 56–79. doi:10.1177/2393957515619719

Makoza, F. (2013). The level of e-Government implementation: Case of Malawi. *Electronic Journal of E-Government, 11*(1), 267–278.

Manetti, G., & Toccafondi, S. (2014). Defining the Content of Sustainability Reports in Nonprofit Organizations: Do Stakeholders Really Matter. *Journal of Nonprofit & Public Sector Marketing, 25*(1), 35–61. doi:10.1080/10495142.2013.857498

Mani, S., & Singh, S. (2016). Sustainable Municipal Solid Waste Management in India: A Policy Agenda. *Procedia Environmental Sciences, 35*, 150–157. doi:10.1016/j.proenv.2016.07.064

Martin Curran, M., & Moran, D. (2007). Impact of the FTSE4Good Index on firm price: An event study. *Journal of Environmental Management, 82*(4), 529–537. doi:10.1016/j.jenvman.2006.02.010 PMID:16678334

Matacena, A. (1991). Responsabilità sociale, cooperativa e sistema informative. *Relazione al Workshop Responsabilità sociale. Bilancio sociale e Cooperativa, 18*.

Matacena, A. (1992). Impresa e ambiente. Il "bilancio sociale". In La cooperazione sociale ed i loro consorzi tra imprenditorialità e solidarietà sociale. Roma, Italy: Istituto Italiano di Studi Cooperativi "L. Luzzati".

Matacena, A. (1984). *Impresa e ambiente. Il "bilancio sociale"*. Bologna, Italy: CLUEB.

Matacena, A. (1987). *Toward a "societal" information system. Economia Aziendale, Rivista dell'Accademia Italiana Di Economia Aziendale*. Milano: Giuffrè.

Matacena, A. (1995). *L'impresa cooperativa come «ideal-tipo» di impresa socialmente responsabile. Giornata di studi economici sulla cooperazione*. Bologna: Printer Editrice.

Matacena, A. (Ed.). (1984). *Impresa e ambiente. Il bilancio "sociale"*. Bologna: Clueb.

Matei, L., & Sandu, C. (2011). *A social entreprise: An empirical Study for Romania*. Paper presented at the 10 International Congress of the International Association on Public and Nonprofit Marketing. Retrieved from SSRN: http://ssrn.com/abstract=1805770

Matei, L., & Sandu, C. (2016). Social Enterprise – an important pillar in Producing and Providing Public goods and services. In L. Matei, M. Meneguzzo, C. Mititelu, & B. Berceanu (Eds.), Business Government relations and social enterprises. Lessons and experiences from South-Eastern Europe (pp. 167-222). Brussels: Bruylant.

Mathews, J. A., Tang, Y., & Tan, H. (2011). China's move to a Circular Economy as a development strategy. *Asian Business & Management, 10*(4), 463–484. doi:10.1057/abm.2011.18

Mathews, M. R. (1995). Social and environmental accounting: A practical demonstration of ethical concern? *Journal of Business Ethics, 14*(8), 663–671. doi:10.1007/BF00871347

Matienzo, M., Roke, E., & Carlson, S. (2017). Creating a Linked Data-Friendly Metadata Application Profile for Archival Description. *International Conference on Dublin Core and Metadata Applications*, 112–116.

Matten, D., & Moon, J. (2008). "Implicit" and "explicit" CSR: A conceptual framework for a comparative understanding of corporate social responsibility. *Academy of Management Review, 33*(2), 404–424. doi:10.5465/amr.2008.31193458

McClusky, J. E. (2007). Re-Thinking Nonprofit Organization Governance Implications for Management and Leadership. *International Journal of Public Administration, 25*(4), 539–559. doi:10.1081/PAD-120013255

McDonald, C. (1999). Internal Control and Accountability in Non-profit Human Service Organisations. *Australian Journal of Public Administration, 11*(22).

McDonnell, D. (2017). Improving Charity Accountability: Lessons from the Scottish Experience. *Nonprofit and Voluntary Sector Quarterly, 46*(4), 725–746. doi:10.1177/0899764017692039

Mehrotra, S., Parida, J., Sinha, S., & Gandhi, A. (2014). Explaining employment trends in the Indian economy: 1993-94 to 2011-12. *Economic and Political Weekly, 49*(32), 49–57.

Mehta, A. (2014). PCMC officials get notice for waste management. *Daily News & Analysis.*

Mehta, D., & Aggarwal, M. (2015). Making Corporate Social Responsibility Mandatory in India-Prospects and Problems. *International Journal of Research in Business Management, 3*(5), 21–30.

Meira, D. (2009). O regime económico das cooperativas no direito português: o capital social. *Vida Económica*. Retrieved from http://recipp.ipp.pt/handle/10400.22/657

Meira, D. A. (2016). *A fiscalizaçao das cooperativas à luz do novo Código Cooperativo português*. Retrieved 6 November 2018, from https://dialnet.unirioja.es/servlet/articulo?codigo=5770310

Meira, D. A., & Ramos, M. E. (2014). *Governação e regime económico das cooperativas*. Porto: VidaEconómica.

Melse, E. (2008). The Financial Accounting Model from a System Dynamics' Perspective. MPRA Paper 7624. Munich, Germany: University Library of Munich.

Mendell, M., & Nogales, R. (2009). Social Entreprises in OECD member countries. What are the financial streams. In A. Noya (Ed.), *The Changing Boundaries of Social Enteprises* (pp. 89–138). Paris: OECD Publishing. doi:10.1787/9789264055513-4-en

Migliavacca, A., Rainero, C., Puddu, L., & Modarelli, G. (2018). Social impact and evaluation: A rational management theory approach. *African Journal of Business Management, 12*(5), 92–102. doi:10.5897/AJBM2017.8458

Millennium. (2005). *Millennium ecosystem assessment synthesis report, a report of the millennium ecosystem assessment.* accessed May 2017 at http://www.millenniumassessment.org/en/Products.Synthesis.aspx

Miller, P. (2001). Governing by numbers: Why calculative practices matter. *Social Research, 62*(2), 379–396.

Milne, M. R. (2002). Positive Accounting Theory, Political Costs and social Disclosure Analysis: A Critical Look. *Accounting, Auditing & Accountability Journal, 12*, 369–395.

Milne, M. R., & Adler, R. W. (1999). Exploring the reliability of social and enviromental disclsures content analysis. *Accounting, Auditing & Accountability Journal, 12*(2), 237–256. doi:10.1108/09513579910270138

Ministério da Solidariedade, E. e S.S. (2014). Decreto-Lei 172-A/2014. *Diário da República, 221*(1). Available at: https://dre.pt/application/conteudo/58900566

Ministério das Finanças e da Administração Pública. (2011). Decreto-Lei 36-A/2011. *Diário da República, 48*(1). Available at: https://dre.pt/application/conteudo/647296

Ministry of Labor and Social Policy Italy. (2008). *Social Reporting (Guidelines for the Social Report of Social Enterprises).* Retrieved from https://www.reportingexchange.com/reportingProvision/1825?entityVersionID=2665

Ministry of Power. (2017). *Power Sector at a Glance - All India.* Government of India.

Ministry of Work, Employment, Professional Training and Social Dialogue, France. (2018). *Social Reporting* (Article R 2323.17 Labor Code). Retrieved from https://www.reportingexchange.com/search?search=social%20report&filters=%5B%7B%22filterName%22:%22entity_type%22,%22filterItem%22:3%7D%5D

Mirshekary, S., & Saudagaran, S. M. (2005). Perceptions and characteristics of financial statement users in developing countries: Evidence from Iran. *Journal of International Accounting, Auditing & Taxation, 14*(1), 33–54. doi:10.1016/j.intaccaudtax.2005.01.001

Mishra, P. N. (2017). *Mismanagement Of Wealth In Shri Padmanabhaswamy Temple: Amicus Seeks SIT Probe, Report on May 3, 2017.* available at: http://www.livelaw.in/mismanagement-wealth-shri-padmanabhaswamy-temple-amicus-seeks-sit-probe-read-report/

Mission, R. (2007). *S-14011/2/2015-SBM, Swachh Bharat Mission (Gramin).* Accessed in Sep 2017 at http://www.mdws.gov.in/sites/default/files/PMC_publication_of_contract_0.pdf

Mitchell, G. (2014). Why Will We Ever Learn - Measurement and Evaluation in International Development NGO's. *Public Performance & Management Review, 37*(4), 605–631. doi:10.2753/PMR1530-9576370404

Mitchell, R. K., Agle, B. R., & Wood, D. J. (1997). Toward a theory of stakeholder identification and salience: Defining the principle of who and what really counts. *Academy of Management Review, 22*(4), 853–886. doi:10.5465/amr.1997.9711022105

MoEFCC. (2016). Plastic Waste Management Rules 2016. New Delhi, India: Author.

Molnar, M. (2004). *Accountability Model and Self-Assessment Initiative for Third Sector Organizations.* Academic Press.

Monzon, J. L., & Chaves, R. (2008). The european social economy: Concept and dimensions of the third sector. *Annals of Public and Cooperative Economics*, *79*(3-4), 549–577. doi:10.1111/j.1467-8292.2008.00370.x

Moody, M., Littlepage, L., & Paydar, N. (2015). Measuring social return on investment: Lessons from organizational implementation of SROI in the netherlands and the united states. *Nonprofit Management & Leadership*, *26*(1), 19–37. doi:10.1002/nml.21145

Mook, L. (2007). *Social and environmental accounting: The expanded value added statement* (Unpublished doctoral dissertation). University of Toronto, Toronto, Canada.

Mook, L. (2014). An integrated social accounting model for nonprofit organizations. In E. Costa, L.D. Parker, & Andreaus, M. (Eds.), Advances in Public Interest Accounting: Vol. 17. Accountability and Social Accounting for Social and Non-Profit Organizations (pp. 197-221). Bingley, UK: Emerald Group Publishing Limited. doi:10.1108/S1041-706020140000017008

Mook, L., Quarter, J., & Richmond, B. J. (2007). What counts: Social accounting for nonprofits and cooperatives (2nd ed.). Medina, OH: Sigel.

Mook, L. (2013). Social accounting for the social economy. In L. Mook (Ed.), *Accounting for Social Value* (pp. 5–28). Toronto: University of Toronto Press. doi:10.3138/9781442694453-003

Moore, M. H. (2003). *The public value scorecard: a rejoinder and an alternative to 'strategic performance measurement and management in non-profit organizations' by Robert Kaplan.* Hauser Center for Nonprofit Organizations, The Kennedy School of Government, Harvard University, Working Paper 18.

Moore, M., & Ryan, W. (2006). *A Framework for analyzing Governance and Accountability Policies and Strategies.* The Hauser Center for Nonprofit Organizations - Harvard University, Working Paper nº 33.3.

Moore, M. H. (2000). Managing for Value: Organizational Strategy in For-Profit, Nonprofit and Governmental Organizations. *Nonprofit and Voluntary Sector Quarterly*, *29*(1), 183–204. doi:10.1177/089976400773746391

Morris, M. (2018). RSL Victoria admits 'inappropriate' gift to former boss partly paid with charity money. *ABC News.* Accessed 13 September 2018, http://www.abc.net.au/news/2018-06-28/former-rsl-victoria-boss-given-inappropriate-gift-probe-finds/9919012

Morrissey, A. J., & Browne, J. (2004). Waste management models and their application to sustainable waste management. *Waste Management, 24*(3), 297-308.

Motwani, R. (2001). *The Sociology of Indian Politics*. Cosmo Publications.

MOUD (2015). *Smart City: Mission Statement and Guidelines*. Author.

Mridula & Sinha. (2016). *Swachh Bharat - A Clean India*. Prabhat Prakashan.

Mueller-Hirth, N. (2012). If You Don't Count: Monitoring and Evaluation in South African NGOs. *Development and Change*, *43*(3), 649–670. doi:10.1111/j.1467-7660.2012.01776.x

Mueller, J., Williams, D., Higgins, A., & Tou, M. (2005). The Measurement of responsible governance and management of NPOs in New Zealand: An evaluation tool for NPOs, donors and government. "If you have no money – you have no mission. *Corporate Governance: The International Journal of Business in Society*, *5*(2), 159–173. doi:10.1108/14720700510562730

Mullins, D. (2006). Competing Institutional Logics? Local Accountability and Scale and Efficiency in an Expanding Non-Profit Housing Sector. *Public Policy and Administration*, *21*(3), 6–24. doi:10.1177/095207670602100302

Münkner, H. (2015). *Co-operative Principles and Co-operative Law* (2nd ed.). Zurich: Lit Verlag GmbH & Co. KG Wien.

Murray, A., Skene, K., & Haynes, K. (2017). The Circular Economy: An Interdisciplinary Exploration of the Concept and Application in a Global Context. *Journal of Business Ethics*, *140*(3), 369–380. doi:10.100710551-015-2693-2

Murtaza, N. (2012). Putting the lasts first: The case for community-focused and peer-managed NGO accountability mechanisms. *Voluntas*, *23*(1), 109–125. doi:10.100711266-011-9181-9

Mustafa, D., & Qazi, M. U. (2007). Transition from Karez to Tubewell Irrigation: Development, Modernization, and Social Capital in Balochistan, Pakistan. *World Development*, *35*(10), 1796–1813. doi:10.1016/j.worlddev.2007.06.002

Nair, G. H., & Rodrigues, L. L. R. (2013). Dynamics of Financial System: A System Dynamics Approach. *International Journal of Economics and Financial Issues*, *3*(1), 14–26.

Nancy, M. P., & Jan, E. (2017). *The Circular Economy – A new sustainability paradigm?* Academic Press. doi:10.1016/j.jclepro.2016.12.048.Abstract

Nandy, B., Sharma, G., Garg, S., Kumari, S., George, T., Sunanda, Y., & Sinha, B. (2015). Recovery of consumer waste in India - A mass flow analysis for paper, plastic and glass and the contribution of households and the informal sector. *Resources, Conservation and Recycling*, *101*, 167–181. doi:10.1016/j.resconrec.2015.05.012

Nannicini, T., Stella, A., Tabellini, G., & Troiano, U. (2013). Social capital and political accountability. *American Economic Journal. Economic Policy*, *5*(2), 222–250. doi:10.1257/pol.5.2.222

Narayana, T. (2009). Municipal solid waste management in India: From waste disposal to recovery of resources? *Waste Management (New York, N.Y.)*, *29*(3), 1163–1166. doi:10.1016/j.wasman.2008.06.038 PMID:18829290

Narwal, M., & Singh, R. (2013). *Corporate social responsibility practices in India: a comparative study of MNCs and Indian companies. Social Responsibility Journal.* doi:10.1108/SRJ-11-2011-0100

Neergaard, U., Szyszczak, E., van de Gronden, J. W., & Krajewski, M. (2012). *Social Services of General Interest in the EU.* Springer Science & Business Media.

Nef. (2008). *Measuring value: a guide to social return on investment (SROI).* Nef.

Neguţ, A. (2013). Social capital, social economy and local development. In *Social economy in the context of local development.* Iaşi: Editura Polirom.

Nesheva-Kiosseva, N. (2018). Aspects of ISO26000 Related to Transaction and Environmental Costs. In S. O. Idowu, C. Sitnikov, & L. Moratis (Eds.), *ISO 26000 - A Standardized View on Corporate Social Responsibility: Practices, Cases and Controversies* (pp. 177–195). Cham, Switzerland: Springer International Publishing.

Neu, D., Warsame, H., & Pedwell, K. (1998). Managing public impressions: Environmental disclosures in annual reports. *Accounting, Organizations and Society*, *23*(3), 265–282. doi:10.1016/S0361-3682(97)00008-1

Nicholls, A. (2009). 'We do good things, don't we?': 'Blended value accounting' in social entrepreneurship. *Accounting, Organizations and Society*, *34*(6-7), 755–769. doi:10.1016/j.aos.2009.04.008

Nicholls, J. (2017). Social return on investment - development and convergence. *Evaluation and Program Planning*, *64*, 127–135. doi:10.1016/j.evalprogplan.2016.11.011 PMID:27919435

Nilsson, M., Baker, T., & Johnston, P. (2009). *DCMI: Interoperability Levels for Dublin Core Metadata.* Retrieved 9 January 2018, from http://dublincore.org/documents/interoperability-levels/

Nistor, L. (2013). *Public Services and the European Union: Healthcare, Health Insurance and Education Services* (2011 edition). The Hague, The Netherlands: T.M.C. Asser Press.

Niven, P. R. (2003). Balanced Scorecard Step-by-Step for Government and Nonprofit Agencies. John Wiley & Sons Inc.

Nobari, J. J. (2015). *Accountability and social impact measurement for a third sector supported housing organisation.* Newcastle University.

Nowland-foreman, G. (2009). The Challenge of Accountability, the Opportunity of Responsibility for Third Sector Organisations. In *6th International Society for Third Sector Research (ISTR) Asia Pacific Regional Conference*, (pp. 2–4). Taipei, Taiwan: Academic Press.

Ntim, C. G., Soobaroyen, T., & Broad, M. J. (2017). Governance structures, voluntary disclosures and public accountability: The case of UK higher education institutions. *Accounting, Auditing & Accountability Journal, 30*(1), 65–118. doi:10.1108/AAAJ-10-2014-1842

O'Brien, E., & Tooley, S. (2013). Accounting for volunteer services: A deficiency in accountability. *Qualitative Research in Accounting & Management, 10*(3/4), 279–294. doi:10.1108/QRAM-09-2012-0037

O'Dwyer, B., & Unerman, J. (2008). The paradox of greater NGO accountability: A case study of Amnesty Ireland. *Accounting, Organizations and Society, 33*(7-8), 801–824. doi:10.1016/j.aos.2008.02.002

O'Rourke, D. (2003). Outsourcing regulation: Analyzing nongovernmental systems of labor standards and monitoring. *Policy Studies Journal: the Journal of the Policy Studies Organization, 31*(1), 1–29. doi:10.1111/1541-0072.00001

Oatley, N. (1999). Developing the Social Economy. *Local Economy, 13*(4), 339–345. doi:10.1080/02690949908726461

OECD. (1999). *Social Enterprises.* Paris, France: OECD Publications.

OECD. (2011). *Together for Better Public Services: Partnering With Citizens and Civil Society.* OECD Publishing.

OECD/EU. (2017). *Boosting Social Enterprise Development: Good Practice Compendium.* Paris: OECD Publishing.

Olsen, S., & Lingane, A. (2003). *Social return on investment: Standard Guidelines* (Working Paper Series). UC Berkeley.

Olson, M. (1969b). Social Indicators and Social Accounts. *Socio-Economic Planning Science*, (2), 334–346.

Olson, M. (1969a). The Plan and Purposes of Social Report. *The Public Interest*, (Spring): 85–97.

Olszak, C. M., & Ziemba, E. (2011). The Stage of E-Government Maturity in a Polish Region -- Silesia. *Journal of Economics & Management, 7*, 87.

Omar, N., & Arshad, R. (2016). Effectiveness, Accountability and Understanding Board Characteristics of Non-Profit Organisations in Malaysia. *Malaysian Accounting Review, 15*(2), 127–150.

Osborne, S. P., & Ball, A. (Eds.). (2010). *Social accounting and public management: Accountability for the public good.* Abingdon, UK: Routledge. doi:10.4324/9780203846070

Othman, R., & Ali, N. (2012). NPO, Internal Controls, and Supervision Mechanisms in a Developing Country. *Voluntas, 25*(1), 201–224. doi:10.100711266-012-9335-4

Oulton, W. (2017). The Role of Activism The FTSE4Good Indices, In: Responsible Investment. In R. Sullivan & C. Mackenzie (Eds.), *Responsible Investment* (2nd ed.; pp. 196–205). New York: Greenleaf Publishing. doi:10.4324/9781351283441-17

Pacioli, L., & Sokolov, I. (Ed.). (2001). Particularis de computis et scripturis. Moscow: Finance and Statistics.

Palley, M. (1977). Social Indicators and Societal Monitoring: An Annotated Bibliography. By Leslie D. Wilcox, Ralph M. Brooks, George M. Beal, and Gerald E. Klongan. (San Francisco: Jossey-Bass Inc., 1972. Pp. 464. *The American Political Science Review, 71*(3), 1162–1162. doi:10.1017/S0003055400265647

Panda, A., & Gupta, R. K. (2007). Call for developing indigenous organisational theories in India: Setting agenda for future. *International Journal of Indian Culture and Business Management, 1*(1-2), 205–243. doi:10.1504/IJICBM.2007.014478

Parker, L. (2005). Social and environmental accountability research: A view from the commentary box. *Accounting, Auditing & Accountability Journal, 18*, 842–860. doi:10.1108/09513570510627739

Parsons, L. M. (2007). The impact of financial information and voluntary disclosures on contributions to not-for-profit organizations. *Behavioral Research in Accounting, 19*(1), 179–196. doi:10.2308/bria.2007.19.1.179

Parthasarathy, R. (1993). *The Cilappatikāram of Iḷaṅko Aṭikaḷ: An Epic of South India.* Columbia University Press.

Patten, D. M. (2002). Give or take on the internet: An examination of the disclosure practices of insurance firm web innovators. *Journal of Business Ethics, 36*(3), 247–259. doi:10.1023/A:1014009229437

Paul, K., Dutta, A., & Krishna, A. P. (2014). A comprehensive study on landfill site selection for Kolkata City, India. *Journal of the Air & Waste Management Association, 64*(7), 846–861. doi:10.1080/10962247.2014.896834 PMID:25122958

PCMC. (2017). PCMC proposes to generate biogas from hotel waste. *Pune Mirror.* Accessed in July 2017 at http://punemirror.indiatimes.com/pune/civic/pcmc-proposes-to-generate-biogas-from-hotel-waste/articleshow/59761295.cms

PCMC. (n.d.). *Pimpri Chinchwad Smart City. PCMC.*

Pearce, J., & Kay, A. (2012). Brief History of Social Accounting and Audit. *Social Audit Network.* Retrieved February 20, 2019, from http://www.socialauditnetwork.org.uk/getting-started/brief-history-social-accounting-and-audit

Peattie, K., & Morley, A. (2008). Eight paradoxes of the social enterprise research agenda. *Social Enterprise Journal, 4*(2), 91–107. doi:10.1108/17508610810901995

Peattie, K., & Morley, A. (2008). *Social Enterprises: Diversity and Dynamics, Contexts and Contributions. A Research Monograph.* ESRC Centre for BRASS, Cardiff University.

Pečarič, M. (2016). Can a group of people be smarter than experts? *The Theory and Practice of Legislation*, 1–25. doi:10.1080/20508840.2016.1259823

Perego, P., & Kolk, A. (2012). Multinationals' accountability on sustainability: The evolution of third-party assurance of sustainability reports. *Journal of Business Ethics, 110*(2), 173–190. doi:10.100710551-012-1420-5

Pérez, C. C., Hernández, A. M. L., & Bolívar, M. P. R. (2005). Citizens' access to on-line governmental financial information: Practices in the European Union countries. *Government Information Quarterly, 22*(2), 258–276. doi:10.1016/j.giq.2005.02.002

Peterson, D. (2010). Agency Perspectives on NGO Governance. *Journal of Management Research, 2*(2), 1–11. doi:10.5296/jmr.v2i2.294

Pfeffer, J., & Salancik, G. R. (1978). *The external control of organizations: a resource dependence perspective.* New York: Harper & Row.

Phillips, M. (2006). Growing Pains: The sustainability of social enterprises. *Entrepreneurship and Innovation, 7*(4), 221–230.

Pidd, M. (2004). *Systems modelling: Theory and practice.* Oxford, UK: John Wiley & Sons.

Piketty, T. (2014). *Capital in the Twenty-First Century* (T. Goldhammer, Trans.). Cambridge, MA: Harvard University Press. doi:10.4159/9780674369542

Piotrowski, S. J., & Van Ryzin, G. G. (2007). Citizen attitudes toward transparency in local government. *American Review of Public Administration*, *37*(3), 306–323. doi:10.1177/0275074006296777

PMC. (n.d.). *Zero Garbage Model*. PMC.

Pollach, I. (2005). Corporate self-presentation on the www strategies for enhancing usability, credibility and utility. *Corporate Communications*, *10*(4), 285–301. doi:10.1108/13563280510630098

Pollach, I., Scharl, A., & Weichselbraun, A. (2009). Web content mining for comparing corporate and third-party online reporting: A case study on solid waste management. *Business Strategy and the Environment*, *18*(3), 137–148. doi:10.1002/bse.549

Pollitt, C., & Bouckaert, G. (2011). *Public Management Reform: A Comparative Analysis - New Public Management, Governance, and the Neo-Weberian State* (3rd ed.). Oxford, UK: Oxford University Press.

Porumbescu, G. A. (2016). Non-profit Accountability in Least Developed Nations: Lesson Learned from West Africa. *Public Administration Quarterly*, *40*(2), 288–315. doi:10.1177/0149206309343469

Powell, A., Nilsson, M., Naeve, A., Johnston, P., & Baker, T. (2009). *DCMI: Abstract Model*. Retrieved 15 November 2018, from http://dublincore.org/documents/2007/06/04/abstract-model/

Prabhune, T. (2018). *Times of India*. Accessed at: https://timesofindia.indiatimes.com/city/ahmedabad/gujarat-tops-in-putting-plastic-to-cleaner-use/articleshow/64954235.cms

Pradhan, V., Sharma, R., & Krishnamurthy, S. (2016). Analyses of Factors Affecting Employee Perception on Organizational Corporate Social Responsibility. *SCIT Journal*, *16*(1).

Prakash, A., & Gugerty, M. K. (2010). Trust but verify? Voluntary regulation programs in the nonprofit sector. *Regulation & Governance*, *4*(1), 22–47.

Pratas, A. (2009). *Dicionário Jurídico* (Vol. 1). Lisboa: Almedina.

Pratas, S. (2007). *Administração aberta e Internet. O caso dos municípios portugueses*. Lisboa: Revista de Administração Local.

Preite, D., & De Matteis, F. (2014). Non Profit Entities and Multi-Stakeholder Relations: Some Highlights on Accountability Management from the Italian "Pro-Loco" Organizations. *Procedia Economics and Finance*, *15*(14), 176–183. doi:10.1016/S2212-5671(14)00474-2

Presidência do Conselho de Ministros. (1977). Decreto-Lei 460/77. *Diário da República*, *257*(1). Available at: https://dre.pt/application/conteudo/277832

Presidência do Conselho de Ministros. (2001). Resolução do Conselho de Ministros n.º 22/2001. *Diário da República*, *49*(1). Available at: https://dre.pt/application/conteudo/384669

Protil, R., & Barreiros, R. (2012). *Strategic Control of Agro-Industrial Cooperatives: A Strategic Map Proposal*. Paper presented at the 30th International Conference of the System Dynamics Society, San Gallen, Switzerland.

Protil, R., & Kugeratski, S. (2012). *Economic Evaluation of Agronomic Research In Agricultural Cooperatives: Proposal of a Dynamic Scorecard Model*. Paper presented at the 30th International Conference of the System Dynamics Society, San Gallen, Switzerland.

Pruthi, R. K. (2004). *Indian caste system*. Discovery Publishing House.

Putman, R. (1995). Bowling Alone: America's Declining Social Capital. *Journal of Democracy*, *6*(1), 65-78.

Raffer, K. (2004). International financial institutions and financial accountability. *Ethics & International Affairs*, *18*(2), 61–77. doi:10.1111/j.1747-7093.2004.tb00468.x

Rajaram, T., & Das, A. (2006). Need for participatory and sustainable principles in India's EIA system: Lessons from the Sethusamudram Ship Channel Project. *Impact Assessment and Project Appraisal*, *24*(2), 115–126. doi:10.3152/147154606781765237

Rana, R., Ganguly, R., & Gupta, A. K. (2015). An assessment of solid waste management system in Chandigarh City, India. *The Electronic Journal of Geotechnical Engineering*, *20*(6), 1547–1572.

Rangarajan, L. N. (Ed.). (1992). *The Arthashastra*. Penguin Books India.

Rao, P., Patil, Y., Bhat, V., & Ketkar, M. (2017). Building Energy, Environment and Sustainability Linkages in Management Education in India—An Innovative Curriculum Based Approach. In Curricula for Sustainability in Higher Education (pp. 61-76). Springer International Publishing.

Rapoport, S. G. (2011). Transparencia y rendición de cuentas. *Revista Mexicana de Sociologia*, *73*(2), 199–229.

Rasche, A., & Gilbert, D. U. (2012). Social Accountability 8000 and socioeconomic development. *Business Regulation and Non-State Actors: Whose Standards? Whose Developments*, 68-79.

Rawhouser, H., Cummings, M., & Newbert, S. L. (2019). Social impact measurement: Current approaches and future directions for social entrepreneurship research. *Entrepreneurship Theory and Practice*, *43*(1), 82–115. doi:10.1177/1042258717727718

Reheul, A.-M., Van Caneghem, T., & Verbruggen, S. (2014). Financial Reporting Lags in the Non-Profit Sector: Empirical Analysis. *Voluntas*, *25*(2), 352–377. doi:10.100711266-012-9344-3

Reich, R. (2016). *Saving Capitalism: For The Many, Not The Few*. London: Icon Books Ltd.

Reich, R. B. (2003). *I'll Be Short: Essentials for a Decent Working Society*. Boston: Beacon Press.

Research Network for Social Enterprise. (n.d.). Retrieved from https://emes.net/

Retolaza, J.L., San-Jose, L., Ruiz-Roqueñi, M., Barrutia, J., & Bernal, R. (2013). *Metodología para la cuantificación del valor social generado por una organización. El caso de Lantegi Batuak*. Bilbao: Universidad del País Vasco e Instituto de Economía Aplicada a la Empresa.

Retolaza, J. L., & San-Jose, L. (2016). Prevención y detección del fraude en la empresa. *Revista Contabilidad y Dirección*, *23*(1), 159–178.

Retolaza, J. L., & San-Jose, L. (2018). Contabilidad social para el bien común. *Revista de Responsabilidad Social de la Empresa*, *29*, 95–122.

Retolaza, J. L., San-Jose, L., & Ruiz-Roqueñi, M. (2015). Monetarizing the social value: Theory and evidence. *Revista de Economía Pública, social y cooperative. C.I.R.I.E.C. España*, *83*(1), 43–62.

Retolaza, J. L., San-Jose, L., & Ruíz-Roqueñi, M. (2016). *Social accounting for sustainability: Monetizing the social value*. Cham: Springer. doi:10.1007/978-3-319-13377-5

Riahi-Belkaoui, A. (1984). *Socio- Economic Accounting*. London: Praeger Pub Text.

Richmond, B. J., Mook, L., & Quarter, J. (2003). Social accounting for nonprofits: Two models. *Nonprofit Management & Leadership*, *13*(4), 308–324. doi:10.1002/nml.2

Robeco, S. A. M. (2018, September 24). *Dow Jones*. Retrieved February 20, 2019, from https://www.robecosam.com/images/review-presentation-2018.pdf

Robeco, S. A. M. (n.d.). *We are Sustainability Investing*. Retrieved February 20, 2019, from https://www.robecosam.com/media/7/3/6/7368ef74b7d48a7e14ff0f22e3b78f57_csa-benefits-of-participation_tcm1011-14469.pdf

Roberts, B. H. (2004). The application of industrial ecology principles and planning guidelines for the development of eco-industrial parks: An Australian case study. *Journal of Cleaner Production*, *12*(8–10), 997–1010. doi:10.1016/j.jclepro.2004.02.037

Roberts, R. (1992). Determinants of corporate social responsibility disclosure: An application of stakeholder theory. *Accounting, Organizations and Society*, *17*(6), 595–612. doi:10.1016/0361-3682(92)90015-K

Rodrigues, A. M. (2016). SNC- Sistema de Normalização Contabilística (3rd ed.). Almedina, Coimbra.

Rodrigues, A. M. (2010). Os novos desafios da Contabilidade para Organizações da Economia Social que aplicam o SNC - As Cooperativas. *Revista Cooperativismo e Economía Social*, *32*, 115–140.

Roelants, B., Dovgan, D., Eum, H., & Terrasi, E. (2012). *The Resilience of the Cooperative Model - How Worker Cooperatives, Social Cooperatives and Other Worker-owned Enterprises Respond to the Crisis and its Consequences*. Brussels, Belgium: CECOP-CICOPA Europe.

Rogers, E. (2003). The Diffusion of Innovations (5th ed.). The Free Press.

Rosa, C. F. (2013). *Desafio de governança à sustentabilidade de organizações sociais: em análise o projeto desenvolvimento de princípios de prestação de contas e transparência da ONG Parceiros Voluntários* (Unpublished master's thesis). Universidade Federal do Rio Grande do Sul, Porto Alegre, RS.

Roslan, N., Arshad, R., Farahah, N., & Pauzi, M. (2017). Accountability and Governance Reporting By Non-Profit Organizations. *International Conference on Governance and Accountability 2016*, *00041*, 1–15. 10.1051hsconf/20173600041

Rotheroe, N., & Richards, A. (2007). Social return on investment and social enterprise: Transparent accountability for sustainable development. *Social Enterprise Journal*, *3*(1), 31–48. doi:10.1108/17508610780000720

Rouf, Md. (2016). Users' Perception on Corporate Voluntary Disclosure in Bangladesh. *Daffodil International University Journal of Business and Economics*, *10*(1), 136–151.

Rumbaugh, J., Booch, G., & Jacobson, I. (2017). *The unified modeling language reference manual*. Addison Wesley.

Rusconi, G. (2009). Stakeholder theory and business economics. *Economia aziendale 2000 web*, 3.

Russel Investment Group. (n.d.). *FTSE Russel Indexes* [Index]. Retrieved February 17, 2019, from https://www.ftse.com/products/indices/home/PageNotFound?aspxerrorpath=/Analytics/Factsheets/temp/4588a59d-deda-4d98-aa7e-cc5b93093f41.pdf

Russian Union of Industrials and Entrepreneurs. (n.d.). *Press room Committees and commissions Positions Analytics Social responsibility Social Charter of Russian Business*. Retrieved February 20, 2019, from http://www.rspp.ru/simplepage/474

Ryan, P. W., & Lyne, I. (2008). Social enterprise and the measurement of social value: Methodological issues with the calculation and application of the social return on investment. *Education, Knowledge & Economy*, *2*(3), 223–237. doi:10.1080/17496890802426253

Sachs, N. (2014, June). Garbage Everywhere: What refuse in India's streets reveals about America's hidden trash problem. *Atlantic*.

Saini, S., Rao, P., & Patil, Y. (2012). *City based analysis of MSW to energy generation in India, calculation of state-wise potential and tariff comparison with EU*. Academic Press. doi:10.1016/j.sbspro.2012.03.306

Saita, M., & Franceschelli, M. V. (2016). Preparing financial statement : the restricted accountability of Non-profit organizations. Academic Press.

Salamon, L. M., Leslie, C. H., & Chinnock, H. (2000). *The nonprofit sector: for what and for whom*. Working Papers of the Johns Hopkins Comparative Nonprofit Sector Project. Baltimore, MD: The Johns Hopkins Centre for Civil Society Studies. Retrieved from https://www.sociedadenaccion.cl/wp-content/uploads/2015/06/Salamon-L.-Hems-L.-Chinnock-K.-2000.-The-Non-Profit-Sector.-For-What-and-for-Whom.pdf

Salamon, L. M., Anheier, H. K., List, R., Toepler, S., & Sokolowski, S. W. (1999). *Global civil society: Dimensions of the nonprofit sector*. Baltimore, MD: The Johns Hopkins Center for Civil Society Studies.

Salani, M. P. (2004). *Il bilancio sociale cooperativo e la responsabilità sociale d'impresa*. Firenze: Il Ponte Editore.

Salomão, A., & Lima, F. (2018). *Análise de crises passadas indica que Brasil vive pior retomada da história. Folha de São Paulo*. Caderno Mercado.

Samuelson, P. A. (1954). The Pure Theory of Public Expenditure. *The Review of Economics and Statistics*, *36*(4), 387–389. doi:10.2307/1925895

Sangole, N., Kaaria, S., Njuki, J., Lewa, K., & Mapila, M. (2014). Community based participatory monitoring and evaluation: Impacts on farmer organization functioning, social capital and accountability. *Journal of Rural and Community Development*, *9*(2), 128–148. Retrieved from http://journals.brandonu.ca/jrcd/article/view/749

San-Jose, L., & Retolaza, J. L. (2015). *La generación de Valor Social como eje vertebrador de la Unión Europea*. Vitoria: Franciso de Landaburu Eurobask.

San-Jose, L., & Retolaza, J. L. (2016). *Contabilidad Social orientada a los stakeholders. Perspectiva de la Administración Pública*. Madrid: Pirámide.

San-Jose, L., Retolaza, J. L., & Freeman, R. E. (2017). Stakeholder Engagement at Extanobe: A Case Study of the New Story of Business. In R. E. Freeman, J. Kujala, & S. Sachs (Eds.), *Stakeholder Engagement: Clinical Research Cases* (pp. 285–310). Cham: Springer. doi:10.1007/978-3-319-62785-4_13

Santayana, G. (1905). Reason in Common Sense. In The Life of Reason (vol. 1, p. 284). Academic Press.

Santos, C., Ferreira, A., Marques, R. P., & Azevedo, G. (2018). EAGLE_Index: Enhancement of an accountability guide for learning E-Government. In Handbook of Research on Modernization and Accountability in Public Sector Management. Academic Press. doi:10.4018/978-1-5225-3731-1.ch006

Santos, J., Raimundo, J., & Lima, R. (2012). *Entidades do setor não lucrativo* (NCRF-ESNL e fiscalidade). Ordem dos Técnicos Oficiais de Contas.

Santos, L., & Amaral, L. (2008a). *Presença Na Internet Das Câmaras Municipais Portuguesas Em 2007 : Estudo Sobre Local eGovernment Em Portugal, DSI - Sociedade Da Informação*. Gávea – Laboratório de Estudo e Desenvolvimento da Sociedade da Informação. Universidade do Minho, Guimarães. Available at: http://hdl.handle.net/1822/8443

Santos, L., & Amaral, L. (2008b). *Presença Na Internet Das Juntas de Freguesia Portuguesas Em 2006 : Estudo Sobre Local eGovernment Em Portugal*. Gávea – Laboratório de Estudo e Desenvolvimento da Sociedade da Informação. Universidade do Minho. Available at: http://hdl.handle.net/1822/8477

Santos, F., Pache, A. C., & Birkholz, C. (2015). Making hybrids work: Aligning business models and organizational design for social enterprises. *California Management Review*, *57*(3), 36–58. doi:10.1525/cmr.2015.57.3.36

Santos, L., & Amaral, L. (2005). *A Presença Na Internet Das Juntas de Freguesia Portuguesas: Estudo Comparativo Entre 2002 E 2004*. Guimarães, Portugal: Gávea – Laboratório de Estudo e Desenvolvimento da Sociedade da Informação. Universidade do Minho.

Santos, L., & Amaral, L. (2006). *A Presença Na Internet Das Câmaras Municipais Portuguesas 2005*. Guimarães, Portugal: Gávea – Laboratório de Estudo e Desenvolvimento da Sociedade da Informação. Universidade do Minho.

Santos, L., Oliveira, J., & Amaral, L. (2003). *Método de Avaliação Da Presença Na Internet Dos Organismos Da Administração Direta E Indireta Do Estado*. Unidade de Missão Inovação e Conhecimento da Presidência do Conselho de Ministros e Departamento de Sistemas de Informação da Universidade do Minho.

Sarukkai, S. (2012). *JRD Tata and the Idea of Trusteeship*. Academic Press.

Sasidharan, K. (2011), A Sree Padmanabhaswamy Sovereign Fund? *Wall Street Journal*. Available at: https://blogs.wsj.com/indiarealtime/2011/07/19/india-journal-a-sree-padmanabhaswamy-sovereign-fund/

Satapathy, S. (2017). An analysis of barriers for plastic recycling in the Indian plastic industry. Benchmarking. *International Journal (Toronto, Ont.)*, *24*(2), 415–430. doi:10.1108/BIJ-11-2014-0103

Sauter, W. (2015). *Public Services in EU Law*. Cambridge, UK: Cambridge University Press.

Saxton, G. D., & Guo, C. (2011). Accountability online: Understanding the web-based accountability practices of nonprofit organizations (First Published July 23, 2009). *Nonprofit and Voluntary Sector Quarterly*, *40*(2), 270–295. doi:10.1177/0899764009341086

Schwartz, R. (2001). *Managing Government-Third Sector Collaboration: Accountability, Ambiguity, and Politics*. Academic Press.

Schwartz, R., & Sharkansky, I. (2000). Collaboration with the 'Third Sector' - Issues of Accountability: Mapping Israeli Versions of this Problematic. *Public Policy and Administration*, *15*(3), 92–106. doi:10.1177/095207670001500308

Schwettmann, J. (2014). The role of cooperatives in achieving the sustainable development goals - the economic dimension. Geneva, Italy: ILO.

Scott, M. (2010). Critical reflections on a decade of third sector modernisation: Another sector is possible. *Local Economy*, *25*(5), 367–372. doi:10.1080/02690942.2010.526793

Searcy, C. (2012). Corporate Sustainability Performance Measurement Systems: A Review and Research Agenda. *Journal of Business Ethics*, *107*(3), 239–253. doi:10.100710551-011-1038-z

Seetharaman, G. (2017, June). India wants to double consumption of cheap material in 5 yrs, what about its plastic waste? *The Economic Times*.

Seldon, A. (2005). *Introducing Market Forces Into 'Public' Services*. Indianapolis, IN: Liberty Fund.

Servera-Francés, D., & Arteaga-Moreno, F. (2015). The impact of corporate social responsibility on the customer commitment and trust in the retail sector. *Ramon Llull Journal of Applied Ethics*, *6*, 161–178.

Shadbolt, N., Berners-Lee, T., & Hall, W. (2006). The semantic web revisited. *IEEE Intelligent Systems*, *21*(3), 96–101. doi:10.1109/MIS.2006.62

Shamasastry, R. (1915). *Kautilya's Arthashastra*. Academic Press.

Sharholy, M., Ahmad, K., Mahmood, G., & Trivedi, R. C. (2008). Municipal solid waste management in Indian cities–A review. *Waste Management, 28*(2), 459-467.

Sharholy, M., Ahmad, K., Mahmood, G., & Trivedi, R. C. (2008). Municipal solid waste management in Indian cities - A review. *Waste Management (New York, N.Y.), 28*(2), 459–467. doi:10.1016/j.wasman.2007.02.008 PMID:17433664

Sharma, V. (2017). India's largest solid waste-to-energy plant launched at Delhi's at Narela. *Hindustan Times*.

Sheldon, E., Wilbert, B., & Moore, E. (Eds.). (1968). *Indicators of Social Change*. New York: Russell Sage.

Shoulders, C. D., & FreeMan, R. J. (2012). Government financial-reporting standards: Reviewing the past and present, anticipating the future. In R. D. Ebel & J. E. Petersen (Eds.), *The Oxford Handbook of State and Local Government Finance*. Oxford, UK: Oxford University Press.

Shuib, N., Said, J., & Atan, R. (2014). The Influence of Financial management Practices, Board Effectiveness and accountability towards Performance: Empirical Test of Non-Profit Organization. *APMAJ Asia-Pacific Management Accounting Journal, 8*(1), 43–63.

Siddhartha, K. (2018). For a Greener Tomorrow. *The Hindu*. Accessed at https://www.thehindu.com/education/for-a-greener-tomorrow/article24953545.ece

Siddiq, K., Meyer, E., & Ashleigh, M. (2013). What is the impact of authentic leadership on leader accountability in a non-profit context? *Proceedings of the International Conference on Management, Leadership and Governance*, 396–399.

Sigma Project. (2003). *Sigma Guidelines: Putting sustainable development into practice - A Guide for Organizations*. Retrieved February 20, 2019, from http://www.projectsigma.co.uk/default.asp

Sillanpää, M. (1998). The Body Shop values report-towards integrated stakeholder auditing. *Journal of Business Ethics, 17*(13), 1443–1456. doi:10.1023/A:1006099731105

Silva, B. (2015). Análise do consumidor consciente e do marketing ambiental: Reflexos do índice de sustentabilidade empresarial (ISE) na imagem das empresas. *REN-Revista Escola de Negócios, 2*(2), 78–97.

Silva, B., & Burger, R. (2015). *Financial vulnerability: an empirical study of Ugandan NGOs*. CIRIEC- Université de Liège.

Silverberg, J. (1968). *Social mobility in the caste system in India*. Academic Press.

Simon Clark Associates. (2002). The Social Economy: A Literature Review, a report to Communities, Simon Clark Associates Ltd, Scotland. In *Social Enterprises: Diversity and Dynamics, Contexts and Contributions. A Research Monograph*. ESRC Centre for BRASS, Cardiff University.

Sinclair, A. (1995). The chameleon of accountability: Forms and discourses. *Accounting, Organizations and Society, 20*(2-3), 219–237. doi:10.1016/0361-3682(93)E0003-Y

Singh, A., & Verma, P. (2014). *CSR@ 2%: A new model of corporate social responsibility in India*. Academic Press.

Singhal, S., & Kapur, A. (2002). Industrial estate planning and management in India—An integrated approach towards industrial ecology. *Journal of Environmental Management, 66*(1), 19–29. doi:10.1006/jema.2002.0571 PMID:12395584

Sitton, J. F. (2010). *Marx today. A Contribution to the Critique of Political Economy*. New York: Palgrave Macmillan.

Sjoberg, F. M., Mellon, J., & Peixoto, T. (2017). The Effect of Bureaucratic Responsiveness on Citizen Participation. *Public Administration Review, 77*(3), 340–351. doi:10.1111/puar.12697

Smith, A. (1976). An inquiry into the nature and causes of the wealth of nations (R. H. Campbell, A. S. Skinner, & W. B. Todd, Eds.). Academic Press.

Smith, S. R. (2010). Hybridization and nonprofit organizations: The governance challenge. *Policy and Society*, *29*(3), 219–229. doi:10.1016/j.polsoc.2010.06.003

Soares, D., Amaral, L., Ferreira, L., & Leal, D. (2014). *Método de Avaliação Da Presença Na Internet Das Câmaras Municipais Portuguesas: Versão 4.0*. Guimarães: Gávea – Laboratório de Estudo e Desenvolvimento da Sociedade da Informação. Universidade do Minho.

Sousa, F. J. M., & Wanderley, L. S. O. (2007). Divulgação da responsabilidade social empresarial: Como os websites empresariais vêm sendo utilizados por empresas de energia e varejo. *Cadernos EBAPE.BR*, *5*(2), 1–13. doi:10.1590/S1679-39512007000200008

Sowa, J. E., Selden, S. C., & Sandfort, J. R. (2004). No longer unmeasurable? A multidimensional integrated model of nonprofit organizational effectiveness. *Nonprofit and Voluntary Sector Quarterly*, *33*(4), 711–728. doi:10.1177/0899764004269146

Spacey, J. (2016, April 13). *8 Examples of Accountability*. Retrieved February 20, 2019, from https://simplicable.com/new/accountability

Spence, C. (2009). Social and the environmental reporting and the corporate ego. *Business Strategy and the Environment*, *18*(4), 254–265. doi:10.1002/bse.600

Spence, C., Husillos, J., & Correa-Ruiz, C. (2010). Cargo cult science and the death of politics: A critical review of social and environmental accounting research. *Critical Perspectives on Accounting*, *21*(1), 76–89. doi:10.1016/j.cpa.2008.09.008

Sprok, J. J. A. (2013). Status attainment in The Netherlands during the period 1851-1890 : The influence of social capital on status attainment in the context of. *Social Cosmos*, *4*(2), 152–166.

Srivathsan, A. (2011, July 7) When the vault was opened in 1931, Kerala. *The Hindu*.

SROI-Network. (2009). *A guide to social return on investment*. Author.

SROI-Network. (2012). *A guide to social return on investment*. Author.

Steccolini, I. (2004). *Accountability e sistemi informativi negli enti locali. Dal rendiconto al bilancio sociale*. Torino: Giappichelli.

Steccolini, I. (2019). Accounting and the post-new public management: Re-considering publicness in accounting research. *Accounting, Auditing & Accountability Journal*, *32*(1), 255–279. doi:10.1108/AAAJ-03-2018-3423

Sterman, J. D. (2000). *Business Dynamics. System thinking and modeling for a complex world*. Boston, MA: Mc Graw-Hill.

Sterman, J. D. (2014). Interactive web-based simulations for strategy and sustainability: The MIT Sloan LearningEdge management flight simulators, Part I. *System Dynamics Review*, *30*(1-2), 89–121. doi:10.1002dr.1513

Stone, W. S., & Wilbanks, J. (2012). Transparency and Accountability: A Look at Non-Profit Internet Website Content. *Insights to a Changing World Journal*, (3), 79–86. Retrieved from http://nuncio.cofc.edu/login?url=http://search.ebscohost.com/login.aspx?direct=true&db=a9h&AN=83529732&site=eds-live%5Cnhttp://content.ebscohost.com/ContentServer.asp?T=P&P=AN&K=83529732&S=R&D=a9h&EbscoContent=dGJyMNHr7ESep7Q4zOX0OLCmr0yep69Ssqa4SreWxWXS&

Strom, S. (2010). Hybrid model for nonprofits hits snag. *New York Times*. Retrieved from https://www.nytimes.com/2010/10/26/business/26hybrid.html

Suárez, D. F. (2010). Collaboration and Professionalization: The Contours of Public Sector Funding for Nonprofit Organizations. *Journal of Public Administration: Research and Theory*, *21*(2), 307–326. doi:10.1093/jpart/muq049

Subramanian, T. S. (2011). Eclectic architecture, exquisite features. *The Hindu*. Accessed in May 2017 from: http://www.thehindu.com/opinion/op-ed/eclectic-architecture-exquisite-features/article2236138.ece

Sueur, A. L., Sunkin, M., & Murkens, J. E. K. (2016). *Public Law: Text, Cases, and Materials* (3rd ed.). Oxford, UK: Oxford University Press. doi:10.1093/he/9780198735380.001.0001

Sugden, J. (2012). Why a Deity Should Be on 'India's Richest' List. *Wall Street Journal*. Available at: https://blogs.wsj.com/indiarealtime/2012/12/25/why-a-deity-should-be-on-indias-richest-list/

Sustainability Accounting Standard Board (SASB). (1997). *SA8000 Standard*. Retrieved February 20, 2019, from http://www.sa-intl.org/index.cfm?fuseaction=Page.ViewPage

Sustainability Accounting Standard Board SASB. (n.d.). *Sustainability Accounting Standards Board*. Retrieved February 20, 2019, from https://www.sasb.org

Sutton, H. (2017). Boost your adult students' progress to degree with CLEP credit. *The Successful Registrar, 17*(6), 1–5. doi:10.1002/tsr.30326

Szyszczak, E., Davies, J., Andenæs, M., & Bekkedal, T. (Eds.). (2013). *Developments in Services of General Interest* (2011 edition). The Hague, The Netherlands: T.M.C. Asser Press.

Tai, M. (2011). *The Nexus of Modernization and Social Capital : A Comparative Exploration of Two Kenyan Villages*. Wesleyan University.

Taleb, N. N. (2014). *Antifragile: Things That Gain from Disorder*. Random House Publishing Group.

Tapsuwan, S., & Asafu-Adjaye, J. (2008). Estimating the economic benefit of SCUBA diving in the Similan Islands, Thailand. *Coastal Management, 36*(5), 431–442. doi:10.1080/08920750802412908

Taysir, E. A., & Taysir, N. K. (2012). Measuring Effectiveness in Nonprofit Organizations: An Integration Effort. *Journal of Transnational Management, 17*(3), 220–235. doi:10.1080/15475778.2012.706736

Teltumbde, A. (2014, November 8). No Swachh Bharat without Annihilation of Caste. *Economic and Political Weekly*.

Tenbensel, T., Dwyer, J., & Lavoie, J. (2014). How not to kill the golden goose. *Public Management Review, 16*(7), 925–944. doi:10.1080/14719037.2013.770054

Terleckyj, N. E. (1981). A Social production framework for resource accounting. In *Social Accounting Systems* (pp. 95–129). New York: Academic Press. doi:10.1016/B978-0-12-392550-3.50009-6

Terleckyj, N. E. (1981). A Social Production Framework for Resource Accounting. In *Social Accounting Systems, Essays on the State of the Art*. Academic Press, Inc.

Theopedia. (2016). *Negative theology*. Retrieved 2 March 2016, from http://www.theopedia.com/negative-theology

Thomson, S. (2015). Towards a social theory of the firm: Worker cooperatives reconsidered. *Journal of Co-operative Organization and Management, 3*(1), 3–13. doi:10.1016/j.jcom.2015.02.002

Thornton, J., & Belski, W. (2010). Financial Reporting quality and price competition among nonprofits firms. *Applied Economics, 42*(21), 2699–2713. doi:10.1080/00036840801964583

Titov, V. N. (2013). The Distribution of Social Capital as a Condition for the Modernization of Russian Society. *Sociological Research, 52*(5), 40–58. doi:10.2753/SOR1061-0154520503

TNN. (2016a, January). Glass waste dumping. *The Times of India*.

TNN. (2016b, January). Nod to zero waste plan in PCMC ward. *The Times of India.*

TOI. (2018). *Times of India.* Accessed at: https://timesofindia.indiatimes.com/business/india-business/no-takers-for-rs-1717-cr-of-csr-funds-in-fy18-report/articleshow/66832211.cms

Tondolo, R. R. P. (2014). *Desenvolvimento de Capital Social Organizacional em um Projeto Interorganizacional no Terceiro Setor* (Unpublished doctoral dissertation). Universidade do Vale do Rio dos Sinos, São Leopoldo, RS.

Tondolo, R. R. P., Tondolo, V. A. G., Camargo, M. E., & Sarquis, A. B. (2016). Transparência no Terceiro Setor: Uma proposta de construto e mensuração. *Espacios Públicos, 19*(47), 7–25.

Tondolo, R. R. P., Tondolo, V. A. G., Longaray, A. A., & Mello, S. P. T. (2017). Implementação da Transparência em Organizações Sociais: Um estudo Multicaso. *Revista Eletrônica de Estratégia & Negócios, 10*(2), 81–98. doi:10.19177/reen.v10e2201781-99

Tondolo, V. A. G., Tondolo, R. R. P., Camargo, M. E., & Guerra, R. M. A. (2018). Capacidades Dinâmicas em Organizações Sem Fins Lucrativos: Uma proposta de mensuração para o terceiro setor. *Revista Eletrônica Científica do CRA-PR, 5*(1), 18–33.

Tooley, S., & Hooks, J. (2010). Public accountability: The Perceived usefulness of school annual reports. *Australasian Accounting. Business and Finance Journal, 4*(2), 39–59.

Torres, L., & Pina, V. (2003). Accounting for Accountability and Management in NPOs. A comparative study of four countries: Canada, The United Kingdom, The USA and Spain. *Financial Accountability & Management, 19*(3), 265–285. doi:10.1111/1468-0408.00174

Tremblay-Boire, J., & Prakash, A. (2014). Accountability.org: Online disclosures by U.S. Nonprofits. *Voluntas, 26*(2), 693–719. doi:10.100711266-014-9452-3

Trussel, J. M., & Parsons, L. (2008). Financial Reporting factors affecting donations to Charitable Organizations. *Advances in Accounting, 23*, 263–285. doi:10.1016/S0882-6110(07)23010-X

Tsui, A. S. (2004). Contributing to global management knowledge: A case for high quality indigenous research. *Asia Pacific Journal of Management, 21*(4), 491–513. doi:10.1023/B:APJM.0000048715.35108.a7

Turkin, S. (n.d.). *How beneficial to be kind: Make your business socially responsible: Social Reporting and Social Audit.* Retrieved February 20, 2019, from http://uchebnik.online/prakticheskaya-psihologiya-treningi/sotsialnaya-otchetnost-sotsialnyiy-46286.html

Turrini, A. (2002). Lo studio dei casi come metodologia di ricerca in economia aziendale. *Azienda Pubblica, 1-2*, 67–85.

UMIC. (2003). *Qualidade e eficiência dos serviços públicos : Plano de acção para o governo electrónico.* UMIC.

UNEP. (2006). *Circular Economy. An alternative model for economic development.* Paris: United Nations Environment Programme.

United Nations Global Compact. (2012). *A Practical Guide to the United Nations Global Compact for Higher Education Institutions: Implementing the Global Compact Principles and Communications.* Retrieved from https://www.unglobalcompact.org/library/5628

United Nations. (1972). *Declaration of the United Nations Conference on the Human Environment* (From Report of the United Nations Conference on the Human Environment, Stockholm, June 1972). Retrieved from http://www.un-documents.net/unchedec.htm

Vaccari, A. (2013). Constructing the social balance: Consumer cooperative, Italy. In S. Zadek, P. Pruzan, & R. Evans (Eds.), *Building Corporate Accountability: Emerging Practice in Social and Ethical Accounting and Auditing* (pp. 171–189). London: Routledge.

Vaculovschi, D., & Antonov, V. (2016). *Developing the social economy in Republic of Moldova by promotion of gender equal opportunities*. Policy Brief, IDIS "Viitorul". Retrieved from http://www.antreprenoriatsocial.md/media/files/Studiu_IDIS_Viitorul_policy_brief.pdf

Valencia, L. A. R., Queiruga, D., & González-Benito, J. (2015). Relationship between transparency and efficiency in the allocation of funds in nongovernmental development organizations. *Voluntas*, *26*(6), 2517–2535. doi:10.100711266-014-9527-1

Van der Laan, S. J., Adikhari, A., & Tondkar, R. H. (2005). Exploring differences in social disclosures internationally: A stakeholder perspective. *Journal of Accounting and Public Policy*, *24*(2), 123–151. doi:10.1016/j.jaccpubpol.2004.12.007

Van Dijk, M. P., & Rabellotti, R. (Eds.). (2005). *Enterprise clusters and networks in developing countries* (Vol. 7). Routledge. doi:10.4324/9780203988114

van Staden, C., & Heslop, J. (2009). Implications of Applying a Private Sector Based Reporting Model to Not-for-Profit Entities: The Treatment of Charitable Distributions by Charities in New Zealand. *Australian Accounting Review*, *19*(1), 42–53. doi:10.1111/j.1835-2561.2008.00039.x

Velamuri, S. R., Priya, A., & Vasantha, K. (2015). *Doing Well to Do Good: Business Model Innovation for Social Healthcare Business Models and Modelling* (Vol. 33, pp. 279–308). London: Emerald Group Publishing Limited.

Verbruggen, A., Fischedick, M., Moomaw, W., Weir, T., Nadaı, A., Nilsson, L. J., … Sathaye, J. (2010). *Renewable energy costs, potentials, barriers: Conceptual issues*. Academic Press. doi:10.1016/j.enpol.2009.10.036

Verité. (n.d.). *Verité | Fair Labor. Worldwide. | Knowledge and Tools to Eliminate Child Labor, Forced Labor, Human Trafficking and Gender Discrimination*. Retrieved February 20, 2019, from https://www.verite.org

Viader, M. I., & Espina, A. M. (2014). Corporate Governance - Are not-for-profits learning form for-profit organizations? A look into governance. *Corporate Governance*, *14*(1), 1–14. doi:10.1108/CG-11-2012-0083

Vidal, I. (2008). The role of social enterprises in Europe: a core element or a distraction in the provision of public services? In S. P. Osborne (Ed.), *The Third Sector in Europe. Prospects and challenges*. Oxon, UK: Routledge. doi:10.4324/9780203932827.pt8

Vij, D. (2012). Urbanization and Solid Waste Management in India: Present Practices and Future Challenges. *Procedia: Social and Behavioral Sciences*, *37*, 437–447. doi:10.1016/j.sbspro.2012.03.309

Vilar, V. (2012). *Divulgação de responsabilidade social na internet – estudo descritivo das páginas de internet dos maiores Bancos mundiais. Dissertação de Mestrado*. Lisboa: Universidade Aberta.

Virmani, B. R. (2005). *Cultural Dilemma in Indian Management*. Academic Press.

W3C. (2014a). *RDF 1.1 Concepts and Abstract Syntax*. Retrieved 21 November 2018, from https://www.w3.org/TR/rdf11-concepts/

W3C. (2014b). *RDF Primer*. Retrieved 10 November 2018, from https://www.w3.org/TR/rdf-primer/

W3C. (2015). *Data - W3C*. Retrieved 31 July 2018, from https://www.w3.org/standards/semanticweb/data

Waddock, S. (2008). The development of corporate responsibility / corporate citizenship. *Organizational Management Journal*, *5*(1), 29–39. doi:10.1057/omj.2008.5

Wanderley, L., Lucian, R., Farache, F., & Filho, J. (2008). CSR information disclosure on the web: A context-based approach analysing the influence of country of origin and industry sector. *Journal of Business Ethics*, *82*(2), 369–378. doi:10.100710551-008-9892-z

Watal, R. P., Advisor, P., & Aayog, N. (2017). *Strategy Paper on Resource Efficiency*. Academic Press.

Water Accounting Standards Board. (2012) *Australian Water Accounting Standards 1 Preparation and Presentation of General Purpose Water Accounting Reports*. Retrieved from http://www.bom.gov.au/water/standards/documents/awas1_v1.0.pdf

Watts, R. L., & Zimmermann, L. (1978). Toward a Positive Theory of the Determination of Accounting Standards. *The Accounting Review*, *54*(1), 112–134.

WEB References Cooperativa António Sérgio para a Economia Social. Lei de Bases da Economia Social - (Lei n.º 30/2013 de 8 de maio) - e Estatuto das IPSS - (DL nº 119/83 de 25.02 (alterado pelos DLs n. os 9/85 de 9.01, 89/85 de 1.04, 402/85 de 1.10, e 29/86 de 19.02). (n.d.). Available at: www.cases.pt (consulted in September 12th, 2018)

Webster, K. (2015). *The Circular Economy: A Wealth of Flows*. Isle of Wight, UK: Ellen MacArthur Foundation.

Weerawardena, J., McDonald, R. E., & Mort, G. S. (2010). Sustainability of nonprofit organizations: An empirical investigation. *Journal of World Business*, *45*(4), 346–356. doi:10.1016/j.jwb.2009.08.004

Weisbrod, B. A. (1988). *The Nonprofit Economy*. Cambridge, MA: Harvard University Press.

Wellens, L., & Jegers, M. (2014). Effective Governance in nonprofit organizations: A literature based multiple stakeholder approach. *European Management Journal*, *34*(2), 223–243. doi:10.1016/j.emj.2013.01.007

West, E. G. (1969). *Adam Smith*. New York: Arlington House.

Williamson, A. L., & Bond, B. J. (2014). Making boston strong: Social capital, collaboration, and accountability lessons for public administrators in the twenty-first century. *Public Administration Review*, *74*(6), 693–695. doi:10.1111/puar.12302

Willis, A. (2003). The role of the Global Reporting Initiative's sustainability reporting guidelines in the social screening of investments. *Journal of Business Ethics*, *43*(3), 233–237. doi:10.1023/A:1022958618391

Wilson, K., & Brownstein, J. S. (2009). Early detection of disease outbreaks using the Internet. *CMAJ : Canadian Medical Association Journal*, *180*(8), 829–831. doi:10.1503/cmaj.1090215 PMID:19364791

Wongthong, P. (2013). *An integrated approach to sustainable management of reef-based SCUBA dive tourism: a case study of Koh Tao, Thailand* (Doctoral dissertation). Retrieved May 1, 2018 from https://hekyll.services.adelaide.edu.au

Wood, D. (1991). Corporate social performance revisited. *Academy of Management Review*, *16*(4), 691–718. doi:10.5465/amr.1991.4279616

Woodward, D., Edwards, P., & Birkin, F. (2001). Some evidence on executive's view of corporate social responsibility. *The British Accounting Review*, *33*(3), 357–397. doi:10.1006/bare.2001.0165

Woolcock, M., & Narayan, D. (2000). Social capital: Implications for development theory, research, and policy. *The World Bank Research Observer*, *15*(2), 225–249. doi:10.1093/wbro/15.2.225

World Business Council for Sustainable Development (WBCSD). (n.d.). *The Reporting Exchange | Global resource for sustainability reporting*. Retrieved February 20, 2019, from https://www.reportingexchange.com/search?search=social%20report

Worrell, R., & Appleby, M. C. (2000). Stewardship of natural resources: Definition, ethical and practical aspects. *Journal of Agricultural & Environmental Ethics, 12*(3), 263–277. doi:10.1023/A:1009534214698

Wu, I.-L., & Chen, J.-L. (2005). An extension of trust and TAM model with TPB in the initial adoption of on-line tax: An empirical study. *International Journal of Human-Computer Studies, 62*(6), 784–808. doi:10.1016/j.ijhcs.2005.03.003

Yadagiri, S. (2018). *Banyan Nation: Living sustainably is the only way forward.* Accessed at http://www.newindianexpress.com/cities/hyderabad/2018/oct/13/banyan-nation-living-sustainably-is-the-only-way-forward-1884733.html

Yaduvanshi, N. R., Myana, R., & Krishnamurthy, S. (2016). Circular Economy for Sustainable Development in India. *Indian Journal of Science and Technology, 9*(46). doi:10.17485/ijst/2016/v9i46/107325

Yamaguchi, K. (2003). *Principle of accounting system dynamics – modeling corporate financial statements.* Paper presented at the 21st International Conference of the System Dynamics Society, New York, NY.

Yang, C., Northcott, D., & Sinclair, R. (2017). The accountability information needs of key charity funders. *Public Money & Management, 37*(3), 173–180. doi:10.1080/09540962.2017.1281649

Yang, Y. T., Horneffer, M., & DiLisio, N. (2013). Mining Social Media and Web Searches For Disease Detection. *Journal of Public Health Research, 2*(1), 17–21. doi:10.4081/jphr.2013.e4 PMID:25170475

Yasmin, S., Haniffa, R., & Hudaib, M. (2014). Communicated accountability by faith-based charity organisations. *Journal of Business Ethics, 122*(1), 103–123. doi:10.100710551-013-1759-2

Yetman, M. H., & Yetman, R. J. (2012). The effects of governance on the accuracy of charitable expenses reported by nonprofit organizations. *Contemporary Accounting Research, 29*(3), 738–767. doi:10.1111/j.1911-3846.2011.01121.x

Yin, R. K. (2009). Case Study Research. In Design and Methods. SAGE.

Young, D. (2011). The Prospective Role of Economic Stakeholders in the Governance of Nonprofit Organizations. *Voluntas, 22*(4), 566–586. doi:10.100711266-011-9217-1

Yunus, M., Moingeon, B., & Lehmann-Ortega, L. (2010). Building Social Business Models: Lessons from the Grameen Experience. *Long Range Planning, 43*(2/3), 308–325. doi:10.1016/j.lrp.2009.12.005

Yusuf, J.-E., Jordan, M. M., Neill, K. A., & Hackbart, M. (2013). For the people: Popular financial reporting practices of local governments. *Public Budgeting & Finance, 33*(1), 95–113. doi:10.1111/j.1540-5850.2013.12003.x

Zadek, S., Pruzan, P., & Evans, R. (Eds.). (1997). Building corporate accountability: emerging practices in social and ethical accounting, auditing and reporting. London, UK: Earthscan.

Zainon, S., Ahmad, S. A., Atan, R., Wah, Y. B., Bakar, Z. A., & Sarman, S. R. (2014). Legitimacy and Sustainability of Social Enterprise: Governance and Accountability. *Procedia: Social and Behavioral Sciences, 145*, 152–157. doi:10.1016/j.sbspro.2014.06.022

Zainon, S., Atan, R., & Bee Wah, Y. (2014). An empirical study on the determinants of information disclosure of Malaysian non-profit organizations. *Asian Review of Accounting, 22*(1), 35–55. doi:10.1108/ARA-04-2013-0026

Zainon, S., Atan, R., Wah, Y., Ahmad, R., Othman, A., & Suhadak, N. (2014). An Integrated Ritual Effectiveness Accountability Reporting System (i-REARs) for Non-Profit Organizations. *International Business Research, 7*(5), 156–165. doi:10.5539/ibr.v7n5p156

Zamagni, V. (2012). Interpreting the Roles and Economic Importance of Cooperative Enterprises in a Historical Perspective. *JEOD, 1*(1), 21–36. doi:10.5947/jeod.2012.002

Zanotti, A. (2013). *Le performance delle cooperative di servizi durante la crisi: un'analisi nel periodo 2009-2011.* Euricse Working Paper, n. 51.

Zevi A., Zanotti, A., Soulage, F., & Zelaia, A. (2011). *Beyond the Crisis: Cooperatives, Work, Finance - Generating Wealth for the Long Term.* Brussels, Belgium: CECOP-CICOPA Europe.

Zhang, X., Song, H., & Huang, G. Q. (2009). Tourism supply chain management: A new research agenda. *Tourism Management, 30*(3), 345–358. doi:10.1016/j.tourman.2008.12.010

Zhu, D., Asnani, P. U., Zurbrugg, C., Anapolsky, S., & Mani, S. (2008). *Improving Municipal Solid Waste Management in India: A Sourcebook for Policy Makers and Practitioners*. World Bank Institute. doi:10.1596/ 978-0-8213-7361-3

Zott, C., Amit, R., & Massa, L. (2011). The business model: Recent developments and future research. *Journal of Management, 37*(4), 1019–1042. doi:10.1177/0149206311406265

About the Contributors

Augusta Ferreira completed her first degree at the Higher Institute of Accounting and Administration of Aveiro; she got her Masters Degree in Business Management Specialization in Corporate Finance at Minho University and she holds a PhD in Accounting at Aveiro University and Minho University. Currently she teaches Accounting within the accounting scientific area at Higher Institute Accounting and Administration of Aveiro (Aveiro University) and she is interested in researching public accounting, accounting information systems, disclosure of financial information and accountability. She has presented and published many articles in national and international journals and conferences.

Rui Pedro Marques received the PhD degree in Computer Science in 2014 from the universities of Minho, Aveiro and Porto, three of the top universities in the north of Portugal. In 2008 he concluded his Masters degree in Electronics and Telecommunications Engineering, at the University of Aveiro, and in 2005 he graduated in the same area, also from the University of Aveiro. His main research interests are related to the integration of Information Systems into organizational topics, contributing with solutions to improve the risk management and the organizational efficiency. He is Professor of Information Systems and Technology since 2007 at the Higher Institute of Accounting and Administration, University of Aveiro, Portugal.

Graça Azevedo has a PhD in Management (scientific field: Accounting) at the Institute of Higher Labor and Enterprise – ISCTE. She has published and presented several articles in national and international journals and conferences as well. She is a member of the Editorial Board of international journal "Accounting and Finance Research". She currently teaches courses in scientific field of Financial Accounting at the Institute of Higher Learning in Accounting and Administration of the University of Aveiro. Her research interests are related to financial reporting, impression management strategies and international accounting standards.

Helena Coelho Inácio has a PhD in Accounting and Management from the University Autonoma the Madrid, a MSc in Economy by the University of Coimbra and a degree in Accounting and Audit by the University of Aveiro. She is Professor in the University of Aveiro, at the Instituto of Accounting and Administration. She lectures under graduated and graduated courses of accounting and audit. She has a book of Internal Control, communications and publications in audit area. She is a member of the research unit on Competitiveness, Governance and Public Policies (GOVCOPP).

Carlos Santos completed his first degree in Electrical Engineering ate the University of Coimbra he got his masters degree in Electrical Engineering Sciences and he holds a PhD in Information Systems and Computer Engineering from the Instituto Superior Técnico (Technical University of Lisbon). Currently he teaches Computer Sciences within the area of scientific computing at Higher Institute for Accountancy and Administration of Aveiro (Aveiro University) and he is interested in researching information systems auditing, accounting information systems and XBRL language. He as presented and published about 50 articles in national and international journals and conferences.

* * *

Corina-Georgiana Antonovici is lecturer at Faculty of Public Administration, National University of Political Studies and Public Administration, Bucharest, being holder of the courses on Public Management, Nonprofit Management, Structures, Mechanisms and Administrative Institutions. She has been involved in several European and national research projects and her most relevant publications approach public management, public organizations, nonprofit organizations, social enterprises, organizational change.

Ana Bandeira is a PhD in Business Administration with a specialization in accounting and Master in Accounting and Management. Professor in the scientific area of Financial Accounting in the Porto Accounting and Business School, in the Polytechnic Institute of Porto. Researcher at CEOS.PP - Center for Organizational and Social Studies of the Polytechnic of Porto. Member of the Portuguese Accounting Standardization Commission.

Claudia Bitencourt, the Dean of the Unisinos Business School, has been working at Unisinos for 22 years. She served as the head of the graduate program in Business Administration from 2013-2017. She received her undergraduate degree from PUCRS (Brazil) and her master's and doctoral degrees from UFRGS (Brazil). She was a Visiting Researcher at the University of Queensland (2000, 2003), the University of Lisbon (2006), Texas Panamerican University (2009, 2011) and, the Thunderbird School of Global Management, as a Fulbright scholar (2009). Her area of interest is in Organizational Behavior, working mainly on the following themes: dynamic capabilities, organizational learning and, social innovation. She has published several academic articles and the following books: "Contemporary management of people" (2004 and 2010), "Competencies management and learning in organizations" (2005) and "On the track of competencies" (2013).

António Cardoso Pinto is graduated in History of Art by the University of Lisbon (Faculdade de Letras) and have a MSc in Corporate Sciences also by the University of Lisbon (ISEG - Lisbon School of Economics & Management), with a thesis about "Accountability & Reporting in the Funding Decision Process of Social Economy". His favorite research subjects in the Social Economy field are related with the quality of reporting, social impact and governance.

Francesca Costanza holds an international PhD in 'Model Based Public Planning, Policy Design and Management' at the University of Palermo (Italy), a MD in Business Economics and Administration and a Msc in Healthcare Management. She was guest researcher at the universities of Bergen and Nijmegen and also conducted EU funded research at the Italian National Council of Research (ICT for Education). Member of the System Dynamics Society, She was teaching assistant in Business Management and Administration at LUMSA University Palermo, where She is currently lecturer of 'Business groups and consolidated financial statements'.

Mariana Curado Malta is an assistant professor of Information Systems at the Accounting and Business school of the Polytechnic of Porto, Portugal. She holds a PhD in Information Systems and Technologies from University of Minho, Portugal. Her research interests are related to the systematic forms of developing Metadata application profiles. In this scope, she is the author of the Me4MAP method. She is the author of several papers and book chapters. For more information see http://maltas.org.

Fabio De Matteis holds a PhD in Business Management and he is researcher of Public and Not for Profit Management at the University of Salento. His research, training and publication activities focus on different fields including accounting and budgeting, programming and control, performance management, accountability and sustainability management.

Pietro Fontana holds a master's degree in Business Economics and Administration and is chartered accountant. He is member of the Provincial Council of Unicoop Palermo, Italy.

Geoffrey Fudurich holds a Master's degree in Environmental Applied Science and Management from Ryerson University, Toronto, Canada. His research interests are environmental certification, waste management, and sustainable tourism. He holds a Bachelor of Commerce from the University of Guelph, Canada, and has worked as a management consultant with Accenture. He is currently working as a Sustainability Consultant in Canada.

Ushi Ghoorah specializes in the financial disclosures, governance, and accountability of nonprofit organizations. Her current research projects include exploring people's perceptions of financial disclosures, the influence of multiple factors on financial disclosures, and the relationship between governance boards and financial transparency within the Australian nonprofit context. Ushi is a board member of the Third Sector Review journal and an advisory panel member of the Australian Accounting Standards Board (AASB). In addition to having worked in Corporate, Insurance, Hospitality and Education, Ushi has completed a Ph.D., two Masters in Accounting (both with distinction), and a BSc (Hon) in Economics & Finance.

Sanja Korac is Assistant Professor and Deputy Head of the Department of Public, Nonprofit & Health Management at the Alpen-Adria Universitaet Klagenfurt, Austria. Her main research interests are performance management and accounting, public personnel management, public service motivation, innovation, and government owned enterprises. Sanja is part of an energetic international group of scholars addressing the topic of financial resilience, active member in the IRSPM Special Interest Group on Accounting and Accountability as well as other international academic groups (IIAS, EGPA, CIGAR, IPMN, VHB). She was visiting professor at the University of Applied Sciences in Technology and Economics Berlin, Germany, as well as short-visit guest professor at the Kristianstad University in Sweden, and the University of Salerno in Italy. In the academic year 2014/2015, she was the Austrian Marshall Plan Foundation Research Fellow at The Johns Hopkins University in Washington, DC. Having a background in public administration practice, Sanja actively engages with practitioners from various organizations in the public and nonprofit sector.

Saravan Krishnamurthy is a graduate in Industrial Management. He has published and reviewed research papers and book chapters in international peer-reviewed journals. He holds keen interests in Sustainability, Renewable Energy, and Social responsibility. He is currently pursuing PhD at Symbiosis International Deemed University, Pune, India. He has taught Sustainability, Business Research, Strategic Management, Operations Management, Globalization and Consumer Behavior.

Larraitz Lazcano is a lecturer at University of the Basque Country (UPV/EHU) in Bilbao (Spain). She is expert in social Accounting and Social Economy. Her research studies are focus on the analysis of the influence and improvement of the implementation of social value systems such as a social Accounting to the social Economy. She has a master degree about Social Economy and she is teaching finance at Economics and Management Faculty.

Ani Matei is professor of public economics at Faculty of Public Administration, National University of Political Studies and Public Administration, Bucharest, specialized on assessing the economic optimum in the public sector, models of local development and evaluation of the economic and social impact of corruption. He is General Editor of Academic Public Administration Studies Archive, as well as member of advisory boards of important journals of economics and social analysis in Lithuania, Romania and India. Author of relevant books and chapters in books, published by L`Harmattan, Paris, France, Lambert Academic Publishing, Germany, Taylor & Francis, UK.

Deolinda Meira is an Assistant Professor of Commercial Law at the Porto Accounting and Business School, of the Polytechnic of Porto, in Portugal. She focuses her current work on the legal framework of cooperative and social economy, which has been the subject of several scientific communications, monographs, book chapters, and articles. Co-editor of the Journal CES (Cooperativism and Social Economy) published by the University of Vigo, Spain. Member of the scientific committee of the CIRIEC España - Revista Jurídica de Economía Publica, Social y Cooperativa, of the Boletín de la Asociación Internacional de Derecho Cooperativo and of the Revista Jurídica Luso-Brasileira (RJLB) Evaluator of scientific papers in peer-reviewed journals. She also develops consulting activities and participates in projects about the legal framework of cooperatives and other entities of social economy. She was a member of the Committee for the Revision of the Portuguese Cooperative Code (revision introduced by the Law no. 119/2015, of 31 August), created within the CNES (National Council for the Social Economy).

Ninel Nesheva-Kiosseva received her Master Degree and PhD in University of National and World Economy, Sofia, Bulgaria. Her habilitation is held at the Higher Attestation Commission to the Council of Ministers of Bulgaria. She has published books in finance, environmental and social accounting, economic theory and history. Teaches at the New Bulgarian University, Sofia

Anna Oppelmayer is university assistant and PhD candidate at the Department of Public, Nonprofit & Health Management, Alpen-Adria Universitaet Klagenfurt, Austria. She has a background in social management and social economy, and has completed her master`s degree in Business and Law, with a specific focus on public management and public law. She has several years of experience in higher education teaching in the field of general business administration, as well as experience in professional training and development in the social and health care services. Anna's main research area is the nonprofit sector. She was involved in the development of a performance measurement system for the Austrian Red

Cross in Carinthia. Currently, Anna is conducting a comprehensive empirical investigation of formal volunteering by children and adolescents in nonprofit organizations. She has been a volunteer in different service areas for the Austrian Red Cross for over thirteen years, and in 2011 she has also joined its regional administration in a formal position.

Wilson José Bernardo Patrocínio holds a master's degree in Accounting and Finance by School of Management and Technology of the Polytechnic Institute of Santarém (Portugal). He worked as an accountant in an accountancy company called Moneris, S.A., between 2013 and 2016. Since 2016, he has been an accountant in another accountancy company called Plurigest, Lda. In his main functions, he has been responsible for managing the accounting data processes of the companies and for guarantying the veracity and reliability of accounting statements, as well as the taxation duties of those companies.

Mirko Pečarič has obtained Master of Science and PhD at the Faculty of Law, University of Ljubljana. He has passed also the national law exam. In 2013 the Government of the Republic of Slovenia appointed him as the State Secretary at the Ministry of Education, Science and Sport. So far, he taught the courses of Administrative Law, Public services, Introduction to Law and the Theory of public administration. He wrote a series of legal opinions, requirements for assessing the constitutionality of laws; he is the author of three monographs and numerous scientific articles.

Daniela Preite is Affiliate Professor of Government, Health and Not for Profit at SDA Bocconi School of Management. She is Aggregate Professor of Business Administration and Management at the University of Salento. She conducted research and training projects with some important public institutions, non-profit organizations and major enterprises. Her research activities focus on various fields, including accounting and budgeting, programming and control, performance management, accountability and social balance, profit/nonprofit and public/nonprofit partnership and human resource management.

Prakash Rao is the Deputy Director and Head of the Energy and Environment Programme at Symbiosis Institute of International Business (SIIB),a constituent of Symbiosis International University, Pune. He has 35 years of experience in the field of energy and environment management with interests in climate change and energy sectors. He holds a Ph.D. from the University of Bombay and has led the Climate Change and Energy Programme at WWF-India for nearly ten years, coordinating its global research, energy policies and community action. Has published around 82 research papers, notes and book chapters in peer reviewed international journals and books and contributes in an advisory capacity to the corporate sector on environmental sustainability issues. He has published four books with a recent publication on 'Environmental Impacts of Tourism in Developing Nations' with IGI Global Publishers, USA.

Jose Luis Retolaza is a Doctor in Economic Sciences, Degree in Philosophy and Psychology (clinical and industrial). Professor of Economics at the Deusto Business School; Scientific Director of GE-Accounting (Global Economic Accounting) and President of EBEN Spain (European Ethics Business Ethics Network). Prior to his academic activity he has worked 20 years in the field of consulting, always in management positions; and has participated in multiple Boards of Directors, Boards of Directors and Patronages.

Rui Robalo holds a PhD in Business Sciences by Faculty of Economics, University of Porto (Portugal). He is Associate Professor of the School of Management and Technology of the Polytechnic Institute of Santarém (Portugal). His teaching covers various accounting topics, in different cycles of studies. He has published research in relevant accounting journals and books.

Leire San-Jose is Associate Professor at University of the Basque Country (UPV/EHU) in Bilbao (Spain), and she is also Visiting Research Fellow at University of Huddersfield (United Kingdom). She is leader of ECRI (Ethics in Finance & Social Value Research group). She was previously a Visiting Scholar at Loyola University Chicago under the supervision of Professor John Boatright and at Darden Business School under the supervision of Professor Edward Freeman. Her most important publications are about ethics in payment to suppliers, social value and social efficiency and stakeholder theory. She has published in impact journals such as Journal of Business Ethics, Sustainability, European Management Journal, Corporate Social Responsibility and Environmental Management and CIRIEC. See www.ehu.eus/leiresanjose and www.ehu.eus/ecri.

Melanie Santos is a post-graduate student in Accounting and Finance at the Accounting and Business School of the Polytechnic of Porto, Portugal.

Carmen Savulescu is lecturer at the Faculty of Public Administration, National University of Political Studies and Public Administration, Bucharest, specialised in e-government, IT for public administration, consultancy and design of programmes in the public sector, human resource management, performance management. She participated in the accomplishment of several research projects financed by national and European research authorities. The most relevant publications approach e-government services, ICT based innovation in the public sector, European and regional comparative studies on e-government.

Pedro Verga Matos is Associate Professor at ISEG – Lisbon School of Economics & Management (Universidade de Lisboa) and researcher of CSG/Advance - Research in Social Sciences and Management. Pedro holds a PhD in Business and Management Studies from Universidade do Porto, an MBA and a Master in Management from Nova School of Business and Economics (Univeridade Nova de Lisboa), and a Licenciatura in Economics from Catolica Lisbon - School of Business and Economics (Universidade Católica Portuguesa). His research interests include corporate governance, public and private partnerships (PPP), social innovation/microfinance, retail and multicriteria analysis.

Index

G

I

L

M

N

O

P

Q

R

S

T

U

V

W

www.ingramcontent.com/pod-product-compliance
Lightning Source LLC
LaVergne TN
LVHW062134300926
849161LV00010B/2530